IBN HAZM

A.G. CHEJNE

KAZI PUBLICATIONS INC.,
1215 West Belmont Avenue,
Chicago, Illinois 60657 (USA).

IBN HAZM

A. G. CHEJNE.

© 1982 by Kazi Publications

All rights reserved
including the rights of reproduction
or translation into anyother language
in whole or in part in any form
without the written permission of
the Author or the Publisher.

Published by:
KAZI PUBLICATIONS INC;
1215 West Belmont Avenue,
Chicago, Illinois 60657 (USA).

Manufactured in the United States of America
1 2 3 4 5 6 7 8 9 10

ISBN   0-935782-03-6   Paper Back

ISBN   0-935782-04-4   Hard Cover

ابن حزم الأندلسي وموقفه من العلوم

تأليف
الدكتور أنور شحنه

١٤٠٢هـ - ١٩٨٢م

Transliteration

TERMINAL	MEDIAL	INITIAL	ALONE	TRANSLITERATION
ا	ا	ا	ا	ʾ
ب	ب	ب	ب	b
ت	ت	ت	ت	t
ث	ث	ث	ث	th
ج	ج	ج	ج	j
ح	ح	ح	ح	ḥ
خ	خ	خ	خ	kh
د	د	د	د	d
ذ	ذ	ذ	ذ	dh
ر	ر	ر	ر	r
ز	ز	ز	ز	z
س	س	س	س	s
ش	ش	ش	ش	sh
ص	ص	ص	ص	ṣ
ض	ض	ض	ض	ḍ
ط	ط	ط	ط	ṭ
ظ	ظ	ظ	ظ	ẓ
ع	ع	ع	ع	ʿ
غ	غ	غ	غ	gh
ف	ف	ف	ف	f
ق	ق	ق	ق	q
ك	ك	ك	ك	k
ل	ل	ل	ل	l
م	م	م	م	m
ن	ن	ن	ن	n
ه	ه	ه	ه	h
و	و	و	و	w
ي	ي	ي	ي	y

VOWELS: short a َ u ُ i ِ   long ā ـَا ū ُو ī ِي

DIPHTHONGS: aw َو   ay َي

CONTENTS

PART I

		Page
PREFACE AND ACKNOWLEDGEMENTS		VII
I.	THE PLACE OF IBN HAZM IN THE INTELLECTUAL HISTORY OF ISLAM: INTRODUCTORY REMARKS	1
	1. A Profile of the Man	
	2. The objective of the Work	
	3. Sources	
	a. Medieval Sources	
	b. Ibn Hazm's Works	
	c. Western Scholarship	
	d. Modern Arabic Works	
	4. Impace of his Ideas	
II.	THE MAN AND HIS TIME	20
	1. His Genealogy and Family	
	2. Social and Political Conditions	
	3. His Political Career and Exiles	
	4. His Views on Society	
III.	THE SCHOLAR — DIALECTICIAN	36
	1. His Intellectual Environment	
	2. His Education and Teachers	
	3. Some of his Ideas	
	4. The Polemicist	
IV.	HIS DOCTRINE OF KNOWLEDGE AND THE COGNITIVE PROCESS	56
	1. Secular Knowledge versus Religious Knowledge	
	2. Conception of Knowledge among Anadlusians	
	3. Ibn Hazm's Conception of Knowledge	
	4. The Source of Knowledge and the Cognitive Process	
	5. Intellect and Faith — Philosophy and Religion	
V.	THE SCIENCES AND THEIR CLASSIFICATION	82
	1. The State of the Sciences	
	2. The Classification of the Sciences before Ibn Hazm	
	3. Classification of the Sciences in al-Andalus	
	4. Ibn Hazm's *Categories of the Sciences (Maratib al-'ulum)*	
	5. The Sciences after Ibn Hazm	
VI.	HIS RELIGIOUS IDEAS AND DOCTRINE	109
	1. God, Prophecy and Miracles	
	2. Qur'an, Traditions, and Consensus	

3. Man's Relation to God
4. The Linguistic Foundation of his Doctrine
5. His Rejection of Human Criteria in Matters of Law
   a. Religious Laws preceding Muhammad
   b. Precaution *(ihtiyat)*
   c. Preference *(istihsan)*
   d. Imitation *(taqlid)*
   e. Opinion *(ra'y)*
   f. Speech Guide *(dalil al-khitab)*
   g. Analogy *(qiyas)*
   h. Causation (ta'lil)
6. Individual Inquiry *(ijtihad)*

VII. BELLES-LETTRES, LANGUAGE, AND HISTORY 132
1. The Writer and Poet
2. On Poetry and Rhetoric
3. On the Arabic Language
4. The Historian and History

VIII. THE PHILOSOPHICAL SCIENCES 153
1. The Legitimate Sciences
   a. Mathematics
   b. Astronomy
   c. Medicine
   d. The Natural Sciences
   e. Logic

IX. THE SPURIOUS SCIENCES 178
   a. Music
   b. Alchemy
   c. Astrology
   d. Magic, Talisman, Dreams and Vision

X. IBN HAZM'S *Maratib al-'ulum* 189
1. Introduction
2. Translation
3. Arabic Edition

NOTES 252
LIST OF PERIODICALS 300
APPENDIX OT IBN HAZM'S WORKS 301
BIBLIOGRAPHY 314
INDEX 327

PREFACE

Ibn Hazm (d. 1064) of Cordova was a humanist *par excellence* and one of the intellectual giants in Islam. He was a belleletrist, poet, historian, theologian, jurist, philosopher and polemecist who is reported to have written four hundred volumes on various disciplines. As a prolific writer, he had a great deal to say about the sciences: religious sciences, grammar and lexicography, poetry, literary criticism, logic, astronomy, astrology, medicine, alchemy, music and others. He recognized the interdependence of the sciences and advocated a broad liberal education combining the secular and the religious disciplines. Besides, he was a critic and an intellectual rebel who raised his voice on the major issues of his time attacking fearlessly the laxity and indifference of religious cholars, jurists and rulers. He was rationalist and devout religious man, who combined a reigorous scientific method with religious criteria clamoring for change and corrective measures in the approach to religious matters and insisting on individual inquiry *(ijtihad)* instead of the hitherto overreliance on old authorities. This fresh approach did not endear him to the secular and religious authorities, which subjected him to ostracism and persecution. In fact, the sale of his books was forbidden and many of them were committed to the fire. Despite these heavy restrictions many of his works survived and had a considerable impact on succeeding generations.

Hence the importance of Ibn Hazm in the intellectual history of Islam. Research on him is hardly commesurate with his talent and great genius. Except for some works in foreign languages, there is hardly a work or monograph on him in English. Thus, it is hoped that this work will fill a gap in the literature about Ibn Hazm by showing his social and intellectual background with main reference to his life and works and with particular emphasis on his classification and conception of the sciences. Though a variety of primary and secondary sources have been consulted, I have used on the core of the study Ibn Hazm's *Categories of the Sciences* on the basis of a new manuscript, which I found in the National Library of Rabat, Morocco, and which was collated with the Istanbul manuscript, edited by Ihsan 'Abbas. The Rabat manuscript is being edited, translated and analyzed with due attention to Ibn Hazm's views on the sciences as they occur elsewhere in his other works. Although Ibn Hazm's approach to the sciences seems to differ from that of other Muslim thinkers, it is deemed relevant to contrast it with: a) his predecessors (al-Farabi, al-Khuwarzımı, the Brethern of Purity); b) contemporary compatriots (Sa'id of Toledo and Ibn 'Abd al-Barr); and c) successors (al-Ghazzali and Ibn Khaldun, among others).

It is hoped that this work will shed some light on the intellectual history of Islam in general and on the position of the sciences in Muslim Spain in particular. In this connection, Ibn Hazm offers a fresh approach to the sciences in which he establishes a heirarchy of the sciences and their interdependence, indicates their utility, and suggests the manner and extent of pursuing each one of them without neglecting even those "spurious sciences" such as astrology and alchemy - the ideal being to enable the individual to discern between right and wrong. One can hardly underestimate the great significance of such approach even in our time in which humanistic studies tend to be relegated to a minor place in favor of technology and vocational disciplines. All in all, it is hopped that this work will make a modest contribution to the field of Arabic studies and will enable the reader to have a better insight to the intellectual perspective of a great medieval thinker.

Minneaplis   A.G.C.
1980

ACKNOWLEDGEMENTS

I wish to express my gratitude to the National Endowment for the Humanities for granting me an Independent Study Fellowship during 1975-76 which enable me to conclude my research and prepare the manuscript for publication. I also wish to thank the office of Research Development of the College of Liberal Art, (U. of Minnesota) for some financial assistance. A special word of thanks goes to Professor George Hourani of New York University at Buffalo, who read the manuscript and offered valuable suggestions and encouragement. I am equally indebted to Professor Assad Busool of the University of Minnesota, who read the galley proofs and offered valuable assistance and suggestions. and to my students Naseef Joussef, Muhammad Abahsayn and Fadl Abdallah for their assistance in collating the Arabic manuscript and offering invaluable suggestions. Last, but not the least, I wish to express my appreciation to Dr. M. Qazi for his interest in the work and for his vigilance and care during the preparation of the manuscript for publication: and to Anne Harbour, who read the manuscript and offered valuable suggestions on the editorial matters. I also wish to thank my daughter Cecila for his assistance in the preparation of the index.

CHAPTER I
THE PLACE OF IBN HAZM IN THE INTELLECTUAL HISTORY OF ISLAM:
INTRODUCTORY REMARKS

1. A Profile of the Man

Ibn Hazm (d. 1064) was a humanist par excellence and one of the intellectual giants not only of Muslim Spain, but of the whole Muslim world. In the Intellectual history of Islam he ranks with al-Ash'ari, al-Ghazzali, and Ibn Taymiyyah in the juridicotheological field; with Ibn Bajjah, Ibn Tufayl, and Averroes in philosophy; and with the great Muslim historians, prose writers, and poets. He as a prolific writer to whom are attributed some four hundred volumes covering a large spectrum of the intellectual disciplines of medieval Islam: poetry, belles-lettres, literary criticism, history, prophetic traditions, theology, ethics, philosophy, and medicine. His work becomes the more important by virtue of its high quality and its imaginative, if not original, approach to these disciplines. Moreover, his writing reveals the brilliant mind of a thinker and reformer who took his scholarship and findings to the common man instead of confining them to the academic setting. As such, he was a sociopolitical activist, an intellectual and religious rebel, and an uncomprosmising critic and polemicist who raised his voice on the major issues of the time, fearlessly attacking what he believed constituted deviations and laxity in religious matters, irrationality with respect to natural phenomena, and indifference of rulers and religious scholars toward the socioreligious problems facing eleventh-century al-Andalus and the whole Muslim world.

In his search for answers to the problems pressing the Islamic community, Ibn Hazm developed and pursued an approach to these problems based on and inspired by the precepts of the religious law and the lucidity and precision of logic. He was consistent and persuasive in his arguments, striving for co-existence between the divine and secular orders. In so doing, he exposed the faults and excesses of the secular and religious leaders of the country, to their great annoyance, and called for corrective measures. As a result, he was ostracized and persecuted — at times, his books were outlawed and even burned.

It may be said that Ibn Hazm lived at the wrong time and in the wrong place. His religio-intellectual perspective was shaped by events that struck at all levels of Andalusian society. At the beginning of the eleventh century, Muslim Spain was torn by political division and internal wars and threatened from the outside by the Christians to the North. Ibn Hazm, who had been born in a golden age to a noble and affluent family, savored some of the splendor and glory of tenth-century Muslim Spain as a child; he came to witness the crumbling of that majestic civilization when he was still in his teens.

After several unsuccessful political ventures, attended by exile, imprisonment, humiliation, and persecution, Ibn Hazm was forced to withdraw from the turmoil of politics, and devoted his life to scholarship and religion. However, he did not become passive or indifferent to the ever-increasing deterioration of his country's stability. Wealth, prestige, and high position were no longer inducements for him, leaving him free to embark on his *jihad* (crusade) with an incisive tongue and a sharp pen. His conviction and temperament would not allow him to remain silent as the splendor, pride, and glory of the past were replaced by lawlessness and social and moral decay. Eleventh-century Muslim Spain was suffering from a lack of strong religious and secular leadership, and the moral fiber of the people was disintegrating. The religious scholars, once the guardians and arbiters of morals, had become wanderers and accommodated the wishes of political and military adventurers who had coined states for themselves, thereby putting an end to the unity of the country and, at the same stime, endangering its Muslim character. Ibn Hazm was fully aware of the imminent danger, and became a vocal critic of the religious and political institutions upon which depended the success or failure of Hispano-Arabic society.

Ibn Hazm entertained the idea of reforming the social, political, and religious institutions of the land, hoping thereby to prevent their total collapse. He was convinced that Muslim Spain was on a self-destructing path and the cause grew from within Andalusian society itself, which had been both complacent and derelict in following the true precepts of Islam. Although he often appeared to be self-righteous and uncompromising, he had a consistency, sincerity, and intellectual integrity which withstood the arguments of his enemies. He had great insight into the major issues of the day, defending his position articulately, with erudition and lucidity. He was intellectually sensitive, yet he defied persecution, indignity, ostracism, and ridicule continuing his work when he could have easily settled for a peaceful life on one of his family's estates or at a small court in al-Andalus.

Ibn Hazm used his genius to fight for the veracity of Islam, which he conceived to be the surest way to happiness and well-being on earth as well as in heaven. Islam is called the truth that has been, was, and is, transcending time, space and vacuum, and remaining through eternity. Although his conception of Islam conformed to the traditional framework, Ibn Hazm felt strongly that Islam was in dire need of being understood on the basis of a new criterion and with a critical approach, thereby eliminating much of what had been accepted as the exclusive norms. He viewed the traditional criteria for arriving at juridicotheological decisions — such as imitation *(taqlid)*, analogy *(qiyas)*, personal opinion *(ra'y)*, preference *(istihsan)*, and interpretation *(ta'wil)* — as innovations *(bida‘)* that should be set aside; instead, decisions should be based upon a new look at the Qur'an, the proven traditions (sunan) of the Prophet, and in the last resort, the consensus *(ijma‘)* of the venerable Companions of the Prophet. In other words, the holy texts *(nass,* pl. *nusus),* comprising the Qur'an and the authenticated traditions, ought to be the sole guiding criteria for arriving at juridico-theological decisions. They should be understood in the context of what they say rather than what they may imply. This can be done by adhering strictly to the apparent meaning *(zahir)* of the text and by conforming to the grammatical and lexical rules of the Arabic language.

This new approach would put an end to some of the legal practices as embodied in the major legal schools —Malikism, Hanafism, Shafi'ism, and Hanbalism — that had wide currency in the Islamic countries. It shocked the religious scholars, particularly those of Muslim Spain, who had slavishly followed the legal doctrine of Malik Ibn Anas. Ibn Hazm was charged with heresy, but he was not deterred. He labelled his critics ignoramuses who had been enchained by old authorities without ever troubling to test the soundness of their practices.

To clarify his point, Ibn Hazm argued that no mortal can add to or subtract from the holy texts *(nusus)* and that the most venerable leaders of Islam, including the companions of the Prophet and the rightly guided caliphs *(al-rashidun)*, are subject to human error. These leaders, like the founders of legal schools and other reputable religious scholars, were virtuous and honorable men who has been rewarded for their individual inquiry *(ijtihad)* whether it resulted in truth or error. However, they could not be given credit for their errors, or be allowed to place themselves on the level of Almighty God and His Prophet. Ibn Hazm delved into Islamic religious history, showing the flimsy foundations of the various Islamic sects that had sprung up in his own time. He also viewed Islam vis-a-vis other world religions — Judaism, Christianity, Zoroastrianism, Buddhism, and Hinduism — showing the superiority of Islam over all of them.

Ibn Hazm emerged from his inquiries with a clear-cut religious perspective that pervaded his thoughts and activity. He was convinced that all worldly things, including the sicences, were subordinate to Islam. Thus, in order for the sciences to have any validity or to serve a useful purpose, they ought to be ancillary and preparatory to the understanding of the divine revelation *(shari'ah)*, which is, the final account,the greatest and noblest of all the sciences. His political ideas were also based on and permeated by religious considerations.he had hoped to bring the faithful to understand and practice Islam as it should be, and he insisted on shifting the political leadership from pretenders and adventurers to the legitimate rule of the caliphate, sanctioned by religious law. He felt, perhaps, that through these means — and only through these means — the golden age of spiritual and political Islam could be revived.

Ibn Hazm had a complex personality that was shaped by the convulsive events surrounding him during most of his life. Those events were overwhelming and frustrating and would have shattered many an insensitive soul. Yet Ibn Hazm survived their impact, and was able to express his scholarly talent as poet, litterateur, literary critic, historian, logician, philosopher, theologian, jurist, and polemicist. Although he was frowned upon by the majority of Muslims, he had many good things to offer in his enormous literary legacy. However great the antagonism against him, and in spite of the heavy restrictions that were placed on the dissemination of his works, his ideas survived to influence some men among succeeding generations.

2. The Objective of the Work

Owing to the wide scope of his learning and his radical approach to the whole religious structure, Ibn Hazm has an important place in the intellectual history of Islam. Nevertheless, he has been relatively neglected until recently by both Western and Eastern scholars. Few studies of his works exist, and there is scarcely anything about him in English. Thus, this work is intended to give a general outline of Ibn Hazm's life and works. Particular emphasis rests on his conception and classification of the sciences, as set forth in *The Categories of the Sciences (Maratib al-'ulum)*. I found a new manuscript of this work in Rabat, Morocco, while working on Hispano-Arabic manuscripts under a Fulbright-Hayes Fellowship. The Rabat manuscript[1] will be edited and collated with an Istanbul manuscript[2] which has already been edited by Ihsan 'Abbas. The edition will be accompanied by an English translation and analysis of its content with due attention to Ibn Hazm's views on the sciences as they are found in his other works.

In his *Categories of the Sciences,* Ibn Hazm sets forth a new approach to the sciences against the bakcground of a long drawn-out controversy as to whether the sciences are in conflict with one another, or as to whether they function in a harmonious and complementary way. Although Ibn Hazm appears to establish a hierrachy of the sciences, he does recognize their interdependence. He indicates the utility of each of the sciences and the manner in which it might be pursued without neglecting even those which he considers "spurious" sciences, such as astrology and alchemy, the idea being to enable the individual to discern between right and wrong. In short, he advocates an ideal liberal arts education to be pursued by everyone to the extent of one's ability. Although the sciences had been discussed by a number of Muslim scholars before Ibn Hazm, it does appear that his categorization of the sciences differs from those of his predecessors, mainly, al-Farabi, al-Khuwarizmi, the Brethern of Purity, and Ibn al-Nadim, and also from those of his contemporary compatriots, Sa'id of Toledo and Ibn 'Abd al-Barr. The main difference between his categorization and those of his predecessors and contemporaries rests on Ibn Hazm's insistence on the harmonization and interdependence of the religious and secular sciences, with the emphasis on the pursuit and study of as many of them as possible within the ability of the individual.[3]

By contrasting Ibn Hazm's views on the sciences with those of his predecessors, contemporaries, and some of his successors, it is hoped that this study will contribute to an understanding of the man and his ideas. It is also hoped that the work will shed some light on the history of ideas in the Middle Ages, not only for medieval Islam, but for European thought as well.

3. Sources

Although Ibn Hazm's views on and his harsh criticism of the socioreligious system of his day were abhorrent to the majority of Muslims, who were committed to existing juridico-theological schools, medieval biobibligraphical data on him is relatively abundant.[4] Information about Ibn Hazm recorded by Hispano-Arabic and, later, by Eastern authors is inadequate in many respects, but medieval sources do offer valuable insights into how the man and his ideas were viewed at that point in the intellectual History of Islam.

However, valuable these sources, they can never be a good substitute for the precious information found in the exant works of Ibn Hazm. Although he was neglected in the past, modern Western and Eastern scholars have in recent times been paying more attention to his works. In fact, they are being revived in the Arab world and Ibn Hazm is looked upon as the epitome of a free thinker and as one of the great luminaries in the intellectual history of Islam. Thus, four types of materials are being used in this work. They are: a) medieval sources; b) Ibn Hazm's works; c) Western works; and d) modern Arabic works.

a) Medieval Sources

Medieval sources are given in a chronoligcal order and in an abbreviated form as follows:[5]

Sa'id (d. 1070), *Tabaqat,* 101-102
Humaydi (d. 1095), *Judhwah,* no. 708
Ibn Khaqan (d. ca. 1140), *Matmah,* 55-56
Ibn Bassam (d. ca. 1147), *Dhakhirah,* I:i, 140-147
Ibn al-'Arabi al-Ishbili (d. 1148), *'Aswasim,* I, 85 and II, 67 ff.
Ibn Bashkuwal (d. 1185), *Silah,* no. 894
Dabbi (d. 1203). *Bughyah,* nos. 412 and 1204
Balawi (d. 1207), *Alif ba',* 383 and 416
Marrakushi (d. 1223), *Mu'jib,* 93-97
Yaqut (d. 1229), *Irshad,* V, 86-97/XII, 235-257 (Cairo ed.)
Shaqundi (d. 1232), *Risalah,* in Maqqari, *Nafh,* III, 192
Ibn 'Arabi (d. 1240), *Futuhat,* II, 519.
Qifti (d. 1248), *Tarikh,* 232
Ibn al-Abbar (d. 1260), *Hullah,* I: 18, 126, 128, 203, 206, 221, 238, 255, 271, 275; II: 2, 8, 13, 71, 128, 366
Ibn Sa'id (d. 1274), *Mughrib,* I, 345-357
Ibn Khallikan (d. 1282), *Wafayat,* III, 13-17
Nuwayri (d. 1332), *Nihayah,* I, 94-95
Dhahabi (d. 1348), *Tadhkirah,* III, 341-
_____ *Siyar,* in *Majma',* X (1941), 433-449
_____ *Tabaqat,* XIV, 15
Yafi'i (d. 1367), *Mir'at,* III, 79-81
Subki (d. 1370), *Tabaqat,* II, 184 ff.
Ibn Kathir (d. 1373), *Bidayah,* XII, 91-92, also XI 247-252

Ibn al-Khatib (d. 1374), *A'mal,* 14, 26, 132, 142, 194
_____ *Ihatah,* I, 216
Ibn Khaldun (d. 1406), *Muqaddimah,* I, 414; II, 60; III, 6
Ibn Hajar al-'Asqalani (d. 1449), *Lisan,* IV, 198-202
Maqqari (d. 1632), *Nafh,* II, 77-84; III, 555
Hajji Khalifah (d. 1657), *Kashf,* I, 346; II, 389 and 522; III, 139 and 617; V, 428 and 486; VI, 278, etc.
Ibn al-'Imad (d. 1679), *Shadharat,* III, 299-300.

Among such medieval authors were Ibn Hazm's own friends — with whom he shared common views, aspirations, and concern for the present and future of al-Andalus. The poet Ibn Shuhayd (d. 134)[6], his companion in youth, dedicated a poem, "What a precious thing I have in Ibn Hazm, who was my succor in my troubles and afflictions." The prince poet 'Ubaydallah b. 'Abd al-Rahman al-Nasir says that Ibn Hazm graces the people like musk and singing guitar *('ud)*[7]; he is the scion of nobility who uses his energy *('ud)* in science; his legal decisions rejuvenate his religious beliefs, and from his gifts sprout his strength *('ud)*[8].

The second, larger group of contemporaries saw Ibn Hazm as a threat to their social position, if not to the whole morale and religious structure of the time. He was accused of being ignorant, weakminded, lacking in discernment, self-righteous and arrogant, a man who had gone beyond the ordinances of the Qur'an and traditions, questioning the companions of the Prophet and every scholar of the past.[9] Ibn Hazm refutes the charges, retorting that his enemies were merely ignorant and had neglected the study of the religious sciences.[10] As for the charges that he was infatuated with the books of the Ancients (philosophers), fatalists and heretics, he challenges his accusers and inquires whether or not they had ever read books on logic, or the works of Euclid and Ptolemy.[11]

Even people congenial to him showed their apprehension about his vocal and radical views. Ibn Hawwat (d. 1058)[12], whom Ibn Hazm considered the best judge he ever knew,[13] appears to have complained in a letter of having been misquoted by Ibn Hazm and also to have stated:

"Had it not been for the fear of the troublemakers and for the calamity of being ruled by ignoramuses, I would write down your utterances and doctrines, would spread them in the world, and would declaim them."[14]

Ibn Hazm was unhappy about his friend's ambivalent stand, and replied that one should fear no one. Ibn Hazm goes on to restate to his "good friend" the fundamentals and validity of the faith that should be defended above any other consideration.

Sa'id, contemporary Andalusian biographer of Ibn Hazm, remarks that Ibn Hazm, besides composing a book on logic, "penetrated quite deeply into the religious sciences, acquiring much more of them than anyone before him in al-Andalus had. He wrote many books with a noble objective."[15] Ibn Hayyan, the great historian of al-Andalus, who does not appear to have much sympathy for Ibn Hazm and his views, acknowledges his wide erudition, saying that "Abu Muhammad knew many sciences such as traditions, jurisprudence, polemics, genealogy, and all that is connected with belles-lettres. In addition, he concerned himself with many of the ancient sciences such as logic and philosophy. He has many works on those sciences, though they contain mistakes and rubbish, particularly his book on logic. This was so because of his audacity of encompassing all the sciences."[16]

In contrast, al-Humaydi, faithful pupil and propagator of Ibn Hazm's works and doctrine, venerated his teacher: "We have not seen his like — may he rest in peace. He combined sagacity, quick learning, nobility of character, and religiosity... Nor have we seen anyone who could improvise poetry more quickly than he did."[17] The biographers Ibn Bashkuwal[18] and al-Dabbi[19] reiterate the statements of Sa'id and al-Humaydi. The historian al-Marrakushi adds:

"And if we introduce this section about this man [Ibn Hazm] which is out of place and far removed from the objective of this work, it is because he is now-a-days the most famous scholar of al-Andalus and the most talked-about man in the assemblies *(majalis)* of leaders and scholars. He is quite renowned because of his opposition to the school of Malik and because of his strict adherence to the Zahirite doctrine. To my knowledge, no one before him had ever attained such a fame among us. His followers among us as well as in al-Andalus have increased now-a-days."[20]

In exalting the excellence of al-Andalus, al-Shaqundi (d. 1232) inquires: "Do you have anyone in the religious sciences like Abu Muhammad Ibn Hazm, who renounced the post of minister *(wizarah)* and wealth, and pursued the path of knowledge, which he considered to be above any other station?"[21]

These statements by his contemporaries, or near contemporaries, from al-Andalus and the Maghrib (North Africa) were, by and large, incorporated in biographical sketches about Ibn Hazm by Eastern authors. The Eastern biographers Yaqut and Ibn Khallikan, for instance, devote ample space in their biographical dictionaries to Ibn Hazm. They were followed by al-Dhahabi (d. 1348), Ibn Kathir (d. 1373), and Ibn al-'Imad (d. 1679), among others. It is significant that the Shafi'ite jurist and historian al-Dhahabi displayed a great interest in Ibn Hazm, with long entries in both his *Siyar* and *Tadhkirah* being devoted to Ibn Hazm:

"He is indeed a leader in Islamic studies; erudite in the transmission of traditions *(naql)* and without equal in spite of his dryness and Zahirite exaggerations with respect to the branches *(furu')* of the law as opposed to its roots *(usul)*.

"He was not only ill mannered in speech with the religious leaders, but used vile language, insulted, and tore people apart. He was penalized accordingly in that the majority of the scholars turned away from him, ignored his works and had aversion to them. In fact, they were committed to fire at one time. Other scholars paid attention to and examined them, criticizing or deriving some benefit from them — either accepting or censuring them. Scholars saw in them either a precious pearl mixed with a firm conviction *(rasf)*, or an insulting query; sometimes they rejoice while at other times they feel astonished. Those who disagreed with him would ridicule and attack him. Perfection is a rare thing; some espouse it while others forsake it, exept the Messenger of God — May God's prayer and peace be upon him.

"He brought a new life to the various sciences; was skillful in the transmission of traditions, and proficient in poetry and prose. He was religious and good; his objectives were noble, and his works useful. He renounced leadership *(ri'asah)* and clung to his home, devoting himself to knowledge. We neither exalt him, nor treat him harshly, for great scholars before us had extolled him. Abu Hamid al-Ghazzali said, 'I found a book on the names of God by Abu Muhammad Ibn Hazm which indicates his great knowledge of the religious sciences *(hifz)* and his fecund mind.' "[22]

Moreover, al-Dhahabi supports and expresses his admiration for the goal Ibn Hazm had set for himself, that is, adherence to the truth and the search for it without commitment to any particular school of thought.[23] Al-Dhahabi addresses himself to this question in language that Ibn Hazm himself might have used. His statement in full is worth quoting:

"Yes, indeed, he who had reached the rank of individual inquiry *(ijtihad)* and is acknowledged by a number of scholars does not swallow imitation easily. Conversely, individual inquiry is never permitted to the beginner and the common people who memorize the Qur'an, or a good portion of it. How could these people engage in individual inquiry? What will they say? On what will they build? How could they fly without having feathers? There is still a third group consisting of highly learned people *(al-faqih al-muntahi)* who are vigilant and discerning traditionists and who had learned in a systematic and summary manner the branches of the law, had studied books on the rules of the roots of the law, and had read grammar. They had added to these virtues the learning of and commenting on the Qur'an, and had the ability of *disputatio.* These are the people who had attained the rank *(rutbah)* of the prescribed individual inquiry *(al-ijtihad al-muqayyad),* and who are qualified to ponder on the proofs presented to them by scholars. Thus, when the truth of a question becomes clear to the individual, attested to by the holy text *(nass),* and practiced by any of the leading scholars such as Abu Hanifah,[24] Malik,[25] al-Thawri,[26] al-Awza'i,[27] al-Shafi'i,[28] Abu 'Ubayd,[29] Ahmad Ibn Ishaq,[30] and others, it ought to be followed and adhered to faithfully, avoiding any licenses. In other words, the individual must be careful, and will not be bound by imitation *(taqlid)* after having presented the evidence *(hujjah).* In this case, however, it may happen that the individual may be afraid that jurists would make trouble for him; he would then conceal the truth and appears not to espouse it. On the other hand, it may happen that his soul may delight with the truth and that he may like to bring it out by virtue of an inner impulse and regardless of the consequences. But how many a man spoke the truth and followed God's commands and upon whom God brought harm because of their bad intention and love for worldly things. This is a secret and current malady in the soul of jurists as it is in the soul of dissipators from among the wealthy people, the leaders of abeyance of rights *(wuquf)*, and those of ornamented tombs...

"O God, make your religion victorious and bestow success on your worshippers. He who seeks knowledge for material utility *('amal)* despises knowledge and will cry over his soul. Likewise, he who seeks knowledge for schooling, legal decisions, glory and service is stupid and deceitful, he harms people and falls into self-conceit..."[31]

With this almost Hazmi language, al-Dhahabi goes one step further and comes to the defense of Ibn Hazm against those who had downgraded and vilified him. He takes issue with Abu Bakr Ibn al-'Arabi,[32] a committed Malikite jurist and the son of a pupil of Ibn Hazm, who could not see any merit in Ibn Hazm and his doctrine. Al-Dhahabi produces a passage from Ibn al-'Arabi in which there is an acid attack on Ibn Hazm, then he rebutts it. The passage and al-Dhahabi's comment follow:

"The advocates of Zahirism constitute a base gang that climbed to a rank which does not belong to them. They spoke words which they do not understand, and which they took from their Kharijite brethren when 'Ali — may God be please with him — was judged during Siffin[33] with the formula: 'there is no decision except that of God *(la hukm illa li-lah).*' The first innovation I encountered in my travels in the East was the esoteric doctrine *(al-qawl bi-l-batin).* When I returned to al-Andalus, I found the exoteric doctrine *(al-qawl bi-l-zahir)* promoted by a stupid man *(sakhif),* known as Ibn Hazm from the district of Seville, who spread the doctrine in the Maghrib. He first espoused the school of al-Shafi'i, then attached himself to the school of Dawud,[34] and threw everything out, becoming an entity unto himself and claiming to be the religious leader *(imam)* of the Islamic community, setting down and exalting things, making legal decisions and legislating. He attributed to the religion of God what is not there, and to scholars things they did not say, thus shunning them. He was led to anthropomorphism and excesses concerning the essence of God *(dhat Allah)* and His attributes. His temperament *(kawn)* found acceptance among people who did not have any sagacity. When they were asked about the proof of any question, they would fumble, Ibn Hazm and his followers would then laugh at them. The authorities tormented him as the result of his behavior, and opposed him according to what seemed to them to be innovation, or prohibition.

"Upon my return from travel, I found the Zahirites in great number. The fire in their error was scorching. Singlehandedly, I made things hard for them but without much success. I also found among them grudgers who conspired against me to the very end. Sometimes, my soul was swept by them; at others, my teeth grimaced at them while opposing, or stirring trouble for them.

"A man brought to me a volume by Ibn Hazm entitled *Nukat al-Islam,* containing artifices *(dawahi),* which I stripped off with interdictions *(nawahi).* Another man brought a treatise of his on belief *(i'tiqad)* which I refuted in a treatise entitled Glory *('izzah).* But the issue is more abominable than refuting it, since the Zahirites maintain that there is no saying except what God had said and that 'we do not follow anyone except the Messenger of God.' That God does not command people to be guided by anyone, or to follow the guidance of any mortal. They should know that they do not have any proof and that their position is a dreadful stupidity. In consequence, I advise you strongly not to be guided by them; you should always insist on proof from them. For the innovator would be contentious and will never come up with the proof when asked."[35]

To this harsh and even distorted assessment of Ibn al-'Arabi concerning the person and doctrine of Ibn Hazm, al-Dhahabi retorts with a rather balanced statement. He says:

"The judge Abu Bakr — may he rest in peace — was not fair to the teacher of his father in the sciences, nor did he speak about him justly. He went at great length to scorn him. In spite of Abu Bakr's great ability in the sciences, he does not come even close to the rank of Abu Muhammad."[36]

Al-Dhahabi adds elsewhere:

"I personally sympathize with Abu Muhammad because of his love for sound traditions and for his knowledge of them. And if I do not agree with him on many points concerning his views on man, causes *('ilal),* and other ugly things with respect to the roots an branches of the law — and while I admit that he is mistaken about more than one question — I do not consider him an unbeliever and misguided, but I wish him and all Muslims forgiveness and indulgence, and I humble myself before his vast intelligence and wide erudition."[37]

b) Ibn Hazm's Works

Medieval sources do acknowledge the wide erudition and sagacity of Ibn Hazm and, at the same time, his seemingly perpetual confrontation with the religious and political leadership of al-Andalus. But the best source of information about the man is Ibn Hazm's own works. They not only substantiate what medieval authors said about him, but contain a mine of information about his character, life, education, works and numerous polemics, not to mention a lucid exposition of his doctrine which Abu Bakr Ibn al-'Arabi attempted to misrepresent. Although the bulk of Ibn Hazm's works have been lost, enough remains for us to assess the man, his doctrine, and intellectual achievement. His literary legacy is enormous. It is reported by his son al-Fadl that he left some four hundred volumes consisting of 80,000 folios. His contemporary, Sa'id,[38] followed by the historian al-Marrakushi,[39] exclaims that such a productivity is unique in Islam excepting, perhaps, the historian-commentator al-Tabari (d. 923),[40] who was considered the most prolific writer in Islam. However numerous his works, only a fraction of them has been mentioned by biographers, and a still smaller number has come down to us.

Asin lists thirty-three works of Ibn Hazm out of the reported four hundred volumes. Many other titles cited by medieval biographers could be added to his list, beside the various editions of works which have appeared after Asin's publication. H. Ritter discovered a *majmu'ah* (collection of miscellanea) of Ibn Hazm in the Fatih Mosque of Istanbul, no. 2704, consisting of 264 folios and containing sixteen treatises,[42] which Asin described subsequently in his *Codice*,[43] and which were for the most part edited by I. 'Abbas in *Rasa'il*,[44] and *Ibn al-Naghrilah*.[45] Also, 'Abbas edited six other treatises in *Jawami'*[46] and the *Taqrib*,[47] an important work on logic. In 1940, al-Afghani[48] listed some fifty-three works by Ibn Hazm along with an edition of Ibn Hazm's treatise, *Mufadalah*,[49] which was followed by an edition of a treatise entitled *Ibtal*.[50] In addition, al-Afghani edited al-Dhahabi's section of his *Siyar*,[51] which lists titles of some seventy works by Ibn Hazm, among which are ten titles on medicine.[52]. Finally, Haqqi edited the *Hijjah*,[53] and Levi-Provencal the *Jamharah*,[54] which was subsequently reedited by Harun, who, in the introduction to the eidtion, listed thirty-seven titles by Ibn Hazm. More recently, Khalifah[55] in his biography of Ibn Hazm gives fifty-four titles.

In the absence of a complete listing of Ibn Hazm's works, an attempt has been made in this work to give as comprehensive a list as possible. Some one hundred forty-six titles have been identified and listed in alphabetical order in the Appendix. However, it is difficult to determine the accuracy of those titles. It should also be noted that the number of titles may be deceiving in that Ibn Hazm, as an active lecturer and polemicist, gave titles to his many lectures, which were later incorporated into the body of his major works, as can be adduced from his *Fisal*.

At any rate, the extant and published works of Ibn Hazm, however few should constitute a solid basis for evaluating his erudition and ability as a scholar. Besides the *Categories of the Sciences*, I have availed myself of virtually all the published works of Ibn Hazm, which include the *Tawq, Fisal, Ihkam, Nubudh, Muhalla, Akhlaq, Taqrib, Nukat, Ibtal, Hijjah, Talkhis, Risalatan*, and other treatises.[56]

c) Western Scholarship

Despite his uncommon intellectual achievement, Ibn Hazm did not receive attention from nineteenth-century Western Orientalism in proportion to his talent and accomplishments. His major works - *Fisal, Ihkam,* and *Muhalla* - are still in need of scholarly editions. Writing in the 1920's the Spanish scholar Asin Palacios lamented the neglect of Ibn Hazm: He placed Ibn Hazm on the level of such philosophers of Muslim Spain as Ibn Bajjah, Ibn Gabirol, Ibn Rushd and Maimonides,[57] and in addition considered Ibn Hazm a gifted theologian, jurist, poet, and literary man.[58]

However his contribution might be assessed, no Arabist could wholly ignore Ibn Hazm in the context of any study of the intellectual history of Islam and, to some extent, in the context of Medieval European thought. In the nineteenth century, the Dutch scholar Dozy[59] gave an account of the life and work of Ibn Hazm, placing, however, too much emphasis on his ethnic background. In addition, Dozy,[60] followed by Wustenfeld[61] and Pons Boigues,[62] dealt with Ibn Hazm in his capacity as a historian. Goldziher[63] and Schreiner[64] dealt with his Zahirite doctrine; Steinschnedier[65] and Friedlander[66] touched upon his polemics.

From the beginning of the twentieth century, more attention was paid to Ibn Hazm's ideas and doctrine, MacDonald,[67] Horten,[68] Tritton[69] and Gardet and Anawati[70] dealt with some aspects of his juridico-theological ideas. But the man most responsible for bringing to the fore the great genius of Ibn Hazm's was Asin Palacios, who made several studies of Ibn Hazm's ideas. After analyzing Ibn Hazm's *Akhlaq,*[71] Asin undertook the translation of the work into Spanish, depicting Ibn Hazm as a moralist.[72] However, Asin's most impressive work was his translation of Ibn Hazm's *Fisal* into Spanish along with an introductory volume on his life, works, and ideas. Although the translation contains omissions and paraphrasing, it constitutes a remarkable achievement. Also, Asin translated into Spanish a chapter from the *Ihkam* which deals with the nature and origin of language.[73] Asin's concern with Ibn Hazm can be matched only by the works of Arnaldez, who, besides his valuable study on the nexus of language and theology in the doctrine of Ibn Hazm,[74] made penetrating studies of Ibn Hazm's polemics,[75] his conception of Holy War,[76] and the place of reason in his system.[77] Finally came Nykl,[78] who devoted an article to *Akhlaq,* and Tomiche, who rendered *Akhlaq* into French along with an edition of the Arabic text and an introduction about the life and works of Ibn Hazm.

However, Ibn Hazm is best known to the West through his literary work, the *the Tawq al-ḥamamah* (The Dove's Ring), dealing with love and lovers. In the nineteenth century, it was noticed by Dozy[80] von Schack,[81] and Pons Boigues.[82] In 1914 the work was edited by D.K. Petrof, and subsequently translated into English by Nykl and Arberry; into Russian by Salie; into German by Weisweiler; into French by Bercher; into Italian by Gabrieli; and into Spanish by Garcia Gomez[83] Each translation is preceded a good introduction. In addition, the *Tawq* has found ample space in general works on Arabic literature by Gonzale Palencia,[84] Peres,[85] Nykl,[86] Gibb,[87] Pellat,[88] Chejne,[89] and others. Although the relation between Arabic lyrical poetry and that of the troubadours is still shrouded by controversies, the *Tawq* is considered to have had a great impact on the lyrical poetry of Spain and Southern France.

Ibn Hazm has been receiving more attention in other areas as well. Seco de Lucena devoted an article to his historical work *al-Nukat,*[90] Bosch[91] studied him as a genealogist; and Rosenthal considered his views on history,[92] knowledge,[93] and the classification of the sciences.[94] Finally some aspects of his polemics have been discussed by Friedlander,[95] Di Matteo,[96]

Garcia Gomez,[97] and Perlmann.[98] Bio-bibliographical information about Ibn Hazm is to be found in Brockelmann,[99] *The Encyclopedia of Islam,* Sarton,[100] and Sezgin.[101] In sum, Ibn Hazm has been regaining his rightful place in the history of ideas. Nicholson calls him "the greatest scholar and most original genius of Muslim Spain."[102] Gibb considers him to be the chief figure of the eleventh century, and his *Tawq* to be "one of the few works in Arabic literature with an immediate and universal appeal."[103] Pellat esteems him as an original poet on a par with Ibn Shuhayd, and certainly one of the most refined and fecund literateurs of Muslim Spain.[104] In 1963, the ninth centennial of Ibn Hazm was observed in Cordova by Spanish dignitaries and numerous Arabists. A number of papers were presented during the celebration, and a modest status of Ibn Hazm was erected in his supposed birthplace.

d) Modern Arabic Scholarship

Lately, Ibn Hazm, has also received a great deal of attention from modern Arab scholars. 'Abbas, al-Afghani,[105] and Hajji, among others, have edited some of his works, and the Arabic presses have printed the major works of Ibn Hazm (albeit in unsatisfactory editions). The University of Damascus has prepared a dictionary of juridical terms used by Ibn Hazm in his massive *Muhalla.*[106] In their general works, Mubarak,[107] Haykal,[108] 'Abbas,[109] Dayah,[110] and others place Ibn Hazm among the major prose writers, poets, and literary critics. Far from being viewed as a heretic, Ibn Hazm is now considered one of the major thinkers of Islam. As al-Afghani states in his biography:

> "Whoever reads the legacy of Ibn Hazm with care will have to admire a great intellect, a fertile mind, a profundity, and an astonishing genius. And whoever studies his life will be overwhelmed by the sanctity of a fighter who elevated the nature of free thought, and applied it to all schools of thought . . .
>
> And if there is nothing else in Ibn Hazm besides being a free thinker and the upholder of truth to the point that good and bad spirits conspired against him, it would be sufficient for a person like me to have the incentive of loving and respecting him."[111]

Abu Zahrah, the biographer of major Muslim jurists, devotes a full study to Ibn Hazm and his juridical views and considers him a reasonable man, but unique among jurists; he distinguished himself as a scholar, traditionist, poet and prose writer.[112] He made use of both the rational method *(al-minhaj al-'aqli)*[113] and the Islamic method *(al-minhaj al-Islami)*[114] to arrive at the truth, thus not differing in objectives with other established legal schools.

Hajiri and Khalifah gave a profile of Ibn Hazm with special reference to his literary activities. Hajiri saw in Ibn Hazm "a very strong personality, a solid and firm intellect, a meticulous and wide knowledge, a firm faith, an enormous capacity for penetrating into the very essence of the questions he dealt with, his power of discerning what could be behind those questions, his ability in debate and disputation, and his power of persuasion and arguments."[115] He concludes:

> "And whatever opinion one may have about Ibn Hazm and his Zahirite school, there is no doubt in the fact that this book of ours shows a man with an independent personality, a powerful and free intellect, and with an open and wide horizon . . . Thus, it behooves us to place him in the highest position among us, to elevate him to the loftiest summit in our intellectual history, and make him a radiant and lofty example with which to guide the young generation that is still beset by social corruption."[116]

Thus, Ibn Hazm is being rediscovered, and his ideas and approach to major religious, social, and educational issues may well have further impact on Muslim thought.

4. The Impact of Ibn Hazm's Ideas

The question of determining the impact of a man's ideas on his contemporaries and succeeding generations is difficult under normal circumstances, and more difficult with a man who was declared a heretic and whose works were suppressed and burned. But ideas cannot be locked in a cell, particularly when they appeal to both the heart and the mind, and convey in some measure the enduring realities in times of distress and dislocation. In spite of the stringent measures imposed, Ibn Hazm was famed in his own time. His ideas were made known through his students, numerous lectures, and many publications and were accessible to a large number of people from within and outside of al-Andalus. This is corroborated by his biographers from East and West, and even admitted by some of his staunchest enemies.

However, not all the people who had access to his ideas had the courage to admit their validity or to acknowledge their indebtedness to Ibn Hazm. Therefore, the impact of his views on succeeding scholars can only be inferred by studying the chronological development of later philosophies, a system which leaves much to be desired. There are many instances of similarites between his views and those of some leading Muslim scholars, who are, by and large, committed to established doctrines. They could not afford to be identified with a well-known and dangerous heretic, let alone with his ideas that cast grave doubt on the validity of almost all the acknowledged juridico-theological schools of the Islamic community.

Nevertheless, evidence of the presence of Ibn Hazm's ideas is attested to by the historian al-Marrakushi,[117] who speaks about the popularity of Ibn Hazm, and his works in the twelfth century, and by Abu Bakr Ibn al-'Arabi,[118] a staunch adversary of Ibn Hazm. Furthermore, Ibn Hazm had a good number of able pupils who were enthusiastic about the master and his doctrine, and some of whom traveled far and wide, spreading his doctrine. Goldziher,[119] followed by Asin Palacios,[120] supplies an impressive list of people who were followers of or influenced by Ibn Hazm's school, known as Hazmiyyah. They include such towering figures as Sa'id of Toledo,[121] Ibn 'Abd al-Barr,[122] al-Humaydi,[123] Abu Muhammad Ibn al-'Arabi, [124] Al-Ghazzali,[125] the great mystic Ibn 'Arabi, [126] the philosopher theologian Ibn Rushd[127] the grammarian Abu Hayyan,[128] al-Dhahabi,[129] al-Sha'rani,[133] and others. Although a great deal of research is needed to determine the extent of Ibn Hazm's influence with regard to specific cases, one may follow some of the persuasive suggestions already made by Asin in this connection, allowing some modifications with respect to some individuals. For instance, Asin lists Sa'id (d. 1070) and Ibn 'Abd al-Barr (d. 1071) as disciples of Ibn Hazm, but all indications are that although they knew Ibn Hazm and his works, these two men do not appear to have espoused Ibn Hazm's doctrine. In the case of Ibn 'Abd al-Barr, the contrary may be the case.[131]

As for al-Humaydi (d. 1095) and Abu Muhammad Ibn al-Arabi (d. 1099), they are known to have been direct pupils of Ibn Hazm, and confessed Zahirites. Both traveled to the East, met leading scholars there, and most probably disseminated the doctrine and works of their master. al-Humaydi studied under Ibn Hazm in Mallorca for a number of years until he and his teacher were impelled to leave the island about 1048.[132] He became one of the most articulate and vocal followers of the master. al-Humaydi not only follows Ibn Hazm's doctrine, but relied on him for much of the historical information in his *Judhwah* and other works. In addition, he made a collection of Ibn Hazm's poems and arranged them alphabetically.[133]

Abu Muhammad Ibn al-'Arabi (d. 1099), the father of the famous theologian Abu Bakr (d. 1148) relates that he accompanied Ibn Hazm for seven years, studying a goodly number of his works.[134] He appears to have remained faithful to his teacher's doctrine. Perhaps his enthusiasm for it did not sit well with his son, who became the archenemy of Ibn Hazm's doctrine, refuting it in several of his works.[135]

The question of the relationship between the ideas of Ibn Hazm and those of al-Ghazzali (d. 1111) is not easy to establish on the basis of the information available — although there are ample indications of an affinity in their ideas and objectives. Chronologically, Ibn Hazm precedes al-Ghazzali. The great Eastern theologian in all probability knew a great deal more about the scholar than his acknowledged familiarity with Ibn Hazm's works on the beautiful names of God;[136] this is likely because of the wide circulation of books and the uninterrupted travel between East and West. In their travels in the East al-Humaydi and Abu Muhammad Ibn al-'Arabi must have made the doctrine and works of their teacher well known among a goodly number of Eastern scholars, including al-Ghazzali himself.

But a definite answer to the relationship of Ibn Hazm and al-Ghazzali must await detailed investigation; collation of texts on particular questions would be one way of arriving at any determination. In the meantime, Asin's suggestions recognizing several similarites between the two men should not be ruled out. Ibn Hazm and al-Ghazzali were enjoined by a similar and intense urge to get at the truth; each had a restless mind and enough valid answers to the many juridico-theological questions facing the Islamic community in matters of beliefs and practice; each was concerned with the relationship between faith and reason, and had a deep commitment to the Qur'an and the authenticated Traditions as the embodiment of the truth. Both appear to attack the excesses of philosophers, or pretenders to philosophy, for their overemphasis on natural phenomena and for ignoring the Divine Revelation, which is, in the final account, the sole container of the truth.[137] Likewise, they ridiculed the limitation of the religious scholars, who more often than not frowned upon the natural sciences and failed to distinguish the natural pheomena from divine acts and will.[138] Although both conceded a great utility to human intellect, they were in agreement that the intellect is not capable of penetrating or grasping the essence and the mystery of Divine Revelation. For both of them, logic was an indispensable tool for elucidating and establishing proofs *(burhan,* pl., *barahin)*, and both wrote popular treatises on logic to facilitate its use and comprehension among a wider audience.[139] Finally, the conception of knowledge, its nature, content, pursuit, and the method of acquiring it were paramount in their thinking.

But though these similarities bring the two men together, there remain some basic differences that separate them. Ibn Hazm revolted against the widely accepted juridico-theological schools by giving form and substance to an almost defunct literalist doctrine (Zahirism), whereas al-Ghazzali remained basically shafi'ite in law. Ash'arite in dogma, and Sufi in morals - all of which were anathema to Ibn Hazm.[140]

The reported popularity of Ibn Hazm during the twelfth century, in which the Almohad dynasty arose (ca. 1121-1269), is significant in connection with three leading figures of the time. They were Ibn Tumart (d. 1130), the founder of the dynasty, and the two great philosophers Ibn Tufayl (d. 1185) and Ibn Rushd (d. 1198). These highly cultured men must have known a great deal about Ibn Hazm, whose doctrine appears to have received encouragement from the Almohad rulers. The plausible tolerance of Zahirism by Almohad leadership may be traced back to Ibn Tumart, who appears to have shared Ibn Hazm's aversion to the rigidity of the Malikite legal school and to the apparent neglect of the study of the Qur'an and Traditions. In consequence, Ibn Tumart hoped, as Ibn Hazm had earlier, to reform and rejuvenate religious beliefs and practices. In about 1107, he emigrated to the East to further his education. There he became acquainted with the teachings of leading jurists and came into contact with great teachers, among whom was probably the aging al-Ghazzali.[141] With his wide exposure to the several legal schools, orthodox theology, Mu'tazilism, Shi'ism, and other juridico-theological currents, Ibn Tumart developed an eclectic doctrine that was not lacking in Zahirite elements. In the manner of Ibn Hazm, Ibn Tumart held that the religious law *(Shari'ah)* was in dire need of being understood properly in accordance with the Qur'an, Traditions, and the consensus of the companions of the Prophet. Although these conceptions were common to all the juridico-theological schools, he insisted on studying anew the religious texts, a requirement that was an essential part of Ibn Hazm's doctrine. Ibn Tumart denounced the imitation *(taqlid)* of the Malikite jurists, and exposed the other legal systems to further scrutiny. He asserted that God's unity *(tawhid)* means complete spiritualizing of the conception of God, an idea which reflects the influence of al-Ghazzali and Ibn Hazm.[142] However, in his capacity as the "infallible imam' *(al-imam al-ma'sum)*, he reserved to himself the prerogative of allegorical interpretation *(ta'wil)* which Ibn Hazm repudiated vehemently.[143]

The Almohads remained faithful to the teaching of Ibn Tumart, continuing the inquiry into the various aspects of religion and reaching conclusions that were in some respects similar to those reached by Ibn Hazm almost a century earlier. The Almohad study of philosophy resulted in the harmonization of faith and reason, an idea propounded earlier by Ibn Hazm, followed by Ibn Tufayl and Ibn Rushd. These two men of great erudition combined the secular and the religious disciplines, excelling as religious scholars, philosophers, and physicians. In his philosophical novel *Hayy,* Ibn Tufayl not only brings to the fore the harmony of faith and reason, but delves into the whole cognitive process, from the knowledge acquired by the senses to that gained from experience; and from the knowledge of worldly existence to the contemplation of the heavens and the universe which will lead one to the conclusion that the world is created and had a primeval Creator. These are some of the verities in the revealed religion of Islam.[144]

It is with Ibn Rushd, however, that more striking similarities can be found. Although Ibn Rushd does not acknowledge his indebtedness, (or aversion, for that matter) to Ibn Hazm for the obvious reason that he was a committed Malikite and a Malikite judge, it would be unlikely that he did not know of Ibn Hazm and his works, particularly at a time when they enjoyed great popularity among the Almohads. The point of similarity between the two men are the disavowal of analogical reasonaing *(qiyas)* and allegorical interpretation *(ta'wil)* for arriving at legal decisions. More significant still is their common approach of the religious scholars for denying the role of Revelation. They also shared the notion that the untutored poeple, who constitute the great majority, are incapable of grasping the philosophical truth because to do so requires sagacity, long study, and continuous individual inquiry. Instead, the untutored must rely on faith alone in the acceptance of the Revelation.[145]

As for the great mystic Ibn 'Arabi, his dependence on Ibn Hazm is specifically acknowledged. Ibn 'Arabi holds Ibn Hazm in great reverence when he relates, "I saw the Prophet - may God's prayer and peace by upon him - in a dream, hugging the traditionalist Abu Muhammad Ibn Hazm; the one was concealed in the other to a point of seeing one only."[146] Moreover, Ibn 'Arabi makes other references to the Cordovan master and to his indebtedness to him. He appears to have studied Ibn Hazm's works and to have abridged his *Ibtal* and *Muhalla*. He was Zahirite in law, and rejected analogy, personal opinion, and imitation.[147] Asin believes that Ibn 'Arabi's indebtedness to Ibn Hazm is unquestionable. Both admitted the limitation of reason in grasping the divine essence, repudiated human authority on matters of adding to or subtracting anything from the holy texts, and advocated complete reliance on the Qur'an, Traditions, and the consensus, yet allowed ample room for individual inquiry *(ijtihad)*. Finally, both held the view that the beautiful names of God are those which appear in the Qur'an. However, they differed in that Ibn Hazm insisted on the external meaning *(zahir)* of the texts, while Ibn 'Arabi advocated their esoteric meaning *(batin)*, which will be grasped not by reason, but through mystical experience along.[148] Later, Ibn 'Arabi had an enthusiastic follower in the Egyptian mystic al-Sha'rani (d. 1441), who also followed Ibn Hazm with respect to the beautiful names of God.[149]

Similarity of ideas and affinity of views are apt to abound in a particular cultural area. But it is quite evident that the legacy of Ibn Hazm had been kept much alive for centuries. We have already seen the attitude of the historian al-Dhahabi (d. 1348) toward Ibn Hazm and his doctrine.[150] al Dhahabi not only displays a great familiarity with the works of Ibn Hazm, but approves of his as a great scholar, agreeing with him in several areas, disagreeing in others. This leads us to consider his contemporary and compatriot Ibn Taymiyah (d. 1328), who was born in Damascus. Ibn Taymiyah suffered a shattered career not unlike that of Ibn Hazm, owing to a similar and equally striking approach to the burning juridico-theological problems of the day. It is no coincidence that his reaction and approach to those problems should be almost identical with Ibn Hazm. Although Ibn Taymiyah belonged to, or was identified with, the Hanbalite school of law, he was a polemicist who combatted Muslim sectarianism, Judaism, and Christianity in language reminiscent of that of Ibn Hazm. He earned many enemies in the process, was imprisoned several times, and finally died in prison. He was an indefatigable fighter of what he considered innovations *(bida')*: Sufi cults, the inertia of the legal schools, and philosophy that was in his opinion the most divisive element in the Islamic community. However, he claimed the prerogative of individual inquiry *(Ijtihad)*, refusing to adhere to any school of thought or doctrine and insisting on going back to the Qur'an and Traditions, and to some degree to the consensus, admitting that even the companions of the Prophet could err as individuals. Moreover, he rejected imitation and interpretation, allowing, however, some room for analogical reasoning.[151]

Finally, a study of the relationship of the ideas of Ibn Hazm with those of the great Tunisian sociologist Ibn Khaldun who knew and made use of Ibn Hazm's works. He found Ibn Hazm's *Fisal* useful for Shi'ism, and recommended that it be consulted.[52] He also relied on him as a transmitter of Traditions,[153] considering him an able interpreter of them[154] and a Zahirite,[155] but disagreed with him with respect to the weight of a dinar.[156] In addition to these acknowledgments, there are a number of areas in which the views of the two men coincide regarding historiography,[157] environmental determinism,[158] and the conception of the sciences,[159] mainly, vision,[160] dream,[161] alchemy,[163] astrology,[164] and music.[165]

It should be emphasised that the impact of Ibn Hazm's ideas on his fellow Muslims is only suggestive, awaiting more detailed and careful research of each case in which such an impact is apparent. In such undertaking, difficulties are apt to be encountered, and many a question may remain unresolved. If this is the case within a cultural sphere, the difficulty is compounded when one attempts to determine the impact of a particular cultural sphere upon another when there is no documentation. Thus any attempt to determine the impact of Ibn Hazm's ideas on Western thought will be at best remain suggestive and provisional. As far as can be ascertained, none of Ibn Hazm's many works is known to have been translated into Latin or other European languages during medieval times, when numerous Arabic works by Eastern and Western Muslim authors were translated, particularly into Latin.

Nevethless, the possibility of a relationship between Ibn Hazm's ideas and their Western counterparts should not be ruled out altogether. There are several, perhaps persuasive reasons to justify the possibility of such a relationship. There are many areas in which striking similarities exist between the ideas of Ibn Hazm and those of later European writers. First of all, Ibn Hazm was one of the greatest polemicists of Islam, who used the scholastic method with great skill and precision.[166] His advocacy of the validity of the intellect for establishing proofs and getting at the truth, his espousal of the harmony of philosophy and faith, his recommendation of a truly liberal arts education, and his insistence on the interdependence and harmony of the religious and secular sciences are significant questions that cannot be overlooked. Moreover, his *Tawq* on love and lovers contains all the ingredients of courtly love which are echoed in Andreas Cappelanus' *Art of Courtly Love* and in the *Book of Good Love* by the Archpriest of Hita.[167] Significantly, some of his arguments against Christianity and Judaism appear in the work of Fray Anselmo Turmeda (fifteenth century)[168] and in some fifteenth and sixteenth-century Aljamiado texts.[169]

There are several ways in which that Ibn Hazm's ideas could have penetrated into Western thought: directly through his spirited controversies with Christians and Jews, and indirectly through the works of his co-religionists whose works were translated into Latin. Research in this area could yield interesting results. In the meantime, an affinity of the views of Ibn Hazm vis-a-vis their Western counterparts should not be surprising, given the fact that Ibn Hazm was, after all, living in Muslim Spain in which continuous interaction between Muslims and European Christians at all levels had been established for centuries.[170]

CHAPTER II

THE MAN AND HIS TIME

1. His Genealogy and Family

Ibn Hazm was born in the golden age of al-Andalus at the turn of the tenth century and lived to witness the political, social, and economic dislocation of the country during the eleventh century. His life was in many respects a microcosm of the life of al-Andalus, sharing some of its splendour and much of its tragedy.

Sa'id gives his genealogy as follows: " 'Ali Ibn Ahmad Ibn Sa'id Ibn Hazm Ibn Ghalib Ibn Salih Ibn Khalaf Ibn Ma'dan Ibn Sufyan Ibn Yazid al-Farisi, a client *(mawla)* of Yazid ibn Abi Sufyan Ibn Harb Ibn Umayyah Ibn'Abd Shams.''[1] His surname *(kunyah)* is Abu Muhammad, but he is generally known as Ibn Hazm. The date of his birth is recorded by Ibn Hazm himself and communicated to Sa'id in writing as having taken place "After the morning prayer and before sunrise in the last day of the month of Ramadan of the year 384"[2] which corresponds to November 7, . 994. His place of birth was Munyat al-Mughirah, located in a fashionable suburb of Cordova. He died on the twenty-eight of the month of Sha'ban in the year 456 (August 15, 1064)[3] in Manta Lisham, the home of his ancestors, located in the Algarve in present day Portugal.

According to the historian al-Marrakushi,[4] the genealogy of Banu Hazm was recorded by Ibn Hazm himself in one of his works. The great majority of his contemporary and later biographers seem to have accepted this version.[5] According to Ibn Hazm, his family had for generations been Muslims attached as clients *(Mawali)* to the Umayyad family from the time of their ancestor Yazid, who became a client of the Umayyad Yazid Ibn Abi Sufyan sometime during the seventh century. In his status as client, Yazid must have adopted Islam. His descendant Khalaf is said to have emigrated to al-Andalus sometime during the eighth century.[6] He settled in the district of Niebla, where he was given the village of Manta Lisham in fief.[7]

This respresentation of the genealogy and the conversion of Banu Hazm to Islam becomes the more significant because it was questioned by the historian Ibn Hayyan (d. 1075), a contemporary of Ibn Hazm, who maintained that the Banu Hazm were neo-Muslims *(Muladies,* Ar. *Muwalladun)* of Spanish ancestry *('ajam),* and that Ibn Hazm's father, Ahmad, was the first member of the family to achieve any prominence in the political and religious life of al-Andalus.[8] Following Ibn Hayyan, the Dutch scholar Dozy[9] denies Ibn Hazm's oriental origin and goes so far as to maintain that his ancestors must have been Spanish Christians by virtue of the exquisite sensitivity of Ibn Hazm, which is not found among Arabs. Moreover, Ibn Hazm was to Dozy "the most Christian" among Muslim poets.[10] Dozy was followed by the Spanish scholar Simonet.[11] Garcia Gomez seems to accept the theory of Christian background and considers Ibn Hazm as "one of the purest incarnation of the soul of Muslim Spain."[12]

On the other hand, Asin Palacios, an ordained cleric and biographer of Ibn Hazm, carefully assesses the question of Ibn Hazm's origin. Although he recognizes Ibn Hayyan's reliability as a historian, Asin raises the question of Ibn Hayyan's prejudice toward Ibn Hazm, owing to poltical and religious differences. He concludes: "The genealogy of Ibn Hazm-be it noble or plebian, Christian or Muslim, Arab, Persian or Spanish - could hardly influence the formation of his mental outlook and character."[13]

Asin's statement takes into account the existence of a cultural environment in which the question of racial origin and religious affiliation does not matter much. At any rate, Ibn Hayyan's assessment of the role of the Banu Hazm in the affairs of al-Andalus appears to conform to the available data. All indications are that the Banu Hazm were settled in the Algarve and that old members of the family, before Ibn Hazm's father, do not appear to have played any significant role in the religious and political life of the Islamic community. In fact, there is little information about Ibn Hazm's grandfather, Sa'id, except that he took the family to Cordova sometime in the tenth century when the provinces were in political turmoil and did not offer security for people with middle or low station in society.[14] However, it can be assumed that Sa'id had the means to give his son, Ahmad the best education available, in addition to a strong commitment to Islam and Arabic culure.

Ahmad,[15] the father of Ibn Hazm, was a highly cultured man and an able public servant. He had a wide education in the Arabic sciences: Arabic Grammar and lexicography, literature, oratory, and religious sciences - all of wich constituted an important part of the requirements for holding an official position. His mastery of the Arabic language was widely acknowledged. He is said to have disdained those who spoke defective Arabic or who wrote with clumsy expressions. In addition, he was an able teacher who taught various disciplines under the reigns of al-Hakam II (961-976) and his son and successor Hisham II (976-1009). He left an array of students who made their mark in the intellectual life of al-Andalus.[16] No doubt his qualifications and ability must have helped him to attract the attention of the court, which took him into its employ. He soon climbed the ladder of success, becoming vizier during the 'Amirid dictatorship (976-1009).[17] Ibn Abi 'Amir al-Mansur (d. 1002), who became the virtual ruler following the death of the caliph al-Hakam II, took Ahmad into his confidence and even entrusted him with the government during his absence in 991. This was done in spite of Ahmad's avowed loyalty to the Umayyad house, which Ibn 'Amir had stripped of nearly all power. Thus, through his great ability and shrewdness, Ahmad survived the suspicion of his patron, who was intolerant of potential pretenders and their supporters, and who did not hesitate to dispose of them. Ahmad enjoyed great influence in his position as vizier, lived in luxury among noble and powerful people, and helped members of the family gain wealth and social prestige.[18]

When Ibn Hazm was born in 994, the family had attained wealth, social status, and enviable contacts. Ibn Hazm was reared in sumptuous palaces and was surrounded by many people, including the ladies of the harem, servants, scholars, and notables. Although it appears that Ibn Hazm's father had many concubines, the data suggest that he did not have many offsprings. Ibn Hazm himself refers to a brother about five years his senior.[19] Although he gives many intimate details about himself, the information about the rest of the family is scanty. In fact, he does not mention his mother at all (she may have been a blond, the coloring preferred by his father, himself, and other courtiers).[20] All indications suggest that he was the second but the favored son of the family. By his own account, his childhood was not a happy one. Overprotected, he spent much time at home in the harem without much access to children of his own age. There, he was exposed to the gossip and machinations of the haremwomen who appear to have taught him the Qur'an, some poetry and writing.[21] He tells us that he was frail and nervous, and had a hardening of the heart, extravagant movement, melancholy, bad mood, and propensity to violent outburst.[22] He also had defective lacrymal glands, caused by having taken incense to cure his heart ailment.[23]

Among other details of his life, he relates that he fell madly in love at a tender age with a sixteen-year-old girl who was living in his house and who had great physical and spiritual endowments. She did not respond to his overtures, but he continued to entertain deep affection for her for many years.[24] Still young, he was exposed to the great talents of the day who attended literary sessions at his home and elsewhere. His pupil al-Humaydi[25] reports that at a literary session, Ibn Hazm listened to the famous Sa'id al-Baghdadi,[26] who was attached to the court of Ibn Abi 'Amir. He also had access to the palaces of rulers, and often attended audience.[27]

Social and Political Conditions

About 1009, when he was fifteen years old, things began to change drastically for Ibn Hazm, his family, and Andalusian society as a whole. It was the beginning of the great *fitnah* (revolt) that came to shatter the whole sociopolitical edifice of al-Andalus. The sociopolitical conditions of the time were so complex that events moved swiftly and had grave repercussions for the future of all al-Andalus and, in turn, the Banu Hazm.[28]

The 'Amirids under Ibn Abi 'Amir al-Mansur (976-1002) had managed to establish a dynasty within the ruling dynasty of the Umayyads. Although Ibn Abi 'Amir bore the title of chamberlain *(hajib)*, he had absolute power over the country, relegating the incumbent caliph, Hisham II, to a ceremonial function. Ibn Abi 'Amir became absolute ruler by purging the government of potential enemies, thereby creating a great deal of resentment among the Arab aristocracy in general and the Umayyad ruling house in particular. The rank and file of the Umayyad house felt, and for good reason, that they had been deprived of the privileges and prerogatives of ruling the country with the dynastic rights sanctioned by the religious law. To counteract potential danger from them and their supporters, Ibn Abi 'Amir reorganized the administration and the army, bringing in loyal and submissive people. He imported a large number of Berbers from the African mainland to man the army, and expelled from the army and the administration those Slavs (Ar. Saqalibah)[29] who did not appear loyal to him. Ibn Abi 'Amir was undoubtedly able and determined, and he ruled the country with an iron hand until his death in 1002. Under his rule prosperity and stability continued in al-Andalus, as they had under the great caliphs 'Abd al-Rahman (912-961) and al-Hakam II. He launched many expeditions against the Christians to the north, and not only kept them at bay but made many of them his tributaries. Ibn Abi 'Amir's policies were followed scrupulously by his son and successor, al-Muzaffar (1002-1008). Although the incumbent caliph Hisham continued to be deprived of any power, al-Muzaffar continued in the manner of his father to show deference to the office of the caliphate and to the person of the caliph, always appearing to act on behalf and with full consent of the caliph, who had shown little or no desire to rule.

The careful, though high-handed policy of Ibn Abi 'Amir and his son al-Muzaffar terminated when 'Abd al-Rahman Sanchol, the brother and sucessor of al-Muzaffar, displayed erratic behaviour and aspired to assume the caliphal throne. In spite of common knowledge that the 'Amirids were not eligible for the exalted office of the caliphate because they lacked the requirements of being descendants of the Quraysh tribe, 'Abd al-Rahman Sanchol impelled Hisham II to nominate him as heirapparent. In so doing, he overlooked the religious sensitivity of the Muslim leadership, which was by and large still traditional and even doctrinaire in religious matters. This sensitivity, added to dormant resentment against the 'Amirids, led to open revolt in 1009, when the inhabitants of Cordova became incensed, rose to open revolt, overthrew the submissive caliph Hisham II, and replaced him with the Umayyad Muhammad al-Mahdi. 'Abd al-Rahman Sanchol was put to death, marking the end of the 'Amirid rule.

The new caliph Muhammad proved lacking in statesmanship in a highly explosive situation. He not only made an indiscrimanate purge of 'Amirids and their supporters from government, but allowed his own supporters, drawn for the most part from the populace, to indulge in looting and wanton killing. He declared Hisham II dead by giving a state burial to a man who resembled the deposed caliph. The scandal was soon uncovered. The lawlessness perpetrated by the new caliph engendered a violent reaction from the 'Amirids and their supporters, mainly the mercenary Berbers, who indulged in equally lawless acts. The city of Cordova was plunged into utter confusion, which spread throughout al-Andalus.

The governors of the provinces were ambivalent in their loyalties, adopted a wait-and-see policy, and attempted to hold onto their domains.

In the badly divided country, three major factions emerged: the Arabs and those identified with them, the 'Amirids and their clients, and the Berbers. For the next twenty years (1009-1031), caliphs were put on the throne by the contending groups, and were removd as easily by overt and covert means in the midst of heated passion, bloody revolts, and destruction of life and property, all of which shook the very foundation of Andalusian society.

As for Ibn Hazm's family, it did not fare well. Ibn Hazm's father, Ahmad, who had served the 'Amirids well and managed at the same time to espouse the legitimist cause of the Umayyad house, was caught in a delimma. His mere association with the 'A ′ds was a good reason for the caliph Muhammad to removing him from his post of vizier and impelling him to move from his palace in the government complex of al-Zahirah to his old residence in the suburb of Balat al-Mughirah in western Cordova. Although he appeared to have received amnesty, he was kept under surveillance and placed under heavy restrictions.

The political agitation gained momentum in November 1009 - barely nine months after the accession of Muhammad al-Mahdi - when the Berbers entered Cordova with Christian help, forced Muhammad al-Mahdi out, and placed on the throne their own candidate, the Umayyad Sulayman al-Musta'in bi-llah. The new caliph was identified with and committed to the Berber cause and, like his predecessor, allowed his supporters to destroy and pillage freely. The inhabitants of Cordova reacted in kind, forced Sulayman out, and allowed Muhammad al-Mahdi to return to Cordova and resume the caliphate. Failing for the second time to bring any semblance of order to the city, Muhammad was put to death after forty nine days of rule. The twice deposed Hisham II was reinstated and ruled for the next three years (1010-1013).

This new development should have given some respite to Ibn Hazm's family, but the contrary appears to be true. Ibn Hazm wrote that even after the proclamation of Hisham, his family was still persecuted with hostility and imprisonment.[31] Cordova continued to be beset by disorder, looting, and killing. The aftermath of destruction and waste left the city a health hazard, and a plague that took many lives, including that of Ibn Hazm's brother. Twenty-two-years-old Abu Bakr,[32] who had served the 'Amirids in the High March, died in 1011; Ibn Hazm's father died in Dhu-l-Qi'dah, June 1012.[33] These blows must have left an indelible impression on the eighteen year-old Ibn Hazm. In addition, he was still suffering from his amorous disappointment, and, in 1013, had to swallow a bitter pill of exile when Hisham II was overthrown and put to death by Sulayman. Sulayman's rule was, according to the dictum of the historian Ibn Hayyan, "extremely troublesome, sinister, and abominable from beginning to end."[34] It was at that time that the Berbers had their full revenge, playing havoc in the city, looting, and confiscating property, which included the home of Ibn Hazm.[35]

His Political Career and Exile

It is likely that Ibn Hazm was involved in the political machinations of the day. If so, this would explain his exile. In 1013, he left his native Cordova and took refuge in Almeria at the court of the 'Amirid client Khayran (d. 1029)[36] who had forged a kingdom for himself as early as 1009. It was a reasonable choice; Ibn Hazm had hoped that the 'Amirid's clients would continue to espouse the 'Amirid cause and accept suitable Umayyad tutelage, thereby salvaging and preserving much of the social, political, and economic status they had enjoyed in the past. But the idealistic young Ibn Hazm appears to have underestimated the political realities of the day and the ambitions of the military and political leaders; these men were content in their status as kings and masters of their newly coined domain, regardless of their public declarations of reinstituting the caliphate on firm foundation. Whatever Ibn Hazm's motivation, he adhered fast to the legitimist cause in the Umayyad house in spite of the fact that the Umayyads themselves were ill-organized and often ambivalent about which member of the caliphal house should assume the exalted office. Because of these weaknesses, the Umayyad house played into the hands of different factions, not to mention the numerous rulers who had aspirations of expanding their rule over neighboring territories. This situation eroded the legitimist cause. Thus, Ibn Hazm's hopes that the 'Amirids and their clients, all of whom owed their power to the Umayyads would agree on a candidate for the Caliphate were frustrated. For one thing, in addition to the ambitions of individual leaders, the 'Amirids were not averse to cooperating with Berbers, whom they had imported to man the army, and hence they were able to forge new alliances. This latitude can be seen in the political behaviour of Ibn Hazm's patron, Khayran, who shifted his loyalties as he saw fit. Khayran first embraced the cause of Hisham, and then that of Sulayman. Soon becoming disenchanted with the latter, Khayran adopted in 1016 the dynastic cause of the Shi'ite Ali Ibn Hammud of Ceuta, whom he encouraged to take Cordova under the pretext of regaining the throne for the deposed and already dead Hisham II (Khayran knew from Ibn Hazm himself that Sulayman killed Hisham in 1013).

Ibn Hazm was a staunch orthodox and could not have consented to have a "heretic" Shi'ite assume the Caliphate. This was probably the main reason for the discord between him and Khayran, who decided to commit Ibn Hazm and his close companion Muhammad Ibn Ishaq to jail where they remained for a few months.[37] In the meantime, 'Ali Ibn Hammud entered Cordova, overthrew Sulayman, and assumed the title of the caliph, thus putting an end to the Umayyad dynasty. The rule of the Hammudids (1016-1027) was to last for almost a decade with some interruption owing to internal strife among the Hammudid leadership and the efforts of other leaders to reestablish the Umayyads. The Hammudids failed to give any semblance of unity to the country, and in fact, in Cordova their rule emphasized divisiveness and political maneuvrings. In 1018, Khayran and other leaders in eastern al-Andalus decided to unseat the Hammudids by espousing the cause of the Ummayad 'Abd al-Rahman al-Murtada, whose proclamation as caliph was received more enthusiastically than Khayran and other supporters had anticipated. Khayran himself met the newly proclaimed caliph in Valencia, as did Ibn Hazm, who had settled in Aznalcazar *(Husn al-Qasr)* following his release from prison. It appears that Ibn Hazm and Khayran became reconciled and joined in their support of the new caliph. In preparation for assuming the throne in Cordova, the caliph decided to pass through Granada with the purpose of making its Zirid ruler render him the oath of allegiance. He was leading a large army supplied to him by his supporters and felt confident that the Zirid ruler would acquiesce to such a show of force. However, the Zirid ruler, who had a strông commitment to the Berber cause, refused to render the oath of allegiance. War ensued in 1018 in which the caliph was killed after he had been abandoned by Khayran and his supporters. Ibn Hazm, who had joined the expedition, was taken prisoner.[37]

It appears that Ibn Hazm was soon released from prison. It was almost six years since he had left Cordova. During those years of exile, he witnessed and participated in major events that had grave repercussions for the future of al-Andalus. In addition to suffering disappointment in politics during his exile, it was probably then that he fell desperately in love with a girl named Nu'm, whom he married; but she soon died, leaving him disheartened and despondent - for seven months he mourned her, refusing even to change his clothes.[38] At this point, Ibn Hazm apparently decided that the caliphal cause was hopeless, and that the Hammudids were in Cordova to stay. He decided to return to Cordova, not without apprehension.

Another possible reason for his decision to return may have been a desire to further his studies. Although he was quite active in politics during his exile, Ibn Hazm always kept abreast of what was going on in Cordova by maintaining correspondence with relatives and friends. In addition, he pursued his scholarly interest and engaged in open debates, becoming acquainted with a wide spectrum of scholars. In Almeria, he frequented literary sessions *(majlis)* and the shop of the Jewish physician Isma'il ibn Yunus (from whom he probably obtained some notion of medicine.)[39] But Cordova still offered the best educational opportunity in spite of disruptions. In 1019, Ibn Hazm departed for Cordova, then ruled by the Shi'ite al-Qasim Ibn Hammud.[40]

It appears that this ruler did not place any restrictions on Ibn Hazm, thus enabling him to live in peace among his many friends and fellow scholars. All indications are that Ibn Hazm devoted most of his time to study, but not without some involvement in political activities. For one thing, Cordova was not the prosperous and serene city he had known as a child, but was full of intrigues and political restlessness. In 1021, the Hammudid al-Qasim was ousted by his nephew Yahya (1021-1023), involving the Berbers and the inhabitants of Cordova in a bloody clash. The deteriorating situation led to the removal of Yahya and the proclamation of the Umayyad

'Abd al-Rahman V, surnamed al-Mustazhir, as caliph. This ruler was about twenty years old, intelligent and highly educated,[41] but inexperienced in coping with a tense and explosive situation. It is probable that the young caliph belonged to the circle of young intellectuals from which he selected his cabinet. They included the twenty-nine-year-old Ibn Hazm, Abu-l-Mughirah, the young erotic poet and cousin of Ibn Hazm, and the thirty-one-year-old Ibn Shuhayd, an able poet and literary critic — an idealistic group that would have done well in better times and in different circumstances. Al-Maqqari makes the following pointed remarks:

> He [al-Mustazhir] elevated some of his friends, who are a cause for astonishment. Each one had his own way of life *(madhhab)* such as Abi 'Amir Ibn Shuhayd, who was engrossed in his passtime *(bitalah);* Abu Muhammad Ibn Hazm who was notorious for refuting scholars and his cousin 'Abd al-Wahhab Ibn Hazm, the erotic poet living in luxury. In so doing, he angered the old viziers and the notables. Al-Mustazhir was also hasty in employing Berbers.[42]

Al-Mustazhir's identification with the Berbers, coupled with his insensitivity to the old Cordovan guard and notables, must have contributed to tensions and uncertainty, and led eventually to his assassination after some forty-five days of rule. He was succeeded by the Umayyad Muhammad al-Mustakfi (1023-1025), a man of mediocre ability and few scruples, whom, in the words of Ibn Hayyan, "The Almighty God has sent us as an afflication and calamity to the people of Cordova."[43] Al-Mustakfi instituted a reign of terror, imprisoning and killing those connected with the caliph al-Mustazhir. Among the imprisoned were Ibn Hazm and his cousin Abu-l-Mughirah. Ibn Shuhayd and others fled to Malaga, probably seeking the intervention of the Hammudid Yahya, who had been ousted from the caliphal throne in 1023. Al-Mustakfi reigned for almost a year and a half. It is not certain whether Ibn Hazm spent all that time in jail. At any rate, he left Cordova once more in about 1025, and headed for eastern al-Andalus, where he settled in Játiva. In the meantime, the Hammudid Yahya entered Cordova for the second time and assumed the caliphal throne (1025-1027). Ibn Hazm's continuing absence from Cordova indicates that he was negatively disposed toward the new ruler.

The city of Cordova did not fare well under the second rule of Yahya. The economic, political, and social problems continued to worsen. Cordova had ceased to be the center of political gravity. Elsewhere in al-Andalus, petty rulers, commonly known as *Muluk al-tawa'if,*[44] were entrenced in their domains, and their rivalries and wars brough the country to a state of anarchy. Yahya's tenuous rule ended with his removal. Once more, Cordova faced a governmental crisis, and its inhabitants made a last attempt to reestablish the Umayyad dynasty. Their choice fell on the Umayyad Hisham III (1027-1031), surnamed al-Mu'ayyad, who was somewhere in eastern al-Andalus, most probably in Alpuente. The new caliph was an old acquaintance of Ibn Hazm's, who had composed a poem praising the prince [45] and who had joined him in the war against the Zirid ruler of Granada during the proclamation of al-Murtada, the brother of the new caliph. It is also likely that Ibn Hazm kept in touch with him while both were living in the kingdom of Valencia. Upon the proclamation of Hisham III in 1027, Ibn Hazm moved from Játiva to Alpuente and served the new caliph in the capacity of adviser and perhaps even vizier.[46] He must have continued in this capacity when the new caliph decided to go to Cordova in 1029, accompanied by a small retinue that included Ibn Hazm. If this is the case, it represents Ibn Hazm's last political aspirations and his last hope of regaining the social, economic, and political status of his family. In 1031, he faced disappointment again when the inhabitants of Cordova decided to abolish the caliphate once and for all.

It was during his second exile in Jativa from about 1025 to 1027 that Ibn Hazm composed his literary masterpiece, the *Tawq al-hamamah* (The Dove's Ring), which is not only a classic on love and lovers, but a political autobiography. Through the *Tawq* as well as Ibn Hazm's treatise describing the excellence of al-Andalus *(fadl)*, which was probably written in Alpuente between 1027 and 1029 shows an ability to discern important facts, to develop abstract ideas, and to organize and systematize. Thus, when he opted for a life of study, Ibn Hazm brought these abilities along with his reflections on life and the ingredients that make it worthy and meaningful.

It is difficult to ascertain the whereabouts of Ibn Hazm following the abolition of the caliphate in 1031. All indications are that he lived in Cordova during the reign of al-Mu'ayyd and remained there until about 1035, when he appears to have been declared heretic by virtue of his Zahirite views and expelled from the city. In all likelihood he headed for eastern al-Andalus and traveled in the kingdoms of Valencia and Denia. It was probably from Denia, then ruled by the enlightened Mujahid (d. 1045), that Ibn Hazm went to Mallorca, also ruled by Mujahid, where he settled until about 1048.[47]

In Mallorca Ibn Hazm found an environment conducive to airing his views openly and freely. The island was incorporated into the kingdom of Denia in about 1014 by Mujahid, himself an able scholar and a patron of learning who attracted to his court the best talents of the day. It was probably in Denia that Ibn Hazm met the great lexicographer Ibn Sidah (d. 1066)[48] and the traditionist Ibn 'Abd al-Barr, both of whom are praised by Ibn Hazm for their outstanding works.[49] Mujahid's liberality to the scholars of his court was also evident at the court of Mallorca, which was ruled by enlightened and able governors, among whom was al-Aghlab (1037-1044). This governor had at his court the cultured secretary Ahmad Ibn Rashiq (d. 1048), a former student of Ibn Hazm's father and a man of vast erudition.[50] It was probably at the prompting of Ibn Rashiq that Ibn Hazm decided to settle on the island, where he received the necessary protection and was given ample freedom to teach, write, and lecture. His debates with Malikite jurists were numerous and spirited and often left his opponents in a state of confusion. He acquired a good number of followers. the most outstanding among whom was al-Humaydi, who became an enthusiastic disseminator of his doctrine both in Mallorca and in the East.

Ibn Hazm enjoyed this freedom for almost a decade, to the annoyance and embarassment of the Malikite reactionaries who had looked for the opportunity to rid themselves of him. Coincidentally, an opportunity arose following his debate with the Malikite jurist Sulayman Ibn Khalif al-Baji (d. 1081),[51] who is said to have been brought to the island by the Malikite jurists to silence Ibn Hazm once and for all just before the death of Ibn Rashiq in 1048. The animated debate resulted in the defeat of Ibn Hazm and, supposedly, in his evenutal expulsion from the island. But what ever the outcome of the debate might have been, the departure of Ibn Hazm from the island must have been prompted by more than a mere debate. For one thing, Ibn Hazm does not appear to hold any grudge against al-Baji, but regards him as a man of great erudition who does honor to the whole Malikite jurisprudence.[52]

A more plausible reason for Ibn Hazm's departure must be sought elsewhere. Indications are that the liberality that prevailed during the reign of Mujahid ended with his death in 1045. Mujahid's successor, 'Ali (1045-1076), spent his youth in captivity, becoming a Christian and speaking Romance. When he was freed and called upon to succeed his father, he had to convert to Islam and to acquaint himself with Arabic and Islamic culture. He had little appreciation for the culture and still less for the religious subtleties. Ibn Sidah and Ibn 'Abd al-Barr, who adorned the court of his father, left it under compulsion and sought broader horizons elsewhere.[53] The reason for their departure is not clear, but it must have had repercussions in the rest of the kingdom, including Malloroca particularly after the death of Ibn Rashiq in 1049. Ibn Hazm lost any form of protection with the death of Ibn Rashiq, and he was compelled to leave the island along with his pupils and followers. It was not a free choice. His pupil al-Humaydi decided to emigrate to the east after 400/1048,[54] whereas Ibn Hazm headed once more to eastern al-Andalus.

It is not known as to how long Ibn Hazm stayed in eastern al-Andalus. By this time, the political map of al-Andalus had assumed a shape, with some kingdoms having emerged. For the reasons stated above, the kingdom of Denia was out of Ibn Hazm's reach. The kingdom of Valencia, where Ibn Hazm had received hospitality in the past — mainly in Jativa and Alpuente — had changed hands many times and remained restive even under its most powerful ruler 'Abd al-'Aziz (d. 1059). Cordova remained unstable and was coveted by more powerful neighboring states. Seville was emerging as the most powerful state of al-Andalus, and had the further attraction of being the site of a fictitious caliph, who had been recognized by the Andalusian party, made up mostly of people who had identified themselves with the Arab cause. Furthermore, Seville was the major cultural center of al-Andalus, succeeding in many ways to the great splendor of tenth-century Cordova. This kind of attraction may have influenced Ibn Hazm to settle in Seville, then ruled by the powerful 'Abbadids (1023-1091). The ruler of the kingdom at the time was al-Mu'tadid (1042-1068), a ruthless but enlightened man, who entertained the ambition of asserting himself over all al-Andalus. Not being eligible for the office of the caliphate, he continued to use the name of the deposed and long dead Hisham II (d. 1013) as the legitimate caliph, a device that had been used by his father Muhammad (1025-1042) as early as 1033. The man impersonating Hisham was harmless, a mat-maker by trade. Yet he received the oath of allegiance from a number of states for their political ends; they thus escaped the danger of facing an actual contender, who would have put an end to their rule. It is almost certain that Hisham II had died twenty years earlier, and Ibn Hazm attests to it.[56]

It is therefore baffling to understand why Ibn Hazm, not known for his discretion, settled in Seville unless he either wanted to expose the farce or entertained a last hope for reviving the caliphate, in spite of having to resort to such a means. If the latter assumption is correct, it did not take Ibn Hazm long to find out that although the party-kings including al-Mu'tadid, were on public record as reviving the institution of the caliphate, they were not willing to implement their repeated declarations. Thus, al-Mu'tadid was displaying the same basic attitude as the various other petty rulers including Ibn Hazm's former patron Khayran.[57] Ibn Hazm soon found himself at odds with al-Mu'tadid, who prohibited him from teaching at the mosque, and from having students inside or outside it. al-Mu'tadid also outlawed his books and ordered them to be burned. These measures made Ibn Hazm more defiant and contemptuous of the ruler, and he retorted with a poem saying that he did not care about the burning of thin paper because its content would stay with him until death.[58]

Since al-Mu'tadid made life unbearable for him, Ibn Hazm's stay in Seville was almost certainly a short one. Now in his sixties, Ibn Hazm decided to settle on the family estate at Manta Lisham, where he spent his last few years living in peaceful surroundings far removed from the animosity of the religious scholars, intrigues, and restlessness which prevailed in the large urban centers. Almost in seclusion, he continued teaching and writing. It was probably then that he wrote his moral treatise, the *Akhlaq,* which contains precious reflections on himself, society, and its value. He was utterly disillusioned, for he had never found congenial surroundings and appreciation after being exiled from Cordova in 1013. He died almost in obscurity in 1064, leaving an extensive literary legacy and three sons.

Ibn Hazm two sons Fadl and Abu Sulayman preserved his writings, and followed to some degree in his footsteps. Fadl (d. 1086) became, paradoxically enough, the vizier and the historian of the 'Abbadids, who had persecuted his father. His *Guide to the Knowledge of the 'Abbadid Geneology*[59] makes interesting reading. His third son Ya'qub (d. 1109) does not appear to have distinguished himself as a scholar.[60]

But Ibn Hazm's greatest legacy consists of his works and thoughts and the impact they had on succeeding generations. Ironically, one of the later 'Abbadid princes espoused Ibn Hazm's doctrine.[61] The great Almohad ruler

Ya'qub (1184-1198) is said to have passed through the village of Ibn Hazm, stopped at his tomb, and made the following remarks: "What a magnificent place is this which produced such a scholar. All scholars are indeed indebted to Ibn Hazm."[62]

His Views on Society

As far as can be ascertained, Ibn Hazm resided in Cordova, Almeria, Aznalcazar, Valencia, Granada, Jativa, Alpuente, Denia (perhaps), Mallorca, Seville, and Manta Lisham, besides the many other places he may have visited during his frequent travels. His unsettled life was filled with anxiety and disillusionment in the midst of animosity and danger. It may be relevant here to single out some of his statements that bear on his state of mind, his character, and his attitude toward and assessment of the major issues of his time.

In the epilogue to his *Tawq,* he reflects on his own condition, saying:

It is only possible to deal with a theme like this [love] when one's hands are free and the heart disengaged. After all the things that have happened to me and fallen upon my shoulders, it is a wonder that a state of mind like mine could have recalled anything, preserved any trace, or invoked the past. For you know quite well that my memory is unsteady, my state of mind is shattered because of the situation in which I find myself: exiled from home; harassed by fate, the tyranny of rulers, disloyalty of friends, adverse conditions, change of fortune, deprivations from inherited and acquired wealth, dispossession of what parents and ancestors had left me, exile and being errant in these lands, loss of wealth and fame, preoccupation with protecting my family and children, longing in despair to returning home, being the toy of fate, and waiting for determination of God's decree.[63]

He adds a poem expressing his resignation and fortitude and setting his goal in life — to defend religion *(din)* and honor *('ird).* In the poem, he states that he made a fortress and a coat of arms out of despair without ever wearing the cloak of the unjust, and that most people are of no consequence for sustaining him as long as his religion and honor are unimpaired. He does not care about what has happened in the past, nor does he care or worry about the unpredictable future.[64]

The goal of defending religion and honor was pursued vigorously and unshakingly for the rest of his life, and permeated all his thinking. Even during the turmoil and frustrations of his political involvments, he appears to have devoted ample time to scholarship, emerging with a new outlook on the religious practices of the time, and with a critical approach to them as well as to the government, rulers, religious scholars, and values of Andalusian society as a whole. A new chapter in his life had begun, moving from political activism to the scholarly arena, in which he gave vent to his convictions with all the force of his mind and the might of his pen. These were his most powerful weapons. He became an intellectual rebel, an indefatigable researcher *(mujtahid),* and a passionate fighter *(mujahid)* who aimed at reforming a society beset by sociopolitical upheavals and moral laxity. There is no indication that he ever relaxed his insistence on those objectives, notwithstanding the danger to his life from the secular and religious leadership of the country. And unlike many scholars of the period, he appears to have resisted the temptation of being attached to any court, except that of the legitimately instituted caliph (or one that apppeared to support reestablishing the caliphate on firm foundations). Although he was quite aware of his superior poetical and literary ability, which could have placed him at any court of his choice if he had been willing to make certain compromises, he held fast to his ideals and came into open conflict with powerful rulers and influential religious scholars.

His *Akhlaq,* written late in life, reflects his attitude toward society and its value. This ethical treatise, written in a stoic vein, proscribes a norm of conduct with a pessimistic and stoic outlook. Ibn Hazm praises justice, fairness, fortitude, and knowledge; he abhors lies, gossip, envy, treason, hypocracy, vanity, and love of fame. For him, personal honor comes before wealth, and generosity and religiosity are qualities to be proud of.[65] His bitter experiences with people led him to think that tranquility of spirit, joy, and health are to be found in solitude, and that people should be treated like fire, "You warm yourself with it, but do not enter its blaze."[66] This thought came to him from recollections that he was persecuted by people, betrayed and abandoned by friends; his own cousin Abu-l-Mughirah, a man who mixed with rulers "like water and wine,"[67] ridiculed him.

In his praise of al-Andalus and its society, he says, "Our al-Andalus is more envious of its good scholars than anywhere else in the world. If a scholar is good, they would say that he is an arrogant plagiarist; and if he is mediocre, they would say, 'Could this be otherwise?' Where did he study and what did he read?"[68] Nevertheless, he himself was not generous with the scholars of the day. He considered them, particularly those who opposed him, as functioning in confusion *(takhlit),* falsehood *(kidhb),* and ignorance *(jahl):* "They would not babble with idle talk were they rational people."[69]

Similarly, for Ibn Hazm, the great revolt of 1009 was an evil. The participants in it were the enemies of God who spread corruption on earth and inflicted grave injustice on Muslims:

> As for the question regarding this revolt *(fitnah),* and regarding the people involved in it and what happened to them, it is a question which we have pondered on for a long time. We beseech God for well-being. Except for those who sought the protection of God, the revolt was an evil that will require detailed elaboration. For one thing, it ruined the religious beliefs in many respects. In brief, every ruler of a city or fortress throughout the width and breadth of al-Andalus was the enemy of God and His Messenger. These rulers pursued corruption on earth. You can see the public confiscation of the property of Muslims; they allow soldiers to indulge in highway robbery in the areas they govern; they exact excise tax *(mukus)* and poll tax from Muslims;

they made the Jews lords for collecting land tax and levy *(daribah)* from Muslims; they give reasons for the necessity of such taxes, which are forbidden by God — thus replacing His commands and prohibitions with their own.

All in all, don't be mistaken about it, and don't be deceived by the dissolute and so-called jurists — those people clothed in sheep skin but with the hearts of lions, who adorn the evil rulers with their own evil, and who vainglory their corruption with their own.[70]

However flamboyantly his statement may be worded, his description of the revolt and its aftermath can be substantiated from other sources. Elsewhere, Ibn Hazm describes in moving terms the desolation that befell his home in Cordova during the revolts;

I inquired about Cordova from a man who had left it. He told me what had happened to our homes in Balat al-Mughith located in the western section of the city. Their traces had been erased, and their vestiges disappeared to the point that one could hardly know where they were. Destruction did away with them; prosperity changed into a desolate desert; people in terrible isolation; beauty in scattered rubbish; and tranquillity in a dreadful array. They are now the refuge of wolves, the plaything of ogres, and the diversion of spirits. . . Their union has been broken and scattered in all directions. Those chambers, which were filled with inscriptions and gorgeous ornaments, shone like the sun, and chased away chagrin by just looking at them; they are now visited by desolation and covered by ruins. All in all, our homes have become like open fauces of ferocious beasts calling attention to the transitional nature of this world; they make you see the end that awaits its dwellers, and make you realize where all of it is going to end.[71]

Perhaps partly because most of his life was spend in divisive society, the office of the caliphate, which was sanctified by the religious law as the only political institution binding all Muslims, was one of the major preoccupations of Ibn Hazm. The caliphate was a casualty of the *fitnah,* but remained for decades one of the most burning questions in eleventh-century al-Andalus. In spite of the futility of reestablishing the caliphate on sound foundations and in spite of Ibn Hazm's failure to achieve that end politically, he continued to adhere to the legitimist cause: the caliphate should prevail as prescribed by the religious law and must be held by a Quraysh descendent (particulary, a member of the Umayyad house). His vocal persistence was a contributing factor in arousing the antagonism of rulers against him, and may have been the main reason for al-Mu'tadid's displeasure. Ibn Hazm labeled the impersonation of the dead caliph Hisham by a mat-maker at the instigation of al-Mu'tadid and other petty rulers an unheard-of scandal *(ukhluqah);*

"a mat-maker *(rajul husri)* appeared twenty-two years after the death of Hisham Ibn al-Hakam al-Mu'ayyad and claimed that he was Hisham. He was rendered the oath of allegiance, and his name was mentioned from all the pulpits of al-Andalus at one time or another.

Blood was shed and armies fought each other concerning these affairs."⁷²

Still another ignominy *(fadihah)* perpetrated at the same time was unheard of in the whole world:

There are four men living three days' journey from each other, each of whom arrogates to himself the title of Commander of the Faithful. They are mentioned simultaneously in the Friday sermons. They are: Khalaf al-Husri in Seville, claiming that he is Hisham Ibn al-Hakam; Muhammad Ibn al-Qasim Ibn Hammud⁷³ in Algecira; Muhammad Ibn Idris Ibn 'Ali Ibn Hammud⁷⁴ in Malaga; and Idris Ibn Yahya Ibn 'Ali Ibn Hammud⁷⁵ in Bobastro. ⁷⁶

Perhaps it was in answer to this kind of lawlessness, confusion, and deceit that Ibn Hazm decided to set down the requirements of the caliphate within the frame work of the religious law. In fact, he devotes a whole section to it in his *Fisal*⁷⁷ and another, lost monographs.⁷⁸ The qualifications expected of a caliph are: being of Quraysh descent; having reached puberty; intelligence; being male; being Muslim; the ability to fulfill the moral precepts of the law; having knowledge of the religious obligations; morals and politics; and being free from mortal sins and scandals. If the incumbent lacks the minimum qualifications, fails to execute the law, or indulges in immorality, he ought to be deposed. As to the manner of succession, the incumbent caliph has the prerogative of handing over the succession to anyone of his choice, within the limits prescribed by law, either through nomination or in concert with the officials of the courts.

Ibn Hazm finds justification for this procedure in the long history of the caliphate in both East and West. In his view, which reflects a long-standing legal tradition, the caliphate is the best and most valid form of government to guarantee the continuity of the temporal and religious power, order, and well-being of the Islamic community as a whole. The procedure of nomination is considered the most effective and practical one. However, if the caliph dies without nominating a successor, any eligible Muslim could proclaim himself caliph and would be acknowledged if his claim were not contested. In this connection, Ibn Hazm offers other alternatives and safeguards: (1) if the incumbent caliph fails to make provisions for the succession, any eligible candidate can proclaim himself immediately after the death of the incumbent; he should be acknowledged even though a more qualified candidate might appear afterward; (2) in the event that two eligible candidates proclaim themselves simultaneously, the one who has better qualifications should be acknowledged; (3) if two pretenders have equal qualifications, the Islamic community should choose one of them, or opt for a third one; and (4) if two pretenders have similar qualifications, preference should be given to the one who possesses the better qualification in political management. Ibn Hazm dismisses the possiblity of elective procedure by the Islamic community as a whole or by the learned men of Islam — although these two procedures might be ideal, they are highly impractical and nearly impossible to execute, which would leave the community to function without a government for an indefinite period of time.⁷⁹

With this strong commitment to the concept of the caliphate and to the Umayyad house, Ibn Hazm could not see any merit in the many petty rulers of al-Andalus, especially those who arrogated to themselves the title of the caliphate:

> "O God, we lodge a complaint about the preoccupation of our Muslim rulers with worldly things at the expense of their religion, such as (1) building palaces that they will soon abandon instead of strengthening the religious law, which will be indispensable for them in the Day of Judgment and in the Hereafter; (2) collecting wealth that is the cause of shortening their lives and the reason for having enemies against them; and (3) avoidance of their religion by means of which they can be powerful in this world as well as attaining success in the Hereafter. They go to the extreme of beholding to vile people, to Christians and Jews, and of allowing the tongues of the infidels and polytheists to be free. . ."[80]

In conclusion, Ibn Hazm defied one and all — be they powerful rulers or religious magnates. He felt destined, or bound, by conscience and religious conviction to assume the role of political and religious reformer and to save his homeland from its moral and political bankruptcy. In the process, he emerged "a vanquished Don Quijote."[81] On the political level, he continued to the very end to embrace the cause of the Umayyad house as prescribed by the requirements of the caliphate, and was convinced that only a resurgence of the Umayyads could bring unity to the country, reviving the most glorious days of tenth-century al-Andalus. On the religious level, he was disquiet about the intolerance and narrow-mindedness of the religious scholars and their blind adherence to old authorities, who lived in different times and under different conditions. Furthermore, he was unhappy about their refusal to admit the validity of rational proofs, about their capitulation to lawless rulers, and about their indifference and inability to redress many of the social evils of the day.

His attitude constantly placed him in difficult situations. But in spite of this and the general erosion of al-Andalus, he had a strong feeling for the country and never left it. His deep sentiment for al-Andalus, in spite of his acknolwedgment of its many defects and misguided leadership, was expressed eloquently when a man from Qayrawan inquired from a friend whether al-Andalus ever produced anything in the intellectual field worth recording. Although the inquiry was not addressed to Ibn Hazm, he answered it in a treatise cataloguing the merits of al-Andalus and its men of letters who were in his estimate worthy of comparison with the intellectual giants of Eastern Islam.[82] Although he does not list himself among the talented Andalusians, he was later convinced of his superior talent, expressed in a poem but he suffered the disillusionment of not being acknowledged in his own country. He considered himself a luminary of knowledge, unappreciated in the West; had he been born in the East, nothing of his fame would have been lost.[83]

CHAPTER III
THE SCHOLAR-DIALECTICIAN

In spite of and deep involvement in politics for two decades, Ibn Hazm appears to have spent every moment available studying, lecturing, and writing. After the abolition of the caliphate in 1031, he devoted himself completely to scholarship. His disheartening political failure proved, in the long run, to be compensated by the scholarly achievement on which his fame rests. Here I shall give a brief account of his scholarly preparation, with reference to his intellectual environment, teachers, and the development of some of his views, with particular emphasis on his position as a dialectician.

Two distinct stages can be discerned in the scholarly preparation of Ibn Hazm: first, a literary preparation which may have extended to about 1031, and which would have enabled him, like his father, to hold a post at the court; and second, a juridico-theological preparation to which he devoted himself completely following his political failures.

His Intellectual Environment

Tenth-century Cordova offered material prosperity, social stability, famous educational centers, and numerous libraries. It was a Mecca for young scholars who came there to enhance their education and to take advantage of the many opportunities available to them. Through Cordova, al-Andalus became one of the most cultured countries in the Mediterranean basin, particularly under the caliphate of 'Abd al-Rahman III (929-961) and the reign of his son and successor al-Hakam II (961-976), down to and including the 'Amirid dictatorship (976-1009). Thus, the generation of Ibn Hazm was brought up in a highly sophisticated culture and educated by men who lived the great moments of Andalusian glory. This generation produced the great poets Ibn Shuhayd and Ibn Zaydun, the historians Sa'id of Toledo and Ibn Hayyan, the able traditionist Ibn 'Abd al-Barr, and the lexicographer Ibn Sidah, as well as Ibn Hazm; these and other scholars lived through a period of transition during which they witnessed the spendor of tenth-century Cordova and its ultimate ruin in the early part of the eleventh century.

Fortunately, the cultural manifestations of the tenth century remained unbroken, and the Revolt of 1009 and its aftermath did not suffocate intellectual pursuits. On the contrary, intellectual life, paradoxically, continued quite vigorously and engendered at the same time a fresh perspective and even self-analysis among the new generation of scholars. Although Cordova remained in utter confusion after the revolt, its cultural legacy was carried on to other Andalusian cities, many of which were by then capitals of new kingdoms. Cities such as Seville, Toledo, Valencia, Malaga, Almeria, Badajoz, and Denia superseded, to some extent, Cordova and preserved and disseminated its culture.

These general remarks have an important bearing on the academic preparation of Ibn Hazm. Education was highly regarded in al-Andalus and eagerly sought by people from all walks of life.[1] Generally, education began at home where parents taught their children reading, writing, and reciting, the Qur'an. If the family occupied a high position in society seasoned and well-known scholars were hired as tutors. In addition, numerous educational institutions were available which offered training at all levels, from an elementary to high and specialized education. Ordinarily, the mosque discharged the function of secondary school and university in addition to being a place of worship; teaching in the mosque was not limited to basic religious instruction, but included highly specialized courses taught by well-known scholars on a variety of subjects. Scholars also held classes in their homes and were sought by students from all over the country. Scholars with specialties would issue a certificate of competence *(ijazah)* to students which would qualify them to teach a particular book or discipline. Travel in search of knowledge or a particular specialty took students all over the Muslim world, not only to Cordova but to Qayrawan in Tunisia, Alexandria in Egypt, Medina in the Arabian Peninsula, Kufah, Basrah, and Baghdad in Iraq. Travelers brought back to al-Andalus not only fresh knowledge acquired at the feet of the great masters of the East, but many books on all conceivable subjects. In consequence, private and public libraries were abundant in al-Andalus, particularly in Cordova, and matched Eastern libraries in content. Tenth-century Cordova was also famous for its numerous bookshops where books were copied not only for scholars, but for average people, who took pride in having libraries at home.[2] In addition, numerous literary sessions *(majalis)* consisting of spirited discussions of all sorts of topics were held periodically at the court of rulers as well as in the homes of scholars and notables.

Ibn Hazm's Education and Teachers

In this cultural environment, Ibn Hazm was exposed early to the best educational facilities of al-Andalus, whether at home or outside it. Being the son of scholar and highly placed official, he had access to good scholars in Cordova, many of whom had studied in the East. His father educated him for a political career; in addition to reading, writing, and reciting the Qur'an, he was introduced to Traditions, Arabic grammar and philology, poetry, wisdom literature, literature in general, and a smattering of the natural sciences. Ibn Hazm was taught reading, writing, and recitation of the Qur'an and poetry by the ladies of the harem.[3] This becomes significant in terms of the educational status of women, some of whom had a preparation that went beyond mere literacy. No doubt, the ladies of the harem were assisted by his father, a well-known teacher.[4] Concurrently, Ibn Hazm was studying various subjects under leading scholars. Thus, by the time he became involved in politics at the age of eighteen, he already possessed a general education that included Arabic, poetry, belles-lettres, history, and the religious sciences - all of which constituted some of the indispensable requirements for holding a position at the court. By the time he was thirty years old, he showed great promise as a litterateur and poet, as can be seen in his literary masterpiece, the *Tawq.*

Judging from the content of the *Tawq,* it appears that at this juncture in Ibn Hazm's life his interest in the religious sciences - Qur anic studies, Traditions, theology and law - was not so great as later in his career, when the religious sciences became his primary concern. However, even then, Ibn Hazm was apologetic about writing on such a "mundane" subject as love and lovers, but offered in his defense that the subject matter of the book was condoned by the experience of many venerable leaders of Islam, if not by the religious law. Althoug he described the vicissitudes and tribulations of love as experienced by himself and other leaders known to him, he always displayed a sense of austerity and piety.

The best insight into the extent of the education of Ibn Hazm is to be found in his works. His treatise on the merits *(fada'il)* of al-Andalus - also written early in his career, about 1027, but not later than 1035 - is significant not only as an anthology of the men of letters up to his own time, but as a curriculum of the man himself. In his *Fada'il,* Ibn Hazm displays a wide knowledge of the works of the men of letters from both the East and al-Andalus. These includes historians, jurists, theologians, commentators of the Qur'an, traditionists, grammarians, lexicographers, poets, rhetoricians, belletrists, scientists, and others. Ibn Hazm included a brief comparative evaluation of their works, indicating the merit and position of the Andalusian men of letters vis-a-vis their Eastern counterparts. In addition, the treatise reveals his familiarity with the "foreign sciences" such as medicine, philosophy, and logic. For instance, he commends his teacher *(ustadh)* Ibn al-Kattani[6] for his several treatises on philosophy, medicine, and the natural sciences; and he praises the work of al-Zahrawi[7] (whom he knew) on surgery, and the work of Ibn al-Haytham[8] on properties, pisons, and drugs.[9] It is only when he mentions mathematical and astronomical works that he suspends judgment admitting his lack of understanding of those disciplines.[10] In light of all this, it is safe to conclude that Ibn Hazm's education was not limited to the so-called Arabic sciences - language, literature, and religious studies - but included the philosophical and speculative sciences as well. This is also attested to by his repeated references to the exemplars of those disciplines and by the facility with which he discussed them.

Furthermore, Ibn Hazm was a defender of philosophy[11] and an advocate of logic. His *Taqrib* was an apologia for the discipline of logic, and perhaps the first attempt in Arabic to popularize the subject; everyday language and familiar examples drawn from the daily life and the law made it comprehensible to the average person as well as to the religious scholars, who opposed it vehemently.

Although he may not have been acquainted with mathematics and astronomy at the time he wrote his *Fada'il* Ibn Hazm came to realize their importance not only as legitimate sciences, but as indispensable tools for understanding and implementing the religious law.[12] He perceived the same validity and utility for medicine, a subject with which he appears to have been more than familiar if we are to accept the ten medical works al-Dhahabi[13] attributed to him. These works cover a variety of topics: prophetic medicine,[14] "happiness," [15] the competence of the physician,[16] the definition of medicine,[17] abridgment of the sayings of Galen concerning acute diseases,[18] cures with dates and raisins,[19] a treatise on the slender,[20] a commentary of the aphorism of Hippocrates,[21] simple drugs,[22] and the cure of the opposite with the opposite.[23]

Unfortunately, none of these works is known to exist today, nor do we have any information that he ever practiced medicine. This, however, may be explained by the fact that Ibn Hazm was always on the move, and did not have the opportunity to practice it. Neverthless, his reported works on medicine, coupled with his repeated references to the discipline and aspects thereof, are sufficient indications that he was proficient in the subject. The men most responsible for teaching him medicine appear to be the Jewish physician Isma'il Ibn Yunus[24] whom Ibn Hazm had met during his exile in Almeria, al-Zahrawi, and Ibn al-Kattani, a prominent man in the speculative and natural sciences.

All indications are that Ibn Hazm had training in the speculative and natural sciences, which were in the medieval conception part and parcel of philosophy. In this connection, he makes repeated references to the "ancients", who include Plato, Aristotle, Hippocrates and Galen, Prophery, Ptolemy, Euclid, and other leading thinkers of antiquity. His familiarity with Muslim philosophers is attested to by his refutation of al-Kindi and al-Razi.[25] Moreover, his *Categories of the Sciences* gives ample evidence of his grasp of the speculative and natural sciences, which he attempted to harmonize with the religious sciences, giving them equal time in the education of the individual, and particularly, in the training of religious scholars. All in all, Ibn Hazm had a broad education in the religious and secular sciences.

It is equally significant to make reference to his linguistic preparation and knowledge of foreign languages. Muslim biographers and historians seldom mention the linguistic proficiency, in spite of the frequent bilingualism and the multiplicity of languages in the Muslim world. This is true of Ibn Hazm; brought up in a bi-lingual environment, he is silent on the subject. However, his writings on the origin of language[26] are revealing in this connection. He not only discerns the existence of a variety of Arabic dialects in al-Andalus, but recognizes that Syriac, Hebrew, and Arabic are closely related, and must have sprung from a mother tongue. In this respect, he precedes nineteenth century semitists by almost eight centuries. He could not have arrived at his conclusion without some knowledge of those languages. In addition, Ibn Hazm most probably knew Romance, commonly used among Andalusians. There are also indications that he had a knowledge of Latin and, to a smaller degree, Greek. Various statements in his *Taqrib* point to a knowledge of these two ancient languages.[27] Furthermore, he makes specific references to having read the Gospels, the Old and the New Testaments, Talmud, the Acts of Martyrs, Christian liturgies, the Acts of the Council of Toledo, and other religious texts, which he subjected to several exgetical criticism.[29] Although translation of the Old and New Testament into Arabic have been available to him, it is doubtful that the other materials existed in Arabic recensions.

Unfortunately, Ibn Hazm's *Fahrasah* did not come down to us; this work listed his teachers and probably the kind of works he was exposed to. However, this loss is compensated for in part by his occasional references to some of his teachers, using the expressions *Shaykh, mu'addib,* and *ustadh,* for teacher. He also uses the term *sahib* for some of them, which may mean colleague or friend. The following paragraphs will give a list of his teachers, particularly those mentioned by him. They are arranged chronologically by the dates of their deaths.[31]

According to the report of al-Humaydi[32] as related to him by Ibn Hazm himself, Ibn Hazm studied history, and probably some Traditions, under Ibn al-Jassur (d. 1010)[33] on or before the year 400/1009, when he was about fifteen. Ibn al-Jassur was an able historian and traditionist who emigrated to the East and studied Traditions and the history of Tabari under various Eastern masters. Upon his return to al-Andalus, he became a renowned teacher, who counted among his students Ibn Hazm and Ibn 'Abd al-Barr. It was probably by Ibn al-Jassur that Ibn Hazm was introduced to the massive history of al-Tabari.

It was probably immediately thereafter that Ibn Hazm studied history and literature under the historian Ibn al-Faradi (d. 1013),[34] who also had studied in the East but returned to Cordova to teach. Ibn al-Faradi left us his valuable biographical dictionary of Andalusian scholars.[35] He was later murdered in his home during the revolt of 1013. Ibn Hazm not only relied on Ibn al-Faradi for the transmission of traditions, but refers to him as "our teacher."[36] He also refers to al-Azdi (d. 1019) an Egyptian emigre who was versatile in language and literature, and who had a good following among students.[37] In all likelihood, Ibn Hazm studied under al-Azdi before his first exile in 1013. Simultaneously, Ibn Hazm may have studied literature under ibn 'Abd al-Warith,[38] to whom he refers as "my teacher" *(mu'addibi).*[39] He also studied literature and language under Ibn Abi 'Abdah (d. ca. 1029),[40] a leading man of letters, who belonged to a prominent family and occupied the post of vizier.

But the man who exerted the greatest influence on Ibn Hazm's scientific training — mainly philosophy, logic, and the natural sciences — was the scientist Ibn al-Kattani (d. 1029),[41] a man of great culture and a scientist whose works on the natural sciences Ibn Hazm commends highly.[42]

Except for Ibn al-Kattani, the expertise of the above-mentioned teachers lay in language, belles-lettres, history, and to a small degree, Traditions. In view of the dates of their deaths, it emerges clearly that Ibn Hazm commenced with a liberal arts education of the belletristic type, with little or no emphasis on religion. The anecdote reported by Muhammad Ibn al-'Arabi that his teacher Ibn Hazm did not know the rudimentary of prayer until the age of twenty-six (that is, until 1020), may be exaggerated,[43] but it does reflect the progression of his scholarly interests. The two men who seem to have influenced profoundly his religious thinking were Ibn Muflit (d. 1034)[44] and Ibn al-Saffar (d. 1037),[45] whom he acknowledges as his teachers.[46] He may have associated with them after his return to Cordova in 1019 until his second exile in 1025; it is almost certain that he was close to them from about 1029 until his third expulsion from Cordova in 1035.

Ibn Muflit was an ascetic and a free thinker who upheld the literalism of the texts,[47] thus appearing to advocate Zahirism, to which Ibn Hazm subsequently devoted himself. Ibn Muflit disavowed imitation *(taqlid)*;[48] for this he was declared heretic, persecuted, and denied a decent burial. At the time of Ibn Muflit's death in 1034, or shortly thereafter, Ibn Hazm was excommunicated and forced to leave Cordova for the third time.

Ibn al-Saffar was a judge and a leading religious scholar in Cordova. Inclined toward an ascetic life, he is reported to have composed various works bearing on Sufism. Thus, Ibn Hazm found two qualities that complemented each other: the analytical and critical approach of Ibn Muflit, and the spiritual resignation and endurance of Ibn al-Saffar. No doubt, it was under their influence that Ibn Hazm formulated his religious thinking after he had studied the legal doctrines of Malik Ibn Anas and al-Shafi'i.

Before his initiation to Zahirism, it is probable that Ibn Hazm studied Malikite law under known authorities. Among those Malikites were Humam Ibn Ahmad (d.1030),[49] al-Talamanki (d. 1037),[50] and Ibn Dahhun (d. 1030),[51] who were known for their deep commitment to Malikism, and who defended it against any deviation. Humam, was in the words of Ibn Hazm, a unique rhetorician of his time and a transmitter of Traditions, which he defined and verified.[52] Al-Talamanki was a famous Qur'anic reader who received his education in the East and returned to Cordova with an enormous store of knowledge pertaining to Qur'anic studies and Traditions. He had a strong commitment to Malikism, and he was like a sword against sectarians and innovators.[53] Ibn Dahhun was popular as a teacher, but uncompromising toward any innovation. If Ibn Hazm did actually study under these men, the rigidity of their stand may have been a factor in Ibn Hazm's abandoning Malikism for Zahirism.

Before discussing Ibn Hazm's conversion to Zahirism, it is important to add the names of some scholars reported to have been his teachers; actually, they were men with whom he came into contact and upon whom he appears to have depended for the transmission of numerous Traditions. They are:

1. **Ibn Nubati** (d. 1010)[54], a teacher of Traditions often cited by Ibn Hazm with the saying: "al-Nubati informed us" *(akhbarana al-Nubati)*.
2. **Ibn Wajh al-Jannah** (d. 1011),[55] a traditionist and pupil of Ibn Hazm's father. al-Humaydi simply says that some scholars related Traditions on his authority, while al-Dhahabi lists him as one of teachers of Ibn Hazm.
3. **Al-Tamimi** (d. 1010),[56] often cited by Ibn Hazm as transmitter of Traditions and whose authority he relies.
4. **al-Wahrani** (d ?),[57] a transmitter of Traditions on whom Ibn Hazm often relies.
5. **Ibn 'Uthman** (d. ?),,[58] a teacher of Traditions on whose authority Ibn Hazm depended.
6. **Ibn Nami** (d. ?),[59] a pious traditionist on whose authority Ibn Hazm transmitted Traditions.
7. **Ibn Asbagh** (d. ?),[60] a traditionist on whose authority Ibn Hazm relied.
8. **Ibn 'Abd al-Barr** (d. 1071),[61] a close colleague *(sahib)* of Ibn Hazm, who transmits numerous Traditions on his auhority.[62]
9. **al-'Udhri** (d. 1056),[63] an able traditionist from Almeria whom Ibn Hazm probably met during his exile in that city.

These names are drawn from the list of teachers given by al-Dhahabi.[64] Although Ibn Hazm appears to rely on most of them for the transmission of Traditions, it is not certain how they influenced his religious thinking. They had a strong commitment to Malikism, which Ibn Hazm later repudiated. In addition to these teachers and colleagues, Ibn Hazm had an array of friends and companions that included princes, poets, scholars, and notable — all of whom made some contributions to the intellectual life of al-Andalus. Only a few names can be mentioned here. There was the prince poet Taliq (d. 1009),[65] whom he knew in his teens and whom he describes as one of the best poets of al-Andalus during the Umayyad dynasty.[66] Likewise, he was the friend of the prince poet 'Ubaydallah Ibn 'Abd al-Rahman,[67] for whom he composed a poem expressing his sincere affection.[68] He also knew Ibn al-Tubni,[69] a man of Maghribi origin, whom he describes as possessing high morals and virtue in addition to being an able religious scholar, poet, and belletrist.[70]

The diverse interests and specialties of these teachers, colleagues, and friends enabled Ibn Hazm to have a broad perspective upon Islamic culture in both its religious and secular aspects. As such, he could be considered a microcosm of Andalusian culture. As a result of his broad education, he was able to shift his interests in a scale of priority and importance — from a belletristic intellectual pursuits to strict devotion to religious studies. The shift appears to have taken place following the vicissitudes of his political fortunes.

His Conversion to Zahirism

It is probable that Ibn Hazm began to take a serious interest in Malikism after his return to Cordova in 1019. During the next five years, he may have studied at *Muwatta'*, the legal codex of Malik Ibn Anas. His curiosity led him to study other legal schools — Hanafite, Shafi'ite, and Hanbalite (which had full acceptance in the East equal to Malikism, but were outlawed in al-Andalus). He was for some time attracted to the Shafi'ite school, but was initiated into the Zahirite doctrine by Ibn Muflit in the late 1020's and early 1030's.

What were the reasons behind his change from Malikism, to Shafi'ism, then to Zahrism? There is no simple answer; if an answer can be found, it would be in his Zahirite doctrine. In light of the sociopolitical disolocation of the country, however, Ibn Hazm may have felt that there was something wrong with the established system and no acceptable answer was given to him by his numerous committed teachers. It was easy for him to become disenchanted with Malikism, which denied to other accepted schools any modicum of validity to the point of persecuting those who studied them or voiced any merit in them. Coupled with this kind of authoritariansim was the reluctance of the religious scholars to concede any merit in philosophy, and particularly in logic, which became Ibn Hazm's yardstick for determining the proof for a particular question. More importantly, the Malikites appeared to him to be basing their legal decisions on assumptions that could not withstand historical scrutiny or logical proofs. Malikite reliance on the Qur'an, Prophetic Traditions, and the consensus *(ijma')* of the companions of the Prophet and his immediate successors would have been acceptable if these authorities were properly understood, but they had been obscured and nullified by excessive reliance on legal precedents handed down from generation to generation. Ibn Hazm saw this subservience to received, fallible human authority as a major obstacle to trying new ideas and undertaking individual inquiry *(ijtihad)* that might dispel old mistakes and set things aright. Moreover, if human authority were to remain unscrutinized, it could ultimately do a great violence to the whole religious edifice.

After abandoning Malikism, Ibn Hazm turned to the Shafi'ite school of law, which appeared for a while to offer intellectual stimulation and individual initiative in that it allowed more room for rational scrutiny in arriving at legal decisions. In addition to its reliance on the Qur'an and the Traditions, the Shafi'ite school gave great weight to analogical reasoning *(qiyas)* and to the consensus of the Islamic community for arriving at legal decisions. Ibn Hazm's initial attraction to the Shafi'ite school may have been inspired by its founder, al-Shafi'i (d. 820), who had been "a critical spectator rather than active participant in the evolving drama of Islamic law."[71] Al-Shafi'i, like Ibn Hazm, had remained uncommitted on legal questions until he was able to understand the complex issues involved in formulating and establishing the principles of the law and its application. Although Ibn Hazm was taken at first by the Shafi'ite critical approach and defended the school vigorously against Malikite jurists who charged him with heresy,[72] he continued his inquiry into the law, studying Qur'anic commentaries and various condices of Traditions with a view to their accuracy and authenticity. With this broadened base of knowledge, he was able to comprehend the basic issues at hand, acquiring thereby an impersonal and critical approach to them. This led him to abandon Shafi'ism on the same grounds as Malikism — that is, human authority given equal credence to divine authority. Consequently, the Shafi'ites' use of analogical reasoning *(qiyas)* for arriving at legal decisions became as abhorrent to him as the Malikites' use of imitation *(taqlid)*.

Henceforth, Ibn Hazm's arguments were no longer based on individual bias or affiliations, but on textual evidence, that is, the holy texts *(nass,* pl *nusus)* by themselves should be the sole criteria in matters of beliefs and practice. He thus freed himself from the strictures and inhibitions of belonging to a particular school of thought. Although he became doctrinaire after having formulated his Zahirite system, he always claimed to follow the truth, to seek it, and not to be bound by any school of thought.[73] This claim notwithstanding, his espousal and advocacy of Zahirism amounted to self-righteousness, which he calls a virtue rather than a defect. He says: "When a thing is established [to be true] I will face anyone as if this meant the whole world."[74]

It is almost certain that Ibn Hazm was introduced to Zahirism by Ibn Muflit between 1027 and 1034. The school had been established by Dawud Ibn Khalaf (d. 883) in Iraq, and was almost defunct by the time of Ibn Hazm in the eleventh century. Dawud [75] was a pupil of al-Shafi'i who disagreed with him for giving too great a role to analogical reasoning *(qiyas)* and the consensus *(ijma')*. Instead, he advocated strict adherence to the literal meaning *(zahir)* of the holy texts — the Qur'an and the Traditions. Essentially, Zahirism advocated that each Muslim rely solely on the Qur'an and traditions and derive legal decisions independently of any established school of law. Even the consensus *(ijma')* must be scrutinized with a view to its conformity or nonconformity with the holy texts. The literal meaning of the holy texts will lead to the actual rather than an implied meaning, thereby putting an end to speculation and to the intervention of human criteria such as imitation, analogical reasoning, personal opinion, interpretation and the like, which are no more and no less than innovations *(bida')* and an affront to the spirit and letter of the religious law *(shari'ah)*.

Although the Zahirite school did not muster enough support to become one of the accepted and established legal schools, it had at one time or another enthusiastic followers, who kept it much alive as a subject of deliberation among legal theoreticians and specialists. Its importation into al-Andalus[76] is credited to certain 'Abdallah Ibn al-Qasim,[77] who had traveled in the East and who entertained Zahrite ideas upon his return. Ibn al-Qasim remained isolated midst ultraconservative Malikites. A few isolated followers of Zahirism did exist from time to time in al-Andalus, but no attempt was made to replace Malikism.

For example, Mundhir Ibn Sa'id (d. 965)[78] was mentioned by Ibn Hazm[79] as a tenth-century advocate of Zahirism. Ibn Sa'id was the chief judge in Cordova under the enlightened reign of al-Hakam II (961-967); he was highly influential and respected for his erudition in law and literature. However, there is no indication that his Zahirite sympathies ever influenced his legal decisions, although some of his legal works — which are not exant — might reveal his Zahirite leaning. Moreover, Ibn Sa'id is not known to have had followers. Still, Zahirism did remain a topic of discussion in academic circles and occasionally attracted committed Zahirites such as Ibn Muflit,[80] who became the mentor of Ibn Hazm.

At first, Ibn Hazm may have regarded Zahirism as an academic curiosity to aid him in his comparatist approach to the existing legal schools. However, he soon was its most articulate and passionate defender, finally disavowing all the existing legal schools on the ground that they had intentionally or unintentionally deviated from the spirit and letter of the holy texts. He became convinced that his Zahirite system had the answers to many of the juridico-theological questions that had caused untold controversies and divisions in the Islamic community.

As developed by Ibn Hazm, Zahirism offered the tools necessary to ascertain the truth which other systems lacked. Essentially a revisionist school, its aim is to understand the holy texts on the basis of Arabic grammar, lexicography, and linguistic intuition. This requires a thorough knowledge of the language, which will permit analysis of the texts with respect to context, internal and terminal vocalizations, subject, object, adverbial clauses, pattern system, and the semantic value of words. All this will require a mental process guided by systematic, if not always logical rules. Furthermore, Zahirism allows ample room for individual inquiry *(ijtihad)* whereby the researcher *(mujtahid)* will determine on the strength of the holy text and logic the validity or invalidity of any question at hand.

The implications of Ibn Hazm's Zahirism for religious doctrine will be discussed below.[81] It is sufficient here to mention that Zahirism, as conceived by him, presented tremendous implications for the established legal schools, which for almost three centuries had striven to establish a system of precedents. The effect of Zahirism would be to take the question of law back to the first century Islam, thereby shattering the very foundations of the whole Islamic legal system. This appears not to be of any consequence to Ibn Hazm. He believed that reassessment of existing schools and revision of old concepts was the right thing to do; this belief, coupled with his intellectual curiosity and restless temperament, gave him the necessary incentive to pursue the truth without inhibitions.

Following the death of his teacher, Ibn Muflit, in 1034, Ibn Hazm devoted himself completely to the formulation and articulation of the

Zahirite system, which permeates most of his writings. Expelled from Cordova upon or shortly after the death of Ibn Muflit, he carried the doctrine with him wherever he went. He was as committed to a cause, so much so that he purged his manual on logic, *Taqrib,* of the term analogical reasoning *(qiyas)* used by the Shafi'ites for determining legal cases.[82] Moreover, he used his vast knowledge to defend Zahirism against powerful and often highly committed opponents. A master dialectician, he insisted on proofs *(burhan)* pl. *barahin)* whether arrived at on the basis of the holy texts *(nass,* pl. *nusus),* through logical demonstration, or both. Ibn Hazm appears to have been self-confident with little patience for his adversaries, be they well-meaning or rabble-rousers.

After this exodus from Cordova, he travelled extensively in eastern al-Andalus, teaching, preaching his doctrine, and acquiring more enemies. Some of his followers, particularly in Mallorca, became strong advocates of Zahirism. He wrote profusely on all sort of subjects, but his major works *Fisal, Ihkam,* and *Muhalla,* as well as his many other treatises, touch upon Zahirism and contain refutations of his adversaries. His *Fisal* and *Ihkam,* in particular, contain his arguments for a true and authentic Islam vis-a-vis not only the various Islamic denominations, but also other religions and philosophies of the world.[83]

Ibn Hazm also delved into the question of faith and reason, asserting their harmoney[84] - although he takes issues with rationalists or pretenders of philosophy who deny the validity of Revelation, and who are more concerned with mathematics, propriety of numbers, position of the stars, the nature of heavenly bodies, astrology, and other natural phenomena.[85] Conversely, he reproaches the religious scholars for slighting the natural sciences and philosophy, and for their condemning logic.[86] Inasmuch as he conceives Zahirism as demanding, he advocates a general education that is all-encompassig, pointing to the interdependence of the sciences.[87]

His Polemics

The works of Ibn Hazm are characterized by a combative spirit and reveal his vast erudition and understanding of a given issue. His systematic method of disputation leads directly to the point under discussion: first, he sets forth the position of his opponents as faithfully as he understands them, and then he proceeds to dissect and refute them with the aid of relevant information drawn from Islamic or non-Islamic sources, depending on the nature of the subject.

Some Prophetic Traditions have it that dialectics and disputation *(jadal wa - munazarah)* are not condoned by the religious law. Ibn Hazm considers those traditions either weak or spurious, and produces numerous traditions in support of the legitimacy of disputation and debate, arguing even that they are obligatory to lead people from error to truth.[88] He admits, however, that there is a blameworthy *disputatio (al-jadal al-madhmum)* in which disputants argue without knowledge and persist in upholding falsehood even after the truth has been demonstrated to them.[89] On the other hand, the *disputatio* that aims at seeking and upholding the truth by showing and destroying falsehood is an obligatory duty. Thus, whoever attaches blame to the search of the truth and the destruction of falsehood is indeed a liar and heretic.[90]

For *disputatio* to be meaningful and constructive, it must follow certain rules with respect to the subject matter, the terms used therein, and to conduct of the disputants. Ibn Hazm was well aware that disputants often entangle the meaning of terms to the point of mixing truth with falsehood.[91] Thus, in order to dispel ambiguity, he offers his definition of terms most frequently used among disputants *(ahl al-nazar)*.[92] He defines: definition *(hadd)*; distinctive quality *(rasm)*; knowledge *('ilm)*; belief *(i'tiqad)* proof *(burhan)*; guide *(dalil)*; evidence *(hujjah);* demonstrator of the reality of things, or guide *(dall)*; the search for conclusive evidence *(istidlal)*; the action of the demonstrator of the reality of things *(dalal);* convincing *(iqna')*; distortion *(shaghab)*; imitation *(taqlid)*; instinct *(ilham)*; prophecy *(nubuwwah)*; divine message *(risalah)*; clarity *(bayan)*; elucidation *(al-ibanah wa-l-tabyin)*; veracity *(sidq)*; truth *(haqq)*; falsehood *(batil)*; lie *(kidhb)*; intellectual or sensory perception *(asl)*; perception derived from a premise *(far')*; the "known", on the basis of either *asl or far' (ma'lum)*; holy text - the Quran and Traditions - *(nass)*; apparent or figurative meaning (*ta'wil)*; universal *('umum)*; particular *(khusus)*; summary *(mujmal)*; explanatory *(mufassar)*; command *(amr)*; prohibition *(nahy)*; obligatory duty *(fard)*; forbidden *(haram)*; obedience *(ta'ah)*; disobedience *(ma'siyah)*; discretionary action *(nadb)*; discerning aversion to *(karahah)*; analogical reasoning without textual justification *(qiyas)*; cause, or the nature of a thing *('illah);* reason for *(sabab);* objective *(gharad)*; a sign agreed upon *(amarah)*; intention *(niyyah)*; condition made *(shart)*; elucidation and explanation *(tafsir wa-sharh)* abrogation *(naskh)*; exception *(istihsan);* disputatio *(jadal wa-jadal)*; attaining one's objective in the search of the truth *(ijtihad)*; opinion not based on proof *(ra'y)*; preference *(isthihsan)*; right *(sawab)*; wrong *(khata')*; obstinacy *('inad)*; circumspection *(ihtiyat)*; caution *(wara')*; ignorance *(jahl)*; rhetorical deduction *(dalil al-khitab)*; the attributes of a thing *(tabi'ah)*; God's legislation through the tongue of His Prophets *(shari'ah)*; lexicons *(lughah)*; locution *(lafz)*; dissention *(khilaf)*; consensus of all the Companions of the Prophet *(ijma');* legislation itself *(sunnah)*; innovation *(bid'ah)*; metonym *(kunayah);* gesture/allusion categorization of a thing *(mufassal)*; deduction of the meaning of a hidden thing *(istinbat)*; legal decision *(hukm)*; faith *(iman)*; unbelief *(kufr)*; polytheism or unbelief *(shirk)*; coercion *(ilzam);*intellect *('aql)*; forthwith action *(fawr)*; lassitude *(tarakhi).*

These terms are given in the order in which they appear in the *Ihkam*; a few will be discussed below. In addition to defining terms used in disputatio, Ibn Hazm, coined popular terminology for his own logic, giving his definition and the old corresponding equivalents.[93] In this and other instances, he aimed at lucidity, one of the most important ingredients for

47

ascertaining the truth or falsity of any question in disputatio. In addition, Ibn Hazm devotes fifteen pages of his *Taqrib*[94] to the etiquette of *disputatio,* giving its rules with respect to the manner of beginning a debate; the way of answering one's opponent; shifting from one point to another during the deliberation; the question of opposing wrong with wrong; and other aspects. A summary of the salient points follows:

1. The two disputants must have two different goals or opposing stands, in which one of the disputants strives for the truth and attempts to convey it to his opponent beyond any shadow of doubt, and the other disputant has not established the truth and is desirous of seeking and arriving at it. This kind of disputatio is good and has laudable consequences; it is pleasing in the eye of God; and anyone who attaches blame to it is stupid and corrupt and deprives himself and others of its benefit.[95]

2. Now if the two disputants *(al-mutanaziran)* are wrong or deceitful - one of them being ignorant but seeking the truth, and the other simply wrong and deceitful - their debate is useless and should not take place, because it would be attended by confusion, great difficulty, shouting, and anger for the simple reason that the ignorant disputant is prone to accept things he has heard from someone without a shred of proof, while his opponent will persist in his deceit.[96]

3. In the course of a debate, the disputants should not be interrupted by a third party, nor should they interrupt each other nor indulge in lengthy and useless talk. Disputants should limit themselves to the task of making themselves clear. Should one of them make a mistake and wish to withdraw it, his opponent should acquiesce; the same should apply when one of the disputants finds that his evidence is unsound and wishes to abandon it in favor of a sounder one. Finally, disputants should not contend ver who should be asking the questions, because this would imply lack of confidence in their ability to win the debate. Thus, in the event of apparent shortcomings, disputants should expand their knowledge first and avoid any debate until they feel prepared; then it does not matter much who asks or responds to the questions. Ibn Hazm prefers to have his opponent choose, but were he given the choice, he would opt for asking the questions. Once the issue of questioner and respondent is settled, the disputants should adhere to their roles. The respondent is expected to answer the questions posed, unless the questioner is unfair or ignorant, or unless he is motivated by the fear of punishment were he to divulge the answer. Ibn Hazm immediately retracts the last part of this statement, saying that fear does not have a place in debates, which ought to be conducted in an atmosphere of safety because they are held in the path of God; thus, no rational Muslim should stoop so low as to not wish, because of fear, to show the triumph of Islam and the truth concerning those questions in which Muslims still differ.[97]

4. If the questioner asks and the respondent answers without further questioning from his opponent, this signifies the end of the debate until it is renewed, unless the respondent has come up with nonsense, impertinence, or irrelevance. In this case, the questioner is more than justified in calling attention to the irrelevant answer.[98]

5. The cessation of a debate takes place only when the proof is demonstrated; it should not end in a rift between the opponents. However, a debate may terminate because of ignorance, fear, or preoccupation, but this should not constitute a rupture of the truth.[99]

6. If one of the disputants terminates the debate because of his inability to answer a question posed to him, he is automatically the loser.

7. The testimony of the audience as to who is the winner in a debate is meaningless because people could simply be sharing the same opinion as the one whom they proclaim the winner. Furthermore, fairness among people in general is quite rare.[100] Proof can never be contradicted; and what is ascertained by proof cannot be contradicted by another proof.[101]

8. It is wrong if one of the disputants will have his opponent speak in order to show that he is wrong, unless he is convinced that his opponent actually is wrong, or suspects that he will come up with the same idea.[102]

8. It is equally wrong to oppose wrong with wrong in *disputatio,* unless doing so is a device for leading the opponent to the right track or for exposing him if his intent is slander, instigation, or rebuke instead of the search for the truth.[103]

10. Abundant evidence is a stgrength in *disputatio.* The disputant should verify all that he hears from his opponent, neglecting not the slightest mistakes or ambiguity.Once everything is made clear, the disputant should ask or answer questions in a clear manner; he should not introduce irrelevant elements in order to cover up his mistakes and weaknesses. Premises, opposite statements, and the conclusions reached by both sides should be scrutinized very carefully; the disputant should not accept from his opponent anything short of the clear truth.[104]

11. The disputant is not expected to do more than clarify and make the truth triumph. Thus, he is not expected to portray what is hidden in the soul, for this is impossible - if a thing does not have a form *(surah),* it is impossible to imagine it as having one. This is a complicated thing, and it is like asking a person endowed with sight to explain colors to a blind person.[105]

12. The disputant should be well informed about the various religious denominations and their adherents. It behooves him to ponder on everything being said and to search diligently for past information. In so doing, he should not be inhibited by the opinions of virtuous people, who are as subject to error as everyone else.[106]

13. If mistakes in fact or judgment are made, they should be retracted even in public without a second thought to the fact that such a confession would mean defeat rather than victory in a debate. The admission of error will earn for the individaul the reputation for fairness, whereas its denial constitutes a despicable act and simple mindedness, making the individual the laughing stock of those who know and aim at the truth.[107]

14. Beware of those who brag about their ability in *disputatio,* claiming that they can turn truth into falsehood and vice versa. These people are liars, vile and contemptible. There is no truth in their claims, for there is no power on earth which could achieve such a stupid pretention.[108]

15. There is no good in ignorance, and knowledge is superfluous if not put into use; in fact, it is worse than ignorance.[109]

16. Beware of imitation or blind reliance on one individual, however right he may have been in some cases, for he could be wrong in others.[110]

17. Convince your opponent that you intend to aid him in attaining the truth, and never remind him of his defeat in a debate, for this will be destructive and will obscure the aim of pursuing the truth.[111]

18. *Disputatio* with people whose goal is not the truth but making noise and differing so as to appear they are winners should be avoided as one would avoid a madman.[112]

19. A disputant should never attribute to his opponent a saying that was not actually said; nor volunteer an answer if not asked; nor speak on behalf of a third disputant; nor talk about a subject without a deep knowledge of it. He should always recognize that the one who knows more has precedence over him.[113]

20 Beware of self-praise, for praise is for someone else to make.[114]

21. Never belittle anyone until you actually know what he has to offer; otherwise, he might surprise you with things you never expected of him; besides, such conduct is characteristic of stupid people.[115]

22. Be careful and gentle with fair-minded people and those who do not understand; do not speak to anyone except when you want to do right for him and to make him understand.[116]

23. Know that no one is able to meet these conditions unless the individual exercises self-control, is oblivious to praise or vilification, and concentrates all his attention on the search for the truth.[117]

Ibn Hazm concludes the section on the conduct of a debate saying that speech differentiates men from beasts and that men without speech would be like donkeys or cattle. However, there are three kinds of men: first, those who are not concerned where their utterances would lead them - whether it be denial, approval, show of arrogance, or statements without proofs; the group includes majority of people; second, those who uphold what they believe in without proofs, and who are not concerned whether they are right or wrong; they believe as the crowds do, or follow imitation and their own inclination; this group of people is quite numerous; and third, those who aim at upholding the truth and suppressing falsehood; this group constitutes a very small minority.[118]

Finally, Ibn Hazm calls attention to the fact that in order to arrive at the reality of things, one must study different opinions and doctrines; scrutinize the nature of things; ponder the evidence of one's opponent; examine religions, sects, and schools of thought; determine people's affiliations and differences; and read their publications. Mastering the scineces has the object of comprehending the realities of things, thereby disavowing falsehood and making truth triumph, and teaching people so as to lead them from ignorance to the right path.[119]

These, then, are the main features governing *disputatio,* which is a praiseworthy and obligatory pursuit with no purpose other than the search for truth. To be valid, *disputatio* ought to be free of coercion, preconceived ideas, or attachment to any particular school of thought. It requires thorough knowledge, not only of the subject under discussion, but also of as many sciences as possible.

Ibn Hazm was well acquainted with the rules governing *disputatio* at an early stage in his career as a scholar-dialectician. This can be inferred from his *Taqrib,* which was probably written during his mentorship in logic under Ibn al-Kattani, who died in 1029. His debate procedures can easily be discerned in most of his extant works, chiefly *Fisal,* and in the numerous treatises that bear the title "refutation of" *(al-radd 'ala).*

Perhaps the most characteristic feature of his polemics is his reliance on analysis of textual material, or exegesis. This method conformed to his Zahirite beliefs and was used profusely whether he was disputing with Jews, Christians, or co-religionists. He used his extensive knowledge of Jewish and Christian religious writings as a great weapon quoting the Old and New Testaments, Talmud, the Acts of Martyrs, liturgies, and others.[120] After minute examination of a text, he proceeded to show the flaws and inconsistencies therein, which led him to conclude that the holy scriptures of the Jews and Christians had ceased to be the authentic revelations; he determined that this was attributable mostly to intentional and malicious alteration through addition or omission, thus resulting in irreconcilable contradictions. This "finding" leads him to the further conclusion that the only authentic revelations that remain are contained in the Qur'an and the Traditions of the Prophet, and, therefore, the only and true religion is Islam.

Ibn Hazm's polemics with Christians, Jew and other non-Muslims extended as well to virtually every shade of opinion and doctrine among his co-religionists from both the East and al-Andalus. He refuted them with the same combative spirit used against non-Muslims. Some of his numerous public debates were recorded on the spot or were incorporated by Ibn Hazm himself into his works.[121] They were held in the major cities of al-Andalus: Cordova, Almeria, Jativa, Alpuente, Valencia, Seville, Mallorca, and wherever he went.[122] Judging from approach, format, and content, one may venture to say that his major work, the *Fisal,* constitutes essentially the polished form of many of his debates.

Owing to the many sensitive issues he discussed, his debates were usually quite heated and did not conform to some of his rules governing the conduct of a debate. Judging by the preserved debates, one finds that he lacked self-control and displayed little patience toward his adversaries. He was a disarming and cruelly blunt debater, of whom it was said:

"He debated with anyone who differed from him concerning his doctrine *('ilm)* and did it without any restraint, saying what came to his mind and revealing his secrets, and always relying on God's covenant that was obligatory on the faithful scholars, whose task was to make the covenant clear and disseminate it among all people so that it will not be kept secret.[123] He never tried to soften his exposition, nor did he proceed gradually, but struck his adversary like a cataract, and made him inhale something hotter than mustard. It was then that kings began to drive him away from their entourage, exiling him from their kingdoms."[124]

This statement made by a contemporary can fairly be substantiated by Ibn Hazm's own extant writings. Ibn Hazm's "Refutation of the One Who Whispers from Afar,"[125] his reply to an anonymous letter, reveals the passion of his enemies and the charges against him. Of course, Ibn Hazm dismisses the charges of stupidity and self-righteousness, retorting: "O Ignoramus, you and your like do not have any need for the Qur'an because of your personal opinion *(ra'y);* nor do you have any need for the *sunan* of the Prophet — may God's prayer and peace be upon him. You no longer interest yourself in the transmission of traditions, or occupy yourself with establishing a verse of the Qur'an, for this is beyond your capability."[126]

To the charges that he was infatuated with the books of the ancients (philosophers), fatalists, and heretics, Ibn Hazm retorted:

"Tell us something about logic, and the books of Euclid and Ptolemy. Have you, or have you not read them, oh babble mouth? If you read them, why should you deny the same to others? Or have you denied them to yourself? Come, tell us about the heresy you found in them — if you are at all familiar with the subject matter therein. But if you have never read them, how can you deny what you do not know? If you have any brain, fear, or shame you would not talk about books concerning which you know nothing."[127]

Undoubtedly, Ibn Hazm strove for lucidity and clarity, important ingredients in his Zahirite system. He was astonishingly consistent in this regard and said what he thought regardless of the consequences - it did not matter whom he was addressing, or what issue he was dealing with. Asin was close to the mark when he characterized Ibn Hazm's polemics as possessing great erudition, but also containing a rigid dialectic, acridity and virulence.[128] It may appear paradoxical that Ibn Hazm, who possessed a masterly command of the Arabic language and an exceptional ability to convey his thoughts, should indulge in perjoratives, name-calling, and vile language toward his adversaries. Yet his "foul mouth" *(mala lengua)*[129] as Asin labels it, became proverbial in his day, and was compared with the sharp sword of the famous viceroy al-Hajjaj.[130] Vulgarity, insults and cruel satires against his opponents - be they Muslims or non-Muslims - are prevalent in virtually all of his extant writings. Asin has singled out from his *Fisal* a number of unbecoming expressions used for his opponents.[131] Terms such as idiotic, jackass, brute, pig, and liar, are not hard to find.

Such sentences as the following are also common: "This villain wanted to escape the dunghill but ended falling in a watercloset full of shit." The author of the Pentateuch is described, "The bull is more discreet than he, and the jackass wiser." The Jews are "the dirtiest, filthiest, and most repugnant race." He describes Biblical and Talmudic accounts as "stories which old ladies relate at night while weaving," or "laughable jokes which are useful only to console the sad one and to dissipate melancholy." In his refutation of Ibn al-Naghrilah, a Jewish financier of Granada who is reported to have questioned the validity of Islam, Ibn Hazm laments what he conceived to be the sorry affair resulting of giving too much power to the Jews. Among the many nasty adjectives used to describe Ibn al-Naghrilah are:" this heretic" *(zindiq)*, "this foolish ignoramus," "this impudent crazy man." and "this contemptible individual." All this leads him to point out the abominations *(qaba'ih)* which the Jews attribute to God, and states that "the Jews are the most slanderous people and most prone to lies. In spite of the fact that I have met many of them, I have found only one in my whole life who avoided ugly lies. I was astonished about that until I discovered their secret in this connection in that they believe out of imbecility and feeble-mindedness that the angels who make reckoning of deeds of the faithful do not know Arabic, or any other language except Hebrew."[132]

In his *Ihkam*, which was probably written later in life, Ibn Hazm continued to show his intemperance using expressions such as "this is the extreme of depravity", "this is a vicious contention"; we shall answer this ignoramus": "how can anyone with an iota of reason think that"; and "anyone who says this possesses great ignorance and has a weak mind."[133]

These kinds of expressions rob much of the dignity from his presentation. However, they should not detract from the merit of his expositions, which are often logical and lucid. Reading his argumentation, one is able to detect an extraordinary and disciplined mind immersed in controversies with rather uncouth and ignorant people - at least, this is how he makes them appear. In view of this, it may be legitimate to pose the question, to what extent did Ibn Hazm remain faithful to the original and actual arguments of his opponents? This is a complex question owing to the fact that only the gist of his opponent's arguments has come down to us. This problem should be subject of careful research and scrutiny. In the interim, Ibn Hazm appears to have been quite careful in this connection, either reproducing his opponents' arguments verbatim or paraphrasing them. However, the religious scholar al-Subki (d. 1370) accuses Ibn Hazm of attributing opinions to other without due study and thereby offending the great Muslim doctors, mainly al-Ash'ari, whom he had accused of heresy.[134] In modern times, Asin tends to believe that Ibn Hazm had some lapses when criticizing Judaism and Christianity,[135] but concludes: "one should not accuse him of a conscious disloyalty or bad faith in his disputes."[136]

Obviously, the man was fallible and became as committed to his doctrine as his many opponents were to theirs. But there is no indication that he indulged in intentional distortion, or that he attempted to fabricate arguments in order to put his thought and conviction in a better light. More often than not, he gave credit when credit was due, even to staunch opponents such as Abu-l-Walid al-Baji, who is reported to have defeated him in debate in Mallorca.[137]

Ibn Hazm's line of argumentation can be appreciated fully only through reading some of his works. For instance, his *Risalatan*,[138] written in the form of questions and answers, illustrates the scope and nature of his controversies. The treatise deals for the most part with real issues with which Muslims had been concerned for generations and to which Ibn Hazm had hoped to find answers and solutions. The treatise is important here in that it shows the polarization of views and ideologies between him and his adversaries. It lucidly conveys some of his views, as contrasting his faith with the beliefs of opponents whom he considers the casualty of confusion *(takhlit)*, falsehood *(kidhb)*, and ignorance *(jahl)*, and who "would not babble with idle talk were they rational people." To the charges launched against him that he used the logical *(mantiqi)* rather than the religious *(shar'i)* method of argumentation, he retorts indignantly that such a charge is a lie and born out of ignorance.[139] He argues that those people are either ignorant about logic, or they know it and cannot demonstrate what is wrong with it; it follows that they should shut up in both instances.[140] He goes on to say that he feels dutybound to show the error and deviations of those who speak as if of a fact when in reality they are oblivious to evidence *(hujjah)* and proof *(burhan)*.[141] To the contention that there are people other than Ibn Hazm who could demonstrate, arrive at the proof, and have evidence, Ibn Hazm retorts:

"This is a point in which doubt cannot be erased with simple words by anyone who examines it. Therefore, it is necessary for the seeker of the truth to listen to the evidence *(hujjah)* of all people *(kull qa'il)*. If the proof is demonstrated, it behooves him to adhere and resort to it, unless he is a godless man *(fasiq)*. For proof cannot be contradicted by another proof, and the truth *(haqq)* cannot be two different things."[142]

All things considered, one cannot afford to belittle Ibn Hazm's erudition and his ability as a dialectician, however intemperate and uncompromising. Armed with the tools of Revelation and logic, he showed an unshakable conviction in the veracity of his stand. There is no reason to doubt his sincerity in pursuing the truth, or what he believed to be the truth, regardless of the consequences. In spite of his disarming rationalism and logical mind, he was absolutely convinced that Islam and only Islam - as viewed within the framework of his doctrine - was the truth embodying all the ingredients that ultimately lead to happiness on earth and eternal bliss in the Hereafter.

The Islam of Ibn Hazm's day, and particularly Spanish Islam, appeared to be facing a grave crisis that manifested itself in the erosion of the political situation as well as in the erosion of public morals and values. This was of utmost concern to Ibn Hazm, who had hoped after his political failures to rescue his society from its predicament. He made al-Andalus his battleground and singlehandedly, without official support or sympathy, tried to alter the juridico-theological thinking of the day in favor of a more rational approach that would satisfy both the heart and mind. He was convinced that he had the solution to the religious problem if only the religious scholars would discard the shackles of traditionalism and look again at the Holy Scriptures. No doubt he was aware that his Zahirite system defied not only Andalusian reactionaries, but the whole juridico-theological traditions of Islam. Nevertheless, he persisted in his audacious stand, disregarding the religious sensitivity of the great majority of Muslims, who could not tolerate his brutal attacks on its past and present leadership, let alone condone the transformation of deeply rooted traditions. As a result, Ibn Hazm paid a heavy price, was rebuffed and ostracized; but he never relinquished his convictions.

CHAPTER IV

IBN HAZM'S DOCTRINE OF KNOWLEDGE AND THE COGNITIVE PROCESS

Secular versus Religious Knowledge

By Ibn Hazm's time, a doctrine of knowledge had been firmly established in Islamic culture. In his thorough study, *Knowledge Triumphant,* Professor Rosenthal has shown that the doctrine of knowledge was rooted in the Qur'an; its full conception evolved and was articulated in the Traditions; and it subsequently was amply treated in Arabic literature,[1] belles-lettres, poetry, and juridico-theological texts,[2] and monographs.[3] Rosenthal concludes that in Islam, "the concept of knowledge enjoyed an importance unparalleled in other civilizations."[4]

The underlying reason for the preeminence of knowledge in Islamic culture is that knowledge was inextricably associated with faith, God, and His creations. In view of its many ramifications, Muslim scholars felt for generations the need to define knowledge, to delimit its scope, to establish its various types in terms of quality and quantity, and to give precedence to some kinds of knowledge over another. For instance, the knowledge of the religious law is an obligation of all believers, for it is not only the noblest pursuit, but the source of all virtues; hence, knowledge is the opposite of ignorance, which is the source of all evil. But though there was consensus on this point, not all Muslim scholars agreed which knowledge should be the ultimate pursuit. The pious Muslim placed the knowledge of the Qur'an and Traditions first, whereas the more secular Muslim, particularly the scientist and philosopher, felt that knowledge of disciplines other than the Qur'an and Traditions was equally important.

In the course of time, there developed the notion of "blameworthy knowledge" *(madhmum)* and praiseworthy knowledge *(mahmud),* and there gradually emerged a seemingly irreconcilable dichotomy between those who held that the religious sciences alone are worthy of pursuit, and the "rationalists," who held that any knowledge is good as long as it meets the dicta of reason and conforms to natural law. During the ninth and tenth centuries, many foreign works, mainly Greek, were translated into Arabic. These works covered all the sciences and introduced many concepts alien to a religion born in the relative isolation of the Arabian desert. Naturally, a cultural shock of this kind produced all sorts of reactions — positive as well as negative.

At first, it appears that, however far removed these sciences were from Islam, they were received with remarkable acceptance. Philosophy, logic, mathematics, astronomy, medicine, and other sciences were avidly pursued along with the religious and philological sciences. This study was encouraged by the caliphal court and was facilitated by an advanced system of education, by an increasing number of publications, and by the establishment of numerous private and public libraries. An interesting pattern emerged whereby religious and philosophical disciplines were developing on parallel line; for a time, they appeared to complement each other, both being useful in this life as well as in the Hereafter. For this reason, perhaps, the term knowledge (*'ilm*) acquired a wide connotation and became all-inclusive in many respects. The pursuit of knowledge in all branches of study became the noblest goal of the faithful: Qur'anic verses, numerous Traditions, and utterances of ancient and Muslim sages were invoked, exalting knowledge in its broadest aspects and urging its dissemination. Although the religious sciences remained implicitly or explicitly at the top of the hierarchy of sciences, the secular sciences were considered just as important. Had this apparently mutual tolerance between pietist and rationalist continued, all the sciences might have been integrated into a unified curriculum. However, this was not to be.

Already in the tenth century, the Eastern scholar al-'Amiri (d. 922)[5] expresses concern about the emerging dichotomy between the religious scholars and philosophers. After defining knowledge and the sciences constituting it, al-'Amiri shows his concern about the attitude of some religious scholars who attacked the philosophical sciences as contradicting the religious sciences. Al-'Amiri took issue with them, saying that the philosophical sciences, like the religious sciences, rest on certain principles conforming to pure reason and are confirmed by valid proof; thus, he could not see any contradiction between them.

The controversy was pronounced in the East, but it was worse in conservative al-Andalus. At first, al-Andalus had accepted the broad definition of knowledge received from the East, but later Anadlusian scholars adopted a definite religious orientation, whereby the philosophical sciences were believed useless, if not harmful, to the religious beliefs. Logic and philosophy, in particular, could be pursued only clandestinely. This does not mean that books on the philosophical sciences did not exist in Muslim Spain; indications are that they were found in abundance among a relatively small number of people who fully appreciated their content and objectives. But the majority of Andalusian scholars had chosen a complete separation of the philosophical and religious sciences, believing that true knowledge resides in the religious sciences and trascends knowledge of all the secular disciplines.

It is against this general background that Ibn Hazm's conception of knowledge and the sciences in general must be viewed. Ibn Hazm's broad education in the philosophical and religious sciences enabled him to appreciate the magnitude of the problem at hand. He proposed a middle course, having to satisfy both pietists and rationalists, but in fact pleasing none. To arrive at such a "compromise", Ibn Hazm relied heavily on the religious texts as well as on philosophical works, but he was careful not to identify himself with any school of thought, either religious or secular. His argument hinged on the question of seeking and ascertaining the truth *(haqq)*, which could be achieved through the Revelation and/or philosophy. After pondering the meaning of knowledge, its scope and significance, and after considering the merit and place of each of the known sciences, Ibn Hazm concluded that the religious sciences and philosophy aim at the same end and, thus, are in complete harmony. Although he remained staunchly religious, he felt that the bonafide secular sciences were not only related to the religious sciences, but offered indispensable assistance in the proper understanding and implementation of the religious law.

Conception of Knowledge among Andalusians

In its time and place, Ibn Hazm's conception of knowledge was audacious. Thus, a review of the conceptions of knowledge current among Ibn Hazm's predecessors and contemporaries may be helpful in understanding how Ibn Hazm came to expound his doctrine of knowledge, in a setting where the pietist had long prevailed over the rationalist outlook.

In all probability, Andalusian traditionalists of the ninth century included a treatment of knowledge in their compilations and abridgments of Traditions. Furthermore, scholars who had been educated in the East may have conveyed the Eastern conception of knowledge to their students through lectures or writing. For example, Yahya Ibn Zakariya (d. 872) is credited a work entitled *On the Merit of Knowledge.*[7]. In *The Unique Necklace (al-'Iqd al-farid)*, the belletrist Ibn 'Abd Rabbihi (d.940) devoted a whole book to the subject of knowledge and education *(al-'ilm wa-l-adab).*[8] Essentially, the *'Iqd* cnsists of Traditions and sayings current in the East, presented in a random order and without any authorical perspective.

Ibn 'Abd Rabbihi defines knowledge and education in a broad sense as 'the pillars upon which rest the axis of religion and worldly affairs. They distinguish man from the rest of animals, and angelic nature from beastly nature. They are food for the intellect, lamp for the body, light for the heart, and a pillar for the soul.''[9]

Knowledge should be disseminated:
"There are two kinds of knowledge: (1) the knowledge that is held back; and (2) the knowledge that is used; whatever is held back is harmful whereas that which is used is beneficial."[10]

Knowledge and action are interrelated:
"Were it not for action, knowledge would not be sought and vice versa."[11]

The intellect plays an important role in the cognitive process, and is defined as "The perception of things in their realities."[12] The intellect is the driver *(sa'iq)* in relation to knowledge, which plays the role of commander *(qa'id);*[13] if a person had no knowledge, he would be devoid of intellect.[14] Evidence shows that the intellect functions in receiving knowledge in the same manner sight receives colors, and hearing receives sounds.[15] In sum, the intellect is the instrument and depository of all knowledge:

"For the Almighty made certain things to support and generate others. Thus, the clarification of the imagination of what is perceived by the senses awakens the desires of memory *(dhikr),* which, in turn, alerts the faculty of thinking to reflect; and reflection stimulates the secrets of volition, and volition, in turn, decides the causes of action leading them to the intellect in which everything will utlimately end . . ."[16]

Prophetic Traditions, and assorted sayings are quoted to exalt the virtue of knowledge, the rewards of acquiring and disseminating it, and the praise and merits of those who devote themselves to it. Some of the traditions and sayings follow: The Prophet is reported to have said, "The virtue of knowledge is better than that accruing from worship."[17] Solomon admonished, "Make knowledge your wealth and education your ornament,"[18] and "Man is not born a scholar, but acquires knowledge through instruction."[19] Knowledge is a continuous process.[21] If a man wishes to become a scholar, he should pursue one discipline only, but if he desires to become an educated person, he should pursue several disciplines.[22] Kings should know genealogy and history; soldiers, warfare and biographies; and merchants, accounting.[23] There are certain subjects that should be pursued in moderation, whereas others should be studied as much as possible. For instance, excessive study of grammar will make a person idiotic; overindulgence in poetry will corrupt him, but extensive study of jurisprudence will ennoble him.[24] Moreover, the individual will waste his time and will be led astray if he searches for things that do not exist; thus, he who searches for religion in philosophy will not escape heresy; the one who seeks wealth in alchemy will not be spared poverty; and the one who looks for rare Traditions will not escape lies.[25]

The sayings reported by Ibn 'Abd Rabbihi come from non-Islamic and Islamic sources on many different periods. Among the profuse quotations, there is no coherent doctrine of knowledge with which Ibn 'Abd Rabbihi could be associated. That was not his purpose; rather, his main concern throughout the *'Iqd* was to select the choicest of literary gems about the various subjects with which he dealt.[26]

However, the eleventh-century Andalusians Sa'id of Toledo, Ibn 'Abd al-Barr, and Ibn Hazm, held definite individual views concerning knowledge, its meaning and content. These towering figures in Andalusian intellectual history all dealt with the subject of knowledge and the sciences in general, and probably knew one another's work quite well. Sa'id and Ibn 'Abd al-Barr were committed Malikites; Ibn Hazm became a staunch Zahirite. Sa'id looked upon the sciences from a secular rather than religious perspective. emphasising geographic determinism and demography as determinants in their occurence and cultivation, and nearly relegating the religious sciences to an insignificant place in the intellectual history of mankind.[27] Ibn'Abd al-Barr maintained a definite religious orientation toward the sciences. Ibn Hazm allowed the coexistence of the religious and philosophical sciences.

It is relevant here to contrast the views of Ibn 'Abd al-Barr with those of Ibn Hazm, and to point to the interaction of their ideas. Ibn Hazm and Ibn 'Abd al-Barr were friends and colleagues and had a great deal in common. Both were natives of Cordova, belonged to highly educated families, and had access to the best education available. Ibn 'Abd al-Barr (978-1071) was the son of a prominent judge and Ibn Hazm's senior by about sixteen years, but in spite of the disparity in age, they studied together under various teachers. But whereas Ibn 'Abd al-Barr hoped to become a prominent judge, like his father, Ibn Hazm had aspired to become a courtier like his father. Because of this, their educational preparations were somewhat different. Ibn 'Abd al-Barr's education encompassed the traditional disciplines - namely, Arabic philology, belles-lettres, Traditions, Qur'anic studies, jurisprudence, and history - whereas Ibn Hazm's education had, at first, a less religious orientation and encompassed Arabic philology, literature, history, and some of the philosophical sciences. This educational disparity separated the two men in their attitude toward knowledge and the sciences in general.

Immediately after the revolt of 1009, Ibn 'Abd al-Barr was forced to leave Cordova for Denia in Eastern al-Andalus. There he served at the court of its enlightened ruler Mujahid and was able to write a number of works, dealing mostly with religious matters, such as jurisprudence, Traditions, and history of the Companions of the Prophet. Ibn Hazm appears to have maintained his association with Ibn'Abd al-Barr and regarded his works with high praise.[28] In fact, Ibn 'Abd al-Barr's *Jami'*, explaining knowledge and its excellence,[29] was known to Ibn Hazm and predates the latter's *Categories of the Sciences*.

The two men's conceptions of knowledge and the science remained almost poles apart, but they shared common ideas on a variety of issues. For example they had contempt for the narrowmindedness of their contemporary jurists for excessive reliance on imitation *(taqlid)*. In this connection, Ibn 'Abd al-Barr almost echoes the sentiment of Ibn Hazm when he says that the religious scholars simply recite and learn some Traditions without understanding them; they combine the lean and the fat, the healthy and the unhealthy, the true and the false, giving credence to one and its opposite at the same time without realizing the contradiction. Some of them more idiotic still and do not even bother to learn the Qur'an and Traditions, but rely blindly on the opinions of authorities; and to add insult to injury, they criticize and ostracize other schools.[30] Although Ibn 'Abd al-Barr did not disavow imitation completely, he entertained reservation with respect to the unreasoned use of personal opinion *(ra'y)*, analogy *(qiyas)*, and guesswork *(zann)*. All these were anathema to Ibn Hazm, who felt they represent an affront to divine power.[32]

What is important here is Ibn 'Abd al-Barr's conception of knowledge. In his *Jami' (Compendium)* elucidating knowledge and its virtues, Ibn 'Abd al-Barr does not attempt to establish a doctrine of knowledge, but compiles traditions that bear on the meaning of knowledge, its virtues, the merit of seeking it, the evidence supporting it, the weakness of utterances about religion without understanding, the permissibility of judgment without evidence, praiseworthy and blameworthy opinion, the limit and permissibility of imitation, and other aspects.[33] Written by anonymous request, the work contains most of Ibn 'Abd Rabbihi's sayings about knowledge in *The Unique Necklace*. Ordinarily, Prophetic Traditions speak for themselves. Reference will be made here to those items ordinarily discussed by Ibn Hazm:

Knowledge is a duty *(faridah)* incumbent upon every Muslim,[34] and ought to be sought even if it were in China; its seekers are warriors in the path of God; God makes the way to Paradise easy for those who search and acquire knowledge;[35] knowledge is the best legacy left after death;[36] it is more meritorious than worship;[37] the scholar is God's trustee on earth;[38] he is taken care of in the Day of Judgment just after the Prophets, but before the martyrs;[39] kings govern people, but scholars govern kings;[40] people are not born scholars - knowledge is acquired through teaching.[41] Knowledge should be pursued at a tender age,[42] and should be imparted only to those who are capable of it, for if it is given to incapable people it is like ornamenting a pig with pearls and gold.[43] Knowledge should not be crowded but given slowly one thing at a time,[44] the steps for acquiring it are; silence, listening, memorizing, implementing, and disseminating it.[45] Knowledge is to be put into action,[46] and should not be acquired for boasting and worldly gains;[47] it ought to be disseminated, and he who conceals it will face the fire of Hell in the Day of Judgment.[48] All in all, he who knows ought to teach, and he who does not know ought to ask.[49]

Knowledge is conceived as light in the darkness,[50] and true knowledge is the knowledge of religion.[51] Whether influenced by the strength of Traditions, or the chaotic conditions of his time, Ibn 'Abd al-Barr cautions scholars not to associate with rulers.[52] particularly unjust rulers; only unworthy people join them, and even Qur'anic readers end in Hell if they frequent such courts.[53] Lastly, the pursuit of knowledge is a means for eternal salvation and not for gaining wealth.[54]

On the basis of these and other utterances, knowledge is tantamount to faith, if not faith itself.[55] There is no satisfactory answer to the question, What knowledge is? Professor Rosenthal has studied the diverse answers of many different people, who define knowledge as a process of knowing, a synonym of gnosis *(ma'rifah)*; finding or obtaining through mental perception; a process of elucidation and discernment; a form; a belief; a remembrance; imagination; image; a vision or opinion; a relative term; a relationship to action; negation of ignorance; and the result of intuition.[56] This same diversity is apparent in Ibn 'Abd al-Barr's *Jami'*. He hedges on a definition of his own saying:

"The definition of knowledge among the theologians is what you ascertain and make clear.[57] Thus, he who ascertains a thing and makes it clear knows that thing. On this basis, the one who does not ascertain a thing but maintains it through imitation among the great majority of scholars is different from adherence to *(ittiba')*, which means that you adhere to something because it is clear to you with respect to the saying of a proponent and the soundness of his doctrine *(madhhab)*, Imitation is when you uphold the opponent's view without knowing him or the aspect and the meaning of his saying. You simply refuse other sayings and attempts to show the error of your proponent. As a result, you persist in following him, fearing to differ from him even if you may know the fallacy of his sayings."[58]

Thus, knowledge is not blind imitation, but that which is ascertainable and varied. There are two kinds, necessary *(dururi)* and self-evident and acquired *(muktasab)*. Necessary knowledge is that which cannot be doubted and is there before the individual has the faculty of thought *(fikrah)* and the ability of demonstration *(nazar)*. It is perceived through sensation *(hiss)* and the intellect *('aql),* such as knowing that a thing cannot be moving and be motionless at one and the same time; that a person could not be standing and sitting at once and that individual could not be healthy and sick at the same time. In the realm of the senses, taste knows the difference between sweet and bitter things, sight differentiates colors, hearing distinguishes sounds, and the like.

Acquired knowledge is that which is gained through the search of evidence *(istidlal)* and demonstration *(nazar)*. This kind of knowledge can either be hidden *(khafiy)* or manifest *(jaliy)* in its relation to necessary or self-evident knowledge - that is, the closer it is to necessary knowledge, the more manifest it is. Finally, the signs *(ma'lumat)* of knowledge are of two kinds, the visible *(shahid)* and the invisible *(gha'ib)*. Visible signs are known by *necessity* as self-evident, whereas invisible signs are known through demonstration *(dalalah)* with the aid of the visible signs.[59]

For Ibn 'Abd al-Barr, as for the great majority of the religious scholars, the roots, reality, and the true meaning of knowledge reside in the knowledge of the Islamic religion. The whole concept is encompassed in the following Prophetic Tradition: "Knowledge consists of three things, and anything beyond them is superfluous. (1) mastering a verse of the Qur'an; (2) a well-supported tradition; and (3) an honest religious obligation."[60] The spirit of this Tradition is reinforced further by another Tradition that says: "One day the Prophet entered the mosque and found a crowd surrounding a man. He asked, 'What is this?' They said: 'O Messenger of God, this is a very learned man *('allamah).'* He said: 'In what?' They replied, 'He is the most knowledgeable in the genealogy of the Arabs, in the Arabic language, poetry, and the quarrels of the Arabs.' Then he said, 'This is a knowledge which does not benefit, and an ignorance of which does not hurt.' "[61] Numerous other Traditions suggest that a true knowledge is the knowledge of the Qur'an and Traditions, and anything beyond that falls under the formula, "I do not know *(la adri)."*

These are the most salient points dealt with by Ibn 'Abd al-Barr in his *Jami'*. Unlike Ibn Hazm, Ibn 'Abd al-Barr simply reports what he considers to be sound and verifiable Traditions, rarely expressing his opinion about any given issue - except perhaps in the process of selection. In this he differs greatly from Ibn Hazm, who may have used some identical sayings and Traditions, but subjected them to careful scrutiny for the purpose of achieving a unified and coherent system of knowledge.

There was also a difference in temperament. Ibn'Abd al-Barr remained the cautious and serene religious scholar, whereas Ibn Hazm displayed his combative spirit in practically every issue he discussed. Armed with the knowledge of logic and a familiarity with the secular sciences, he showed his contempt for the abysmal ignorance of the religious scholars in matters affecting faith and their attitude toward the secular disciplines. It was with this attitude that Ibn Hazm defended the secular discipline and attempted to reconcile them with the religious sciences.

Ibn Hazm's Conception of Knowledge

Knowledge, its origin, value, acquisition, dissemination, and classification were major concerns of Ibn Hazm, and constitute an integral part of his juridico-theological doctrine. They are discussed in several of his works: *Taqrib,*[62] *Fisal,*[63] *Ihkam,*[64] *Akhlaq,*[65] *Tawqif,*[66] and *Maratib al-'ulum*[67] - indeed, the *Maratib al-ulum* is devoted exclusively to the subject of knowledge and the sciences. In his treatment of knowledge, Ibn Hazm combines the religious and philosophical concepts of knowledge, finds the two to be harmonious and complementary, and defends his position with acumen and insight, presenting a wealth of information to show the intricacy of the subjects and the various opinions concerning it. In discussing knowledge, he takes into consideration faith, reason, sensation, and other means for arriving at cognition. He comes to the happy conclusion that knowledge can be arrived at through faith and reason in different ways, but with the same result.

Deriving his inspiration and information from the religious texts and secular writing, Ibn Hazm comes up with a coherent system reflecting his views on the intricate subject of knowledge. To him, knowledge is the certainty *(tayaqqun)* of a thing as it is.[68] It is the opposite of ignorance *(jahl),* which precludes the reality of a thing in the soul.[69] It is associated with the four cardinal virtues: justice *('adl),* understanding *(fahm),* courage *(najdah),* and generosity *(jud).* Ignorance is associated with the three capital vices of inequity *(jawr).* cowardice *(jubn),* and avarice *(shuhh)*[70] It is the ornament of the intellect, which would be a barren soil without knowledge.[71] This brings the intellect and knowledge close to each other in the pursuit of virtues. Knowledge is a multi-faceted thing, but the noblest knowledge is that which brings the individual closer to his Maker.[72]

Knowledge, like faith, is a passport to happiness in this life and in the Hereafter.[73] As depositories of knowledge, faith and reason — although differing in nature — have an identical aim in Ibn Hazm's thinking, that is, the attaintment of virtues *(fada'il)*. This approximation with faith and reason becomes more evident in his broad conception of knowledge. Inasmuch as knowledge is related to the state of individual happiness on earth as well as in Heaven, it should be sought incessantly and disseminated; its seeker, however, should not boast about it because it is a gift from God.[74] He should always be humble with whatever knowledge he may have because someone else could have more knowledge than he.[75] Finally, knowledge should be put into practice, otherwise the ignorant person would appear better off than the scholar.[76] In fact, knowledge and action *(al-'ilm wa-l-'amal)*[77] go together and are inseparable, particuarly with regard to the performance of the religious duties. In consequence, the greatest virtue along with the practice of goodness is to teach and implement knowledge.[78]

In addition to these and similar statements found throughout his *Akhlaq*, Ibn Hazm devotes a special section to knowledge which deserves translation:[79]

31. The virtue of pursuing knowledge would be a good and compelling reason to make the ignoramuses respect you, and the scholars like and honor you. Furthermore, how about other virtues that accrue from it in this world and in the Hereafter?

32. The disadvantage of ignorance makes it a good and compelling reason to abandon it, if only because the ignorant man envies the scholar and rejoices with his fellow ignoramuses. Moreover, how about other vices that are detrimental in this world and in the Hereafter?

34. If the scholar were to ponder for a time on the satisfaction that knowledge brings with respect to the humiliation of the ignoramuses and their preoccupation with not knowing the secret of the realities of things, in addition to the happiness he will experience with regard to the knowledge of hidden things that are not known to others, he will certainly multiply his thanks to God - may He be glorified and exalted - and will be happy with the knowledge he has which he will desire to increase.

35. He who occupies himself with the low sciences *(adna)* and abandons the lofty ones *(a'la)* of which he is capable is like the farmer who sows corn in soil suited for wheat, and like the planter who sows barley where dates and olive trees thrive.

36. Dissemination of knowledge among people not suited for it is destrucive. It is like giving honey and sweets to those suffering from a burning fever; and musk and amber to inhale to those suffering from headache resulting from excess of bile.

37. The one who is greedy with his knowledge is more blameworthy

than the one who is greedy with his money, because the latter fears the loss of what he has, whereas the former is simply avaricious about something which is not expendable, and which is loss if not used.

38. Whoever has a vocation for a given science - though it may be less lofty than another - should not abandon it for another because this would be like a man planting coconuts in al-Andalus and another planting olive trees in India. They will not bear any fruit in either case.

39. The noblest of knowledge is that which will bring you closer to the Almighty God, and will help you to please him.

40. Compare yourself in wealth, position, and health with those who have less than you, but compare yourself in religion, knowledge, and virtues with those who have more than you.

41. Recondite sciences are like strong medicine; they help people with strong constitutions, but destroy those with weak bodies. Similarly, they will greatly enrich and purify the vigorous intellect, b ut they will destroy the weak one.

42. If the fool were ever to immerse himself in intellectual pursuits in the same manner that he is immersed in his foolishness, he would emerge wiser than Hasan al-Basri, Plato of Athens, and the Persian Buzur — jumhir.

43. Intellectual inquiry will be useless if it is not supported by the good fortune of religion and by that of [the sciences] of the world.

44. Do not hurt yourself to experiment with vitiated opinions in order to demonstrate their fallacy, for in this way you will perish. The upholder of a vitiated opinion will end blaming you for differing with him! Thus you are better off being free of abominable things than repenting after you have fallen into them.

45. Beware of pleasing someone whom your soul considers evil and concerning whom there is no compelling obligation to please from the vantage point of the law and virtue.

46. True science unveils the ignorance concerning the attributes of God - may He be glorified and exalted.

47. There is no greater harm to the sciences and their pursuers than the harm coming from ignorant intruders and outsiders, who claim that they know it all and who believe that they are doing good when actually they bring harm.

48. Whoever wishes the benefit of the Hereafter, the wisdom of this world, moderation of conduct, possession of all moral qualities, and the practice of all virtues, should follow the example of Muhammad, the Messenger of God - may God's prayer and peace be upon him - and should put into practice his moral qualities and conduct as much as he can. May God help us to follow His example and fulfill His wish. Amen, Amen.

49. Ignorant people annoyed me twice during my lifetime; once when they spoke about things they did not know when I was still ignorant; and the second time when they shut up in my presence when I became learned. They always shut up when it is beneficial to them, and speak up when it is not.

50. Scholars made me happy twice during my lifetime: when studying while I was ignorant, and when conversing with me after I became learned.

51. One of the virtues of knowledge and asceticism is that God - may He be glorified and exalted - bestows them only on the right and deserving people. And the defect of high positions, wealth and prestige in this world is that they are often found among people who are neither entitled to nor deserving of them.

52. He who seeks virtue associates himself with people of virtue only, and joins the best companions among the people of equity, piety, honesty, nobility, patience, fidelity, loyalty, magnanimity, clean conscience, and true friendship.

53. He who seeks fame, wealth, and pleasure befriends only people who are like rabid dogs and deceitful foxes, and joins on the road the enemies of belief and those whose nature is vitiated.

54. The utility of knowledge in the practice of virtue is enormous, for through it one will be able to know the beauty of virtue which will never escape him; he will also be able to know the ugliness of vices, avoiding them except upon rare occasions; he will take heed of nice praise and will wish something like it for himself; he will also take heed of damnation and will attempt to avoid it. On these grounds, it is necessary to conclude that knowledge has a great deal to do with every virtue, and that ignorance has its share in every vice. Moreover, no one will ever achieve virtue without learning the sciences - excepting those who posses pure natures and virtuous constitutions. To this category belong the Prophets - may God's prayer and peace be upon them; this is so because God Almighty has taught them all goodness *(khayr)* without the intervention of man.

55. I have seen some common people who possess moderation and excellent characters in a measure exceeding those of wise and self-assured scholars. This is rare, however. On the other hand, I have seen people who have pursued the sciences, have learned the covenants of the Prophets - may God's prayer and peace be upon them - and have known the admonitions of the wise men *(hukama),* but had characters such that no one could surpass them in wicked conduct, in public and secret depravity. This happens very often. In light of this, I have come to the conclusion that moral qualities are bestowed on some people and denied to others by Almighty God."

This section from the *Akhlaq,* written late in Ibn Hazm's life, represents the gist of this reflections and conclusions concerning the subject of knowledge. His last statement (no.55) appears to be in contradiction to other statement that virtues are associated with the degree and quality of knowledge, but it is consistent in that it expresses his belief that God bestows knowledge and virtues on whoever He wishes. In statement 55, as elsewhere, Ibn Hazm shows his religious perspective, even at the risk of contradiction, saying that some average and untutored individuals could be equal and even superior to some scholars in matters of moral qualities. This question must, however, be viewed within the context of faith and reason - both instruments and depositories of knowledge. No virtue can ever be achieved except by the grace of God, for virtue is associated with and depends upon knowledge in the same manner that vice is associated with and is the result of ignorance. Prophets belong to a special category, receiving knowledge directly from God without human mentorship.

In sum, knowledge is indispensable for all people; it must be pursued to the fullest extent and according to one's ability; but it should never be entrusted to those who are inept or incapable of understanding its significance and implications. Knowledge is something acquired through teaching and the use of human faculties. But for knowledge to fulfill its noblest goal it must be channeled, not toward the acquisition of wealth and prestige, but toward the search for truth, which will enable the individual to come closer to the Almighty God. In essence, knowledge consists of comprehending God's revelations, practicing moral virtues, and knowing the realities of things in this world. The object of knowledge is to please and be close to the Almighty and to attain a world order encompassing humanity at large.

The Source of Knowledge and the Cognitive Process

Ibn Hazm's maxims and aphorisms are inspired by previous collections of sayings and Traditions. As such they do not represent anything new, but they become significant within the context in which Ibn Hazm uses them. The following paragraphs are intended to reveal that context.

Ibn Hazm had a strong commitment to religion and upheld the view traditional among Muslim scholars that God is the teacher and the source of all knowledge.[80] He says that it is impossible to find a single individual in time or space who has any knowledge including language or any other science,[81] which is not taught to him by someone else. Furthermore, man is endowed with certain faculties, gifts of God which enable him through research or personal inquiry *(ijtihad)* to ascertain the realities of things, to comprehend and reaffirm divine knowledge, and at the same time, to distinguish between right and wrong. Through human faculties, particularly the intellect, man will be able to ascertain the truth; knowledge of the creation of the world; the necessity of having a Creator; the unicity of God; and the necessity of the existence of revelation, prophecy, and most important, the reality of the Revelation handed down to the Prophet Muhammad.[82] In his quest for these verities, man is assisted by the science of logic. Although logic constitutes the pillar of and is ancillary to all the sciences, no science, however humble or even doubtful, should escape the attention of the student.

Given human limitations, however, no one should devote himself completely to a base science, neglecting the lofty. This explains in greater part Ibn Hazm's hierarchal categorization of the sciences according to their nobility and utility. Despite this, Ibn Hazm insists that for a full comprehension of the religious sciences, no one can dispense with the more "noble" secular sciences. He places intellect *('aql)* and faith *(iman)* at almost the same level because both aim at the same thing - that is, philosophy and religion have a common ground. Owing to human limitations, not everyone can be a philosopher and ascertain the truth by himself. Here, faith plays its most important role because it is available to all. But faith alone may not be the answer to all human problems pertaining to this world and the Hereafter. It must be reaffirmed and taken out of the realm of confusion, doubts, and superstitions. For this, education becomes paramount and indispensable, requiring teachers who are made and found in urban centers, not in uncivilized places such as the lands of the Slavs, Black Africa and the desert.[83]

Aside from the divine origin of knowledge and the need for teachers to impart it, Ibn Hazm develops a theory of acquisition of knowledge which is basically similar to the one developed among Greek philosophers. To him, knowledge is closely related to the state of the soul and the degree of its awareness of its surroundings. The soul is assisted by sensation *(hiss)*, assumption *(zann)*, imagination *(takhayyul)*, and the intellect *('aql)*. These faculties lead the soul to think and decide in accordance with what they convey to it.[84] Thus, if the soul has forgotten something it had stored, it will with the help of those faculties seek to recollect the forgotten thing in the same manner that an owner will search for his tool when it is lost. However, not all the faculties of the soul can be relied on with the same degree of certainty. Assumption *(zann)* is the least reliable because it can deceive - for instance, assuming an armed and stout man to be courageous when he may actually be a coward. Imaginaion can also be unreliable - as when one imagines hearing a voice when actually there is none, or when one imagines seeing a man when in reality there is no such man. Only the intellect can be relied on to determine the accuracy of cognitions gathered by the senses. The intellect is defined as "faculty by means of which the soul is able to discern all existing things*(mawjudat)* as they are categorized, and to perceive the true qualities of things, denying only those qualities which are not applicable to them. This is the true meaning of the intellect, which has also the power of discernment. Discernment is the cognition of the intellect without which there is no cognition *(idrak)*. Moreover, the intellect has the added power to make use of obedience *(ta'at)* and virtues, and of avoiding disobedience and vices."[85]

The intellect is not the same as discernment *(tamyiz)*; it goes beyond discernment. For discernment consists of the ability to distinguish a thing by virtue of a quality peculiar to that thing; it can be achieved by any rational being. Thus, every rational being *('aqil)* is discerning, but not every discerning person is a rationalist.[86] Discernment functions as an agent of the soul and a catalyst for ascertaining the knowledge of things as they are. Its relation to the soul is explained by Ibn Hazm in the following manner. He says that there are two things in the world: (1) that which subsists by itself; sustains others, occupies a place, has length, width, and depth; and is called body or substance *(jawhar);* and (2) that which subsists in another thing and not by itself, and is an accident *('arad)* that lacks dimensions; to this category belong colors, taste, odor, movement, and the like. To him, body and substance are one and the same thing; and to the contention that substance is neither a body nor an accident, he retorts that this is impossible because existence consists of a Creator and creation only, and there cannot be anything in between. Within this context, he moves to define the soul and the intellect.

Ibn Hazm considers the whole concept of the soul as it had been understood by those schools of thought which questioned whether or not the soul exists, and whether it is an accident, a mixture of humors, a breath that enters or leaves the body, or a substance that is not a body nor an accident, but the ruling agent *(al-fa''alah al-mudabbirah).* which is man himself. Discounting these views he maintains that the soul is synonymous with spirit *(ruh),* and that it is a body having length, width, and depth; occupying a place; living; possessing the faculties of sensory perception, rationality, and discernment; knowing all things except itself; and being the ruling agent of the body.[87] As such, the soul constitutes the core of the cognitive process with the intellect *('aql)* as one of its faculties - in other words the intellect is an accident or agent of the soul.[88] Therefore, it can be contrasted with stupidity *(humq).*[89] Linguistically, he says that the intellect means interdiction and serves to discern things and to employ obediences and virtues.[90]

> "The intellect does not make anything forbidden or obligatory; it is one of the accidents found in the soul; it is impossible for accidents to decide on things or legislate. Therefore, the intellect is only the knowledge of things as they are with respect to their qualities and quantities, no more, no less."[91]

Thus, the intellect does not decide to change the order of things or their nature, particularly in religious matters - it cannot , for instance, decide whether eating pork should be forbidden or permitted, because this is already legislated in the Holy Texts. The intellect's role is limited to helping the discerning soul: "The intellectual faculty *(quwat al-'aql)* is that which helps the discerning soul to make justice triumph, to choose what sound understanding dictates and to be convinced of it, and to make it manifest with the aid of the tongue and other bodily movements in action."[92]

Neverthless, Ibn Hazm reiterates the preeminent role of the intellect in the attainment of knowledge, in ascertaining the proof *(burhan)* and in demonstrating the truth *(haqq).*[93] In his preoccupation with separating true knowledge from mere opinions or assumptions, he insists that the intellect is that which distinguishes right from wrong. He refutes those who deny such a role and who claim that knowledge emantes only from (1) instinct/inspiration *(ilham)*; (2) history *(khabar)*; or (3) imitation *(taqlid)*. Ibn Hazm considers each of these to be wicked distortion lacking any foundation in fact. As instinct *(ilham)* "is a knowledge that makes an impression on the soul without any proof, demonstration, persuasion, or imitation; it is simply a natural act *(fi'l al-tabi'ah)* proper to irrational and some rational animals, such as the spider weaving its web and the bee building its honeycomb."[94] As inspiration, *ilham* cannot be ascertained by proof, or be accepted as a miracle; it is mere pretension, which anyone could claim. Imitation, which is the belief *(i'tiqad)* in something on the strength of someone's having said it, is equally faulty because one person may imitate someone who is wrong and another, someone who is right.[95] Knowledge transmitted through history must be scrutinized to determine whether the information is right or wrong; this will require proofs, which can be achieved only through the evidence *(hujjah)* of the intellect.[96] In short, "since all the means - instinct/inspration, imitation, and history - which are claimed by our adversaries for arriving at the realities of things cannot lead to a sound knowledge on their own strength, it follows that the right thing to do is to resort to the evidence of the intellect and conclusions; it also follows that the intellect actually discerns the qualities of existing things, guiding and leading the researcher to the realities of the conditions of things."[97]

Ibn Hazm brings out in another context the primary role of the intellect in the cognitive process. He addressed himself to the question, already discussed by his predecessors and contemporaries, whether knowledge is the outcome of necessity/self-evidence *(bi-idtirar)*, of acquisition *(bi-iktisab)*, or of both necessity and acquisition.[98] Ibn Hazm defends the view that knowledge is *necessary*/self-evident and that only the method of attaining it is acquired. He delves into the question at some length, showing how the necessary knowledge is acquired.[99] He states that man *(insan)* lacks both intellectual perception and knowledge at the time of birth,[100] supporting this contention on the basis of the Qur'anic verse, "God brought you forth from the womb of your mother without knowing anything."[101] However, the child at birth possesses sensation *(hiss)* and voluntary movement *(harakah iradiyah)* as do other animals.[102] The child folds and extends his feet; moves his limbs in all directions, experiences pain when cold, hungry, or pinched; seeks food and uses his mouth to find the breast of his mother. These functions - life, sensation, movement, and growth - are natural endowments common to all animals. However, though animals will continue to act uniformly and unchangeably by virtue of instinct *(ilham)*,[103] as the child grows, he will act in varied and innovative ways. The bee will make its honeycomb and the spider its web with constancy guided by instinct, which is an innate faculty and *necessary* nature *(tabi'ah daruriyyah)*.[104] On the other hand, man uses all sort of innovation in the manufacture of textiles; he makes embroideries, golden strings and the like; learns the crafts; and practices the sciences, such as architecture, astronomy, medicine, algebra, eloquence, and theology.[105]

Thus, though the faculty of instinct *(ilham)* remains the constant determining factor in the acts and behaviour of animals, it is not the same with human beings. As the child grows, his instinct is soon overshadowed by other faculties. He will acquire rationality when his rational soul *(nafsuhu al-natiqah)* becomes strong, familiar and at home with his surroundings and when the humidity begins to dry. It is then that the soul will begin to discern things.[106] This faculty of discernment *(tamyiz)*, which is peculiar to man, will enable him to distinguish between aromatic and fetid smells, to differentiate colors, sweet and bitter tastes, sharp and rough sounds, and the like. All these discernments fall in the domain of the senses; to the senses is added intuitive knowledge *('ilm bi-l-badihiyat)*, by means of which the soul will take cognizance of truths: that a part is smaller than the whole, that a person cannot be sitting and standing at the same time, that things exist in time and are endowed by certain characteristics and quiddities *(taba'i'wa-mahiyah)*, that actions are produced by an agent, and that information *(khabar)* can be true or false. "All of this can be seen in all people while growing and constitutes the first stages of intellectual perception, which no rational being can dispute.... Only crazy and ignorant people, who do not know the realities of things *(haqa'iq al-ashya')*, will ask for a demonstration."[107]

Along with sensation, discernment, and intuitive knowledge, God created in man the faculty of reflection *(quwat al-tafkir)*, which enables him to make use of the senses *(isti'mal al-hawas)* for seeking demonstration *(istidlal)*, and the faculty of understanding *(fahm)* that which the senses perceive. Finally, the soul is endowed by God with the faculty of the intellect, which determines the realities of things through inferences from premises *(bi-muqaddimat raji'ah)* based on the first intellection and sensation. Thus, demonstration leads ulitmately to establishing the proofs concerning the realities of things. In the whole ascending process of cognition, knowledge is found to be necessary/self-evident *(idtirariyyah)*: "All cognitions *(ma'arif)* are necessary because that which is not known with certainty is assumption *(zann)*, and because that which is known by assumption is neither a science nor knowledge."[109] On the other hand, the process of seeking and demonstrating the realities of things is called acquisition.[110]

The attainment of proofs for ascertaining the realities of things through the intellect is not always easy, and requires complete education and possession of deep understanding. Thus, the attainment of the realities of things through scientific demonstration, where the intellect plays an important role, is easy if the truth to be demonstrated is close to the premises, but more difficult if the truth is remote from them. For instance, it is easier to achieve the addition of small numbers without errors than the addition of much larger numbers. This does not imply, however, that addition of large numbers would be wrong, the difference lying only in the degree of skill.[111] All in all, it is though the intellect that the truth is demonstrated and that right is discerned from wrong.[112] Thus, it is false to argue that knowledge can be attained through instinct, inspiration, imitation, or historical information. However, Ibn Hazm concedes that the soul may possess true knowledge of past or invisible things through history *(khabar)*, but historical information can be accepted only if verified and reaffirmed by reliable witnesses;[113] the intellect remains important for ascertaining the veracity or falsity of the information.[114]

Intellect and Faith - Philosophy and Religion

Clearly Ibn Hazm attaches great significance to the intellect, considering it as the major instrument of knowledge and the sole agent for attaining and reaffirming the reality of a thing. However, the intellect cannot change the nature and reality of things, nor is it able to perceive or penetrate their essence, particularly God's essence; nor is it able to add or subtract anything from the Divine Revelation; nor is it able to make lawful or unlawful ordinances in contravention of the ordinances of God and His Prophet.[115] This is quite clear from his discussion of God's knowledge *('ilm Allah)* and human knowledge *('ilm al-khalq)*.[116] He asserts that Divine knowledge and human knowledge are two different things, in that the former is uncreated, whereas the latter is God's creation.[117] God's knowledge is nothing other than God Himself.[118] As such, knowledge is eternal and identical with Him. This view contrasts with that held by the rationalist Mu'tazilites, who conceive God's knowledge metaphoriclly as not having a reality. Ibn Hazm's view also conflicts with the Orthodox view that God possesses knowledge in reality and not metaphorically.[119] He objects to both views, saying that Mu'tazilah's contention means that God's knowledge is created and that the Orthodox view means that God *is* knowledge: "Whoever maintains the createdness of God's knowledge commits a grave enormity,"[120] and those who designate God as knowledge err because God never chose that designation for Himself.[121] In short, to delve into Divine essence is beyond human faculties, including the intellect.

It remains to look into the relation between faith and intellect, which is crucial to the relation between religion and philosophy. This extremely important element in Ibn Hazm's system bears on his conception of knowledge and the sciences in general. He contrasts the intellect with belief *(i'tiqad)* and faith *(iman)* in the cognitive process. Although different, and they are similar to the intellect but not identical with it. Despite their shortcomings, they are indispensable for the great majority of people as a good substitute for the intellect. To be sure, such people are recipients of knowledge without proof, which the intellect alone can bring out:

> "Belief *(i'tiqad)* is the firm establishment of a judgment in the soul either by way of proof or following someone whose doctrine has been attested by a proof; it is then a true knowledge, without doubt, it is also the establishment of a judgment either by way of convincing, in which

case it is a sure knowledge and can be right or wrong, or without convincing or proof, in which case it can be either right by mere luck or wrong by bad luck."[122]

Belief is, thus, true knowledge if it is ascertainable. This becomes important with respect to who is believing - if the believer posseses the ability of scientific demonstration, he can ascertain the veracity or falsity of a belief and act accordingly; but if he happens to be an untutored individual, he is left at the mercy of those who are supposed to know.

Ibn Hazm tackles the question of faith in similar manner, displaying remarkable consistency and allowing dispensations for those unable to ascertain proofs by themselves. The intellect is an accident of the soul and serves to ascertgain the reality of a thing, and it is within the reach of the few who have the ability of scientific demonstration; faith is the recipient and depository of knowledge for the great majority, and it is within the reach of all people from all walks of life, learned or not. The average individual may accept that knowledge by faith *(iman)*, which "is an attestation by both the tongue and the heart."[123] He can stop right there, perform his religious duties, and receive all the benefits accrueing therefrom, because he will be pleasing God, Who in His wisdom "does not make it obligatory on people to ascertain knowledge, except in affirming it with their tongues, invoking Islam and the belief therein, and in carrying out the invocation in their hearts, thus being exempt from producing proofs for ascertaining knowledge.[124] By its very nature, then, faith depends in all acts pertaining to divine commands and prohibitions, the fulfillment of which constitutes the basic requisites for the good life in this world and in the Hereafter.

Ibn Hazm realizes, however, that people are prone to believe all sorts of things which may be contradictory and even absurd. Since not everyone has the intellectual capacity and the necessary preparation to ascertain the truth by himself, the common people have to rely on the dicta of their learned peers. God himself has created different degrees of faith: (1) an initial faith that can be equated with the intuitive knowledge *('ilm al-badihiyat)* by means of which the individual is able to perceive that the whole is larger than a part; this initial faith may also constitute the highest form when given to angels and prophets; (2) a faith resulting from information handed down by informants, such as the early converts to Islam; (3) a faith resulting from demonstration and proofs, such as witnessing a miracle; and (4) a faith bestowed on all people for no particular reason, which is common to all untutored people.[125]

Ibn Hazm appears to equate the origin of knowledge with that of faith; both are a gift *(mawhibah)* from God[126] and should be channeled in the path of God.[127] Both faith and intellect in different ways, aim at one and the same thing; the acceptance of the totality of obedience *(ta'at)* and virtues *(fada'il)* as ordained by God in the Qur'an and the sound Traditions. This close relationship between faith and reason is apparent in one of his definitions of knowledge, in which he means the same thing as cognition *(ma'rifah)* that is, the certainty of a thing as it is, as the result of a necessary proof; the testimony of the senses and/or the first intellection; or simply following what the Almighty God ordered to be followed, which is the same as the truth not requiring the search for demonstration *(dun istidlal)*.[128] Here Ibn Hazm places the intellect and faith on almost equal footing. This becomes more apparent when he says that he was a believer on the strength of faith before his education, and he remained faithful after it. The intellect does not alter the reality of things which faith affirms without the need of demonstration and proof. The faith that accepts the reality of things is readily available to women, merchants, peasants, and the masses in general. Although these people lack the education to ascertain the proofs by themselves, they are moved by the grace of God to know through faith the realities of things, mainly, the existence of one God and belief in His Revelations as handed down to His Messenger Muhammad.[129]

To the question whether faith should be put to the test of proof or rationalized, Ibn Hazm replies that it is feasible indeed among those whose have the ability of demonstration, but attempts among the majority would lead only to doubt and confusion. For the common people to demonstrate the validity of faith would be an exacting task requiring a lifetime of study to arrive at the necessary proofs. Furthermore, God in His wisdom would not impose such an exacting task upon his worshippers when He expects only the confession of Islam with their hearts and tongues.[130] Ibn Hazm appears here to be quite condescending toward the masses, but he goes further elsewhere, stating that the great majority of people are stupid, weakminded, and incapable of determining the truth for themselves. Only the learned few can achieve that,[131] and not all of them are qualified to perceive the realities of things, for this would require complete detachment from any kind of inclination, a thorough study of all doctrines without personal involvement in any one of them, and self-analysis with respect to character, inclination or imitation.[132]

In summary, an intellectual elite is capable of demonstrating the truth, leaving the majority to receive the truth as embodied in religion through faith.[133] The end result is that God bestows the same knowledge on both groups without distinction. Thus, study and education help to demonstrate what is already there, the only difference being that they allow the individual to see the truth through personal endeavor and to sharpen his mind against false opinions and innovations that have been imposed on the Divine Revelation.[134] In either case, he who believes in God and obeys his commands is faithful and knows the truth whether he demonstrates it or not.[135] Conversely, he who follows the authority of someone other than God and His Prophet is equivocal, and a rebel against the Almighty God.[136]

Concomitantly, Ibn Hazm displays great impatience and even contempt toward the elitist group that comprised the religious scholars and the philosophers. These two groups actually had identical goals — that is, the search for and adherence to the truth — but the complete misunderstanding of their respective fields, the religious scholars frowned on philosophy and logic, and the philosophers denied the validity of Revelation. In so doing, they rendered a great disservice not only to each other but to the very disciplines they represented. The religious scholars who disavowed the usefulness of philosophy and logic on the ground that they lead to doubt and unbelief were far removed from scholarship. The theologians *(al-mutakallimun)*, in particular, brought untold harm to religion, creating divisiveness and unbelief in the Islamic community through their idle talk that had no head nor tail, consisting of rigamarole, confusion, and corrupt and contradictory propositions.[137] These people do not deserve the name of scholars, for the true scholar is one who knows the certainty of things in themselves, and failing this, it cannot be said that he knows nor has the knowledge of a thing; he has mere assumptions.[138] Ibn Hazm lists three classes of people who do not meet the requirements of true scholarship: first, the negligent people who are preoccupied with trivia such as earning a living or looking after honor and prestige; second, the followers of old authorities who do not ponder on the veracity or falsity of the thing they espouse, even to the point of rejecting a clear proof when presented to them; and third, those who deny in words the dictates of their hearts for fear of upsetting their social rank or the potential for gaining more wealth. He concludes with chagrin that these classes predominate among the mass of men.[139] To show the error of the religious scholars concerning their belief that philosophy is detrimental to religion, he states that his own experience proves the opposite; after having believed through faith before his education, his faith was strengthened when he became a scholar equipped to undertake scientific demonstration.[140]

Ibn Hazm displays equal displeasure toward the extreme rationalists, who became victims of their own traditionalism.[141] These people were concerned solely with mathematics, propriety of numbers, position of the stars, the nature of the heavenly bodies, astrology, and other natural phenomena, neglecting altogether the religious sciences. In so doing, the rationalists had committed the same error as the religious scholars, allowing themselves to be influenced by the shortcomings of the religious scholars, and deciding without previous examination, that religion has no validity or claim to the truth. As a consequence, the philosophers plunged into unbelief, becoming libertines, pleasure-seekers, drunkards, adulterers, and followers of many other abominable things.[142]

Ibn Hazm looks upon the gulf separating the religious scholars and the philosophers with deep concern. Giving credit where credit is due, he exposes the enormity of their error, hoping to strike a middle course between the two diametrically opposed groups. The narrow-minded religious scholars' forbidding the study of dialectics is refuted and declared false on the basis of Qur'anic verses[143] and some Tradtions. Moreover, Ibn Hazm urges the faithful to study and reflect on the creation of the heavens and earth, assuring them that doing so will reaffirm the truth. At the same time, he invites the philosophers to ponder on God and His Will as manifested in His revelation, also assuring them that the truth brought about by their discipline is not different from that found in the Revelation. He concludes with the felicitous statement that Revelation and philosophy aim, after all, at one and the same thing, that is, the search for and adherence to the truth. They both aim at orderly management of human affairs, right conduct, and the upholding of virtues — all of which will contribute to the attainment of happiness and well-being on earth as well in Heaven.[144] His words follows:

"Philosophy in its meaning, result, and objective actually consists of the improvement of the soul, permitting it to use virtues and right conduct during its worldly existence in order to attain salvation in the Hereafter. This is exactly the meaning and objective of the religious law (shari'ah). Philosophers and religious scholars are in agreement concerning this.

One may argue with the person who makes pretension to philosophy and denies the Revelation that he ignores in reality the essential thing and is far removed from its objective and meaning. Is philosophy not, according to the consensus of philosophers, the science that distinguishes virtues from vices, and the science that establishes the proofs (barahin) which differentiate right from wrong? The answer must be in the affirmative. One may ask further of the pretender of philosophy, have not the philosophers maintained that the improvement of the world rests on two things — one internal (batin) and the other external (zahir)? That the internal consists of the use of legal precepts (shara'i') by the soul which forbid injustices of people against each other and shameful deeds? And that the external consists of building fortifications and the use of weapons to repel the enemy who intends to tyranize and undermine the people? In addtion to what we have mentioned concerning the improvement of the soul, the philosophers have also included the improvement of the body through medicine. Once more, the answer must be in the affirmative. One may inquire further: does not the well-being of the world consist of preventing people from killing that leads to the loss of life; from adultery that corrupts lineage and destroys inheritance; from injustice that harms people, their wealth and property; from vices such as violence, envy, lies, laziness, avarice, calumny, fraud, treason, and the like? Is it not true that all this is accomplished through religious precepts that forbid all that? The answer again must be in the affirmative.

"If this were not the case, negligence in which evil resides would be the order of the day concerning all that we have mentioned. In consequence, had it not been for that [the religious law and philosophy], the whole world and the sciences would be vitiated, and man would be deprived of the virtue of understanding, speech and intellect, and would be like a beast. From all this, one may conclude that the religious precepts constitute one of two things: (1) either they are true emanating from God — may He be glorified and exalted — who is the Creator and Manager (mudabbir) of the world as it is conceived by the religious scholars; or (2) they eixst by virtue of the agreement of the most virtuous men for the purpose of managing the affairs of people and preventing them from committing injustices and vices. If those stupid people maintain that the religious precepts are arrived at by the agreement of the most virtuous people, we must then conclude that what is made obligatory on people to follow is just lies, lacking any foundation, a contrived truth and obligation imposed without authority, an error, and with rewards and punishments constituting lies. If this is the case, then lies which constitute the vilest depravity and the greatest evil will prevail, and the well-being of the world which is the object for seeking virtues will never take place. If this is the case, truth is not distinguished from falsehood, veracity becomes depravity, falsehood would appear as truth and veracity, lies as virtues, thereby depriving the world of any sustenance except through falsehood; lies will become the consequence of truth, falsehood the fruit of veracity; deceit, fraud, and treason would constitute virtues and friendly admonitions, all of which will constitute an utter impossibility and an absurdity that cannot be accepted by the intellect.

"And the opponents may argue that if the truth of the mundane origin of religious precepts is revealed to the common people, there is the danger that they may not wish to practice virtues, and for this reason, it is necessary to use threats for making them practice virtue, and to lie to them as to children, and as you Muslims permit, according to your religious law, the husband to lie to his wife for harmony's sake and people to deny their religion under tyranny and time of war. In consequence, we will impose on you what you had imposed on us, saying that lies constitute truth and virtues in their religion."[145]

Although Ibn Hazm admits the existence of such "white lies" in Islam — which are condoned by the religious law — he argues that they are made for practical purposes, and there is more benefit for them than harm. However, if goodness and virtues were to be accomplished through falsehood and lies, it would nullify both religion and philosophy altogether, particularly if the legal precepts were to be conceived as mere human convention *(mawdu'ah)*. This is so because the thing agreed upon by one man may be different from that is agreed upon by another man, thus constituting a blatant contradiction that will be rejected by the intellect. For "we know by virtue of the intellect and its *necessity*/self-evident that the truth is not found in different and contradictory doctrines, but in one only, the rest being false"; it follows that human contentions, whether applied to philosophy or religion, are without foundations in fact — leaving one inescapable alternative in that the religious precepts are true in themselves, and emanate from God, Who is the Creator and Manager of the world.[146]

Once Ibn Hazm arrives at the conclusion that legal precepts emanate from an Originator *(munshi')* and not from human conception, he poses the question of which of the established religions is the true one. Consistent with his belief in one truth and one religion, he argues that anyone with common sense *(kull dhi hiss salim)* will have to admit that of all the existing religions there must be one and only one that is true and the rest must be false. In consequence, it behooves all rational people to seek and adhere to that religion and abandon the rest. In that religion — Islam, of course — resides the well-being of the soul for all eternity; outside, the soul will endure perdition for all times.[147]

The implication here is quite clear. The world must have an orderly system that will function harmoniously and free from contention. To achieve this goal, it must be guided by precepts that will guarantee its well-being, and will direct the conduct of its inhabitants toward happiness on earth as well as in heaven. Although Ibn Hazm believes Islam to be the only doctrine capable of achieving that purpose, he admits that philosophy in its metaphysical and natural aspects has the same objective as religion. The basic difference separating the two is that religion emanates from God, whereas philosophy is a human manifestation resulting from endowments bestowed on man by the same Creator. Moreover, the true religion contains the ultimate and infallible truth, whereas philosophy searches for and attempts to demonstrate and adhere to that universal truth. For the rest, faith and reason or revelation and philosophy are almost on an equal level, complementary without contradiction. It is this conviction that leads Ibn Hazm to advocate a truly broad liberal education including the study of both the religious and the secular sciences. In so doing, Ibn Hazm set the stage for a school of thought having portentious significance, whose impact was echoed later by the two great Andalusian philosophers Ibn Tufayl and Ibn Rushd.[148]

Intellect *('aql)* is identical with faith *(iman)* in that it signifies the use of obediences *(ta'at)* and virtues *(fada'il)*.[149] It is the opposite of stupidity *(humq)*,[150] which signifies disobedienct *(ma'asi)* and vices *(radha'il)*.[151] And it is useless if it is not supported by the good fortune of religion.[152] It does not flatter for personal and worldly gains but seeks the truth; people who use their intellect for flattery possess cunning *(daha')* and not intellect.[153]

Unquestionably, the intellect plays an important part in the cognitive process in Ibn Hazm's thinking. This becomes important in the long history of skirmishes surrounding the position of the intellect among Muslim intelligensia — some denying it any role in the cognitive process, others assigning to it great importance in the acquisition of knowledge and in ascertaining the truth. To the rationalist Mu'tazilites, the intellect is the guide by means of which man is able to decide what is good and bad, and the whole concept of justice is based on what reason dictates.[154] To the philosopher, the intellect is an emanation of the First Intellect, which is God. It is through the intellect that rational arguments establishing the proofs are arrived at, as contrasted with traditional arguments *(sam'i)* that have their sources in the Qur'an and Traditions.[155]

To Ibn Hazm, both rational and traditional arguments appear equally valid and present no contradiction. In fact, he devotes a whole section[156] to establishing the validity of the intellect *(ithbat hujaj al-'uqul),* pointing to the elements that integrate it, such as demonstration *(istidlal),* evidence *(hujaj),* proofs *(barahin),* and necessity of praiseworthy dialectics *(al-jadal al-*

mahmud) — all of which constitute the foundations for distinguishing right from wrong and for arriving at the truth. Aside from the religious texts, there is no other source of knowledge that can achieve this goal, including historical information *(khabar)*, imitation *(taqlid)* and instinct inspiration *(ilham)*, which have ultimately to be subjected to rational proofs.[157]

Nowhere does Ibn Hazm suggest that the intellect — except for the ability of demonstration — supersedes faith *(iman)*, nor does he consider the rationalizer *('aqil)* to be superior to the faithful *(mu'min)*. On the contrary, the *'aqi* would not deserve the name were he an unbeliever. Furthermore, *'aql* is, like faith, a gift from God. One should not lose sight of the fact that Ibn Hazm followed the traditional philosophy established in the ninth century by al-Kindi (d. 865), who maintained that philosophy taught the unity of God and the pursuit of happiness, and who concluded that "the acquisition of all those things is the very essence of what the true messengers have brought us from God."[158] Al-Kindi adds that the utterances of Muhammad and the Revelation handed to him are ascertainable by intellectual processes and that only people devoid of reasoning would reject them.[159] Also, one should not overlook the fact that Ibn Hazm had the unshakable conviction that the absolute truth resides in the Revelation and the teaching of Muhammad, thus making of the intellect no more than a tool for demonstrating and bringing to the fore the realities of things — mainly, the existence of God, Revelation, and prophecy.

The intellect has, however, its limitations, such as theology *(kalam)* and discursive reasoning *(nazar)*, and is limited solely to finding the realities of things as they are without going into such questions as the essence of God and other things belonging to the world beyond. In this respect, Ibn Hazm's views have great affinity to those held by al Ghazzali — at least, before the latter chose the Sufi path, which is said to lead to certainty *(yaqin)* through the bestowal of divine illumination on the heart of the believer. In fact, al-Ghazzali confesses in his *Munqidh* the agony of a mental crisis resulting from the unsatisfactory way of attaining certainty through theology, esoterism *(batiniyyah)*, or philosophy. Nevertheless, al-Ghazzali did not overlook the important role of the intellect and discussed its nobility, kinds, and role.[160] To him the *'aqil* (rationalizer) is not different from the *mu'min* (the faithful,in that he is the one who believes in God and His prophets and obeys His commands.[161] It may be added that the Hanbalite theologian Ibn 'Aqil (d. 1119) conceived the intellect as the most excellent of God's gifts, whose "fruit is the obedience of God in what He commands and forbids."[162] This would make the nexus between Ibn Hazm and Ibn 'Aqil quite likely.[163]

The intellect for both Ibn Hazm and al-Ghazzali is a more reliable means for attaining the reality of things than either belief *(i'tiqad)* or imitation *(taqlid);* these two means are incapable of achieving the reality of things since they accept a thing without examination or research.[164] Ibn Hazm rejects *taqlid* altogether in the application of the religious law;[165] al-Ghazzali concedes that it can be true or false, but sees it as useful for the common people.[166] As for inspiration *(ilham)*, al-Ghazzali regards it as common to all people, especially to God's friends *(walis)*, but as different from revelation *(wahy)*, which is bestowed on prophets only and involves a direct and actual seeing and hearing of an angel.[167]

Furthermore, a careful scrutiny of the views of Ibn Hazm and al-Ghazzali on the position of theology and philosophy as a means of attaining knowledge will reveal striking similarities even in the area of the relation between philosophy and revelation. Ibn Hazm was a staunch opponent of al-Ash'ari and Ash'rites in general, whom he often refutes and labels as misguided individuals if not heretics. Although al-Ghazzali did not go that far, he looked upon theology *(kalam)* and theologians *(mutakallimun)* with great reservation, saying that *kalam* is wanting in achieving certainty because it is limited to defending the Muslim creed against innovators. As such, it is a defective tool and can lead, as it actually did, to divisiveness, useless talk, envy, vainglory, and innovations.[168] The same is true of philosophy when it ignores or encroaches upon the divine order.

To Ibn Hazm, intellect and faith aim at the same thing, obedience of God's commands and perception of the truth, which is one, indivisible and infallible. However, there are two different ways of attaining the truth, through prophecy and through philosophy. The philosopher al-Kindi had already pointed to the difficulty attending the philosopher, which requires studying many sciences, whereas the religious sciences can be possessed without seeking, effort, or research. In other words, the truth is attained by the philosopher with hard work, while it is comprehended by a prophet in a single flash of inspiration.[169] The truth contained in the Revelation was taught by Muhammad to mankind for its well-being on earth and for achieving eternal bliss in the Hereafter. God chose Muhammad and informed him about things he did not know by way of a power or special faculty lacking in other creatures.[170] This is prophecy bestowed on special persons, who are God's prophets and messengers.[171] In his capacity as prophet-messenger Muhammad is infallible by virtue of the infallibility of the knowledge bestowed on him, which transcends the knowledge of any other mortal — be he a rationalist *('aqil)* or faithful *(mu'min)*. Ibn Hazm agreed with this position, and so, largely, did al-Ghazzali.

With this premise, Ibn Hazm tackled the problem of the relationship between philosophy and Revelation by insisting with some qualifications[172] that they are in complete harmony and without contradictions. In so doing, he allowed ample room for rationalists to reflect and ponder on the realities of things on the basis of proofs, believing that the truth can be arrived at on the basis of demonstration and proofs as well as on the basis of the *dalil* (guide) of the holy texts. Although Ibn Hazm appears to endorse the unquestionable validity of philosophy for arriving at the truth, he does, like al-Ghazzali, entertain grave doubts about what he conceives to be philosophizers along with dualists, Brahmans, Jews, and Christians. They are: (1) the sophists who deny the existence of every reality;[173] (2) those who uphold the eternity of the world and deny that it has a manager;[174] (3) those who maintain that the world is eternal but has a manager;[175] (4) those who maintain that the world has primeval creator but uphold the concept that vacuum and duration are eternal;[176] and (5) those who deny the validity of revealed religion and conceive it to be the work of impostors.[177]

In this connection, Ibn Hazm and al-Ghazzali concur. As strongly committed to Revelation as Ibn Hazm, al-Ghazzali recognized the validity of some components of philosophy such as mathematics, astronomy, logic, and the natural sciences as long as they remained confined to their respective limits. This is clear from his *Munqidh*,[178] al-Ghazzali singles out and refutes three major groups (1) the atheists *(dahriyyun)* who deny the existence of God; (2) the naturalists *(tabi'iyyun)* who deny life in the Hereafter; and (3) the deists *(ilahiyyun)* who err in matters pertaining to God, notwithstanding their contributions to mathematics, logic, the natural sciences, metaphysics, politics, and ethics, all of which may be valid but which cannot supersede what is contained in the Revelation.

In conclusion, one basic difference remains between Ibn Hazm and al-Ghazzali. Whereas Ibn Hazm remained convinced of the unquestionable validity of the intellect for demonstrating the truth, al-Ghazzali late in life conceived the intellect insufficient for that purpose and selected for the Sufi path as the surest way of having communion with the Almighty and of apprehending the certainty of God and of things in the Hereafter.[179] This belief led to a negative attitude toward philosophy and philosophers, and in his *Tahafut,* he emphasized the damage over the benefit coming from them.[180]

CHAPTER V

THE SCIENCES AND THEIR CLASSIFICATION

The State of the Sciences

No conception of knowledge would be complete without reference to the subject matter it covers. This fact, together with the great interest in the meaning and dimensions of knowledge in Muslim society, perhaps is why Muslim scholars began to divide, identify, and categorize the various disciplines as early as the ninth century. The inclusion or omission of a particular discipline in any classification was in itself significant of the extent of the sciences, their place in the curriculum, their respective merits and precedence, and perhaps ignorance of a particular science. More significant still was the order assigned to each discipline in the hierarchy of the sciences. Key words in the titles of works - such as *division (aqsam), inventory (ihsa'), key* or *introduction (miftah),* and *categories (maratib)* - ordinarily reveal the intent and the intellectual perspective of the author.[1] In other words, any classification of the sciences must, of necessity, reflect either the intellectual perspective of individual author or the intellectual mood of his time and environment.

In classical Islam of the ninth and tenth centuries, translating and borrowing from "the foreign sciences," mainly Greek, had reached enormous proportions. The incorporation and cultivation of some of these sciences developed in parallel and were accepted with the "Arabic sciences," comprising Arabic philology in general and the developing of religious sciences. Later, this distinction between foreign sciences and the Arabic sciences was to have implications for the desirability or undesirability of a particular science being included in the family of sciences.

Early Muslim philosophers of the ninth and tenth centuries, whose education was laced generously with Greek thought, appear to have followed the Greek precedent in the classification of the sciences. Consciously or unconsciously, they placed a strong emphasis on the philosophical sciences merely acknowledging Arabic philology and the Islamic sciences. This is evident in the classification of the sciences made by the philosopher al-Farabi, and perhaps al-Kindi, who were followed by Ibn Sina in the eleventh century. From the tenth century, the even handed classification of al-Khuwarizmi and, to some extent, those of Ibn al-Nadim and the Brethren of Purity pay as much attention to the Arabic sciences as to the foreign sciences. Although the Brethren of Purity lean toward the philosophical and natural sciences, al-Khuwarizmi and Ibn al-Nadim appear simply to relate the state of the sciences in their own time. In fact, both al-Khuwarizmi and

Ibn al-Nadim list the sciences without passing judgment upon which would take precedence; neverthless, the mere fact that they begin with the religious sciences may in itself by significant. At any rate, nowhere in their classifications is there any indication that some sciences are harmful and should be avoided, whereas others are beneficial and should be pursued.

Also during the ninth and tenth centuries, a strong religious orientation toward the sciences was developing parallel to the secular orientation of the phihlosophers. The secular and religious sciences were moving toward extreme polarization during Ibn Hazm's lifetime. By then, in the eleventh century, the secular sciences were looked upon by some religious circles with mistrust and were even considered detrimental to the religious sciences. The philosopher al-'Amiri (d. 992) expressed an early concern toward this attitude.[2] After classifying the sciences into two main categories - the religious sciences and the philosophical sciences[3] - giving each its due, he calls the attention of the religious scholars to their assumption that the philosophical sciences contradict the religious sciences, saying such an assumption has no foundation because the phihlosophical sciences rest on certain principles not different from those of the religious sciences. In fact, revelation is in harmony with pure reason and demonstration, hence there could not be any contradiction between religion and philosophy. The philosophical sciences in their three main branches - mathematics, natural science and metaphysics - are not only noble in their own right but have the distinct advantage of enabling the individual to know the realities of things and to exercise virtue; to have an insight into God's creations; and to be able to defend himself against false doctrines without ever falling into disbelief. It appears that al-'Amiri's main concern was to defend the philosophical sciences against attack by some religious scholars. This becomes quite clear when he dismisses the religious sciences as consisting of three branches without specifying what they are, but describes at great length each branch of the philosophical sciences, showing their respective merits in a language that reflects his own philosophical bias. Al-'Amiri's conception of the sciences becomes the more significant when contrasted with that of Ibn Hazm, who shared the same idea, but who, unlike al-'Amiri, was more inclined to the religious than to the philosophical sciences.

The Eastern philosopher al-'Amiri and the Andalusian thinker Ibn Hazm lived a century apart, but a possible relationship between the ideas of the two men should not be ruled out. On the other hand, the issue of the religious versus the philosophical sciences was much alive during Ibn Hazm's time, and it is possible that Ibn Hazm arrived independently at similar conclusions. Regardless, the classification of the sciences was paramount in Ibn Hazm's thinking and occupied ample space in some of his works. Suffice it to say that Ibn Hazm made a comprehensive classification of the sciences in a historical context, ranking each science in the family of the sciences.

In spite of Ibn Hazm's religious bias, which he eloquently expresses, he attempts to build a bridge between the religious and philosophical sciences, defying in many ways the pervasive ultraorthodoxy of his Andalusian contemporaries. He seldom overlooked any of the sciences. Those omitted, such as astrology and alchemy, he disallowed not because they presented a danger to religion, but because they failed to satisfy the rules of logic, the natural law, and the necessary conditions for experimentation *(tajribah)*. However, the attempt of al-'Amiri and Ibn Hazm to harmonize the religious and secular sciences remained unheeded, and the dichotomy between the two major categories widened as time went on. Eventually the religious scholars succeeded in asserting their point of view. Even in the eleventh century, the great theologian al-Ghazzali, a man of famed erudition in both the religious and philosophical sciences, gave a comprehensive classification of the sciences, but looked with suspicion upon philosophers and naturalists, who by design or neglect (as he saw it) attempted to explain natural and metaphysical phenomena at the expense of religion.

Although philosophy continued to have its defenders in Ibn Tufayl and Ibn Rushd in th twelfth century, philosophy and its cognates were heading for worse times.By the thirteenth century, the attitude of the Muslim scholars toward them was, by and large, marked by omission. In his *Key of The Sciences,* the Turkish scholar al-Sakkaki (1160/228) indicates the state of the sciences during his time. Limited to the Arabic sciences with little attention to the philosophical (foreign) sciences, his division included the following disciplines: syntax, grammar, rhetoric, meaning *(ma'ani),* style, flowery style, the science of demonstration *('ilm al-istidlal),* and poetry. In the fourteenth century, the sociologist Ibn Khaldun, in his attempt to give legitimacy to his new "science of culture."[5] classified the sciences with equal space given to the religious and the philosophical sciences, even though he showed some apprehension toward philosophy.[6] His classification was most comprehensive since the time of Ibn Hazm, and the last attempt to reintroduce classicism to its rightful place in Islamic culture. Whatever his motivation may have been, his endeavor met with failure. Subsequently, the philosophical sciences were by design, neglect, or ignorance ommitted from any classification of the sciences. The prolific scholar al-Suyuti (d. 1505), credited with hundreds of works, paid little or no attention to the philosophical sciences. In his division of the sciences, he included religion, commentaries, Traditions, jurisprudence, laws of inheritance, syntax, grammar, calligraphy, style, flowery style, and Sufism, adding only surgery and medicine as worthy of pursuit.[7]

The preceding remarks are intended to show the general attitude of Muslim scholars toward the sciences. It is within this overall context that Ibn Hazm's classification must be viewed for a better understanding of the fundamental question that occupied Muslim teachers for centuries. In order to focus more precisely upon Ibn Hazm's contribution with regard to the sciences, the next section analyzes the classification of the sciences by his leading predecessors in the East, and the following section, that of his predecessors, and contemporaries in al-Andalus.

The Classification of the Sciences before Ibn Hazm

Muslim philosophy developed and took final shape around the works of Aristotle, which had been translated into Arabic. Aristotle, highly revered and frequently quoted by the Ancients, was held in great esteem among Muslim scholars and was referred to as the first teacher *(al-mu'allim al-awwal)*, who was closer to attaining the truth than any scholar before or after him. His encylopedic knowledge became a model for students aspiring to wisodm. Muslim scholars emulated his division of the sciences, modifying it to incorporate the Islamic religion and the Arabic Language.

Aristotle divided the sciences into three major categories: (1) the theoretical or speculative sciences, including mathematics, physics, and philosophy; (2) the practical sciences comprising ethics, economy, and politics; and (3) the poetical sciences, comprising arts, poetry, music, and rhetoric.[8] This classification was followed in its broader outlines by early Muslim scholars, who paid little attention to the Arabic sciences. al-Kindi, who is credited with some two hundred seventy works dealing mostly with the secular sciences,[9] seems to have followed the Aristotelian model in his two reported treatises on the nature and classification of the sciences.[10] The titles of his works, suggests that al-Kindi had a strong philosophical orientation; making it unlikely that he included the religious sciences in his division. Thus, those treatises presumably dealt with philosophy, logic, astronomy, mathematics, medicine, astrology, alchemy, physchology, politics, and other disciplines.

This tendency to omit sufficient and specific provisions for the Arabic sciences appears also in the work of the tenth century philosopher al-Farabi (d. 950). In his *Inventory of the Sciences,*[11] al-Farabi gives five categories of the sciences, each with subdivisions; he defines each science and states its purpose. His categorization contains no specific reference to the Arabic sciences:

1. Language *('ilm al-lisan):* grammar *('ilm qawaniniha),* lexicography *('ilm al-alfaz),* the art of writing *('ilm qawanin al-kitabah),* the art of reading *('ilm qawanin al-qira'ah),* and prosody *('ilm qawanin al-ash'ar).*

2. Logic *('ilm al-mantiq):* describing its components following the *Organon* of Aristotle and giving justification for its validity and utility, saying that it "straightens the intellect and leads the individual to the road of certainty and truth."[12]

3. Mathematics *('ilm al-ta'alim):* the science of number *('ilm al-'adad),* geometry *('ilm al-handasah),* optics *('ilm al-manazir),* astronomy *('ilm al-nujum),* music *('ilm al-musiqa),* weight *('ilm al-athqal),* and mechanics *('ilm al-hiyal).*

4. The natural sciences and metaphysics *(al-'ilm al-tabi'i wa-l-'ilm al-ilahi):* heaven and earth, generation and corruption

(al-kawn wa-l-fasad), meteorology *(al-athar al-'ulwiyyah),* mineralogy *(ma'adin),* botany *(al-nabat),* zoology *(hayawan),* psychology *(nafs),* and the metaphysical world *(ma ba'd al-tabi'ah).*

5. Politics *('ilm al-madani),* jurisprudence *(fiqh),* and theology *(kalam).*

In his *Inventory of the Sciences,* al-Farabi's stated purpose was "to enumerate the generally known sciences one by one and to give a general survey of each one of them." This is significant in that he apparently deems the religious sciences of Islam unworthy of being described as a "known science." This omission becomes even more significant when one realizes that the work is intended to enable the individual to appreciate the sciences and to pursue them knowingly, not blindly, with due regard to their respective merit, utility, weakness, and strength; to enable him also to uncover who is a mere pretender and who is not; to assist him in knowing what should be studied of each of the sciences; and to help those who wish to resemble scholars and appear as one of them.[13]

By and large, al-Farabi gives a descriptive listing of the sciences without opinion about a proper hierarchy, with the exception of logic. When he speaks of language, he does so in general terms, avoiding specific reference to Arabic and its background in the sense that it contains the Qur'an and the Traditions. Also, he places politics, jurisprudence, and theology under a single heading without reference to them in an Islamic context. Thus, his treatment of the sciences has a secular approach, and his political philosophy is Platonic, as attested to by his two important works, *The Ideal City* and *City Management.*[14]

While al-Kindi and al-Farabi were taking a secular approach to the sciences, others attempted to provide for the newly developing Arabic sciences. During the tenth century, a secret society, known as the Brethren of Purity *(ikhwan al-safa'),* divided the sciences and described their respective merits. Their *Rasa'il* emphasizes and elevates the philosophical and natural sciences, but there is sufficient material on the religious sciences to justify their inclusion. To the Brethren, knowledge is the representation *(surah)* of the known in the soul of the scholar, and is the opposite of ignorance *(jahl),* which is the absence of that representation: "Know that the souls of scholars are erudite in actuality *(bi-fi'l),* and the souls of students are erudite in potentiality *(bi-quwwah);* learning and teaching are nothing but bringing out that which is in potentiality and translating it into action."[15] The pursuit of knowledge is the noblest virtue, "for the Almighty ordered the faithful to do many things, and forbade them to do others, but there is nothing more imperative, more virtuous, more glorious, more noble, and more useful to the faith . . . than knowledge, its pursuit, and teaching."[16] Furthermore, knowledge will earn for the scholar many praiseworthy qualities such as nobility, glory, wealth, strength, generosity, and others.[17] From this, the Brethren's purpose in dividing and describing the sciences becomes clear: it is to guide the student in selecting from the many available disciplines. "For the desire of the soul for the different sciences and the arts is like the appetite of the body for the various foods with respect to taste, color and smell."[18] The Brethren remained uncommitted whether religious or secular knowledge should take precedence.

They discern three categories of the sciences:

I. THE PRACTICAL OR LITERARY SCIENCES (al-'ulum al-riyadiyyah, aw-ilm adab): aiming mostly at making a living and improving life. They consist of nine disciplines: (1) writing and reading; (2) lexicography and grammar; (3) arithmetic and commercial transactions; (4) poetry and prosody; (5) divination ('Ilm al-Zajr wa-l-fa'l) and the like; (6) magic, talisman, alchemy, mechanics, and the like; (7) trades and crafts; (8) mechanising, agriculture, and animal husbandry; and (9) biography and history.

II THE RELIGIOUS SCIENCES, aiming at healing the soul and attaining life in the Hereafter. There are six disciplines: (1) Revelation; (2) allegorical interpretation of the Qur'an; (3) Tradition (hadith); (4) jurisprudence, ordinances, and legal decisions; (5) exhortations, predication, asceticism and mysticism; and (6) dream interpretation.

III. THE PHILOSOPHICAL SCIENCES, consisting of: (1) mathematics-arithmetic, geometry, astronomy, and music; (2) logic - poetics rhetoric, disputation, demonstration, and sophistry (3) the natural sciences - corporeal principles, heaven and earth, generation and corruption, meteorology, mineralogy, botany, zoology, medicine, veterinary medicine, animal husbandry, agriculture, and the crafts already included under the practical sciences; and (4) the metaphysical sciences — knowledge of God, angelology, the science of the soul, politics and eschatology.[19]

It was also in the tenth century that the scientist al-Khuwarizmi included both the religious and the philosophical sciences in his comprehensive *Keys to the Sciences*. Unlike the classification discussed thus far, al-Khuwarismi's division lacks definite conception of knowledge and has no preference for either religious or philosophical sciences. Al-Khuwarizmi simply lists the sciences and explains their vocabularies in order to facilitate the use of the sciences by cultural persons.[20] His straightforward presentation contains two sections, the first devoted to the Arabic sciences (al-'ulum-al-'arabiyyah) and the second to the foreign sciences ('ulum al-'ajam).[21] This sharp distinction between "Arabic"and "foreign" marks a significant point in the long skirmish between the philosophers and the religious scholars:

I. THE ARABIC SCIENCES: (1) jurisprudence; (2) theology; (3) grammar; (4) writing or correspondence (kitabah); (5) poetry and prosody; and (6) history.

II. THE FOREIGN SCIENCES: (1) philosophy; (2) logic; (3) medicine; (4) arithmetic; (5) geometry; (6) astronomy/astrology; (7) music; (8) mechanics; and (9) alchemy.

Ibn al-Nadim (d.988), a contemporary of al-Khuwarizmi wrote his *Fihrist* with the purpose of cataloguing books on known disciplines. In sodoing, Ibn al-Nadim indicates the extent of the sciences during the tenth century, but does not offer a philosophy of knowledge or an attitude toward the secular or religious sciences. The ten chapters listing authors and their works, are each devoted to a particular discipline: (1) language and sacred books; (2) grammar and lexicography; (3) history, literature, biography, and genealogy; (4) poetry; (5) theology; (6) jurisprudence and Traditions, (7) philosophy and the ancient sciences (natural sciences, logic, mathematics, music, astronomy, and medicine); (8) night chats, fables, divination, magic, astrology; (9) doctrines and beliefs; and (10) alchemy.[22]

In the eleventh century, the versatile philosopher/physician Ibn Sina (d. 1037), wrote some ninety-nine works on philosophy, logic, metaphysics, medicine, geometry, astronomy, theology, and philology.[23] He popularized the philosophical sciences in his encyclopedic work *al-Shifa'*, abridged under the title of *al-Najah*. Like the philosopher al-Kindi and al-Farabi, Ibn Sina has a secular and philosophical perspective, which is quite evident in his *Shifa', Najah, Isharat,* and *Danesh-name*. In *Danesh-name*, he divides the philosophical sicences *(al-'ulum al-'aqliyyah),* into theoretical and practical sciences: the theoretical sciences aim at attaining the truth and include medicine, astrology, physiognomy, dream interpretation, talisman, divination, alchemy, mathematics, geometry, astronomy, music, and metaphysics; the practical sciences aim at achieving the good for society and comprise ethics, economics, and politics. From these two main categories, Ibn Sina arrives at four principal sciences in ascending order: (1) logic (2) physics, (3) mathematics and (4) metaphysics; each science has its subdivisions. He relegates the religious sciences to a minor place in his system and conceives knowledge as consisting of two kinds, a concept *(tasawwur)* and an attestation of act of judgment *(tasdiq)*[24] with no reference to its divine origin or its relation to Revelation. However, Ibn Sina recognizes that the sciences are interrelated and that all of them receive their principles from the "first philosophy"[25] - logic serving as an instrument for all of them.[26]

The Classification of the Sciences in Al-Andalus

In al-Andalus, the works of Ibn Juljul,[27] Sa'id,[28] and Ibn Hazm himself[29] offer a good picture of the intellectual life with respect to the philosophical and natural sciences. The foreign sciences (philosophy, logic, medicine, pharmacology, mathematics, geometry, astronomy, and astrology) were cultivated side by side with the Arabic sciences (grammar, lexicography, Qur'anic studies, Traditions, jurisprudence, theology, history, prosody, and belles-lettres). However, considering their orthodoxy, it may be assumed that the Andalusians of the ninth and tenth centuries overtly favored the religious sciences. Not until the eleventh century did any Andalusians even attempt to classify the sciences; then, coincidentally, three who were well acquainted attempted the task. They were Ibn 'Abd al-Barr, Sa'id of Toledo, and Ibn Hazm.

Herein, their clasification of the sciences will be reviewed to determine their attitudes regarding the religious sciences and the philosophical sciences, their conception of knowledge, and the relation between their attitudes and those of their Eastern counterparts. The relationship between Ibn 'Abd-al-Barr and Ibn Hazm has already been noted.[30] In his *Jami'*, dealing with the various aspects of knowledge, Ibn 'Abd al-Barr classified the sciences considering opinions of religious scholars and philosophers.

He reported that the religious scholars, divided the sciences into three categories: the lofty knowledge *('ilm a'la)*, the middle knowledge *('ilm awsat)*, and the base knowledge *('ilm asfal)*. Lofty knowledge is knowledge of religion that does not admit any discussion beyond what God has explained in the Qur'an and the Traditions of the Prophet. Middle knowledge is knowledge of the sciences of the world, such as medicine and geometry. Base knowledge is the acquisition and performance of crafts.

Within an Islamic context, Ibn 'Abd al-Barr specifies that lofty knowledge comprises three aspects: (1) the special knowledge of the faith and Islam, God's unity, and devotion as prescribed in the Qur'an; (2) the knowledge of the sources of information concerning legislation, the Prophet, his companions, and religious scholars; and (3) the knowledge of Traditions and legal decisions. He quotes a Tradition on the authority of Abu Ishaq al-Hufi[32] which says: "The sciences are three kinds: (1) the knowledge of this world, such as medicine and astronomy; (2) the knowledge of the Hereafter, the Qur'an, Traditions, and jurisprudence; and (3) the knowledge which is not of this world nor of the Hereafter, such as poetry."

He reports three kinds of sciences among the philosophers as well: the loftiest analogical reasoning *('ilm al-qiyas)*, concerned with spiritual matters; the middle knowledge with corporeal things; and the base knowledge with skills performed by the organs.

Ibn 'Abd al-Barr's statement in full follows:

"The sciences among all people of faith comprise three kinds: (1) Lofty knowledge, (2) base knowledge, and (3) middle knowledge. The lofty knowledge among them does not leave room for anyone to talk about anything beyond what God has explained in His Books according to the text handed down by Him to his Prophets - may His prayers be upon them. The middle knowledge is the cognition of the sciences of the world in which the knowledge of a thing is like the knowledge of something resembling it, and it can be identified by its kind and species, as in the knowledge of medicine and geometry. The base science is the acquisition of the crafts and the different kinds of work, such as swimming, horsemanship, clothing, decoration, calligraphy, and similar works, which cannot be encompassed and described in a book. They are acquired through the training of the organs.

"This division of the sciences among the religious scholars is the same as the one among the philosophers, except that the philosphers consider analogical reasoning to be the loftiest science, bearing on the heavenly sciences that are beyond nature and the celestial sphere and dealing with the creation of the world, its duration, anthropomorphism and its denial, and other questions, none of which can be perceived by observation and the senses . . . The middle and base sciences among the philosophers are the same as among the religious scholars, except that the middle knowledge is divided into four parts that are considered to be basic sciences *(ru'us al-'ulum)*. They are mathematics, astronomy, medicine and music. The meaning of music consists of composition of tunes, regulating sounds, measurement of beats, *(wazn al-anqar),* and the establishment of different kinds of amusements are discarded and repudiated among the religious scholars in conformity with the religious law.

"In mathematics, they consider the following to be sound: the knowledge of numbers, multiplication, division, denominations, *(tasmiyah),* the extraction of roots, the knowledge of the totality of numbers, the meaning of line, circle, dot, and the extraction of figures and the like. Mathematics is indispensable for all the sciences.

"Astronomy, its fruit and benefit among the religious scholars, consists of the knowledge of the movement of the celestial bodies, the journey of planets, the rise of the signs of the zodiac, knowledge of daytime and night, the Sagitta of night from the Sagitta of day in each country, the day, the distance of countries from the Equator, from the North Pole and from the eastern and western horizons; the birth and appearance of the crescent; the warning of the stars about storms and other phenomena; the trajectory, position, longitude, and latitude of the stars; eclipse of the sun and the moon, its duration and scope in each country; and the meaning of the brilliance of the sun, moon, and stars. There are some scholars who deny some of the things we have described on the ground that no one knows through the stars *(najamah)* about the hidden, nor does anyone ever know it with certainty unless he is a prophet whom God endows with a special quality with which he is able to see what is not possible to perceive. They maintain that only deceitful, beguiled, deficient, and ignorant people claim for certain the knowledge of the hidden; it is so because they consider that the occurence [of astrological phenomena] cannot take place except over a long period of time, thus making the allegations of knowing things through the stars like those who fabricate lies through prognostication *('iyafah),* augury *(zajr),* palm reading *(khutut al-kaff),* looking through the shoulder *(al-nazar fi-l-katf),* birthmarks *(fi mawadi'qard al-farufi al-khaylan),* curing by cogitation *(al-'ilaj bi-l-fikr),* possession by the devil *(mulk al-jinn)* and the like - all of which are rejected by the intellect, cannot be proved, and none of which is true. This is so because if they happen to be right in one instance, they may be also wrong in similar instances - all of which is apart from the flimsy basis of their assertion. Thus, asserting in one instance and erring in many others shows the incorrectness of their pretentions. In reality, there is nothing sound except what the Prophets - may God's prayers be upon them - had come forth with. It was related to us . . .[33] that 'Umar said,'learn about the stars that guide you in the darkness of the land and the sea and stop right there.' 'there is nothing wrong in learning about the stars insofar as it will guide you.' The Messenger of God - may God's prayer and peace be upon him - said, 'He who aquires a knowledge of the stars will acquire a part of magic in proportion to what he had learned about them.' 'Verily God had purified this land from polytheism even though the stars did not lead them astray.' 'After me, I fear that three things will happen to my community: the injustice of the scholars, the belief in the stars, and denial of divine decree *(al-takdhib bi-l-qadar).*'

"Medicine [the natural sciences][34] aims at understanding the nature of the plants of the earth, its trees, waters, minerals, precious stones, foods, aromas, knowledge of the elements, the basic principles, the characteristics of animals, the nature of bodies, natural dispositions, organs, the occurence of disasters, the nature of time and countries, the benefit of motion and repose, the several kinds of cure, friendliness, and politics. This is the second and middle knowledge and consists of the knowledge of bodies; the first and lofty knowledge is the knowledge of religion; and the third and low knowledge is what the organs are trained to do.

"The religious scholars agree that the lofty knowledge is the knowledge of religion. Muslim scholars are in agreement that the knowledge of religion rests on three parts: first, the cognition of the essence *(khassah)* of faith *(iman)* and Islam, that is, the knowledge of God's unity and sincerity *(ikhlas).* It is only through the Prophet - may God's prayer and peace be upon him - that one may attain that knowledge; it is so because of His Will. It is also through the Qur'an that such a knowledge is attained with respect to God's creation, which is attested to by his creatures; the proofs of His unity and eternity; and the affirmation and attestation of all that is in the Qur'an with respect to angels, scriptures and messengers. Second is the knowledge of the source of information with respect to religion and legal precepts, about the Prophet - may God's prayer and peace be upon him - for through him and his tongue God legislated His religion; about the religious scholars who transmitted that on the authority of the Prophet; about the men who carried that to you up to your own time; and about the manner of establishing clearly the continuity of the Prophetic Traditions. And third is the knowledge of the Traditions *(sunan)* with respect to their obligatory nature and study, the determination of legal decisions requiring information about reliable witnesses; and knowledge of what is incumbent from what is supererogatory, of legal rights, allegations, and the exceptions that prevailed among the Consensus. The religious scholars maintain that the knowledge of jurisprudence is not feasible without the knowledge of all that. Success comes from God.[35]

As suggested earlier Ibn 'Abd al-Barr does not offer a solution to the dichotomy that separated the religious scholars and the philosophers. His *Jami'* was limited to mere reporting with no interjection of personal opinion; however, given his reliance on traditions going back to the Prophet, one may reasonably assume that Ibn 'Abd al-Barr's approach to the sciences was influenced by religious considerations.

On the other hand, Sa'id of Toledo had a secular perspective, relying much on topographical and demographic considerations in which the facts of history are important. Sa'id was born in Almeri'a and studied, according to Ibn Bashkuwal, under Ibn Hazm. However, Sa'id, Ibn Hazm's biographer does not mention having studied under Ibn Hazm, though familiar with his works. In any case, Sa'id's training consisted of both the secular and the religious sciences, in which he excelled. Sa'id served the Banu Dhi al-Nun of Toledo as judge and wrote a work on astronomy and two on history (dealing with the biographies of Arab and non-Arab scholars[37] and with the history of mankind.[38]

Although these works are not extant, their titles appears to confirm the universal outlook of Sa'id's small yet valuable work entitled *Categories of Nations*.[39] In this work that Sa'id places nations in a hierarchial order according to the sciences they had produced. The sciences are, according to him, influenced by and dependant upon a suitable geographic environment, which causes the inhabitants of a nation to be either stupid or intelligent. There is some hint of this geographic determinism in Ibn Hazm's thinking,[40] and a great deal of it in the thinking of Ibn Khaldun.[41]

To Sa'id, nations differ because of conduct *(akhlaq)*, physiognomy *(suwar)*, and language *(lughah)*.[42] He states that anyone who is familiar with the history of mankind will find that seven nations gave rise to all others; they are the Persians, Chaldeans, Greeks, Turks, Indians, Copts and Chinese. And there are two categories of nations: those which cultivated the sciences and produced several kinds, and those which came up with no science and who handed down no useful scientific knowledge. Eight nations concerned themselves with the sciences: Indians, Persians, Chaldeans, Hebrews, Greeks, Romans, Egyptians, and Arabs. The rest of mankind - consisting of the Chinese, Gogs and Magogs, Turks, Khazars, Berbers, Negroes, Slavs, Russians, and others are devoid of science.

Among the people who do not concern themselves with the sciences are some who possess knowledge of skills only. The Chinese mastered the practical crafts, and the Turks show a great dexterity in warfare and in handling weapons.[43] But these skills are the product of instinct rather than intelligence and may be compared with the honeycombs of bees and to the web of spiders. Their courage in war may be compared with the courage of lion or a tiger.[44] The others in this category, particularly the inhabitants of the extreme north and south resemble beasts more than human being. The northerners, who live on the fringes of the civilized world, suffer from cold mixtures; they are voluminous, rude, white complexioned and stupid. The southerners suffer from hot mixtures, are black, lack perception, and indulge in frivolity and ignorance.[45] Sa'id was quick to realize that the Berbers and the Galicians (inhabitants of the "civilized world") are behind in the sciences, but their lack of accomplishment is explained in that God has determined their fate!

On the other hand, the people who cultivate the sciences are the quintessence of God's creatures on earth, because they devote themselves to the attainment of the virtues of the rational soul *(fada' il al-nafs al-natiqah)* and disdain the mere skills of the Chinese and courage of the Turks.[46] In spite of their black complexion, which is puzzling to Sa'id, the Indians had taken a great interest in the sciences and made considerable contributions to astronomy, mathematics, geometry, medicine, preparation of drugs, metaphysics, politics, music, and ethics, much of which reached Islam. On this account, they are the fountainhead of wisdom, and the source of justice and sound political management.[47] Similar praise is bestowed on the Persians for their excellent political management, and for having cultivated medicine, astrology, astronomy, mathematics, and astronomical observatories.[48] The Chaldeans excelled, likewise, in astronomy, the construction of astronomical observatories, "the secrets of the stars," motion and astrology.[49] The Greeks call their scholars philosophers, which means "lovers of wisdom." Sa'id says: "Greek philosophers occupy the loftiest position among men, and are the most exalted people among scholars by virtue of their true concern with the various arts *(funun)* of wisdom, such as mathematics, logic, the natural sciences, metaphysics, domestic management, and politics."[50] He mentions specifically Empedocles, Pythagoras, Socrates, Plato, Appolonius, Archimedes, Euclid, Ptolemy, Galen, and Aristotle with reference to the accessibility of their works among Muslims.[51] The Romans, whose language is Latin, fell heir to the Greeks and had many scholars in the various branches of philosophy.[52] Finally, the Egyptians cultivated mathematics, the natural sciences, metaphysics, talisman, alchemy, astronomy, and astrology, before and after the Flood, and excelled in them.

After this interesting background material, Sa'id deals with the Arabs,[53] to whom he devotes a good portion of his work. He says that the pre-Islamic Arabs were nomadic people and had some notion of the stars and medicine, but God did not grace them with the knowledge of philosophy.[54] Only al-Kindi in Islamic times is known to be a philosopher. During the reign of the 'Abbasid caliph al-Ma'mun (813-833), the philosophical sciences were pursued in earnest, after many foreign works had been translated into Arabic. Those sciences included philosophy, logic, mathematics, geometry, astronomy, astrology, music, medicine, and other sciences. Many Muslims, such as al-Kindi, al-Farabi, and al-Razi, excelled in them. Their legacy was transmitted to al-Andalus, and many works on the sciences were written by Andalusians. During the time of Ibn Abi al-Mansur (d. 1002), that the caliphal library of Cordova was purged of scientific works to appease the common people.[55]

Sa'id's account reveals not only the state of the sciences in al-Andalus and his familiarity with the philosophical sciences in antiquity and Islamic times, but his own bias toward the sciences, in particular the philosophical sciences. Obviously, language, physiognomy, and moral code do not matter much in connection with the merit of a nation, what matters most is the kind of sciences that nation has produced, and especially, those sciences connected with philosophy. To him, it is the philosopher rather than the religious scholar who occupies the loftiest position among God's creatures and, by implication, it is the foreign philosophical sciences rather than the Arabic Sciences that actually count.

On the whole, Ibn 'Abd al-Barr and Sa'id show the attitude of the Anadalusians toward the sciences. It should be noted, however, that Ibn 'Abd al-Barr's moderate, impersonal attitude is not representative of the extreme attitude of the religious scholars, who object to philosophy and logic on the ground that they are detrimental to religion. In fact, Ibn 'Abd al-Barr criticizes some religious scholars who imitate old authorities with little scrutiny. Be that as it may, the attitudes of Ibn 'Abd al-Barr and Sa'id toward the sciences reflect the dichotomy that had been building up over the ninth and tenth centuries between philosophers and religious scholars. In the midst of this, Ibn Hazm formulated his conception of the sciences, addressing himself particularly to extremists who, through ignorance or design, attempted to ignore or distort the two principal sources of the truth — that of Revelation and that of philosophy.

Although he remained deeply religious in outlook and had an unshaken commitment to Islam as the sole embodiment of the truth, Ibn Hazm recognized that the concept of knowledge had many ramifications and could be understood properly only in the context of the totality of the experience of mankind in both its spiritual and scientific aspects. He built his doctrine of knowledge around the relationship of the universe to God and vice versa, bringing in the interaction of the visible and the invisible, or the physical and philosophical sciences, on the one hand, and the divine sciences, on the other. It is this kind of thinking, perhaps, that influenced Ibn Hazm to believe that no science, however modest or rudimentary, should be overlooked. The interaction of God with the universe should not remain in the realm of theory, but should be implemented through a philosophy of education which aims at guiding the individual to a well-rounded education with due attention to both the religious and secular disciplines. By this means, Ibn Hazm forged a synthesis and an integration of all the sciences, including even the pseudosciences. And if Ibn Hazm places limitations on the pursuit of a well-rounded education, it is because he realizes that life is short and that the capacity of individuals is not the same, requiring them to pursue a minimum curriculum, or to take up a lofty instead of a base science.

In short, he defends philosophy against the extremism of the religious scholars as he defends religion against the extremism of the philosophers. His approach to the sciences and their classification is unique in Islam and goes beyond al-'Amiri's defense of the philosophical sciences; the slanted divisions of al-Farabi, Ibn Sina and Sa'id, who favor the philosophical sciences; the noncommittal divisions of al-Khuwarizmi, Ibn al-Nadim, the Brethren of Purity, and to some extent, Ibn 'Abd al-Barr. Ibn Hazm's classification constitutes a blueprint for reconciliation of the sciences. Although the religious sciences occupy in his system the apex of the scientific pyramid on the ground that they are more lasting and more useful for man's well-being on earth as well as in Heaven, they would fall short without a basic knowledge of language, history, mathematics, astronomy, medicine, and logic, the fundamental science for determining what is right and wrong.

Besides his *Categories of the Sciences,* which will be analyzed in the next section, Ibn Hazm delved into the question of the sciences, in some of his other works and with the same remarkable consistency. In his *Tawqif,*[56] a treatise written in reply to an inquiry addressed to him regarding the two categories of the sciences (the sciences of the Ancients *('ulum al-awa' il)* and knowledge contained in prophecy *('ilm ma ja' at bi-hi al-nubuwwah),* Ibn Hazm attempted manner to give a succinct answer so as to leave no doubt. He says that the sciences of the Anciencts (philosophers) consist of philosophy and the rules *(hudud)* of logic. Philosophy is a lofty and good science because it contains the cognition *(ma'rifah)* of the whole world and what it contains regarding genera *(ajnas),* species *(anwa'),* particulars *(ashkhas),* substances *(jawahir),* and accidents *(a'rad),* and because it leads to the establishment of proof *(burhan)* without which nothing can be regarded as truth. Logic also discerns what is believed to be truth but actually is not; its utility is enormous in determining the realities of things.[57] Mathematics, geometry, medicine, and astronomy are, likewise, good demonstrative sciences and very useful in this world.[58] As for astrology,[59] it is false because it lacks demonstrative proof.

However useful these and other siences are in this world, they cannot supersede what prophecy brought forth. The merit and utility of prophecy reside in three things. The first is improvement of the spiritual character and the upholding of justice, generosity, continence, truthfulness, courage, patience, clemency, mercy, and avoidance of all things. (In essence, prophecy leads to the cure *(mudawah)* of the soul, which takes precedence over the cure of the body.[60] In this connection, it is impossible for philosophy to improve the character of the soul without the aid of prophecy for the simple reason that philosophy would require obedience to someone other than the Creator, and besides, philosophers differ among themselves with respect to the fixation of moral qualities.[61]) The second is repulsion of injustices, protection of personal property, and security from invasions.[62] In sum, prophecy tells us that the world is created, has a beginning and an end, and that time and space are finite.[64]

This "clarification" being made, Ibn Hazm takes up the question of the growth of the individual, his education and subsistence — all of which are impossible without language. But language requires again, teaching, for no science can exist without teaching. For this reason that countries such as those of the Slavs, Turks, Daylamites, and Black people are devoid of science because they follow the course of nature without teaching. Through teaching and learning the language and the crafts, the individual will be able to inquire about the existence of God, His creation and Revelation, thus arriving at the truth contained in His religion as handed down to His Prophet Muhammad.[65] He will also realize that the religious law of Christians and Jews is adulterated, as are the laws of Zoroastrians and Manichaeans.[66] This being the case, it follows that the individual ought to pursue the sciences and interest himself in them according to their stated objectives. But under no circumstances should the study of the religious law be undertaken for the purpose of gaining high position and wealth, for this leads to perdition only.[67]

In his *Taqrib,* a work of logic written relatively early in his life, Ibn Hazm not only exalts the merit and utility of logic.[68] but gives a summary of the sciences:

"The sciences which are current among people nowadays and which are pursued are twelve — from which two extra sicences are the result. This category [of dividing the sciences] is different from that which was current among the Ancients [philosophers]. Thus, we limit ourselves with the help and power of the Almighty to those sciences which are beneficial to people at all times and by means of which people arrive at perceiving other sciences. They are the sciences of the Qur'an, Traditions, denominations *(madhahib),* legal decisions *(futya),* logic, grammar, lexicography, poetry, history, medicine, mathematics, geometry, and astronomy. The sciences of dream interpretation *('ibarah)* and rehtoric *(balaghah)* result from these sciences.

"The science of the Qur'an is divided into five parts: (1) reading, (2) vowel endings *(i'rab),* (3) rare expressions *(gharib),* (4) commentary *(tafsir),* and (5) legal decisions *(ahkam).* The source *(al-marju' ilayh)* of Qur'anic reading resides in premises that go back to known and reliable readers, who trace their version back to the Prophet—may God's prayer and peace be upon him—and about whom there are proofs regarding the soundness of their transmission as emanating from him. Vowel endings are based on premises that are true if the expression conforms to certain vowels and form which constitute its source. Lexicography is that which agreed upon in the Arabic language. Legal dcisions are arrived at through clearly defined expressions and their elucidation by the Prophet — may God's prayer and peace be upon him.

"Tradition is divided into two parts, the sciences of transmission *(riwayah)* and the science of establishing its veracity *(ihkam)*. The source of the transmission of Traditions rests on premises, transmitted on the authority of trustworthy people whose fairness, proofs, and witnesses are duly verified. The source of transmission is also derived from premises taken from the text of the Qur'an whose soundness we have already mentioned. The source of establishing the veracity of Traditions is derived from the meaning of the expressions contained therein and their mutual understanding, as we have explained elsewhere.

"The source of denomination outside the Islamic religions is derived from premises going back to the first intellection *(awa'il al-'aql)* and sensation, as we have mentioned in the *Fisal*.

"The source of legal decisions consists of premises derived from the Qur'an, Traditions which are true on the basis of proofs, and premises going back to the consensus of virtuous scholars whose decisions are confirmed by the Qur'an, as we have demonstrated in our books.

"The source of grammar consists of premises arrived at through the authority of the Arabs, whose understanding and knowledge of meanings in their language is great. As for grammatical causation *('ilal)*, it is highly unsound.

"The source of lexicography consists of premises going back to what was heard from the Arabs and transmitted through known and trustworthy authorities. After all, Arabic is their language.

"The source of poetry consists also of premises based on what has been heard from the Arabs with respect to meters *(awzan)* — and with no consideration to meters used by other people because people call poetry only that which encompasses metrics, as Ibn al-Nadim mentions in his book. The source of what is good or bad in poetry goes back to things agreed upon by people who transmitted a great deal of it and who dedicated themselves to examining its meaning with respect to easy and sweet expressions and meaning that encompasses nicety, right metaphors, sweet allusions, and beautiful versification.

"The source of history *(khabar)* consists of premises that guarantee the continuity and soundness of transmission without leaving doubt concerning the existence of famous countries, famous kings, battles, and other information about them.

"The source of medicine consists of premises which experience has verified with respect to the beginning and appearance of the degree of diseases, the disturbance of mixtures that cause them, and the counteracting of all that through the power of drugs. All goes back to the first intellection and sensation.

"The source of mathematics and geometry consists of premises going back to the first intellection.

"Astronomy is divided into two parts. The first is knowledge of the form of the stars; disconjunction *(qat')*[69] of the stars, sun, moon, and the heavens; and the division of the celestial sphere and its position. The source of this division consists of premises derived from mathematics, geometry, first intellection, and sensation. The second is the influence *(qadaya)* of the stars resulting from the positions of the stars, sun, and moon in their motion through the signs of the zodiac, and from facing each other. If experience *(tajribah)* confirms anything of that, it may be considered true; otherwise, they are limited to the sayings of old authorities.

"Rhetoric will be mentioned in its proper place, God willing.

"The source of dream interpretation is derived from things related by the Messenger of God — may God's prayer and peace be upon him — and by virtuous men in this science.

"The prerequisites of these two sciences [rhetoric and dream interpretation] consist of extending one's knowledge in all the sciences and in relation to nature and in conformity with the origin of Creation."[70]

In this succinct and descriptive division, Ibn Hazm states the objective and the source of each one of the sciences; only elsewhere does he offer an opinion of their respective merits, interrlationships, pursuits, and disseminations. In his *Talkhis*,[71] a treatise on eight questions posed to him by friends, he takes up the subject of the sciences, offers a curriculum, and considers devotion to learning to be the best lifetime pursuit, along with the practice of justice and the fight *(jihad)* in the path of God.[72] Although his curriculum aims at enhancing a religious education, it contains various of the secular sciences. He suggests the memorization of the Qur'an or portion thereof, the study of the seven Qur'anic readings, Traditions, grammar, and lexicography — all of which are obligations incumbent upon all Muslims; and further, an acquaintance with poetry, mathematics, medicine, books on denominations *(ahl al-ra'y)*, and other subjects. [73] These and other pursuits should be undertaken for salvation and improvement of moral charcter, but under no circumstances for attaining leadership and prestige.[74] This point is reiterated and emphasized again and again in his other works.[75] Finally, he points out that a distinction should be made between the lofty and base sciences, and that the individual should set priorities when pursuing them.

Ibn Hazm's Categories of the Sciences
(Maratib al-'ulum).

The subject of the sciences in their various aspects occupied a prominent place in Ibn Hazm's thinking throughout his career. Ample space is given to them in his *Taqrib, Tawqif, Talkhis,* and the *Fisal,* and others written at different states of his career. In many respects, these works contain the raw material for the formulation of his definitive ideas on the subject, which he articulated and systematized in his *Categories of the Sciences,* apparently written late in life.[76] It contains his theories regarding the meaning, merit or demerit, classification, interdependence, and manner and degree of pursuing the sciences. The Arabic edition and translation of the work appears elsehwere in this study, so it will be discussed only briefly here.[77]

Ibn Hazm remained faithful to the full title of the treatise, which reads: "The Categories of the Sciences, the Manner of Studying them, and Their interrelationship." He begins by saying that God has placed man above many of His creatures, endowing him with the faculty of discernment *(tamyiz)* by means of which he is able to engage in the sciences and the crafts. God's trust should not be wasted, but should be used in full measure. It is pointless to study magic, talisman, music, and alchemy, which do not deserve the name of sciences; instead, study those sciences whose learning is feasible and useful according to their importance and the degree of their utility. Man has two abodes, this world and the Hereafter, and his education should fullfil the needs of both. It follows that the pursuit of sciences in order to acquire wealth and prestige is futile, a waste of time and talent. The best sciences *(afdal al-'ulum)* are those which will lead to salvation in the Hereafter.

After this preamble, Ibn Hazm says that any rational being will realize that he cannot attain the sciences without study and that study requires listening, reading, and writing. A child should start writing about the age of five and should make sure that his handwriting is straight, clear, and without embellishment, unless he intends to join rulers and unworthy people and waste his time drafting documents that are full of lies. As for reading, he should acquire the necessary competence to read any book that may fall into his hand.[78]

Thereafter, he should study grammar and lexicography to the point of acquiring the necessary knowledge, without studying grammatical causation *('ilal),* which is useless. To reinforce his linguistic ability, the student should recite that kind of poetry that contains wise and moral sayings, avoiding poetry on themes of love, war, separation, satire, praise, and eulogy, which are detrimental to moral edification.[79]

After the study of grammar and lexicography, the student should take up mathematics, geometry, and astronomy, astrology is not a bonafide science.[80] Then he should take up logic in order to discern what constitutes a proof and what does not, and to be able to judge between right and wrong.[81]

Following the study of logic, he should look into the natural sciences *(al-tabi'iyyat),* atmospheric conditions, composition of the elements, zoology, botany, minerals and anatomy *(tashrih).*[82]

While he is pursuing these disciplines, he should not neglect the study of both ancient and contemporary histories.[83]

Having studied all of these sciences, the student then will be prepared to seek proof of whether the world is created or uncreated. If he finds out, as he must, that the world is created, he will inquire further whether the world has a creator, and, in turn, whether this creator is one or more than one. Once he finds out that there is one single creator, he will look into prophecy and will ask whether it is feasible. He will conclude that it is feasible on the basis of necessary/self-evident information *(akhbar daruriyyah)*. Once he is satisfied with the feasibility of prophecy, he will have to admit the validity of the Prophecy of Muhammad, and God's covenants as revealed to him in the Qur'an.[84]

It is extremely significant that Ibn Hazm has so far offered a *strictly secular* curriculum devoid of any religious training. He believes it to be sufficient for the individual to find out for himself that the world is created, has a creator, and that prophecy is one of the creator's manifestations. Once the validity of prophecy is affirmed, he brings his argument to the happy conclusion that the Prophecy of Muhammad must of necessity be valid one, and that anyone who ignores this reality, or the reality of the existence of the religious law *(shari'ah),* will inflict great harm on himself by neglecting its study or espousing a base and less useful science. For after all, the main purpose of education is to derive the utmost benefit for both this world and the Hereafter; this can be achieved only by studying the religious law.[85] He goes on to say that learning and teaching a particular discipline is acceptable, but learning it for the purpose of joining an unjust ruler or seeking praise, wealth, and prestige will bring calamity.

In sum, education for mundane purposes is self-defeating and constitutes a waste of time, talent, and energy since "knowledge requires sagacity, understanding, research, memory, and perseverance; it also requires toil, expenditure, and as many books as possible."[86] Speaking about books, Ibn Hazm is of the opinion that the more books there are the better,

No book is devoid of usefulness, in fact, a book is an increase of knowledge which the individual will find if and when he needs it, for there is no way for the individual to retain all the knowledge in which he specializes. And since there is no way to accomplish this, it follows that books are delightful storehouses for the individual seeking knowledge. Had it not been for books, the sciences would have been lost and could hardly be found. Thus, he who decries the abundance of books errs; and were one to follow his opinion, the sciences would have been ruined, and ignoramuses would make contention and claims as they wish. Had not been for the testimony of books, the claim of both the scholar and the ignoramus would be on a par. It is through books that haughtiness is tumbled through reiterating the opinions of scholars, adhering to what is heard, and collecting it. Thus, the individual should cling wholeheartedly to the inkstand and paper; to people of civilized countries where knowledge flourished; and to confronting contenders and facing polemicists. It is through this that realities will emerge before him. For the one who speaks on his own authority and on the basis of what he thinks is not the same as the one who speaks on the authority of someone else. A bereaved mother is not the same as a hired mourner."[86a]

After his attempt to establish the validity of the religious law and the necessity of studying and adhering to it, Ibn Hazm proceeds to define and divide the sciences. Of the seven universal and ageless sciences, three — religion, history, and language — distinguish one nation from another whereas the remaining four — philosophy, astronomy, numbers, and medicine — are the same among all people. He then elaborates upon his major division, limiting himself to the Islamic experience with respect to religion, language, and history and following, on the whole, the traditional division of the philosophical sciences:

I. RELIGIOUS LAW *(shari'ah):*
 1. Reading *(qira'ah)* and Meanings *(ma'ani).*
 2. Prophetic Traditions *(hadith):* text *(matn)* and chain of transmitters *(ruwah).*
 3. Jurisprudence *(fiqh):* Qur'anic ordinances *(ahkam),* hadith ordinances, consensus *(ijma'),* and the knowledge of proofs concerning the soundness or unsoundness of their agreements.
 4. Theology *(kalam):* the knowledge of the doctrines of theologians and the proof concerning them.

II. LANGUAGE:
 1.. Grammar *(nahw).*
 2. Lexicography *(lughah).*

III. HISTORY *(akhbar),* having five categories *(maratib):*
 1. Dynastic.
 2. Annalistic.
 3. Countries.
 4. Classes *(tabaqat).*
 5. Genealogy *(nasab).*

IV. ASTRONOMY *('ilm al-nujum);*
 1. Astronomy proper *('ilm al-hay'ah).*
 2. Astrology *(qada').*

V. NUMBERS *('ilm al-'adad).*

VI. LOGIC *('ilm al-mantiq):*
 1. Rational *('aqliy)* logic.
 2. Sensory *(hissiy)* logic.

VII. MEDICINE *('ilm al-tibb):*
 1. Spiritual medicine *(tibb al-nafs).*
 2. Corporeal medicine *(tibb al-ajsam);*
   a. The knowledge of the nature of corporeal things.
   b. The knowledge of the composition of the organs.

    c. The knowledge of diseases and their causes.
    d. Surgery.
    e. Preventive medicine.

As an afterthought, he adds poetry *(shi'r)* and says that there are two other sciences - rhetoric *(balaghah)* and dream interpretation *('ilm al-'ibarah)* - which are offshoots of the sciences mentioned above, or the result of two or more sciences. He concludes, "These are the arts *(afanin)* that are designated as knowledge *('ilm)* and sciences *('ulum)* in ancient and modern times."[87] and adds that upon reflection anything that is known can be called knowledge, including crafts; however, crafts aim solely at gaining a livelihood without having anything to do with the real objective of knowledge, which consists of the attainment of salvation in the Hereafter.[88]

Some of the above sciences are discussed elsewhere in this book. It remains here to discuss Ibn Hazm's view on the inter-relationship of the sciences. In his judgment, the sciences are inter-related, and none can dispense with the others.[89] In other words, the religious scholars are in need of the philosophical and natural sciences as much as the philosophers are in need of the religious sciences. This theory leads Ibn Hazm to devise an integrated education in which the humanities, the natural sciences, and the religious sciences unite to produce true understanding of this world and the causes behind its very existence. Ibn Hazm maintains the profound conviction that through the study of language, mathematics, astronomy, logic, the natural sciences, and history, the individual will be able to perceive that the world is created and it has a Creator, Who is also the Giver of Law containing His commands and prohibitions which regulate man's conduct in this life and prepare him for a blissful life in the Hereafter. This may be one of the unique features of Ibn Hazm's conception of the sciences.

There are religious as well as sociological implications to Ibn Hazm's approach to the sciences and education which impose an obligation on the individual to contribute his share to society. He quoted his teacher Ibn al-Kattani as asking, "How is it possible that a man should remain idle without noticing that everyone else is doing something, e.g., the plowman tilling the soil, the miller grinding grain, and the like.[90] Also, in order to have security and social order, there must be a law *(shari'ah)* that guarantees the safety of society through rewards for good deeds and punishment for acts of lawlessness. There is no way out, except the presence of and occupation with the law,[91] which will guarantee the individual safety from injustices perpetrated by rulers, the nobility, or the common people.[92]

In short, law is a necessity for an orderly society and viable political organization as well as of religious significance for life in the Hereafter. For these two reasons, religious law takes precedence over other sciences, which are limited to the affairs of this world only, and it cannot be ignored by anyone who makes claim to scholarship. By the same token, however meritorious religious studies are, they could never be complete without studying all the sciences having relevance to religious practices and beliefs (such as determining inheritance, the time of prayer, fasting, and pilgrimage) and without a knowledge of foods, drinks and the state of health - all of which require a basic knowledge of mathematics, astronomy, medicine, and other relevant disciplines. In addition, the Qur'an cannot be understood fully without a knowledge of the Arabic language and the Prophetic Traditions. Anyone who attempts to make a legal decision without such a knowledge places himself on the level of a donkey, whether he arrives at that decision on his own or imitates someone else whose decision he will never be sure is right.[93] In the same manner, those who devote themselves solely to grammar, lexicography, prosody, and the like, neglecting the religious sciences, are like those who have salt without the food.[94] Ibn Hazm is careful to say that he is minimizing the importance of specialists for failing to relate their specialties to other sciences, particularly the religious sciences. In sum, all the sciences are interdependent, contributing together to an understanding of the connection between the universe and its Maker.[95]

As already suggested, Ibn Hazm offers a coherent and systematic division of the sciences not for the purpose of mere listing, which had been done before, but for the purpose of articulating a new doctrine. The lack of such a doctrine had separated Islamic religious scholars and philosophers. The categorizations of the sciences by Ibn Hazm's predecessors and contemporaries tended to emphasize either the philosophical or religious side with no attempt to reconcile the differences between two seemingly antagonistic groups. Al-'Amiri came close when he defended the philosophical sciences as being harmonious with the religious sciences, but he did not take into consideration the extremism of some scholars, nor did he propose an educational plan whereby the two groups might work in unison toward the single truth which Ibn Hazm conceives to be the subject of both religion and philosophy. This is an extremely important point which deserves further study.

The Sciences after the Time of Ibn Hazm

There are indications that both al-Ghazzali and Ibn Khaldun knew some of the works of Ibn Hazm and even praised them.[96] Moreover, a close look at the careers of the three men and their ideas reveals interesting similarities and almost identical motivations. Al-Ghazzali, whose work flourished in the second half of the eleventh century, shortly after Ibn Hazm's death, displayed as much concern for the truth as Ibn Hazm before him.Both were concerned with the fate of Islam and entertained the hope of reinterpreting and reviving the religious law, thereby saving it from the narrow-minded religious scholars as well as from the extreme rationalism of the Philosophers. Both assumed the role of reformers and hoped to establish Islamic theology and jurisprudence on firm foundations. This caused them to ponder on the various aspects of knowledge and on the relationship of the physical world to a primeval and eternal creator. In so doing, they took into consideration the various sciences, their respective merits and utility, and made of logic a powerful tool for combatting misguided theologians and jurists. In the final account, they succeeded in devising a coherent system of theology and law. Although Ibn Hazm's system failed to earn support, that of al-Ghazzali prevailed among the majority of Muslims, making him the venerable theologian of Islam that St. Thomas Aquinas is of Christianity.

Al-Ghazzali formulated his religious ideas after a long period of hesitation and skepticism that took him from theology to the imitation of a leader *(taqlid al-imam),* to philosophy, and finally to mysticism.[97] Throughout this long trajectory, he was hoping to attain the knowledge of the reality of things *('ilm haqa' iq al-umur)* with certainy *(bi-'ilmin yaqiniyin),*[98] but failed to satisfy his inner desire. For him, things perceived by the senses as well as those perceived by the intellect were not free from error and thus could not lead to the certain knowledge he had hoped for. However, he persevered and came to perceive the reality of things through the light that the Almighty cast in his chest. It is the light *(nur)* that became the key to the major portion of knowledge.[99]

In this respect, al-Ghazzali differed from Ibn Hazm, who conceived the intellect *('aql)* to be the key to knowledge, although his objective was almost the same. Al-Ghazzali turned to mysticism after an emotional crisis brought about by the confusion among the major schools of thought. "When the Almighty God, by virtue of His grace and great bounty, cured me from this disease, I was able to discern four groups of people who sought the truth: (1) the theologians, (2) the esoteric *(al-batiniyyah)* or those who followed the infallible leader *(al-imam al-ma'sum),* (3) the philosophers, and (4) the Sufis."[100] Not unlike Ibn Hazm, he was disenchanted with the claims and methods of the theologians and with the pretension of the esoterics and philosophers, who had strayed from the main objective of ascertaining the truth. He believed that the *sufi* way *('ala tariq al-sufiyyah),* which combines knowledge and action, leads to the elimination of obstacles before the soul, thereby freeing it from blameworthy qualities and wicked attributes.[101]

However great the differences between the two men in their search for the ultimate truth, there are a number of areas in which their views coincide. Al-Ghazzali's attitude toward theologians and philosophers does not differ much from that of Ibn Hazm. Neither one appears to loathe theology and philosophy per se, but they question the methods and pretension of philosophers and theologians, each group arrogating to itself the key to the truth.[102] Similarly, their views coincide with respect to the imitation of leader, which does not lead to certainty *al-'ilm al-yaqin),* nor is it a sure means of determining right from wrong.[103] The truth should stand on its own strength and not because someone said it. "For, the rational being *(aqil)* would ponder on a question; if he finds it to be true he must accept it whether its proponent is a liar or truthful person."[104] Moreover, al-Ghazzali was a strong advocate of individual inquiry *(ijtihad)* for verifying the truth or falsity of a particular question.[105]

With respect to the sciences, al-Ghazzali and Ibn Hazm arrived at certain similar conclusions. They conceived the religious sciences to be the embodiment of the truth and the manifestation of divine wisdom, deserving to be placed at the apex of the scientific pyramid and pursued as much as possible. The worldly sciences such as mathematics, logic, metaphysics, and politics are legitimate and should be heeded and pursued by the faithful; but they should not give license to the philosophers to denigrate the religious edifice, nor should they be the cause of skepticism and disbelief.[106]

These are some of the salient points of al-Ghazzali's *Deliverer from Error,* an autobiographical work written late in life, containing the gist of his mature thinking after a long emotional crisis similar to that of St. Augustine. But his *Revivification of the Religious Sciences*[107] constitutes his *opus magnum* and contains his important religious ideas. In it al-Ghazzali discusses knowledge and its virtue; teaching and learning; knowledge expectd of the individual *(fard 'ayn)* and knowledge expected of the community at large *(fard kifayah);* misconceptions and praiseworthy and blameworthy knowledge *('ilm mahmud* and *'ilm madhmum),* the damage resulting from *disputatio,* the etiquette of teacher and student, the damage resulting from knowledge and scholars, the issues separating the philosophers and the religious scholars, and the intellect[108] - all of which were of great concern to Ibn Hazm.

Al-Ghazzali begins his treatment of knowledge and the sciences by citing numerous traditions exalting knowledge, scholars, teaching, and learning.[109] Knowledge leads to action and is the means of attaining eternal bliss in the Hereafter and happiness on earth, thus making it the best and noblest pursuit.[110] It is the instrument that leads to the Almighty God. It includes the crafts, political management, and the philosophical and religious sciences, which are placed in hierarchical order according to their nobility and complexity.[111] People differ about which science should take precedence - theologians say theology; jurists, jurisprudence; the commentators, the Qur'an, the traditionists, Traditions; and so forth. Al-Ghazzali gives precedence to, first, the science of transaction *('ilm al-mu'amalah),* that is, the relationship of man to God which consists of belief *(i'tiqad),* action *(fi'l),* and abandonment of forbidden things; and second the science of uncovering secrets *('ilm al-mukashafah)* that leads to the knowledge of the hidden which is the expression of the light that appears in the heart at the time of its purification.[112] He adds that knowledge, which includes all the philosophical and religious sciences, is incumbent upon the Islamic community. This leads al-Ghazzali to divide the sciences into two major categories:

I. THE RELIGIOUS SCIENCES *(al-'ulum al-shar'iyyah),* which are not attained by the intellect, experience, and hearing; they are praiseworthy and consist of four kinds: (1) roots *(usul)* comprising of Qur'an, Traditions, and the Consensus; (2) branches *(furu'),* which are derived from the roots and comprise law and the knowledge of the conditions of the heart *('ilm ahwal al-qalb);* (3) the ancilary sciences *(muqaddimat),* comprising grammar and lexicography which are the instruments for knowing the Book of God; and (4) the complementary sciences *(al-mutammimat)*, comprising Qur'anic readings, commentary and history.[113]

II. THE NON-RELIGIOUS SCIENCES *(al-'ulum ghayr al-shar'iyyah)*, comprising geometry, mathematics, logic and the natural sciences, all of which are praiseworthy.

On the whole, al-Ghazzali's structure of the sciences suggests a rapproachment between the religious and secular sciences, but it lacks the elements of integration and interrelationship on which Ibn Hazm insists. Significantly, al-Ghazzali makes some qualifications in his division of the sciences. He says that theology does not merit inclusion among the religious sciences because it is contained in the Qur'an, and that which came to be known as theology is no more than a blameworthy *disputatio (mujadalah madhmumah)*[114] And if some wonder, says he, that we included law *(fiqh)* among the secular sciences, our reply is that law, by its very nature, deals with worldly questions, thus justifying its inclusion among the worldly sciences.[115] His exclusion of philosophy from the secular sciences is explained in that philosophy is not a discipline per se, but comprises the totality of the secular sciences,[116] and as such it is a praiseworthy science. On the other hand, history is permissible *(mubah);* so is poetry as long as it does not contain stupid things.[117] Finally, he dismisses magic, talisman, astrology, and soothsaying from the category of the sciences on the same grounds as Ibn Hazm - they do not constitute a form of knowledge and are harmful to both their pursuers and those who believe in their credibility.[118]

However great the similarities between Ibn Hazm and al-Ghazzali, al-Ghazzali obviously limits the role of the intellect in ascertaining the truth, substituting the "light" from above, that is, adopting the Sufi path. In so doing, the problem of the sciences and their relationship remains where Ibn Hazm left it. Ibn Hazm's synthesis establishing an interdependence among the philosophical and religious sciences was soon forgotten, and the debate continued. It was Ibn Rushd who attempted for perhaps the last time to establish a harmony between Revelation and reason, religion and philosophy.[119]

Detailed and careful study is needed to determine whether the ideas of Ibn Hazm concerning the division and integration of the sciences had an impact on men such as the Andalusian philosophers Ibn Tufayl and Ibn Rushd, who were staunch proponents of the harmony of faith and reason, or religion and philosophy. Like Ibn Hazm, Ibn Rushd had a well-rounded education in the philosophical and religious sciences. He excelled as philosopher, theologian, and jurist. Although Ibn Rushd may not be considered an intellectual rebel and reformer in the manner of Ibn Hazm, he spoke just as eloquently and courageously for the philosophical sciences. He did not camouflage his thought in his capacity as a Malikite judge, thanks to the benign and tolerant attitude of the Almohad rulers whom he served. When discussing the relationship between religion and philosophy in his *Fasl,*[120] *Tahafut,*[121] and *Manahij,*[122] he did so openly and vigorously in a language reminiscent of that used by Ibn Hazm. Moreover, the following points pursued by Ibn Rushd are similar if not identical to those elaborated upon by Ibn Hazm. Ibn Rushd recognizes three levels of knowledgeable people: the philosophers, who have the ability of demonstration; the theologian/dialecticians, who innvovate and the rhetoricians, who persuade the great majority of people.[123] It is the philosophers who have the ability of demonstrative reasoning and who are able to show the harmony between Revelation and philosophy; for says Ibn Rushd,"Truth does not contradict truth, but agrees with it, and is a witness to it."[124] He concludes elsewhere that "philosophy is the companion of the law and its twin sister."[125]

After the fall of the Almohad dynasty in the thirteenth century, and subsequnt socio-political dislocation throughout western Islam,the problem of the sciences appear to have been deemed unimportant. In the latter part of the fourteenth century, it was discussed by the Tunisian thinker Ibn Khaldun, in a time of confusion and political turmoil not unlike that prevailing in the time of Ibn Hazm. Like Ibn Hazm, Ibn Khaldun had a broad education in the philosophical and religious sciences, and a frustrating political career ending in utter failure. Thereafter, Ibn Khaldun abandoned politics and devoted himself to writing a universal history, prefaced by his monumental *Muqaddimah* containing his reflections and philosophy about the Islamic experience in its manifold aspects. Perhaps, hoping to rescue Western Islam from its predicament, he offered an assessment of, if not a solution to, the grave political, religious, and intellectual crises facing the Islamic community. However, he was not explicit on many points and lacked the forward and vigorous approah of Ibn Hazm. At any rate, Ibn Khaldun, pondered the development, growth, and decline of society as reflected in its various institutions, including intellectual life. From the long history of mankind in its brilliant and dark moments, Ibn Khaldun drew conclusions to formulate a new science of culture.[126] The best representatives of Islamic thought - including al-Ghazzali, Ibn Hazm, Ibn Rushd and others - were known to him, as were the great and mediocre leaders of the Islamic community. Crucial issues that had faced the Islamic community for generations, received a good deal of his attention, including the problem of the sciences.

Ibn Khaldun appears on the surface to describe the state of the sciences and to divide the religious sciences *(al-ulum al-naqliyyah al-wad'iyah)* and the philosophical sciences *(al-'ulum al-tabi'iyyah al-falsaifyah)*. The religious sciences- Qur'anic commentary, Qur'anic readings, jurisprudence, the roots of the law, controversial questions and dialectics, theology, Sufism, and dream interpretation - are derived from the religious law as commanded by God and do not involve the intellect, nor are they subservient to it except in relating problems of details with basic principles. In other words, they contain the unalterable truth as handed down by God to His Prophet. On the other hand, the philosophical sciences - mathematics, geometry, astronomy, logic, physics, medicine, agriculture, metaphysics, sorcery and talisman, the secrets of letters, and alchemy - are sciences with which man became acquainted through his ability to think and to discern between right and wrong.[127]

However, a close look at this total approach reveals something else which in many ways resembles the approach of Ibn Hazm. In the manner of Ibn Hazm, Ibn Khaldun prefaces his chapter on the sciences with a discussion of man's ability to think, the relationship of thought to action, the experimental intellect, man's knowledge, angels, prophets, the acquisition of knowledge, the crafts, and teaching, he concludes that the sciences are the prerogative of man and are acquired through teaching.[128] Ibn Khaldun excludes the various crafts from the sciences, although he considers them to involve an act of the mind and the ability to think just as the sciences do.[129] He devotes a separate chapter to them, placed just before the one on the sciences.[130] He gives the same reason for their original exclusion as Ibn Hazm had - the crafts are meant to make a living and consist of services rendered by a servant, judge, mufti, teacher, preacher, or government employee; they increase or decrease according to supply and demand[131] and are so numerous as to defy any enumeration.[132]

Like the crafts, the intellecltual sciences are not limited to any particular religious group and can be cultivated by all people who are able to learn them.[133] But the religious sciences are different, and distinguish people from one another - Islam being the only true religion. Ibn Khaldun recognizes that the religious and the bonafide philosophical sciences are valid in their own right. The degree of perception, however, constitutes a basic difference between the two groups of the sciences. Although man is able through his intellectual faculties to comprehend the causes that are natural and obvious and presented in an orderly manner,[134] he is not able to comprehend all existing things and their causes, or to know all the details of existence.[135] For the intellect has its limitations - although the intellect is a correct scale that leads to certainty, it is not able to go beyond its own level to comprehend God and His attributes.[136] Furthermore, the essence of spiritual things is unknown, hard to get at, and cannot be proved by logical arguments.[137] This is in agreement with Ibn Hazm's view that philosophy is able to establish the realities of things, but cannot go beyond into the divine realm.[138] In the last resort, it is faith that is the source of all religious obligations. Faith is the affirmation by the heart of what the tongue says.[139]

CHAPTER VI

HIS RELIGIOUS IDEAS AND DOCTRINE

In his categorization of the sciences, Ibn Hazm places the religious sciences - the Qur'an, Traditions, jurisprudence, and theology - at the apex of the scientific pyramid, and views them as the expressions of God's will and His truth handed down to man to enable him to achieve happiness on earth and to prepare him for a life of bliss in the Hereafter.[1] They are intimately related to each other and constitute the *Shari'ah*, which of all the religious laws of mankind, is the only true one containing the unadultered truth that should be known and followed without the slightest deviation. As such, their pursuit is incumbent upon all mortals, who aspire order and well-being on earth and immense reward in the Hereafter. For this reason, they merit precedence over all the sciences, and ought to be pursued in their totality. However perfect and complete, the religious sciences cannot be fully comprehended without studying the worldly or philosophical sciences.[2] As already indicated, Ibn Hazm reasons that the sciences are related to one another and no science, however, praiseworthy and complete, can dispense of the other sciences. Within this context, an attempt will be made in this chapter to explore some of the juridico-theological ideas of Ibn Hazm.

Ibn Hazm wrote numerous juridico-theological works, which elucidates his literalist doctrine, Zahirism, against the background of the various systems of Muslim law and theology that had developed over the preceding four centuries. In separate treatises, he dealt with the Qur'an[3], its miraculous nature,[4] its reading,[5] abrogating and abrogated verses,[6] and other relevant questions. He developed various works to the Traditions with respect to their accuracy and made comprehensive collection,[7] an abridgment[8], and a commentary on them.[9] Concomitantly with the Qur'an and Traditions, which are the source of the religious law, he also discussed at length the consensus *(ijma')* of the Islamic community,[10] defining its role and the different categories of consensus.[11] These studies led him, in turn, to explain the reality of faith,[12] acts leading to salvation or damnation,[13] prayer,[14] pilgrimage,[15] death,[16] and the soul.[17] He also dealt with other topics, such as singing.[18] A large number of works are devoted to the various legal schools in the form of refutation,[19] some of which contain refutation of Judaism and Christianity.

Although many of his works have been lost, his *Fisal, Ihkam,* and *Muhalla* contain the gist of his religious ideas and doctrine. There is a good reason to believe that these three are comprised of shorter works with little alteration, and as a result, constitute the most reliable source of information concerning the religious ideas and the Zahirite doctrine of Ibn Hazm. In addition, his *Nubadh,* a manual based largely on his *Ihkam,* gives a capsular account of his ideas and deals with the roots *(usul)* of the law.

The *Fisal*.[21] in five parts, comprises the theology of Ibn Hazm. Written over a long period of time, the polemical work aims basically at presenting his version of a true Islam, vis-a-vis other Muslim denominations and other world religions and philosophical systems. As such, it covers most of the juridico-theological and philosophical issues that had occupied Muslim scholars for generations. His *Ihkam*, in eight parts, establishes the roots *(usul)* of the law in Zahirism, as contrasted with other legal schools; he pays special attention to the various criteria for arriving at legal decisions. The *Muhalla*, in eleven volumes, sets down in a comparatist way Ibn Hazm's Zahirite legal system, showing its validity over the legal schools of Malik, Abu Hanifah, and Shafi'i. Consisting of 2,308 queries *(mas'alah)*on law in theory and practice, it is an encyclopedia of Islamic law in all kinds of situations pertaining to obligatory, permissible, and forbidden acts; articles of the faith with respect to the belief in God and His unity; the various religious duties expected of the faithful, and human transactions pertaining to marriage, divorce, family affairs, inheritance, purchase and sale, slavery, food, clothing, and the like. Intended for the initiate and as a refresher, the *Muhalla* is a commentary on his abridgment of the *Mujalla*, which was based on his large work, the *Khisal*, commented on in his massive lost work, the *Isal*. Al-Dhahabi reports that the *Muhalla* was highly regarded and considered unique along with the juridical work *al-Mughni* by Ibn Qudamah.[22] The late modern religious reformer Rashid Rida[23] said that the printing of the *Mughni* of Ibn Qudamah and the *Muhalla* of Ibn Hazm would let him die in peace without concern for the fate of Islamic law.[24]

1. God, Prophecy, and Miracles

Ibn Hazm's works are permeated by an unswerving belief in an Almighty God and by an unshaken conviction in the veracity of Islam as the only true religion. His faith is not something he received passively, but is based on a wide knowledge of most of the religio-philosophical systems known in his time; he confesses that he arrived at the ultimate trush as contained in the Revelation through both faith and demonstrative reasoning.[25] This conviction led him to reconcile the truth reached by philosophy and that already contained in the Revelation,[26] and to embark on a vehement attack against the extremism of both philosophers and pietists as without foundation because faith and reason are in harmony.[27] God exists whether looked at from the vantage point of philosophy, or through God's Revelation as handed down to his Prophet Muhammad, in turn, three fundamental principles — God, Revelation, and Prophecy — are realities that must be accepted without deviation. Hence, Ibn Hazm reproaches the Sophists for denying any reality; the atheists for their incredulity; the dualists for failing to recognize the unicity of one God; the deists for denying Divine Revelation; and the Zoroastrians, Jews, and Christians for not recognizing the reality of the Prophecy of Muhammad.[28]

God is one, eternal, unique, and having all the attributes with which He designates Himself. He created the world from non-existence, without a preexisting paradigm, impelling reason, or previous decree. He ordered things without any help, difficulty, or effort. He made His creation when He wanted and as He wanted it. He acts or does not act as He wishes. He is the Truth which He made manifest to His prophets, who are people who did not have any apprenticeship, study, or research, but were endowed with excellent qualities.[29] He is the Teacher without whom the sciences, arts, and language cannot be acquired.

Prophets are his children, having fathers and mothers like everybody else, except for Adam, who was created from dust, and Jesus, who appeared in the womb of his mother without sexual intercourse *(min ghayr dhakar)*.[30] God chose the prophets to propagate His Revelation, Muhammad being the Seal of the Prophets. He is the instrument behind all phenomena, able to change the nature of things through miracles *(mu'jizat)*, performed through by His prophets, such as converting a stick into a serpent and resurrecting the dead. The divine mission of Muhammad is verified by many miracles, among which are the inimitability of the Qur'an, supplying a large army with water from a small cup, and defeating a whole tribe with a handful of dust.[31] Miracles are, thus, the acts of God, and intimately associated with prophecy; they cannot be produced by any other mortals inclduing saints, spirits, or jinns.[32] Miracles, like prophecy, are within God's power and the expression of His will. To say that they can be discharged by any mortal or even an animal is the highest of absurdity.[33] In this connection, Ibn Hazm refutes violently those who suggest such a thing[34] as well as those who uphold the concept of transmigration of the soul.[35]

Ibn Hazm considers prophecy and miracles to be inseparable. He defines prophecy as bestowing "God's Revelation *(wahy Allah)* on some one who did not know it before."[36] Its recipients, messengers *(rusul)* or prophets *(anbiya')*, are the chosen people and the best of God's creatures, including men and spirts *(al-ins wa-l-jinn)*. Messengers occupy the highest places in Paradise, followed by Prophets. Muhammad is a messenger who occupies a lofty place in Paradise, followed by his wives, after whom come his Companions.[37] It is an obligation to believe in all the prophets, because they are the carriers of God's Revelation and are able to bring forth miracles,[38] a power based not on assumption *(zann)* but on God's commands.[40] Being the last prophet, Revelation, which only unbelievers oppose,[41] ends with Muhammad.[42]

To Ibn Hazm, the historicity of both prophecy and miracles cannot be questioned because they were verified by eyewitnesses and transmitted by a good number of people throughout the centuries. In consequence, their truth must be accepted in the same manner that historical events about kings, scholars, and nations are universally acknowledged. Denial of their historicity would be tantamount to denying that anything had ever happened before one's time.

2. Qur'an, Traditions, and Consensus

The Qur'an, prophetic Traditions *(hadith)* and consensus *(ijma')* constitute the roots *(usul)* of the religious law *(shari'ah)*, which contains God's commands and prohibitions. They express divine will in complete harmony, despite apparent contradictions. They are the sole source of the law, and any human criterion superimposed upon them will constitute a serious deviation, if not heresy.

The Qur'an contains God's revelation; it is a miracle beyond human imitation; it is co-eternal with and inseparable from God.[43] Ibn Hazm conceives the Qur'an as the Word of God *(kalam Allah)* and His own knowledge *('ilmuh)*. In fact the terms Qur'an and the Word of God meanthesame thing, aside from the phonetical diference. The Qur'an is not an attribute *(sifah)* as the Mut'tazilah content, nor a quality of the same essence as conceived by the Ash'arites — these would make the Qur'an something other than God[44] and constitute impiety. As the container of the divine Truth, the Qur'an is the consummation of eloquence, the Word of God in reality with no metaphorical connotations.[45] Its style, content, and pronouncements are clear and inimitable for all eternity. No mortals, spirits, or jinns could ever approximate its superior qualities.[46] This being the case, no single letter should be amended,[47] and its absolute integrity must be maintained. Alteration in any shape or form will contribute to the loss of its miraculous nature.[48] In sum, it must be accepted as it is and in full concerning all that it contains about prophets, suffering, joy, commands, and prohibitions. It is the truth as it is *('ala zahirih)* without artifice or symbolism.[49]

Were the Qur'an to be translated into a foreign language, or some of its expressions replaced by other Arabic expressions, it could no longer be called Qur'an, thereby losing its miraculous nature.[50] He who reads such a translation would be reading something other than the Qur'an.[51] Furthermore, even prayer would be invalid, were the Qur'an recited in a foreign language.[52] This does not apply, however, to an oath rendered in one's own language.[53]

In short, the Qur'an is crystal clear and complete and constitutes the root of the law. Its clarity *(bayan)* is unquestionable. Ibn Hazm is unwilling to admit the presence of contradictions, although he concedes that some verses may appear to be unclear or to contradict others. However, these can be elucidated in three ways: first, some verses are quite explicit and self-contained and do not need clarifications; second, others express general ideas whose elaborate meanings can be derived on the basis of other relevant verses; and third, some verses' general concepts can be specified with the aid of Traditions, which are also the expression of divine will.[54] He concludes:

"Since proofs *(barahin)* and miracles make clear that the Qur'an is God's covenant to us and since He commands us to adhere to and act according to it, and since its transmission is sufficiently sound and beyond any doubt and is in book form and well known in all regions, it is incumbent upon us to carry out its content, which is the source to go back to, as stated in the Qur'anic verse: 'We have not overlooked anything in the Book.'[55] In consequence, it is an obligation to abide by it concerning any command or prohibition contained therein."[56]

In Ibn Hazm's view, the historicity of Muhammad and the authenticity of the Qur'an as God's Revelation cannot be doubted because they are proved by a long and uninterrupted tradition handed down by virtuous men and scholars for many generations. Next he turns to the deeds and sayings of Muhammad as embodied in the large collection of *sunan,* or *hadith,* and contrasts them with the Qur'an, saying that whereas the Qur'an is a recited revelation *(wahy matluw)* handed down by God to Muhammad, the deeds and sayings *(sunan/hadith)* of Muhammad are revelations related *(wahy murwi)* by a chain of authorities who witnessed or heard them.[57] As such, they are an appendage to the Qur'an and enjoy equal validity once they are proved sound[58], a signifcant qualification because many Traditions were fabricated or lacked proof of authenticity. Ibn Hazm raises questions regarding the authenticity of many Traditions accepted as authentic by earlier jurists and theologians. He examined the existing collections of Traditions and dismissed many he considered spurious; these included the *mursal,* or Traditions having a break in the chain of transmission; Traditions transmitted by a witness lacking in moral character; and the *munqati',* or traditions which cannot be traced back to the Prophet himself. His new codex contained the sound Traditions *(al-khabar al-sahih),* those which emanated from the Prophet and express God's will; they complement the Qur'an and constitute the same decree.[59]

As with the Qur'an, the Traditions ought to be preserved without any change in wording because this would imply faulty speech *(lahn)* on the part of the Prophet, whose eloquence has been proved beyond reproach. For this reason the student of law must learn Arabic grammar and Arabic lexicography, without which he would be unable to arrive at the legal decisions.[60]

Ibn Hazm does not admit the charge that some Traditions contradict one another and, at the same time, contradict some verses of the Qur'an. In his view, they are in complete harmony and constitute certainty *(yaqin)* transcending any doubt or opinion *(zann wa-shakk).* He maintains that those apparent contradictions turn out, upon examination, not to be contradiction at all, and resolves the problem through the application of the principle of exception *(istithna')* — that is, singling out or particularizing the general, which may constitute a small or great part of the thing stated.[61]

In short, the Qur'an and the authenticated Traditions are self-contained and perfect and embody the infallible truth and the perfection of religion *(ikmal al-din).* Anything beyond them is sophistry, charlatanry, and lies.[62] They are the sole foundation of the religious law *(shari'ah),* which should be understood as it is and in its literal meaning with no interpretation, personal opinion, analogical reasoning, or any other human criterion. They constitute the *dalil* (guide), to the law. In the attempt to understand the true or literal meaning of the texts, Ibn Hazm cautions that particular care should be taken to establish the general *('umum)* or particular *(khusus)* meaning of words; the next step is to arrive at the actual meaning of a given religious prescription.[63]

Ibn Hazm does not question the veracity of the Qur'an in any way; in this, he is in complete agreement with his predecessors, except in the manner of reading and understanding it. In the area of Traditions he differs markedly from other juridico-theological scholars, rejecting many of the Traditions they had accepted. Likewise, he differs with them concerning the consensus *(ijma')* and its composition. Ibn Hazm limits the composition of a consensus to the Companions *(sahabah)* of the Prophet, and even here, he makes certain stipulations. There is one alternative only in religious matters, either a total agreement *(ijma')* or disagreement *(ikhtilaf)*, nothing in between;[64] to be valid a decision of the consensus must be unanimous. Although he considers the Companions of the Prophet to be the "best men," under no circumstances should their decisions bypass the law as established in the Qur'an and Traditions; this prerogative belongs to God and His Messenger alone. In his treatise comparing the Companions,[65] Ibn Hazam categorizes their precedence and virtuosity, Abu Bakr being the "best man," 'Umar the next best, and so on; in consequence of this difference among the Companions, only the certain and sound agreements *(al-ijma' al-sahih al-mutayaqqin)* based on the Qur'an and Traditions[66] which the Companions arrived at and upheld without a dissenting voice are an obligation on the faithful.[67] Any subsequent agreement not conforming to the agreements of the Companions is utterly wrong;[68] their agreements alone are incumbent upon us *(muftarad 'alayna)*.[67] However, Ibn Hazm does not close the door to agreements reached by the Companions' successors, provided that they conform to the truth and are based on evidence *(hujjah)*,[70] which resides in the Qur'an and the authenticated Traditions.[71] In case of difference among the consensus, recourse should be made to the Qur'an and Traditions only, but under no circumstances to any particular school or region, whether the inhabitants of Medina or any other place.[72] In short, any legislation *(shar')* not based on the text *(nass)* is unbelief *(kufr)*.[73] And the Qur'anic verse requiring obedience to the "men of authority among you" *(uli al-amr minkum)*[74] does not give license to anyone to assume a role belonging to God and His Prophet, and is valid and obligatory only as long as it conforms to God's commands, and to the deeds and sayings of the Prophet.[75] For the consensus cannot be valid if it espouses wrong.[76]

Ibn Hazm raises serious questions regarding the validity of numerous Traditions, and some of the agreements reached by the consensus. On the other hand, he never doubts the absolute integrity of the Qur'an. The truth being one and indivisible, it follows that the body of Traditions and the agreements of the consensus must conform to and agree with the Qur'an. Anything outside of that truth constitutes assumptions, innovations *(bida')*, and unbelief *(kufr)*. Thus, it behooves the faithful to accept and understand the truth in the Qur'an and in the *authenticated* Traditions and *sound* agreements of the consensus; the faithful may be guided by specific rules which he prescribes in great detail when explaining his Zahirite doctrine.

3. Man's Relation to God

For a better insight into his religious ideas, it is helpful to consider Ibn Hazm's conception of man in relation to God. There appears to be some predeterminism in his system. God, Who is the Creator of all things, the Giver and the Source of the Sciences, bestows the truth on some people and denies it to others.[77] Man is subservient to God to Whom he owes all his faculties *(quwah)* including justice *('adl)*, understanding *(fahm)*, discernment *(tamyiz)*, logic *(mantiq)*, and intellect *('aql)*.[78] These faculties are mere tools to know and understand the reality of things, including the Divine Truth, but are in no way capable of passing a judgment on, penetrating into, adding to or subtracting anything from the Revelation. They are simply meant to enable the individual to believe in, accept, and be guided by God's commands and prohibitions as prescribed in the Qur'an and the authenticated Traditions. God created knowledge and language so that man could learn that God exists and is the Truth, the Qur'an and Traditions give ample evidence of this and, as such, constitute the sole source of the Truth.

Ibn Hazm holds to this theocentricity with rigid and unbending religiosity. The Qur'an and Traditions constitute the point of departure and *the principal basis* for understanding man's position in the universe and his relation to God and the rest of His creation. Already having warned the pietists against blind acceptance of old authorities, Ibn Hazm here warns the rationalists of the limitations of their faculties for explaining the mystery of Revelation.

4. The Linguistic Foundation of His Doctrine

Once the veracity of the Holy Scriptures—the Qur'an and Traditions—is established beyond any doubt, there remains the problem of understanding them *as they are and for what they are*. This problem led to the establishment of various schools of thought, each with different criteria. Drawing his inspiration from the ninth-century Zahirite doctrine, Ibn Hazm was convinced that the Holy Texts could be understood properly in context merely be following the literal meanings of words. On the surface, the system appears simplistic and quite restrictive, particularly to an inquiring mind like his. However, it does involve steps and an intense mental process, requiring a thorough knowledge of the Arabic language and possession of a *linguistic intuition*. There are three steps for achieving the desired results: first, understand the meaning of words through linguistic intuition and/or the aid of a lexicon; second, determine the place and value of a word in a sentence; and third, give each word its proper connotation within the context of a given text.

However simple this may seem, there are a number of difficulties to which Ibn Hazm addresses himself. One of them is the handling of parallel texts. He suggests discernment for determining the appropriate meaning. If a text offers a general proposition *('umum)* and another one a particular *(khusus)* limiting the first, the latter should be adopted. Also, it is valid to apply the future tense to the past tense on the ground that the word of God is timeless and cannot be limited by time or space.[79]

His advocacy of the integrity and veracity of the scriptural texts *(nass* pl. *nusus)* constitutes the cornerstone of Ibn Hazm's system. To be understood properly, the system must be placed within the framework of the nature of the Arabic language. As developed, his doctrine was not limited to legal problems, but included the whole of Islamic theology. Arnaldez[80] has analyzed the linguistic foundations of Ibn Hazm's doctrine, his arguments related to the nature of God, His attributes, and other questions pertaining to the implementation and interpretation of the religious law.

In this connection, it is relevant to mention some of the issues which concerned Ibn Hazm and many of his predecessors. The anthropomorphists before the time of Ibn Hazm adhered strictly to the letter of the Qur'an and Traditions and conceived God in the form of man. Their opponents, the rationalist Mu'tazilah, interpreted the Holy Scriptures in a metaphorical sense, denying God all atrributes that can be applied to man; they also conceived God as an impersonal and abstract entity. There were, of course, many other shades of opinion as well which caused heated controversies, charges and countercharges of heresy, and resulted in various sects and denominations. In the tenth century there emerge the theological school of al-Ash'ari, who attempted to bridge the gap between the anthropomorphists and the Mu'tazilites. Al-Ash'ari maintained that God's actions and attributes are similar to those of man, but differ in essence from them. He disavowed the imitation *(taqlid)* of the pietists and, at the same time, held that the Qur'an had the answer to a given question, thereby limiting the extreme rationalism of the Mu'tazilah. Al-Ash'ari condoned the use of analogy *(qiyas)*, but held fast to the concept that any interpretation should be based on the external meaning of the text *('ala zahir al-ayah)*.[81] Finally, al-Ash'ari maintained that all names referring to God and their derivatives constituted God's attributes. Thus, the word *'alim* (knower), derived from *'ilm* (knowledge is as good an attribute as *'alim* (knowing), which is found in the Qur'an.

Arnaldez[82] sees, and reasonably so, much similarity between the views of al-Ash'ari and those of Ibn Hazm. Although al-Ash'ari attempts to establish a middle course between the anthropomorphists and the Mu'tazilites - an attempt not unlike that of Ibn Hazm - Ibn Hazm launched a vehement attack on the man and his school, known as Ash'arism. His attack centered on the derived attributes of God, which in Ibn Hazm's opinion could not possibly be applied to God because He did not choose them for Himself. Thus, a derivative which does not occur in the Qur'an, could not be equal to that which does occur.[83] And if they ask the difference between knower and knowing, says Ibn Hazm, we shall reply, "What is the difference between omnipotent *(jabbar)* and acting powerful *(mutajabbir)*."[84] Moreover, Ibn Hazm rejects the Ash'arite notion of knowing the essence of God's attributes, contending that human reason is limited to knowing the existence and unicity of God, and is incapable of knowing God's essence. Consistently with this thinking, he also rejects the Ash'arite use of analogy, maintaining that such a use would place man on the level of God and would allow him to legislate, when actually God is the only legislator. He reiterates a statement he often makes, that human faculties are limited to the acceptance and understanding of the Revelation and, thus, are deficient in passing judgment on it, let alone adding to or subtracting anything from it.[85]

All in all, Ibn Hazm is as much opposed to the application of human criteria — analogy, personal opinion, preference, imitation, interpretation — in jurisprudence as he is to their application in theology. To him, these criteria were innovations long time after the death of Muhammad and his Companions and, as such, infringe upon God's wisdom.

As already stated, Ibn Hazm derives the strength of his doctrine from the nature and structure of the Arabic language. Language, not necessarily Arabic, is a divine behest *(tawqif)* as opposed to human convention *(istilah)*,[86] because were language something conventional, it would imply that full exercise of reason and knowledge of the sciences were innate, but these cannot be acquired except through teaching. Thus, man could not have attained the knowledge of the original language without the help and teaching of God. Language is a root *(asl)* given to man at the time of his creation, without which he could not have existed. Only after the bestowal of teaching of the original language was man able to devise new languages by mutual agreement with his fellow men. It appears that Ibn Hazm means by "language" the faculty of speech. This could explain why he did not specify which language was the oringal language of mankind. Furthermore, he grants that any or all languages are capable of receiving Divine Revelation and of expressing the truth; the allegation that one language is better than another is nonsensical. This position separates him from many of his Muslim predecessors and contemporaries, who considered Arabic a privileged language with extraordinary and even divine attributes. Nevertheless, Arabic has a portentous significance in that it contains the Revelation, the deeds and sayings of the Prophet.

In short, language is a reality created by God, a science, and the vehicles of the sciences. But in order for it to serve as a viable instrument of communication, a language must be fixed, clear, and not requiring any new act of the mind. To Ibn Hazm, Arabic fulfills these requirements and has the special endowment of containing the perfect and clear Qur'an and the almost equally eloquent sayings of the Prophet. This quality makes the Arabic language a unique instrument of communication by means of which meanings can be understood easily and unequivocally. Hence, Ibn Hazm advocated strict adherence to the apparent meaning of the text and a limitation to what the text says, rather than to what it might imply:

"The proof of what we said concerning the fact that expressions carry their meaning on the basis of their externality *(min zahiriha)* is the saying of the Almighty God, 'In a clear Arabic tongue.'[87] and also His saying, 'We have not sent a messenger except with the tongue of his people so that he may make things clear to them.'[88] It follows that we have clarity *(bayan)* in which the expressions of the Qur'an and Traditions carry their meanings as they appear in their external form and according to their position. Thus, whoever departs from this and makes interpretation without a text or the consensus will be slandering the Almighty God and His Prophet, will be contradicting the Qur'an, will be making claims, and will be taking expressions out of their context."[89]

Ibn Hazm explains his doctrine by drawing examples from Arabic grammar and lexicography. With reference to the imperative *(amr)* as it is used in grammar, he explains the divine commands *(amr,* pl. *awamir)* and prohibitions *(nahy,* pl. *nawahi)* as they appear in the Qur'an and the Traditions. Both commands and prohibitions are specific orders and, as such, constitute obligatory actions requiring immediate execution. They do not admit interpretation *(ta'wil)*, laxity or delay.[90] To the allegation that expressions have different meanings even in the case of commands, in that color can be white, black, or something else or in that *'ayn* may mean "eye," "fountain," or "letter of the alphabet," Ibn Hazm retorts:

"Every accident *('arad)* and body *(jism)* has its particular name that distinguishes it from other things so that a mutual understanding can take place and so that the listener knows what the speaker is saying. If this were not so, there would not be any understanding, and the utterance of God to us would be meaningless. . . It follows that were it not for the fact that each meaning *(ma'na)* has its own particular name *(ism)* and clarity, it would be nonexistent because of ambiguity resulting from the mixing of meanings. In consequence, the origin *(asl)* — as we have indicated — rests on the necessity of reason *('aql)* and the text *(nass)* of the Qur'an. As they mention, we find indeed in the language many names signifying several things as we find many others signifying specific things. However, since we all know that the purpose of language is to make things clear and not to confuse, it becomes necessary for us to adhere to the root *(asl),* which is the particularization of each meaning by a name and without associating it with anything else."[91] In sum, commands and prohibitions in the language are specific and clear orders, constituting an obligation *(wujub)* to be carried out unless there is a *dalil* (guide) to the contrary.[92] They should be understood in a general way *('umum)* unless there are specific injunctions to the contrary. Ibn Hazm illustrates his point with numerous examples. In the injunction that everything inebriating is forbidden, it must be understood to mean that all alcoholic beverages are inebriating, whether they are made of grape, fig or barley, and thus forbidden.[93] He who denies this "will nullify the dicta of language, reason and religion."[94] Likewise, when it is commanded to perform the ablution with water, it simply means water and not some special kind of water, as some jurists would insist, for restricting the divine order constitutes unbelief. On the other hand, in cases where commands are given in the masculine, they must be understood to include women also by virtue of the spirit of the language and its usage.[95] Women are not excluded from religion, and are expected to perform all the religious obligations, including that of holy war *(jihad)*. This is true of freemen and salves as well.[96]

In addition to grammatical rules and semantics, there is also linguistic intuition, which is on a par with sensory and rational faculties. Linguistic intuition enables the individual to discern the actual meaning of words within a particular context. A word with several meanings actually refers to different things in usage, this aspect does not in any way affect the reality of the word. Through the faculty of linguistic intuition, the individual is able to distinguish between the apparent *(zahir)* and inner *(batin)* meaning of such a word. Whereas the apparent meaning leads to something concrete, the inner meaning may lead to unyielding interpreations. In this connection, Ibn Hazm opposes the use of metaphor *(majaz)* unless specified by scriptural evidence, arguing that human imagination could not exceed divine power.[97] God and God alone gives words their proper and figurative meanings, by virtue of being the First Inventor *(al-muwaqqif al-awwal)* of language.[98] On the question of eloquence *(balaghah)*, Ibn Hazm maintains that the most eloquent person is the one who knows and pursues the divine law, not the one who innovates. Muhammad is, of course, the most eloquent man because the Word of God was revealed to him, thus making him the most knowledgeable. This makes his ordinances not unlike those of God — they are obligatory unless there is the option for an alternative *(takhyir)* or recommendation *(nadb)*.[99] Next to him in eloquence are the nomads, whose linguistic intuition could never be substituted by any other human faculty. For this reason, Ibn Hazm attaches great importance to the testimony of the nomads and to the soundness of the descriptive method used by the renowned grammarian Sibawayh (d. ca. 800) in his famous *al-Kitab (The Book)*, as opposed to the analogical method used by other philologists.[100]

In sum, commands and prohibitions as supported by many Traditions should be understood in a literal sense *('ala zahiriha)*[101]:

119

"Any rational being knows that God — may He be exalted and glorified — arranged languages and provided them with clarity. They consist of expressions resting on clear meanings of designated things. The Almighty God said, 'We have not sent any messenger except with the tongue of his people so that he may make things clear to them.'[102] The tongue is the language, and there is no disagreement about that. But if speech did not clarify meaning, what things do the deserters of God and His Prophet understand, or with what do they understand each other?"[103]

He continues by asking how one can know the meaning of a thing said by someone if he means something other than what he appears to be saying? In this connection he rebukes the Rawafid (an extremist Shi'ite group) for their interpretation of the command about killing a cow as not meaning a cow, buth 'A'ishah, the young wife of the Prophet.[104]

In conclusion, once words are defined according to their external reality and their context, nothing more is needed to attain their actual meanings. Wordings of the Holy Scriptures are clear and simple; only impostors, liars and sophists try to inject confusion into them.[105] Human faculties (senses, discernment, reason, and linguistic intuition) serve as useful tools for affirming the existing eternal verities — no more, no less. They are incapable of passing judgment on divine decisions or penetrating divine essence, but as tools, they are helpful in searching for the *dalil* (guide) of the texts and for the proofs.[106] To the charges that he equates the *dalil* with analogy *(qiyas)*, Ibn Hazm protests vehemently that his *dalil* has nothing to do with human criteria, but constitues the evidence, which is contained in the Scriptures.[107]

5. His Rejection of Human Criteria in Matters of the Law

Ibn Hazm's religious doctrine emerges clearly in his discussion and refutaion of the criteria used by the other juridico-theological systems. Mainly in the *Fisal, Ihkam, Muhalla, Nubadh, Ibtal,* and the *Talkhis,* Ibn Hazm devotes much space to these criteria — 448 pages in his *Ihkam* alone.[108] He lists and discusses those criteria as follows:

a. Religious laws *(shara'i')* preceding Muhammad.
b. Precaution *(ihtiyat)*.
c. Preference *(istihsan)*.
d. Imitation *(taqlid)*.
e. Opinion *(ra'y)*.
f. Speech guide *(dalil al-khitab)*.
g. Analogy *(qiyas)*.
h. Causation *(ta'lil)*.

Each one of these concepts could fill a separate study by virtue of the wealth of information Ibn Hazm uses in his arguments, counterarguments, and refutations. Suffice it here to state that Ibn Hazm considers them all to be invalid, incapable even of aiding to understand and implement the letter and spirit of the religious law. On the contrary, they are not only divisive elements, but work in direct opposition to God's commands and prohibitions. Furthermore, they are not condoned by the Qur'an and Traditions in spite of the claims of their advocates. He argues that God made everything according to an orderly plan, and His commands and prohibitions are clearly prescribed in the Holy Texts. What God has ordered cannot be opposed or altered, and what He has prohibited cannot be made permissible, things for which there is no command or prohibition are neutral *(mubah)*, that is, neither obligatory nor reprehensible.[109] In other words, what God has left in silence is outside the law *(fa-huwa maghfur ghayr dakhil fi hukm)*.[110] It is not binding and is of little or no consequence *(saqit)*.[111]

a. Religious Laws Preceding Muhammad[112]

Scriptures, mainly those revealed to Jews and Christians, can be relied only insofar as they are reflected in the Qur'an because they are, for the most part, adulterated almost beyond recognition. In this state, they cease to be genuine and could not be in harmony with the Qur'an and Traditions. Moreover, revelations handed down to Jews and Christians became abrogated with the Qur'an in the same manner that Christianity abrogated Judaism. Ibn Hazm illustrates his contention by profuse examples showing the discrepancy between the Judeo-Christian scriptures and the Qur'an, and points, as he does in his *Fisal*,[113] to the malicious alterations of the Old and New Testaments by misguided followers.

b. Precaution *(ihtiyat)*[114]

The exercise of precaution rests on not doing something in order to avoid doing a forbidden thing. To the contention that there are similarities *(mushtabihat)* between what is permissible *(halal)* and what is forbidden *(haram)*, he retorts that such an argument is not valid, and leads to something beyond the Qur'an and Traditions, amounting to correcting God in things clearly stipulated in the religious law.[115] Were *ihtiyat* to be valid, anything could be judged by it including prayer and the like, thus overlooking God's decisions concerning what is certain *(yaqin)* with respect to what is permissible and what is forbidden — to the point of making what is permissible forbidden, and vice versa. This kind of ambivalence cannot be applied to decisions that have been made with certainty *(la hukm illa li-l-yaqin wahdah)*. It follows that *ihtiyat* is no more than a suspicion, an insinuation *(tuhmah)*, or an assumption *(zann)* — all of which are far removed from the truth.[116] He concludes that when we suspect a forbidden thing, it is better to suspend judgment (tawaqquf) until we find out whether it is actually forbidden or permissible.[117]

c. Preference *(istihsan)*[118]

Preference became current in the third/ninth century among some legal experts.[119] It is similar to *istinbat* (deduction)[120] and opinion *(ra'y)* in that a decision *(hukm)* is made by a person on the basis of what he considers to be the most preferable decision with respect to consequence *('aqibah)* and condition *(hal)*. Malikite and Hanafite jurists used preference in many cases, whereas the Shafi'ites denied its validity. Advocates justify its use on the basis of the Qur'anic verse, "Those who listen to a testimony and follow the best of it as those whom God guides, and are the most understanding."[121] Ibn Hazm says that this verse is evidence against rather than in support of preference because the verse does not say that they should follow what they *consider* best *(ma istahsanu)*, but "what is best" *(ahsana)*. It follows that the best testimony *(ahsan al-aqwal)* is that which conforms to the Qur'an and Traditions, not what may be considered best. The consensus *(ijma')* agrees on this, and anyone advocating the contrary is not a Muslim. Furthermore, it is impossible that the truth lies in what we like *(ma istahsanna)* without proofs.[122] Were it so, the realities of things would be void, and textual evidence *(dala'il)* and proofs *(barahin)* would contradict each other. This would also mean that the Almighty God had ordered us to differ when He actually prohibits us from doing so. Moreover, it is impossible that all scholars would like the same thing, considering the difference in their inclination, nature and objectives. All things considered, he says, "The truth is the truth *(al-haqq haqq)* even if all people don't like it, and wrong is wrong *(al-batil batil)* even if all people like it... It follows that *istihsan* is a passion *(shahwah)*, the following of one's inclination, and an error *(dalal)*. Moreover, we may ask the upholder of *istihsan* 'What is the difference between what you like and what someone else does not like, and vice versa, and which one of the two is more deserving of the truth?' "[123]

d. Imitation *(taqlid)*[124]

Imitation is defined as "believing in something because someone else has said it before him, but without a proof which supports that saying,"[125] or adopting a legal decision because so-and-so did earlier. Inasmuch as the practice of imitation was common among the Malikites of al-Andalus during his time, Ibn Hazm devotes a large section to it, refuting its advocates forcefully and passionately. He says the whole concept is wrong because it cannot be supported by any textual evidence, and is doubly wrong because it means following someone other than the Prophet,[126] or arriving at decisions that may be outside the prescriptions of the Qur'an and Traditions.[127] He goes on to show its fallacy:

"The belief of the individual in one, two, or more sayings about which people of discernment and scholars differ is wrong in one of two ways: (1) either believing in something on the basis of proof that the individual had ascertained, or (2) believing without a proof at his disposal.

"Now if he believes in something on the basis of a proof he had ascertained, one of two things could be wrong: either (1) he is believing in something on the basis of a true and sound proof per se *(fi dhatih)* or (2) he is believing in something which he thinks he has proof for, when actually he has only contention *(shaghab)* and distortion *(tamwih).* In the latter case, where contention is believed to be a proof and it is not, it takes different forms: analogical reasoning *(qiyas)* or acceptance of an incomplete chain of transmission *(al-akhdh al-mursal),* report based on weak transmission, the abrogated, the particularized *(al-mukhassass),* and other abominable questions presented in a distorted way.

"As for the individual who believes in something without a proof at his disposal, one of two things could be lacking. Either he believes in something he likes by virtue of his inclination — and in this category fall opinion, preference, and the pretext of inspiration *(da'wa al-ilham),* or he believes in something on the basis of the saying, 'I entrusted the question to someone,' *(qalladtu fulanan al-amr),* that is, 'I hang a necklace on his neck.' Some advocates of imitation are ashamed to be identified with this meaning, denying it, and allege, 'We do not imitate but follow.' In consequence, they never free themselves from this kind of distortion concerning the ugliness of their deeds in upholding the forbidden, giving it a name of their own choosing, and in accepting it because someone other than the Prophet has said it. In so doing they disobey the Almighty God, following what God did not command them to follow. It is sufficient to ask the blind imitator concerning the falsity of imitation, 'What is the difference between you and the one who imitates someone else? By your own admission, did he imitate someone who is more knowledgeable and better than he?' Were he to reply that by imitation is meant the imitation of every scholar, he would be placing religion to one's device and would make obligatory the contradictions in legal decisions.'"[128]

Ibn Hazm argues, further, that to accept what so-and-so related on the authority of so-and-so is wrong because no one after the Prophet, including his Companions, the Orthodox caliphs, and other virtuous men, is deserving of credence because they were not recipients of the divine revelation. Even the Islamic community as a whole is not deserving of this prerogative. To the allegation that imitation is unavoidable, because one imitates a butcher when he mentions God's name, Ibn Hazm expresses his indignation, saying that such an imitation places its advocates on the level of asses as far as their ignorance goes. Were they to follow the butcher, they should by the same token follow the dissolute *(fasiq),* every proponent, as well as Jews and Christians.[129] To emphasize his point, he brings in the pitfalls of imitating even the most venerable men in Islam. He asks what is the difference between those who imitate the caliphs 'Umar and 'Ali and those who imitate the jurists Malik and Abu Hanifah. In either case imitation is wrong, and the question of precedence of 'Umar and 'Ali over Malik and Abu Hanifah is not a sufficient justification for upholding imitation.[130] This is so because the Companions of the Prophet including 'Umar and 'Ali, differed among themselves, and to follow or imitate them is, therefore, indefensible.[131] Ibn Hazm inquires, how could imitation of different people be permissible if some people are right and others are wrong?[132] Imitation of scholars, particularly by the common people, is also wrong if the imitation consists of following a particular scholar of his views, and justifiable only if the imitation of a scholarly judgment is in consonance with God's commands and the sayings and deeds of the Prophet.[133] He concludes:

"We forbid anybody to imitate anyone except the Prophet, and to imitate without proof; we make it obligatory to follow what the proof makes it obligatory, and we advise not pay any attention to those who mix up the meaning of words by calling imitation truth *(al-haqq taqlidan).*"[134]

He adds elsewhere:

"Know now that accepting the sound Traditions of the Prophet, what the Qur'an made obligatory on the basis of the text and its apparent meaning, and what the community agreed upon is not imitation, and it is not permissible to call it imitation, because this would be tantamount to deceit, ambiguity, and confusing right with wrong. For imitation is actually the acceptance of the saying of someone other than the Prophet, and it is done without a proof."[135]

In sum, imitation of human authority is illicit in both jurisprudence and theology because it infringes upon divine authority. Whoever subjects himself to the authority of a mortal or to a school of thought offends God, and is a sinner.[136]

e. Opinion *(ra'y)*[137]

Ibn Hazm says that opinion took inception as early as the time of the Companions of the Prophet in the first century of Islam. However, the Companions never condoned it,[138] although its advocates would like us to believe that they did. Furthermore, the allegation of its supporters that opinion is condoned by the Qur'an and Traditions has no foundation in fact; on the contrary, the Qur'an disavows it in the verse, "I have today completed your religion for you."[139] Thus, opinion is illicit, and one who wishes to find out about religion should not seek the views of the upholders of opinion.[140] Ibn Hazm considers opinion and preference to be the same thing, and for this reason he lumps them together in his discussion. The Qur'anic verse; "Their affair is a matter of consultation among them,"[141] purportedly supporting opinion, is grossly misunderstood because the verse in question does not give license to tamper with the divine revelation. Also, the Traditions produced in support of opinion are at best weak, or unauthenticated Traditions. To the contention that prayer, fasting, pilgrimage, and other religious duties were arrived at by way of opinion and consultation *(mushawarah),* Ibn Hazm retorts that the upholders of such a view are liars and unbelievers,[142] for the simple reason that were such a procedure valid, there would not be any difference between legislating by way of opinion and divine legislation.[143] The Qur'anic verse, "Their affairs is a matter of consultation among them" simply means the use of discretion *(tasarruf)* in mundane matters such as the nomination of someone to a public office or asking one's neighbor for a good tailor. And the search of opinion *(ijtihad al-ra'y)* means to consult scholars on matters conforming to the precepts of the scriptures, but does not give license to follow a particular scholar or his opinion.[144] In consequence, whoever follows Malik or Abu Hanifah is disobeying God's commands.[145] "Opinion is simply passing a decision on religious matters without textual evidence, and it is done by a legal expert *(mufti)* on the belief that such a decision is more encompassing and more just concerning commands and prohibitions."[146] "And whoever gives a legal decision on the basis of his personal opinion will be making decisions without knowledge, for there is no knowledge about religious matters outside the knowledge of the Qur'an and the Traditions."[147]

f. Speech Guide *(dalil al-khitab)*[148]

Speech guide is defined as a procedure of making a decision on what has been passed over in silence *(al-maskut 'anhu)* as opposed to what is decided on the basis of a text *(al-mansus 'alayh)*.[149] Essentially, it is a rhetorical argument that adduces a judgment from a text beyond what the text means. Ibn Hazm says that it is an area where enormous errors and abominable things take place.[150] He says that to treat what has been passed over in silence on the same level as what has been prescribed by the text is to arrogate to oneself a function belonging to God and His messenger alone. The individual must limit himself to what the text says, for to derive meaning by implication is a subjective interpretation having no linguistic basis and, thus, constitutes an affront to the Almighty and His law. He says, "Every address *(khitab)* and proposition *(qadiyah)* conveys to you what is there in them, but does not give you decisions on something that is not in them, nor does it suggest that what has been passed over in silence either conforms to or differs from them."[151]

g. Analogy *(qiyas)*[152]

Ibn Hazm devotes the largest space to analogy, and he refutes it with great vehemence. Analogy was used mainly by Shafi'ites for arriving at legal decisions in cases not specified in the Qur'an and Traditions. To its advocates, it was a procedure often used by the Prophet and his Companions and condoned by the Qur'an and Traditions; subsequent use was based on the belief that the Prophet would have acted in such a manner where decisions about similar but not specified things could be arrived at on the basis of decisions prescribed for specified and similar things. To Ibn Hazm, the procedure is totally wrong. He says that the advocates of analogy sometimes refer to it as "extracting" *(istinbat)* in the sense that "water surfaces" *(inbattat al-ma')*, that is, it is extracted from the soil and stones. At any rate, it is a procedure by which a decision is arrived at on the basis of an expression *(lafz)* whose meaning is remote from what it actually conveys. This makes the procedure wrong, and its advocates are misguided for extracting meanings from the sayings of the Prophets which are not there and which are contrary to the spirit and nature of the Arabic language.[153] This is principal reason that he condemns its use and declares it an innovation *(bid'ah)* that does a great violence to the religious law. And contrary to the claim of its advocates, Ibn Hazm maintains that there is no justification for analogy in either the Qur'an and Traditions, and if there is one, it does not specify when, how, and with regard to what one should use it. Thus, to arrive at legal decisions without texts is an impossibility, and any claim to the contrary constitutes a pretension without foundation in proof.[154] The use of analogy in language[155] is not valid, particularly for arriving at legal decisions, because the Arabic language ought to be understood as spoken by the Arab nomads and the Holy Scriptures ought to be understood in their true meaning as indicated by the rules of Arabic grammar and Arabic lexicography.

In his refutation of analogy, Ibn Hazm enlists the support of the jurist Abu Hanifah, who is reported to have said, "It is preferable to adhere to a broken *(al-khabar al-mursal)* or weak *(da'if)* Tradition than to analogy." He discerns three kinds of analogy: first, the most similar and impelling *(al-ashbah wa-l-awla),* where a decision made for one thing is applied to a similar thing; second, a similar situation *(mithl),* in that if expiation is required for having had intercourse in the month of Ramadan, the same is required of the one who breaks fasting; or if it is obligatory to wash a vessel seven times after it has been used by a dog, the same would be required if used by a pig; and third, the least similar *(al-adna),* where if urine nullifies the ablution, so does blood; or if touching the penis nullifies ablution, so does touching the backside. To this usage of analogy and its purported usefulness, he says:

"There is no usefulness in adding or subtracting anything from the commands of God. To the contrary, it is a calamity, a dangerous situation, an affront to God's ordinances, an inequity and falsehood."[156]

With this categorical disavowal of analogy, Ibn Hazm proceeds to defend his Zahirite system against the charges launched against it by the analogists. He does it satirically in the following anecdote:

"Some advocates of analogy have charged our predecessors [the Zahrites], saying our jurisprudence *(fiqh)* in following the literal meaning is like the actions of a servant whose master has ordered him to bring in a washbowl and a pitcher. The servant brought them in, but without any water in the pitcher. His master asked, 'Where is the water?' Then the servant replied, 'You did not order me to bring in water, but a washbowl and a pitcher, and here they are; for I do not do anything beyond what you order me to do.'

"We shall answer them with God's help. Your jurisprudence actually resembles the action of the servant when his master instructed him: 'If I order you to do something, do also what is similar to it.'

The master, thus, taught him analogy as it is, and the servant learned it well and accepted it. One day the master had a fever and asked the servant, 'Bring me a physician, for I feel a disorder.' The servant in fear did not hesitate and brought in all that was associated with the doctor. The servant was then asked, 'Who died?' He replied, 'No one.' Then he was asked, 'Why then the washerman, the washtub, the bier, the gravedigger at the door?' Afterward, the master called in the servant and asked, 'Who are those people at the door?' The servant replied, 'Did you not tell me that if you order me to do something I should also do what resembles it?' The master said, 'Yes.' Then the servant continued, 'You ordered me to bring in a physician because of your disorder; thus, nothing resembles death more than an illness and a physician, and for this I brought in the washerman, the bier, the gravedigger, and all that resembles them as you ordered me to do.'

"To all this, we may conclude that the servant who had brought in an empty pitcher had a better excuse in carrying out the order of his master than the servant who brought in the gravedigger, the washerman, and the bier as an analogy of illness and the physician. The master who had ordered his seveant to bring in the pitcher may have wished to show the pitcher to someone, or to sell it."[157]

After a long expose of arguments and counterarguments regarding the invalidity of analogy, Ibn Hazm concludes:

"Analogy constitutes an error, disobedience, and innovation. Its use is not permissible for arriving at legal decisions regarding any aspect of the religion. . . He who arrives at legal decisions related to the religion of God with disregard to God's utterance and that of His Prophet is a sinner."[158]

h. Causation *(ta'lil)*[159]

The subject of causation occupies the last portion of his *Ihkam*. Ibn Hazm defines cause *('illah)* as the nature of a thing elucidated by its attribute *(sifah)*, which is inseparable from it. In other words, cause and effect are interwoven, as in the case of fire being the cause of burning, and ice the cause of refrigeration.[160] He says that causation was a way by which a legal expert deduced the cause *('illah)* of a decision for which there is a text; such a procedure is wrong because it implies that God legislated on an issue by virtue of a cause.[161] He restates the use of *ta'lil,* saying that if God stipulates that He made a thing a reason for *(sabab)* a given decision, it would mean that whenever the cause of a thing is found, the decision for it would also be found.[162] In short, the advocates of *ta'lil* contend that God and His Prophet made decisions for certain things because of something else.[163] In upholding such views, the individual becomes a sinner by virtue of the fact that he is abandoning the external meaning of the text and attributing something else to it.[164]

To illustrate the fallacy of the whole concept, he says that the Prophet's interdiction of slaughter with a nail is construed by the advocates of *ta'lil* to mean that slaughter with any bone is forbidden, because a nail is a bone. Ibn Hazm retorts that this is wrong because, had the Prophet meant all bone, he would not have singled out the nail. He also gives the example of the shabby man who entered the mosque while Muhammad was preaching, and was ordered by Muhammad to prostrate twice. To the advocates of *ta'lil,* prostrating at that time was unseemly, and the order was meant only to attract the attention of the audience so that they would pay more attention to what he was saying.[165] To Ibn Hazm, this is distortion, at best.

Moreover, causation becomes more grievous when it has bearing on the actions performed by God. To Ibn Hazm, God never makes a decision because of a cause, for when He decides because of a cause, it is always stated in the text.[166] To the contention that decisions take place because of causes in the same manner that derivations are arrived at in the language, he retorts that there is no connection between causation and derivation.[167] Furthermore, he does not favor the principle of derivation in the language — although he concedes that coining new words is legitimate as long as they conform to the quality of the thing from which a word is coined. For instance, a thing can be called white only when the quality of whiteness possessed by that thing.[168] By the same token, we cannot say that *khayl* (horse) is derived from *(khayala'* (pride), or vice versa, since both terms may have coexisted independently. Otherwise, were *khayl* derived from *khayala',* it could be argued, why should not the lion be called by that name? The same can be said of the word *bazi* (falcon), which is supposed to be derived from height. Why not, then, call the eagle, the mountain, and the sky all by the same name?[169]

Ibn Hazm denies categorically that God acts because of a cause, he does concede that certain decisions are made for a reason *(sabab)* — which is quite different from *'illah* (cause). Even here, the *reason for* must be accepted as long as there is a text supporting it.[170] To him, there is a distinct difference between *cause* and *reason for,* in the same manner there is a distinction between sign *('alamah)* and objective *(gharad).* His explanation of these four terms — cause *('illah),* reason for *(sabab),* sign *('alamah),* and objective *(gharad)* follows:

"Cause is the name for every quality that imposes itself by necessity on a thing; it is not separate from its effect *(ma'lul),* such as the nature of fire having burning as its effect, and ice being the cause of refrigeration. Thus, fire and burning, and ice and refrigeration cannot exist apart from each other, nor do they precede or come after each other.

"*Reason for* is every action done by a person freely on account of something else; if he wishes, the individual may desist from doing that action-as in the case of anger that may lead to revenge, anger being the reason for revenge.Thus, if the avenger does not wish to avenge, he does not avenge. It follows that *reason for* is not by necessity imposed on the thing resulting from it *(al-musabbab)*, and does precede the action caused by it.

"The objective of revenge is the relinquishing and removal of anger.

"Sign is something two individuals agree on; if one of them sees it, he would know about the things agreed upon, and would act accordingly."[171]

He concludes that there is no denial that God has made certain things for reasons or for any other objective.[172] But under no circumstance should one construe that God is constrained by such actions, for He transcends both cause and efect. Moreover, God is not in need of a compelling reason when legislating. His commands speak for themselves, and must be taken as they are and in conformity with the spirit of the Arabic language.

On the basis of this summary of the religious ideas and doctrine of Ibn Hazm, it is clear that no human criterion could ever serve as an adjunct to, let alone a substitute for, the divinely revealed Qur'an and the Traditions of the Prophet. These are the roots of the law and the pillars of the truth to which nothing can be added or subtracted. The consensus of the Companions of the Prophet may serve as an adjunct to them as long as their agreement is unanimous and within the framework and spirit of the law. Therefore, legal decisions *(qada', or hukm)* outside of the Qur'an and Traditions do not leave any room for analogy, imitation, personal opinion, preference, causation, or any other human criteria, including the dicta of the venerable Companions of the Prophet and the most learned leaders of the Islamic community. God acting through His Prophet is the sole legislator.[173] All being equal, scholars, women, slaves, bastards, and even non-Muslims could arrive at legal decisions, but these would be meaningless if reached outside the religious law.[174] In short, legal judgments must be based on and are meant to carry out God's precepts, but they cannot make the forbidden permissible, and vice versa.[175]

6. Individual Inquiry *(Ijtihad)*[176]

In light of these restrictions on human authority, one may inquire where individual inquiry fits into Ibn Hazm's system. Or to put it differently, is the individual helpless before that which is established for him? To Ibn Hazm, this kind of question does not appear to present any problem because the truth and the realities of things have always been here, and it is up to the individual to discover and accept them as they are. Moreover, there is a world order which has been created and managed by an Almighty God whose will, power, and wisdom are beyond human power to comprehend. Nevertheless, man, who has been endowed with sensation, reason, linguistic intuition, and other faculties, can still reach for and is able to find the realities of things, besides the realization of the existence of God and His manifest will as contained in the Scriptures. On the other hand, human faculties, however valuable they may be, are the mere creation of God and subservient to His will and knowledge. Although they are capable of gaining awareness of the existence of God, they fall short in penetrating His divine essence. Undoubtedly human faculties are useful tools in searching for and to understanding divine commands and prohibitions, but they are not capable of passing judgments on God and His legislation. The intellect *('aql)* is able to discern things as they are, to establish proofs, and to seek the guide *(dalil)*, but it cannot establish or legitimize new things.[177]

In spite of these limitations, individual inquiry and the insistence on the pursuit and acquisition of knowledge occupy an important place in Ibn Hazm's system. They are meant solely to help learn the realities of things, physical or metaphysical. He says:

"If they ask us when personal inquiry *(ijtihad)* is allowed to delve into the guide *(dalil)*, we shall reply, 'At all times, for the *dalil* is the text *(nass)*.' And individual inquiry is to seek God's decisions in the Qur'an and the Traditions *(sunnah)* only."[178]

Individual inquiry is an attempt to the limit of one's ability to learn what God has made obligatory on the faithful in His religion so that His decrees may be obeyed.[179]

This endeavor is incumbent upon every Muslim. It will lead to the truth, which is one and not admitting contradicion.[180] Individual inquiry is no more than the desire of the soul to release its faculties for arriving at decisions already prescribed in the Qur'an and Traditions,[181] and that the individual researcher *(mujtahid)* ought to operate within this framework. In his endeavor to find the truth, the *mujtahid* ought to begin his search without preconceived ideas or commitment to any particular school, and must proceed in good faith. He cites the Tradition of the Prophet to the effect that he who endeavors, decides, and proves to be right will receive two rewards in heaven; if he endeavors, decides, and proves to be wrong, he will still receive one reward.[182] However, the one reward is granted not for being wrong, but for his inquiry *(ijtihadih)*, which is the right thing to do when seeking the truth.[183]

In his search for the truth, the *mujtahid* should always circumscribe himself to the Scriptures, and should not come up with opinions of his own, for after the Prophet Muhammad there is no evidence *(hujjah)* in support of following the deeds and saying of anyone else. Admittedly, many venerable Muslims, such as Malik Ibn Anas, and Abu Hanifah, searched for the truth and urged the faithful to uphold it, but they were not always right: "This is the lot of every scholar throughout the ages. They are right sometimes, and wrong others. Thus, there is no reason to follow them in all instances."[184] He adds: "No doubt, the researcher who errs *(al-mujtahid al-mukhti')* is better and more deserving of reward than the imitator who is right *(al-muqallid al-musib)*, for the latter is a sinner *(athim)* for imitating and undeserving of reward even though he may be right, whereas the researcher who errs is deserving of reward for his research, and is not a sinner because of his error."[185]

Of course, Ibn Hazm does not expect everybody to be a *mujtahid*, although he insists that everyone should try. He makes provisions for the common people and suggests that they should indeed avail themselves of scholars for information about the Scriptures, but under no circumstance should they espouse the scholars' personal opinions,or advocate their particular points of view.[186] In other words, *Ijtihad* should not give license to anyone to legislate beyond what is in the Qur'an and the Traditions.[187] *Ijtihad* means only the search for the reality of things which are in consonance with the Scriptures. It is no more and no less than seeking the *dalil*, and hence, is synonymous with *istidlal* - that is, the search of the *dalil* or evidence.[188]

CHAPTER VII

BELLES-LETTRES, LANGUAGE, AND HISTORY

1. The Writer and Poet

Ibn Hazm's numerous religious writings overshadow his accomplishments as a gifted man of letters and poet. Nonetheless, his literary masterpiece, the *Tawq,* is well known. Although small, his literary production possesses such excellence that he is one of the foremost writers of eleventh-century al-Andalus and, perhaps, one of the greatest of the whole Muslim world.

Ibn Hazm's early education consisted mainly of the study of language, belles-lettres, and poetry - the most important requirements for a career at court. These interests gradually deferred to the religious sciences, to which he devoted most of his life. One may speculate that had he succeeded in a political career, his literary production would have been much larger. But, as he was to reflect late in life, quite possibly life at court would not have enabled him to exercise independent judgment or to satisfy his conscience for at court he would have had to cater to the vanity of the ruler and the sensitivity of ignoramuses. Fortunately for scholarship, Ibn Hazm was saved by circumstance - he remained true to himself to the very end and expressed himself without the heavy restrictions ordinarily imposed by the self-serving ruling class and the highly opinionated scholars of the day. But the religious scholar Ibn Hazm remained to the very end the litterateur Ibn Hazm in that lucidity and clarity became the main characteristics of his style. Even when dealing with difficult religious topics, he continued to display a remarkable ability in handling the language.

All indications are that Ibn Hazm wrote most of his literary works before 1035, when he became almost totally devoted to religious studies. Until then he was quite active in literary circles, and with his close friend Ibn Shuhayd (d. 1034) belonged to a literary school which assessed the literary merit of al-Andalus and initiated literary criticism. Ibn Hazm and Ibn Shuhayd, the chief critics, were both concerned with clarity *(bayan),* rhetoric *(balaghah),* versification *('arud),* and the essential ingredients for good prose and poetry. Both seem to have had an aversion to the pendantry of philologists, who were more concerned with memorization of rare expressions and hair splitting answers to some grammatical problems than with clarity of presentation. In consequence, they reacted adversely to traditional philology as represented by Ibn al-Iflili (d. 1049), whom Ibn Shuhayd ridicules,[1] and whom Ibn Hazm criticizes in his *Ta'aqqub*[2] in this work Ibn Hazm takes issue with Ibn al-Iflili in connection with the latter's commentary of al-Mutanabbi's *Diwan*. Both men were gifted and quite concious of their literary virtuosity, which they did not hesitate to boast about. In his

Tawabi', Ibn Shuhayd felt equal and even superior to some leading Eastern poets and litterateurs.[3] For his part, Ibn Hazm not only exalted the literary talents of his Andalusian compatriots vis-a-vis their Eastern counterparts,[4] but spoke of himself as a shining sun in the literary firmament, noting with chagrin that he had not been accorded due recognition in the wilderness of his homeland.[5]

At any rate, Ibn Hazm wrote a number of works with both historical and literary interest. Some have been lost, such *Eloquence and Rhetoric*,[6] *Prosody*,[7] *Poets at the Court of Ibn Abi 'Amir*,[8] *Book of Poetry*,[9] *Categories of Scholars*,[10] and two linguistic treatises dealing with the emphatic letters *Dad and Za"*[11] and *Sad and Dad*,[12] respectively. These works would indeed be valuable for apprising Ibn Hazm's actual literary standing. On the other hand, we are fortunate to have three of his works which give us an insight into his literary stature. *The Excellence of al-Andalus*, the *Treatise on Good Conduct*, and *The Dove's Ring*.

The excelllence of al-Andalus[13] shows his great erudition and discernment of the major literary productions known in the Arabic language up to his own time. In it Ibn Hazm displays a wide knowledge of pre-Islamic and Islamic poetry in its classical, neoclassical, and contemporary trends and, at the same time, shows his appreciation of the various styles of prose writings. The treatise is meant to show the standing of Andalusian authors vis-a-vis their Eastern counterparts; it is significant in revealing not only the state of Andalusian literary activities before and during the time of Ibn Hazm, but also his ability as a literary critic to discriminate good or bad in Arabic literature.

His *Treatise on Good Conduct*[14], written late in life, is a collection of 394 sayings and maxims reflecting his philosophy and personality. The treatise falls into the category of ethics, but it also forms an integral part of belles-lettres *(adab)* in that it instructs and moralizes. However,. its sober execution lacks the elements of humor and entertainment which ordinarily are found in belletristic writings. His personal views on numerous subjects drawn from first hand experience are presented austerely, with a religious emphasis on the way to attain happiness in this world and in the Hereafter. The twelve division of the work deal with the cure of soul; intellect and repose; knowledge; right conduct; companions, friends, and admonitions; the various aspects of love; the different forms of physical beauty; practical morals; corrupt characters; characteristics of the soul; the eagerness of man to know; and etiquette of literary assemblies.

Ibn Hazm's literary masterpiece is his *Dove's Ring*, which alone is sufficient to place him among the great Arabic litterateurs for all time. In the *Tawq*, Ibn Hazm combines his poetical compositions with prose in a masterly fashion, appearing always to be more concerned with clarity than with conventions and formal expressions. Although his style at times is cumbersome, the work flows smoothly. Except for the citation of some Traditions to clarify or justify his point, nowhere does he seem constrained by rigid patterns and conventions particularly in the use of language. This is most apparent in his prose and poetry, where archaic and sonorous expressions are generally avoided. His wealth of ideas and deep understanding of the subject (love) were such that he did not feel the need of quoting his predecessors on the subject, or indulging in excessive ornamentation, unusual imagery, or rhymed prose *(saj')* where the meaning is ordinarily sacrificed to fit rhymes into a block. This is also true of his poetry where the form is subordinated to the content so that it can be read and understood with ease. As such his poetry is spontaneous, constituting the true expression of the author, and conforming to his own environment rather than to a fictitious or unknown place. In the words of Garcia Gomez, the *Tawq* is "an Andalusian elegy"[15] and "his best work and the best in all Hispano-Arabic literature."[16]

The significance of the *Tawq* rests not only on its subject and literary merit, but also on the wealth of information it contains about the author and Andalusian society during the early part of the eleventh century. The *Tawq* was written at the request of a friend probably during Ibn Hazm's second exile from Cordova between 1025 and 1027, while he was residing in Jativa.[17] Although it has some platonic elements [18] and may have been inspired by the *Book of Flower (Kitab al-zahrah)* of the anthologist Ibn Dawud (898-910),[19] the son of the founder of Zahirism, the *Tawq* is not an academic dissertation on the subject of love. Unlike the *Book of Flower,* it is not a compilation of relevant materials on the subject of love by preceding poets and authors. Rather the *Tawq* narrates the joys and tribulations of love based mostly on Ibn Hazm's own inner feelings, experiences, and observations. Consequently, the work shows a remarkable originality transcending conventions and stereotyped situations. Garcia Gomez describes this eloquently,"What was being said in Baghdad with subtle prose and borrowed verses, the author says in Jativa warmly and humanly from himself and his friends in Cordova."[20]

The *Tawq* consists of thirty chapters and an epilogue and deals with love, its causes, accidents, and what occurs in it and by it: origin, essence, various kinds, signs, falling in love in dreams, by word of mouth, or long association; the messenger, correspondence, the keeping of secrets, separation, oblivion, and other aspects. In spite of its worldly theme the *Tawq* reveals the austerity and religious sensitivity of the author. In fact, he introduces the work with an apologetic note, fearing that he will be accused of frivolity for delving into such a topic. He quotes the Qur'an in his defense and mentions many respectable Muslims who had experienced love. After this rather cautious introduction, Ibn Hazm develops his theme, remaining faithful to a plan of work in which spiritual love and an ascetic and religious attitude prevail.

To Ibn Hazm, love is something that resides in the very essence of the soul, having an abstraction that possesses it and does not abandon it until death. Therefore, true love is a spiritual choice of the soul.[21] At worst, it is a sickness whose remedy is in itself.[22] For love to be lasting, certain natural qualities must be common to both the lover and the beloved. Interestingly enough, however, Ibn Hazm does express a preference for blondes shared by his father and many of the Umayyad princes and rulers.[23] He tells about his own experience of love and confesses in moving terms how he suffered when his slave girl Nu'm died, leaving him despondent for months. To him, she was the ideal lover and had all that one wanted of spiritual and physical beauty.[24]

The *Tawq* has great significance for Arabic literature in general and for the development of courtly love in Europe. There is no evidence whether the work was known to medieval Europeans, though a comparison with some of its European counterparts reveals many common elements.[25] Be that as it may, the work on its own merit deserves a place among world classics. It is written in a masterly fashion, attesting to the author's ability as a prose writer and poet. It is almost unique in Arabic literature by virtue of its form, content, thematic unity, and comprehensiveness on the subject of love. The style reveals not only the sensitivity, moral character, and idealism of the man, but also the disciplined mind, austerity, and restraint that were later to characterize him as a sincere, if not uncomnpromizing, religious scholar. The *Tawq* sets the tone and the manner of his future writings, which are clear and organized. His use of rhymed prose coming into vogue under the influence of the Eastern prosist Badi' al-Zaman (d.1008),[26] was minimal and never sacrificed meaning. He also avoided the use of literary artifices, hidden meanings, double entendre, contrived situation, and old conventions. He was direct and to the point and addressed himself to questions about which he had a wide knowledge through his training, experience, and observations, or through information gotten from eyewitnesses. In his *Tawq* he states, as he often does in his other works, that he is relating the known truth.[27] This along with his insistence on authority, proof, and guide *(dalil)* - marked his approach to juridico-theological problems. Although similes and metaphors are not lacking in his *Tawq*, he disavowed them altogeter in later writings. Eventually, his candidness and bluntness toward his adversaries became so extreme that they proved embarrassing to his audience and even damaging to his credibility. As already indicated,[28] he came to use fiery and blunt language to the point of cruelty. His frequent use of perjoratives against his enemies, even when his point was made clearly and eloquently, robbed much of the dignity from his otherwise superb and expressive style.

Most of these elements of directness and lucidity in his prose can also be found in his poetry. His knowledge of versification and ability to express his ideas clearly without being encumbered with rare expressions are also significant. His pupil al-Humaydi says of him, "We have not seen anyone who could improvise poetry more spontaneously than he."[29] Ibn Hazm himself was not bashful in boasting about his poetical dexterity when he said that he was able to contrast two things with another two in the same verse, a talent much appreciated in rhetoric. Not only that, he was able to contrast three things with another three in the same verse, and four and five things, which he consideres exraordinary. He illustrates the contrast of five with five in the following verse:

> I, she, the cup, white wine, and darkness
> resembled earth, rain, pearl, gold, and jet

and concludes proudly that the use of quintuple metaphors is beyond the ability of just anyone.[30]

During his youth, Ibn Hazm wrote numerous poems on a variety of themes. Unfortunately, the collection made by his pupil al-Humaydi is lost, but a good number of his peoms are found in his *Tawq* as well as in the works of his biographers.[31] Ibn Khayr (d. 1180), who studied the works of Ibn Hazm, mentions one *Qasidah* (ode) in *mim* (rhyming with the letter *m*), consisting of seventy-three verses, and another rhyming in *ba'* of seven verses.[32] Al-Subki[33] has preserved a poem of 179 verses rebuking the Byzantine Emperor Nicephorous for his attack on Islam.

Ibn Hazm's poems deal for the most part with love and its tribulations, praise of princes and friends,eulogy, and exaltation to God. Many are autobiographical, expressing his sentiments as a lover and conveying some of his qualities and philosophy of life. A poem composed following the bur ning of his books by al-Mu'tadid of Seveille shows his defiance and indignation when he says that the paper can be burned but that which was written thereon will remain in the heart until death.[34] There are other poems expressing his loyalty to friends,[35] lamenting the envy of his enemies toward him,[36] giving admonitions,[37] and complaining about fate.[38]

On Poetry and Rhetoric

Ibn Hazm was an incisive literary critic. Although there is no evidence that he abandoned poetry altogether when he became emersed in religious studies, he did develop an ambivalent attitude toward poetry and its usefulness, particularly that poetry containing themes of love, separation, war, satire, panegyric, and elegy. Realizing the importance of poetry in Arabic culture and its value for clarifying linguistic problems, Ibn Hazm concedes that the student would be served by learning poetry which contains wise maxims and good things *(hikam wa-khayr)*, such as the poetry of Hassan Ibn Thabit,[39] Ka'b Ibn Malik[40] 'Abdallah Ibn Ruwahah,[41] Salih Ibn 'Abd al-Quddus,[42], and others.[43] But he argues:

"It is necessary to avoid four kinds of poetry:

1. Love and sentimental poetry *(al-aghzal wal-l-raqiq)*, that provokes desires, invites infatuation, incites chivalry, leads the soul to dissipation and pleasure, makes easy the occupation in deceit and passion, and denies realities to the point of even leading to viciating religion and the world; to extravagant spending for objectionable pursuits; to destruction of honor; to disappearance of manliness; and to the loss of respon-

sibility. Listening to sentimental poetry, particularly love poetry, about males, description of wine and licentiousness, will certainly destroy the constitution of the individual to a point of requiring treatment and cure. In all, this kind of poetry facilitates corruption, makes disobedience easy, and is generally harmful.

2. Poetry dealing with vagabondry and wars such as the poetry of 'Antarah,[44] 'Urwah Ibn al-Ward,[45] Sa'd Ibn Nashib,[46] and the like. For these poetical compositions agitate the soul, stir nature, and make it easy for the individual to resort to destructiveness without any reason and even to needless self-destruction; they will also lead to the loss of the Hereafter besides the kindling of revolts, facilitating crimes, abominable conditions, avidity for injustice, and the shedding of blood.

3. Poetry of separation, description of desert and abandoned dwellings, which makes departures and separation easy and which may needlessly lead the individual to a situation from which it is difficult to escape.

4. Satirical poetry *(hija')*, which is the most viciating kind of poetry for it will make it easy for the individual to be in the condition of insolent people such as street sweepers, dealers of wind instruments, and those who make their living by means of insults, depravity, baseness, the shredding of people's honor, the singling out their defects, and the sanctity of parents. In this lies destruction in the world and in the Hereafter."[47]

To this Ibn Hazm adds that there are two kinds of poetry which may be neither prohibited completely nor recommended: panegyric and elegy. "Their permissibility resides in that they may contain the virtues of the person who is elegized or those of the one who is being praised. This requires the reciter of such poetry to have the desire for describing the likeness of such a condition. On the other hand, our dislike for them rests on the fact that there are many lies in these two kinds of poetry, and there is no good in falsehood."[48] Similarly, excessive recitation of poetry intended to making a livelihood is also a blameworthy pursuit, because it is a false and superfluous way and not the way leading to truth and virtues. Furthermore, he quotes the saying that everything is adorned with some truthfulness except the caluminator and the poet;[49] that the Ancients maintained that poetry is a lie;[50] that God informed us that poets act contrary to what they say; and that Muhammad forbade indulgence in poetry with the exception of that containing wise sayings and exhortations.[51]

Ibn Hazm is quick to remind the reader that he is not criticizing the content of poetry out of ignorance or lack of ability in versification, but simply calling attention to some of its harmful effects if pursued indiscriminately:

"Let no skeptic think that we belittle this discipline (poetry) out of ignorance. Anyone from among our contemporaries having had contact with us and having heard about our stature in the field will know how extensively we delved into the recitations of poetry, how well acquainted we have been with its meanings, how our standing has been regarding all kinds of poetry, the nicety, meaning, and division of poetry; how able we have been in its composition, how well we achieved it in both odes and short poems, and how easy it was for us to make long and short compositions. But the truth is more important than what is being said."[52]

With this concern in mind, Ibn Hazm would make a provision for poetry in the curriculum as long as its content is edifying and as long as the student bears in mind the following: (1) that a full devotion to poetry is sinful *(haram)*; (2) that indulging in it to excess is undesirable but not sinful; and (3) that taking a portion of it is desirable and necessary, for the Prophet himself made use of poetry and recognized that there is some wisdom in it.[53] In sum,

"He who uses poetry for wisdom and asceticism will do well and will have his reward; and he who uses it in scolding or corresponding with a friend, lamenting a wrong deed of one of his brethren, or praising fairly a deserving person, is not a sinner and his poetry is not distasteful. But he who uses poetry for defaming a Muslim, praising untruthfully, or flirting with the harem of Muslims, is a dissolute."[54]

It may seem paradoxical that Ibn Hazm should disavow many of the poetical themes with which he had dealt in his own compositions. But the religious scholar Ibn Hazm is speaking now, and his reflection on the demerits of poetry belongs to a later stage in his intellectual development. Statements from his early works such as the *Tawq, Fada'il* and *Taqrib* (probably written before 1031) bear witness to his early positive attitude toward and even enthusiasm for poetry. He expresses admiration for leading poets with little consideration for the themes they dealt with. When he mentions the two leading Eastern poets Abu Tammam[55] and al-Buhturi,[56] he says that they had far-reaching theories and inventiveness regarding the subject of poetry, each advancing his own ideas, but "I do not wish to compare my poetry with theirs because they have the merit of precedence and priority, leaving us harvesting what they have sowed."[57] Abu Nuwas[59] and others censured the wailing over ruins, but praised those who were given to pleasure. Abu Nuwas prided himself in pleasure and did it with masterly style and excellent language, though he was a crafty traitor.[59] Moreover, Ibn Hazm's wide knowledge of poetry extended to Andalusian poets, in whom he saw as much merit as that of leading Eastern poets:

"And even if our leading poets were only Ahmad Ibn Muhammad Ibn Darraj al-Qastalli[60] who does not fall behind Bashshar,[61] Habib,[62] and al-Mutanabbi,[63] now then, and we have in addition to him Ja'far Ibn 'Uthman al-Hajib,[64] Ahmad Ibn 'Abd al-Malik Ibn Marwan,[65] Aghlab Ibn Shu'ayb,[66] Muhammad Ibn Shukhays,[67] Ahmad Ibn Faraj,[68] and 'Abd al-Malik Ibn Sa'id al-Muradi,[69] each of whom is a stallion with a blaze on his forehead."[70]

Moreover, Ibn Hazm considers poetry as a science consisting of transmission, meaning, virtue, defect, parts, meters and versification. He had pondered on the art of prosody and the elements required for producing good poetry. Whether or not he was influenced by Ibn Shuhayd, whom he mentions, [71] it appears that he shares his views with respect to the innate talent required for producing excellent poetry:

"Poetry is divided into three parts: (1) the art of composition *(sina'ah)*, (2) natural disposition *(tab')*, and (3) excellence *(bara'ah)*.

"The art of composition consists of borrowing things and giving them meaning and metaphors. The leader of this category among the Ancients was Zuhayr Ibn Abi Sulma[72] and among the moderns, Habib Ibn Aws.[73]

"Natural disposition is that in which affectation is lacking; its expressions are commonly known and not exceeding their meanings to the extent that if you wish to express these meanings in prose you could not come up with smoother and more succinct expressions. The leader of this category among the Ancients was Jarir[74] and among the moderns, Al-Hasan.[75]

"Excellence is the ability to get at subtle and remote meanings and come up with sufficient number not already known among people; it is also the ability to make the right comparison and to embellish the subtle meaning. The leader of this category among the Ancients was Imru'al-Qay[76] and among the moderns, 'Ali Ibn 'Abbas al-Rumi.[77]

"The poetry of all people falls under and is made up of the divisions we have mentioned. Whoever wishes to get the expertise in the various divisions of poetry, in what is best in it, and in the techniques of delving into its nicety should consult the book of Qudamah Ibn Ja'far,[78] which deals with *Criticism of Poetry (Naqd al-shi'r)*, and the books of Abi 'Ali al-Hatim,[79] which are the most comprehensive on the subject. Poetry is a power, which is not acquired *but* innate,[80] even though we urge poets to increase their knowledge of and reflect on poetry."[81]

Ibn Hazm's views on good writing hinge on the concept of rhetoric *(balaghah)*, In his *Taqrib*,[82] a section on rhetoric summarizes his thinking about the subject. After mentioning the writings of Aristotle, Ja'far Ibn Qudamah, and Ibn Shuhayd he says that rhetoric differs from one language to another according to what different people conceive to be good expressions. He holds the view that rhetoric aims at simplicity and understanding; it should be devoid of unusual expressions and must be succinct, prolix, or repetitious, depending on the composition and kind of audience. Its primary concerns are clarity and instructiveness, for the Almighty God has arranged languages and provided them with clarity and expressions with clear meanings for designated things.[83] In consequence, rare expressions should be kept at a minimum.

"We maintain that rhetoric is that which the common people understand as the elite does; it is done with wordings that awaken the average person who is not acquainted with such arrangement and meaning; it is also that in which all intended meaning is grasped without adding anything to or subtracting anything from what is needed for the thing sought; it is that which makes the understanding of the listener easy whereby the remote expressions having several meanings become clear and familiar, thereby facilitating memorization because of its brevity and the easiness of its expressions. The essential prerequisites for all are brevity for those who are able to understand, explanation for those who do not understand, and avoidance of repetition for those who do not comprehend, refuse to listen or are negligent.

"The aforementioned is divided into two parts:one is related to familiar expressions current among the common people, such as the rhetoric of 'Amr Ibn Bahr al-Jahiz,[84] and the other is connected with expressions unfamiliar to the common people, such as the rhetoric of Hasan al-Basri[85] and Sahl Ibn Harun.[86] There is a third part which takes a little from both sides, such as the rhetoric of Ibn al-Muqaffa'[87] the translator of *Kalilah wa-Dimmah*, and others. All in all, the rhetoric of people falls under the categories we have mentioned."[88]

Unlike peotry, rhetoric is acquired through training and is the result of two or more disciplines - Qur'anic studies, Traditions, history, lexicography, poetry and so forth.[89] It is recommended that the individual read the books of al-Jahiz in particular for the purpose of acquiring rhetoric as a second nature, for natural disposition *(tab')* is useless without widening one's knowledge of the science.[90]

Like poetry, rhetoric is either good or harmful, depending on whether it is used in the path of God or not. Ibn Hazm says, "Rhetoric is a praiseworthy science if its pursuer directs it to invoking God - May He be glorified and exalted - to elucidating the knowledge of realities, and to teaching the ignorant. On the other hand, if its pursuer were to direct it to contrary purpose, he will be empty handed in that he will trouble himself and spend his life in something having evil consequences for himself. May God save us from such a misfortune."[91]

As already indicated,[92] Ibn Hazm adheres to the generally held concept that the Qur'an is unique, perfect, and consummation of eloquence. The Almighty God revealed it and made it beyond any human power to produce anything like it as to style, wording, pronouncements, and content.[93] It is a miracle *(mu'jiz)* impossible to imitate by Arabs or non-Arabs, men or jinn. Its superiority is universally acknowledged by believers and unbeliev rs. Its unique qualities defy any description. Thus, to say that it represents the pinnacle of eloquence *(balaghah)* would be wrong because this would imply that someone at one time or another could come up with a similar composition. This would indeed compromise its very divine nature.[94] Ibn Hazm's conviction regarding the uniqueness of the Qur'an in form and content and his insistence on its clarity constitute an important part of his Zahirite doctrine.

3. The Arabic Language

Although Arabic is not conceived by him as the "mother of all tongues" as it was by many of his Muslim predecessors, Ibn Hazm does grant its intimate relationship to Islam. In fact, Arabic and the Scriptures are intrinsic to his Zahirite doctrine. It is for this reason that Ibn Hazm insists on the necessity of profeciency in the Arabic langauge, without which no proper understanding of the Scriptures could be possible. Studying Arabic grammar and lexicography is incumbent upon all Muslims *(fard 'ala al-kifayah)*[95] because the Qur'an is revealed in a "clear Arabic."[96] He who does not know Arabic grammar and Lexicography "is not able to know the language in which God revealed our religion and in which He spoke to us; and he who does not know Arabic grammar and lexicography does not know his religion, and he who does not know his religion is duty bound to learn it."[97] If this is incumbent upon the ordinary faithful, it is more so upon the student of the law:

"It is incumbent on the jurist to know the Arabic language so that he may be able to understand what God and His Prophet have said; he should know grammar, which is the arrangement of words as used by the Arabs, and by means of which he may be able to understand the meanings of words through the different vowels and their position in a sentence. He who is ignorant of lexicography, which consists of expressions designating things, does not know the language in which the Almighty God spoke to us. He who does not know the language is not permitted to pass legal decisions, for he would be making decisions about things he does not know."[98]

He reiterates the same idea in various connections and adds that it is likewise forbidden that Muslims consult and accept legal decisions from those who arrogate to themselves the title of scholars and jurists, but who are ignorant of grammar and lexicography.[99] He emphasizes again and again that the Qur'an and Traditions must be studied in the original, or Islam would be obliterated. Those who study the language will have a great reward *(ajr 'azim)* and will enjoy high esteem. He inquires how anyone could pass judgment on ablution or almsgiving without knowing the corresponding Arabic terms or the function of the case endings, which determine subject, object, and prepositional clauses. Aside from the religious significance of Arabic, he points out in somewhat a temporizing way the usefulness of Arabic for gainful purpose as long as it is not done for perpetuating injustice, carrying out oppressions, determining excise taxes and liabilites *(mukus wa-qabalat)*, or associating with corrupt rulers. Studying and using the language for such purposes will bring a great loss and the curse of the Almighty.

The study of Arabic is not an end in itself but a means to an end, namely, the acquisition of the necessary knowledge that will enable the individual to understand the Qur an and Traditions. In this way, the individual will be able to enjoy a happy life in this world and prepare himself for a blissful life in the Hereafter. Ibn Hazm does not demand a thorough study of Arabic philology, but offers a syllabus of knowledge sufficient to implement the religious duties. After learning to read and write, the young student should take up the study of Arabic grammar and lexicography — to enable him to read correctly and to understand what he reads. For this purpose, he recommends the grammatical work *al-Wadih (The Clear One)* by his compatriot philologist al-Zubaydi (d. 989),[101] the abridged grammar *al-Mujiz* by the Eastern grammarian Ibn al-Sarraj (d. 929)[102] or any similar text; reading *The Book (al-Kitab)* of the great Eastern grammarian Sibawayh would have an added usefulness. Any grammatical study beyond such works would be superfluous because the time could be put to a better use.

Ibn Hazm cautions against the study of grammatical cause *('ilal)*, a curiosity leading nowhere.[103] He does not place many restrictions on the pursuit of lexicography, arguing that unlike theoretical grammer, it explains the realities of expressions that denote designated things, thereby eliminating doubt or ambiguity. Therefore, the more one learns of them the better. He recommends the lexical work *al-Gharib al-musannaf* by the Eastern lexicographyer Abu 'Ubayd (d.837),[104] who is reported to have spent forty years compiling it. He also recommends the *Abridgment of Kitab al-'ayn* by al-Zubaydi, which is based on the work of al-Khalil Ibn Ahmad (d. 786),[105] the father of Arabic lexicography and teacher of leading philologists of Basrah. If the student wishes to penetrate more deeply, he could use the lexical works of the Eastern philologists Thabit Ibn Thabit,[106] Ibn al-Anbari (d. 940),[107] and Ahmad Ibn Dawud al-Dinawari (d.895).[108]

In sum, the Arabic language comprising grammar and lexicography occupies a preeminent position in his classification of the sciences, and a prominent place in his curriculum. As a language, it is God's creation and His gift without which a Muslim would be unable to attain well being on earth and to prepare himself for a life of bliss in the Hereafter. It is a source *(asl)* in its religious connotation possessing clear and fixed rules that point to accurate meaning of words in a given context. As such, the Arabic language constitutes the foundation of his literalist doctrine as embodied in Zahirism.

4. The Historian and History

Ibn Hazm has a deep historical consciousness, which extended to both secular and religious matters. Revelation, miracles, and prophecy are events as credible as those related to nations, kings, and scholars.[109] Islamic history is, of all the histories of mankind, the most reliable.[110] He undertook the study of Islam in its historical context, displaying special interest in the historical reality of Islam and the people responsible for its dissemination. This preoccupation led him to study the Qur'an with respect to its accuracy, considering the chronological order of the abrogating and the abrogated things *(al-nasikh wa-l-mansukh)*, not to mention the philological factors that help its understanding. Similarly, he undertook a critical study of Traditions to determine their soundness and accuracy. He established a method whereby he was able to declare certain commonly accepted Traditions to be without foundation.

Ibn Hazm's search for facts or the reality of things drove him to explore the various aspects of Islam as a religion and Islam as a polity. To establish the veracity of Islam, or his own version of it, Ibn Hazm undertook not only the study of the major Muslim sects and the various Islamic juridico-theological systems, but also the study of the major world religions and philosophies as they were known to the Greek and Muslim philosophers. He contrasted the various religious doctrines and philosophical theories with Islam and arrived at his own conclusions, set down in the *Fisal*. This is the only historical information in which Ibn Hazm takes a universal approach, considering though polemically the beliefs and dogmas of the people outside of the Islamic religion. His other historical works are based on the Islamic experience and include a wide range of subject.

Most of Ibn Hazm's numerous historical works are lost. However, those we have give insight into the writing of history and into his historical perspective. His historical writings were valuable enough for succeeding historians to use them as source material, either directly or through his pupils — mainly al-Humaydi, who kept the historical tradition of the master much alive. In this connection, it should be mentioned that some treatises attributed to him are too succinct; they constitute abridgments or notes handed down or written by students. His biography of Muhammad[111] is a case in point. As it stands, the biography presents the bare facts about the genealogy and birth of Muhammad, with cryptic references to his companions, secretaries, servants, messengers, wives, and children. In addition, it has information about Muhammad's first encounter with the angel Gabriel; early converts, their persecution, and flight to Ethiopia; Muhammad's ascent to the seven heavens; the institution of the five daily prayers; his flight to Medina and activities there, his raids, and the martyrs who fell in the battlefield; legislation such as the institution of almsgiving and the prohibition of wine; Arab delegations to foreign countries; and Muhammad's farewell address and death. Rather than Ibn Hazm's usual dialectical approach taken in most of his religious writings, the work is written in complete detachment and without any attempt to pass judgment, criticize, or refute. Furthermore, there are no references to sources, nor to the objective of the work.

In contrast to this general biography of Muhammad, his *Farewell Pilgrimage*[112] is relatively long and replete with Traditions supported by corresponding chains of transmitters. The account covers some ten days of the daily activities of Muhammad during his last pilgrimage to Mecca. It consists of a minute description of Muhammad's journey from the moment he left Medina until he reached Mecca and his return. It appears clear from his introduction that Ibn Hazm wanted to dispel some of the alleged contradictions surrounding the last days of Muhammad by relying on the "most authenticated Traditions." He states his reason for writing it:

> "Traditions having bearing on the description of the activities of the Messenger of God — may God's prayer and peace be upon him — during his farewell pilgrimage have abounded and come down to us from different sources and with different connotations. Details of that

holy deed had been described with a great deal of information, but with no coherence — to the point that the abundance of information was one of the reasons that the majority of people could not understand it; and many other saw a great deal of contradiction in that information. In consequence, many people have avoided consulting works on the subject."[113]

Ibn Hazm arranged the information briefly but clearly and supplied the necessary chains of transmission tracing them back to the Prophet himself in his own wording, or the wording of his Companions, who had witnessed him do a thing, or had heard that he made this or that statement. Thus, he hoped to set the record straight by producing clear proofs for all who have a modicum of fairness and discernment so that the allegation of conflicting and contradictory reports is terminated once and for all. He continues:

"We do not make hasty decisions on things we have not been able to demonstrate, nor do we venture to detruncate that which does not glitter before our eyes, nor do we pass judgment on things whose realities we have not determined. Were we to do this, we would be simply making opinions. God forbid, for this would be the path of ignominy which no man of religion or reason would desire for himself."[114]

Ibn Hazm was equally interested in the lives and deeds of the Companions of the Prophet, about whom he wrote three works which survive. The *Names of Companions-Transmitters According to the Number of Traditions Transmitted*[115] lists the Companions according to the number of Traditions attributed to them in the order of 2000, 1000, 100 down the line. It is merely a listing of their names under the numerical headings such as *ashab al-alfayn* (those who transmitted two thousand Traditions), those of the one thousand, and so on. For instance, Abu Hurayrah, one of the close Companions of Muhammad, is credited with 5374 Traditions supposedly transmitted on his authority. Similarly, in *Companions Who Made Legal Decisions*[116] Ibn Hazm lists the early Companions and their immediate successors from Mecca, Medina, Basrah, Kufah, Damascus, and other cities, who had given their legal opinions on a variety of issues. His work *Precedence among the Companions*[117] attempts to place the Companions on a scale according to their respective virtues and in relation to the Prophet Muhammad. After reviewing the various opinions on the subject, Ibn Hazm advances his own preference, based on the degree of relationship to Muhammad: at the top of the scale are 'A'ishah and Khadijah, the two favorite wives of Muhammad, who are followed by Abu Bakr, the first caliph of Islam, whom he considers far superior to 'Ali, the son-in-law of the Prophet, and more knowledgeable and more virtuous than he. He lists the rest of the Companions in a downward scale according to individual merit. The tone of the treatise is polemical. He concludes that the Islamic community is the most virtuous community *(afdal al-umam)* of all the people in the world and that a mosque is a better place than any other.

There is a fragmentary work dealing with the Islamic conquests,[118] some eleven pages containing the names of countries conquered along the names of generals who conquered them and the names of caliphs under whom the conquests were carried out. In connection with conquests, Ibn Hazm also wrote a treatise dealing with the expeditions of Ibn Abi 'Amir al-Mansur,[119] whom Ibn Hazm's father served as vizier.

Ibn Hazm wrote four books on the institution of the caliphate, presumably dealing with its theoretical and practical significance. His treatise on the Imamate[120] may contain the same material that appears in the *Fisal*, on requirements of the office.[121] Another work entitled the *Imamate and Politics*,[122] deals with the biographies of caliphs, their hierarchical order by merit and virtue, information about the officials of the court and national and international policies.

His *Names of Caliphs*[123] contains sketchy biographies of the Orthodox caliphs of Medina, the Umayyad caliphs of Damascus, and the 'Abbasid caliphs of Baghdad. He gives a few facts about each caliph, mentioning the principal events of his reign, giving the name of his mother, or noting whether a caliph died naturally or was assassinated.

Finally, the *Speckle of the Bride*[124] is an unusual history of the Umayyad rulers of al-Andalus and Eastern caliphs arranged under such heading as : honorific names *(laqab)* given to rulers; caliphs who ascended to the throne by virtue of nomination; heirs apparent who were not able to assume office; caliphs who were elected; caliphs who acquired the office by force; pretenders to the office; people who assumed the caliphate having older brothers; when the caliphate was held by four or three brothers; caliphs who assumed the office while under age; those who assumed it at the ages of sixty, fifty, forty, and thirty; the oldest and the youngest caliphs; caliphs ousted, blinded, or killed; those who held it for days and months and those who held it for more than twenty years; caliphs who had some defects; those who had children, and those who did not; those who killed their fathers, sons, brothers, or were killed by slaves.

His treatise dealing with the duration of the tenure of emirs[125] is assumed to contain the names of governors of al-Andalus, and may have a format similar to the works dealing with the caliphs. The work may contain also the names of famous governors of the East with reference to their preeminent position and relationship to the central government.

Ibn Hazm also wrote two noted works on genealogy, one dealing with the Arabs,[126] and the other with the Berbers.[127] The massive genealogy of the Arabs catalogues Arab tribes and individuals who settled in various parts of al-Andalus and also some of the neo-Muslim families prominent in Andalusian affairs. The section on some of the Berber tribes is brief presumably, it was expanded upon in his lost genealogy of the Berbers. Both are invaluable with respect to the distribution of the Andalusian population.

In the field of literary history, Ibn Hazm is credited with five histories, of which only *The excellence of al-Andalus*[128] survives. This anthology includes major men of letters from both East and al-Andalus. We may assume that his *Book on Poets*[129] was writen in the same vein and dealt with

Andalusian poets and their poetical compositions. A more specialized work dealt with the poets at the court of Ibn Abi 'Amir al-Mansur.[130] His *Categories of Scholars*[131] is believed to have been a comprehensive work classifying Andalusian men of letters by field and by scholarly standing. Finally, his catalogue[132] of the names of his teachers would be invaluable for better insight into his education and associates.

The *Fisal* contains valuable information about Muslim and non-Muslim denominations and Ibn Hazm's views on multiplicity of theological problems and the writing of history. Ibn Hazm recognized many authors before he had written about the religious and philosophical systems of mankind, but he believed their works were either too prolix and diffuse or too concise. He wanted to present the various religio-philosophical issues on the basis of tangible evidentce and proofs. He says, "We shall not assume anything to be true until it is demonstrated by proofs on which the truth rests." In addition, the *Fisal* gives a good insight into Ibn Hazm's historical method and historical criticism. An example is where he questions the accuracy of the reported 600,000 able fighting Jews under twenty years old who were in the Sinai Peninsula after they had left Egypt.[133] This number was questioned with a similar argument by Ibn Khaldun more than three centuries later.[134]

Historians such as Ibn Sa'id, al-Marrakushi, Ibn al-Abbar, Ibn al-Khatib, Ibn Khaldun, and Eastern historian al-Sakhawi, among others, cited Ibn Hazm's authority on rulers, men of letters, and other subjects. Although Ibn Hazm was considered partial to the Umayyad dynasty, which he regarded as the noblest of Islamic dynasties,[135] he did not lose sight of the defects and abuses of some of its rulers. To him, the emir al-Hakam I (796-822) was one of those overt sinners and shedders of blood among us.[136] The emir 'Abdallah (888-912) was also a murderer, who conspired against his own brother, killed his two sons and a brother, and others.[137]. On the other hand, Hisham I (788-796) was a pious and just ruler.[138] Muhammad I (852-886) was a lover of knowledge; a man of good conduct, fair and sensitive to the feeling of traditionists; and protector of Baqiy Ibn Makhlad against the harassment of the religious scholars.[139] Al-Hakam II (961-976) was a man of great learning who had an enormous library.[140] Al-Mustazhir (reigned in 1023), under whom Ibn Hazm served as a vizier, was the epitome of intelligence, eloquence and sensitivity, and a great belletrist.[141] Under the Hammudids, who ruled Cordova from 1016 to 1027, there was in the course of three days an ignominy without equal - the existence of four caliphs.[142]

In addition, Ibn Hazm's authority was cited upon men of letters. The scholar Mundhir Ibn Sa'id al-Balluti (d. 966) is said to have entertained Zahirite ideas.[143] The *Nawadir,* a belletristic work by al-Qali (d. 967), is equated with the famous belletristic work *al-Kamil* by the Eastern philologist al-Mubarrad (d. ca. 897).[144] Information about the philologist al-Zubaydi,[145] Ibn Abi 'Amir al-Mansur,[146] and other Andalusian figures is often given on the authority of Ibn Hazm. Finally, al-Sakhawi (d. 1497) refers to several of Ibn Hazm's works: the *Maratib al-'ulum,* a biography of Muhammad, the *Fisal,* and a work on Traditions.[147]

Unlike many of his predecessors, Ibn Hazm gives prominent place to history in his classification of the sciences. To him, history *('ilm al-khabar)* is one of the seven universal and ageless sciences common to all people; yet it differentiate nations from one another.It is a science of unquestionable validity, is based on premises that guarantee the continuity and soundness of transmission without leaving doubt concerning the existence of famous countries, rulers, scholars, religious denominations, different schools of thought, political institutions, and other human activities, but not excluding some of the divine manifestations such as the appearance of revelation, prophecy and miracles.[148] Because of its immediate relevance to the rise of Islam and the Islamic experience over the centuries, history is edifying and instructive, and occupies an important place in the education of the individual. It is a must for the student, who is encouraged to relegate it to a time of leisure when he is tired from studying other sciences, " For history is a very easy, stimulating, entertaining and pleasurable disciple."[149] However, its relegation to a time of leisure is not intended to minimize the important role of history in education. To the contrary, history enables the individual to learn about the experience of people in the past with respect to their good and bad deeds; about the tyranny and excesses of rulers; and about scholars and virtuous men. As such, history will enable the individual to emulate the good deeds of his ancestors and to avoid the bad ones. Ibn Hazm states:

"If the individual attains proficiency during his initiation in the sciences, he should not neglect the study of the history of ancient people and those who succeeded them, nor should he neglect reading ancient and contemporary histories in order to acquaint himself with the disappearance of those nations, the destruction of civilized countries, and the obliteration of famous cities that were firmly established and fortified; he should also be acquainted with the passing of their inhabitants and their vicissitudes; the passing of kings, who killed and oppressed people and who accumulated a great deal of money, armies, and weapons to perpetuate the rule for themselves and their offspring, but which did not remain. On the contrary, those kings vanished along with their legacies; their offspring have gone and disappeared, leaving behind them misdeeds, blemishes, and ugly remembrances befitting their souls in the Hereafter and their mentioning in this world. With this realization, asceticism and indifference will result, leading the individual to look down on kings because of the enormity of afflictions that had befallen them and their descendants. Such a realization will also lead him to praise God-fearing people for their virtues, thereby wishing them for himself, and will enable him to hear their censuring of vices, thereby avoiding them himself. He will come close to ascertaining the soundness of history and its aid on the basis of a given narration, notwithstanding the long distances and time of those who collected it, and to see clearly the efforts, the different religions, and the various schools of thought of people; he will then become certain that the information is sound, not admitting any doubt. On the other hand, he may come across different versions and will then realize that it is muddled. He will also perceive information about scholars and pious men and would strive to be in a similar condition and to add his name to their if and when he will conduct himself as they did by imitating their examples and deeds. Likewise, he will become acquainted with the deeds of corrupt people on earth and the bad things said about them and what bad names they left behind, thereby abhorring their path and avoiding being mentioned among them."[150]

Moreover, history will help the individual to see the success or failure of dynasties and the vicissitudes of nations, which are caused by human actions and not the stars, as astrologers would like us to believe.[151] The implications here is quite clear. To Ibn Hazm, history is no more and less than recording human actions, and reflects human responsibility with respect to the good or bad deeds of man. Ibn Hazm appears to believe that historical facts can be ascertainable without any doubt, and could not be possibly concealed or altered no matter what attempts are made to distort the actual situation. This historical perspective permeates his historical writings and is reflected in his conception of the sciences where importance is placed on the degree of utility of each one of the sciences. History is, thus, important as an invaluable lesson that guides the individual to have a great perception of human experience in its positive and negative aspects thereby leading him to the road of virtue which is commendable for this world and in the Hereafter. Finally, Ibn Hazm does not appear to express any preference about the manner of writing history. He simply says that history may be written according to dynasties, annalistic treatment, countries, categories, genealogy, or mixed form.[152]

Genealogy also forms an important part of historical writings. In his *Jamharah* on the genealogy of the Arabs who settled in al-Andalus, Ibn Hazm defends genealogy as indispensable for determining the facts about the background of Muhammad, for determining inheritance, for ascertaining the eligibility of people for the Caliphate, for identifying the paternity of children, and the like. After mentioning that the Prophet Muhammad and his Companions approved it and considered it important in religious matters, he says:

"Indeed, the knowledge of genealogy is a significant and lofty science by means of which mutual acquaintance is made. The Almighty God has made use of part of it. Therefore, no one can ignore learning it ... The knowledge of genealogy is obligatory because it will enable the individual to know that Muhammad - May God's prayer and peace be upon him - was the one whom God sent with the religion of Islam to men and spirits *(al-ins wa-l-jinn);* that he is Muhammad Ibn 'Abdallah al-Qurayshi al-Hashimi, who was brought up in Mecca and emigrated to Medina. Whoever doubts that Muhammad was not a Qurayshite, but a Yemenite, Tamimi, or non-Arab is an unbeliever and barren of knowledge about his religion."[153]

It follows that those who deny the validity of genealogy consider its knowledge to be a useless and superfluous error.[154]

Ibn Hazm's conception of history is inspired by and based on the Islamic experience, which of all the experience of mankind is ascertainable in the revelation as handed down to the Prophet Muhammad, in the miracles of the Prophet, in the authentic Traditions, in the merit of the wives and Companions of the Prophet, in the presence of Islamic community, and in the superiority of Islam over all other world religions. This historical outlook is reflected in his religious and historical writings. For him, the history of Islam and of the Islamic peoples is the most reliable of the histories of all the nations of the world - including the histories of the Jews, Persians, Chinese, Indians, Copts, Syrians, Edomites, Amorites, Moabites, and other people. As for the history of the northern people inhabiting the cold zone and the Black people inhabiting the torrid zone, it is almost non-existent because these people lack the sciences, books and historical writings. Aside from his religious bias, Ibn Hazm appears to be influenced by the data available to him whereby he had ample material on the Islamic period, on the one hand, but little, if any, about other people. His reasoning follows:

"The most reliable history among us is the history of the Islamic community; its beginning, conquests, information about its caliphs, kings, and those attached to them; its scholars and other things connected with it. The history of the Israelites is sound for the most part, although some of it contains visible interpolation and obvious corruption; its information is sound from the time the Israelites went to Syria up to their last exodus and not before that. The History of the Greeks is reliable from the time of Alexander and not before that time. The History of the Persians is reliable from the time of Darius Ibn Darius and still more reliable from the time of Ardashir Ibn Babak; as for the time before that, it consists of superstitions containing obvious lies. As for the Turks, Khazars, the Northern people and the Black countries, they have neither sciences, nor histories. This holds true for the history of North Africa and al-Andalus before the coming of the Muslims. The histories of the Copts, Syriac people, Yemenites, Ammonites, Moabites, and others have perished completely with nothing left except fabrications and superstitions. As for India and China their histories have not reached us as we would have liked. However, they are two nations possessing science, records, publications, and collections. Thus the student of history should occupy himself only with things whose veracity we have shown, lest he should become disheartened when he finds out by himself what is false."[155]

In light of this statement, Ibn Hazm closes the door of research about non-Muslims. For his purpose, the Islamic experience alone would be sufficient for edifying and instructing. Moreoever, he pleads eloquently that revelation, prophecy, and miracles have been, like mundane historical facts about rulers, scholars, and nations, accepted on reliable testimony, and transmitted from generation to generation by a good number of virtuous people. All things being equal, he inquires, why should Revelation, Prophecy, and miracles be doubted where historical events about rulers and other people are accepted? If someone maintains that people do not deny historical facts but deny the existence of miracles, his answer would be that if the majority of people do not know the facts of history about their own country, this does not prove that those facts do not exist or should be declared false.[156]

Of course, reported facts are subject to verification by eyewitnesses, proper and reliable transmission, and written documentation. Ibn Hazm discusses this problem in his *Fisal*[157] and *Ihkam*[158] in connection with the determination of the accuracy and soundness of the Prophetic Traditions. Aware of the possibility of forgery and suppression of facts, Ibn Hazm states that facts may be tampered with for a variety of reasons. For instance, some people suppress facts to erase the tyranny and injustice inflicted by their ancestors. To Ibn Hazm, such an attempt is futile because these people could not with all the power that might be available to them succeed in erasing the truth of history, nor could they eliminate the virtue of other people. The Umayyads of Damascus attempted to tarnish the good reputation of the fourth caliph, 'Ali, but failed. Prophets had their mortal enemies, were ridiculed and denigrated but prevailed in the end. Such evidence leads him to conclude that the infallible signs attending the mission of Muhammad are beyond dispute and are ascertainable as other historical facts. In this respect he puts the moral and positive value of human authority into play, placing a substantial reliance on trustworthy witnesses regardless of their number. By definition, he assumes that a trustworthy witness cannot possibly lie and gives examples to illustrate his contention. If two trustworthy witnesses, who have never met, report the same fact verbatim, such a report must be accepted as true, for it is impossible that there should be exact wording if they were lying. The same would apply in the case of a single individual reporting the death of someone, either in person or in writing. The validity of such testimonies is the same as that conceded to reports handed down by an uninterrupted chain of witnesses. He argues that the truth is not contingent upon number and that many or the few can either lie or tell the truth, depending, of course, on the moral qualities of the individuals involved.

Next, Ibn Hazm turns to reports handed down from generation to generation. This takes him to the heart of the question regarding the numerous reports about the deeds and sayings of the Prophet Muhammad as contained in the several codices of Traditions. To Ibn Hazm, reports handed down through an uninterrupted chain of transmitters *(khabar mutawatir* going back to Muhammad and preserved by Muslim scholars for centuries are unquestionable and must be accepted as true. Although this kind of information was not witnessed personally by all the transmitters, it must be accepted in its entirety. "And whoever denies it will be in the position of the one who denies what he perceives with the senses, no more, no less. Thus, he would be impelled not to believe because there was a time before him and in that his father and mother were preceded him, or having been born from a woman."[159]

To the contention that in order for information to be accepted it must have the concurrence of all people from East and West, or at least the concurrence of three hundred, seventy, fifty, or a minimum of three persons, Ibn Hazm retorts that such allegations have no foundation in fact, for the veracity of a thing is not subject to magic numbers. He remarks,"It is inconceivable that there should be any difference between what is transmitted by twenty or nineteen persons, or between seventy and sixty-nine persons.[160] He concludes that the testimony of two or one person will do as long as the persons involved are honorable and trustworthy; but under no circumstances should the testimony of anyone be accepted unless the transmitter is just, knowledgeable, and accurate in his written transmission.[161] Likewise, information handed down with a break in the chain of transmission, or not traced back directly to the Prophet, may be considered doubtful and even rejected.[162]

CHAPTER VIII

THE PHILOSOPHICAL SCIENCES

In spite of his strong commitment to Islam, Ibn Hazm did not condemn philosophical sciences, as did many Muslims who saw in them threat to religious belief. Having the advantage of a broad education, Ibn Hazm was able to assess the merit of the philosophical sciences in relation to the religious sciences. Furthermore, he used the "logical method" and applied it rigorously and quite persuasively to religious questions. In fact, his preparation in and writing on some of the philosophical disciplines are sufficient to place Ibn Hazm - despite his vocal religious bias - among the major Muslim philosophers. After defining and stating the objective of each one of the sciences, he advocated combining the various Arabic and foreign sciences into a wholesome curriculum that he conceived to be the best preparation for an understanding of the physical world as well as for a life of bliss in the Hereafter.

The philosophical sciences were generally understood to include all those disciplines which were translated from Greek into Arabic; they comprised three main branches - mathematics, the natural sciences, and metaphysics - with logic serving as a tool for all of them.[1] To Ibn Hazm, however, the universal sciences are four: astronomy, mathematics, medicine, and philosophy.[2] He defines philosophy as a discipline which "is the knowledge of things as they are according to their definition, from the highest genera to particulars, as well as the knowledge of divine matters." In another context, he refers to the philosophical sciences as the sciences of the Ancients *('ulum al-awa'il),* which he defines as follows:

"Know - may God help us and you in what it pleased Him - that the sciences of the Ancients consist of philosophy *(falsafah)* and the definitions of logic *(hudud al-mantiq)* with which Plato, his pupil Aristotle, Alexander[4], and those who followed their path dealt. It is a good and lofty science because it contains the knowledge of all the world in all aspects pertaining to genera, species, individual substances, and accidents. It also enables the individual to arrive at the proof *(burhan)* without which nothing can be certain, and which discerns what is believed to be a proof from what is not. The usefulness of this knowledge is great for discerning the realities from non-realities."[5]

Furthermore, some aspects of philosophy in an Islamic context were almost undistinguishable from some of the theological questions pertaining to the existence of One and a Supreme Being, creation, duration of the world, right conduct, attainment of happiness, political management and the like. Ibn Hazm attempted to find answers to such questions by means of philosophy and Revelation; however, philosophy is limited in that it deals with only the affairs of this world[6] and cannot by itself and without the aid of prophecy improve the character of the soul[7] or lead to salvation after death.[8]

Ibn Hazm had his formal training in the philosophical and natural sciences under the scientist Ibn al-Kattani.[9] His philosophical writings - though few in comparison with his religious works or the philosophical works of the great Muslim philosophers such as al-Kindi, al-Farabi, Ibn Sina and Ibn Rushd - are substantial and significant enough to place him among Muslim philosophers. An examination of his works shows his grasp of the major philosophical issues that had occupied Muslim thinkers for centuries, and his familiarity with leading Greek philosophers such as Plato, Aristotle, Hippocrates, Porphyry, Euclid, Ptolemy, and Galen. In spite of his commitment to the religious sciences and his belief in their ultimate finality, he regards the philosophical sciences as disciplines deserving an important place in education. In fact, he urges the student and the jurist as well to read them and also the books of Euclid and Ptolemy and some work on surgery.[10] Moreover, he defends himself passionately against those enemies who charge him with overindulgence in the books of the Ancients.[11] To him, philosophy is the twin sister of religion, which cannot be understood fully without philosophy. Both aim at one and the same thing.[12] Reason and faith are accidents of the soul and complementary to each other.[13] Logic is the elucidation of every science.[14] Mathematics, astronomy, and medicine are important on their own merit, without mentioning their significance and utility in the application of the religious law.[15]

Ibn Hazm's philosophical works include ten treatises on medicine[16] and other treatises, of which five are extant. His *Akhlaq,* an ethical treatise, has received the attention of various scholars.[17] Its objective is to correct the vitiated soul and to cure its maladies.[18] Reflecting Ibn Hazm's experience and his views, the treatise consists of numerous aphorisms which can be traced to both ancient and Islamic backgrounds. Essentially, it deals with character *(akhlaq)* in its positive and negative manifestations, always calling attention to qualities that lead to right conduct and virtuous life through practising good deeds and conforming to the prescriptions of both the religious law and philosophy. Justice, generosity, courage, fortitude, sincerity, friendship, and love of knowledge and its pursuits are some of the many aspects of virtuous life.

His *Taqrib* is perhaps the first attempt by a Muslim thinker to popularize logic by replacing technical with popular terms and using examples from daily life and the law. His *Maratib,* classifying the sciences has the distinct merit of integrating the religious and philosophical sciences, emphasizing their interdependence and the necessity of pursuing most, if not all, of them. In his short treatise on the soul,[19] Ibn Hazm conceives the soul to the manager of the body, living, rational, discerning and knowing all things except itself. His numerous polemics cover a wide range of subjects in which he refutes the religious doctrinists, sophists, pretenders to philosophy, and others.[20] In one he takes issue with his co-religionist philosopher al-Kindi[21] on a number of questions related to cause and effect, intellect, soul, and the beautiful names of God. Likewise, he refutes the philosopher physician al-Razi[22] on cosmology, eternal duration, absolute vacuum, and the dualist doctrine of good and evil.

Not all the philosophical sciences can be called legitimate and useful because some lack the necessary requirements of being sciences. In consequence, the philosophical sciences comprise two categories: first, the legitimate sciences comprising logic, mathematics, medicine, and astronomy, which are demonstrative sciences, and second, the spurious sciences comprising magic, talisman, music, alchemy, and astrology, which are not demonstrative *(ghayr burhaniyy)*.

As a general premise, Ibn Hazm believes that anything known can be called knowledge or a science,[23] and this may include carpentry, weaving and the rest of the crafts. He defines the sciences according to their objectives and categorizes them as being "lofty" or "base" in proportion to the degree of their utility in this world and in the Hereafter - all of them being legitimate. The legitimacy of a science does not reside in the degree of its utility, but in certain criteria for calling a science a science: the process of cognition (sensation, intuition, intellect, discernment), a scientific method, and result that can be verified by proof or experimentation. Logic, mathematics, astronomy, medicine, and their subdivisions meet these requirements, whereas alchemy (as opposed to chemistry) does not because it attempts to change the nature of a thing, which miracles alone can accomplish. No scientific method or proof is involved. Likewise, astrology (as opposed to astronomy) lacks repeated experimentation *(tajribah)* under identical conditions - the element of time leaves the result unverified.

1. The legitimate Sciences

a. Mathematics ('ilm al-a'dad)

Mathematics, or the science of numbers, was cultivated widely among Muslims and enjoyed a prominent place in Islamic culture, with no indication of controversy. Although mathematics was not foreign to the Near East, Muslim scholars acknowledged their indebtedness to the Greeks. The importance of mathematics in religion, state affairs, and daily life could hardly be denied given its unquestionable validity, applicability, and utility. It is for these reasons that Ibn Hazm gives mathematics a prominent place in his division of the sciences. Its neglect in the education of the individual - be he pious or layman - was of great concern to him.

Ibn Hazm states the nature and purpose of mathematics as ascertaining the rules of numbers, establishing their proofs, and implementing them for measuring and other purposes.[24] "Andrumakhish,[25] the author of the book on arithmatic *(Kitab al-arithmatiqi)*, and his followers dealt with the nature of numbers. It is a good, sound, and demonstrative science except that its utility concerns this world only, with respect to the division of property among people and similar matters. The utility of all things in this world is rather small and insignificant owing to our swift exodus from it and the impossibility of remaining in it. And everything which ceases becomes nonexistent."[26] In spite of this qualification, the mathematical sciences are among the lofty sciences,[27] derived from premises based on the first intellection.[28] They are valuable not only on their own merit, but for religion as well; their pursuit is incumbent upon all Muslims *(fard 'ala al-kifayah)*. Thus, it behooves the student to pursue them in order that he may acquire a knowledge of multiplication, division, addition, and subtraction.[29] He should also take up surveying *(misahah)*, which is also a good and demonstrative science studied by Euclid and his followers, and which is helpful in transporting water, lifting weights, designing buildings, and constructing instruments.[30] Finally, the student should be acquainted with arithmetic, which is the knowledge of the nature of numbers.

b. Astronomy *('ilm al-nujum)*.

Closely related to mathematics and also cultivated widely in Islam, astronomy was regarded as a noble science and never fell into disfavor; its sister, astrology, however, was both influential and controversial in Muslim society. Ibn Hazm took a strong stand with respect to the merit or demerit of the science of the stars.[31] He says:

"Astronomy *('ilm al-hay'ah)* was discussed by Ptolemy, Lunakhas[32] before him, their followers, and earlier, the people of India, Nabataeans, and Copts. It is a good, sensory *(hissiyy)*, and demonstrative science. It consists of the knowledge of the celestial bodies, their revolution, intersection, position, and their distances. It also deals with the stars, their motion, size and distance, and their satellites. The utility of this science is to arrive at the principles of creation and the majesty of the wisdom of the Creator, His power, His design, and His will. This utility is a very lofty one, specially for matters concerning the Hereafter."[33]

Thus, one reason astronomy should be pursued is that it is a convincing proof of the act of creation and its Maker. The student should familiarize himself with the works of Euclid and Ptolemy. Ptolemy's *Almagest* will enable him to acquire a knowledge of eclipses, the width and length of countries, time, the length of days and nights, the ebb and flow of water, the positions of the sun, moon, and planets. Astronomy, along with the mathematical sciences, is indispensable to religion for determining the position of the individual toward the *Qiblah,* or facing Mecca during the time of prayer and division of inheritance, booty, and the like without which religion would never be complete. Moreover, even if the individual studies astronomy and mathematics for gainful purposes, he is deserving of reward *(ma'jur)* as long as he does not use them for iniquity.[34]

c. Medicine

"Prophetic medicine" *(al-tibb al-nabawi)*, based on the supposed practice of the Prophet, encouraged Muslim scholars to cultivate medicine on a scientific basis, as practiced among the ancient Greeks. In consequence, medicine occupied a prominent place among the sciences in Islamic culture, attested to by the enormous medical literature in Arabic. By the eleventh century, medicine had reached the pinnacle of its development, and appears to have constituted an integral part of scientific or philosophical education. The ten medical works attributed to Ibn Hazm by al-Dhahabi[35]; Ibn Hazm's praise for the medical works of al-Zahrawi, Ibn al-Haytham, and his teacher Ibn al-Kattani[36]; and Ibn Hazm's statement on medical matters scattered throughout his writings[37] all suggest that Ibn Hazm was knowledgeable in the subject of medicine. Moreover, Ibn Hazm assigns an important place to medicine in his classification of the sciences, and considers it among the obligatory subjects in the curriculum.

For him, medicine is a lofty science with the dual purpose of caring for the body and implementing the religious law. He states its background, objective, and nature as follows:

"Medicine, which Hippocrates, Galen, Dioscorides, and their followers studied, is a science concerned with the cure of bodies from maladies in this life. It is a demonstrative and good science whose utility resides in this world only. However, it is not a universal occupation *(sina'ah 'ammah)* because we have observed that the inhabitants of the desert and most countries are cured from their maladies without the aid of a physician, and because their bodies regain health without treatment just the same as, and even more than, those who have been treated. They attain a life span as long or short as that of those who have been treated . . . But if someone alleges that they use medical treatment, our answer to that is that their medical treatments do not conform to the rules of medicine and are frowned upon by the physicians. In fact, all that they do through spells has no room among physicians."[38]

The knowledge of medicine is inferred from the first intellect and sensation[39] and derived from premises that are confirmed by experience *(tajribah)* with respect to the appearance and causes of illness owing to the disturbance of mixture and with resepct to counteracting illnesses through the power of drugs. Ibn Hazm defines it as follows:

"The science of medicine consists of two parts: the medicine of the soul, which is the result of the science of logic; it is concerned with the improvement and correction of moral conduct *(akhlaq)* by preventing it from excess and dereliction and placing it in a position of moderation. The medicine of the body consists of the knowledge of the nature of bodies, the knowledge of the constitution of organs; the knowledge of illnesses, their causes and response to drugs; and the determination of the power of drugs and food. The medicine of the body also consists of two parts: practical and surgical means such as setting broken bones, slitting *(batt)*, cauterization, and amputation; and the elimination of the power of maladies through the power of drugs. It is further divided into two parts: the preservation of health by preventing the occurrence of diseases, and the treatment of diseases when they occur."[40]

Inasmuch as medicine has a direct bearing on the improvement of the moral character as well as the well-being of the body, Ibn Hazm considers knowledge of medicine to be a necessity in the application of the religious law, particularly in matters pertaining to serious defects, such as madness, that affect both the behavior and the legal capacity of the individual.[41] Thus, pursuing it is an absolute duty.[42] However important in preventing illness and preserving health and however indispensable in the execution of the religious law, medicine would be useless were it to be placed above the rest of the sciences since it is, by itself, quite limited and even superfluous as attested by its absence among the inhabitants of the desert and other backward countries. Nonetheless, physicians are the guardians of health and moral conduct and in such capacity they should avoid the company of rulers, who often demand the impossible from them: "We indeed dislike that a virtuous man should associate himself with the ruler in matters connected with medicine because ignorance, intemperance, and impatience get the better of kings when they are deprived of pleasure. This situation is not conducive to administering the regimen of healthy people and the treatment of the sick ones. Habitually, rulers trouble the physician to revive the dead and regard him inadequate if he fails to achieve this goal. In other words, if the physician were to follow their whims, he would be deceiving them, and were he to advise them properly, they would disobey and find him troublesome."[43]

d. The Natural Sciences

The natural sciences, which are derived from premises based on sense perception, appear to constitute a separate category among the sciences distinguishing them from astronomy, medicine, mathematics, and other cognate sciences. Philosophers, such as al-Farabi and Ibn Sina, made provision for them in their classification of the sciences and contrasted them with their counterpart, metaphysics. Although Ibn Hazm does not assign them a prominent place among the sciences and considers them as separate from medicine and astronomy, he does not totally overlook them. To him, they are important in understanding physical phenomena and the world about us. In consequence, they deserve a place in the curriculum. In fact, the student should, after the study of logic, pay attention to "the natural sciences" *(tabi'iyyat),* atmospheric conditions, compositions of the elements, zoology, botany, and mineralogy; and should read books on anatomy in order to perceive the masterly creation and the role of the Creator; the formation of the members of the body; the will, wisdom, and power of the Creator.[44]

e. Logic

It is to the subject of logic that Ibn Hazm devotes an ample space. Arabic logic *('ilm al-mantiq)* occupied an important place in Islamic culture, and received the attention of a good number of writers over the centuries.[45] However, no sooner had logic developed fully than it became the object of heated controversies within the general context of the sciences. As a result, it had both ardent supporters and uncompromising opponents. To its advocates, logic is a noble science and an indispensable tool *(alah)* for all the sciences. To its opponents, it is not only useless, but detrimental to religious beliefs in that it leads to doubt and diminution of faith.[46] This dichotomy of views which had its locus in Eastern Islam reached al-Andalus with all the attending consequences. Due to the ultra conservative posture of Andalusians toward issues affecting religious beliefs and practices, logic appears to have been condemned at the outset by pietists, who were for long time the guardians of an unadulterated orthodoxy. This notwithstanding, the free circulation of books from the East and the frequent travel of scholars from al-Andalus to the East and vice-versa were important factors in making logic and other unpopular disciplines known to the curious student. Under the circumstances, logic was pursued in a clandestine manner in al-Andalus, and had its early supporters prior to the time of Ibn Hazm in the eleventh century.

Ibn Hazm was convinced of the significance of logic, pointed to its utility in all disciplines including the religious sciences and viewed it as a remedy fit for intelligent people. He emphasized the value of logic within the context of both the religious and secular sciences,[47] and was its staunch defender throughout his career even when he became devoted almost wholly to the study of the religious disciplines. His work on logic, *Facilitating the Understanding of the Rules of Logic and Introduction Thereto (al-Taqrib li-hudud al-mantiq wa-madkhaluh),* was written early in his career between 1025 and 1029.[48] The work is not only an apologia for logic, but a lucid treatment of the subject with the declared intention of simplifying it using new vocabulary, and examples derived from the religious law and every day experience hoping, thereby, to make the discipline readily comprehensible to a large audience.[49] It was this new approach, perhaps, that led some of his Andalusian contemporaries to criticize Ibn Hazm and accuse him of deviating from Aristotelian logic and of dabbling in things beyond his capability.[50] This assessment was followed uncritically by Eastern biographers,[51] who appear to have failed to consult Ibn Hazm's *Taqrib* in order to evaluate his attitude to and competence in logic. Moreover, they also appear to have overlooked his other works, mainly, *Fisal,*[52] *Ihkam,*[53] *Tawqif,*[54] and *Maratib al-'ulum,*[55] where Ibn Hazm emphasizes the importance of logic and directs the reader to his *Taqrib.*

It is within this framework that Ibn Hazm's views on logic will be considered on the basis of his *Taqrib* and other statements found in his other works in order to show his commitment to, and his grasp of logic, which he used as an important tool in his many polemics with Muslims, Jews, and Christians. Attempt will be made to place his views and works in a historical context with reference to the views and works of some of his predecessors.

Arabic logic was based on Aristotle's *Organon* and Porphyry's *Eisagoge,* both of which were known to the Arabs through the original Greek and later commentaries on them.[56] Post-Aristotelian commentators expounded on the *Organon* adding to it Stoic and neo-Platonic elements.[57] Muslim scholars appear to have relied on both the original and the commentaries, and produced a recension incorporating their format and content. The *Organon* and the *Eisagoge* were translated several times into Arabic, abridged, commented and super-commented on by several generations of Muslim scholars. More often than not, they were combined into one single work with the *Eisagoge* serving as an Introduction *(madkhal)*, followed by the *Organon* in eight parts: Categories *(maqulat)*, Hermeneutics *('Ibarah)*. Analytics *(qiyas)*, Apodictics *(burhan)*, Topics *(jadal)*, Sophistics *(mughalatah)*, Rhetoric *(khitabah)*, and poetics *(shi'r)*[58]

The task of arriving at a final Arabic recension was a long drawn process, and involved generations of translators and commentators. Ibn al-Muqaffa' (d.757),[59] Hunayn b. Ishaq (d.877),[60] his son Ishaq (d.916). Matta b. Yunus (d. 940), and Yahya b. 'Adi (d. 974),[63] were among the principal translators. Among the commentators and authors were al-Kindi (d. 873),[64] his pupil al-Sarakhsi (d. 899),[65] al-Farabi (d. 950), [66] al-Razi (d. 925),[67] and Ibn Sina (d. 1037),[68] who wrote on some sections or on the whole of the *Organon*. These Eastern scholars, among others, exerted an enormous influence on the development of Arabic logic, and were instrumental in forging an important place for logic among the Arabic sciences. As a result, logic came to permeate Arabic philology, theology, jurisprudence, rhetoric, and dialectics.[69]

In its important place in Islamic culture, logic could hardly be ignored by those Andalusians, who depended for education on Eastern masters, and who were familiar with Eastern logicians whose works were imported into al-Andalus during the ninth-tenth centuries. In spite of the conservative outlook of Andalusians, logic appears to have been pursued by a large number of scholars. The scientist-historian Sa'id of Toledo supplies valuable information about the state of the secular sciences in al-Andalus with particular reference to logic. Sa'id refers to the great library of the caliph al-Hakam II (961-76) and says that many people were driven to read the Books of the Ancients *(kutub al-awa'il)*, and to learn the various schools of thought contained therein.[70] Sa'id also gives the names of scientists who concerned themselves with or wrote on logic. More often than not, those scientists were physicians, mathematicians, astronomers, and philologists. Muhammad b. 'Abdun (d. ca. 990) was an able physician, who studied in the East and introduced Aristotelian logic into al-Andalus.[71] 'Abd al-Rahman b. Isma'il b. Zayd (10th.c.), known as Euclid, was knowledgeable in geometry, and wrote a book abridging the eight books on logic. He also traveled to the East where he died[72].Muhammad b. Isma'il, known as the philosopher *(al-hakim)*, was an expert in both logic and mathematics.[73] Ibn Sidah (d. 1065), the great lexicographer of al-Andalus, is credited with a comprehensive work on logic in which he followed the method of the Eastern Logician Matta b. Yunus.[74] His contemporary al-Hasan b. 'Abd al-Rahman, known as Ibn al-Jallad, was an expert in geometry, astronomy, motion of the stars, logic and the natural sciences.[75]

Abu-al-Walid Hisham b. Ahmad b. Khalid al-Kinani, known as Ibn al-Waqshi, was an expert in geometry, logic, and the secular sciences.[76]

Thus, by the time of Ibn Hazm in the eleventh century, logic was not only known among a goodly number of Andalusians, but cultivated as well. In his *Fadl*, an anthology exalting the excellence of al-Andalus and written about 1027, Ibn Hazm refers to two Andalusian scientists and credits them with several works on philosophy.[77] They are: Sa'id b. Fathun al-Saraqusti (d.ca.1010),[78] known as al-Hammar, and Abu 'Abdallah Muhammad b. Hasan al-Madhhiji (d. 1029), known as Ibn al-Kattani.[79] Ibn Hazm appears to have had an intimate knowledge about these two men, who most probably influenced his scientific preparation. Al-Humaydi quotes a poem by Ibn Fathun on the authority of his teacher Ibn Hazm in which Ibn Fathun deplores and even ridicules the attitude of his contemporaries toward logic:

1. They inflict injustice on logic when describing it
   With things that are not there; for they are ignorant of it;
2. Were they aware of its merit, they would not deny it;
   And were they aware of its virtue, they would like it.
3. But by God they lie even if they knew it
   And would persist in all what they impute to it.[80]

It is not clear whether Ibn Hazm studied logic under Ibn Fathun, but there is reason to believe that he was familiar with his works and his views on logic, which he echoed in his *Taqrib*. On the other hand, Ibn Hazm's relationship with Ibn al-Kattani was that of a pupil, which he acknowledges with deference when he refers to Ibn al-Kattani as "our teacher" *(Shaykhuna)*.[81] Furthermore, he considers Ibn al-Kattani as an able scientist and an expert in medicine, logic, aphorisms - on all of which he wrote numerous and well known works.[82] Sa'id acknowledges the scientific expertise of Ibn al-Kattani, and refers to his training by quoting from Ibn al-Kattani's writings that he (Ibn al-Kattani) studied logic under Muhammad b.'Abdun,[83] 'Umar b. Yunus b. Ahmad al-Harrani,[84] Ahmad b. Hafsun b. 'Abdallah b. Ibrahim al-Asimi,[85] Abu 'Abdallah b. Mas'ud,[86] Muhammad b. Maymun,[87] and others.[88]

Whether or not these men can be considered logicians is hard to tell in the absence of their works. However, one can gather from their biographical sketches that they covered the gamut of Arabic culture, poetry, philology, the religious and the secular sciences. This is the more significant in that logic had a fertile soil in al-Andalus, was pursued rather actively, and followed a trajectory similar in many ways to that in Eastern Islam. In consequence, Ibn Hazm was a beneficiary of both Andalusian and Eastern legacies, had a sufficient background about the evolution and development of Arabic logic, and was quite familiar with the manifold problems facing it, mainly, the polarization of views with respect to its merit or demerit, the difficult format of presentation, the lack of easily understood examples, and the technical but disparate vocabulary. These problems had already their tolls in Eastern Islam during the ninth-tenth centuries, and contributed to the formation of deep rooted attitudes toward logic resulting in a seemingly two irreconcilable stands: that of the scientist-philosopher supporting logic, and that of the jurist-theologian denigrating it.

This polarization of views has an enormous repercussions. Theologians had developed their theological dialectics consisting of arguments, counteragruments and conclusion.[89] Their method, which was developed by the theologian al-Ash'ari (d. 935), remained essentially apologetic an *argumentum at hominem* aiming at defending one's position and triumph over the adversary by all means available.[90] As such, it lacks the rigor and precision of Aristotelian methodology. It is for this reason, perhaps, that Ibn Hazm, who was followed by al-Ghazzali, and Ibn Rushd (d. 1198), viewed the dialectic of the theologians as falling short of demonstrative reasoning *(burhan)* and of attaining certainty *(yaqin)*.[91] Aware of the shortcoming of the theological dialectics, Ibn Hazm attempted to put Greek logic at the service of Islamic theology and jurisprudence with his insistence on thorough individual inquiry *(ijtihad)* and investigation *(bahth)* for ascertaining the truth.[92] As a consequence, Ibn Hazm, revolted against theological dialectics, and the end result hinged on the validity of the Aristotelian method versus the dialectics of the theologians.

The skirmish between the philosophers and the religious scholars concerning the merit or the demerit of logic was, in full swing during the tenth century, was articulated in writing, and often aired in private and public debates. It remained unabated during the time of Ibn Hazm, who was decidedly on the side of the philosophers - notwithstanding his deep commitment to the religious sciences. For a full appreciation of his stand, it may be relevant to point to some of the arguments of his predecessors which were advanced in public debates and in writing. One such a celebrated debate took place between the Christian logician Abu Bishr Matta b. Yunus (d. 940) supporting logic, and the philologist Abu Sa'id al-Sirafi (d. 979) denigrating it.[93] The lengthy debate dealt, among other things, with the relation of logic to language. To the contention of Matta that logic is the instrument *(alah)* of speech, al-Sirafi retorts that it may be so for the Greek language, but has nothing to do with the Arabic language.[94]

The philosopher Abu Hasan al-'Amiri (d. 992) conveys the attitude of theologians and traditionists toward logic when he says that they despise logic and argue that works on logic do not contain but obscure words and strange phrases and had their authors been blessed with any ideas that correspond to the truth, they would surely have taken great pains to clarify them. They further argue that any intelligent person is able to draw logical conclusion without the formal study of logic. Finally, theologians and jurists considered logic detrimental to religious beliefs, and for this reason they came under the attack of the philosophers.[95] This antagonism to logic remained unabated up to the time of Ibn Hazm, and continued undiminished long after his death resulting in the saying: "He who espouses logic espouses heresy" *(man tamantaqa tazandaqa.)*[96]

On their part, philosophers and scientists, who had their training in the secular sciences — medicine, mathematics, astronomy, and others — were staunch supporters of logic. More often than not, they made provision for it in their division of the sciences. The philosopher al-Kindi, who wrote works on the subject, considered logic an important science deserving a place among the philosophical sciences.[97] Al-Khuwarizmi (d. ca. 990), who was concerned with explanation of technical terminology of the various sciences, included logic among the sciences, and devoted nine paragraphs to it explaining Porphyry's *Eisagoge* and the eight books of the *Organon*.[98] The great philosopher al-Farabi wrote on logic and considered it one of the five groups of sciences.[99] The Brethren of Purity, a secret and eclectic society which attempted to harmonize the religious and secular sciences, regarded logic as one of the four philosophical sciences.[100]

While the scientist-philosopher assigns an important place to logic in the classification of the sciences, there is no consensus of opinion as to whether logic is a "science" (*'ilm*), a craft *(sina'ah)*, or an "instrument" *(alah)* as the Greek term *Organon* may convey; or as to whether logic is an integral part of philosophy, or merely its tool. After dividing philosophy into theoretical and practical, al-Khuwarizmi states the problem succinctly: "Some consider logic as a third branch of philosophy; others as part of theoretical philosophy; a third group considers it an instrument of philosophy; and a fourth group regards it as part and tool of philosophy."[101] In his *Inventory of the Sciences (ihsa' al-'ulum)*, Al-Farabi refers to logic as a craft *(sina'ah)* that supplies the rules for right thinking and the attainment of the truth. As such, it is extremely useful and should be pursued.[102] His contemporary al-'Amiri considered logic as an invaluable instrument of the philosophical sciences, "which alone properly enables the rational soul to distinguish between truth and untruth in speculative problems and between good and evil in practical problems. . . Logic controls question and answer as well as contradiction, contrast and fallacy. It helps to resolve doubt, expose misleading statements and supports ideas. . ."[103] Al-'Amiri's views were reiterated by the Nestorian 'Isa b. Ishaq b. Zur'ah (d. 1008), a pupil of the famous logician Yahya b. 'Adi, who offers an apologia for logic. Ibn Zur'ah maintains that "only through the application of logic in philosophical reasoning do we learn what is possible and what is impossible in the nature of things."[104] He adds that logic "is a discipline whose objective includes discrimination of truth from falsehood in discourse, and distinguishing the good from evil in action..."[105]

These tenth-century views of leading scholars were echoed and articulated in the eleventh century by the great philosopher-scientist Ibn Sina, who devoted an ample space to logic in several of his works that are written in a popular language and constitute veritable encyclopedias of the secular sciences.[106] Ibn Sina conceives logic as a science by means of which one is able to derive knowledge from the unknown to the known; to arrive at true knowledge; to know what approximate the truth, and what is an error. Furthermore, logic is a scale that determines the usefulness of the rest of the sciences.[107] Ibn Sina's influence on future generations was enormous, but it is not certain that Ibn Hazm knew of his works at the time he wrote his *Taqrib*. However, Ibn Sina's views were echoed among others, by the great theologian al-Ghazzali (d. 1111), who viewed logic as a scale by means of which one is able to discern right from wrong. Furthermore, it is the servant of the sciences and the truth, which are the conditions for happiness.[108] In sum, logic has a primary importance in explaining words and determining their relationship to meaning. More importantly, it has the purpose of establishing a methodology by means of which the veracity or falsity of a given issue can be determined with a modicum of accuracy. In such a role, logic could not have been overlooked in the evaluation of Islamic culture.

It is within this historical framework that Ibn Hazm's views on logic should be considered. It appears that Ibn Hazm realized fully not only the prominent role of logic in Islamic culture, but was quite familiar with its evolution, development, and the manifold problems facing it. He pondered on all these questions in his *Taqrib* and set out to formulate his ideas about the significance of logic and its place among the sciences.

In his introduction to the *Taqrib* which is a comprehensive treatise on logic, Ibn Hazm refutes the adversaries of logic indicating its merit, importance, and the reasons behind writing the work. The arguments of adversaries have no foundation in fact since logic is meant: 1) to elucidate existing and ascertainable things; 2) to give them forms and attributes that are reaffirmed by the intellect; and to 3) designate them by sounds or by means of signs *(isharat)*.[109] He refers to Aristotole's eight Books of the *Organon* pointing to their purpose of arranging and designating things under names conveying meaning, thus making them comprehensible for elucidating things.[110] Being this the purpose of logic, the argument of adversaries to the effect that logic lead to unbelief *(kufr)* and the triumph of heresy is utterly wrong.[111] Ibn Hazm states categorically that there is nothing wrong with logic *per se,* except perhaps the manner in which it had been written. He complains that books on logic lacked clarity through the use of letters and symbols *(huruf wa-rumuz)*, and the use of examples that are removed from religion and alien to every day experience.[112] Consequently, he proposes to remedy this difficulty by replacing letters and symbols by examples derived from the religious law, and by changing or explaining the technical jargons hitherto used in treatises on logic. Ibn Hazm does not give an inkling about the works of his Islamic predecessors where such a difficulty of presentation occurs. However, he often refers to the Ancients *(awa'il)* and predecessors *(mutaqaddimun)* without specifying who they were.[113] On the other hand, he mentions the Greek source of logic and its two leading paragons: Aristotle and Porphyry.[114] Ibn Hazm also calls attention to the deficiency of translations of works on logic without specifying again any particular translation. In sum, Ibn Hazm intends to rewrite the works of Artistotle and Porphyry with no apparent objective, except simplification in order to put an end to "the complication in translation, and to the presentation of this science with an uncommon expressions."[115] Another principal objective of his is to correct the apprehension of people toward the discipline, to expose the error and the myopic attitude of its opponents, who "have been asserting confidently through vicious assumptions and without any certainty that can be arrived at on the basis of research that philosophy and the rules of logic contradict the religious law. Thus, our main purpose, intention and knowledge are to illuminate this darkness."[116]

On the whole, Ibn Hazm succeeded in bringing out a lucid treatment of logic remaining faithful to Porphyry's *Eisagoge* and Aristotle's *Organon* with respect to format and content. However, he often digressed refuting the methodology of theologians and jurists with respect to imitation *(taqlid)*, analogical reasoning *(qiyas)*, and other means.[117] For the rest, he shows a great enthusiasm for logic and considers it an invaluable science having an indispensable application for all the sciences. To him, logic *('ilm al-mantiq)* is the interpretation *('ibarah)* of all the sciences.[118] He assigns to it a prominent place in his classification of the sciences, and divides it into rational and sensory: the rational consisting of metaphysical and natural, and the sensory consisting of the natural only.[119] He also assigns to it a prominent place in the curriculum, and urges the student to pursue it as soon as he has a knowledge of reading, writing, grammar, lexicography, some poetry, number and astronomy. It is significant to note that Ibn Hazm places logic in the curriculum before the pursuit of the religious sciences. He emphasizes its utility in that logic will enable the student to have a knowledge of genera, species, simple expressions, propositions, premises, and conclusion, thus, preparing him to know what is proof *(burhan)* and what is contention; it will also enable the individual to avoid what is believed to be a proof, but is not. It is through logic that the individual will arrive at the reality of things, and will discern falsehood without any shred of doubt.[120] It is through it that proof can be ascertained regarding creation and the certainty of the existence of a sole Creator.[121] Moreover, logic is the best weapon in disputation and debate *(al-munazarah wa-l-jadal)* for combating and exposing sophistry and contention.[122] It is also useful in Qur'anic studies, Traditions, denominations, grammar, lexicography, poetry, rhetoric and, particularly, in legal opinions *(futya)* concerning lawful, unlawful, obligatory, and permissible acts. In sum, it is helpful in understanding all things on which God legislates, on their meanings, designations, homonyms, and synonyms. "In consequence, all experts should know that the individual who does not understand the value of logic is removed from what the Almighty God and His Prophet — May God's prayer and peace be upon him — had prescribed; that such an individual should not be permittd to pass legal judgment between two individuals because of his ignorance of definitions of words *(hudud al-kalam)*, their structure, the formulation of premises, and of drawing conclusions on which rests the proof that is always certain; nor he will he be able to discern between true and false premises."[123]

To Ibn Hazm, logic is measured by the degree of its utility, which is enormous having an immediate and broad application. However important and useful, the pursuit of logic for its own sake would be a futile endeavour, since logic is essentially a means to an end: "To those who attain the fundamentals of logic and claim expertise in it, we say: "You have acquired a knowledge that has no benefit except within the framework of the rest of the sciences. You are like the one who gathered materials for building, but failed to use them for that purpose, thus, leaving them idle and meaningless."[124] In other words, logic ought to be put into practice in conformity with its true objective, that is, serving the rest of the sciences.

In addition, Ibn Hazm devotes ample space refuting the arguments of the opponents of logic. The following passages reveal his thinking. To the question that the ancestors *(salaf)* did not cultivate, or have any need for logic, Ibn Hazm retorts:

> "If an ignoramus were to ask us: "Did anyone of the pious ancestors deal with this discipline?" The answer will be that this science is imbedded in the soul of anyone who possesses understanding *(lubb)*. The bright intellect can arrive at the utility of this science in proportion to the degree of understanding God has provided him. The tailed *(munkasi')* ignoramus is like the blind person and you have to caution him. This is true of all the sciences. None of the pious ancestors — may God be pleased with them — dealt with grammatical questions. However, when ignorance became rampant among people owing to the use of different vowels that denoted different meanings in the language, scholars wrote books on grammar, eliminating thereby the wrong use of voweling. This was very helpful for understanding the utterances of God — may He be glorified and exalted — and those of His Prophet — may God's prayer and peace be upon Him. The writing of grammar was truly a good deed by scholars, who will receive their reward. The same is true regarding the composition of books on lexicography and jurisprudence.

> "The pious ancestors did not have any need for all that for the simple reason that God provided them with virtue and the advantage of witnessing Prophecy with their own eyes. However, those who followed them were poverty stricken regarding all that. In consequence, it emerges as a matter of common sense that the shortcomings of those who do not study or read those books [grammar, lexicography, jurisprudence] are quite apparent. In fact they are like animals. This is also true regarding logic. For he who ignores logic will not be able to see the composition of the utterances of God — may He be glorified and exalted — nor that of His Prophet — may God's prayer and peace be upon him. Surely confusion will take place to a point that he will not differentiate between it and the truth, nor will he know his religion except by imitation, which is blameworthy."[125]

Ibn Hazm rebukes three major groups in order to clarify his point regarding the validity of logic:

> "There is one group which condemns books on logic without having any information about their purpose and meaning and without having read them. They maintain that they contain unbelief and lead to heresey... We find it extremely rewarding to eliminate this falsehood from their perplexed souls which judge before ascertaining, consent without knowledge, and jump to conclusion without proof..."[126]

"There is a second group which considers these books [on logic] to be a laughing matter and idle talk. As a rule, the majority of people are quick to oppose things of which they are ignorant and to denigrate what they do not know. As a result, we have also deemed it an act of piety to explain the merit of the discipline, and made it easily understood to those unaware of its scope...

"In the third group are people who have read books on logic, but with an unbalanced understanding, sickening inclination, and short-sightedness. Their hearts are impregnated with a cistern of scorn; they sail the ship of incapacity, contaminate the transmission of the law, accept the ignoramuses, and claim that they understand everything when in reality they are of all people the farthest removed from logic or any knowledge of it...

"In the fourth group are people who perceive things with clear intelligence and wholesome thinking, who are removed from any inclination and have sound minds. The people were enlightened by logic, understand its objective, and are guided by its lighthouse. The unity of God is reaffirmed among them with the necessary proofs, which are there. They also see the division of the created things, the impact of the Creator on them and His management of them. They find these lofty books [on logic] a pious friend, counseling confidant, and a true companion who does not give up in adversity and who can always be found in time of distress. Moreover, whenever they undertake any branch of knowledge, they will find these books *[on logic]* lying before and with them."[127]

It is because of the maladies *(balaya)* that affect the masses that Ibn Hazm resolved to compose his book in a simple language and to call attention to the value of logic, not only on its owm merit but as an indispensable ancillary to all the sciences—hoping thereby to facilitate its understanding to people of all walks of life. He considers it a duty to share and disseminate the knowledge of logic by all means possible: through popularization, prediction in the streets and assemblies, financial support and rewards for those who pursue and acquire the knowledge of logic. This notwithstanding, Ibn Hazm reflects that not all people are capable of pursuing logic, which he compares to a strong drug. If such a drug is taken by a healthy and strong person, it will benefit him enormously; but if taken by a sick and weakling individual, it will increase his malady and will lead even to death. He says:

"When we became aware of all that and the harm that leads to those maladies we have mentioned, we concluded that the difficulty lies in the translation and in the use of uncommon expressions, which are employed in them. Furthermore, not every concept *(fahm)* has the appropriate expression. In consequence, we sought the help of God — may He be glorified and exalted — to help us write within the limits of our ability, a work explaining meanings in simple and easy expressions in order to facilitate — God-willing — their understanding by the average person, the elite, the knowledgeable, and the ignorant as well...[128]

"For, indeed, the task of the individual who befriends knowledge and knows its virtue is to endeavor to make it, to the best of his ability, familiar and as light as humanly possible. This should be done even if it were possible for him to rush with knowledge into the open road, call for it in the public streets, and call out for it in the roving assemblies. Were it also possible for him, he should grant money to its students, reward the one who acquires it, increase the reward for its seekers, and increase the station of those engaged in it. Doing all that patiently, with toil and trouble, will constitute a great fortune, an excellent deed, a noble and gratifying endeavor...

"We have found these books [on gloic] to be a strong drug, which, if taken by a person with strong health, sound nature, firm composition, and good mixture, will benefit him, will purify his constitution will strengthen his senses, and will straighten his condition. On the other hand, if it is taken by a sick person whose mixture is disturbed and whose constitution is frail, it will overcome him, increase his malady, and perhaps, will cause him to perish and die. The same is true with these books on logic. If they are consulted by an intelligent and perceptive person — and however he may change or act — they will never ceases to benefit him and render him a luminous guidance, shining clarity, success in every science he may undertake, and good things in the Hereafter and now. On the other hand, if they are consulted by a simple-minded man, they will paralyze him; and if consulted by a man of weary understanding, they will make him stupid and perplexed. All in all, each individual should partake according to his ability. Our success rests with God alone — may He be glorified and exalted."[129]

Ibn Hazm's strong plea for the importance of logic as a tool for establishing proof *(burhan),* besides his defense of it against the onslaught of its opponents, mainly, the religious scholars, permeates the pages of his *Taqrib,* a summary-analysis of which follows:

A Summary-Analysis of the *Taqrib*

The following paragraphs were intended to give a general idea about the manner in which Ibn Hazm approached logic indicating some of the innovative ways introduced within the framework of Aristotelian logic and the works of his Muslim predecessors.

A summary-analysis of his *Taqrib,* a work of logic, reveals that Ibn Hazm was a major logician to be reckoned with. In fact, logic appears to permeate most of his works in that he often give preference to the use of Aristotlian (syllogism) over the dialectical method of arguments and counter-arguments of the theologians. This tendency appears early in his works which indicates that the *Taqrib* was composed at an early stage of his career by about the same time he composed his literary masterpiece, the *Tawq,* and his literary anthology, the *Fadl al-Andalus* — both of which were written in all probability between 1025 and 1030.[130] However, his reference to the *Fisal* in his *Taqrib*[131] and to the *Taqrib* in his *Fisal*[132] poses a problem of chronology as to which precedes the other. A plausible answer may be found in that the *Fisal,* being a large composition and consisting of a multiplicity of subjects, may have been written during a long span of time, which justifies such a cross reference.

In view of his passionate defense of logic and of his many references to it in his major works,[133] it is easy to assume that logic had an enormous impact on the formation of his intellectual perspective. On the other hand, it is difficult to determine the extent of the dissemination of the *Taqrib* and its possible impact on Arabic logic. Although the majority of Ibn Hazm's biographers cite the *Taqrib* as one of his principal works, they often denigrate it, with the exception of al-Humaydi (d. 1095), Ibn Hazm's pupil, who says: *"Facilitating the Definition of Logic and Introduction Thereto* is written in popular language with juridical examples. He undertook the task of elucidating it, eliminating misconception about it, and refuting the lies of swindlers concerning it. As far as we know, no one before him had written such a work in this manner."[134]

On the other hand, his contemporary Sa'id (d. 1070) of Toledo says that Ibn Hazm, "concerned himself with the science of logic, and composed a book on it which he called *Facilitating the Definition of Logic.* He was prolix explaining the manner of attaining knowledge and using extensive juridical examples drawn from the religious law. He differed from Aristotle, the founder of this science, with respect to some of the fundamentals of logic in the way of the one who did not understand Aristotle's aim, nor having accepted this book. For this reason, his book was full of mistakes."[135] Another contemporary, the historian Ibn Hayyan (d. 1075), reiterates the statement adding that Ibn Hazm,"has written many books on logic and philosophy which are full of mistakes and rubbish. This is so, because of his audacity of delving into these sciences, specially logic."[136] These statements by two of Ibn Hazm's contemporaries were incorporated almost verbatim by Ibn Sa'id al-Maghribi (d. 1274),[137] and the Eastern scholars: Yaqut (d. 1348), Qifti (d. 1248),[139] Ibn Khallikan (d. 1282),[140] and Dhahabi (d. 1348).[141]

This general antagonism to the work must be understood within the context of Ibn Hazm's tense relationship with the religious scholars, whom he attacked vehemently, and who in turn declared him heretic and frowned upon his works. Thus, it emerges clearly that his biographers simply incoroprated the statement of a contemporary without scrutiny, and without having had a first hand information about the actual content and purpose of the *Taqrib.* Moreover,they failed to take into account Ibn Hazm's commitment to and defense of the philosophical sciences in general, and his insistence of reconciling them with the religious sciences, in particular. As a result, such a negative evaluation remained uncontested for centuries, and even continued current among modern scholars,[142] some of whom were to dismiss the value of the work and to attribute to al-Ghazzali (d. 1111) some of its innovative approach, mainly, popularizing the discipline and providing it with new examples and new terminology.[143] These notions, however, became outmoded with the publication of the *Taqrib* in 1959, by Ihsan 'Abbas, who edited it on the basis of a manuscript of the Zaytunah Mosque of Tunis (Ahmadiyyah Collection, no. 6814).

Ibn Hazm starts the *Taqrib* with a preamble refuting the opponents of logic, indicating its importance and the reasons behind writing the work.[144] After these preliminaries, he procceds with a systematic treatment of logic following Porphyry's *Eisagoge* and Aristotle's *Organon*.

I. Porphyry's *Eisagoge* (Madkhal)

Ibn Hazm attaches a great importance to the *Eisagoge,* and remains faithful to its subject matter concentrating on the *quinque voces* (the five terms) : genus *(jins),* species *(naw'),* difference *(fasl).* particular *(khassah),* and accident *('arad).* He places a great emphasis on definition *(hadd)* and description *(rasm),* and considers them the key *(miftah)* of the whole book. He takes up attribution *(haml)* and subject *(wad'),* and shows the difference separating substance *(jawhar)* and accident maintaining that they constitute the two and only categories of existing things. He elaborates on these notions by examining the nature of sound *(sawt),* as having or lacking a meaning. Meaningless sounds are such as those uttered by a parrot, or any other animal,[145] while meaningful sounds are expressions *(alfaz)* designating existing things by themselves, or qualifying other things, that is, they denote either a substance, or an accident.[146] Here Ibn Hazm establishes a great difference between substance and accident maintaining that substance exists by itself independently of anything else, while an accident does not and is dependent on something else. Substance and accident apply to all God's creation, except God Himself, Who is neither a subject, nor an attribute.[147] Similarly, all things, except God, are determined in two ways: either by a definition *(hadd)* specifying the nature of a thing, or by a description *(rasm)* differentiating a thing from another. This difference is important in Ibn Hazm's view, for it facilitates mutual understanding. Thus, attempting to obscure the true intent of expressions is the occupation of babblers, stupid and ignorant people.[148]

Ibn Hazm proceeds to explain the principal terms of *Eisagoge*. Genus encompasses two or more species - being substance the highest genus *(jins al-ajnas)* that can be applied to all things.[149] Species, called *surah* by the ancients in conformity with the linguistic usage in Greek, is a substratum of genus comprising a group of things that agree in definition and description. Species in its various kinds *(naw al-anwa')* have in common a single definition, a single nature, and the same differentiation, but differ in accidents only.[150] Below the species are individual things *(ashkhas).*[151] Thus, all created things are classified under genera, species, and things -- being difference *(fasl),* particular *(khassah),* and accident *('arad)* mere attributes *(sifat)*. Thus difference is the differentiation of one nature from another, or a distinction between one species and another; the particular is equal to what is particularized and constitutes a definition thereof; and accident applies to and differentiates species, generea and individual things, but its absence does not constitute the disappearance of the thing which it qualifies.[152]

II. Aristotle's *Organon*

Ibn Hazm adheres closely to Aristotle's *Organon* with respect to arrangement and content. However, he reduces the eight headings of the *Organon* into five, but lumping *Qiyas,, jadal* and *safsatah* under the heading of *burhan,* which constitutes the core of his system. His arrangement follows:

1. *al-Asma' al-mufradah* (Categories)

Ibn Hazm explains this coinage as corresponding to the Greek Qatighuriyas and to the Arabic *Maqulat* consisting of ten expressions. He divides the Book into two sections: one dealing with simple expressions, and the other with the different parts of speech. Simple expressions comprise: unequivocal words *(al-asma' al-mutawati'ah,* equivocal *(al-asma' al-mukhtalifah),* homonyms *(al-asma' al-mushtarakah)* synonyms *(al-asma' al-mutaradifah),* and derived words *(al-asma' al-mushtaqqah).* Speech consists of independent words conveying more than one thing, and consisting of five kinds; a proposition *(khabar),* inquiry *(istikhbar),* exclamation *(nida'),* desire *(raghbah),* and command *(amr).* The last four kinds do not admit of truth or falsity, while a proposition does.

Ibn Hazm then proceeds with a lengthy discussion of the ten expressions: substance *(jawhar),* quantity *(kammiyyah),* quality *(kayfiyyah),* relation *(idafah),* time *(zaman),* place *(makan),* position *(nusbah),* possession *(milk),* action *(fa'il),* and passion *(munfa'il).*[153] He concludes with a discussion of "similar", "opposite", "Contradictory", and contrasting statements, and takes issue with some of his predecessors with regard to the misuses of certain expressions, or misinterpretation of fundamental principles. He says that theologians had misused the word *qadamah* when applying *qadim* to God when He actually is the First.[154] Similarly, the Ancients also erred by maintaining that the genus precedes the species arguing that it is impossible that the whole could precede its parts. The same can be said about cause and effect *(al-'illah wa-l-ma'lul),* which are simultaneous and inseparable.[155] He concludes discussing motion and its various kinds.

2. *Kitab al-akhbar* (Hermeneutics).

Ibn Hazm says that it corresponds to the Greek Bari Arminiyas, but does not mention the Arabic equivalent, *'Ibarah,* often used by some of his Muslim predecessors.[156] He says that the term *akhbar* (pl. of *khabar)* was used by the grammarians in the sense of predicate, and by the historians in the sense of information.[157] However, he hardly mentions that the term was used by some of his Muslim predecessors in its meaning as a proposition. He reiterates a previous statement that *khabar* is the only part of speech that can be either true, or false.[151] Specifically, the Book deals with parts of speech: noun *(ism)* verb *(kalimah)*, called *nu'ut* by grammarians and *sifat* (attributes) by theologians; statement *(qawl)* expressing a complete thought; and elements *('anasir)* conveying what is obligatory, permissible, possible, or impossible. He concludes with a discussion of the different kinds of propositions *(qadaya,* pl. of *qadiyah):* affirmative *(mujibah),* negative *(nafiyah),*[159] conditional *(shartiyyah),* determinate *(dhat al-aswar),*[160] indeterminate *(muhmalah),* special *(makhsusah),* and a qualifier *(sur),*[161] that is, a proposition introduced by "every", "each", and the like.

3,4,5,6. Kitab al-burhan (Apodictics).

It corresponds to the Afudiqtiqa, or the Fourth Book of the *Organon*, which establishes the criteria for demonstration. As such, it occupies an important place in the *Organon* and in Ibn Hazm's *Taqrib* as well. In fact, Ibn Hazm gives *burhan* precedence over *qiyas* (Analytics) in so far as it was used by Muslim jurists and theologians, who are believed to have carried *qiyas* to the extreme and with unyielding results, thus, causing heated controversies and division in Islam. Moreover, he does not believe that *qiyas* possesses the rigor and precision of syllogism and, as such, could serve as a substitute for *burhan,* which is alone the surest way to certainty. This notwithstanding, he remained faithful to the format of the *Organon,* and provided ample room for *qiyas, Sophistics,* and *Disputatio,* but not without expressing grave reservations concerning their validity:

"We combined in this part of our work the things contained in Aristotle's Third Book on logic called *Anulutikiya* (Analytics), his Fourth Book called *Afudiqtika* (apodictics) to correspond to them since the object of both is to elucidate the manner and conditions of proof. . . We have also added to it Aristotle's Fifth Book called *Tubiqa* (Topics) dealing with disputatio, to which we added the conditions that are indispensable for disputants seeking the realities of things. Essentially, this book deals with the conditions of establishing the proof and things ancillary to it.

We have also added Aristotle's Sixth Book called *Sufistiya* (sic) (Sofistics) dealing with the quality of wranglers, who turn away from the realities of things, and advocate the triumph of ignorance and jugglery. The reason for such inclusion is that it is necessary for the seekers of the realities of things to know the quality of such people and be prepared for them."[162]

Although Ibn Hazm considers analogical reasoning, and sophistry as false methods for establishing the realities of things, he reasons that ignoring them would do a great violence for establishing the proof. "For our object is to establish the proof and to correct the manner of demonstration *(tashih al-istidlal)* in all differences and disagreements occurring among disputants."[163]

To Ibn Hazm, the essential ingredients of proof are: proper demonstration, definition, and the proper formulation of syllogism *(jami'ah)*. Ibn Hazm attaches enormous importance to establishing the proof through syllogism which consists of two propositions*(qadiyatan)* or premisses *(muqaddamatan)*, and a conclusion *(natijah)*.[165] A single proposition does not convey more than what it contains, and constitutes a union *(qarinah)* when combined with another proposition. He devotes ample space to the different kinds of arriving at the proof *(ashkal al-burhan)*,[165] pointing to the validity,[166] or fallacy of propositions.[167] Unlike his predecessors, he makes ample use of propositions bearing on the religious law for arriving at legal decisions.[168] He also delves into the theory of the acquisition of knowledge concluding that truth and falsehood are absolute terms not admitting any degree of intensity: "It is impossible that a truth could be truer than another truth, or a falsehood more false than another."[169] In all, while the senses, the intellect, and transmission *(naql)* may lead to a true knowledge the same cannot be said about *ilham* (divine inspiration) when claimed by people other than prophets.[170] And from the vantage point of logic, he conceives three methods of reasoning as invalid for establishing the proof. They are a) *qiyas,* b) *Safsatah,* and c) *al-jadal wa-l-munazarah.*

a). *Qiyas* (Analytics).

Ibn Hazm disavows *qiyas* from the vantage point of Islamic dogmatics and logic, pointing to its fallacy in that *qiyas* is the belief in a proof when actually there is none.[171] In fact, it was the object of heated controversies among Muslim jurists and theologians some supporting its use while others disavowing it. Its advocates used it profusely, and fell into enormous errors by arriving at the knowledge of the universal through the particular. While the religious scholars called it *qiyas,* the Ancients called it *istiqra'* (induction), who also misused it thereby arriving at the wrong conclusion. This is shown in their premise that an agent is a body, thus concluding, that the First Agent, which is God, is also a body.[172] Such a procedure is as bad as the method used by theologians and jurists which aims at arriving at the knowledge of the hidden on the basis of the visible *(al-istidlal bi-l-shahid 'ala al-gha'ib)*. This is utterly wrong, "because had its advocates done their research *(bahth),* they would have known that the hidden to the senses concerning existing things is not hidden to the intellect but is as manifest as that which is perceived by the senses, no more no less. . . Thus, there is no such hidden things concerning known things *(ma'lumat),* for that which is hidden to the intellect is impossible to be known."[173] Ibn Hazm illustrates his point saying that even the blind knows about the existence of colors in the same manner a person with sight does; and that people admit the existence of elephants, even if they had never seen one. He concludes: "As for the things, which are neither affirmed nor denied, by the nature of the intellect, we shall accept those if and when we find them, and we shall not interdict those which we cannot find.[174]

Another reprehensible method to Ibn Hazm is the following of one's appetites *(shahawat)* through the use of unbridled similarities *(mushtabahat)* whereby decisions are arrived at by attributing to God things not found in texts emanating from Him, but on the basis of similarity through the application of ordinances for specified things to unspecified things, thereby creating untold erosion in the application of the religious Law.[175] Similarly, Ibn Hazm ponders on the question of relationship between cause and effect *(al-'illah wa-l-ma'lul)*, and refutes those who maintain that cause must have an impelling reason for its effect. He argues that such a view would compromise God's intent, and would subject Him to strictures, for the Almighty acts voluntarily as He wishes, and does things for no cause. Aside from this religious consideration, Ibn Hazm conceives cause and effect intertwined and always acting interdependently: "It is impossible that a cause could ever be found in time without having an effect." This is true for both ordinary things and legal ordinances.[176]

After showing the flaws of *qiyas* in its various ramifications, Ibn Hazm concludes: "know that liberality *(musamahah)* in seeking the realities of things is absolutely inadmissible; there is either truth, or falsehood, and it is impossible that a thing can be true and false at one and the same time."[177] He maintains that there is no discrepancy between the religious ordinances and the way of proof *(burhan)*.[178] However, the analogists *(al-qayyasun)* had distorted the whole concept of *qiyas* converting it into trickery and sophistry:

"Know that the Ancients *(al-mutaqaddimun)* called the premises *qiyas;* then came the trickery of our brethern, the analogists, who used it as a sophistical and weak ruse for arbitrariness and sophistry. They called *qiyas* the arbitrary way reached through the reprehensible induction *(al-istiqra' al-madhmum)* arriving at decisions in the absence of scriptural texts in the same way as when texts exist; and they do so on the basis of certain similar features found in two different things."[179]

b. *Safsatah* (Sophistics)

Ibn Hazm considers sophistics as an extension of *qiyas,* and launches in the manner of Aristotle a vehement attack against it. Sophists *(ahl al-shaghab)* indulge in confusion and double talk with intent to deceive, and deviate people from the truth. Their method is built on false premises. He says: "Deception is the greatest weapon of the confounder and advocate of falsehood."[180] This deception may take place by affirming what cannot be affirmed; falsifying a syllogism; cleaving to a homonym; and particularizing or generalizing for things qualities applied to other things. He illustrates their method with copious examples, and concludes with reflections on the superiority of the intellect over the senses[181] for grasping the reality of things that can be attained with investigation alone,[182] and arrived at with the proper evidence.[183]

c. *al-jadal wa-l-munazarah* (Topics)

Ibn Hazm tackles *Disputatio* and debates against an Islamic background, but using the material in Aristotle's Topics. *Disputatio* and debates had became current in Islamic society and, at the same time controversial some supporting their validity while other opposing them, but always through the invocation of Prophetic Traditions. On his part, Ibn Hazm considered *disputatio* a praiseworthy endeavour as long as it follows a strict method of demonstration, and a rigorous set of rules that would govern all its aspects including the etiquette, qualifications, and the moral integrity of disputants. In so doing, he integrated Aristotlian logic with the hitherto unyielding Islamic dialectics that consisted of arguments, counterarguments, and conclusion, but remaining essentially apologetic and an *argumentum at hominem,* having the object of defending one's side and triumphing over the opponent.[184] Aware of these pitfalls, Ibn Hazm made use of logic, and insisted on thorough individual search *(ijtihad),* investigation *(bahth),* and evidence for establishing the truth regardless of the consequences.[185] In short, Ibn Hazm gives an unqualified support of *disputatio* that is based on rigorous rules,[186] and condemns trickery in debate, and fighting wrong with wrong.[187] He spells out the conditions governing debates; considers sheer ignorance the claim of those who purport to turn the true into false, and viceversa; warns against blind imitation of the Ancestors and over-reliance on reputable authorities;[188] and disavows obscurantism in debate concluding with an exaltation of knowledge and the pursuit of the sciences, which alone lead to establishing the realities of things.

4. *Kitab al-balaghah* (Rhetoric)

It corresponds to *Rituriqa,* the Seventh Book of the *Organon,* and to the Arabic *Khitabah* commonly used by Muslim logicians. It is a succinct treatment of Rhetoric, with general reference to Aristotle, Qudamah b. Ja'far,[189] Hasan al-Basri,[190] Sahl b. Harun,[191] Ibn al-Muqaffa',[192] and Ibn Shuhayd.[193] Ibn Hazm says that a knowledge of rhetoric requires two or more sciences, and its merit resides in avoiding excessive use of rare expressions, and in making things understood by both the average person and the elite.[194]

5. *Kitab al-shi'r* (Poetics)

It also consists of a brief treatment calling attention to the works of Qudamah b. Ja'far and of Abu 'Ali al-Hatimi for further information. He simply says that all things contain some elements of truthfulness except those expressed by a slanderer or a poet, adding that the ingredients of poetry are three: craftmanship *(sina'ah),* innate ability *(tab'),* and excellence *(bara'ah).*[195]

On the whole, the format and content of the *Taqrib* conform to those of Aristole's *Oreganon.* The inclusion of Porphyry's *Eisagoge* as an Introduction *(madkhal)* appears to have been optional among Ibn Hazm's Muslim predecessors, as the following table shows:

	Kindi[196]	Khuwar-izmi[197]	Farabi[198]	Ibn al-Nadim[199]	Ibn Hazm
I. Porphyry's *Eisagoge*	---	*Madkhal*	---	---	*Madkhal*
II. Aristotle's *Organon*					
1. Categories	*Maqulat*	*Maqulat*	*Maqulat*	*Maqulat*	*al-Asma' al-mufradah*
2. Hermeneutics	*Tafsir*	*Tafsir*	*'Ibarah*	*'Ibarah*	*Akhbar*
3. Analytics	*'Aks*	*'Aks*	*Qiyas*	*Tahlil al-qiyas*	*Burhan:* a. *qiyas* b. *Safsatah* c. *jadal*
4. Apodictics	*Idahah*	*Idah*	*Burhan*	*Burhan*	---
5. Topics	*jadaliyah*	*jadal*	*jadaliyah*	*jadal*	---
6. Sophistics	*Mughalatah* ı	*Tahakkum*	*al-Hikmah al-mumawwahah*	*Mughalitun*	---
7. Rhetoric	*Balaghah*	*Khitabah*	*Khitabah*	*Khitabah*	*Balaghah*
8. Poetics	*Shi'r*	*Shi'r*	*Shi'r*	*Shi'r*	*Shi'r*

While Ibn Hazm compresses the Eight Books of Aristotle's *Organon* into Five Books remaining faithful to its content, he adds numerous examples drawn from everyday experience and the religious law. His choice of terminology for the different books appears to have been derived for the most part from primitive terminology such as *balaghah* (rhetoric) which had been used by the philosopher al-Kindi. He also appears to rely on some of al-Farabi's explanation who referred to the *maqulat* as *mufradat* and to the *'ibarah* as *aqwal basitah*. He also appears to have been influenced by the grammarians in the use of *khabar* (predicate of a nominal clause).[200] Moreover, the significance attached to proof *(burhan)* was already echoed by Al-Farabi who considered it as having precedence and primacy over the rest of the *Oreganon* since the object of logic is to accomplish the goal of *burhan* being all the rest of the *Organon* mere ancillaries to it with the first three books serving as preliminaries and the following four books as aid and tool.[201] As a result, Ibn Hazm disavows *qiyas* as used among religious scholars; condemns Sophistics altogether; elevate *disputatio* to the level of *burhan*,[202] and makes provisions for rhetoric and poetics with a modicum of tolerance.

A further distinctive feature of the *Taqrib* is the careful attention given to definition *(hadd)* of terms, which he considers paramount. He often goes at great length elucidating terms, and giving their equivalents in logic, grammar and theology. He says that the word *kalimah* is meant "verb" to the philosopher, attributes *(nu'ut)* to the grammarian, and qualities *(sifat)* to the theologian.[203] He often gives Greek equivalents to Arabic terminology:

two premises *(qadiyatan)* and a conclusion *(natijah)* are called *sullugismus* in Greek and *(jami'ah)* in Arabic.[204] He finds Latin better equipped language than Arabic for discerning the difference between quality and quantity.[205] Finally, he gives new terminology to hitherto used Arabic terms, when these appear to him obscure or misleading. He says that the term *did* (contrary) and *naqid* (contradictory) hitherto used by predecessors *(mutaqaddimun)* tend to lead to confusion and, for this reason, he proposes *nafi 'amm,* or *naqid 'amm* for universal denial, and *nafi khass* or *naqid khass* for particular denial.[206] He also replaces *kull* (universal) and *juz'* (particular) by *'amm* and *khass,* respectively.[207]

In conclusion, an examination of his *Taqrib* and other statements on logic in his other works show that Ibn Hazm had a great insight into, a grasp of, and a deep commitment to logic. He appreciated the value of logic for demonstrating the realities of things in both the secular and religious fields. He appears quite conversant in the works of Aristotle and Porphyry whom he considers the paragons of the discipline, and often refers to his Muslim predecessors *(al-mutaqaddimun)* but without specifying who they were. As a result, he emerges not only as a knowledgeable and enthusiastic logician, but a staunch defender of the discipline against attacks by co-religionists. He makes it crystal clear that there is nothing wrong with the discipline *per se*, but perhaps in the manner it had been presented by predecessors. Consequently, he proposed to present it in an easy language thereby eliminating the confusion surrounding it. Thus, he hoped that his co-religionists will cease opposing it and would begin to appreciate its value even in religious matters.

In this connection, Ibn Hazm was in full agreement with his Islamic predecessors - the philosphers-scientists - and at great odd with the religious scholars, who looked upon the philosophical sciences in general with great mistrust. This position was consistent with his conception of the sciences, their relationship, and their interdependence, which he articulated in his *Maratib al-'ulum.* Here as elsewhere, he disavowed the dichotomy of views separating the philosopher and the religious scholar, called for their harmonization, and insisted on offering a combined curriculum that would do justice to both the secular and religious sciences. He conceives this to be the only sure way that would lead to a true comprehension of the physical world and the divine mission of Muhammad.

Moreover, Ibn Hazm complains not only about the onslaught against logic, but about those who accused him of heresy for having been an avid reader of the books of the Ancients *(kutub al-awa'il)*,[208] and about those who denigrated his works without having read them.[209] This antagonism to the man and his works is also reflected by the majority of his biographers, who also acknowledged his wide erudition. Under the circumstances, it is difficult to gauge the impact of his works on succeeding generations. This notwithstanding, it is significant to note that Ibn Hazm's conception of logic, and his attempt at simplifying and popularizing it should coincide with those of the Eastern theologian al-Ghazzali (d. 1111), who attempted in his *Mihakk* and *Mi'yar* to show not only the invaluable utility of logic, but to make it easy and palatable to a large audience through simplification and the use of examples drawn from the religious law.[210] Finally, Ibn Hazm was a towering figure in an Andalusian context, and a worthy predecessor of his compatriots - the great philosophers Ibn Bajjah (d. 1138), Ibn Tufayl (d. 1181), and Ibn Rushd (d. 1198),[213] who gave the intellect and demonstrative reasoning a deserving place in the search for the truth.[214] Moreover, there is no indication that anyone in al-Andalus before the time of Ibn Hazm had attempted to defend the discipline publicly. His successors - Abu-l-Salt of Denia, Ibn Bajjah, Ibn Tufayl and Ibn Rushd do not appear to speak for the discipline as forthrightly as Ibn Hazm did. Not until more than a century and a half after the death of Ibn Hazm did Ibn Tumlus (d. 1223) of Alcira write his treatise on logic, defending it in language similar to that used by Ibn Hazm. Ibn Tumlus was appalled by the neglect of logic by the scholars of his day and by their simultaneous antagonism toward and ignorance of it.[215]

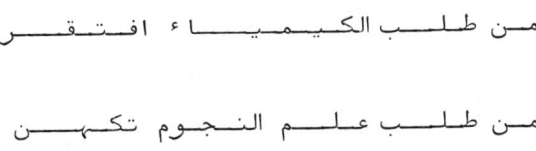

IX. THE SPURIOUS SCIENCES

The spurious sciences consisting of sorcery, magic, divination, talisman, alchemy, and astrology were not only pursued in Islam, but found no small a place among the legitimate sciences even among some great thinkers of Islam. The Brethren of Purity, Ibn al-Nadim and Ibn Khaldun, among others, made provision for them in the division of the sciences. Thus, by the time of Ibn Hazm in the eleventh century, they appeared so common that Ibn Hazm felt impelled to make reference to them and to call attention not only to their spuriousness but to the enormous harm they could inflict on religious beliefs and practices. In fact, Ibn Hazm took special care of pointing out that sorcery, magic, talisman, alchemy, and astrology are blameworthy sciences not only because they lead to corrupt morals, dissipation, and deceit, but most importantly because they are based on false premises, lack a scientific method, and lack proof.[1] "Know, may God give you success, whomever you see espousing music, melody, and talisman is a swindler, liar, and shameless juggler. The same is true for the one who busies himself in alchemy, for he has added to these blameworthy qualities we have mentioned the greed for robbing people of their money, for making forfeit money lawful, and for inflicting injustice on people with whom he deals.[2]

This statement was made in a society in which most of these subjects not only found a place in the divisions of the sciences, but exerted portentous influence in Islamic culture. They were controversial disciplines, with staunch advocates and opponents. Although music was not totally sanctioned by the religious law, it flourished and had an enormous literature.[3] Alchemy, an offshoot of chemistry, appears to have had an early start[4] and was pursued earnestly by philosophers such as al-Kindi and al-Farabi. Likewise, astrology made its inroads into the courts and high places, where the astrologers occupied a prominent place, often deciding the outcomes of wars even before they had been fought. Sorcery, talisman, and magic remained in the folklore of the people, and served as entertainment, creating wonders and excitement.[5]

a. Music

Without discussing the merit of music as a valid science, Ibn Hazm does not provide for it in the categorization of the sciences, nor does he consider it one of the seven basic philosophical sciences to which Ibn Khaldun refers.[6] In fact, he appears to condemn it by considering it conjectural, particularly three kinds of music which create artificial states in the individual - making the cowardly person courageous, making the avaricious magnificent, or making the soul either friendly or repulsive.[7]

This position is quite a departure from that of his predecessors, who considered music to be a legitimate and viable science under the rubric of philosophy and the subheading of mathematics. Ibn Hazm passes over this precedent in silence. However, he could not wholly ignore music in his own environment and had to face the issue from the vantage point of the religious law. In his short treatise on singing,[8] he poses the question whether entertainment and singing are permissible or forbidden. After quoting some Traditions pro and con, he concludes that these Traditions condemning singing because it creates hypocrisy and because the voice of a songstress is considered cursed as that of a wailing women are not authentic. Thus, singing, amusement, and dancing are permissible during the feast breaking the Ramadan fast *('id al-fitr)* and during the feast of Immolation *('id al-adha)*, even if conducted in the mosque.[9] Furthermore, singing is commendable if the intent is to animate the soul and to strengthen it for obeying God, and if the singer has the purpose of attaining piety. In addition, singing is permissible even if the singer does not intend to obey God. In this case, the singer may be foolish, but he is definitely dissolute if he sings for disobeying God.[10]

Similar regulations are applied to musical instruments. Lutes *('idan)*, wind instruments *(ma'azif)*, pipes *(mazamir)*, and drums *(tanabir)* may be used, purchased, and sold.[11] Their use however, should be constructive and not mere pasttime. The training and purchasing of singing girls, are also lawful. As for other amusements, he condones the use, purchase, and sale of chess *(shitranj)*,[12] but condemns the game of chance *(maysir)*[13] and the use, purchase, and sale of backgammon.[14]

b. Alchemy

Some leading Muslim scientists and philosophers wrote on alchemy, considering it a legitimate science and within the realm of possibility. In fact, some of them were enthusiastic alchemists. The philosopher al-Kindi is reported to have been a practitioner of alchemy and wrote treatises on the subject. He was followed, among others, by his pupil al-Sarakhsi, al-Farabi, and Ibn Sina, who also wrote about alchemy and practiced it, in addition al-Farabi and Ibn Sina included chemistry in their divisions of the sciences. In al-Andalus proper, the scientist al-Majriti (d. ca. 1007), to whom is attributed the *Rutbat al-hakim*[15] on alchemy, appears to have practiced alchemy. He had enthusiastic pupils in Abu Bakr Ibn Bishrun[16] and Asbagh Ibn Muhammad Ibn al-Samh (d. 1035), who also wrote on the subject. It would be interesting to know the attitude of Ibn al-Kattani, Ibn Hazm's teacher, toward the discipline. In the absence of information, it cannot be ascertained whether or not Ibn Hazm was echoing his views.

To Ibn Hazm, alchemy leads not only to swindling, lies, insolence, forgery, and depravity, but "is void and nonexistent, and has never been proved valid even for one single hour. This is so because it is absolutely impossible to convert one species *(naw')* into another. Moreover, there is no difference between converting copper and gold, and between converting a man into a donkey and vice versa. This is the case for all species, because it is absolutely impossible to convert one species into another.[17] There is no point in occupying oneself with a nonexistent science; the individual should pursue a science which can be learned and from which benefit can be derived.

Significantly, the great sociologist Ibn Khaldun (d.1406) reiterates the substance of Ibn Hazm's views. After defining the purpose of alchemy and giving a historical sketch of its development with reference to its major leaders in East and West.[18] Ibn Khaldun observes that most of the expressions used by alchemists "tend to secret hints and puzzles, scarcely to be explained or understood., This is proof that alchemy is not a natural craft.[19] He continues that alchemy is in the realm of miracles or, at best, sorcery[20] pursued by people who are unable to make a living and who are prompted by greed.[21] In spite of the numerous attempts, alchemists have failed to create gold and have forged official coins, thus cheating people with impunity.[22] After mentioning the arguments of al-Farabi and Ibn Sina in its favor, Ibn Khaldun concludes, "We, however, have another starting point for refuting the alchemists. It shows that the existence of alchemy is impossible and that the assumptions of all (who defend alchemy), not only Tughra'i and Avicenna, are wrong."[23]

c. Astrology *(Ahkam al-nujum, or al-qada' bi-l-kawakib)*

Ibn Hazm mentions astrology as a part of the science of stars,[24] and devotes ample space to it in his *Maratib* as well as in his *Fisal*. He conceives astrology to be futile and useless, opposing the view held be leading predecessors such as the philosophers al-Kindi, al-Farabi, and Ibn Sina, who wrote various works on the subject.[25] Al-Farabi[26] saw it as a branch of astronomy and defined it as the science of the signs concerned with what will happen in the future. In contrast, Ibn Hazm distinguishes between astronomy and astrology: astronomy leads to knowledge of the marvel of creation and its Creator, whereas astrology, a pseudo science is based on claims and experience *(tajribah)* that are impossible to verify. He says, "The influence of the stars is false because it lacks proof; it consists of claims only. We cannot reckon on the basis of our observation the many lies concerning the decisions of the astrologers. And if you wish to verify this yourself, try, for you will find that the majority of those decisions are like those of the magician and the soothsayer as to accuracy, no more and no less."[27] After this outright condemnation of astrology, Ibn Hazm refutes several other notions about the nature of the stars and their motion. Those who maintain that the stars are rational beings and the managers of the cosmos with or without God are polytheists and unbelievers, because such a claim is unfounded.[28] And to the contention that the circular movements of the stars are the most perfect, he demands proof, inquiring why a circular movement should be better than a rectilinear one, or why a motion from west to east should be better than repose? To him, these are mere allegations, but those who uphold the view that the stars are the managers of the world with or without God should be given capital punishment as prescribed by the religious law.[29]

On the other hand, those who believe that the stars are created and lack intelligence but who insist that the stars have influence on the course of events are not unbelievers but in error. To Ibn Hazm, they are misled by certain experience, such as the occurence of the high and low tides which take place when the moon is half and full and passing through the meridian. This kind of occurrence has nothing to do with the predetermination or influence of the stars and can be verified by the senses; the same is true of the impact of the rays of the moon on the growth of squash, cucumbers and hair. Similarly, the rays of the sun exert an influence on the humor of the eyes of cats at different hours of the day. All this is verifiable and must be accepted. Only those things beyond verification must be rejected.[30]

Ibn Hazm argues that for an experiment to be valid and to have a universal acceptability, it ought to have the same result through repeated experiments — hence, the soul can confirm the result in the same manner it confirms that if a man stays under water for three hours, he will surely die. If this kind of experiment is repeated again and again, the result will be the same.[31] This is not the case with experiments related to the influence of the stars. If at all possible, they will take hundreds of years to be verified. Thus, horoscopes showing or pretending to show future events are not credible because what they predict would take thousands of years to verify. There is no record showing that one single kingdom has ever lasted during one tenth of a revolution of a star, let alone the whole of it. Moreover, history does not go back that far, and there is no evidence that a single nation existed that long or had observatories for recording one revolution, let alone the many other revolutions. His opinion is worth quoting in full:

> "Occupation with astrology is meaningless. It is inescapable that what is said about the influence of the stars is either right or wrong, and there is no third alternative. If the influence of the stars is right, it has no usefulness except hastening anxiety, grief, misfortune, and trouble such as the occurrence of illness, tragedies, death of loved ones, shortening of life, and the knowledge of offspring's corruptibility.

> "If the advocates of astrology maintain that it is possible to repel all that, they will then contradict themselves in that astrology will have no reality of its own, for indeed, there is no way of rescinding the decreed truth. And if astrology is wrong, there is no point in occupying oneself with it.

> "Abu Muhammad said: we shall make a firm and sound declaration so that intelligent people will know and counsel themselves that there is no way of changing the species and altering the nature of things. He who occupies himself with anything pertaining to these two sciences [astrology and alchemy] will be disappointed and bereft, and will be searching for things he will never find. On the whole, astrology is not a science of proof, but consists of claims to experiences. If it is so, it is then false without any doubt. Experiences are never valid unless the condition of a thing is repeated many times on the basis of a single quality. The complete horoscope *(nasbah)* of the planets is completed only after ten thousand years. There is no way to confirm such an experience as this except through an uninterrupted succession of people who would observe the horoscopes. We know for certain that no kingdom from the beginning of civilization had ever lasted one tenth

of a rotation, let alone the whole rotation. And if a kingdom disappears, it does so because of wars, invasions, bad conditions, corruption of the country, and other happenings. All this will cause the disappearance of the sciences of that kingdom, its classes, observatories, and most if not all the information about that kingdom. In light of all this, there is no way to make continuous observation during this time, let alone to repeat it for one rotation after another. Moreover, we have no history older than the Old Testament, which goes back only about three thousand years. Where, then, does what we want take place? We do not have enough reliable information about the history of the Persians except from the time of the Sasanids, and this less than one thousand years. This is also true of the history of the Romans. As for the history of the Copts, Assyrians, Yemenites, Adomites, Ammonites, Moabites, and their duration, there is no information or trace of them. How, then, can observations remain during all that time? As for India and China, information about them has not reached us as we would have liked. Perhaps they have old observatories since they have been spared destruction in the course of centuries. However, the Chinese have not been people of science, but of crafts. Perhaps, this may exist in India; but if it is not so, then its non-existence is certain in the world.

"Abu Muhammad said: these are some of the conditions governing astrology concerning its qualities that cannot be overlooked by anyone claiming its knowledge — mainly, the knowledge of the orbit of Aquila, the position of the luminary stars, the dark and bright signs of the zodiac, the dark spots, the stairs of the zodiac, the characteristics of the rotating stars in each sign of the zodiac, the fixed stars, and other data concerning which astrologers are not able to give their due on the basis of the principles they advocate. If this is the case, the realization concerning their knowledge about the influence of the stars is impossible to attain. We have not reckoned, as we have shown them, those influences which are ascertainable and agreed upon by good people concerned with this science and who dealt with it in their books. Only an insignificant amount of astrology is credible and even here, as in the case of birth, it can be arrived at by opinion and calculation better than through astrology. As for weather conditions, change of time, and small conjunction, we have not seen astrologers through the years assert in one single instance — and God — may He be glorified and exalted—knows. We have found only that most of their utterances are based on opinion and guesswork only. There is nothing in their utterances except what they claim in that the planet Saturn appears in such a sign of the zodiac and descends in some other. This is the case concerning the rest of the bright stars and concerning locations and other superstitions... They never come up with any proof, convincing argument, or contention concerning that except saying, 'Listen, shut up, and believe the prince.' In concesquence, anything with such a method should not be pursued by any rational being claiming it to be a science. However, the seeker of the realities of things should not avoid examining it so that he may know the objectives of astrologers, put himself at ease through acquaintance with it, to be on the watch against their claims and superstitions, and to eliminate any preoccupation by knowing that astrology lacks any usefulness."[32]

Ibn Hazm reiterates the same points in his *Fisal* and raises specific objections to the claims of the astrologers.[33] Among these objections are: (1) the requirements of the astrologers are so complicated that it is impossible to attain them; (2) that when the astrologer is figuring out the position of a given planet, he would be missing the positions of others; (3) that the suppositions that the temper of Saturn is cold-dry, that of Mars is warm-dry, and that of the moon cold-humid are based upon qualities proper to the four elements of the earth and not applicable to the planets; (4) the contention that the division of the earth follows the influence of the stars, or the foundation of a city is owing to the influence of the horoscope is totally false; (5) the contention that the death of animals such as hens by decapitation is also owing to the influence of the stars is eqully false; and (6) the contention that castration should take place only in the first and seventh zones lacks any validity.

Ibn Hazm considers these and similar claims to lack proof, for experience tells him that man is capable of contradicting the decree of the stars, thus invalidating any such claim. This being the case, the so-called decrees of the stars are more conjectures and guesswork. Astrologers' predictions could never constitute prophecy or even the science of the occult. Moreover, even if astrology is valid, it is still harmful since it brings distress and unhappiness. If the astrologer insists that he can counteract all that, then astrology must have no validity at all because there is no way of counteracting the inevitable. In conclusion, astrology should be avoided altogether, particularly in one's association with the ruler: "As for associating oneself with rulers in matters of astrology, no one with any brain will ever concern himself with that since the one who is involved in astrology takes upon himself things that are not in his power to deliver. The astrologer would spend his time in continuous lies, contradictory promises, continual deceit, shame and disgrace. All in all, let the aim, effort and ability of the one who associates himself with the ruler be directed fully to improve the character of the ruler, to incite him to piety, and to prevent him from sin."[34]

Ibn Hazm's elaborate refutation of astrology is no doubt motivated by scientific considerations as well as by his concern that astrology could assume the function of prophecy, which is in the hand of God alone. Moreover, in astrology, the divine orderly plan of the universe is replaced by the caprice of celestial elements - which would, indeed, be inconsistent with Ibn Hazm's conception of God, Prophecy, and the free will of man.

In this connection, it is of interest to contrast Ibn Hazm's views on astrology with those of Ibn Khaldun. who was familiar with some of Ibn

Hazm's works, particularly the *Fisal.* Ibn Khaldun follows the traditional division of the sciences and includes astrology among the mathematical sciences.[35] He gives due recognition to the fact that astrology was cultivated along with sorcery and talisman by some Muslim scientists.[36] After explaining the nature and practice of astrology, he refutes it in a language reminiscent of that used by Ibn Hazm. Ibn Khaldun summarily dismisses astrologers' allegation that the knowledge of astral power and influence is acquired through experience, saying that all human lives combined could not be able to attest to such an experience because such a long period of time is required to have it repeated.[37] In consequence, the achievement of astrology is flimsy and the result of conjecture and guesswork.[38] Actually, no one can tell the particular power of each one of the stars, nor is it possible to calculate their positions. Furthermore, it is wrong to assume that the stars exercise an influence on the world and that they are agents, because there is no agent except God.[39] In sum, astrology is worthless from the vantage point of religion and reason. It is harmful to civilization, hurts the faith of the common people, and creates expectations which are detrimental to stability and order. For these reasons alone, astrology should be forbidden by all civilized people.[40] Ibn Khaldun concludes that even if astrology were in itself sound, no Muslim could ever acquire it, because the religious law does not sanction it; besides it is a very difficult, if not impossible, subject to master.[41]

d. Magic, Talisman, Dreams, and Vision

Magic, talisman, incantation and dream interpretation had been placed among the sciences by some Muslim scholars,[42] although there were some reservations about their validity and merit. For this reason, Ibn Hazm took pains to evaluate them. Like astrology, they had serious implications with respect to religion; were they valid, they would do violence in the divine plan. To Ibn Hazm, magic "consists of tricks and confusion and cannot possibly transmute the nature of a thing. Were the magician able to transmute nature, there would not be any difference between him and a prophet.[43] In consequence, anyone who sanctions it will be an unbeliever."[44] In his *Fisal,*[45] he discounts the validity of magic and talisman. He says that it is the height of absurdity to consider for one moment that magic is capable of transmuting the nature of things. Not even saints are able to do this. Only God has the power to change the nature of things, and this is done by miracles through His Prophets. All things that exist in the world are ordained by God according to essential differences, thus making species and genera absolutely unchangeable. Therefore, to say that a magician or a saint has the power to fly in the air, walk over water, change a man into a donkey, and the like lacks foundation. In other words, to equate human tricks *(hiyal)* with miracles *(mu'jizat)* is untenable. In sum, were the transmutation of things possible to the magician and saints, it would be possible to everybody, creating an infinite number of pretensions.

Ibn Hazm admits two kinds of "magical" power *(quwah)* which are quite different from the nature of miracles: First the power of talisman is the result of astral or natural phenomena, but does not change the nature or essence of a thing. This kind of power can be witnessed and attested to. For example if a scorpion is engraved on a ring when the moon is in the zodiac zone, the holder of the ring will be free from scorpion stings. Certain amulets will prevent locusts or hail from ever entering a town. These powers, according to Ibn Hazm, are God's powers and counteract the effect of other powers in the same manner that heat is repelled with cold and vice versa, or like the power of music which is capable of harmonizing or disharmonizing the order of things.[46]

The second kind of magical power is incantation *(ruqyah)*, which consists of utterances drawn from certain letters and which causes certain powers of association which excite the nature of certain things, thereby repelling the power they have. Several times he witnessed a person who was able to cure an abcess through incantation, causing the abcess to dry and disappear on the third day following the utterances of the incantation. He says that such an occurence cannot be denied because it can be witnessed and verified by personal observation. Such results are not different from those caused by incense in repelling cardiac weakness. Moreover, certain things produce effects by virtue of their own natural properties, as in the case of magnets, which attract iron. None of these phenomena can be classified among or equated with miracles in which the essential attributes of things are transmuted, such as splitting the moon, dividing the sea, or creating ex-nihilo food and water. Only God can perform such deeds and manifest them through His Prophets.[47] On the other hand, the magician may be able to produce some effect through trickery, but he is never able to alter the essence of things. His power actually is not different from that produced through the eloquence of poets. Ibn Hazm quotes a Tradition of the Prophet, "Certainly, eloquence has something of magic, which sometimes exerts an influence on the soul exciting or muting it and, thereby, leading it to motley purposes."[48]

The subject of vision and dream interpretation has also occupied Muslim religious scholars, and has been, on the whole, regarded with high esteem insofar as vision and dreams are related to divine inspiration and transmission of prophecy. To Ibn Hazm, vision *(ru'ya)* is a real phenomenon and constitutes, according to prophetic Tradition, one forty-sixth part of prophecy.[49] This being the case, it is indispensable to have a knowledge of dream interpretation, which is a natural gift possessed by the one who also has had a mastery of the sciences.[50] However, not every dream is based on divine inspiration, nor can it be considered true. Many absurd things can be seen in a dream such as being alive when decapitated, or dreaming that a person is in China when actually he is in al-Andalus. These kinds of dreams are contrary to sensory perception and reason, and may have their inspiration from four different sources: (1) dreams emanating from the devil, which are characterized by confusion and incoherence; (2) dreams reflecting a preoccupation, such as meeting a feared enemy or a beloved person; (3) dreams resulting from physiological conditions, as in the case of a sanguinary person who sees flowers, light, and red colors, or a person, suffering from biliousness who sees fires and the like; and (4) dreams emanating from God, which inspire the soul of the dreamer to convey a knowledge of the future or to reveal the hidden things *(mughayyabat)*. Such dreams are found at several levels and degrees, depending on the purity of the soul. They are good dreams and constitute according to prophetic injunction one twenty-sixth, forty-sixth, or seventieth part of prophecy. They are always true if they happen to prophets, and can be true or false if they happen to others.

The views of Ibn Hazm on magic, talisman, dream interpretation, and vision coincide in many respect with those of Ibn Khaldun. The fact that these two great thinkers each devotes ample space to them is in itself significant. Ibn Khaldun recognizes the existence of magic, talisman, dreams, and vision in antiquity and among Muslims, and admits, as Ibn Hazm does, that they possess certain verifiable manifestations. However, both emphasized that those manifestations result from natural phenomena and are quite different in nature from those emanating from a divine power.[51] To confuse them or to associate manifestations resulting from those disciplines with miracles and prophecy is unbelief,[52] and as such is forbidden by the religious law.[53] Once this distinction is made, both men describe magic and talisman giving each its due. To Ibn Khaldun, magic and talisman show that the ordinary human soul may be able to influence upon the world of the elements.[54] The soul of a prophet, which receives its inspiration from God, has the unique quality of perceiving actual divine knowledge[55] in contrast with the soul of a sorcerer which has the quality of attracting "the spirituality" of the stars and influencing upon created things.[56] However, the influence of sorcery is either the result of physical conditions or the inspiration of Satan. In sum, the soul has three degrees of magical ability: (1) that which exercises its influence through mental power; (2) that which exercises its influence through the aid of the tempers of the spheres, the elements, or property of numbers; and (3) that which exercises its influence upon the faculty of imagination by planting images and pictures.[57]

Within these limitations, the efficacy of magic, talisman, and sorcery is admitted. Their result can be attested to by personal observations. Furthermore, Ibn Khaldun says that Muhammad is known to have been put under magical spells.[58] He testifies that he witnessed a sorcerer put a person under a spell and also make the guts of animals fall out of their bellies.[59] The so-called loving numbers, 220 and 284, are said to effect friendship and love.[60] A seal on which is engraved a lion, a snake, and a scorpion will give its owner to have enormous power over rulers.[61] This notwithstanding, sorcery is evil, derived from the elements and the devil, and practiced by evil people, whereas miracles are derived from divine power and performed by virtuous men.[62]

Ibn Khaldun devotes a whole section to vision[63] and considers it one of the religious sciences. To him, vision is supernatural perception through which even revelation may begin. However, dream visions may be either true or confused, depending on whether perceptions come from the brain, and then are transmitted by the imagination to the senses or they come from memory. If they are perceived by the brain, they are true and timelss; if perceived by memory, they are hazy and subject to forgetfulness. After recognizing the different kinds of good and bad dreams, Ibn Khaldun concludes, "Dream Interpretation is a science resplendent with the light of prophecy, because prophecy and dreams are related to each other."

PART TWO

TRANSLATION AND ARABIC EDITION OF *MARATIB AL-'ULUM*

CHAPTER X

Ibn Hazm's *Maratib al-'ulum:*
The Manuscript

1. Introduction

A brief account of the content of the *Maratib al-'ulum (The Categories of the sciences)* has been given above.[1] Although the treatise is relatively small alongside other voluminous works of Ibn Hazm, it did not escape the attention of the majority of Ibn Hazm's medieval biographers from both the Western and Eastern parts of the Islamic world.[2] Its mere listing by the several biographers indicates the significance attached to the *Maratib* and, probably, familiarity with it. However, the *Maratib* was lost to modern scholarship until recently. In 1927 Asin Palacios[3] speculated that the content of the *Maratib* might be similar to the division of the sciences by the philosopher Ibn Sina, (this proved to be not entirely correct). Subsequently, in the early 1930's, H. Ritter discovered in the Fatih Mosque in Istanbul a miscellanea *(majmu'ah)* containing various treatises by Ibn Hazm, among which was the *Maratib*. The miscellanea bearing the number 2704 consists of 264 folios, of which folios 253-264 are devoted to the *Maratib*. Asin gave a full description of the miscellanea in his "codice."[4] He recognized the importance of the *Maratib* and expressed his intention of translating it into Spanish, but unfortunately he was unable to do so.[5]

The manuscript was neglected until 1952 when 'Abbas edited the *Maratib* on the basis of the Istanbul manuscript, along with other treatises of Ibn Hazm.[6] Subsequently, Mu'nis[7] gave a brief account of its contents and was followed by Chejne.[8] And Rosenthal[9] translated that portion of the *Maratib* which deals with the division of the sciences.

The author recognized the significance of the treatise and for some time entertained the idea of translating it into English. However, he had hoped to find another manuscript that would make the translation more accurate and complete. The opportunity offered itself when the author discovered a manuscript of the *Maratib* in the General Library of Rabat. The *Maratib* was part of a miscellanea in the Awqaf Collection bearing the number 209. The manuscript is written in a Maghribi script and consists of sixteen folios (folios 231-247), each of which contains twenty-seven lines except for the first and last folios. In excellent condition and quite legible, the manuscript was prepared by an unnamed scribe on the twenty-eighth of the month of Ramadan in the year 1001 A.H.

A collation of the Rabat manuscript with the Istanbul manuscript and with 'Abbas' edition shows that both manuscripts conform substantially to each other in spite of numerous minor additions and omissions that can be attributed to scribes' inadvertent mistakes. In this connection, the two manuscripts complement each other. Although the Rabat manuscript was not available to him, some of 'Abbas' suggested corrections of lapses in the Istanbul manuscript conform to the renderings of the Rabat manuscript, thus, dispelling any doubt about what might be the original. Furthermore, the Rabat manuscript offers some peculiar features. A new thought or paragraph is ordinarily introduced with "Abu Muhammad said" and ends with an open circle with a dot in the center. The *hamzah* is ordinarily substituted for *ya (sayir* for *sa'ir);* the undotted *ya* for *alif;* and the long *ta (ta tawilah)* for the hooked *ta (ta' marbutah).* In addition, a preposition and a particle are written separately instead of joined - thus, *fima* is written as *fi ma.* Finally, words such as *lakin, hadha* and *kadhalika* are written as *lakin, hadha,* and *hakadha* - that is, with *alif* instead of a dagger which ordinarily is not written. These minor points do not detract much from the value of the manuscript. Here the text is collated and reconstructed in a new edition upon which the English translation is based.

Finally, a few words should be said about the translation. No matter what method of translation is used, the translator is apt to be uneasy about his rendering, particularly of some difficult passages. This is especially true of the *Maratib*, a terse and compact treatise which contains a multiplicity of ideas. It appears that Ibn Hazm recorded the essence of his ideas in the form of reflections and saw no need for elaborating on some of them. Having examined some of those points dealt with at some length in other works of Ibn Hazm, the translator was tempted to render a free translation. But in view of the fact that many of the points have been discussed in the body of this book, he decided to render an almost literal translation, preserving much of the manner in which Ibn Hazm expressed himself. It is thus hoped to approximate the original in form as well as in content.

Translation

[231] In the name of God, the Merciful and Compassionate. May God's prayer be Upon our Lord Muhammad, Upon his Family and Companions, and May He grant them Salvation.

Book on the Categories of The Sciences, The Manner of Studying Them and Their Relation to Each Other - The Composition of the Teacher and Religious Scholar Abu Muhammad 'Ali Ibn Ahmad Ibn Sa'id Ibn Hazm al-Andalusi al-Zahiri, May the Almighty God Have Mercy Upon Him and be Pleased with Him, and May He Benefit us From it.

The jurist, the Imam, and the religious scholar Abu Muhammad 'Ali Ibn Hazm - May God have mercy upon him - said, Praise be to God, the Lord of the worlds, Who bestowed on us bountiful benefits and granted us lofty faculties. Praise be to Him that He may be pleased with us and grant us many of his benefits and noble gifts. May God have prayer on our Lord

Muhammad, who is His best creature and the purest offspring from among Adam's descendants, and who was sent with guidance to rescue those who follow him from the darkness of unbelief and the blindness of ignorance in order to lead them to the light of faith and the triumph of knowledge.

Now to our topic. Verily God - May He be Glorified and Exalted - showed a special deference to the sons of Adam, and preferred them over many of His creatures. He distinguished them from the rest of His creation with the faculty of discernment, thereby enabling them to engage in the sciences and the crafts. Thus, it is incumbent upon the individual not to squander the trust given to him by his Creator, nor to neglect the gift his Savior had placed at his disposal; it is also incumbent upon him to protect and use them, to encompass and disseminate them in all what he was called upon to do.

Henceforth, there is a saying for every season. The ancestors had sciences, devoted themselves assiduously to teaching them, and bequeathed them to posterity. Afterward, some of the sciences remained and so the need for them, whereas the record of others was studied but their leaders were vanquished and forgotten remaining in name only. Among these are the sciences of magic and the science of talisman, whose remains are quite evident but whose knowledge is conjectural. This is true of music and its three kinds, which the Ancients have described that there is a kind of music which makes the coward courageous and is called *al-lawiyy*[10] a second kind that makes the avaricous person munificent, and I believe it is called *al-taniniyy*[11] and a third kind that makes the soul either friendly or repulsive. All these qualities are nonexistent in the world today. Then know - May God help you - that whomever you see claiming the knowledge of music, melody, and talisman is indeed a swindler, a liar, a conjurer, and an insolent person. This is also the case if you find anyone dealing with alchemy, for he would add to these blameworthy qualities just mentioned the greed for stealing people's money, legitimizing the forgery of currency, injustice to those with whom he deals, and beguiling his soul and his appearance besides the depravity he inflicts upon himself. The two sciences first mentioned (magic and talisman) have been in existence for centuries in spite of being nonexistent (invalid) and disconnected. As for this science (alchemy) whose advocates claim the conversion of the essence of nonprecious metal, it is still void and nonexistent as a science; it has never been proved valid even for one single hour. This is so because it is absolutely impossible to convert one species into another. Moreover, there is no difference between converting copper into gold and vice versa, and between converting a man into a donkey and vice versa, and for all species; it is absolutely impossible to convert one species into another. Success comes from the Almighty God. I derive my support from Him. There is no God except Him.

[232] Abu Muhammad said: There is no purpose in occupying oneself with a science that is obsolete and nonexistent. On the other hand, if is incumbent upon the individual to interest himself in the sciences that are possible to learn and which are beneficial at the right time. He should

choose those sciences and proceed gradually with those that are indispensable for their attainment, that is, he should take up the important first, then the most important; the useful and then the most useful. Thus, were he to aspire to the highest science without having mastered those sciences aiding to achieve them, he would be like the one who wants to climb to a well-built, dark and open upstairs room without bothering to use the stairs and the entry without which the room cannot be reached.

Abu Muhammad said: The individual has only two abodes: the worldly abode and the abode in the Hereafter when he departs from this world. We know for certain that the length of stay in this world is a matter of days only. It follows, thus, that the effort of the individual in science that are useful in this world only constitutes an ominous outlook and a hopeless persuit for the simple reason that the sciences that are useful in this world aim only at either the acquisition of wealth, or the preservation of the health of the body. There is no third alternative to these two. The purpose of the sciences meant for the acquisition of wealth is a very narrow one because the acquisition of wealth can be attained without knowledge, more easily and expeditiously than increasing one's knowledge, by joining a ruler or engaging in real estate or business. In fact, we find that the ignoramus is more successful in these pursuits than the adept scholar. If this is the case, the task of seeking knowledge as a means of acquiring wealth along with the toil involved therein is both troublesome and devious because the pursuer would add two gross blemishes: one in which he had abandoned the shorter and easier of two ways for attaining his desire and purpose in favor of the thornier road involving more toil and less usefulness; and the other in which he used the supreme quality that distinguishes him from reptiles and beasts to acquire stones about which he does not know when they will leave him and vice versa. Such a person would be like the one who toiled hard and spent his nights and long toil to make a precious and sharp Indian sword, and to build an elegant and well-proportioned mansion with profuse decorations and strong foundations. When the sword and the building were completed as he wanted them, he used the sword for breaking bones and cutting herbs, and the mansion for throwing in whatever waste was swept. Is there a worse loser than this one?

As for the knowledge aiming solely at preserving the health of the body, the one who toils and exerts himself to attain and limit himself to it will never achieve its perfection except containing illness without knowing for certain whether or not his objective of curing or not curing an illness will be accomplished. Even if he succeeds, he is not sure that the disease will not reappear even strong than before, nor is he certain of the occurrence of a similar illness for which he had exhausted his effort to cure, or the occurrence of a still more pernicious illness defying any cure. What is certain and inescapable is that the physician is not able to repel death when it occurs, nor is he able to treat a chronic illness when it becomes ingrained. Perhaps, this may happen in an instant to the one who toils to cure it.

He who ponders on what we have said will realize that the usefulness of the pursuit of the sciences for their ephemeral utility only is very small, and on the whole, has a meager benefit. Although the two purposes of the sciences for acquiring wealth and preserving health have some degree of benefit, they entail little gain and small reward in relation to the toil of acquiring knowledge as their cause. In fact, an incurable malady, a grave censure, and a ruinous loss will be the lot of the one who acquires the loftiest sciences and spends his knowledge for the purpose of acquiring wealth and not for the purpose for which they are intended. Indeed, the state of ignorance is better for its bearer than that of the one who had learned a science in the context we have mentioned. We beseech God's succour, and may He protect us from desertion.

CHAPTER

Abu Muhammad said: If this is the case as we have mentioned, the best sciences [233] are those which lead to salvation in the Hereafter and to the attainment of success in the Eternal abode. The student of these sciences having this purpose in mind will be compensated with eternal tranquility, but with little effort; he will have a good bargain and a successful effort in which he endeavored little but gained a lot and in which he gave a little but received a great deal in return; he will also be the one who will know what is transitory, thereby frowning on it, and will discern what is lasting and will go after it. We beseech God's grace so that He may place us among this kind of people. Amen.

Abu Muhammad said: Any person with sound intelligence will know with certainly that he will not be able to attain the sciences without study, and that study is not possible without listening, reading, and writing. There is no short cut to these three means, nor is there another way for attaining the sciences without them. If this is the case, let us deal now with the help of the Almighty God with the manner of attaining the sciences, with the elucidation of those having the best quality and the loftiest value, with the tangible and great need people have for them, with the minimum extent of pursuing them, and with the ultimate goal of the sciences.

Abu Muhammad said: It is incumbent upon those who train their offspring and others to initiate them from the first moment they become strong and able to understand and reply to what they are being addressed, that is, at the time when the child is about five years old; they should be then entrusted to a teacher, who will instruct them in writing and letter formation of words. If the child becomes skilled in that, he should be able to write and read. When learning to write, the student should limit himself to having his handwriting with the letters straight to make it clear and without misspelling. If the handwriting does not meet these requirements, it would be very difficult to read. As for enhancing the beauty of handwriting, it is not a virtue but a pretext perhaps toward attaching oneself to a ruler, thereby consuming all his time either inflicting injustice upon people, or drafting documents with items far removed from the truth and replete with lies and distortions. He would, thus, spend his life-time in vain, would have a poor bargain and would like to repent when repentance is of no avail. He would be like a man who possesses a great amount of musk, but ceased to use it for scenting and treating the soul with its aroma and fragrance and turned it to sweeten the beasts and spill it wastefully on the road until all of it is gone. This is the extent of learning how to write.

The extent of learning to read consists in that the student should become proficient in reading any book that should fall into his hand in his mother language which he uses to communicate with people. He should be good at it. In addition, he should learn the Qur'an by heart because he would acquire through it many useful aims such as drill in reading and the exercise of the tongue when reciting it. Moreover, he would become to some degree eloquent besides achieving the meritorious obligations and the noble admonitions contained therein which he will find a precious tool before and when he needs them.

When he becomes successful in writing and reading as we have indicated, he should take up simultaneously the study of grammar and lexicography. The meaning of grammar is the knowledge of the changes of consonants and vowels, which will show the difference of meaning as the *u* ending indicating the subject, the *a* ending the object, the *i* ending the prepositional clause, the vowelless ending command and prohibition, the use of *y* for the dual and plural in both accusative and genitive, the use of *alif* for the dual nominative and the *waw* for the sound plural in the nominative, and so on. If the student does not know this science, he will find it impossible to understand what he reads in any of the sciences.

Lexicography consists of expressions that convey meanings and require a knowledge of grammar in all things used in communication with people and their published works. Moreover, a knowledge of lexicography is required in expressions most frequently used. Also a minimum knowledge of grammar is required as contained in the *Clear Book* by al-Zubaydi[12] and similar works such as the *Abridgment* of Ibn al-Sarraj[13] and similar compilations that are light and comprehensive. On the other hand, delving deeply into the study of grammatical causation is superfluous and lacks any utility [234] because it is a distraction from the well-known and is removed from the most obligatory and important. Moreover, grammatical causation constitutes lies, and there is no point in occupying oneself in something having this quality. For the object of studying grammar is to understand dialogues and to meet the need of the individual for unfolding books collected on the sciences. Thus, he who wants to increase his knowledge in this science and delve into grammatical principles contained in *The Book* of Sibawayh[14] will do well, although occupying oneself with something else would be better and more important because there is no usefulness in going beyond the limit we have indicated except for the one who wishes to make the study of grammar a means of livelihood. This is a noble goal because it is a part of knowledge in any case.

Two books on lexicography will suffice: one is the *Gharib al-musannaf* of Abu 'Ubayd,[15] and the other is the *Mukhtasar al-'ayn*[16] of al-Zubaydi, which will enable the student to acquaint himself with common expressions and uncommon ones that will act as a tool for any need that might arise at any time when found in books he may read. If the student wishes to penetrate deeply into lexicography, he should master the *Khalq al-insan* and the *Firaq* of Thabit,[17] the *Mudhakkar wa-l-mu'annath* of Ibn al-Anbari,[18] *al-Maqsur wa-l-mamdud wa-l-mahmuz* of Abu 'Ali al-Qali,[18] *al-Nabat* of Abu Hanifah Ahmad Ibn Dawud al-Dinawari,[20] and the like; he will do well contrary to what we have said regarding grammatical causation. This is so because lexicography is in its entirety a reality having sound conventions and expressions conveying meanings. The more extensive lexicography is for having a name for every meaning in the world, the better it is for a more lucid understanding, freer from doubt and nearer to clarity. However, limiting oneself to the acceptable extent, as we have mentioned, and engaging in the most important and surest of the sciences are more imperative.

Abu Muhammad said: If we were to recite some poetry in addition to what we have mentioned, it should consist of peoms containing maxims and good things such as the poetry of Hassan Ibn Thabit,[21] Ka'b Ibn Malik,[22] and 'Abdallah Ibn Ruwahah[23] - May God be pleased with them-and such as the poetry of Salih Ibn 'Abd al-Quddus[24] and the like, for their poetry is an excellent aid for alerting the soul. However, it is necessary to avoid four kinds of poetry:

1. Love and sentimental poetry *(al-aghzal wa-l-raqiq),* that provokes desire, invites infatuation, incites racketeering, leads the soul to dissipation and pleasure, makes easy the occupation in deceit and passion, and denies realities to the point of even leading to vitiating religion and the world; to extravagant spending for objectionable pursuits; to destruction of honor; to disappearance of manliness, to the loss of responsibility. Listening to sentimental poetry, particularly love poetry, about males, description of wine and licentiousness, will certainly destroy the constitution of the individual to a point of requiring treatment and cure. In all, this kind of poetry facilitates corruption, makes disobedience easy and is generally harmful.

2. Poetry dealing with vagabondry and wars such as the poetry of 'Antarah,[25] 'Urwah Ibn al-Ward,[26] Sa'd Ibn Nashib,[27] and the like. For these poetical compositions agitate the soul, stir nature,and make it easy for the individual to resort to destructiveness without any legitimate reason and to needless self-destruction; they will also lead to the loss of the Hereafter besides the kindling revolts, facilitating crimes, abominable conditions, avidity for injustice, and the shedding of blood.

3. Poetry of wandering, description of deserts, and abandoned dwellings, which makes departure and separation easy and which may lead the individual needlessly to a situation from which it would be difficult to escape.

4. Satirical poetry *(hijā)*, which is the most vitiating kind of poetry for its pursuer; for it will make it easy for the individual to be in the condition of insolent people such as toilet sweepers, dealers of wind instruments, and those who make their living by means of insults, depravity, baseness, the shredding of people's honor, the singling out of their defects, and the defilement of the sanctity of parents. In this lies destruction in this world and in the Hereafter.

[235] There are also two kinds of poetry which may not be prohibited completely, nor do we recommend them; they are in our view among those things that are permissible but reprehensible, and include panegyric and elegy. Their permissibility resides in that they may contain the virtues of the person who is elegized or those of the one who is being praised. This requires the reciter of such poetry to have the desire for describing the likeness of such a condition. On the other hand, our dislike for them rests on the fact that there are many lies in these two kinds of poetry, and there is no good in falsehood.

Excessive recitation of poetry intended for making a livelihood is also a blameworthy acquisition, because it is a false and superfluous way and not the way leading to truth and virtues. Let no skeptic think that we belittle this discipline (poetry) out of ignorance. Anyone from our contemporaries having had contact with us and having heard about our stature in the field will know how extensively we delved into the recitations of poetry, how well acquainted we have been with its meanings, how our standing has been regarding all kinds of poetry, the nicety, meaning, and division of poetry; how able we have been in its composition, how well we achieved it in both odes and short poems, and how easy it was for us to make long or short compositions. But the truth is more important than what is being said.

If the individual attains a knowledge of grammar and lexicography to the extent we have indicated, he should turn to the science of numbers and become proficient in multiplication, division, addition, subtraction and fractions. He should also take up plane geometry and become acquainted with arithmetic, which is the knowledge of the nature of numbers. He should be able to read and understand Euclid's book, become acquainted with its objective, and know its meanings. It is a lofty science by means of which he will be able to arrive at the knowledge of the signpost of the earth and its surface; the composition of the celestial bodies, their rotations, positions, and distances; and the proofs concerning all that and concerning the rotations of the planets and disjunctions in the sign of the zodiac. Moreover, this is a very lofty science by means of which the individual will become acquainted with the reality of the termination of the world and with the evidence concerning God's workmanship of the world. Thus, it will remain for him to contemplate the Maker only. He will also observe the workmanship, management, and composition through his acquaintance of what we have indicated and through the *Almagest*,[28] which will also enable him to know the eclipses, the width and length of countries, time, the lengthening and shortening of days and nights, the rising and ebbing of tides, the rising and setting of the sun, moon, and bright stars. Penetrating deeply into the study of geometry will be useful for bringing in water, lifting weights, designing buildings, and setting up scientific instruments.

Occupation with astrology is meaningless. It is inescapable that what is said about the influence of the stars is either right or wrong, and there is no third alternative. If the influence of the stars is right, it has no usefulness except hastening anxiety, grief, misfortune, and trouble such as the occurrence of illness, tragedies, death of beloved ones, shortening of life, and the knowledge of offspring's corruptibility.

If the advocates of astrology maintain that it is possible to repel all that, they will then contradict themselves in that astrology will have no reality of its own, for indeed, there is no way of rescinding the decreed truth. And if astrology is wrong, there is no point in occupying oneself with it.

Abu Muhammad said: We shall make a firm and sound declaration so that intelligent people will know and counsel themselves that there is no way of changing the species and altering the nature of things. He who occupies himself with anything pertaining to these two sciences [astrology and alchemy] will be disappointed and bereft, and will be searching for things he will never find. On the whole, astrology is not a science of proof, but consists of claims to experiences. If it is so, it is then false without any doubt. Experiences are never valid unless the condition of a thing is repeated many times on the basis of a single quality. The complete horoscope *(nasbah)* of the planets is completed only after ten thousand years. There is no way to confirm such an experience as this, except through an uninterrupted succession of people who would observe the horoscopes. We know for certain that no kingdom from the beginning of civilization had ever lasted one tenth of a rotation, let alone the whole rotation. And if a kingdom disappears, it does so because of wars, invasions, bad conditions, corruption of the country, and other happenings. All this will cause the disappearance of the sciences of that kingdom, its classes, observatories, and most, if not all the information about that kingdom. In light of all this, there is no way to make continuous observation during this time, let alone to repeat it for one rotation after another. Moreover, we have no history older than the Old Testament, which goes back only about three thousand years. Where then does what we want take place? We do not have enough reliable information about the history of the Persians except from the time of the Sasanids, and this is less than one thousand years. This is also true of the history of the Romans. As for the history of the Copts, Assyrians, Yemenites, Adomites, Ammonites, Moabites, and their duration, there is no information or trace of them. How then can observations remain during all that time? As for India and China, information about them has not reached us as we would have liked. Perhaps, they have old observatories, since, they have been spared destruction in the course of centuries. However, the Chinese have not been people of science, but of crafts. Perhaps, this may exist in India; but if it is not so, then its non-existence is certain in the world.

Abu Muhammad said: these are some of the conditions governing astrology concerning its qualities that cannot be overlooked by anyone claiming its knowledge, mainly, the knowledge of the orbit of Aquila, the position of the luminary stars, the dark and bright signs of the zodiac, the dark spots, the stairs of the zodiac, the characteristics of the rotating stars in each sign of the zodiac, the fixed stars, and other data concerning which astrologers are not able to give their due on the basis of the principles they advocate. If this is the case, the realization concerning their knowledge about the influence of the stars is impossible to attain. We have not reckoned, as we have shown them, those influences which are ascertainable and agreed upon by good people concerned with this science and who dealt with it in their books. Only an insignifcant amount of astrology is credible and even here, as in the case of birth, it can be arrived at by opinions and calculations better than through astrology. As for weather conditions, change of time, and small conjunction, we have not seen astrologers through the years assert in one single instance, and God — May He be glorified and exalted — knows. We have found only that most of their utterances are based on opinion and guesswork only. There is nothing in their utterances except what they claim in that the planet Saturn appears in such a sign of the zodiac and descends in some other. This is the case concerning the rest of the bright stars and concerning locations and other superstitions. They never come up with any proof, convincing argument, or contention concerning that, except, "Listen, shut up, and believe in the prince." In consequence, anything with such a method should not be pursued by any rational being, claiming it to be a science. However, the seeker of the realities of things should not avoid examining it so that he may know the objectives of astrologers, put himself at ease through acquaintance with it, to be on the watch against their claims and superstitions, and to eliminate any preoccupation by knowing that astrology lacks any usefulness.

Our teacher, the judge Abu-l-Walid Yunus Ibn 'Abdallah[29] told me, "I heard the ascetic Yahya Ibn Mujahid al-Fazari say the maturity of my studies was reached when my understanding became strong and when my will became fortified." I said to him: "Show us the way so that we may attain that during our lifetime through your advice." He said, "Yes. I used to take a bit of each science because hearing people disucss things without knowing what they were saying was a great grief." He said this or something to this effect. Abu Muhammad said: He was right, indeed. May God have mercy upon him.

Abu Muhammad said: If the individual attains what we have indicated, he should begin the study of the definitions of logic — the knowledge of genera, species, simple nouns, logical propositions, premises, syllogism, and conclusions — so that he may be able to know what is a proof, convincing argument, and what is a contention, and how to be cautious regarding what is believed to be a proof but is not. It is through this science that the individual can arrive at the realities of things and distinguish them without a shred of doubt from falsehood.

The student should look into the natural sciences, atmospheric conditions, composition of the elements, zoology, botany, and mineralogy. He should read books on anatomy in order to perceive the masterly creation [237] and the role of the Creator; the formation of members of the body; the will, wisdom, and power of the Creator.

If the individual attains proficiency during his initiation in the sciences, he should not neglect the study of the history of ancient people and those who succeeded them, nor should he neglect reading ancient and contemporary histories in order to acquaint himself with the disappearance of those nations, the destruction of civilized countries, and the obliteration of famous cities that were firmly established and fortified; he should also be acquainted with the passing of their inhabitants and their vicissitudes; the passing of kings, who killed and oppressed people and who accumulated a great deal of money, armies, and weapons to perpetuate the rule for themselves and their offspring, but which did not remain. On the contrary, those kings vanished along with their legacies; their offpsring have gone and disappeared, leaving behind them misdeeds, blemishes, and ugly remembrances befitting their souls in the Hereafter and their mentioning in this world. With this realization, asceticism and indifference will result, leading the individual to look down on kings becaue of the enormity of afflictions that had befallen them and their descendents. Such a realization will also lead him to praise God-fearing people for their virtues, thereby wishing them for himself, and will enable him to hear their censuring of vices, thereby avoiding them himself. He will come close to ascertaining the soundness of history and its aid on the basis of a given narration, notwithstanding the long distances and time of those who collected it, and to see clearly the efforts, the different religions, and the various schools of thought of people; he will then become certain that the information is sound, not admitting any doubt. On the other hand, he may come across different versions and will then realize that it is muddled. He will also perceive information about scholars and pious men and would strive to be in a similar condition and to add his name to theirs if and when he will conduct himself as they did by imitating their examples and deeds. Likewise, he will become acquainted with the deeds of corrupt people on earth and the bad things said about them and what bad traces they left behind, thereby abhorring their path and avoiding being mentioned among them. The student should relegate this science particularly to a time of leisure and when he is tired from studying other sciences. For history is a very easy, stimulating, entertaining and pleasurable discipline, and no one should neglect any vestige, nor that information requiring evidence that is truly indispensable to knowledge of establishing the truth, but he should be in the position of the one who values the fact that knowledge did not begin with him.

If the student becomes proficient in what we have indicated, the most important things for him are the knowledge of what is expected of him in this world and what is expected of him thereafter should he depart from this world. He should proceed with that before the end of the duration of his journey in this world, which is very short. There is nothing more certain for him than this. Besides, misery, comfort, pleasure, wealth, leadership, poverty, apathy, and adversity are transitory things and pass quickly. We do not refer to death, which is inescapable, but to old age and the vicissitudes of fate whose capriciousness with people cannot be trusted for a moment.

If the individual becomes proficient in what we have indicated, it will be necessary for him to look into seeking the proof on the basis of the necessary sciences we have mentioned. He should inquire whether the world is created or uncreated. If he concludes that it is created — and this is evident through the calculation of its duration, the number of its individual species — he should then inquire whether or not it has a creator. If he concludes that it has a primal creator — and this is evident by virtue of attribution as a part of the definition of logic — he should then inquire whether the Creator is one or more than one. If he concludes that the Creator is one — and this is evident through the aforementioned numerical calculation — he should inquire whether prophecy is possible, necessary or impossible. If he concludes that it is possible per force by virtue of the fact that Creator of the world has a free will and is able to perform anything, and if he then concludes that prophecy exists by virtue of necessary information, he should look into all prophecies about which denominations have differed. If he concludes that prophecy is ascertainable in more than one person, it would be necessary by the same token to ascertain the prophecy of the one who is like him and to accept what had been transmitted on his authority in the same manner it had been accepted of the other. He will then ponder that and will have to concede to the one whose prophecy is attested by proofs and who speaks on behalf of God — May He be glorified and exalted — and relays His covenants. Once this is realized, the individual will then inquire into all things that are lawful or unlawful, will act accordingly, and will not accept any command or prohibition from anyone who is not confirmed by the Revelation of God — May He be glorified and exalted. This is the road to deliverance, the avenue of salvation, and the foundation of success. Whoever deviates from it will be bewildered, wavering and helpless; his roads will be many and he will perish as a failure and penitent, hoping to gain salvation by luck like the one who finds a morsel without search. We seek God's help from such tribulations.

Abu Muhammad said: This road we have described will lead to the confirmation of the Prophecy of Muhammad - May God's prayer and peace be upon him - and will require studying what is in the Qur'an, the covenants of God - May He be glorified and exalted. It also requires the studying of the authenticity of the covenants of the messenger of God - May God's prayer and peace be upon him - thereby distinguishing what is sound or unsound among them and accepting and adhering to them accordingly. Except for the Islamic religion, none of this is existent in other denominations. As for idol worshippers or the followers of the Brahmins who deny prophecies, there is no way of ascertaining a religious law for them since they deny the existence of an authentic Legislator and the way leading to Him, thereby having people follow their utterances in futility and without having any deterrent against inequity and abomination. As for Manichaeism, confusion is quite apparent in their doctrine that conceives the Maker as having created things in Himself. This will deny the requirements concerning the creation of the world, as we have demonstrated in our book entitled *Differences of Religions, Sects and Denominations*.[30] As for the religious law of the Christians, its followers affirm that their laws are not the outcome of the revelation of the Almighty God, but are the result of convention by King Zakarias and the rest of the patriarchs; this is a thing which reason shows that it is not binding since proof does not make it so. As for Zoroastrianism, its followers admit that two thirds of their book did not come down, and that their laws were in that lost portion; it follows that is an absurdity to have the Almighty God commission people to do things about which they do not know and which has disappeared. The Zoroastrians further admit that Ardhashir Ibn Babak set down laws other than those which were obligatory on them. Only an ignoramus believes this, and only an idiot adheres to it. As for Judaism, the Jews recognize that they have not had access to most of the necessary laws since the time they left Zion; that the rabbinical laws which they practice today are other than those required of them in the Torah and that their scholars made compensation for that, making it obligatory upon them to acknowledge the soundness of what the leading scholars maintain at the same level they acknowledge what emanates from their prophet - May peace be upon him.

Abu Muhammad said: When the neglector of reality occupies himself with a science other than the religious science, he will indeed be undiscerning and will inflict harm upon himself, since he will have shown a predilection for the base and least useful over the loftiest and most useful. Were someone to argue that the science of numbers, astronomy, and logic consist of the knowledge of things as they are, we shall respond that this is well and good, provided that the individual aims by means of them at seeking the evidence pointing to the Maker of things through His creation so that he may advance through that toward attaining success, salvation and deliverance from suffering and misfortune. It is on this basis that we have made the categorization in the order of priority. In consequence, if the objective of knowledge is the knowledge of present things as they are only, then the student of those sciences - as the one whose main purpose is the knowledge of the characteristics of countries as they are, the characteristics of the inhabitants of each country, and their mode of living - can be described by officiousness and stupidity rather than as a man of true knowledge; since the reality of knowledge, as we have seen, is to seek it for one's benefit and for the benefit of others in this transitory world as well as in the Eternal Abode that is his permanent dwelling and the place of eternal life. We seek the help of the Almighty God.

Abu Muhammad said: If the individual is engaged in a sufficient and satisfying mode of living, he should thank God - May He be glorified and exalted; - he should be content and should also work toward the Permanent Abode. He should not indulge in unlawful things and traversal which he will abandon or they will abandon him. If he is in need and it is possible to make his livelihood from knowledge, he will do well as a teacher of orthography, for it is a great virtue because it is a means of knowing and from which everyone learns something; he will receive a double reward to eternity from every person who has learned from him in that he was the reason behind their lifeblood. The individual will also do well as a teacher of grammar, mathematics, or medicine. In any of these pursuits [239], he should be sincere and increase his knowledge as much as possible so that it may become the means of goodness for instructing ignorant people and eradicating with God's help their maladies. He should never consent to deceit and distortion whereby he would vitiate his character, livelihood, life to come and, thus, lose his contractual obligations. He should endeavor to exercise moderation. And were he to be afflicted by the company of the ruler - he would have indeed the greatest affliction and will be faced with the abominable danger of losing his religion and his soul besides preoccupation and anxiety - he should not enjoin him in any forbidden thing even if that meant his own ruin. For it is better for him to remain ruined, oppressed, deserving of expecting reward, and a praiseworthy person, than to become an oppressor, pernicious, evil, and a blameworthy person. Perhaps his ruin is swift even if it were delayed for a while, for it is unavoidable. This notwithstanding, he should know that if the ruler sees that he is concerned with his religion and that he is a counselor of his regarding what does not harm him in the Hereafter, he will put great trust in him and will regard him highly. On the other hand, if the ruler sees in him that he is greedy and that he gives precedence to worldly things over the affairs of the next world, he will have a bad opinion about him, will not trust him concerning his person, and will dispose of him whenever the opportunity presents itself.

Abu Muhammad said: We indeed dislike that a virtuous man should assocate himself with the ruler in matters connected with medicine because ignorance, intemperance, and impatience get the better of kings when they are deprived of pleasure. This situation is not conducive to administering the regimen of healthy people and the treatment of sick ones. Habitually, rulers trouble the physicians to revive the dead and regard him as inadequate if he fails to achieve this goal. In other words, if the physicians were to follow their whims, he would be deceiving them, and were he to advise them properly, they would disobey and find him troublesome. As for associating oneself with rulers in matters of astrology, no one with any brain will ever concern himself with that since the one who is involved in astrology takes upon himself things that are not in his power to deliver. The astrologer would spend his time in continuous lies, contradictory promises, continual deceit, shame, and disgrace. All in all, let all the aim, effort and ability of the one who associates himself with the ruler be directed fully to improve the character of the ruler, to incite him to piety, and to prevent him from sin.

Abu Muhammad said: The pillars of knowledge are a well-rooted desire in which knowledge takes precedence over all worldly accidents such as pleasure, wealth and fame. Hence, the pursuit of true knowledge is to dissociate himself from the other irrational animals. As such, the individual should not use it for acquiring wealth and boasting. Knowledge requires sagacity, understanding, research, memory, and preservance; it also requires toil, expenditure, and as many books as possible.[31] No book is devoid of usefulness; in fact, a book is an increase of knowledge which the individual will find it and when he needs it, for there is no way for the individual to retain all the knowledge in which he specializes. And since there is no other way to accomplish this, it follows that books are delightful storehouses for the individual seeking knowledge. Had it not been for books, the sciences would have been lost and could hardly be found. Thus, he who decries the abundance of books errs; and were one to follow his opinion, the sciences would have been ruined, and ignoramuses would make contention and claims as they wish. Had it not been for the testimony of books, the claim of both the scholar and the ignoramus would be on a par. It is through books that haughtiness is tumbled through reiterating the opinions of scholars, adhering to what is heard, and collecting it. Thus, the individual should cling wholeheartedly to the inkstand and paper; books are his indispensable tools. He should interest himself in people of civilized countries where knowledge flourished; and in confronting contenders and facing polemicists. It is through this that realities will emerge before him. For the one who speaks on his own authority and on the basis of what he thinks is not the same as the one who speaks on the authority of someone else. A bereaved mother is not the same as a hired mourner. And he who listens to one scholar only will get almost nothing; he would be like the one who persists drinking from one well containing turbid salt, having abandoned sweet and fresh water were he to drink from other wells. Engaging one's equal and opposing enemies in debates that truth can be discerned from falsehood. There is no other way.

He who seeks knowledge in the manner we have mentioned will almost succeed in his objective, will not waver in his effort, and will attain a great benefit in a short time. On the other hand, he who deviates from this path will have greater toil and less benefit. He who limits himself to one science and does not acquaint himself with another will be a laughingstock and will be missing more from his own specialty than what he knows of it because of the relationship of the sciences to one another as we have mentioned. For the sciences are stairs connected with each other as we have described. He who seeks to encompass all the sciences [240] is almost detruncated, removed from knowledge, and unable to achieve anything; he would be like a procurer without any goal since a lifetime falls short of attaining that. On the other hand, the individual should take up a little of each science if only to the extent of knowing the objective of each one of them. Afterwards, he should take up what is most indispensable as we have described. It is only then that he should devote himself to the science in which he excells with all his natural inclinations, heart, and all means at his disposal, and should master it to the best of his ability. This may mean two, three, or less sciences, depending on the degree of his natural sagacity, his power of understanding, his persistent inclination, and his devotion to study. All this is feasible with the help of God - May He be glorified and exalted; for were it dependent on the will of the individual, each man would hope to be the best of mankind. For understanding and devotion, too, are divided as are wealth and condition in the saying: "fortune is already allotted; therefore, do your best in what you seek."

He who seeks knowledge in order to boast about it, to be praised for it, or to gain means of it wealth and fame is far removed from success, because his object is not the realization of knowledge, but something else. The self and the eye of man crave for his own objective only no matter how it was pursued and as long as he attains the goal which he sets for himself.

Abu Muhammad said: The prevailing science today are divided into seven, and are the same among all people in all places and at all times. They are: (1) the religious law of every nation, which is always there, since every nation believes in something, either affirming or denying it; (2) science of history of a nation; (3) the science of language of a nation. Nations differ from one another by virtue of these three sciences. As for the remaining four sciences, they are common to all nations and consist of: (4) philosophy, which is the knowledge of things as they are and according to their definitions from the highest genera to particulars; it also include the knowledge of metaphysics; (5) astronomy; (6) numbers; and (7) medicine, which deals with the care of the body.

We have already demonstrated that every religious law *(shari'ah)* - except the religious law of Islam - is false. Thus it is incumbent to limit oneself to the law of the truth, and to avail oneself of all the means for a thorough knowledge of it. The science of the religious law of Islam is divided into four parts: the science of the Qur'an, the science of Traditions, the science of jurisprudence, and the science of theology.

The science of the Qur'an consists of the knowledge of its reading and the knowledge of its meaning.

The science of Traditions consists of the knowledge of the texts and the knowledge of transmitters.

The science of jurisprudence consists of legal precepts as contained in the Qur'an and Traditions; of what all Muslims agreed or disagreed on and of the knowledge of what is sound or unsound concerning the various demonstrations.

The science of theology consists of the knowledge of the doctrines of theologians, and of the knowledge of their arguments and what is sound or unsound concerning them on the basis of proof.

The science of grammar consists of old traditional transmission and the newly established causes.

The science of lexicography is based entirely on oral transmission. The science of history consists of categories with respect to arrangements according to dynasties, annalistic treatment, countries, categories, mixed arrangement. The most reliable history among us is the history of the Islamic community: its beginning, conquests, information about its caliphs, kings, and those attached to them; its scholars and other things connected with it. The history of the Israelites is sound for the most part, although some of it contains visible interpolation and obvious corruption; its information is sound from the time the Israelites went to Syria up to their last exodus and not before that. The history of the Greeks is reliable from the time of Alexander and not before that time. The history of the Persians is reliable from the time of Darius Ibn Darius and still more reliable from the time of Ardashir Ibn Babak; as for the time before that, it consists of superstitions containing obvious lies. As for the Turks, Khazars, the Northern people and the Black countries, they have neither sciences, nor histories. This holds true for the history of North Africa and al-Andalus before the coming of the Muslims. The histories of the Copts, Syriac people, Yemenites, Ammonites, Moabites, and others have perished completely with nothing left except fabrications and superstitions. As for India and China, their histories have not reached us as we would have liked. However, they are two nations possessing science, records, registry, and literary compositions.

Thus, the student of history should occupy himself only with things whose veracity we have shown, lest he should become disheartened when he finds out by himself what is false. Success come from God. Furthermore, he should not waste his time in useless things, particularly in those things that are false and about which we have spared him all effort. However, if the individual wanted to exert himself in such pursuit, he will arrive at the same conclusion as we did. Instead, he can use his effort better by devoting himself to the material we have recommended. Success comes from God.

Genealogy is a part of the science of history.

The science of the stars consists of the knowledge of astronomy and the basis of its proof, and what they refer to as the influence of the stars.

The science of numbers consists of ascertaining the rules of numbers, of establishing the proof, and their implementation in measuring and other purposes.

The science of logic consists of a rational and sensory part. The rational part is concerned with metaphysical and natural things, while the sensory part is concerned with natural things only.

The science of medicine consists of two parts: the medicine of the soul, which is the result of the science of logic; it is concerned with the improvement and correction of moral conduct by preventing it from excess and derelection and placing it in a position of moderation. The medicine of the body consists of the knowledge of the nature of bodies, the knowledge of the constitution of organs; the knowledge of illnesses, their causes, and response to drugs; and the determination of the power of drugs and food. The medicine of the body also consists of two parts: practical and surgical means such as setting broken bones, slitting *(batt),*[32] cauterization, and amputation; and the elimination of the power of maladies through the power of drugs. It is further divided into two parts: the preservation of health by preventing the occurrence of diseases, and the treatment of diseases when they occur.

The science of poetry consists of its transmission, meaning, virtue, defect, parts, meters, and versification.

Abu Muhammad said: There are also two sciences which are the outcome of the combined sciences we have mentioned and/or the result of two or more sciences. They are the science of rhetoric and the science of dream interpretation.

Rhetoric is a praiseworthy science if its pursuer directs it to invoking God - May He be glorified and exalted - to elucidating the knowledge of realities and to teaching the ignorant. On the other hand, if its pursuer were to direct it to contrary purpose, he will be empty-handed in that he will trouble himself and spend his life in something having evil consequences for himself. May God save us from such a misfortune.

Dream interpretaion is a natural gift possessed by the interpreter who is aided by a previous knowledge. Dream interpretaion cannot be reliable without the interpreter having before hand natural gifts and previous mastery of the sciences.

Abu Muhammad said: We recommend these arts *(afanin)* which are designated in ancient and modern times with the name of knowledge and sciences. Moreover, on verification and close examination, anything which is known may be called knowledge. This includes, commerce, tailoring, weaving, navigation, agriculture, forestry, horticulture, construction, and other crafts. This notwithstanding, these crafts are relevant to this world in that people need them for their livelihood. As for the sciences which we have described before, they have for their object the attainment of salvation in the Hereafter. For this reason, they merit precedence and should be preferred over other sciences. Success comes from the Almighty God.

Abu Muhammad said: We advise the student not to belittle what he does not know, for this would constitute an indication of his shortcomings and assertion about things without knowledge; nor should he be conceited about what he knows, for in so doing he would do violence to the merit of his own discipline, and would deserve detestation from God, Who had bestowed it on him as a gift. He should not envy anyone who is more knowledgeable than he and attempt to belittle him. These are two major blemishes. However, if he envies someone without disparaging him, but does it out of a desire to attain what the envied one has, he would do well, since the desire leads to good things. He should not belittle those who are less knowledgeable than he and should remember that he has been himself in that position before he acquired what he knows. He should not withhold what he knows, thereby placing himself at the level of the one who does not know, in that both do not make use of knowledge nor do they disseminate it. He should not talk about any science without a previous knowledge of it so as to avoid embarrssment; nor should he seek with his knowledge worldly goals, thereby exchanging the lofty for the base thing. All in all, he should devote himself to the Almighty God overtly and covertly for He is the ornament [242] and embellishment of the world. Success comes from God.

Abu Muhammad said: The sciences we have mentioned are related to one another, and are mutually interdependent. We have demonstrated from the outset that the raison d'etre of our existence in this world and the goal of learning the sciences is the knowledge of what the Almighty God wanted from us, the knowledge of what He had made us of, and the knowledge by means of which the pious would know our sorrowful, cruel, and vitiated position that is filled with evil and all sorts of misfortunes and perditions, and which is surrounded by all kinds of calamities and destruction. In other words, it is knowledge of the religious law, its dissemination and practice according to its requirements. If this is the case, there is no way out of the true knowledge of the religious law, and the need of the individual to know its reality through proof, that is, the knowledge of the roots of beliefs, the knowledge of what is obligatory upon him, the knowledge of what is forbidden, and the knowledge of what is permissible. This cannot be achieved without the knowledge of the dicta of the Almighty God as revealed to us in His Book; nor can it be achieved without the knowledge of what the Messenger of God- May God's prayer and peace be upon him - has ordered and communicated to us; nor without the knowledge of what the religious scholars have agreed or disagreed upon. This cannot be arrived at without the knowledge of the transmitters of those admonitions and without the knowledge of their time, names and genealogy to distinguish them in conformity with the proper designation of things, the knowledge about those who are accepted or rejected, the knowledge about those who had been met or not met and on whose authority Traditions have been transmitted, and the knowledge of famous Qur'anic readings in order to arrive at the agreement or disagreement concerning meanings that may lead to different decisions. All this, in turn, could not be accomplished without the knowledge of lexical usage, case endings that differentiate meanings according to different and similar situations. Moreover, it is necessary to relate lexicography and declension, to some aspects of poetry as it is necessary to have a knowledge of genealogy by means of which the individual is able to know who is or is not eligible for the Imamate; to have a knowledge as to who were the helpers whom we are urged to follow their good deeds and to avoid their bad ones; and to have knowledge as to who were the best relatives, who are not required to pay the voluntary charity *(sadaqah)*. It is also necessary to have some knowledge about mathematics in order to determine the position of the *qiblah,* the setting of the sun and the moon, and the different times of prayer. One cannot arrive at the reality of this without a knowledge of astronomy, nor can one arrive at the veracity of proof concerning that without acquainting oneself with the definitions and meanings of speech and logic. Knowledge of mathematics is also necessary in determining the division of personal possessions and measuring land in connection with inheritance and booty. The determination of all this is surely a necessary religious obligation. Likewise, it is required by the religious law to know the defects that should be taken into consideration, such as being possessed by madness. We were commanded on the authority of the Messenger of God- May God's prayer and peace be upon him - to practice the treatment of the sick. Thus, it is necessary to know how to treat the sick, and this is based on two premises requiring a knowledge of illness and their cure and constitutes the science of medicine.

The invocation of God - May He be glorified and exalted - is a duty and cannot be fulfilled without a degree of clarity, rhetoric, and a knowledge of beautiful expressions and clarity of meanings which appeal to the heart. All this is not possible without a knowledge of the religious law, lexicography, case endings, eloquence, and the proper use of both prose and poetry.

Vision is valid and constitutes one forty-sixth part of prophecy. The knowledge of its interpretation is necessary and cannot be achieved without the mastery of the aforesaid sciences.

One has to be acquainted with astrology in order to realize its falsity, for wrong cannot be known from right without a knowledge of astrology.

Abu Muhammad said: This is one aspect of the interdependence of the sciences and their need for one another. On the other hand, if the individual is not able to encompass all the sciences, he should, as we have indicated, have some acquaintance with them, however small this may be. Furthermore, people should cooperate with one another in the sciences for carrying on their duties in the same manner people cooperate with one another in building a home, which necessarily requires for its completion builders, workers who carry the stones and lay the clay, makers of roof tiles, woodcutters, carpenters and nail makers. This is also the case of other pursuits where people need the cooperation of one another as in agriculture, and the like, which cannot be carried out without the cooperation of making and using tools. It is this kind of cooperation that leads to salvation and attainment of the eternal world. In short, pleasing the Creator is the most imperative and noblest pursuit; we seek the support of the Almighty God.

Abu Muhammad said: Among the repulsive things for the individual is to remain idle all his life in this world, spending all the time in foolishness, inactivity, disobedience, and inequity when the individual could spend his time in something better and more important. I heard our teacher Muhammad Ibn al-Hasan[33] say to me and others, "It is indeed astonishing that an individual should remain in this world without cooperation in a matter of common good. Does he not see the plowman plowing for him, the miller grinding for him, the weaver weaving for him, the tailor sewing for him, the builder constructing for him, the butcher slaughtering for him, and other people doing some work from which he benefits and which he needs? Would he not be ashamed to be a burden on all those people without contributing anything to the general welfare?" By my life, his utterance is good and sound embodying maxims that stir up the dormant effort for what is intended here. Still more, what better utterance than **His saying** concerning cooperation among people, for the Almighty God warned his servants in the verse, "Cooperate with each other in piety and Godliness."[34] In fact, everything in which the individual participates in a commom welfare *(maslahah)*, whether pertaining to religion or anything useful to him in this world, is piety and godliness as long as the individual avails himself of what God commanded and urged him to do. After fulfilling what the Almighty God has made obligatory on the individual to learn his beliefs in words and action, the next best thing he does in this world is to teach people their religion for which they were created, thereby leading them to pleasing God -

May He be glorified and exalted - bringing them out by the grace of the Almighty Creator from the **blinding** darkness to pure light and from a deadly and narrow alley to a vast expanse; thereby exercising justice, avoiding inequity, and defending their possession with the zeal of warriors against corrupt and inequitable people; making them abide by the goal for which they were created concerning the performance of religion which the Almighty God made obligatory on them; and aiding them to acquire what we have mentioned with respect to records, safekeeping, distribution, determining individual rights, collection of obligatory money, and so forth. This should always be the case in helping people in all things requiring cooperation, including the crafts which are indispensable for them.

Abu Muhammad said: Know that there are among people of discernment (1) those who believe in the soundness of the Hereafter and in reward after death; (2) those who are doubtful about that; and (3) those who deny the existence of the Hereafter and reward believing in life of this world only. It is incumbent upon those who believe in the Hereafter and reward to exert themselves and make every effort in every possible way to escape damnation in the Hereafter. If the individual were to occupy himself in something else, he would forfeit that in which his salvation resides in the Hereafter, and would not only be undiscerning, stupid, blameworthy, and suicidal, but would be in the worst condition among crazy people and irrational francolins. No one is saved in the Hereafter without having studied the religious law of the truth and without having adhered to its obligations; nor would he be saved without having placed it above any science and without having practiced it over any action. Were he to neglect the religious law, his condition in this transitory world will be that of repentant. If he doubts the Hereafter, it will then be incumbent upon him to exert himself and abandon any distracting situation that would take him away from investigating the soundness as to whether the Hereafter is real or not. Were he to occupy himself in something else, he would then be without any doubt undiscerning, a loser of contractual obligation, beguiling himself, and **avoiding an issue on** which his great misfortune or happiness rests. All in all, he will never arrive at the knowledge of the Hereafter and reward without studying the religious law and without searching for the proof in it so as to perceive the reality concerning that.

Finally, if the individual does not believe in the soundness of the Hereafter but believes only in this world, there is one of two alternatives, not admitting a third one. The one alternative is the one in which he does not see the soul beyond, being plunged in appetites, its heedlessness in pleasure, and its addiction to inclinations. In this case, there is nothing important for the individual beyond this. This kind of posture would impel him not to retaliate against the one who takes pleasure in killing him, stealing his property, divulging his secret humiliating him in things pleasing others and harming him in things delighting the like of him. There is no greater looser than the one who he does not see except this abode in which his lot is nothing but misfortune, toil, trouble and perdition. [244] It may also be the case in which the individual upholds politics as a guarantee for his safety and that of others onerning blood, wives, skin, property, attainment of health, improvement of conditions, and self-sufficiency. This can never come about and is nonexistent without the use of the religious law as a deterrent in the Hereafter and as a means of punishment of disobident people in this world. Thus, if there is no other way for safety except through the religious law, it follows then that occupation with it should be the aim and deviation from it will constitute a vitiated opinion.

Moreover, he who occupies himself with the religious sciences will attain the safety of the ruler, the elite, and the masses, and will achieve high position and benefit in this world. On the other hand, he who opposes the religious law will earn the opposition of the ruler, the elite, and the masses, and will be exposed to misfortune concerning his blood, property, and condition. He who does not recognize the Hereafter but this world only is the most stupid, the least discerning, the most unfortunate, and will have the poorest way of life. Moreover, he will be exposed not only to misfortune and perdition during his lifetime, but will endure harm, and horrors, will deem suffering and harm easy, and will be exposed to perdition, suffering and calamity. The one who thinks that if he leaves this world he will attain eternal life, eternal happiness, and eternal joy is indeed stupid and a madman. We have said this in order to show through necessary, sensory and rational proof that preference of the religious law over all the sciences is incumbent upon all - upon those who do not recognize or doubt the Hereafter as well as upon those who do recognize the Hereafter. There is no difference in this. We beseech the Almighty God for the help that pleases Him; the work that brings us nearer to Him; the leisure that brings us close to him; and the aversion to what is lacking in purity and reward. Amen, Amen.

Abu Muhammad said: Some people - whose ignorance is overwhelming, whose minds are weak, and whose nature is vitiated - think that they are scholars, but actually they are not. There is no greater harm to the sciences and to true scholars than the harm from this group we have just mentioned. It is so because they took a meager part of some of the sciences, missing a much larger portion than what they had grasped. Moreover, their search for knowledge was not the search for the knowledge of the Almighty God, nor was their aim to escape the darkness of ignorance but to overwhelm people with vanity, and admiration, to stir trouble and discord, and to pride themselves arrogantly and vaingloriously that they are scholars when in reality they are not. This path leads nowhere because its pursuers have not achieved the reality of things and because they squandered all the necessary prerequisites, thereby increasing their wickedness. Their aim along with their disdain for other people is not but contempts for the sciences and their shortcomings, on the false belief that there is no valid science other than the one they pursue. This often happens to a beginner learning a science while he is still immature and in the prime of his youth, except that these initiates are expected to be cured from this malady through long observation and lengthy elucidation.

Our purpose now is to demonstrate to those people who have this quality one of two things: either (1) the shortcoming of their science which they boast about as being above other sciences, or (2) the need of their science for other sciences in that if they do not add to it others will remain wanting without much usefulness, and perhaps, will bring them great harm. We have found some people who have studied the religious sciences, but who denigrated the rest of the sciences. This is a great defect because the religious science does not benefit its pursuer until he knows the language which the lawgiver used to communicate with the people and until he knows and understands the science of numbers with respect to the distribution of the shares of an estate, inheritance, the time of the rising of the sun and moon which determines the times of prayers, the start of the month of fasting (Ramadan), and the time of **pilgrimage**.. Moreover, if the individual does not know the harmfulness of food and drink, he would be on the verge of partaking that which would hurt and harm him - and this is forbidden. The Messenger of God - May God's prayer and peace be upon him - ordered medication, thus making it a duty to follow his command. Therefore, learning medicine is an obligatory - duty incumbent upon Muslims, and he who neglects its study is negligent in his religious duty. Moreover, the Qur'an is Arabic, and there is no way for anyone to know it without a knowledge of grammar and lexicography. The same is true especially of the person who takes up one branch of the religious sciences; he will be wanting, will inflict harm on his soul, and will lead it to perdition. Moreover, were he to take up the Qur'anic science, for instance, without mastering the science of the say**ings and needs of the Prophet, he would be empty-handed** concerning religion and would not have the evidence on his side. By the same token, he who has command of the sayings and deeds of the Prophet without a mastery of the science of the Qur'an would not know what reading is permissible and what is not, nor would he know what the Almighty God did or did not reveal. Furthermore, were he to make legal decisions without expertise in the sciences of the Qur'an and the sayings and deeds of the Prophet, he would be equal to a donkey; his legal decisions are not acceptable because he does not know what he is deciding on, nor does he know whether his decisions are right or wrong. He simply passes legal decisions imitating someone whom he does not know as to whether he is right or wrong and, except by guesswork, he does not know what is incumbent upon him, or whether his decision or deed is a part of religion or outside it. Finally, were he connected with speculative theology and without a knowledge of the sayings and deeds of the Prophet, **he will surely perish on account of his** negligence of the reality of the religious law with which the Almighty God **had entrusted him, obligated him to fulfill, and commanded him to adhere to.**

We have also found people who have studied only the Arabic sciences such as grammar, lexicography, poetry, and prosody, and showed contempt for the rest of the sciences. This people are in the same position as the one who does not possess any food except salt, and no weapons except polisher for cleaning weapons. They will be oblivious to the religious sciences without which our coming to this world is meaningless and without which he will not have salvation and peace when departing from this world. They will also be far removed from the knowledge of realities.

We have likewise found people who have studied the sciences of the Ancients *('ulum al-awa'il),* or a branch thereof, and who looked upon the rest of the sciences [245] with ridicule. A case in point is that of the one who undertakes the study of medicine and who does not see any other science beyond it. One would tell this specialist in medicine, Do you not think that there are people who do not need treatment, nor do they know about medicine, yet there are among them people with healthier bodies and live longer than those who concern themselves with medicine, such as the people of the desert, the masses, and the inhabitants of countries who do not master medicine? No one can deny this, for it can be observed quite clearly. Then one may inquire, what is the utility of medicine? The object of the students of medicine is to repel illness and preserve health. Physicians are not more successful in this objective than other people. Similarly, there are geometricians and astronomers who look scoffingly and as though it were nonsense upon the sciences outside their own. One would tell them, what is the difference between the knowledge of the traversal of this or that star, or between the knowledge of the characteristic of this or that sign of the zodiac, or the distance of a given planet from the earth? Or what is the difference between the knowledge of the characteristic of a given city; the movement of a lady from that of so and so. For this reason, they have to admit that there is no way for them except that which leads to salvation, because all what they say about certain things in the world is information only having no usefulness except the knowledge of things in their aspects and, by means of which, the demonstration of a Maker and a Manager of the world. If the individual turns to astrology, he will entertain false claims and unverifiable superstitions that are invalidated by proof as we have demonstrated in another place, mainly, their failure to present evidence, except alleged experimentation. The claim of the astrologers to experience is false because those experiences cannot be verified owing to the fact that they take place over a long period of time, there is no way in which a dynasty lasts that long, nor is there a permanent condition for people to live in happiness and peace for that long time. Then, we shall ask the astrologers: If what you have at hand is true, as you assert, concerning birth and marriage, we also find that rams are born, live, are slaughtered, and eaten in a matter of minutes. [246] Afterward, leather is made of their skin, some of which becomes parchment used for writing and lasting a long time, while other parts are tags in the form of pieces and waste. Nothing of that leather comes to life and grows. Moreover, astrologers have failed in religious science, which is the truth.

We also tell those who have grasped the definitions of logic and who have denigrated the rest of the sciences: **You have acquired an instrument,** which is useless and unprofitable, if not put at the service of the rest of the sciences. You are like the one who gathered tools for construction, but did not use them for that purpose, thereby making your tools idle and useless.

Were those specialists to respond that those sciences are meant for livelihood and profit, we shall retort by saying that those sciences are the least profitable and very limited for gaining a livelihood. Thus if your objective is the acquisition of livelihood, then commerce, agriculture, and joining the ruler are more profitable and have a greater potential for wealth than those sciences you have embarked on.

Abu Muhammad said: We do not intend to belittle anything in these sciences. God forbid if we did. Were we to do this, we would be entering the company of those whom we censure and we would follow a contemptible path. On the contrary, we belittle only those who intend with their specialized discipline to find fault in and denigrate the rest of the sciences. As for the one who studies a given science without the Almighty God having opened the door for him to pursue another science, but who acknowledges the merit of the rest of the sciences, the limitation of his own discipline, and his own shortcomings, he is indeed beneficient, praiseworthy, and virtuous for having achieved balance in equity, justice, and truthfulness with respect to what he lacks. He will have achieved the blessing of recompense. No blame can be attached to him for what the Almighty God did not disclose to him. As for the individual who takes up what he needs from each one of the sciences and uses what he knows as it should be, he is indeed the most virtuous person, because he has attained the glory and sufficiency of the soul in this world and success in the Hereafter. Indeed, he has avoided the path of the ignoramuses and those who failed to make use of what they know and contrary to these conditions.

To sum up, had it not been for the search for salvation in the Hereafter, the study of any part of the sciences would be meaningless, because it is tiresome for the soul and the body, and because it is hard work that hampers the way to the pleasure of the transitory world concerning drink, food, diversion, foolishness, promotion to high positions, thirst for revenge, following one's inclination, and accumulation of wealth. And had it not been for the Hereafter which leads to the knowledge of the way of attaining success in it through the search of the sciences, the individual who occupies himself with knowledge would be in the worst possible condition. If this is the case, all the sciences are interdependent, as we have already demonstrated, and in need of each other; their objective is solely the knowledge of what lead to success in the Hereafter, that is, the knowledge of the religious law. Success lies in the Almighty God; He is my Guardian and Protector.

THIS IS THE END OF THE CATEGORIES OF THE SCIENCES. PRAISE BE TO GOD, THE LORD OF THE WORLD; HIS PRAYER AND PEACE BE UPON MUHAMMAD, THE LORD OF THE MESSENGERS AND THE SEAL OF THE PROPHETS, UPON HIS COMMUNITY, HIS COMPANIONS, WIVES, AND ALL HIS BRETHREN MESSENGERS TO THE DAY OF JUDGMENT.

IT WAS EXECUTED WITH THE HELP OF THE POWER OF GOD ON THE 28TH OF THE MONTH OF GLORIOUS RAMADAN IN THE YEAR 1001. MAY GOD GRANT US HIS BLESSING.

ARABIC EDITION

رمــــوز

أ : جامع فاتح في استنبول نمرة ٢٧٠٤
ر : مخطوطة الأوقاف نمرة ٢٠٩ المكتبة العمومية في الرباط
° ° : مثبتة في أ ناقصة في ر ٠ الا في حالة كلمة واحدة .
( ) : مثبتة في ر ناقصة في أ ٠ الا في حالة كلمة واحدة .
ع : إعداد عباس

(بسم الله الرحمن الرحيم)
صلى الله على سيدنا محمد وعلى آله وصحبه وسلم تسليما

كتاب مراتب العلوم وكيفية طلبها وتحلق بعضها ببعض، تأليف الشيخ الامام الحافظ أبي محمد علي بن احمد بن سعيد بن حزم الأندلسي الظاهري رحمه الله تعالى و رضي عنه ونفعنا به)(1).

" قال الفقيه الامام الحافظ أبو محمد على بن سعيد بن حزم ، رحمه الله "(2) الحمــد لله رب العالمين الذى أفاض علينا النعم الجزيلة ، ومنحنا القوى(3) الرفيعة حمـــدا برضيه عنا ، ويقتضي لنا المزيد من آلائه(4) ومواهبه السنية ، وصلى الله على سيدنــا(5) محمد ، خيرته من الانس وصفوته من ولد آدم ، المبعوث بالهدى لاستقاذ من اتبعــه من ظلمات(6) الكفر(وعمى الجهل الى نور الايمان و بصر العلم)(7).

أما بعد ، فان الله عز وجل(8) كرم بني آدم وفضلهم على كثير ممن خلق تفضيلا(9) ، وخصهم دون(10) خليقته بالتمييز الذي مكنهم به من التصرف في العلوم و الصناعـــات فواجب على المرء ألا يضيع ودية خالقه عنده وأن لا يهمل عطية باريه لديه ، بل فرض عليه أن يصونها باستعمالها فيما له خلق ، و أن يحوطها بتصريفها(11) فيما دعي اليه .

وبعد ، فان لكل مقام مقالا ، ولكل زمان حالا ، وان السالفين قبلنا كانت لهــم علوم يواظبون على تعليمها ، ويرثها الماضي منهم الآتي . ثم أن من تلك العلوم ما بقــى وبقيت الحاجة اليه ، ومنها مادرس رسمه ، ودثرت أعلامه وأنبت(12) فلم يبق الا اسمه . فمن ذلك علم السحر وعلم الطلسمات فان بقاياها ظاهرة لائحة ، وقد طمست(13) معرفة علمها ، ومن ذلك علم الموسيقى وصنوفها(14) الثلاثة ، فان الأوائل قد(15) يصفــون أنه كان منها نوع(16) يشجع الجبناء وهو اللوي ، ونوع ثان يسخى البخلاء وأظنــه الطنيني ، ونوع ثالث يؤلف بين النفوس وينفر . وهذه صفات معدومة من العالــم

---

(1) في أ : بسم الله الرحمن الرحيم وصلى الله على سيدنا محمد وآله رسالة فى مراتب العلوم . (2) . (3) ناقص في ر مثبت فى أ . (3) ر : القوة . (4) كذا فى ر ، فى أ ، الاله ، ع : آلائه . (5) ناقص في ر مثبت في أ . (6) ر : ظلمت . (7) أ : وعمى الجهل الى نور العلم . (8) أ : تعالى . (9) ناقصة فى أ . (10) أ : وخصهم على سائر . (11) أ : في تصريفها . (12) كذا فى ر ، فى أ : وأبنت ، ع : وأنبت . (13) أ : طمس . (14) أ : وأصنافها . (15) أ : الأوائل يصفــون . (16) أ : منها يشجع ، ع : منها ما يشجع .

اليم جملة ، فاعلموا أسعدكم الله بتوفيقه أن من رأيتموه يدعي معرفة (١٧) علم الموسيقى واللحون ، وعلم الطلسمات ، فانه مخرق كذاب ومشعوذ وقاح ، وكذلك من وجدتموه يتعاطى علم الكيمياء (١٨) فانه قد (١٩) أضاف الى هذه الصفات الذميمة التي ذكرنـا الطمع (٢٠) استئكال (٢٠أ) أموال الناس واستحلال التدليس في النقود وظلم من يعامل فـي ذلك والتخوير بروحه وبشرته في جنب ما يجاني من هذه الرذيلة . فان العلمين المذكورين أولا ، وان كانا قد عدما وانقطعا البتة ، فقد (٢١) كانا موجودين دهورا . وأما هــذا العلم الذي يدعونه من قلب جوهر (٢٢) الفلز (٢٣) فلم يزل عدما غير موجود . وباطــلا لم يتحقق ساعة من الدهر ، اذ من المحال الممتنع (٢٤) قلب نوع الى نوع ، ولا فرق بــين قلب (٢٥) نحاس الى أن يصير ذهبا أو قلب ذهب الى أن يصير نحاسا ، وبين قلب انسـان الى أن يصير حمارا ، أو قلب حمار (٢٦) الى أن يصير انسانا . وهكذا سائر الأنواع كلهـا وهذا محال (٢٧) البتة ، وبالله تعالى التوفيق "ومنه أستمد، ولا آله الا هو" (٢٨) .

(قال أبو (232) محمد) (٢٩) فلا وجه للاشتغال بعلم قد دثر وعدم ، وانمـا الواجب أن يهتم (٣٠) المرء بالعلوم المكن تعلمها التي قد (٣١) ينتفع بها في الوقت ، وأن يؤثر منها بالتقديم ما لا يتوصل الى سائرها (٣٢) الا به، ثم الأهم فالأهم والأنفــع فالأنفع ، فان من رام الارتقاء (٣٣) الى أرفع العلم دون معاناة ما لا يوصل اليه (٣٤) الا به كمن رام الصعود الى علية مفتحة مظلمة أنيقة البناء دون أن يتكلف التنقل اليها فـي الدرج والمراقي التي لا سبيل الى تلك العلية الا بتكلفها (٣٥) .

(قال أبو محمد) (٣٦) وليس للمرء الا داران : دار الدنيا ودار معاده اذا فــارق الدنيا ، وبيقين ندري أن مدة المقام في هذه الدنيا (٣٧) انما (٣٨) هي أيام تلائــــل ، واجهاد المرء نفسه فيما لا ينتفع به من العلم الا في هذه الدار رأي فائل (٣٩) وسعي (٤٠) خاسر (٤١) لأن المنتفع به في هذه الدار من العلم ، انما هو ما اكتسب به المــــال ،

___

(١٧) ناقصة في أ . (١٨) ر : الكيميات ، ا : الكيمياء . (١٩) ناقصة في ر .
(٢٠) ناقصة في أ . (٢٠أ) ا : في استئكال ع : استئكال . (٢١) ر : قد (٢٢)
ر : لجوهر . (٢٣) كذا في ر ، ا : الفكر ، ع : الفلز . (٢٤) ناقصة في أ .
(٢٥) ا : أن يقلب . (٢٦) ر : حمارا . (٢٧) ا : ممتنع . (٢٨) ناقص في ر .
(٢٩) ناقصة في أ . (٣٠) ر : يهمم . (٣١) ناقصة في ر . (٣٢) ا : سائرة .
(٣٣) ر : الارتقا . (٣٤) ناقصة في ر . (٣٥) ا : الأبهما . (٣٦) ناقصة في
أ . (٣٧) ا : الدار . (٣٨) ر : وانما . (٣٩) كذا في ا ، ع : قاتل ع :
فائل . (٤٠) ر : معنى . (٤١) كذا في ر لكن ا : واجهاد المرء نفسه فيما
لا ينتفع به الا في هذه الدار من العلوم رأي قاتل وسعي خاسر .

أو ما (٤٢) حفظت به. صحة الجسم فقط "فهما وجهان لا ثالث لهما" (٤٣) فأما العلوم التي يكتسب بها المال فان وجه الكسب بها ضيق غير متسع ، واكتساب المال بغير العلم أجدى وأشد (توصيلا الى المراد (٤٤) من) التوسع في العلم (¹⁴⁴) لكسب (٤٥) المال كصحبة السلطان وعمارة الأرض والتقلب في التجارات . وهذه الوجوه كلها قد نجد الجاهل الاغتم أنفذ (٤٧) فيها من العالم النحرير، فان ذاك كذلك ، فالشغل بطلب العلم ليكون سببا الى كسب المال والتحبب فيه بهذه النية عناء وضلال ، وفاعله قد جمع عيبين عظيمين ؛ أحدهما أنه (٤٨) ترك أخصر الطريقين الى مطلوبه وأسهلهما في التوصل الى غرضه ، وركب أوعرهما مسلكا وأطولهما تعبا وأقلهما فائدة وأبعدهما منفعة . والوجه الثاني أنه استعمل الفضيلة التامة التي بان بها عن الحشرات والبهائم في اقتناء أحجار (٤٩) لا يدري متى تدعه أو يدعها (٥٠) ، وكان كمن أتعب نفسه ، وأسهر ليله وأطال كده في اقامة سيف هندي قاطع نفيس، وبناء دار سوية (٥١) أنيقة البنيان (٥٢) محكمة النقوش (٥٣) ، موثقة الأساس، فلما تم له كما أراد جعل يستعمل السيف في كسر العظام وقطع البقل، وأوقف الدار لطرح ما يكنس فيها من الحشوش (٥٤) ، فمن أخسر صفقة من هذا. وأما العلم الذي ليس فيه الا حفظ صحة الجسم فقط فان المتعب فيه ببدنه (٥٥) المجهد لنفسه في تلقيه (٥٦) وتقييده لا يحصل من تمامه لديه الا على الحصر (٥٧) في معاناة مرض لا يدري أن يتم له غرضه من برئه أم لا يتم (٥٨) ، ثم ان تم فليس على ثقة من عودة (٥٩) ذلك الداء بعينه أشد مما (٦٠) كان ، أو حدوث داء آخر مثل الذي استفد طوقه في معاناته (٦١) أو أعضل (٦٢) منه . وأما المضمون المحتم فانه

---

(٤٢) ر: وما . (٤٣) ناقص في ر . (٤٤) ناقصة في أور ، زيادة لازمة . (٤٤أ) : توصلا الى العر' . (٤٥) ر : كسب. (٤٦) ر :فقد . (٤٧) انفسد ؛ ع : انغذ . (٤٨) ناقصة في أ . (٤٩) أ : حجارة . (٥٠) ر : ويدعها . (٥١) أ : وينىء دارا سرية . (٥٢) ا : البناء . (٥٣) ا : النفوس، ع : النقوش . (٥٤) ا : ما يكنس من الحشوش فيها . (٥٥) ناقص في ر . (٥٦) ا : تتقينه، ر : تثقيفه، ع : تلقيه . (٥٧) ا ، ر : الحصر،ع : البصر . (٥٨) ناقص في ر . (٥٩) ا : عود . (٦٠) ا : ما . (٦١) ا : استنفذ ظونه في معاته. ع : استنفد طوقه في معاناته . (٦٢) ا : واعضل .

لا يقدر على دفع الموت اذا حل ، ولا على علاج الزمانة اذا استحكمت ، ولعل ذلــــــك يحدث بمن أتعب نفسه في مداواته في أسرع من كر (٦٣) الطرف .
فمن تأمل ما ذكرنا علم ان المنفعة بما قصد به من العلم الى المنفعة الحاضرة (٦٤) فقط (٦٥) ، قليلة جدا وضعيفة الفائدة (٦٦) جملة . الا أن هذين الوجهين (٦٧) وان كانا وتحي النفع قليلي الاجزاء لكل من حاطبهما (٦٨) بالتعب في اقتناء العلم الذي هــــو سببها ، فلهما (٦٩) حظ من النفع . وانما الداء (٧٠) العباء والذم الكامل و الخســـارة المحضة ، حال (٧١) من اقتنى أرفع العلم ليحصل به على كسب مال من غير وجهـــــــه ، وصرف ما علم في غير (٧٢) طريقه ، فان حال الجهل (٧٣) افضل لعليله (٧٤) من حال من تعلم العلم لما (٧٥) ذكرنا ، ونسأل الله التوفيق ونعوذ به من الخذلان .

(قال أبو محمد) (٧٦) فاذا الامر كما ذكرنا فأفضل العلوم (٢٣٣) مــا أدى الى الخلاص في دار الخلود ووصل الى الفوز في دار (٧٧) البقاء . فطالب هـــذه العلم بهذه (٧٨) النية هو المستعيض بتعب راحة الابد ، وهو ذو الصفقة الرابحـــة والسعي النجح (٧٩) الذي بذل قليلا واستحق كثيرا ، وأعطى (٨٠) تافها وأخذ عظيمــا وهو الذي يعرف مالا يبقى معه فزهد فيه ، وميز مالا يزايله فسعى له ، نسأل اللــــه أن يجعلنا في (٨١) عدادهم بمنه آمين .

(قال أبو محمد) (٨٢) وباليقين يدري كل ذي حس (٨٣) سليم أنه لا يتوصــل الى العلم الا بطلب ، ولا يكون الطلب الا بسماع وقراءة وكتاب ، ولابد من هــــــذه الثلاث (٨٤) خصال والا فلا سبيل دونها الى شيء من العلم البتة . فان ذلك كذلــك

---

(٦٣) أ : كذع ع : كر . (٦٤) أ : الخاصة . (٦٥) ناقصة في : أ . (٦٦) أ : العائدة . (٦٧) أ : الا أن هذا من الوجهين ع ، الا أن هذين هذين الوجهين . (٦٨) أ : قليلي الاجزاء لا تحاصلبا ، ع : قليلي الاجزاء لاتصالهما . (٦٩) أ : فلهذا . (٧٠) ر : الدواء . (٧١) ناقصة في ر . (٧٢) ر : من غير . (٧٣) أ : الجاهل . (٧٤) أ : لحامله أمل ، ع : الخاملة أجل . (٧٥) أ : من حال العلم . (٧٦) ناقصـــة فـــي أ . (٧٧) ر : محلة . (٧٨) أ : لهذه . (٧٩) أ : النجح . (٨٠) ر : اعطــــــــا . (٨١) ر : من . (٨٢) أ : ناقصة في أ . (٨٣) ناقصة في أ ع ، لب . (٨٤) ر : الثلاثة .

فلنتكلم بعون الله تعالى على وجه التوصل الى العلوم وبيان أفضلها صفة وأعلاها قــدرا ،
والذي بالناس اليه الضرورة الماسة ، والفاقة الشديدة والحد الذي لا يجزى(٨٥) مـنـــه
مادونه والنهاية التي لاوراء لها منه . (قال أبو محمد)(٨٦) فالواجب على من ساس صغار
(أهل نوعه من ولده أومن غيرهم)(٨٧) أن يبدأ عند أول اشتدادهم وفهمهم ما يخاطبون بـه ،
وقوتهم على رجع الجواب وذلك يكون في خمس سنين أو نحو ذلك (٨٨) من مولد الصبي فيسلمهم
الى   (من يعلمهم الخط)(٨٩) وتأليف الكلمات من الحروف فاذا درب الغلام في ذلــك
كتب (٩٠) وقرأ . والحد الذي لاينبغي أن يقتصرالمتعلم (٩١) على أقل منه أن يكــون
خطه (٩٢) قائم الحروف بينا صحيح التأليف الذي هوالمجزىء فان الخطان لم يكــن
هكذا لم يقرأ الابتعب شديد فاما (٩٣) التزيد في جمال (٩٤) الخط فليس فضيلة (٩٥) بـل
لعله داعية الى التعلق بالسلطان ، فيفنى دهره اما في ظلم الناس و اما في تسويـــد
القراطيس وتواقيع بعيدة (٩٦) من الحق مشحونة بالكذب والباطل فيضيع زمانه باطــلا
ويخسر (٩٧) صفقته ويندم حين لاينفعه الندم ، وكان كانسان ملك مسكا كثيرا فتــرك
أن يصرفه في التطبيب (٩٨) به ومداواة النفوس يريحه وقوته (٩٩) وأقبل يطيب به البهائم ،
ويصبه في الطريق حتى فني في غير فائدة . فهذا حد (٩٩أ).
وحد تعلم القراءة أن يمهر في قراءة كل (١٠٠) كتاب يخرج الى (١٠١) يده بلغته
التي يخاطب بها اهل (١٠٢) صقعه وينفذ فيه ويحفظ مع ذلك القرآن فانه يجمع بذلــك
وجوها عظيمة (١٠٣) من المنفعة (١٠٤) أحدها التدرب في القراءة (١٠٥) وتمرين (١٠٦)
اللسان على تلاوته فيفصح (١٠٧) من ذلك حدا الى ما يحصل عنده من عهوده الفاضلة (١٠٨)
ووصاياه الكريمة ، ليجد هاعد ة عنده مدخرة لد به قبل حاجته اليها (١٠٩) يوم حاجته اليها فاذا (١١٠)

---

(٨٥) ريجز" . (٨٦) ناقصة في ١ . (٨٧) ١ : فالواجب على من ساس صغــار
ولد انه وغيرهم . (٨٨) ١ : او نحوها . (٨٩) ١ : في تعليم الخط ،ع : الى موئ ب
في تعليم الخط . (٩٠) ١ : ودرب ع : درس . (٩١) ١ : المعلم . (٩٢) ١ :
الخط . (٩٣) ١ : واما . (٩٤) ١ : حسن . (٩٥) ١ : فليس هو فضيلة . (٦
٩) ر : بتفاقيع بعيدة ، ١ : بعيد ،ع : بعيدة . (٩٧) ١ : وتخسر . (٩٨
١ : التطبيب . (٩٩) كذا في ر ، وا ،ع : وفعوته . (٩٩أ) ناقصة في أ ،ع :
حد . (١٠٠) ١ : من . (١٠١) ١ : القراءة لكل . (١٠٢) ناقصة في ١ .
(١٠٣) ١ : وجوه كثيرة عظيمة . (١٠٤) ناقصة في ١ . (١٠٥) ١ : في القراءة
له . (١٠٦) كذا في ر ، ١ : وتمييز ،ع : وتمرين . (١٠٧) ١ : فيحصـل .
(١٠٨) ر : الفاصلة . (١٠٩) ١ ، ر : اليه ،ع : اليها . (١١٠) ١ ،ر : اليه
،ع : اليها

أنفذ(١١١) في الكتابة(١١٢) والقراءة كما ذكرنا ، فلينتقل(١١٣) الى علم النحو وعلم(١١٤) اللغة معا .

ومعنى النحو هو معرفة تنقل هجاء اللفظ وتنقل حركات الذي يدل كل ذلك على اختلاف المعاني كرفع الفاعل ونصب المفعول وخفض المضاف ، وجزم الأمر والنهـــي ، وكالياء في نصب(١١٥) التثنية والجمع وخفضهما(١١٦) ، وكالألف في رفع التثنيـــة والواو في رفع الجمع وما أشبه ذلك . فان جهل هذا العلم(١١٧) عسر عليه فهم(١١٨) ما يقرأ من العلم .

واللغة : هي الالفاظ(١١٩) التي(١٢٠) يحبر بها عن(١٢١) المعاني فيتقصى(١٢٢) من علم النحو كل(١٢٣) ما يتصرف في مخاطبات الناس وكتبهم المؤلفة ، ويتقصى(١٢٤) اللغة المستعمل الكثير(١٢٥) التصرف واحط(١٢٦) ما يجزئ من النحو ، فكتــاب(١٢٧) الواضح للزبيدي أو ما نحا نحوه كالكتاب الموجز(١٢٨) لابن السراج ، وما أشبـــه هذه(١٢٩) الأوضاع الخفيفة الكافية(١٣٠) ، وأما التعمق في علل(١٣١) النحـــو ففضول ولا منفعة (٢٣٤) لها(١٣٢) بل هي مشغلة عن الأوكد ومقطعة عـــن(١٣٣) الأوجب الأهم(١٣٤) وانما هي تكاد يبيّن ما وجه الشغل بما هذه صفته وانما الغـــرض بهذا(١٣٥) العلم فهم(١٣٦) المخاطبة وما بالمرء حاجة اليه من فك(١٣٧) الكتــب من(١٣٨) المجموعة في العلوم فقط . فمن تزيد(١٣٩) في هذا العلم الى إحكام كتـاب سيبو يه نحسن به الا أن الاشتغال بغير ذلك(١٤٠) أولى وأفضل لأنه لا منفعة للتزيد علــى

---

(١١١) أ : نفذ . (١١٢) أ،ر : الكتاب . (١١٣) ر : فلننتقل . (١١٤) ناقصة في أ . (١١٥) ناقصة في أ . (١١٦) زيادة اقتضاها السياق ، في أ : وكالياء في التثنية والجمع فـي النصب وخفضهما . (١١٧) مكررة في ر . (١١٨) أ (١١٩) أ : علم . (١٢٠) أ : الفاظ . (١٢٠) ناقصة في أ . (١٢١) أ . (١٢٢) أ : عن . (١٢٢) أ : فيتقضي . (١٢٣) ناقصـة فـى ر . (١٢٤) أ : ويتقضى . (١٢٥) ر : الكبيرة . (١٢٦) أ : واقل . (١٢٧) أ : كتـاب . (١٢٨) أ : كالموجز . (١٢٩) ناقصة في أ . (١٣٠) أ : الحقيقة . الكافية ناقصـة في أ . (١٣١) أ : علم . (١٣٢) أ : لا منفعة بها . (١٣٣) أ : دون . (١٣٤) أ : والأهم . (١٣٥) أ : من هذا . (١٣٦) أ : فهمي . (١٣٧) أ : قل ، ع : في قراءة . (١٣٨) ناقصة في أ . (١٣٩) أ : يزيد . (١٤٠) أ : هذا .

المقدار الذي ذكرنا الا لمن أراد أن يجعله معاشا فهذا وجه فاضل لأنه باب من العلم على كل حال .

والذي يجزئ $^{(141)}$ من علم اللغة كتابان $^{(142)}$ أحدهما الغريب المصنف لأبي عبيد ، والثاني مختصر العين للزبيدي ليقف على المستعمل منها $^{(143)}$ ويكون ما عــــــدا $^{(144)}$ المستعمل منها $^{(145)}$ عدة لحاجة إن عنّت يوماما $^{(146)}$ في لفظ مستغلق فيما يقــــرأ من الكتب فان أفضل في اللغة $^{(147)}$ حتى يحكم خلق الانسان لثابت والفرق له و المذكـر والمؤنث لابن الانباري، والمقصور والممدود $^{(148)}$ والمهموز لأبي علي القالي و النبـــــات لأبي حنيفة أحمد بن داود الدينوري وما أشبه ذلك فحسن بخلاف ما قلناه $^{(149)}$ في علــــل النحو لأن اللغة كلها حقيقة وذات أوضاع صحاح وعبارات عن المعاني ولو كانت اللغة أوسع حتى يكون لكل معنى في العالم اسم مختصره لكان أتم $^{(150)}$ للفهم وأجلى للشــــك وأقرب للبيان الا أن الاقتصار على المقدار الجاري ما ذكرناه $^{(151)}$ والانصراف الى الأهــم والأوكد من سائر العلوم أولى .

(قال أبو محمد) $^{(152)}$ وان كان $^{(153)}$ علينا مع ما ذكرنا رواية شئ من الشعر فــــلا يكن $^{(154)}$ الا من الأشعار التي فيها الحكم والخير كشعر حسان بن ثابت وكعب بن مالــك ، وعبدالله بن رواحة رضي الله عنهم ، وكشعر صالح بن عبدالقدوس ونحو ذلك فانها نعـــم العون على تنبه النفس. وينبغي أن يجتنب $^{(155)}$ من الشعر أربعة أضرب أحدهــــــا : الاغزال والرقيق فانها تحث على الصبا $^{(156)}$ وتدعو $^{(157)}$ الى الفتنة ، وتحض على الفتــوة وتصرف النفس الى الخلاعة $^{(158)}$ واللذات $^{(159)}$ وتسهل الانهماك في الشطارة و العشـق وتنمى عن الحقائق حتى ربما أدى ذلك الى افساد الدين $^{(160)}$ والدنيا وتبذير المال فـي الوجوه الذميمة وأخلاق العرض وذهاب $^{(161)}$ المروءة وتضييع الواجبات. وان سماع شعــــر

---

(141) ر : يجزئ . (142) أ : كتابان . (143) أ : بهما . (144) ر : عــدى . (145) أ : منهما . (146) ناقصة في ر . (147) أ : علوم اللغة . (148) أ : والممدود والمقصور . (149) أ : ما قلنا . (150) أ : أبلغ . (151) أ : ذكرنا . (152) ناقصة في أ . (153) أ : وان كان ه ر : وان علينا . (154) ر : يكون . (155) أ : يتجنب . (156) أ : الصبابة . (157) ر : تدعوا . (158) ر : الخالفة . (159) أ : الذات . ع : اللذات . (160) أ : الى الهلاك والفساد في الدين . (161) أ : واذهاب .

رقيق لينقضي بنية المرء الرائق نفسه(١٦٢) حتى يحتاج الى اصلاحها ومعاناتها برهة لاسيما ماكان منها(١٦٣) في الغزل(١٦٤) بالمذكر وصفة الخمر والخلاصة فان هذا النوع يسهل الفسوق ويهون المعاصي ويردي جملة .

والضرب الثاني : الأشعار المقولة في التصعلك وذكر الحروب كشعر عنترة وعروة بن الورد وسعد(١٦٥) بن ناشب وما هنالك فان هذه أشعار تثير النفوس وتهيج الطبيعة وتسهل على المرء موارد التلف في غير حق وربما أدته (الى ذهاب نفسه ضياعا)(١٦٦) في غير واجب(١٦٧) ، والى خسارة الآخرة مع اثارة الفتن وتهوين الجنايات والاحوال الشنيعة(١٦٨) والنزوع الى الظلم وسفك الدماء .

والضرب الثالث : أشعار التغرب وصفات المفاوز والبيد والمهامه فانها تسهل التحول والتغرب وتشتت(١٦٩) المرء فيما ربما صعب عليه التخلص منه بالمعنى .

والضرب الرابع ، الهجاء ، فان هذا الضرب أفسد الضروب لطالبه لأنه(١٧٠) يهون على المرء الكون في حال(١٧١) أهل السفه من كاسي الحشوش(١٧٢) والمعاناة(١٧٣) لصنعة الزمر(١٧٤) المكتسبين(١٧٥) بالتسافه(١٧٦) والنذالة والخساسة وتمزيق الاعراض وذكر العورات(١٧٧) وانتهاك حرمة(١٧٨) الآباء والأمهات وفي هذا حلول الدمار فـي الدنيا والآخرة .

(235) ثم صنفان في الشعر(١٧٩) لا نُنْهى(١٨٠) عنهما نهيا تاما ولا نحض(١٨١) عليهما بل هما عندنا من المباح المكروه وهما المدح والرثاء ؛ فاما اباحتهما فلأن فيهما ذكر فضائل المرثي(١٨٢) والممدوح وهذا يقتضي للراوي(١٨٣) ذلك الشعر الرغبة في مثــل

_____

(١٦٢) أ : لنفسه . (١٦٣) كذا في ر ، أ : يُنهى ، ع : يُجنى . (١٦٤) ناقصة في أ .
(١٦٥) كذا في ر ، أ : سعيد ، ع : سعد . (١٦٦) أ : الى هلاك نفسه في غير حق .
(١٦٧) أ : حق . (١٦٨) ر : الشيعية . (١٦٩) أ : تنشب . (١٧٠) أ : فانه .
(١٧١) أ : حالة . (١٧٢) كذا في ر ، أ : كاني الحسوس ، ع : كاسي الحشوش .
(١٧٣) ر : المعانت . (١٧٤) أ : الزبير . (١٧٥) أ : المتكسبين . (١٧٦) أ : بالسفاهة
(١٧٧) ر : العورات . (١٧٨) أ : حرم . (١٧٩) أ : من الشعر . (١٨٠) أ : لا ينهى .
(١٨١) أ : ولا يحض . (١٨٢) أ : الموت . (١٨٣) أ : للراوي .

ذلك الحال ، وأما كراهتنا لهما فلان (١٨٤) أكرماني هذين (١٨٥) النوعين الكــذب ولا خير في الكذب ٠

وأيضا فان الاكثار من رواية الشعر ، (ربما ادى بصاحبه الى التكسب بالشعر (١٨٦) هو كسب غير محمود ، لانه من (١٨٧) طريق الباطل والفضول ، لا من طريق الحـــق والفضائل ٠ ولا يظن ظان أن هذا علم جرّدناه فذممناه فقد علم من داخلنا وبلغه (١٨٨) أمرنا (من أهل زماننا) (١٨٩) كيف توسعنا في رواية الاشعار وكيف تمكنا (١٩٠) مــــن الاشراف على معانيها ، وكيف وقوفنا على آفانين الشعر ومحاسنه ومعانيه وأقسامـه ، وكيف قوتنا على صياغته (١٩١) ، وكيف تأتي مقصده ومقطوعه لنا (١٩٢) وكيف سهولــة نظمه علينا من الاطالة فيه (١٩٣) والتقصير ولكن (١٩٤) الحق أولى بما قيل (١٩٥) ٠

فاذا بلغ المرء من النحو واللغة الى الحد الذي ذكرنا فلينتقل الى علم العـــدد ، فليحكم الضرب والقسم والجمع والطرح والتسمية ولياخذ طرفا من المساحة ، وليشرف (١٩٦) على الارثماطيقي ، وهو علم طبيعة العدد ٠ وليقرأ (١٩٧) كتاب اثليدس قراءة متفهم لــه ، واقف على أغراضه ، عارف بمعانيه ، فانه علم رفيع ، به يتوصل الى معرفة نصيب الارض ومساحتها وتركيب الأفلاك ودورانها ومراكزها وأبعادها والوقوف (١٩٨) على براهين كل ذلك وعلى دوران الكواكب وتقطعها في البروج ، وهذا (١٩٩) علم رفيع جدا يقف بـــه المرء على حقيقة تناهي جرم العالم وعلى آثار صنعة الباري تعالى (٢٠٠) في العالـــم فلا يبقى له الا مشاهدة (٢٠١) الصانع فقط ، وأما الصنعة والادارة (٢٠٢) والتركيب فقد شاهد كل ذلك بوقوفه على ما ذكرنا وبمطالعة (٢٠٣) كتاب المجسطي يعــــرف (٢٠٤) الكسوفات وعروض البلاد وأطوالها والاوقات وزيادة الليل والنهار ونقصهما (٢٠٥) والمد (٢٠٦) والجزر ومنازل الشمس والقمر والدراري ٠ وأما الاشغال في الساحـــة فمنفعته في جلب المياه ورفع الاثقال وهندسة البناء واقامة الالات الحكمية ٠ وأما الاشتغال

ــ

(١٨٤) أ : فلان ٠ (١٨٥) ر : هاذين ٠ (١٨٦) ناقصة في أ ٠ (١٨٧) كذا في ر ، ناقصة في أ ، ع : ٠ (١٨٨) أ : أضافها ٠ (١٨٩) أ : أبلغه ٠ ناقصة فــي ر ٠ (١٩٠) ر : تمكنا ٠ (١٩١) أ : صناعته ٠ (١٩٢) ناقصة في ر ٠ (١٩٣) أ : فــي الاطالة ٠ (١٩٤) ر : ولاكن ٠ (١٩٥) ر : ماقيل ٠ (١٩٦) ر : ويشرف ٠ (١٩٧) ر : واليقرأ ٠ (١٩٨) ر : والوقف ٠ (١٩٩) أ : فهذا ٠ (٢٠٠) ناقصة في أ ٠ (٢٠١) في ر : مشاهدات (٢٠٢) ر : والارادة ٠ (٢٠٣) أ : وبمطالعته ٠ (٢٠٤) ر : ويعرف ٠ (٢٠٥) ناقصة في أ ٠ (٢٠٦) ناقصة في ر ٠

بأحكام النجم فلا معنى له ولا يخلو(٢٠٧) وأن يكون(٢٠٨) مايحتكون من قضاياها حقــا
أو باطلاء ولا سبيل(٢٠٩) الى قسم ثالث فان كانت(٢١٠) حقا فما لها فائدة الا استعجــال
الهم والغم والبؤس والنكد كتوقع(٢١١) المرض والنكبات وموت الأحبة وانقطاع كمية العمر
ومعرفة فساد المولد .

فان قالوا أنه قد يمكن دفع مايتوقع من ذلك فقد ناقضوا(٢١٢) بأنها لا حقيقة لها ٠
اذ الحق الحتم لا سبيل الى رده٠ وان كان(٢١٣) باطلا فاهل(٢١٤) ألا يشتغــل به ٠
(قال أبومحمد)(٢١٥) ٠ ونقول قولا صحيحا متينا ليعلم كل ذي عقل ينصح نفسه
بأنه لا سبيل الى قلب الأنواع واحالة الطبائع،فمن اشتغل بشيء من هذين العلميــن
فانما هو انسان محروم مخذول يطلب مالا يجد أبدا٦(٢١٦) ٠ وبالجملة فليس القضـــاء
بالنجوم علم برهان وانما هى دعاوى(٢١٧) تجارب وان هى كذلك فهى باطل بلا شك(٢١٨)
لأن التجارب لا تكون الا بتكرار(٢١٩) الحال مرارا كثيرة جدا على صفة واحدة لا تستحيــل
البتة(٢٢٠) ٠ والنصبة التامة من الكواكب لا تعود الا الى عشرة آلاف من السنين(٢٢١) ،
ولا سبيل الى ضبط تجربة مثل هذه(٢٢٢) الا بتداول قوم متعاقبين لرصد النصــب
و باليقين ندرى(٢٢٣) أنه لا يبقى فيما(٢٢٤) انحدر عن شرق المعمور(٢٢٥) ، مملكــة
عشر الدور فكيف الدور كله واذا ذهبت المملكة لم تذهب الا بحروب وغارات وسوء حــال
وفساد بلاد وحدوث آخره وهذا كله يذهب بعلم تلك المملكة وترتيبها وأرصادها وأكثر اخبارها
بل كلها ،فلا سبيل(٢٢٦) مع هذا (236) الى اتصال رصد هذه المدة كلها ،فكيف
أن يمكن تكرار التجربة دورا بحد دور)(٢٢٧) ٠ وما عندنا تاريخ أبعد من تاريـــخ

_____

(٢٠٧) ر : يخلوا ٠ (٢٠٨) أ : يخلو من أن يكون ٠ (٢٠٩) أ : اذ لا سبيـــل ٠
(٢١٠) ر : كان ٠ (٢١١) أ : لتوقع ٠ (٢١٢) أ : فقد قضوا ٠ (٢١٣) ر : كانت ٠
(٢١٤) فاهل مكررة مرتين فى ر ٠ ا : أهل ٠ (٢١٥) غير موجودة فى أ ٠ (٢١٦)
غير مثبت فى ر ٠ (٢١٧) ا : وانما هي تداعى ابدا وبالجملة تجارب٠ ع : تراعـــى ٠
(٢١٨) أ : وانهي كذلك فباطل بلا شك ٠ (٢١٩) أ : بتكرير ٠ (٢٢٠) أ : أبـــدا ٠
(٢٢١) ر : لا تعود الى عشرات آلاف من السنين ٠(٢٢٢) ر : هذا ٠ (٢٢٣) ر : ندرى ٠
(٢٢٤) ر : فى ما ٠ (٢٢٥) أ : الجمود ٠ (٢٢٦) أ : مع ذلك ٠ (٢٢٧) أ : فكيــف
أن يمكن دوام التجربة تكرارا دورا بحد دور ٠

التوراة (٢٢٨) وليس له (٢٢٩) الا نحو (٢٣٠) ثلاثة آلاف سنة فقط ، فاين يقع
مما (٢٣١) نريد ؟ واما تاريخ الفرس فــ(٢٣٢) عندنا اخبار لهم فاشية محققة الا مـــن
عهد ملوك الساسانية وذلك اقل من الفعلم وكذلك تاريخ الروم . واما تاريخ القبط(٢٣٣)
والسريانيين واليمن (٢٣٤) وأدم (٢٣٥) وعمون ومؤاب (٢٣٦) وسائر تلك الأمـــم
فما لهم اليوم (٢٣٧) فى الدنيا خبر ولا اثر ، فكيف تبقى ارصاد المدة المذكـــورة ؟
واما الهند والصين فلم تبلغنا اخبارهم (٢٣٨) كما نريد ، ولعل لهم ارصادا قديمـــة .
فانهما مملكتان سلمتا من الآفات على مر الدهور . على أن أهل الصين ليسوا أهل علم
البتة وانما هم اهل صناعات ، فلعل هذا يكون بالهند . فان لم يكن فمضمون عدمـه
من العالم . (٢٣٩)

(قال أبو محمد) (٢٤٠) هذا الى مافى شروط (٢٤١) علم (٢٤٢) القضاء مـــن
الصفات التى لا سبيل لمن يدعى علمها الى استيفائها من معرفة مواقع السهــام (٢٤٣)
ومطارح الشعاعات والبروج (٢٤٤) النيرة والمظلمة والقتمة والآبار (٢٤٥) وخو اصا الدرارى
فى كل برج . والكواكب البابانية (٢٤٦) وغير ذلك مما لا يمكنهم توفيته حقه على اصولهـــم ،
فاذ ذلك كذلك (٢٤٧) ، فتحقيق علمهم فى القضاء لا سبيل اليه البتة ولا نحصى (٢٤٨)
كم شاهدنا لهم من القضايا المحققة المتفق عليها من اهل الاحسان لهذا العلم علــى

_____

(٢٢٨) ر : التورتة . (٢٢٩) ر : لها . (٢٣٠) ناقصة فى أ . (٢٣١) ر ، ع : فاين
يقعان مما اريد . ع : فاين يقع ما نريد . (٢٣٢) كذا فى ر ، ناقصة فى أ ، ع :
اضافها . (٢٣٣) ر : واما تاريخ الفرس فماعندنا القبط . (٢٣٤) ناقصة فـــى أ .
(٢٣٥) ناقصة فى ر . (٢٣٦) ر : مؤات . (٢٣٧) ناقصة فى ر . (٢٣٨) أ : آثارهم .
(٢٣٩) غير مثبت فى ر . (٢٤٠) ناقصة فى أ . (٢٤١) ر : شرط . (٢٤٢) ناقصة فى ر .
(٢٤٣) أ : من مواقع السهـام . (٢٤٤) أ : والدرج . (٢٤٥) كذا فى ر ، أ : والقيمة
والآثار . ع : والقتمة والآبار . (٢٤٦) أ : البنيانية . (٢٤٧) أ : فاذا كان ذلــك
كذلك . (٢٤٨) أ : ولا يحصى .

مافي كتبهم ، فما صدق (٢٤٩) منها شيء الا الاقل النزر الذي (٢٥٠) يصدق بالـــرأي
والتقدير (٢٥١) اكثر منه من المواليد (٢٥٢) التي لا شيء في علمهم أحق منها ، وامــــا
المناخات وتحاول (٢٥٣) السنين والقرانات الصغار فيعلم الله (عز وجل) (٢٥٤) اننــــا
ما رايناهم صدقوا منها ولا (٢٥٥) في قضية ابدا ، كل سنة رأينا ، وما وجدنا اكثر كلامهم
في ذلك الا على ظاهر الرأي والتقدير فقط ، ولو لم يكن من ظاهر الدعوى الا قولهــــم
زحل يشرف في برج كذا ، ويسقط في برج كذا ، وكذلك سائر (٢٥٦) الدراري ودعواهـم
في وجوه المطالع وسائر وجوه الخرافات ، (٢٥٧) فانهم لا يأتون على ذلك ببرهان (٢٥٨) ولا
باقناع ولا بشغب وانما هو " اسمع و اسكت وصدق الامير " وما كان هذا سبيله فلا ينبغــى
ان يشتغل به عاقل اشتغال ممتد به علما ، الا انه لا ينبغي لطالب الحقائق ان يخلــو مــن
النظر فيه ليعرف أغراضهم ويمنع نفسه من تطلعها الى الوقوف عليها (٢٥٩) وليفيق مــن
دعاويهم ومخرقتهم ، ويزيل عن نفسه الهم اذا عرف انه (٢٦٠) لا فائدة فيه .

ولقد (٢٦١) حدثني شيخنا القاضي ابو الوليد يونس بن عبد الله (٢٦٢) قال: سمعت
يحيى بن مجاهد الفزاري الزاهد يقول : هذا كان أوان طلبي للعلم اذ قوي فهمــــي
واستحكمت ارادتي .

قال (٢٦٣) فقلت له : فعلمنا الطريق ، لعلنا ندرك ذلك بوصاتك ، فــي
استقبال اعمارنا ، فقال (٢٦٤) نعم كنت آخذ من كل (٢٦٥) علم طرفا ، فان سمــاع
الانسان (قوما يتكلمون في علم وهو لا يدري) (٢٦٦) ما يقولون ، غمة عظيمة . أو كلاما هــــذا
معناه ، (قال أبومحمد) (٢٦٧) ولقد صدق رحمه الله .

---

(٢٤٩) أ : فما صدق . (٢٥٠) ر : التي . (٢٥١) أ : يصدق بالتقدير . (٢٥٢) ر : المواليد
أ : نحنى من المواليد . (٢٥٣) ر : تحاول . (٢٥٤) ناقصة في أ . (٢٥٥) ناقصة في أ .
(٢٥٦) أ : وكذا سائر . (٢٥٧) أ : تلك الخرافات . (٢٥٨) أ : لا برهـــــان
(٢٥٩) ر : عليه . (٢٦٠) ر : بانه . (٢٦١) ر : فلقد . (٢٦٢) أ : ولقد حدثني شيخنــا
يونس بن عبد الله القاضي . (٢٦٣) ناقصة في أ . (٢٦٤) أ : قال . (٢٦٥) كذا في
ر ناقصة في أ ، ع . (٢٦٦) أ : أضافها . (٢٦٧) قوما يتحدثون وهو لا يدري . (٢٦٧) ناقصة
في أ .

(قال أبومحمد)[268] : فاذا بلغ الانسان حيث ذكرناه أخذ في النظر في
حدود المنطق وعلم الأجناس والأنواع والأسماء المفردة والقضايا والمقدمات والقرائن[269]
والنتائج ليعرف المرء ما البرهان وما الإتباع[270] وما الشغب ، وكيف التحفظ
مما يظن أنه برهان "وليس يبرهان"[271] ، فبهذا العلم يقف على الحقائق كلها
و يميزها من الاباطيل تميزا لا يبقى معه ريب ، وينظر في الطبيعيات وهو ارض الجو
و تركيب[272] العناصر ، في الحيوان والنبات[273] والمعادن ، و يقرأ كتب التشريح
ليقف على محكم الصنعة وتأثير الصانع وتأليف الاعضاء[274] واختيار (237)
المدبر وحكمته[275] وقدرته فاذا أحكم ذلك في خلال ابتدائه بالنظر في العلوم
فلا يكن منه اغفال لمطالعة أخبار الأمم السالفة و الخالفة وقراءة التواريخ القديمة
والحديثة ليقف من ذلك على فناء[276] الممالك المذكورة[277] وخراب البلاد
المعمورة ، ودثور المدائن[278] المشهورة التي طالما حصنت وأحكمت مبانيها وذهاب من
كان فيها ، وانقطاعهم ، وتقلب الدنيا بأهلها "وذهاب الملوك الذين قتلوا النفوس
وظلموا الناس واستكثروا من الأموال والجيوش والعدد ليستديموها لهم[279] ولا عقابهم
فمادامت[280] لهم ، بل ذهبوا وانقطعت آثارهم ، ورحل بنوهم وضلوا ، و بقي
ما تحملوا من الاثام والذم والذكر القبيح لازما لأرواحهم في المعاد ولذكرهم في الدنيا"[281]
فيحدث له فيها بذلك زهد وقلة رغبة وليشرف على اغترار الملوك بها ، وعظيم[282]
الحسرات النازلة بهم وبمخلفيهم ، وليقف على حمد المتقين[283] الاخبار للفضائل
فيرغب فيها ، ويسمع ذمهم للرذائل فيكرهها[284] ، ويفي[285] على تيقن الصحيح
منها بما[286] يرى من تناصر التواريخ على تباعد اقطار

----

(268) ناقصة في أ . (269) ر : للقرائن . (270) ناقصة في أ . (271) ناقص في ر .
(272) ر : ترك . (273) أ : وفي الحيوان والنبات ر : في الحيوان أو النبات .
(274) ر : الاعضا . (275) ناقص في ر . (276) كذا في ر ، أ : ختا ، ع : فناء .
(277) ناقص في ر . (278) ر : البلاد . (279) أ : ليستدموا ماهم ولا ، ع : ليستديموها
لهم . (280) أ (281) أ : دام ع : دامت . (281) ناقص في ر . (282) أ : لعظيم .
(283) ر : المتقين . (284) أ . (285) ر : يوفي . (286) أ : النصح . (286) أ : لما .

جامعها (٢٨٧) وتفاوت أزمانهم وتباين هممهم واختلاف أديانهم وتفرق مذاهبهم على نقل قصة ما ، فيوقن أنها حق لا شك فيه ، و يسمع بخلاف (٢٨٨) نقلهم في قصة ما ، فيدري أنها مضطربة ويرى أخبار العلماء والصالحين ليحرص (٢٨٩) على مثل حالهـم و يرغب في لحوق (٢٩٠) اسمه بأسمائهم اذا سلك طريقهم وحذا حذوهم وعمل عملهـم و يطالع آثار المفسدين في الأرض وسوء الثناء (٢٩١) عليهم وما أبقوا من الآثـار (٢٩٢) الذميمة فيمقت طريقهم ويجتنب أن يكون مذكورا فيهم ، ويجعل هذا العلم خاصة وقـت راحته و سآمته من تعلم غيره من العلوم، لأن (٢٩٣) هذا العلم سهل جدا و منشـط و منتزه ولذة ، ولا ينبغي (٢٩٤) لأحد أن يخلو منه أثرا (٢٩٥) ولا ماتقوم به الحجة من الاخبار التي يضطرالى العلم بها حقيقة بل يكون بمنزلة من قدّران العلم (٢٩٦) لـم يكن الا منذ كان هوفاذا أحكم ماذكرنا، فأولى الأشياء به معرفة ماله خرج الى هذا العالـم وما اليه يرجع اذا خرج من هذا العالم (ويبادر بذلك قبل انقضاء) (٢٩٧) أيام سفره فانهـا قليلة جدا فلا شيء أوكد عليه من هذا لأن ماعدا (٢٩٨) ذلك من بؤس ونعيم ولذة ومسـال ورياسة و فقر وخمول ونكد فمنقض كله في أسرع وقت . لسنا نقول بالموت الذي لابد منـه فقط بل (٢٩٩) بالهرم وعوارض (٣٠٠) الدهر الذي لا يؤمن تحوله (٣٠١) بأهله قبـل كر الطرف .

فيلزم (٣٠٢) المرء أن ينظر اذا أحكم ماذكرنا (٣٠٣) أن يطلب البرهان مـن العلوم الضرورية التي ذكرنا هل العالم (٣٠٤) محدث أم لم يزل (٣٠٥) ، فاذا حصل لـه أنه محدث وذلك قائم من احصاء (٣٠٦) العدد لازمانه وعدد أشخاص أنواعه (٣٠٧) ، نظر هل له (٣٠٨) محدث أولا محدث له فاذا حصل له أنه محدث (٣٠٩) لم يـزل ،

---

(٢٨٧) ٢ : حاملها . (٢٨٨) أ : بخلاف . (٢٨٩) أ : فيرى الحرص . (٢٩٠) ٢ : الحاق . (٢٩١) أ : الآثار . (٢٩٢) ٢ : الاسماء . (٢٩٣) أ : فان . (٢٩٤) أ : لا ينبغي . (٢٩٥) ٢ : فلا يدري منه أثرا . (٢٩٦) أ : العالم . (٢٩٧) أ : وبيان ذلك بيان انقضاء . (٢٩٨) ر : ماعدى . (٢٩٩) ر : بلى . (٣٠٠) ر : معـارض . (٣٠١) أ : تقلبه . (٣٠٢) كذا في ر ، أ : فيلزم ٤ ع : ظليلزم ، ا : ذكريا في . (٣٠٣) ر : ذكرنافي . (٣٠٤) أ : على هل العالم . (٣٠٥) أ : أول يزل . (٣٠٦) أ : في احصـاء . (٣٠٧) أ : وعدد أشخاصه وأنواعه . (٣٠٨) مثبتة في ر ، ساقطة من أ ، ع : أضافها . (٣٠٩) ر : أن له محدثا .

وهذا قائم من باب الاضافة (٣١٠) من حدود (٣١١) المنطق ، نظر هل المحـــدث
واحد أو اكثر من واحد فاذا حصل له أنه واحد وهذا قائم من باب الاحصاء المذكور فـــي
العدد نظر (٣١٢) هل النبوة ممكنة أو واجبة أو ممتنعة فاذا حصل له أنها ممكنة بالقـــوة
بما يوجبه المحدث للعالم (٣١٣) مختار لا يعجز عن شيء ، ثم اذا حصل له أنها (٣١٤)
قد وجدت بالاخبار الضرورية نظر في النبوات التي قد (٣١٥) افترقت عليها الملــــل
فاذا حصل له أن كل ما (٣١٦) ثبتت به نبوة واحد منهم فوجب (٣١٧) أن تثبت بمثلـــه
نبوة من نقل عنه مثل الذي نقل عن غيره منهم وقف عند ذلك وسلم الأمر الى مـــــن
صحت له (٣١٨) البراهين بنبوته ، وأنه عن الله عز وجل يتكلم ،وعن عهوده يخبــر ،
ويبحث حينئذ (٣١٩) عن كل ما أمر به او نهي عنه فاستعمل نفسه به ولم يقبل من انســـان
مثله لم يؤيد بوحي من الله عز وجل أمرا ولا نهيا فهذا طريق (٣٢٠) الخلاص (٣٢١)
و شارع النجاة (٣٢٢) وحجة الفوز (٣٢٣) التي من عاج عنها طال تحيره وتـــــردد ،
وتلدده (٣٢٤) ،و افترقت به السبل (٣٢٥) حتى يهلك خاسرًا نادمًا ،(238)
ليونقا (٣٢٦) بالبخت ، كمن وجد لقطة باذ طلب (٣٢٧) بالله من البـــساء ،
(قال أبو محمد) (٣٢٨) ، وهذه الطريق التي (٣٢٩) وصفنا مؤدية الى الاقــرار
بنبوة محمد صلى الله عليه وسلم وموجبة (طلب ما في القرآن) (٣٣٠) من عهود الله عــز
وجل (٣٣١) (وطلب تصحيح عهود رسول الله صلى الله عليه وسلم) (٣٣٢) وتمييــــز
صحيحهما (٣٣٣) مما لم يصح منها (٣٣٤) ،والاخذ بكل ذلك والتمسك به فان هـــــذا

_____

(٣١٠) أ : الفضائل . (٣١١) ر : حدوث . (٣١٢) مثبتة في ر ،ساقطة من أ ،ع :
أضافنا . (٣١٣) ناقصة في أ . (٣١٤) أ : أنه . (٣١٥) ناقصة في أ . (٣١٦) ر :
كلما . (٣١٧) أ : فواجب . (٣١٨) ناقصة في ر . (٣١٩) أ : تبحث . (٣٢٠)
كذا في ر ، ناقصة في أ ، ع ، أضافناها . (٣٢١) ر : المخلص . (٣٢٢) ر : النجات .
(٣٢٣) أ : ومحلة الفوز . (٣٢٤) ناقصة في أ . (٣٢٥) ر : وافترقت السبل به . (٣٢٦)
أ : مونيا . (٣٢٧) مرفيا . (٣٢٨) ،ونحون . أ . (٣٢٩) ناقصة في أ . (٣٣٠) كذا في ر ، أ : الذي
ع . التي . (٣٣٠) أ . (٣٣١) لطلبنا في القران . (٣٣١) أ : تعالى . (٣٣٢) أ : وطلب
عهوده عليه السلام . (٣٣٣) أ . صحيحهما . (٣٣٤) أ : منهما .

معدوم في جميع الملل «حاشا»(٣٣٥) ملة الاسلام ؛ لأن ملة من عبد الأوثان او دا ن بقول البراهمة المبطلين للنبوات فانه لاسبيل الى اثبات شريعة لهم اذ (٣٣٦) قــــد اعدموا المثبت الشارع واعدموا الطريقة (٣٣٧) الموصلة اليه فيبقى الناس (٣٣٨) علـــى قولهم سدى لا زاجر لهم عن ظلم ولا عن فاحشة وأما دين المنانية فظاهر التخليـــط بقولهم (٣٣٩) ان الصانع صنع في نفسه وهذا يبطل (٣٤٠) بما يوجب حدوث العالـــم على ما بيناه في كتابنا الموسوم(بالفصل في الملل والاهواء والنحل)(٣٤١) . وأما شريعـــة النصارى فانهم مُقرُّون ان شرائعهم (٣٤٢) ليست وحي من الله تعالى (٣٤٣) وانمـــا هي (٣٤٤) من وضع زكريا (٣٤٥)الملك وسائر البطارقة وهذا شيء (٣٤٦) تشهــــد العقول انه (٣٤٧) لايلزم اذا لم يجب الزامه برهان . وأما ملة المجوس فهم معترفـون بان ثلثي كتابهم ذهب وأن في ذلك الذاهب كانت الشرائع ، ومن الباطل الممتنـــع ان يكلف الله تعالى الناس أن يحملوا بشيء لايدرونه ،وقد ذهب عن أيديهم ويقـرون أن ازدشير بن بابك (٣٤٨) وضع لهم شرائع غير التي كانت لازمة لهم ،وهذا (٣٤٩) لايعتقده الا جاهل ولايدين به الا مخذول .

وأما ملة اليهود فيعترفون (٣٥٠) ان اكثر شرائعهم اللازمة لهم لاسبيل لهم اليهــا اذ (٣٥١) خرجوا عن صهيون · وان شرائع الربانيين منهم التي هم الآن عليها هي غـــير شرائعهم التي اتوا بها في التوراة ،وان علماءهم عوضوهم عن تلك هذه ، ويلزم الاقرار بمن (٣٥٤) صح عنه من الاعلام مثلما صح عن نبيهم(صلى الله عليه وسلــم)(٣٥٥) .

_____

(٣٣٥) ر :حاشى . (٣٣٦) ر: وان . (٣٣٧) ا : الطريق . (٣٣٨) ا : فيبقـى .
(٣٣٩) ا : لقولهم بأن . (٣٤٠) ا : مبطل . (٣٤١) ا : بالفصل بالملل والنحل .
(٣٤٢) ر : شرايعهم . (٣٤٣) ا : ليست من وحي الله تعالى . (٣٤٤) ا : هنَّ .
(٣٤٥) ر : من وضع زكريــــــا . (٣٤٦) ا : ناقصة في ا . (٣٤٧) ا : بانه .
(٣٤٨) ر : باك . (٣٤٩) ا : فهذا . (٣٥٠) ا : فمعترفون . (٣٥١) ر : اذا .
(٣٥٢) غير مثبت في ر . (٣٥٣) ا : ويلزمهم . (٣٥٤) ر :على . (٣٥٥) ا :عليه السلام .

(٣٥٦) (قال أبومحمد) : (٣٥٧) متى (٣٥٨) اشتغل مغفل للحقيقة عــــن علم الشريعة بعلم غيره فقد أساء النظر وظلم نفسه اذ آثر الأدنى والأقل منفعة علــى الأعلى والأعظم منفعة ؛ فان قال قائل إن في علم العدد والهيئة والمنطق (٣٥٩) معرفة الأشياء على ماهي عليه . قلنا أن هذا حسن اذا قصد به الاستدلال علـــى الصانع للأشياء بصنعته ليتدرج بذلك الى الفوز والنجاة (٣٦٠) و الخلاص من العذاب و النكد (وعلى هذا رتبنا الترتيب للتقدم) (٣٦١) وأما ان لم يكن الغرض الا معرفــة الأشياء الحاضرة على ما هي عليه فقط ، فطالب تلك (٣٦٢) العلـــوم (٣٦٣) ومـــن جعل وكده معرفة صفات (٣٦٤) البلاد على ماهي عليه ، وصفات (البــــــلاد على) (٣٦٥) سكان أهل كل بلده (٣٦٦) وماهي عليه وصورهم ســـــواء (٣٦٧) ومن كان هذا غرضه (٣٦٨) فقط ، فهو الى أن يوصف بالفضول والحماقة أقرب منــه الى أن يوصف بالعلم اذ حقيقة العلم هو ما قلنا أن يطلب (٣٦٩) لينتفع به طالبــه وينتفع به غيره في داره العاجلة ، و داره الأجلة ، و التي (٣٧٠) هي محل قـــراره ، ومكان خلوده وبالله تعالى نتأيد .

(قال أبو محمد) (٣٧١) فان كان المرء العامل (٣٧٢) في كفاف مـــــــن المعاش (٣٧٣) من وجه مرضى ، فليحمد الله عزوجل وليقنع به ، وليعمل لدار القـــرار ولا ينره الى الاستكبار (٣٧٤) من أحجار وخرق يتركها عما قريب أو تتركه . و إن كــان في حاجة ، فإن أمكنه أن يجعل مكتسبه من العلم فحسن ، أما أن (٣٧٥) يكون معلمـــا هجاء فتلك (٣٧٦) فضيلة عظيمة (لأنه سبب الى معرفة ؟) (٣٧٧) كل من تعلم منــــه

──────────────

(٣٥٦) ناقصة في أ . (٣٥٧) أ : فان . (٣٥٨) ناقصة في أ . (٣٥٩) كذا في ر ، ع : لمنطق ، ع : والمنطق . (٣٦٠) ر : النجات . (٣٦١) ناقصة فــي أ . (٣٦٢) أ : هذه . (٣٦٣) ر : نطالب تلك العلوم سواء . (٣٦٤) أ : صفــة . (٣٦٥) ناقص في أ . (٣٦٦) أ : بلد . (٣٦٧) ناقصة في ر . (٣٦٨) أ : ومن كان هذا هو غرضه . (٣٦٩) أ : انه يطلبه . (٣٧٠) أ : التي . (٣٧١) ناقصفي أ . (٣٧٢) أ : العالم . (٣٧٣) أ : العيش . (٣٧٤) أ : ولايسره الاكـــــبار . (٣٧٥) ر : اما فان . (٣٧٦) أ : فهي . (٣٧٧) أ : لأنه سبب كل من تعلم . ع : لأنه سبب حيـاة .

شيئا ، وله الاجر المضاعف من كل من يتعلم ممن علّمه هو الى انقضاء الابد ، بان (۳۷۸)
كان سبب حياة نفوسهم،أو معلم (۳۷۹) نحو أوحساب (۳۸۰) أو طبيا ، فان كـــان
في أحد هذه السبل (۳۸۱) فلينهج في صناعته (239) تلك ، وليطلب التزيـد
من العلم (۳۸۲) ما أمكنه (۳۸۳) ليكون سببا الى الخير (۳۸٤) في تعليم الجهال (۳۸٥)
وابراءالادواء باذن الله تعالى ،ولا يرض (۳۸٦) بالغش والتمويه فيفسـد
خلقه ومكسبه ومعاده (۳۸۷) ، فتخسر (۳۸۸) صفقته ، وليستعمل القناعة جهـده
فان (۳۸۹) ابتلي بصحبة سلطان "فقد ابتلي بعظيم البلايا وعرض للخطر الشنيــع
في ذهاب دينه ، وذهاب نفسه ، وشغل باله ،وترادف همومه" (۳۹۰) فلا يشاركـه
في محظور البتة ،وان اداه ذلك (۳۹۱) الى التلف فلأن يتلف مظلوما مأجـــورا
محتسبا (۳۹۲) محمودا ، افضل من ان يبقى ظالما مسيئا آثما مذموما ، ولعل تلفـه
سريع وان تأخر مدة فلابد له من التلف (۳۹۳) وليعلم ان السلطان اذا رأى (۳۹٤) منه
اشفاقا على دينه ونصيحة له على مالا يريد (۳۹٥) في معاده ، فانه يتزيد ثقة بــه ،
ويجل في عينه ، واذا رآه (۳۹٦) شرها مؤثرا لعاجلته (۳۹۷) على آخرته (۳۹۸) ســاء
ظنه به ، فلم (۳۹۹) يأمنه على نفسه اذا رأى الحظ له في اهلاكه (٤۰۰).

(قال ابومحمد) (٤۰۱) ، ولقد نكره للفاضل ان يصحب السلطان بعلم الطــب ،
فان الغالب على الملوك الجهل والسبعية (٤۰۲) ، وقلة الصبر على ماتقطع بهـــم
عن لذاتهم وتدبير الأصحاء (٤۰۳) ومعاناة (٤۰٤) المرضى ولا يحتمل هذا ، فهـــم

_____

(۳۷۸) ر: فانه . [(۳۷۹) ر: مؤدب . (۳۸۰) أ: مؤدب حساب . (۳۸۱) ر: فــان
كان في هذا أحد هذه السبل . (۳۸۲) ر: من علمها . (۳۸۳) أ: بما أمكنـــه .
(۳۸٤) أ: للخير . (۳۸٥) أ: الجاهل . (۳۸٦) ر: ولا يرضى . (۳۸۷) ا:
فيفسد خلقه ومتاعه ومكسبه . (۳۸۸) أ: فيخسر . (۳۸۹) أ: وان . (۳۹۰) ناقص
في ر . (۳۹۱) ناقصة في ر . (۳۹۲) ر: محسنا . (۳۹۳) أ: فلابد من التلـف .
(۳۹٤) ر: رأء . (۳۹٥) أ: ونصيحة له فيما لا يؤذيه . (۳۹٦) ر: واذا رءاه .
(۳۹۷) أ: عاجلته . (۳۹۸) ر: أخراه . (۳۹۹) أ: ولم . (٤۰۰) أ: هلاكـه .
(٤۰۱) ناقصة في أ . (٤۰۲) كذا في ر، أ: والمتعية ع: السبعية . (٤۰۳)
ر: الاصحا . (٤۰٤) ر: معانات .

دأبا يكلفون الطبيب إحياء الموتى، ويستقعدونه (٤٠٥) دون هذه المنزلة فان اتبــــع
أهواءهم غشهم وان نصحهم عصوه واستثقلوه ، واما صحبتهم بالنجوم فلا يدخل في ذ لـك
ذو مسكة عقل البتة لانه يتعاطى ما لا يعرفى توته الوفاء به ، فهو دهره في كذب متصل
ومواعيد مختلفة (٤٠٦) ، وخدائع متصلة ،وفضائح متواترة وخزايا متتابعــــة (٤٠٧)
وللكن (٤٠٨) وكد (٤٠٩) من اتصل بسلطان اصلاح أخلاقهم وحملهم على الصــبر
وصرفهم عن المآثم (٤١٠) جهده وطاقته .
(قال أبو محمد) (٤١١) : ودعائم العلم شهوة (٤١٢) مستحكمة يؤثرها العلـم
على سائر أغراض (٤١٣) الدنيا من اللذات والمال والصوت ، ثم قصد الى عــين (٤١٤)
العلم ليخرج به عن جملة أشباه البهائم فقط ، لا يجعله مكسبة (٤١٥) ، ولا ليمـدح
به ،وذكاء ،وفهم وبحث (٤١٦) وذكر وصبر على كل ذلك . وعلى التعـب (٤١٧)
وانفاق المال عليه والاستكثار من الكتب ، فلن يخلو كتاب من فائدة (٤١٨) وزيادة
علم يجدها فيه اذا احتاج اليها ولا سبيل الى حفظ المرء لجميع علمه الذي يختص به ،
وان لا سبيل (٤١٩) الى ذلك ، فالكتب نعم الخازنة له اذا طلب ولولا الكتب لضاعـت
العلوم فلم توجد (٤٢٠) .(وقد أخطأ من ذم) (٤٢١) الاكثار منها ولو أخذ برأيــه
لتلفت العلوم ولجاذبهم الجهال فيها ،وادعوا ما شاءوا ، فلولا شهادة الكتب لاستوت
دعوى العالم والجاهل وسقوط الانفة في التكرار (٤٢٢) على العلماء وتقيد مــــا
يسمع (٤٢٣) وجمعه ، وملازمة المحبرة والكتب بيده وكبه ، وسكنى حاضرة فيهـــا
للعلم (٤٢٤) نفاق (٤١٥) ،ولقاء المتنازعين (٤٢٦) وحضور المتناظرين ،فبهــذا
تلوح له الحقائق) (٤٢٧) ، فليس من تكلم عن نفسه وما يعتقد كمن تكلم عن غــيره ،
وليست الثكلى كالنائحة (٤٢٨) المستأجرة (٤٢٩) ،ومن لا يسمع الا من عالــــم

ـــــــــــــــــــــــــــــــــــــــ

(٤٠٥) ر ع ا : يستقصروهم ، ع ، (٤٠٦) : يستقعدونه . (٤٠٧) ر : مختلفة . (٤٠٧)غير مثبت
في ر . (٤٠٨) غير مثبت في ا . (٤٠٩) أ : وكدّ . (٤١٠) ر : المشاتم . (٤١١)ناقصة
في ا . (٤١٢) أ : مشهورة . (٤١٣) ا : أغراض . (٤١٤) ر : الى غير العلم . (٤١٥)
ا : مكسبة . (٤١٦) غير مثبت في ر . (٤١٧) ا : والتعب فيه . (٤١٨)غير مثبت في ر.
(٤١٩) ا : فان لا سبيل . (٤٢٠) أ : ولم توجد . (٤٢١) أ : وهذا خطأ ممـن ذم .
(٤٢٢) أ : التكرار . (٤١٣) كذا في ر ، ناقصة في ا ع ، (٤٢٤) أضافها : العلم .
(٤٢٥) ناقصة في ا . (٤٢٦) ر : متنازعين . (٤٢٧) ا : فبهذا تلوح الحقائق .
(٤٢٨) غير مثبت في ر . (٤٢٩) ر : كالمستأجرة .

واحد أوشك الا (٤٣٠) يحصل على طائل (وكان كمن لم يزل يستقي من بئر واحد) (٤٣١) (ولعله انما يشرب الملح الكدر) (٤٣٢) وقد ترك العذب الصافي (٤٣٣) ومع اعتراك الاقران ،(ومعارضة الخصوم يلوح الحق من الباطل) (٤٣٤) ، ولابد ، فمن طلب العلم (٤٣٥) كما ذكرنا أوشك (٤٣٦) أن ينجح مطلبه وأن لا يخفق سعيه ، وان يحصل في المدة اليسيرة على الفائدة العظيمة ، ومن تعدى هذه الطريق كثر تعبه ، وقلت منفعته ، ومن اقتصر على علم واحد ولم (٤٣٧) يطالع غيره ، أوشك أن يكون ضحكة ، وكان ماخفي عليه من علمه الذي اقتصر عليه أكثر مما أدرك منه لتعلق العلم بعضها ببعض ، كما ذكرنا ولأنها (٤٣٨) درج بعضها الى بعض كما وصفنا ، ومن طلب الاحتواء على كل علم أوشك أن ينقطع ويتحسر (٤٣٩) ولا يحصل (240) على شيء ، وكان كالمحضر الى غير غاية ، إذ (٤٤٠) العمر يقصر عن ذلك وليأخذ (٤٤١) من كل علم بنصيب ، ومقدار ذلك معرفته بأغراض ذلك العلم فقط ،(ثم يأخذ ما به الضرورة الى مالابد منه) (٤٤٢) كما وصفنا ، ثم يعتمد العلم الذي يسبق (٤٤٣) فيه بطبعه وبقلبه (٤٤٤) ، ومخيلته (٤٤٥) ، فسيكثر منه ما أمكنه ، فربما كان ذلك(منه في علمين أو أكثر أو أقل على قدر ذكاء طبعه وقوة فهمه) (٤٤٦) ، وحضور خاطره ،واكبابه على الطلب وكل ذلك بتيسير الله عز وجل (٤٤٧) فلو الى ارادة (٤٤٨) المرء كان ، لكان مُنى كل أحد أن يكون أفضل الناس .

والفهم والعناية مقسومان (بقسمة الأموال والأحوال) (٤٤٩) والحظ مقسم فأجمل في الطلب ، ومن طلب العلم (٤٥٠) ليفخر به أو ليمدح فيه (٤٥١) أو ليكتسب (٤٥٢) به مالا أوجاها فبعيد عن الفلاح ، (لأنه ليس غرضه التحقيق فيه) (٤٥٣) ، وانما غرضه شيء آخر غير العلم ، ونفس الانسان وعينه طامحتان (٤٥٤) الى غرضه فقط ، فلا يبالي كيف

___

(٤٣٠) أ : ان لا . (٤٣١) أ : وكان كمن يشرب من بئر واحدة . (٤٣٢) أ : ولعله اختار الملح الكدر . (٤٣٣) ناقصة في أ . (٤٣٤) أ : ومع اعتراك الاقران ومعارضتهم يلوح الباطل من الحق . (٤٣٥) ر : فمن طلبه كما ذكرنا . (٤٣٦) غير مثبت في سي . (٤٣٧) أ : لم . (٤٣٨) أ : أنها . (٤٣٩) أ : ينحسر . (٤٤٠) كذا في ر ، أ . اذا في ع ، أ : اذ . (٤٤١) ر : لاكن يأخذ . (٤٤٢) ر : ثم يأخذ ما به الضرورة اليه مالابد له منه . (٤٤٣) كذا في ر ، أ : ينشق . ع : يسبق . (٤٤٤) ر : ويقبله . (٤٤٥) أ : وبخيلته . ر ، أ : بجلته . (٤٤٦) أ : منه في علمين أو ثلاثة أو أكثر على قدر ذكاء فهمه وقوة طبعه . (٤٤٧) أ : تعالى . (٤٤٨) أ : بارادة .
(٤٤٩) أ : قسمة المال والحال . (٤٥٠) كذا في ر ، ناقصة في أ . ع : أضافها .
(٤٥١) أ : به . (٤٥٢) أ : ليكتسب . (٤٥٣) أ : لأنه ليس له غرض في التحقيق فيه .
(٤٥٤) أ : طامحان .

كان طلبه اذا حصل على مراده الذى اياه قصد .

(قال ابو محمد)⁽⁴⁵⁵⁾ والعلوم⁽⁴⁵⁶⁾ (القائمة اليوم)⁽⁴⁵⁷⁾ تنقسم اقساما سبعة عند كل امة وفى كل مكان وكل زمان ،⁽⁴⁵⁸⁾ وهى : علم شريعة كل امة ،"فلا بد لكل امة"⁽⁴⁵⁹⁾ من معتقد ما ⁽⁴⁵⁹⁾ اما اثبات واما ابطال . وعلم اخبارها وعلم لغتها، فالا مم تتميز فى هذه العلوم الثلاثة . واما العلوم الاربعة الباقية تتفق فيها الا مم كلها ، فهى الفلسفة : وهى معرفة الاشياء على ما هى عليه "من حدودها من اعلى الاجناس الى الاشخاص ومعرفة الهيئة"⁽⁴٦٠⁾ ومعرفة الهيئة ، ومعرفة العدد ومعرفة الطب وهى معاناة الاجسام ⁽⁴٦١⁾ وقد بينا ان كل شريعة سوى الاسلام فباطل ، فالواجب ان يقتصر⁽⁴٦٢⁾ على شريعة الحق وعلى كل ما اعان على التبحر فيها⁽⁴٦٣⁾، فعلم⁽⁴٦٤⁾ شريعة الاسلام ينقسم اقساما اربعة : علم القرآن ، وعلم الحديث ، وعلم الفقه ، وعلم الكلام .

فعلم القرآن ينقسم الى معرفة قراءاته ومعانيه ، وعلم الحديث ينقسم الى معرفة متونه ومعرفة رواته ، وعلم الفقه ينقسم الى احكام القرآن واحكام الحديث وما اجمع عليه وما اختلفوا فيه ،⁽⁴٦٥⁾ ومعرفة(وجوه الادلة و ما يصح⁽⁴٦٦⁾ منها ومالا يصح ، وعلم الكلام ينقسم الى معرفة⁽⁴٦٧⁾ مقالاتهم والى⁽⁴٦٨⁾ معرفة حجاجهم وما يصح منها بالبرهان وما لا يصح ⁽⁴٦٩⁾ وعلم النحو ينقسم الى مسموعه القديم وعلله المحدثة ، وعلم اللغة مسموع كله⁽⁴٧٠⁾ وعلم الاخبار ينقسم على مراتب⁽⁴٧١⁾ اما على

---

(٤٥٥) ا : غير مثبت فى ا . (٤٥٦) ا : فالعلوم . (٤٥٧) غير مثبت فى ا . (٤٥٨) ا : فى كل زمان وكل مكان . (٤٥٩) غير مثبت فى ا (٤٦٠)، ر : من يعتقد.. (٤٦١) ا : والعلوم الاربعة الباقية تتفق فيها الا مم كلها وهى : علم العدد والطب وهو معاناة الاجسام ، وعلم الفلسفة وهى معرفة الاشياء على ما هى عليه من حدودها من اعلى الاجناس الى الاشخاص ومعرفة الهيئة . (٤٦٢) ا : الاقتصار . (٤٦٣) ا : فى علمها . (٤٦٤) ا : وعلم . (٤٦٥) ر : الناس . (٤٦٦) ا : وجوه الدلالة وما صح . (٤٦٧) ا : ومعرفة . (٤٦٨) ناقصة فى ا . (٤٦٩) غير مثبت فى ر . (٤٧٠) ا : كله فقط . (٤٧١) ر : الى مراتب .

۲۳۷

الممالك (٤٧٢) واما (٤٧٣) على السنين و اما على البلاد واما على الطبقات أو منشورا (٤٧٤) فأصح التواريخ عندنا تاريخ (٤٧٥) الملة الاسلامية ومبدؤها وفتوحها واخبار (٤٧٦) خلفائها وملوكها والمتزين بذلك منهم وعلمائها (٤٧٧) وسائر ما انتظم بذلك وأما تاريخ بني اسرائيل فأكثره صحيح وفي بعضه دخل (٤٧٨) (ظاهر وفساد لائح) (٤٧٩) وانما يصح منه ،اخبارهم منـذ صاروا الى الشام الى أن خرجوا عنها الخرجة الاخيرة (٤٨٠) لا ما قبل (٤٨١) ذلك .

واخبار الروم انما تصح من عهد الاسكدر لما قبل ذلك أصلا (٤٨٢) . واخبـار الفرس انما تصح من عهد دارا بن دارا (٤٨٣) واصحها ما كان من عهد أزد شير بن بابك . و اما قبل ذلك فخرافات ظاهرة الكذب ، و اما الترك والخزر وأم الشمال وممالك السـودان فلا علوم لهذه الأمم ولا تواريخ ، واخبار افريقية والاندلس قبل دخول المسلمين بها واخبار القبط والسريانيين واليمن وعمون و مؤاب و سائر الأمم ، فقد بادت آثارها جملة فليس فيها الاتكاء يب و خرافات ، و اما الهند والصين فلم تبلغنا اخبارهم (٢٤١) كما نريد لهـما انما أمتا علم وضبط وتقيد وتأليف فينبغي لطالب العلم (٤٨٤) الاخبار أن لا يشتغل الا بما أعلمناه بصحته والا فسينقطع قلبه فيما يلح له في آخر الامر بطلانه ، وبالله تعالى التوفيق (٤٨٥)

" ولا ينبغي له قطع وقته بما لا يجدي عليه نفعا بما اخبرناه ببطلانه فقد كفينـاه التعب في ذلك وان احب التعب وقف على ما وقفنا عليه من ذلك " . (٤٨٥ا) .

──────────

(٤٧٢) كذا في ر أ ؛ ممالك ع ؛ الممالك . (٤٧٣) أ ؛ أو . (٤٧٤) ر ؛ أو منشـور . (٤٧٥) غير مثبت في ر . (٤٧٦) ر ؛ وفتوحها وفتوحها وخلفائها . (٤٧٧) أ ؛ وعلمائهـم . (٤٧٨) ر ؛ داخل . (٤٧٩) غير مثبت في أ . (٤٨٠) أ ؛ الاخرة . (٤٨١) أ ؛ لا من قبل . (٤٨٢) ناقصة في أ . (٤٨٣) ر ؛ دار بن دار . (٤٨٤) ر ؛ العلم . (٤٨٥) ثمة اختلاف ظاهر بين نسخة أ ، ر فيما يتعلق بنص الفقرة المبدوءة ؛ وعلم الاخباره ففي نسخة ا يـرد النص على النحو التالي : (وعلم الاخبار ينقسم على مراتب ؛ أما على الممالك أوعلى السنين واما على البلاد واما على الطبقات أو منشورا . فأصح التواريخ عندنا تاريخ الملة الاسلاميــة و مبدؤها وفتوحها و أخبار خلفائها و ملوكها والمتزين عليهم والمتين عليهم وعلمائهم وسائر ما انتظم بذلك . واما تاريخ بني اسرائيل فأكثره صحيح وفي بعضه دخل وانما يصح منه اخباره الى بالشام الى ان خرجوا عنها الخرجة الاخرة ، قبل ذلك . واخبار الروم انما تصح من عهـد الاسكدر لما قبل ذلك . واخبار الترك والخزر وسائر أم الشمال وأم السودان فلا علم لهـذه الامم ولا توالیف ولا تواریخ . ولم تبلغنا أخبار الهند والصين كما نريد . الا انهم أمتا علم وضبط توالیف وجمع . وأما الأمم الدائرة من القبط اليمانيين والسريانيين والاشمانيين وعمون وموآب وسائر الأمم فقد بادت أخبارهم جملة ، فلم يبق منها الا الاتكاء يب وخرافات . وأما الفرس فلا يصح شيئ من أخبارهم الاماكن من عهد دارا بن دار فقط . واصح اخبارهم ما كان من عهد أزد شير ابن بابك فقط فالطالب للأخبار ينبغي له ألا يشتغل الا بما أعلمناه بصحته ولا ينبغي له قطع وقته بما لا يجدي عليه نفعـا ـ لما أخبرناه ببطلانه فقد كفيناه التعب في ذلك . وإن أحـب التعب وقف على ما وقفنا عليه من ذلك) . (٤٨٥ا) غير مثبت في ر .

وعلم النسب جزء من علم الخبره وعلم النجوم ينقسم الى معرفة نصبة الهيئة(٤٨٦) والتعديل
ببرهانه(ثم الى الذي يذكر فيه من القضاء)(٤٨٧) وعلم العدد ينقسم الى ضبط قوانينه ثــم
برهانه ثم العمل بذلك في المساحات وغير ذلك . وعلم المنطق ينقسم الى عقليّ وحسيّ ،
فأما (٤٨٨) العقلي فالا هي و طبيعي وأما الحسي فطبيعي فقط .
وعلم الطب ينقسم قسمين : (٤٨٩) طب النفس ، وهو من نتيجة علم المنطق باصـــلاح
الأخلاق ومداواتها (٤٩٠) وصرفها عن الافراط والتقصير واقامتها على الاعتدال : و طــــب
الأجسام : وهو ينقسم الى معرفة الطبائع الجسمية ومعرفة تركيب (٤٩١) الأعضاء ، و معرفة
العلل و اسبابها (وماتعارضه به)(٤٩٢) و تمييز القوى (من الأدوية والاغذية)(٤٩٣) و ينقسم
ايضا قسمين (٤٩٤) ، عمل باليد كالجبر و البط والكي والقطع وعمل في صرف قوى العلــــل
بقوى الادوية ، و ينقسم أيضا قسمين : حفظ الصحة لئلا يحدث المرض ثم معاناة المـرض .
وعلم الشعر : ينقسم الى روايته ومعانيه و محاسنه و معايبه وأقسامه ووزنه (٤٩٥)
و نظمه (٤٩٦) .

(وقال ابومحمد)(٤٩٧) : وهاهنا علمان انما يكونان (٤٩٨) نتيجة العلوم الــــتي
ذكرنا اذا اجتمعت أو من نتيجة اجتماع علمين منهما فصاعدا ، وهما علم البلاغة وعلم العبارة .
فأما علم البلاغة ؛ فان صرفه صاحبه (في الدعاء)(٤٩٩) الى الله عَزَّ وَجَلَّ والى (٥٠٠) تبيين
علم (٥٠١) الحقائق و تعليم الجهال فهو (٥٠٢) فضيلة حسنة (٥٠٣) وان صرفه
(٥٠٤) في ضد ذلك فقد خسرت صفقتـــه (٥٠٥) .

---

(٤٨٦) ١ : علم الهيئة . (٤٨٧) أ : ثم الذي يذكرونه من القضاء . (٤٨٨) ١ : أما .
(٤٨٩) ر : ينقسم الى عقلي قسمين . (٤٩٠) كذا في ر ، أ : مداراتها ، ع :
مداواتها . (٤٩١) ر : تركب . (٤٩٢) أ : وماتعارضه به من الأدوية . وتمييز القوى
من الادوية . (٤٩٣) أ : للاغذية . ع : الاغذية . (٤٩٤) ر : قسمين حفظ الصحــة
(٤٩٥) غير مثبت في ر . (٤٩٦) ر : ونظمه ونثره . (٤٩٧) ناقصة في أ . (٤٩٨) ر ، أ :
يكونا . (٤٩٩) غير مثبت في أ . (٥٠٠) غير مثبت في أ . (٥٠١) غير مثبت في ر .
(٥٠٢) أ : فهي . (٥٠٣) غير مثبت في أ . (٥٠٤) أ : واما ان صرفه . (٥٠٥) غير
مثبت في أ .

اذ أتعب نفسه وأفنى دهره (٥٠٦) فيماهو وبال عليه ، ونعوذ بالله تعالى (٥٠٧) مــــــن البـــلاء .

وأما علم العبارة : فهـو طبع في المخبر مع عون العـلم عليه ولا يقطع بصحته الا بعد ظهــور ذلك عليه لا قبله . (قال أبو محمد ونحن نوصي بهذه) (٥٠٨) الأثانين وهــــي (٥٠٩) التي يطلق عليها في قديم الدهر وحديثه اسم العلم والعلوم . وعند التحقيــــق وصحة النظر فكل ما (٥١٠) علم فهو علم ؛ فيدخل في ذلك علم التجارة والخياطة والحياكة وتدبير السفن وفلاحة الأرض وتربية (٥١١) الشجر وما ناتها وغرسها (٥١٢) والبنــاء وغير ذلك (٥١٣) (من الصناعات) الا أن هذه انما هي للدنيا خاصة فيما (٥١٤) بالناس اليه الحاجة في معايشهم والعلوم التي قدمنا فالغرض (٥١٥) منها (٥١٦) التوصل الى الخلاص في المعاد فقط ، فلذلك استحق التقديم والتفضيل وبالله تعالى التوفيق .

(قال أبو محمد) (٥١٧) : ونحن نوصي طالب العلم بأن لا يذم ما جهل منهـــا فهو دليل على نقصه وقوله بغير معرفة وأن لا يعجب بما علم (فيطمس فضيلة علمه) (٥١٨) ، ويستحق المقت من الواهب له ما وهب ، وأن لا يحسد من فوقه حسدًا يؤدي به الـــى تنقصه (٥١٩) ، فهذه رذيلتان ، واما ان حسده ولم ينتقصه (٥٢٠) وكان ذلك رغبة منه في الوصول (٥٢١) الى ما وصل اليه محسوده فحسن ، وهو رغبة في الخير وأن لا يحقر من دونه فقد كان في مثل حاله قبل أن يعلم ما علم ، وأن لا يكتم ما علم (٥٢٢) فيحصل هو ومن لا علم له في منزلة واحدة ، اذ كلاهما غير مستعمل للعلم ولا مظهر له وأن لا يتكلم في علم قبل أن يحكمه فيخزى وأن لا يطلب بعلمه غرض الدنيا (٥٢٣) نبيت ل الأفضل بالأدنى (٥٢٤) وأن يستعمل تقوى الله تعالى (٥٢٥) في سره وجهره فهو زيـــن

---

(٥٠٦) أ : عمره . (٥٠٧) غير مثبت في أ . (٥٠٨) غير مثبت في أ . (٥٠٩) غير مثبت في أ . (٥١٠) ر : فكلما . (٥١١) أ : تدبير الشجر . (٥١٢) غير مثبت في ر . (٥١٣) غير مثبت في أ . (٥١٤) ر : في مـــا . (٥١٥) أ : الغرض . (٥١٦) كذا في ر ، ناقصة في أ ، ع ؛ أضافناها . (٥١٧) ناقصة في أ . (٥١٨) أ : فتطمس فضيلته . (٥١٩) أ : تنقيصه . (٥٢٠) ر : يتنقصــــه . (٥٢١) أ : رغبة في الوصول . (٥٢٢) أ : علمه . (٥٢٣) أ : عرض الدنيا . (٥٢٤) ر : في الأدنى . (٥٢٥) غير مثبت في ر .

(٥٢٧)"وبالله التوفيق" (٥٢٦) العالم وحليته (٢٤٢)

فصل (٥٢٨) (قال أبو محمد(٥٢٩)) : والعلم التي ذكرنا متعلق (٥٣٠) بعضها ببعض لا
يستغني (٥٣١) منها علم عن غيره ،فأول ذلك أننا(٥٣٢) قد أبنّا أن غرضنا في الكون فـــي
الدنيا والمطلوب بتعلم العلم انما هو تعلم (٥٣٣) علم ما أراد الله تعالى منا(وما لـــه
اخترعنا(٥٣٤) و ما به يكون المخلصون هو(٥٣٥) مكاننا المكدر(٥٣٦) المظلم المشــوب
بالآفات المملوء من أنواع المتالف والمهالك ، المحفوف (٥٣٧) بأصناف البلايـــا(٥٣٨)
والمعاطب وهو المعرفة بالشريعة والاعلان بها والعمل بموجبها، فاذا الأمر كذلك ، فــلا
سبيل الى صحة المعرفة بها . (واستحقاق المرء لأن يكون عالما بحقيقتها بالبرهـــان
الا بمعرفته بأصول الاعتقادات وما يجب عليه حتما ، وبما يحرم عليه ، وبما هو مباح له ،
وهذا لا يكون الا بمعرفة أحكام عهد الله تعالى الينا في كتابه المنزل (٥٣٩)) وبمعرفـــة
ما وصّانا به (رسول الله صلى الله عليه وسلم) (٥٤٠) "وبلغه الينا(٥٤١) وما أجمع
علماء الديانة عليه وما اختلفوا فيه و لا يوصل الى هذا الا بمعرفة الناقلين لتلك الوصايـــا
و أزمانهم وأسمائهم وأنسابهم للفرق فيما (٥٤٢) اتفقت فيه الأسماء ، وبمعرفة المقبول بــين
من غيرهم ومعرفة . (٥٤٣) من لقوا فحدثوا عنه ممن (٥٤٤) يلقوه فيبلغهم عنه (٥٤٥)
وبمعرفة القراءات المشهورة ليقف بذلك على ما اتفق فيه المعاني مما تختلف فيحـــدث
باختلافها (٥٤٦) حكم ما (٥٤٧) ،وكل هذا لا يتم الا بمعرفة مستعمل اللغة و موا قــــع
الاعراب الذي (٥٤٨) تختلف المعاني باختلافه مثله (٥٤٩) و أشكاله ولا بد في اللغـــة

_____

(٥٢٦) غير مثبت في أ ، (٥٢٧) غير مثبت في ر ، (٥٢٨) غير مثبت في ر ، (٥٢٩) غيـر
مثبت في أ ، (٥٣٠) أ : يتعلق ، (٥٣١) أ : ولا ، (٥٣٢) أ : انا ، (٥٣٣) غير مثبت
في ر ، (٥٣٤) كذا في ر ، أ ، ع :وما به أخبرعنا ، (٥٣٥) ر : من هو ، (٥٣٦)
أ : الكدر ، (٥٣٧) أ ، (٥٣٨) ر : والمحفوف ، (٥٣٨) ر : البلاء ، (٥٣٩) أ : واستحقاق حقيقتها
ا بمعرفة أحكام الله عز وجل وعهوده الينا في كتابه المنزل ، (٥٤٠) أ : محمد عليه السلام ،
(٥٤١) غير مثبت في ر ، (٥٤٢) أ : بينما ، (٥٤٣) ر : المعرفة بين المقبولين وغيرهـم
والمعرفة ، (٥٤٤) ر : لمن ، (٥٤٥) ر:عنهم ، (٥٤٦) ر : باختلافه ، (٥٤٧) ر :
حكما ما ، (٥٤٨) ر : التي ، (٥٤٩) أ : أمثلته .

والاعراب من التعلق بطرف من علم الشعر ، ولابد من المعرفة بالنسب ليــدري (٥٥٠) المرء(من تجوز الامامة فيهم ومن لاتجوز فيهم)(٥٥١) . ومعرفة (٥٥٢) من هم الانصار الذين امرنا (٥٥٣) بالاحسان الى محسنهم والتجاوز عن مسيئهم ومن هم اولــو القربى الذين حرمت عليهم الصدقة ولابد ان يعرف من الحساب ما يعرف به القبلـــة والزوال وأوقات(٥٥٤) الصلوات(٥٥٥) ، ولا يو قف على حقيقة ذلك الا بمعرفــة الهيئة ولا يعرف حقيقة البرهان في ذلك الا من وقف على حدود الكلام والنطق (٥٥٦) (و لابد ان يطلب من الحساب ايضا كيف يعرف قسمة المواريث)(٥٥٧) في الامـــوال ومساحة الارض المقسومة في المواريث(٥٥٨) وفي الغنائم(٥٥٩) فان تحقيق ذلــك فرض لابد منه ، ولابد في الشريعة من معرفة العيوب التي " تجبّ التكليف كعاهـــة الجنون المتملكة "(٥٦٠) (وامرنا بالتداوي على لسان رسول الله صلى الله عليــــه وسلم ، فلا بد من معرفة ما يكون به التداوي)، وهاتان مقدمتان يقتضيان معرفة العلــل ومداواتها وهو علم الطب)(٥٦١) . (٥٦٢) والدعاء الى الله تعالى واجـــب ولا سبيل اليه الا بالحظ (من البيان)(٥٦٣) والبلاغة ومعرفة ما تستجلب به القلوب من حسن اللفظ وبيان المعنى ، ولا يكون هذا الا(المعرفة بالشريعة)(٥٦٤) وباللغــــة وبالاعراب وبما لفصاحة وحكم المنثور والمنظوم (٥٦٥) . والرؤيا حق وهي (٥٦٦) جزء من ستة واربعين جزءا من النبوة ، ولابد (٥٦٧) من معرفة عباراتها ، ولا تكـــون عباراتها الا بالتمكن في العلوم المذكورة . واما القضاء بالنجم فلا يعرف بطلانه الا مــن

---

(٥٥٠) أ ؛ بما يدري . (٥٥١) أ ؛ من تجوز الامامة من لا تجوز فيهم . (٥٥٢) غــــير مثبتة في ا . (٥٥٣) كذا في ر ،ناقصة في ا ، ع ؛ أضافها . (٥٥٤) أ ؛ الى أوقات (٥٥٥) ر ؛ الصلاة . (٥٥٦) غير مثبتة في ا . (٥٥٧) أ ؛ ولابد ان يعرف من الحساب ايضا كيف قسمة المواريث . (٥٥٨) ناقصة في ا . (٥٥٩) أ ؛ والغنائم . (٥٦٠) ر؛ يجب بها الرد في الحيوان المتملك . (٥٦١) أ ؛ وقوام الآفات والأدواء ، فلابد مـــن معرفة العلل ومداواتها وهو علم الطب . (٥٦٢) أ ؛ عزوجل . (٥٦٣) ناقصة في ا . (٥٦٤) أ ؛ بالمعرفة الشرعية . (٥٦٥) أ ؛ المنظور والمنثور . (٥٦٦) غير مثبت في ر . (٥٦٧) أ ؛ فلابد .

أشرف عليه ولا يحرف(568) الخطأ(569) من الصواب الا بمعرفته بها(570).

(قال أبو محمد)(570) : فهذا وجه تعلق العلوم بعضها ببعض، وافتقار بعضها الى بعض، وان لم يمكن(571) المرء الاحاطة بجميعها فليضرب في جميعها بسهم(572) ماءو إن قلّ ــ كما قدمنا ــ وليكن الناس فيها بالترتيب في تعاونهم على اقامة الواجب من ذلك عليهم كالمجتمعين لاقامة منزل ، فانه لا بد من بناء وأجراء ينقلون الحجر ويدوسون(573) الطين ، ومن صناع(574) القرمد وقطاعي الخشب (أو القصب)(575) وصناعي الابواب والمسامير حتى يتم البناء وكذلك سائر ما بالناس الحاجة اليه من الحرث وغيره(576) فانه لا يتم الا بالتعاون على آلاته "والعمل بها"(577) "وكذلك التعاون"(578) على ما به تكون النجاة والترقي الى عالم الخلود ، ورضى الخالق أو جب والزم(579) ، وبالله تعالى نتأيد•(580).

(قال أبو محمد)(581) : ومن السمج القبيح أن يبقى(582) الانسان فارغا • في مدة اقامته•(583) في هذه الدار(584) مغنيا تلك المدة فيما غيره(585) أولى به وأحسن منه في حماقة وبطالة أو معصية أو ظلم(586) وقد سمعت شيخنا محمد بن الحسن(587) يقول لي ولخيري : ان من العجب من يبقى في هذا العالم دون(588) تعاون(589) على مصلحة ، اما يرى الحراث يحرث له ، ، والطحان يطحن له والنساج ينسج له ، والخياط يخيط له(590) ، والبناء يبني له والجزار يجزر له(591) وسائر الناس كل يتولى(592) شغلا له فيه مصلحة وبه الضرورة • أفمــا

---

(568) ر : الخطا • (569) ا : الخطأ والصواب الا بمعرفتهما معا • (570) ناقصة في ا • (571) ا : يكن ، ع : تمكن • (572) ر : بنصيب • (573) ا : ينقلون • (574) ر : صانع • (575) ناقصه في ا • (576) ناقصة في ا • (577) غير مثبت في ر ، ا : بالتعاون على بآلاته ، ع : بالتعاون على القيام بآلاته • (578) ر : والتعاون • (579) ا : واكرم • (580) غير مثبت في ر • (581) كذا في ر ، ا • (582) ا : فصل • (583) ا : بقاء • (584) غير مثبت في ر • (585) مطموس ما بعد ها في ر • (586) غير مثبت في ر • (587) كذا في ر ، ا : أبو الحسن ، ع : بن الحسن • (588) كذا في ر ، ناقصة في ا ، ع : أضافها • (589) ا : محاونة لنوعه • (590) غير مثبت في ر • (591) ا : والجزار يجزر له والبناء يبني له • (592) ا : متول •

يستحيى أن يبقى $^{(593)}$ عيالا على كل من في العالم ، الا $^{(594)}$ يعين هو أيضا بشىء من المصلحة ولعمرى $^{(595)}$ (إن كلامه هذا لصحيح حسن) $^{(596)}$ و $^{(597)}$ " إن فى كلامه من الحكم لما يستثير الهم الساكنة الى ماهيئت له . وأى كلام فى نوع هذا أحسن من كلامه فى تعاون $^{(598)}$ الناس $^{(599)}$ وقد نبه الله تعالى عباده $^{(600)}$ بقوله ؛ وتعاونوا على البر والتقوى فكل مالمخلوق فيه مصلحة فى دينه أو فى مالا غنى به عنه $^{(601)}$ فى دنياه فهو بر وتقوى ٠ اذا استعان به على ما أمر الله وحض عليه ، وأفضل ما استعمله المرء $^{(602)}$. (فاعلا ما تكلفه) $^{(603)}$ فى دنياه بعد أداء ما يلزمه لله $^{(604)}$ تعالى فى نفسه من تعلم" اعتقاده من قول وعمل $^{(605)}$ بأن $^{(606)}$ يعلم الناس دينهم الذى له خلقوا ، فيقودهم الى رضى الله عز وجل "و يخرجهم بلطف خالقه تعالى من الظلمة" $^{(607)}$ العمية $^{(608)}$ الى النور الخالص، ومن الضيق $^{(609)}$ المهلك الى السعة الرحبة ، ثم الحكم بالعدل $^{(610)}$ ، والمنع من الظلم ، والذب عن $^{(611)}$ الحوزة بجهاد أهل الحرب والمحاربة $^{(612)}$ وأهل البغى واقامة الناس $^{(613)}$ على ماخلقوا له $^{(614)}$ من اقامة الدين الذى افترضه الله تعالى عليهم ثم احراز ما ذكرنا بكتابة واختزان $^{(615)}$ وقسمة واقامة حد وقبض مال واجب قبضه وغيرذلك ، ثم هكذا أبدا كل مافيه عون على ذلك حتى يبلغ الامر الى الصناعات التى لاغنى بالناس عنها .

---

(593) أ : يكون . (594) أ : على كل العالم لا . (595) أ : ولقد صدق ولعمرى . (596) غير مثبت فى أ . (597) زيادة لازمة . (598) أ : كلام فى نوع ، ع : كلام فى تعاون . (599) غير مثبت فى ر . (600) ر : عليه . (601) أ : أوبما لا غنى للمرء عنه . (602) غير مثبت فى ر . (603) غير مثبت فى أ . (604) أ . (605) ر : اعتقاد قول وعمل . (606) أ : ان . (607) ر : و يخرجهم من الظلمة . (608) أ : العمية . (609) أ : المضيق . (610) أ : بالحق . (611) ر : على . (612) ر : وأهل المحاربة . (613) كذا فى ر ، ناقصة فى أ ، ع أضافها . (614) ر : على ماله خلق . (615) أ : واحتراز .

(قال أبو محمد)(٦١٦)، (٦١٧) اعلم أن كل أحد من الناسمن له تمييز صحيح فانه لا يخلو من أن يكون موقنا بصحة المعاد بعد الموت وبالجزاء، أو يكون شاكًا في ذلك، أو يكون معتقدا أن لامعاد له(٦١٨) ولا جزاء، وانما هي(٦١٩) هذه الحياة الدنيا(٦٢٠) فقط. فان كان ممن يوقن بالمعاد والجزاء فاللازم له اجهاد نفسه واستفراغ طوقه فيما يخلص(٦٢١) به من الهلكة في معاده، ويكون حينئذ ان(٦٢٢) اشتغل بغير ذلك وضيع ما فيه نجاته وخلاصه في الأبد، فاسد التمييز سخيف العقل مذموما مملكا لنفسه، بل في أسوأ(٦٢٣) حالة من المجانين والحيوان الدراج(٦٢٤) غير الناطق. ولا مخلص في المعاد الا بالبحث عن شريعة الحق(و التزام موجباتها)(٦٢٥) وايثار تعلمها(٦٢٦) على كل علم (والعلم بها على كل عمل وان اخر ذلك فحاله في دنياه السريع فنادما وان كان شاكا في المعاد(٦٢٧) فالواجب عليه اجهاد نفسه وترك كل حال شاغلة له(٦٢٨) عن البحث عن صحة الأمر في أن(٦٢٩) المعاد حق (أو في أنه غير حق)(٦٣٠) وإن(٦٣١) اشتغل عن ذلك بشيئ(٦٣٢) غيره فهو بلا شك فاسد التمييز، خاسر الصفقة، (مغرور معرض)(٦٣٣) عن الأمر الذي فيه عظيم البلاء عليه أو كثير(٦٣٤) السعادة له. ولا يصل الى علم ذلك الا بالبحث عن الشرائع وطلب البرهان فيها حتى يقف(٦٣٥) على حقيقة الأمر في ذلك. وان كان غير معتقد لصحة المعاد ولم يكن عنده شيئ غير هذه الدار، فلا يخلو(٦٣٦) من أحد وجهين لا ثالث لهما، (أن يكون لا يرى)(٦٣٧) الا(٦٣٨) امراج(٦٣٩) النفس في الشهوات واهمالها في اللذات واطلاقها على اتباع الهوى، فان كان هكذا(٦٤٠) فليس أولى بذلك "فيه من غيره"(٦٤١) وهذا رأي يقتضي(له أن لا ينتقم ممن يلتذ)(٦٤٢) بقتله

ـــــــــــــــــــ

(٦١٦) ناقصة في ا. (٦١٧) ا: واعلم. (٦١٨) ناقصة في ا. (٦١٩) غير مثبت في ر. (٦٢٠) ر: غير مثبت في ر. (٦٢١) ا: يتخلص. (٦٢٢) ا: اذا. (٦٢٣) ا: بل اسوأ. (٦٢٤) كذا في ر، ع: الدارج. (٦٢٥) ع: عن شريعة الحق وتعلمها. (٦٢٦) ع: وايثار تعلمها. (٦٢٧) ا: ونجاته في دنياه، ع: واحراز نجاته في دنياه الآجلة. (٦٢٨) ر: شاغلة عن البحث. (٦٢٩) ا: عن أن. (٦٣٠) ا: أو شيئ غيره حق. (٦٣١) ا: واذا. (٦٣٢) ا: بذلك عن شيئ. (٦٣٣) ا: مخبر بنفسه. (٦٣٤) ر: كبير. (٦٣٥) ا: يقع. (٦٣٦) ر: يخلوا. (٦٣٧) ا: أن لا يكون يرى. (٦٣٨) ناقصة في ا. (٦٣٩) كذا في ر، ع: امراح. (٦٤٠) أ: فان كان هذا هكذا. (٦٤١) ر: في غيره من غيره نبه، ا: في غيره. ع: فيه من غيره. (٦٤٢) ا: له أن لا يظلم ممن تلف.

و أخذ مالَه وهتك^(٦٤٣) سترَه ، وتسخيرَه^(٦٤٤) فيما يلذ به غيرهُ ، واشقائه فيما ينعـم به من سواه^(٦٤٥) ، ولا اخسر صفقته ممن يرى الا^(٦٤٦) (دارَله إلا هـــــذه الدار^(٦٤٧))ثم لا يكون حظه فيها^(٦٤٨) الا الشقاء والتعب والكد^(٦٤٩) والهلكة .

(٢٤٤) او يكون ممن يقول^(٦٥٠) بالسياسة التي جماعها الأمن له من غـيره ولغيره منه على دمه وحرمته وبشرته و ماله وشمول العافية^(٦٥١) وصلاح الحال والكفاية ، وهذا لا يصح البتة ولا يوجد الا باستعمال الشريعة الرادعة^(٦٥٢) بالوعيد فــــــي الآخرة^(٦٥٣) والعقاب في الدنيا لأهل المعاصي^(٦٥٤) فان لاسبيل^(٦٥٥) الـــى ذلك الا بالشريعة فالاشتغال بها هو الغرض ، والاشتغال عنها رأي فاسد . وايضـا فان المشتغل بعلم الشريعة محصِّل الأمن من السلطان والخاصة والعامة(متصل بعلو^(٦٥٦) الحال في الدنيا والصلاح فيها ومن خالفها فمحصل^(٦٥٧) (للمخافة من السلطان^(٦٥٨) والخاصة والعامة ، متعرضللبلاء في(دمه ومالـه وحالـه)^(٦٥٩) ، فلا أضعف عقلا^(٦٦٠) ولا أسوأ تمييزاً (ولا أتم منحسة)^(٦٦١) ولا أنكد^(٦٦٢) عيشا مــــن^(٦٦٣) لا يقر بالمعاد ،ولا يعرف الا هذه الدار، ثم هو متعرض فيهـــا^(٦٦٤) للبلاء والهلكة^(٦٦٥) مدة حياته ، وانما يتحمل الاذى^(٦٦٦) والمخــاوف (ويستسهل العذاب والاذى)^(٦٦٧) ويتعرض للهلكة والأذى^(٦٦٨) والبلاء^(٦٦٩) من يرى انه (ان خرج عن)^(٦٧٠) هذه الدار صار الى الحياة الابدية والنعيم السرمدي

---

(٦٤٣) ا : اوهتك . (٦٤٤) كذا في ر، أ ،وتسخير ع ، وتسخيره .(٦٤٥) ا : به سواه . (٦٤٦) ا : ان لا . (٦٤٧) ا : سوى هذه . ـ (٦٤٨) ا : منهــــــا . (٦٤٩) ا : العاقبة ع أ : ناقصة في أ . (٦٥٠) أ : يقوى . (٦٥١) كذا في ر، أ (٦٥٢) أ : الداعية . (٦٥٣) أ : بالاخرة .(٦٥٤) أ : لاجل المعصية . (٦٥٥) ر : والاذا فانه لاسبيل . (٦٥٦) أ : متصل لعلو . (٦٥٧)أ : فحصــــل (٦٥٨) أ : للمخالفة للسلطان . (٦٥٩) أ : في دمه وحاله و ماله . (٦٦٠)ا:حالا (٦٦١) غيرمثبت في أ . (٦٦٢) أ : ولا أضعف . (٦٦٣) كذا في ر، أ : لمــن ع : ممن . (٦٦٤) غيرمثبت في أ . (٦٦٥) غيرمثبت في أ . (٦٦٦) غيرمثبــت في ر . (٦٦٧) غيرمثبت في أ . (٦٦٨) غيرمثبت في أ . (٦٦٩) كذا في ر، أ : ولبلاء ع : البلاء . (٦٧٠) أ : اذا خرج من .

والسرور الخالد (٦٧١) والا فهو أحمق مجنون ، وانما قلنا هذا لـــنرى (٦٧٢) بالبرهان العقلي الحسي الضروري أن ايثار علم الشريعة على كل علم واجب علــــى من (٦٧٣) لا يقر بالمعاد (٦٧٤) وعلى من يشك بالمعاد ، كوجوبه على من يقـــر بالمعاد (ولا فرق . ونسأل الله تعالى عونا على ما يرضيه وشغلا بما يزلف لديــه ، وفراغا لما يقرب منه ونفارا مما لابر فيه ولا اجرا آمين آمين) (٦٧٥) .

(قال أبو محمد) (٦٧٦) ، وان قوما قد (٦٧٧) قوي جهلهم وضعفت عقولهم وفسدت طبائعهم ، يظنون أنهم من أهل العلم وليسومن أهله ولا شيء أعظم آفة على العلوم وأهلها الذين هم أهلها بالحقيقة من هذه الطبقة المذكورة لأنهم تناولوا طرفا من بعض العلوم يسيرا ،وكان الذي فاتهم من ذلك العلم (٦٧٨) اكــــــثر مما أدركوا منه ولم يكن طلبهم لما طلبوه (٦٧٩) من العلم لله تعالى ولا ليخرجوا به (٦٨٠) من ظلمة الجهل ، لكن (٦٨١) ليزدروا بالناس (٦٨٢) زهوا وعجبـــا وليماروا به لجاجا (٦٨٣) وشغباء وليفخروا بأنهم من أهله تطاولا ونفخا ، وهــذه طريق مجانية الفلاح لأنهم لم يحصلوا على الحقيقة وضيعوا سائر لوازمهم فعظمــــت خبيثتهم (٦٨٤) ولم يكن وكدهم مع الازدراء (٦٨٥) بغيرهم (٦٨٦) الا ازدراءا بسائــر (٦٨٧) العلوم وتنقصها (٦٨٨) لظنهم الفاسد أنه لا علم الا الذي طلبوه (٦٨٩) فقط. وكثيرا ما يعرض هذا للمبتدئ (٦٩٠) في علم من العلـــــوم في (٦٩١) عنفـــوان الصبــــا (٦٩٢) وشره الحداثــــــــــــة (٦٩٣) الا أن هــــــــــــــؤلاء

_____

(٦٧١) ر : الخالص ، أ : الخالدى ، ع : الخالد . (٦٧٢) ناقصة فــي أ .
(٦٧٣) أ : على كل من . (٦٧٤) غير مثبت في ر . (٦٧٥) غير مثبت فـــــي أ .
(٦٧٦) ناقصة في أ . (٦٧٧) ناقصة في أ . (٦٧٨) ناقصة في أ . (٦٧٩) أ : طلبوا . (٦٨٠) ناقصة في أ . (٦٨١) ر : لاكن . (٦٨٢) ر : الناس .
(٦٨٣) أ : ليماروا لجاجا . (٦٨٤) أ : خيبتهم . (٦٨٥) أ : أيضا مع الازدراء.
(٦٨٦) ر : على غيرهم . (٦٨٧) أ : الازدراء بسائر . (٦٨٨) أ : وتنقيصهــــا .
(٦٨٩) أ : طلبوا . (٦٩٠) ر : للمبتدي . (٦٩١) أ : وفي . (٦٩٢) ر : الصبى.
(٦٩٣) أ : وشدة الحداثة .

يرجى(٦٩٥) لهم البرء من هذا الداء مع طول النظر والزيادة فى التبيين(٦٩٤) ، فقصدنا الى أن نُري(٦٩٦) كل من هذه صفته "احد وجهين"(٦٩٧) ، إما نقص علمــــه الذي يتبجح به عن غيره من العلوم ، أوفاقة(٦٩٨) علمه ذلك الى غيره مـــن العلوم ، وأنه(إن لم يضف اليه غيره من العلوم)(٦٩٩) كان ناقصا لاينتفع به كبير منفعة بل لعله يستضره(٧٠٠) جدا ، فمن ذلك أنا وجدنا قوما من أهل (طلب علـــم الديانة)(٧٠١) ، يزرون على سائر(٧٠٢) العلوم ، وهذا نقص شديد(٧٠٣) (لأن علــم الشريعة)(٧٠٤) لاينتفع به صاحبه (الا حتى يعرف اللغة التي بها خاطب النـــاس صاحب الشريعة)(٧٠٥) (وحتى يعرف من العدد ما يفهم به قسمة الفرائـــــض والمواريث)(٧٠٦) وأن يعرف من المطالع ما يعرف به أوقات الصلوات(٧٠٧) ودخـــول شهر الصوم(٧٠٨) ووقت الحج ، (وأيضا فانه)(٧٠٩) ان لم يعرف مضار المآكــــل والمشارب(٧١٠) أوشك أن يتناول ما يؤذيه(٧١١) ويضربه ، وذلك محرم عليه (٧١٢) وقد أمر رسول الله صلى الله عليه وسلم بالتداوي (245) فاتباع أمره فرض ، فتعلم الطب فرض على الكفاية ومضيعه(٧١٣) مضيع فرض ، والقرآن(٧١٤) عربي فلا سبيل الـى أن يعلمه من (لايعلم النحو واللغة)(٧١٥) ولاسيما إن كان المذكور لم يتناول مـــن الشريعة الا علما واحدا من علومها ، فهذا انسان ناقص مسيئ الى نفسه مهلك لهـا ، لأنه ان تناول"علم القرآن"(٧١٦) ولم يحسن(٧١٧) علم السنن كانت يده من الديــن

_____

(٦٩٤) أ : لايرجى ، (٦٩٥) أ : السن ، (٦٩٦) أ : فقصدنا أن نـــــــري ، (٦٩٧) غير مثبت في ر ، (٦٩٨) كذا في ر و أ ، بانه ، ع ، فاقة ، (٦٩٩) أ : وان لم يضف غيره من العلوم الى علمه ، (٧٠٠) كذا في ر، أ : يستصربه ، ع : يستضربه ، (٧٠١) أ : طلب العلم ، أعني الديانة ، (٧٠٢) أ : يزرون بسائـــــر ، (٧٠٣) أ : نقص عظيم شديد ، (٧٠٤) غير مثبت في أ ، (٧٠٥) غير مثبت في أ ، (٧٠٦) أ : في قسمة الفرائض والمواريث ، (٧٠٧) ر : الصلاة ، (٧٠٨) أ: شهر رمضان ـ شهر الصوم ، (٧٠٩) ناقصة في أ ، (٧١٠) أ : المشرب ، (٧١١) ر : ما نيه يؤذيه ، (٧١٢) ناقصة في أ ، (٧١٣) ر : مضيعه ، (٧١٤) ر : والقراءان ، (٧١٥) أ : لم يعلم العربية ، (٧١٦) ر : القرءان ، (٧١٧) أ : ولم يتناول ،

صفرا ، وكان علمه حجة (٧١٨) عليه لا له . وان أحسن (٧١٩) علم السنن ولـــم
يحسن علم القرآن (٧٢٠) لم يعرف (٧٢١) مايجوز (٧٢٢) به القراءة مالاتجوز (٧٢٣) ،
ولا ما أنزل (٧٢٤) الله تعالى ما لم ينزل . وان تعلق بالفتيــا دون
(أن يكون عالما) (٧٢٥) بالقرآن (٧٢٦) والسنن فهو والحمار سواء ، ولا يحـــل
له (الفتيا لأنه لايدري بما يفتي أبحق أم بباطل) (٧٢٧) وانما يفتي مقلدا لمن لا
يدري هل أصاب أم (٧٢٨) اخطأ (٧٢٩) ، ولايعرف ماهو عليه أهو من الديـــن
أم هو من (٧٣٠) غيرالدين الا ظنا . وان تعلق بالكلام دون أن يعرف السنن
كان هالكا ، لمغيبه عن حقيقة الشريعة التي كلفه الله تعالى اياها ، وأمـــره
بالتزامها (٧٣١) .

ووجدنا قوما طلبوا علوم العرب فازروا (٧٣٢) على سائر العلوم كالنحو واللغة
والشعر والعروض ، فكان هؤلاء بمنزلة من ليس بيده (٧٣٣) من الطعام الا الملـــح
ومن ليس (٧٣٤) معه من السلاح الا المصقلة (٧٣٥) التي بها (٧٣٦) يجلــــى
السلاح فقط (٧٣٧) وكان غائبا (٧٣٨) عن علم الشريعة التي لامعنى لخروجنـــا
الى هذا العالم غيرها ، ولا خلاص لنا ولا سلامة عند خروجنا من الدنيـــا
الا بها . وكان بمعزل عن علم الحقائق . ووجدنا قوما طلبوا علوم الأوائل أوعلمـــا
منها ، فاتخذوا (٧٣٩) سائر العلوم سخريا مثل من تعلق بالطب فلم يرعلما (٧٤٠)
غيره . فيقال له انك " لاتشك أنه " (٧٤١) قد يكون فيمن لا يتعانى ولايحسن الطب
(من هم أصح أجساما) (٧٤٢) وأطول أعمارا من المعتنين (٧٤٣) بالطب (٧٤٤)
كأهل البادية والعامة والبلاد التي لايحسن أهلها الطب ، هذا أمر لاينكره منكر ،

ـــــــــــــــــ
(٧١٨) أ : ناقصة في أ . (٧١٩) أ : ومن أحسن . (٧٢٠) ر : القرآن . (٧٢١) أ : لم
يعلم . (٧٢٢) أ : مايجوز . (٧٢٣) أ : لايجوز . (٧٢٤) أ : وما أنـــزل .
(٧٢٥) أ : دون علم . (٧٢٦) ر : بالقرآن . (٧٢٧) أ : أن يفتي لأنه لايفـــتي
أحق أم باطل . (٧٢٨) أ . (٧٢٩) أو . (٧٣٠) ر : اخطأ . (٧٣٠) أ : أم مـــــن .
(٧٣١) أ : والتزم اياها ع : والزمه اداءها . (٧٣٢) أ : فازدروا .
(٧٣٣) أ : في يده . (٧٣٤) أ : وليس . (٧٣٥) ر : المصقلة . (٧٣٦) غيرمثبت
في ر . (٧٣٧) غيرمثبت في أ . (٧٣٨) ر : غايبا . (٧٣٩) أ : واتخـــذوا .
(٧٤٠) ر : ان علما . (٧٤١) ر : لاشك في أنه . (٧٤٢) أ : أحسن أجسامـــا .
(٧٤٣) أ : المتعنين . (٧٤٤) ناقصة في أ .

فان هذا عيان مشاهد ، فما فائدة الطب اذن؟ و لا غرض لأهله (745)(الا ازالــة العلل واستعمامة الصحة) (746) فلم (747) يحصلوا من هذا الغرض الا على اقــل مما حصل عليه غيرهم · ومثل قوم من أهل الهندسة وعلم الهيئة لايرون ماعداذلك من العلوم الا هذرا (748) ولغوا فيقال لهم (749) ماالفرق بين معرفــــة قطع كوكب كذا ۠ وكوكب كذا ۠ (750) وصفة برج كذا ۠ وبرج كذا ۠ (751) ، (ومساحــة كوكب كذا) (752) من الأرض وبين صفة مدينة كذا ، ٠وحركات ملك فلانـــــة أو حركات فلان وفلان ، وهذا لاسبيل لهم الا المخلص منه ، لان كل ذلــك خبرعن بعض مافي العالم فقط لا يفيد فائدة ۠ (753) الا المعرفة بما عرف مـــن كل (754) ذلك أنه (755) على هيئته ، والاستدلال بكل ذلك على الصانع و المدبر (756) سواء (757) ٠

فان صار الى علم القضاء لم يحصل الا على دعاوى كاذبة و خرافات لاتصح ، بل البرهان قائم (758) على بطلان هذه الدعاوى (759) بما قد أحكمناه في غــــير هذا الموضع (760) ، ومن ذلك أنهم لا يذكرون (761) على ذلك دليلا أصـــلا الا تجارب يذكرونها و هذا باطل لأن تلك التجارب لا يمكن اثباتها البتة (762) لأنها لاتكون الا في مدد طوال ، ولاسبيل الى بقاء دولة ولا الى (763) استرار (حالة قوم على سرور وسلامة) (764) ، مقدار تلك المدة أبدا ، ونقـــول لهم : ان صح (765) ما بأيديكم ، باقراركم ، المواليد والقرانات ، ونحن نجــد الكبش يولد ويعيش وينتج وهو يباشر أكله (766) وفي دقيقة واحدة ثم يعمــل

ــــــــــــــــــــــــــــــــــ

(745) ر: لاهلبه ٠ (746) أ : الا تصحيح الاجسام ودفع الأمراض المخــوف للموت ٠ (747) أ : ولم ٠ (748) ر ، هزءا ٠ (749) غير مثبت فـــي ر ٠ (750) غير مثبت في ر ٠ (751) غير مثبت في ر ٠ (752) غير مثبت فـــي أ ٠ (753) ر ، و حركة فلانة وحركة فلان ، أو مساحة مابين مدينة كذا و مدينة كذا ، وهل كل ذلك الا خبر و خبر ، وهذا ما لاسبيل لهم الى التخلص منه ، لأنه لا فائدة لكل ماطلبوا وما نظروا فيه ٠ (754) غير مثبت في ر ٠ (755) غير مثبت فــي ر ٠ (756) أ : المدبر ٠ (757) غير مثبت في ر ٠ (758) ر : قائم ٠ (759) ر : ابطالها ٠ (760) ر : المكان ٠ (761) أ : يدعون ٠ (762) ناقصة في ر ٠ (763) ناقصة في أ ٠ (764) أ : حالة على سلامة ٠ (765) أ : أصح ٠ (766) ر : كله شقي ، أ : ناشر كله ، ع ، يباشر أكله ٠

من جلده أديم ، فبعضه رق (٧٦٧) يُنسخ فيه ، وتطول مدة بقائه (٧٦٨) وبعضه
رقاع (٧٦٩) تقطع وتهلك (٧٧٠) ، ولم يتقدم في الوجود والنشأة بعض ذلك الأديم
بعضا ، وأيضا فانهم خابوا من علم (246) الشريعة الذي هو الحقيقة .

وطائفة حصلت على علم حدود المنطق (وغابوا ما سواه) (٧٧١) فنقول لهم :
انكم لم تحصلوا الا على آلة (٧٧٢) العلوم التي لا منفعة لها ولا فائدة (٧٧٣)
الا بتصريفها (٧٧٤) في سائر العلوم فأنتم (٧٧٥) كمن جمع آلة البناء ولم يصرفها
في البنيان فهي معطلة لديه لا معنى لها ، فان قالوا إن لهذه (٧٧٦) العلوم
معايش ومكاسب ، قلنا هي أضعف المكاسب وأقل المعايش سعة ، فان ليسغرضكم
الا هذا ، فالتجارة والزراعة وصحبة السلطان أجدى في المكسب (٧٧٧) وأوسع
في الوفر (٧٧٨) حظا مما أنتم عليه .

(قال أبو محمد) (٧٧٩) : ولم نورد شيئا من هذا تنقصا (٧٨٠) لشيئ من
هذه العلوم ، ومعاذ الله من هذا ولو قصدنا (٧٨١) ذلك لدخلنا في جملة من نذم ،
ولركبنا الطريقة (٧٨٢) الخسيسة لكن (٧٨٣) تنقصا لمن قصد بعلمه ذم سائر العلوم
وتنقصها (٧٨٤) وأما من طلب علما ما لم يفتح الله تعالى (٧٨٥) له في غيره وهو
مع ذلك معترف بفضل سائر العلوم ، "ونقص ما حصل عليه (٧٨٦) ونقص (٧٨٧)
حاله ان قصر (٧٨٨) عنها ، فهم محسن محمود فاضل قد (٧٨٩) تعوض الانصاف
والعدل والصدق ما فاته منها فنعم العوض (حصل عليه) (٧٩٠) ، ولا ملامة

---

(٧٦٧) ر ، أ : ورق ، ع : رق . (٧٦٨) ر : بقايه . (٧٦٩) أ : بطائق ، ع :
نطائق . (٧٧٠) أ : وتحفن . (٧٧١) غير مثبت في أ . (٧٧٢) غير مثبت في أ :
(٧٧٣) ر : فايدة . (٧٧٤) أ : تصريفها . (٧٧٥) كذا في ر ، أ : فانت ، ع :
فانتم . (٧٧٦) ر : هذه . (٧٧٧) أ : بالمكسب . (٧٧٨) أ : بالدفر ، ع :
بالوفر . (٧٧٩) غير مثبتة في أ . (٧٨٠) أ : تنقيصا . (٧٨١) أ : ولو فعلنا .
(٧٨٢) أ : المدة ، ع : الملة . (٧٨٣) ر : لاكن . (٧٨٤) ر : وتنقصا .
(٧٨٥) غير مثبت في ر . (٧٨٦) غير مثبت في ر . (٧٨٧) ر : وبنقص .
(٧٨٨) أ : اقصر . (٧٨٩) غير مثبت في ر . (٧٩٠) غير مثبت في أ .

عليه فيما لم يفتح ° الله تعالى° (٧٩١) له فيه ، وأما من أخذ من كل علم ماهو محتاج اليه واستعمل ماعلم كما يجب فلا أحد أفضل منه ، لأنه (٧٩٢) قد حصل على عز النفس وغناها في العاجل وعلى الفوز في الآجل ، ونجا مما حصل فيه أهل الجهل، ومن لم يستعمل ما علم من اضداد هذه الأحوال .

وجملة الأمر أنه لولا طلب النجاة في الآخرة لما كان لطلب شيء من العلوم معنى لأنه تعب (للنفس والجسم وشغل) (٧٩٣) قاطع (٧٩٤) عن مسرات (٧٩٥) الدنيا المتعجلة من المشارب والمآكل والملاهي والسفاء (٧٩٦) والاعتلاء والتشفي (٧٩٧) واتباع (٧٩٨) الهوى ، (وجمع المال) (٧٩٩) فلو لم تكن (٨٠٠) آخرة يؤدي (٨٠١) (الى معرفة طريق الفوز فيها) (٨٠٢) طلب (٨٠٣) العلوم ، لما كان أحد أسوأ حالا من المشتغل بالعلم ، وإن (٨٠٤) الأمر كذلك فالعلوم كلها (٨٠٥) متعلق بعضها ببعض (محتاج بعضها الى بعض كما بينا قبل) (٨٠٦) ولا غرض لها الا معرفة ما أدى الى الفوز في الآخرة فقط وهو علم الشريعة ، وبالله تعالى التوفيق ، وهو حسبي ونعم الوكيل . ° (٨٠٧)

(آخر مراتب العلوم ، والحمد لله رب العالمين وصلواته وسلامه على سيد المرسلين وخاتم النبيين محمد وأمته وصحبه وأزواجه أجمعين وعلى جميع اخوته من الرسل والى كل منهم الى يوم الدين) . (٨٠٨)

نجز بحول الله وقوته لتاريخ الثامن والعشرين من شهر رمضان المعظم عام الواحد وألف عرفنا الله خيره .

─────────

(٧٩١) غير مثبت في ر .
(٧٩٢) ر : لا . (٧٩٣) غير مثبت في أ . (٧٩٤) أ : وقاطع . (٧٩٥) أ : لذات . (٧٩٦) غير مثبتة في ر . (٧٩٧) ناقصة في أ . (٧٩٨) ر : والتباع . (٧٩٩) ناقصة في أ . (٨٠٠) أ : يكن . (٨٠١) ر : يودى . (٨٠٢) ناقصة في أ . (٨٠٣) أ : اليها طلب . (٨٠٤) أ : فاذ . (٨٠٥) أ : كذا في ر ، أ ، فالأمر كله ع ، فالعلوم كلها . (٨٠٦) أ : كما بينا قبل محتاج بعضها الى بعض . (٨٠٧) ر : والغرض ماذكرنا والله الموفق . (٨٠٨) أ : تمت الرسالة الموسومة بمراتب العلوم والحمد لله رب العالمين وصلاته على سيدنا محمد وعلى آله وصحبه وسلم تسليما كثيرا .

NOTES

CHAPTER I:
THE PLACE OF IBN HAZM IN THE INTELLECTUAL HISTORY OF ISLAM

1. Awqaf Collection no. 209, folios 231-246, General Library of Rabat, Morocco.
2. Fatih Mosque of Istanbul, no. 2704, folios 253-264.
3. Ibn Hazm, *Maratib al-'ulum*, 81/242. Pagination refers to 'Abbas' edition and to the Rabat manuscript.
4. For details on full titles, place, and date of publication, see bibliography under the respective authors.
5. On Ibn Shuhayd, see his *Diwan;* Dickie, *Ibn Shuhayd;* Peres, *Poesie*, 95-96; Nykl, *Poetry* 103-105; and Monroe's introduction to his translation of Ibn Shuhayd's *Tawabi*; 1ff.
6. Maqqari, *Nafh*, III, 362.
7. On 'Ubaydallah Ibn 'Abd al-Rahman al-Nasir, see **Nykl,**. *Poetry,* 63.
8. Maqqari, *Nafh*, III, 588. The word *'ud* in the poem appears in its several shades of meaning.
9. Ibn Hazm, *Hatif* see Appendix, Cf. Chapter III, note 125.
10. *Ibid.*, 8-9. Cf. Chapter III, 126.
11. *Ibid.*, 10-11. Cf. Chapter III, 127.
12. He is 'Abd al-Rahman Ibn Khalaf al-Ma'arifi. See Humaydi, *Judhwah*, no. 590; Dabbi, *Bughyah*, no. 997.
13. Ibn Hazm, *Tawq*, 272. Reference to the Spanish translation by Garcia Gomez is made here.
14. Ibn Hazm, *Iman*, 21.
15. Sa'id, *Tabaqat*, 101-102.
16. As quoted by Ibn Bassam, *Dhakhirah*, I:i, 140 and Yaqut, *Irshad*, V, 92.
17. Humaydi, **Judhwah,** 307.
18. Ibn Bashkuwal, *Silah*, no. 894.
19. Dabbi, **Bughyah,** no. 1204.
20. Marrakushi, *Mu'jib*, 96-97.
21. Shaqundi, *Risalah*, in Maqqari, *Nafh*, III, 192.
22. Dhahabi, *Siyar*, in *Majma'*, 402-403; Ibn **'imad, Shadharat**, III, 299. On al-Ghazzali's remarks, see Ghazzali, *Maqsad*, 126.
23. Dhahabi, *Siyar*, 406, quotes Ibn Hazm as saying: *"Ana atba' al-haqq wa-ajtahid wa-la ataqallad."*
24. Abu Hanifah flourished in Iraq and was the founder of a legal school named after him. He died in 767. On him see *SEI;* Schacht, *Introduction*, **40f.**
25. Malik Ibn Anas (d .795) was a Medinese jurist and founder of a legal school named after him. He is the author of the famous legal codex *al-Muwatta'*. His doctrine became the sole legal school in al-Andalus. On him, see *SEI*.
26. He is, perhaps, Sufyan al-Thawri (d. 778), who was a traditionist and religious scholar in Kufah, Iraq.
27. al-Awza'i (d. 774) was a Syrian jurist, who established a school of law which had currency for a time under the Umayyads in the East and **al-Andalus**.

28. Shafi'i (d. 820) was a jurist and founder of a legal school named after him. He flourished in Iraq; his doctrine appears in his *Risalah*.
29. Abu 'Ubayd (d. 931) is, perhaps, 'Ali Ibn al-Husayn Ibn Harb, a jurist from Baghdad.
30. Ahmad Ibn Ishaq (d. 957) was a Shafi'ite jurist known as al-Sibghi (cf. Zirikli, *A'lam*, I, 91).
31. Dhahabi, *Siyar*, 406-407. Cf. Chapter VI, on imitation and *Ijtihad*.
32. Abu Bakr Ibn al-'Arabi (d. 1148) was a prominent Malikite judge in Seville. It should be added that Ibn Zarqun al-Ansari (d.721/1321), a staunch Malikite, composed his *Mu'alla* in refutation of Ibn Hazm's juridical work, *al-Muhalla* (see Ibn Farhun, *Dibaj*, 286).
33. The Battle of Siffon took place in 657-659 between the fourth caliph 'Ali and the future Umayyad caliph Mu'awiyah (661-680) and polarized - the partisans of 'Ali (Shi'ah) and "Orthodoxy". The Kharijites, formerly partisans of 'Ali, seceded from him to form their own group, which opposed the established government for centuries. On the Kharijites, see Salem, *Khawarij*, and also, *SEI*.
34. Dawud Ibn Khalaf (d. 884) was the founder of the Zahirite school that was revived and articulated by Ibn Hazm. See below, Chapter III, and *SEI* under *Zahiriya*.
35. Dhahabi, *Siyar*, 404-405.
36. *Ibid.*, 405.
37. *Ibid.*, 439-440.
38. Sa'id, *Tabaqat*, 102.
39. Marrakushi, *Mu'jib*, 94.
40. He is the author of the universal history entitled *Akhbar*, and of a commentary of the Qur'an in thirty volumes entitled *Tafsir*. Ibn Hazm was familiar with both works.
41. Asin, *Abenhazam*, I, 245-278.
42. The treatises are: **Usul-furu', Iman, nafs, Durrah, Tawqif, Ibn al-Naghrilah, Hatif, Kalb, Risalatan, Akhlaq, Imamah, Alam, Ahl al-shaqa; Ghina' Talkhis,** and *Maratib al-'ulum*. They are here abbreviated. For full titles and other information see under Ibn Hazm in the Appendix.
43. Asin, *Codice*, in *al-Andalus*, 2(1934), 1-56.
44. See the content of *Rasa'il* under 'Abbas in the Bibliography.
45. See content of *Ibn al-Naghrilah* under 'Abbas in the Bibliography.
46. See the content of *Jawami'* under 'Abbas in the Bibliography.
47. See the full title of *Taqrib* under Ibn Hazm in the Appendix.
48. Afghani, *Ibn Hazm*, 51-59.
49. See full title of *Mufadalah* under Ibn Hazm in the Appendix.
50. See the full title of *Ibtal* under Ibn Hazm in the Appendix.
51. Dhahabi, *Siyar*, 433-436.
52. *Ibid.*, 436.
53. See the full title of *Hijjah* under Ibn Hazm in the Appendix.
54. See the full title of *Jamharah* under Ibn Hazm in the Appendix.
55. Khalifah, *Ibn Hazm*, 128-134.
56. For full details on these works see under Ibn Hazm in the Appendix.
57. Asin, *Abenhazam*, I, 5-6; Asin, *Ibid*, I, 6, attributes the neglect of Ibn Hazm to his acid attack on his co-religionists and his equally violent attacks on Judaism and Christianity.
58. *Ibid.*, I, 9.
59. Dozy, *Histoire*, II, 326-332.
60. In the introduction to his edition of Ibn 'Idhari's *Bayan* (Leiden, 1848), 65-67.
61. Wustenfeld, *Geschichteschreiber*, 202.
62. Pons Boigues, *Ensayo*, 130-138.
63. Goldziher, *Zahiriten*, 166ff.

64. Schreiner, in *ZDMG*, (1898), 464-486.
65. Steinschneider, *Literatur*.
66. Friedlander, *Komposition*, I, 267-277; and in *JAOS*, (1907).
67. MacDonald, *Theology*, 209-212; and 245-48.
68. Horten, *Systeme*, 564-593.
69. Tritton, *Theology*, index; and in *BSOS*, 12(1047), 1-4.
70. Gardet-Anawati, *Introduction*, 147-150.
71. Asin, in *CE*, (1909), 41-61 and 517-540.
72. The *Akhlaq* was translated under the title of *Los caracteres y la conducta*. See *Akhlaq* under Ibn Hazm in the Appendix.
73. Asin, in *al-Andalus*, 4(1936-39), 253-281.
74. Arnaldez, *Grammaire*.
75. Arnaldez, *Controverse*.
76. Arnaldez, *Guerre*.
77. Arnaldez, *Raison*.
78. Nykl, in *AJSLL*, 49(1923), 30-36.
79. See *Akhlaq* in the Appendix.
80. Dozy, *Histoire*, III, 341ff.
81. Schack, *Poesie*, 114ff; and Valera's Spanish translation, I, 123-129.
82. Pons Boigues, *Obras*, 509-523; cf. his *Ensayo*, 130ff.
83. For the scholarly history of the *Tawq*, see Garcia Gomez translation, 319-321.
84. Gonzalez Palencia, *Historia*, 155-173.
85. Peres, *Poesie*, 77-79.
86. Nykl, *Poetry*, 73-103.
87. Gibb, *Literature*, 114.
88. Pellat, *Litterature*, 126.
89. Chejne, *Muslim Spain*, 185ff., 168ff.; also his *Arabic* 10, 35, 73.
90. Seco de Lucena, *Naqt*, in *al-Andalus*, 6(1941), 357-375.
91. Bosch, *Ibn Hazm*.
92. Rosenthal, *History*, 26ff. and 112ff.
93. Rosenthal, *Knowledge*, 120-122; 234-237 and the index.
94. *Heritage*, 58-61; Mu'nis, *Clasificacion;* Chejne, *Muslim-Spain*, 169ff.
95. Friedlander, in the introduction of his *Heterodoxies*.
96. di Matteo, *Pretese*.
97. Garcia Gomez, *Ibn al-Naghrilah, al-Andalus*, 4(1936-1939), 1-28.
98. Perlmann, in *PAASR*, 18 (1949).
99. Brockelmann, *GAL*, I, 505ff., and Suppl. I, 692-697.
100. Sarton, *Introduction*, I, 713.
0. Sezgin, *Geschichte*, index.
102. Nicholson, *History*, 426.
103. Gibb, *Literature*, 114.
104. Pellat, *Litterature*, 122 and 126.
105. See above, notes 44ff.
106. See *Mu'jam* in the bibliography.
107. Mubarak, *Nathr*, II, 166-178.
108. Haykal, *Adab*, 324-330.
109. 'Abbas, *Tarikh*, 303-322.
110. Dayah, *Naqd*, 307-328.

111. Afghani, *Ibn Hazm*, 4-5.
112. Abu Zahrah, *Ibn Hazm*, 4.
113. *Ibid.*, 148.
114. *Ibid.*, 177ff.
115. Hajiri, *Ibn Hazm*, 6.
116. *Ibid.*, 7-8.
117. For Marrakushi's statement, see above, note 20; cf. Ibn al-Athir, *Kamil*, XII, 61; Asin, *Abenhazam*, I, 280.
118. See above, note 32.
119. Goldziher, *Zahiriten*, 193-195.
120. Asin, *Abenhazam*, I, 282-328, lists some thirty-six scholars who were influenced by the ideas of Ibn Hazm.
121. *Ibid.*, 284-289. It is doubtful that Sa'id was his pupil. Cf. below, Chapter, V, Notes 36ff.
122. *Ibid.*, 285-289. All indications are that Ibn Hazm and Ibn 'Abd al-Barr were co-disciples and that Ibn Hazm is more dependent on his senior Ibn 'Abd al-Barr than the reverse. Cf. below, Chapter IV, 28ff,
123. *Ibid.*, 291-293. He is Muhammad Ibn Fattuh al-Humaydi. On him, see Dabbi, *Bughyah*, no. 257.
124. *Ibid.*, 295-296. He is Abu Muhammad 'Abdallah Ibn al-'Arabi (d.1099), the father of Abu Bakr. He traveled to the East where he died. See Yaqut, *Irshad*, V, 89-90.
125. *Ibid.*, 297-300. Al-Ghazzali (d.1111) was the leading orthodox theologian.
126. *Ibid.*, 311-314. Muhiyy al-Din Ibn 'Arabi is one of the leading mystics of Islam and author of numerous works, among which is the *Futuhat*. See Afifi, *Ibnul 'Arabi*; Corbin, *Ibn 'Arabi*.
127. *Ibid.*, 314-316. Ibn Rushd (d.1198), known to the Latin West as Averroes, was a philosopher, physician, theologian, and jurist, and served at the Almohad court where the influence of Ibn Hazm is said to have been great. He was a great commentator on the works of Aristotle, and a great advocate of the harmony of faith and reason. See his *Fasl*. See Gautier, *Ibn Rochd*.
128. *Ibid.*, 318-319. He was a Granadine philologist who traveled to the East, where he died in 1345. See Hadithi, *Abu Hayyan*, 315ff. and 371ff.
129. *Ibid.*, 322-323. Al-Dhahabi (d.1348) was a famous traditionist-historian who expressed great sympathy for some of the ideas of Ibn Hazm. See above, notes 22ff.
130. *Ibid.*, 323-324. Al-Sha'rani (d.1442) was an Egyptian mystic and a great defender of Ibn 'Arabi.
131. See below, Chapter III, notes 28ff.
133. Asin, *Abenhazam*, I, 29ff.
133. Humaydi, *Judhwah*, no. 708. In fact, the *Judhwah* is replete with information derived from the authority of Ibn Hazm.
134. Dhahabi, *Siyar*, 437.
135. Mainly, Abu Bakr Ibn al-'Arabi's *Qawasim*; cf. note 32.
136. Ghazzali, *Maqsad*, 125, ponders the question of the beautiful names of God and appears to accept the Tradition on the authority of Abu Hurayrah, a companion of Muhammad, to the effect that God possesses ninety-nine names. However, he admits the difficulty of determining them, and concludes by giving a great credit to Ibn Hazm's attempt and conclusions.
137. Ghazzali, *Tahafut*, 36ff., states that the purpose of his work was not disavowal of philosophy per se but certain erroneous views held by some philosophers and theologians. Cf. Chatper IV on intellect and faith.
138. In this connection, al-Ghazzali, *Tahafut*, 44, distinguishes between the physical and the metaphysical sciences, saying that mathematics, astronomy, and the like have nothing to do with metaphysics *(al-ilahiyat)*.

139. Ibn Hazm's *Taqrib* and al-Ghazzali's *Mihakk* should constitute a starting point for a comparison of the ideas of the two men. It is interesting to note that al-Ghazzali, *Tahafut*, 45, states that logic is certainly valid, but is not the sole patrimony of philosophers.
140. Asin, *Abenhazam*, I, 300.
141. Tourneau, *Almohad*, 6-7.
142. MacDonald, *Theology*, 246.
143. For a full appreciation of Ibn Tumart's doctrine, see Ibn Tumart, *Livre;* MacDonald, *Theology*, 245-249; Asin, *Abenhazam*, I, 305-306; Brunschvig, *Ibn Tumart*.
144. For a full appreciation for Ibn Tufayl's philolophy, see his *Hayy*.
145. Asin, *Abenhazam*, I, 307-327. For more details on these points, see Ibn Rushd, *Fasl*, 30; and his *Tahafut*, I 27.
146. Ibn 'Arabi, *Futuhat*, II, 519.
147. MacDonald, *Theology*, 261.
148. Asin, *Abenhazam*, I, 311-314.
149. MacDonald, *Theology*, 280.
150. See above, notes 31ff.
151. See Ibn Taymiyyah, *Naqd*, 17, where he refers to Ibn Hazm's *Fisal*. On Ibn Taymiyyah, see *SEI;* Goldziher, *Zahiriten*, 188-192; MacDonald, *Theology*, 275 and 283; and Laoust, *Ibn Taymiyyah*. Cf. Chapter VI on imitation.
152. Ibn Khaldun, *Muqaddimah*, I, 414.
153. *Ibid.*, II, 171.
154. *Ibid.*, II, 463.
155. *Ibid.*, III, 6.
156. *Ibid.*, II, 60.
157. *Ibid.*, I, 16ff. For his part, Ibn Hazm, *Fisal*, I, 165/II, 309ff., points to the exaggerated number of Jews in the Sinai peninsula after their exodus from Egypt. Numbering after the slant refers to Asin's translation of the *Fisal*.
158. Ibn Hazm, *Maratib al-'ulum*, 79/240; also his *Fisal*, I, 109, where he conceives the Black and the Northern peoples to be devoid of the sciences, a notion well articulated by Sa'id, *Tabaqat*, 8ff., and Ibn Khaldun, *Muçaddimah*, I, 168ff.
159. Ibn Hazm, *Maratib al-'ulum*, 83/243, insists on the need for cooperative effort in the sciencies in the same manner that society's success depends on the cooperation of all its components — a notion that constitutes the basis of Ibn Khaldun's sociological doctrine. Furthermore, the comprehensive treatment of the sciences by both men betrays a similar, if not identical outlook.
160. See below, Chapter VIII, note 141.
161. *Ibid.*
162. See below, Chapter VIII, note 130.
163. See below, Chatper VIII, notes 93ff.
164. See below, Chapter VIII, note 115.
165. However, Ibn Khaldun, *Muqaddimah*, 111, 112, considers music to be part of the mathematical sciences. One may add Ibn Qayyim al-Jawziyah, who often mentions Ibn Hazm in his *Rawdah* dealing with love.
166. On this point, See Chejne, *Role, 112;* Makdisi, *Scholastic Method*.
167. The subject of courtly love and its relation with the troubadours is still controversial among scholars. The pros and cons may be found in the following works: Nykl, *Influence, his Poetry* (Ch. VII) and his *Troubadors*, Castro, *Espana*, 396ff.; Garcia Gomez in his introduction to the translation of *Tawq*, 69-77; Denomy, *Arabic Influence*, "*Fin amors*", and *Heresy*, Jeanroy, *Poesie*.
168. Fray Anselmo Turmeda, *Tuhfah,* (ed. by de Epalza). In fact, Turmeda names Ibn Hazm, *Tuhfah*, 194, 99-101.
169. See Cardaillac, *Polemique*, I, 132ff. cf Chejne, *Moriscos*.
170. Chejne, *Islamization*.

CHAPTER II:
THE MAN AND HIS TIME

1. Sa'id, *Tabaqat*, 101; cf. Yaqut, *Irshad*, V, 86, who omits Ibn Ma'dan, whereas Ibn Khallikan, *Wafayat*, III, 13 says, "mawla yazid Ibn Abi Sufyan Sakhr Ibn Harb." Ibn Hazm's pupil al-Humaydi, *Judhwah*, no. 708, does not give his full genealogy and simply says: "Ali Ibn Ahmad Ibn Sa'id Ibn Ghalib Abu Muhammad asluh min al-Furs". Al-Humaydi was followed by al-Dabbi, *Bughyah*, no. 1204 and to a certain extent by Ibn Bashkuwal, *Silah*, no. 894, who says: " 'Ali Ibn Ahmad Ibn Sa'id Ibn Hazm Ibn al-Farisi." In all these cases, however, no question was raised concerning the genuineness of his Persian origin.
2. Sa'id, *Tabaqat*, 102 Yaqut, *Irshad*, V, 86, who derives his information from Sa'id says that he was born in the last day of Ramadan in the year 383. On the other hand, Ibn Bashkuwal and Ibn Khallikan, *Wafayat*, III, 15, give the same date as Sa'id.
3. *Ibid.* Again Yaqut, *Irshad*, V, 88, puts the date of his death *Jumada al-ula*, 457, where as Ibn Bashkuwal and Ibn Khallikan, among others, reproduce the date given by Sa'id. On the other hand, it is interesting to note that al-Humaydi, *Judhwah*, 309, does not seem to know the exact date of the death of his teacher, saying that he died after the year 450.
4. Marrakushi, *Mu'jib*, 93.
5. Mainly, Humaydi, *Judhwah*, 305; Sa'id, *Tabaqat*, 101; Yaqut, *Irshad*, V, 86; Ibn Khallikan, *Wafayat*, III, 13.
6. Ibn Khallikan, *Wafayat*, III, 13.
7. *Ibidem.*, cf. Yaqut, *Irshad*, V, 87.
8. Ibn Bassam, *Dhakhirah*, 1:i, 142; also quoted by Yaqut, *Irshad*, V, 93. Cf. Asin, *Abenhazam*, I, 19ff. It should be noted that the term *'ajam* designated people of non-Arab ancestry and was applied, as a rule, to Persians.
9. Dozy, *Histoire*, II, 326, says that the family of Ibn Hazm was Christian until the time of his great grandfather Hazm and that the family was ashamed of its Christian origin, claiming a Persian ancestry. If this is the case it is indeed surprising that Ibn Hazm's numerous enemies did not use such information to discredit him. Moreover, if his ancestry was actually controversial, Ibn Hazm, who was famous for his many controversies, would have taken up the issue. In fact, there is silence on his part on this point, and it is rather surprising that no mention of his genealogy is made in his important genealogical work, the *Jamharah*.
10. *Ibd.* II, 331ff.
11. Simonet, *Historia*, 642
12. Garcia Gomez in his introduction to his Spanish translation of the *Tawq*, 50.
13. Asin, *Abenhazam*, I, 23. Modern Arab scholars are divided on the question of Ibn Hazm's origin. Abu Zahrah, *Ibn Hazm*, 26, and Khalifah, *Ibn Hazm*, 22, are inclined to accept Ibn Hazm's oriental origin, but Hajiri, *Ibn Hazm*, 16ff. discounts it, giving weight to Ibn Hayyan's version.
14. The settlement of Banu Hazm in Cordova cannot be ascertained with any precision. However, it may be assumed that it took place just before or shortly after the accession of the caliph 'Abd al-Rahman III (912-967), when the situation in the provinces was extremely unstable.
15. On Ahmad Ibn Hazm, see Humaydi, *Judhwah*, no. 215; Dabbi, *Bughyah*, no. 412.
16. Ahmad Ibn Rashiq (d. 1048), secretary at the court of Mallorca, appears to be one of Ahmad's pupils. See Hajiri, *Ibn Hazm*, 34, who suggests several important people who may have been among his students.
17. On the 'Amirids, see 'Inan, *Dawlah;* Dozy, *Histoire*, II, 28ff. and Levi-Provencal, *Histoire*, II, 192-272.

18. One may mention his nephew Ahmad Ibn 'Abd al-Rahman, whose son Abu-l-Mughirah, achieved great prominence as courtier and poet. On Abu-l-Mughira, see Ibn Bassam, *Dhakhirah,* I:i, 147ff. Cf. below, note 42.
19. Ibn Hazm, *Tawq,* 259.
20. *Ibid,.* 130.
21. *Ibid.,* 249ff.; cf. Asin, *Abenhazam,* I, 41
23. Ibn Hazm, *Tawq,* 112.
24. *Ibid.,* 249ff.; cf. Asin, *Abenhazam,* I, 43.
25. Humaydi, *Judhwah,* 241.
26. Sa'id al-Baghdadi (d. 1026) was a prominent Baghdadi poet and belletrist who emigrated to al-Andalus and was attached to the court of al-Mansur Ibn Abi 'Amir. On him, see Humaydi, *Judhwah,* no. 509; Dabbi, *Bughyah,* no. 852; Blachere, *Sa'id.*
27. Ibn Hazm, *Tawq,* 195, says: "I walked on carpets of caliphs and attended audience at the courts of kings, but I have never seen a veneration comparable to the one the lover feels for his beloved."
28. On the events leading to the great revolt and its aftermath, see Dozy, *Histoire,* III, ff.; Levi-Provencal, *Histoire,* II, 200, Chejne, *Muslim Spain,* 38ff.
29. The Slavs were slaves of European origin introduced by the caliph 'Abd al-Rahman III as praetorian guards. They attained prominence and political power during the reign of al-Hakam II.
30. Ibn Hazm, *Tawq,* 250.
31. *Ibid.*
32. *Ibid.,* 259.
33. *Ibid.,* 250.
34. Ibn Bassam, *Dhakhirah,* I:i, 25 and 32.
35. Ibn Hazm, *Tawq,* 251.
36. *Ibid.,* 260.
37. *Ibid.,* 261
37a. Handler, *Zirids,* 27ff.
38. Ibn Hazm, *Tawq,* 223.
39. *Ibid.,* 114.
40. *Ibid.,* 262. Qasim ruled from 1018 to 1021.
41. Ibn Bassam, *Dhakhirah,* I:i, 40.
42. Maqqari, *Nafh,* I, 489. Cf. Ibn Bassam, *Dhakhirah,* I:i. 36.
43. Ibn Bassam, *Dhakhirah,* I:i, 38.
44. On the party kings, see Prieto y Vives, *Reyes,* and 'Inan, *Duwal.*
45. Ibn Hazm, *Tawq,* 203.
46. Yaqut, *Irshad,* V, 87 Hajiri, *Ibn Hazm,* 15, is inclined to think that Ibn Hazm served Hisham III in the capacity of vizier. This is quite probable since Ibn Hazm knew Hisham III; in addition, there was his commitment to the caliphal cause.
47. For more detail on Ibn Hazm's stay in Mallorca, see Asin, *Abenhazam,* 195-210.
48. Ibn Sidah was a leading lexicographer and the author of the valuable lexical works *al-Muhkam* and *al-Mukhassas.* On him see Humaydi, *Judhwah,* 709; Dabbi, *Bughyah,* no. 1205.
49. *Ibn Hazm, Fada'il,* in Maqqari, *Nafh,* III, 170.
50. On Ahmad Ibn Rashiq, see *Judhwah,* no. 215; Dabbi, *Bughyah,* no. 400.
51. On al-Baji, see Ibn al-Abbar, *Hullah,* II, 128; Ibn Sa'id, *Mughrib,* I, 404; and Maqqari, *Nafh,* II, 67.
52. Ibn Hazm, *Fisal,* I, 88. An interesting dialogue is reported to have taken place between Ibn Hazm and al-Baji. It runs as follows: "Al-Baji: excuse me, I have studied in a dim light; to which Ibn Hazm replied: I also beg your pardon since most of my study was

done on a silver and golden platform" (implying that wealth is more of a deterrent to the search of knowledge than poverty). (Yaqut, *Irshad*, V, 88).

53. For tne departure of Ibn Sidah and Ibn 'Abd al-Barr from Denia, (see Khuli's introduction to his edition of Ibn 'Abd al-Barr's *Bahjah*.
54. Dabbi, *Bughyah*, 113.
55. For the history of Valencia at that time,see Huici Miranda, *Valencia*,III, 165ff
56. Ibn Hazm, *Fisal*, I, 59.
57. See above, note 36.
58. For the Arabic text of the poem, see Yaqut, *Irshad*, V, 96; Peres, *Poesie*, 406; Nykl, *Poetry*, 102.
59. Ibn al-Abbar, *Hullah*, II, 34. The Arabic title of the work is : *al-Hadi ila ma'rifat al-nasab al-'abbadi*.
60. Ibn Bashkuwal, *Silah*, no. 1522,
61. Ibn al-Abbar, *Hullah*, I, 71.
62. Maqqari, *Nafh*, 238, CF. Asin, *Abenhazam*, I, 243.
63. Ibn Hazm, *Tawq*, 309. The translation is based on an undated Beirut edition, 245.
64. *Ibid.*, 310.
65. For all these points, see Ibn Hazm, *Akhlaq*, nos. 43, 90, 97, 113, 114, 208, 217.
66. *Ibid.*, nos. 63; cf. nos. 64, 215, and 306.
67. Ibn Bassam, *Dhakhirah*, I:i, 111.
68. Ibn Hazm, *Fada'il*, Maqqari, *Nafh*, III, 166-167.
69. Ibn Hazm, *Risalatan*, 85ff.
70. Ibn Hazm, *Talkhis*, 173-174. The poll tax *(jizyah)* and the land tax *(kharaj)* were taxes traditionally collected from Christians and Jews, commonly known as the "protected people" *(ahl-al-Dhimmah)*. The excise tax *(mukus)* and levy *(daribah)* were also extraordinary taxes not required for Muslims.
71. Ibn Hazm, *Tawq*, 227. The translation is based on undated Beirut edition, 148-49.
72. Ibn Hazm, *Nuqat*, 83; Ibn Hazm, *Fisal*, I, 59.
73. Muhammad Ibn al-Qasim Ibn Hammud was proclaimed caliph in 439/1047 while he was governor of Algeciras. See Ibn Khatib, *A'mal*, 142.
74. Muhammad Ibn Idris Ibn 'Ali Ibn Hammud was the ruler of Malaga and assumed the caliphate in about 438/1046. See Ibn Khatib, *A'mal*, 141.
75. Idris Ibn Yahya Ibn 'Ali Ibn Hammud was proclaimed caliph in 434/1042, but was ousted by his cousin Muhammad Ibn Idris in 438/1046. See Ibn al-Khatib, *A'mal*, 141.
76. Ibn Hazm, *Nuqat*, 83-84.
77. Ibn Hazm, *Fisal*, F. 167ff.
78. His *Imamah-Siyasah* (see Appendix) may contain the same material as the section in his *Fisal*.
79. For details on the procedures of succession in Islam, see Chejne, *Succession*.
80. Ibn Hazm, *Ibn al-Naghrilah*, 45.
81. Garcia Gomez in his introduction to his Spanish translation of the *Tawq*, 47.
82. Ibn Hazm, *Fada'il*, 156-179.
83. For the Arabic text of the poem, see Ibn Bassam, *Dhakhirah*, I:i, 145, Cf. Peres, *Poesie*, 49; Nkyl, *Poetry*, 102.

CHAPTER III:

THE SCHOLAR - DIALECTICIAN

1. On Muslim education in Spain, see Ribera, *Ensenanza*. For an insight into education in the East during the eleventh century, see Makdisi, *Muslim Institutions*. On education in general, see Shalaby, *History;* Tritton, *Materials*.
2. For the pride of the Andalusians in their private libraries, see the anecdote in Chejne, *Muslim Spain*, 156-157.
3. Ibn Hazm, *Tawq*, 165 and 272.
4. Dabbi, *Bughyah*, no. 412.
5. Ibn Hazm, *Fada'il*, in Maqqari, *Nafh*, III, 156-178.
6. He is Muhammad Ibn al-Hasan al-Madhhijji known as Ibn al-Kattani (d. 1029). Cf. below, note 41.
7. He is Khalaf Ibn 'Abbas al-Zahrawi (d.ca. 1036). He was born in the governmental complex al-Zahra, was a famous surgeon and served as court physician to the caliph al-Hakam II. Ibn Hazm is quoted as saying (Humaydi, *Judhwah,* 421) that al-Zahrawi's sayings and works in the natural sciences and on the setting of broken bones would place him among the great physicians even if he composed no works on general medicine.This statement, besides his recommendation that the student read books on surgery (his *Maratib al-'ulum,* 71/236) indicates that Ibn Hazm had more than a mere familiarity with medicine. In addition, Ibn Hazm, *Fada'il,* 175) mentions having known al-Zahrawi and refers to his surgical works with praise. On al-Zahrawi, see Humaydi, *Judhwah,* no. 421; Dabbi, *Bughyah,* no. 715; Ibn Abi Usaybi'ah *'Uyun,* II, 52ff.
8. He is al-Hasan Ibn al-Hasan Ibn al-Haytham (d. ca. 1039), known to the Latin West as Alhazen, a famous scientist at the Fatimid court in Egypt; he wrote numerous works on mathematics, astronomy, philosophy, and medicine. On him, see Ibn Abi Usaybi'ah, *'Uyun,* II, 91ff.; Qifti, *Tarikh,* 167-168. Cf. Brockelmann; *GAL,* I, 469ff.*Suppl.* I, 851
9. Ibn Hazm, *Fada'il,* 175.
10. *Ibid.,* 176, where Ibn Hazm says that, as for mathematics and astronomy, "We have not sufficient knowledge of them, nor have we examined them. Consequently, we are not able to discern the good or bad authors and, thus, we have to rely on the opinion of people whom we trust." This notwithstanding, Ibn Hazm appears to have acquired a deeper understanding of those disciplines at a later stage of his intellectual development and gave them great importance in the education of the young and in the preparation of religious men. See his *Maratib al-'ulum,* 67/235.
11. On Ibn Hazm's stand on philosophy and logic, see his *Fisal,* I, 158; and his *Taqrib,* 8ff.
12. Ibn Hazm, *Taqrib,* 202; and his *Maratib al-'ulum,* 89/241.
13. Dhahabi, *Siyar,* 436. In addition, Ibn Khallikan, *Wafayat,*III,14, followed by Ibn Kathir, *Bidayah,* XII, 92, acknowledged that Ibn Hazm was a physician and wrote treatises on medicine. Cf. Ibn Hazm, *Tawq,* 110 and 113, where he discusses the symptoms of love which had been dealt with by ancient and medieval Arab physicians. On this point, see Garcia Gomez, *Medicina;* and Samso, *Medicina.*
14. Ibn Hazm, *Tibb.*
15. Ibn Hazm, *Sa'adah.*
16. Ibn Hazm, *Bulghah.*
17. Ibn Hazm, *Hadd al-tibb.*
18. Ibn Hazm, *Jalinus.*
19. Ibn Hazm, *Tamr.*

20. Ibn Hazm, *Nuhhal.*
21. Ibn Hazm, *Sharh-fusul.*
22. Ibn Hazm, *Adwiyah.*
23. Ibn Hazm, *Shifa!*
24. Ibn Hazm, *Tawq,* 114.
25. Ibn Hazm, *Kindi* and *Razi.*
26. Ibn Hazm, *Ihkam,* I,. 28ff.; cf. Asin, *Origen.*
27. Ibn Hazm, *Taqrib,* 15, 36, 52, 54.
28. Ibn Hazm, *Fada'il,* 166.
29. Ibn Hazm, *Fisal,* I, 48ff./149ff. However, one cannot discount the possibility that the Mozarabs, who remained Christians and appeared to be arabized, may have translated some of those religious tracts into Arabic.
30. Ibn Hazm, *Fahrasah;* see Appendix. Ibn Khayr, *Fahrasah,* 429, mentions having studied Ibn Hazm's *Fahrasah* under Shurayh Ibn Shurayh (d.1143), who was one of Ibn Hazm's followers. On Ibn Shurayh, see Dabbi, *Bughyah,* no. 849.
31. For a comprehensive list of Ibn Hazm's teachers, see Dhahabi, *Siyar,* 400-401. Cf. Asin, *Abenhazam,* I, 99-102; Hajiri, *Ibn Hazm,* 70ff.
32. Humaydi, *Judhwah,* 106.
33. He is Ahmad Ibn Muhammad Ibn Sa'id, known as Ibn Jassur. See Humaydi, *Judhwah,* no. 181; Ibn Bashkuwal, *Silah,* no. 37; cf. Ibn Hazm, *Ihkam,* 249 and 556; Dabbi, *Bughyah,* no. 336; Dhahabi, *Siyar,* 400; and Asin, *Abenhazam,* I, 98.
34. He is 'Abdallah Ibn Muhammad Ibn Yusaf. See Ibn Bashkuwal, *Silah,* no. 273; Dabbi, *Bughyah,* no. 888.
35. Ibn al-Faradi, *Tarikh.*
36. Ibn Hazm, *Fada'il,* 170.
37. Ibn Hazm, *Tawq,* 196, 197, 260, and 272. He is Abu-l-Qasim 'Abd al-Rahman Ibn Abi Yazid al-Azdi. See Asin, *Abenhazam,* I, 102; Hajiri, *Ibn Hazm.* 73.
38. He is Ahmad Ibn Muhammad Ibn 'Abd al-Warith; see Humaydi, *Judhwah,* no. 180; Ibn Bashkuwal, *Silah,* no. 28; Dabbi, *Bughyah,* no. 335.
39. Ibn Hazm, *Taqrib,* 192; cf. Dabbi, *Bughyah,* no. 335.
40. He is Hassan Ibn Malik Ibn Abi 'Abdah. See Humaydi, *Judhwah,* no. 380; Dabbi, *Bughyah,* no. 662. Cf. Ibn Hazm, *Ihkam,* IV, 400 and VIII, 1124.
41. He is Muhammad Ibn al-Hasan al-Madhhiji, known as Ibn al-Kattani. See Humaydi *Judhwah,* no.35; Dabbi, *Bughyah,* no. 81; cf. Asin, *Abenhazam,* I, 100.
42. Ibn Hazm, *Fada'il,* 147; cf. his *Maratib al-'ulum,* 83/243, where he refers to Ibn al-Kattani as our teacher *(shaykhuna).*
43. Yaqut, *Irshad,* V, 89; Dhahabi, *Siyar,* 437; cf. Asin, *Abenhazam,* I, 106.
44. He is Abu-l-Khiyar Mas'ud Ibn Sulayman Ibn Muflit. See Humaydi, *Judhwah,* no. 814; Ibn Bashkuwal, *Silah,* no. 1352; Dabbi, *Bughyah,* no. 1361; Dhahabi, *Siyar,* 400ff.; cf. Asin, *Abenhazam,* I, 336-339.
45. He is Yunus Ibn 'Abdallah Ibn Mughith known as Ibn al-Saffar. See Humaydi *Judhwah,* no. 910; Ibn Bashkuwal, *Silah,* no. 1512; Dabbi, *Bughyah,* no. 1418; cf. Asin, *Abenhazam,* I, 109. Ibn Hazm himself acknowledges him as his teacher (see his *Maratib al-'ulum,* 70/236 and his *Iman,* 22; cf. *Ihkam,* 208, 521.
46. Ibn Hazm, *Tawq,* 242, mentions Ibn Muflit, and in his *Maratib al-'ulum,* 70/237, he refers to Ibn al-Saffar; cf. his *Iman,* 23.
47. Humaydi, *Judhwah,* 350, says that Ibn Muflit "yamil ila al-ikhtiyar wa-l-qawl bi-l-zahir."
48. Ibn Bashkuwal, *Silah,* 618, says "Wa kana dawudi al-madhhab la yara al-taqlid."
49. On Humam, see Ibn Bashkuwal, *Silah,* no. 350; Dabbi, *Bughyah,* no. 677; Dhahabi, *Siyar,* 400; cf. Asin, *Abenhazam,* I, 99. Cf. Ibn Hazm, *Ihkam,* 194, 294, 523.

50. He is Ahmad Ibn Muhammad al-Talamanki. See Ibn Bashkuwal, *Silah*, no. 92; Dabbi, *Bughyah*, no. 347; Dhahabi, *Siyar; cf.* Asin. *Abenhazam*, I, 100. Cf. Ibn Hazm, *Ihkam*, 497, 519, 539.
51. He is 'Abdallah Ibn Yahya Ibn Ahmad, known as Ibn Dahhun. See Ibn Bashkuwal, *Silah*, no. 590; cf. Asin, *Abenhazam*, I, 109.
52. Ibn Bashkuwal, *Silah*, no. 350.
53. Ibn Bashkuwal, *Silah*, no. 92.
54. His is Muhammad Ibn Sa'id Ibn Hubat. See Humaydi, *Judhwah*, no. 66; Ibn Bashkuwal, *Silah*, no. 1136; and Dabbi, *Bughyah*, 134. Dhahabi, *Siyar*, 400, considers him as a teacher of Ibn Hazm, whereas al-Humaydi simply says that Ibn Hazm transmitted traditions on his authority *(rawa 'anhu).* Cf. Ibn Hazm, *Ihkam*, 145, 248, 327, 519, 549, 560, 574.
55. He is Yahya Ibn Mas'ud Ibn Wajh al-Jannah. See Humaydi, *Judhwah*, no. 146; Dabbi, *Bughyah*, 1481; Dhahabi, *Siyar*, 400. Cf. Ibn Hazm, *Ihkam*, 535.
56. He is 'Abdallah Ibn al-Rabi' Ibn 'Abdallah al-Tamimi. See Humaydi, *Judhwah*, no. 551; Dhahabi, *Siyar*, 401; cf. Asin, *Abenhazam*, I, Ibn Hazm, *Ihkam*, 244, 245, 250, 267, 272, 414, 518.
57. 'Abd al-Rahman Ibn 'Abdallah Ibn Khalid al-Wahrani (n.d.). See Ibn Hazm, *Ihkam*, 370; Humaydi, *Judhwah*, no. 604; Dhahabi, *Siyar*, 401.
58. He is 'Abdallah Ibn Muhammad Ibn 'Uthman (n. d.). See Humaydi, *Judhwah*, no. 531; Dhahabi, *Siyar*, 401.
59. He is 'Abdallah Ibn Yusuf Ibn Nami (n. d.). See Humaydi, *Judhwah*, no. 575; Dhahabi, *Siyar*, 401. Cf. Ibn Hazm, *Ihkam*, 272, 273, 284, 299, 326, 328, 398, 517, 541.
60. He is Ahmad Ibn Qasim Ibn Asbagh (n. d.). See Humaydi, *Judhwah*, no. 243; Dhahabi, *Siyar*, 401. Cf. Ibn Hazm, *Ihkam*, 203, 520.
61. On Ibn 'Abd al-Barr, see Humaydi, *Judhwah*, 368.
62. Ibn Hazm, *Ihkam*, 766, 779, 809, 810, 857, 881, 929.
63. He is Ahmad Ibn 'Umar Ibn Anas al-'Udhri. See Humaydi, *Judhwah*, 236. *Cf.* Ibn Hazm, *Ihkam*, 198, 391, 545, 560.
64. Dhahabi, *Siyar*, 400-401. Ibn Hazm also transmits traditions on authorities such as al-Muhallab (d. 1030), *Ihkam*, 198 and 271; Yahya Ibn 'Abd al-Rahman Ibn Mas'ud, *Ihkam*, 327 and 425; and 'Abd al-Rahman Ibn Salamah, *Ihkam*, 202.
65. He is Marwan Ibn 'Abd al-Rahman Ibn 'Abd al-Nasir (ca. 961-1009). See Peres, *Poesie*, 57; Nykl, *Poetry*, 61-67; Vernet, *Literatura*, 89.
66. Ibn Hazm, *Tawq*, 131.
67. He is 'Ubaydallah Ibn 'Abd al-Rahmam Ibn al-Mughirah Ibn al-Nasir. See Nykl, *Poetry*, 63.
68. Ibn Hazm, *Tawq*, 90.
69. He is Muhammad Ibn Husayn Ibn Muhammad al-Tubni. On him, see Ibn Bassam, *Dhakhirah*, I:i, 261; Nykl, *Poetry*, 61.
70. Ibn Hazm, *Tawq*, 259-260.
71. Coulson, *Law*, 53.
72. The famous jurist Baqi Ibn Makhlad fell victim to the accusation of heresy because of his Shafi'ite sympathies. In fact, Ibn Hazm, *fada'il*, 168, expressed a great admiration for Ibn Makhlad and considered him on a par with the great Eastern commentator al-Tabari.
73. Dhahabi, *Siyar*, 406.
74. Ibn Hazm, *Akhlaq*, no. 106.
75. See *SEI* under *Zahiriya*.
76. On the introduction of Zahirism into al-Andalus, see Asin, *Abenhazam*, I, 131ff.
77. On 'Abdallah Ibn al-Qasim, see Humaydi, *Judhwah*, no. 536; Dabbi, *Bughyah*, no. 886.
78. On Mundhir Ibn Sa'id, see Humaydi, *Judhwah*, no. 811; Dabbi, *Bughyah*, no. 1357.
79. Ibn Hazm, *Fada'il*, 169.
80. See above, note 44.

81. The implications of Zahirism is the object of a separate section having bearing on Ibn Hazm's disavowal of the criteria of imitation, personal opinion, analogical reasoning, interpretation for arriving at legal decisions. See his *Ibtal, Ihkam,* and Chapter VI.
82. It should be pointed out that *qiyas* (analogical reasoning) was an integral part of Aristotle's *Organon* and remained so among the great majority of Muslim logicians.
83. Ibn Hazm, *Fisal,* I, 8ff.
84. Ibn Hazm, *Ihkam,* 14-28.
85. Ibn Hazm, *Maratib al-'ulum,* 82/242.
86. *Ibid.,* 71/237; also, his *Hatif,* 10.
87. Ibn Hazm, *Maratib al'ulum,* 63ff./232ff.
88. Ibn Hazm, *Ihkam,* I, 19ff. It appears quite clear from the extensive treatment of *jadl wa-munazarah* (dialectics and disputation) by Ibn Hazm that the subject was not only important, but was controversial because difference, or contention *(khilaf),* among Muslims was not condoned by the Qur'an and Traditions. This notwithstanding, works on *khilaf* made their appearance as early as the ninth century, suggesting an early development of dialectics and disputation. Their purpose was, however, marred by some showmanship and hence were subjected to strictures and prohibition. See **Makdisi,** *Scholastic Method, 649 and 650, note, 45.)*

In this connection, it may be relevant to call attention to al-Ghazzali's views on the subject. Al-Ghazzali, *Ihya',* 37-40 distinguishes between blameworthy and praiseworthy disputations, pointing out that misguided *disputatio* carries with it untold harm, but praiseworthy *disputatio* is highly commendable since it aims at seeking and ascertaining the truth. After giving the background of its appearnce following the death of Muhammad and his immediate successors, he says that succeeding rulers did not have enough qualifications to decide on religious matters, and had to rely on the services of scholars whom they honored with high positions and rewards. Subsequently, scholars became eager to hold official positions for glory and prestige, vied with one another, and indulged in debates that resulted in disparate views, each claiming to uphold religion and defend the Sunnah. This led to abominable fanaticism, animosity, confusion, and serious differences — besides the desire of scholars to win victory in debates, to dumbfound people, and to display virtuosity and boastfulness.

Ibn Rushd, *Fasl,* 23, maintains that discursive reason *(nazar)* is necessary and condoned by the law in order to extract the hidden from what is known. Finally, Ibn Khaldun, *Muqaddimah,* III, 30-34, devotes a whole section to dialectics and controversial questions *(al-jadal wa-l-khilafiyat),* pointing to the differences resulting therefrom because of the use of different data and the outlook of particular scholars.

For the development of the scholastic method in Islam and its possible impact on Western scholasticism, see the incisive article, *Scholastic Method,* by Makdisi; see also his *Dialectique.* On the general history of the scholastic method, see Grabmann, *Geschichte.*
89. Ibn Hazm, *Ihkam,* I, 23.
90. *Ibid.,* I, 26.
91. *Ibid.,* I, 34, Al-Ghazzali, *Ihya',* 28-29, was also aware of the problem of giving terms different connotations. He says: "Know that the inception of the confusion between the blameworthy sciences and religious sciences resides in the alteration of praiseworthy nouns, their change and use for vile purposes other than the meanings intended for them by the pious ancestors." *(Ibid,* 28). He reiterates the same idea in his *Tahafut,* 41, where he says that one of his three major differences with the philosophers is that concerning the use of terms *(alfaz),* such as designating the Maker of the World *(sani' al-'alam)* as a substance *(jawhar).*
92. Ibn Hazm, *Ihkam,* I, 34-36. His lost *Hadd (Definition)* and *Hudud (Definitions)* — see Appendix — may have relevance on the subjcet of definition of terms.
93. See below, Chapter VIII, notes 60ff. It should be noted that al-Ghazzali, *Mihakk,* 30 and 38, adopted new logical terminology for the purpose of clarity and for making the discipline of logic palatable to a large audience. Madkour, who published his

Organon before the edition of Ibn Hazm's *Taqrib*, was not able to refer to Ibn Hazm's new terminology and appears to credit al-Ghazzali for it (see his *Organon*, 243). Similarly, Jabre, *Certitude*, 108, whose work appeared about the same time as the edition of the *Taqrib*, refers to the change of logical terminology by al-Ghazzali with no mention of the precedent established by Ibn Hazm.

94. **Ibn Hazm, *Taqrib*,** 185-200. Realizing some of the negative aspects of disputation, **Al-Ghazzali,** *Ihya'*, 1, 38-40, calls attention to both negative and positive aspects, saying that *disputatio* is not intended to arouse passion and win people to one's side, but to seek and establish the truth. He says: "our purpose in *disputatio* is to investigate the truth so that it may become clear, since the truth is being sought." *(Ibid,* 1, 38).

But in order to arrive at the truth, cooperation and observation of eight rules are necessary: (1) the disputant should first and above all concern himself with and fulfill his duty *(fard 'ayn)* before preoccupying himself with communal obligation *(fard kifayah);* were he to engage in the latter at the expense of the former, he would be a fraud and would be like the one who abandons prayer and gathers clothes instead, with the pretense of covering up those who happen to be naked while in prayer; (2) should the disputant conceive that communal obligation is more important in disputation and act differently, he is certainly a sinner; (3) the disputant must be a researcher himself *(mujtahid)* who would be able to make a decision on the basis of his research and not because so-and-so had made it previously; (4) the disputant should debate those issues that have happened or are about to happen; (5) disputation is better in privacy than at public gatherings among notables and rulers; (6) the disputant should be persistent in his search for the truth, and should not look upon his "helper" and "companion" (that is, opponent) as an enemy — his opponent succeeds in showing him **his error** and the truth, he should be thankful; (7) the disputant should allow his "helper" to shift from one kind of evidence to another; and (8) the disputant should engage in debates only with those who are devoted to knowledge.

Ibn Rushd, *Fasl*, 29-30, argues strongly for discursive reason *(nazar)*, saying that the fact that there are dabbling, unintelligent, disorganized, dissolute, and uneducated people who engage in disputation should not constitute a reason for preventing intelligent, well-educated, virtuous, and just people from taking up disputations. Similarly, Ibn Khaldun, *Muqaddimah*, III, 31ff., says that involvement in controversial questions is a useful discipline as long as it conforms to certain rules governing the behaviour of the disputants. It is because disputants let themselves go in their argumentation that authorities on the subject had to lay down rules for proper behavior concerning rejection and acceptance, asking and replying, admitting defeat, interrupting and contradicting, and the like. Interestingly enough, Ibn Khaldun credits later authorities for having compiled the rules of debates, such as Muhammad Ibn Muhammad al-'Amidi (d. 1218) and 'Umar Ibn Muhammad al-Nasafi (d. 1142).

95. Ibn Hazm, *Taqrib*, 185.
96. *Ibid.*, 186.
97. *Ibid.*, 187.
98. *Ibid.*, 188.
99. *Ibidem.*
100. *Ibidem.*
101. *Ibidem.*
102. *Ibid.*, 190.
103. *Ibidem.*
104. *Ibid.*, 192.
105. *Ibidem.*
106. *Ibid.*, 194.
107. *Ibidem.*

108. *Ibid.*, 195.
109. *Ibidem.*
110. *Ibidem.*
111. *Ibid.*, 196.
112. *Ibidem.*
113. *Ibidem.*
114. *Ibidem.*
116. *Ibidem.*
117. *Ibidem.*
118. *Ibid.*, 197-98. The three classes of people given by Ibn Hazm would correspond to Ibn Rushd's (1) the people of proof *(burhan);* (2) dialecticians; and (3) rhetoricians. See his *Fasl,* 31.
119. *Ibid.,* 198-199.
120. Ibn Hazm, *Fisal,* I, 116ff./II, 238ff.
121. Yaqut, *Irshad,* V, 94; cf. Asin, *Abenhazam,* I, 188.
122. Ibn Hazm, *Fisal,* 1, 3, 7, 19, 106, 142; II, 9, 15, 41; III, 8; IV, 27; V, 3, 4, 11. For more details, see Asin, *Abenhazam,* I, 187ff.
123. Qur'an 3:187.
124. Ibn Sa'id, *Mughrib,* I, 355; Ibn Bassam, *Dhakhirah,* I:i, 149; cf. Asin, *Abenhazam,* I, 207. On Ibn Hazm as a polemicist, see Asin, *Indiferencia;* his *Abenhazam,* I, Chapter XIV; Di Mateo, *Pretese;* Perlman, *Ibn Hazm;* Garcia Gomez, *Polemica;* Arnaldez, *Controverse.*

   Virtually most of his works are permeated by polemics and had a wide range of subjects comprising the views of many individuals and the gamut of jurisprudence, theology and various philosophical systems. Among such works are: *Fisal, Ihkam, Muhalla, Anajil, Tabdil, Ibtal, Ikhtilaf, I'rab, Izhar, Jawab, Kashf, Nukat, Hatif,* and others refuting predecessors and contemporaries such as Ibn Hafsun, Ibn al-Iflili, Ibn Ishaq, Ibn al-Naghrilah, Ibn al-Rawandi, Khawlani, Kindi, Razi, and others.
125. Ibn Hazm, *Hatif;* see Appendix.
126. *Ibid.*, 8-9.
127. *Ibid.,* 10-11.
128. Asin, *Abenhazam,* I, 188.
129. *Ibid.*, 191.
130. Al-Hajjaj was the viceroy of the Umayyad caliph 'Abd al-Malik (685-705) and was known in the Traditions as a bloodthirsty individual. Cf. Ibn Khallikan, *Wafayat,* III, 15.
131. Asin, *Abendhazam,* I, 191-193. Cf. Ibn Hazm, *Fisal,* I, 127, 129, 138, 148, 153, 179, 202; II, 12, 15, 24, 35; IV, 100, 108, 218.
132. Ibn Hazm, *Ibn al-Naghrilah,* 64ff., cf Garcia Gomez, *Polemica.*
133. For these and similar expressions, see Ibn Hazm, *Ihkam,* 447, 575.
13. Subki, *Tabaqat,* 1, 43; cf. Asin, *Abenhazam,* I, notes 221, 191.
135. Asin, *Abenhazam,* I, 189-190.
136. *Ibid.,* I, 191.
137. See above, Chapter II, notes 51ff.
138. Ibn Hazm, *Risalatan,* 85-135.
139. *Ibid.*, 87.
140. *Ibid.*, 101-102.
141. *Ibid.*, 85.
142. *Ibid.*, 114.

CHAPTER IV

HIS DOCTRINE OF KNOWLEDGE AND THE COGNITIVE PROCESS

1. Rosenthal, *Knowledge*, 70ff.
2. *Ibid.*, 252ff.
3. *Ibid.*, 277ff.
4. *Ibid.*, 334.
5. He is Abu-I-Hasan Muhammad Ibn Jusuf al-'Amiri. See Zirikle, *A'lam*, VII, 21-22.
6. 'Amiri, *I'lam*, 84ff. Rosenthal, *Heritage*, 63ff.
7. His ***Kitab fada'il al-'ilm'***; cf. Rosenthal, *Knowledge*, 279. See Ibn Farhun, *Dibaj*, 354-355; Sezgin, *Geschichte*, I, 473.
8. Ibn 'Abd Rabbihi, *'Iqd*, Book VI, 206-493.
9. *Ibid.*, II, 206.
10. *Ibdem*.
11. *Ibid.*, II, 22.
12. *Ibid.*, II, 249.
13. *Ibid.*, II, 207.
14. *Ibid.*, II, 206.
15. *Ibidem*.
16. *Ibidem*.
17. *Ibid.*, II, 214.
18. *Ibid.*, II, 209.
19. *Ibid.*, II, 211.
20. *Ibid.*, II, 209,
21. *Ibid.*, II, 211.
22. *Ibid.*, II, 208.
23. *Ibid.*, II, 207-208.
24. *Ibid.*, II, 208.
25. *Ibidem*.
26. For a brief account of the *'Iqd*, see Chejne, *Muslim Spain*, 205ff.
27. For Sa'id's division of the sciences, see below, Chapter V, notes 36ff.
28. Ibn Hazm, *Fada'il*, 169-170; cf. Humaydi, *Judhwah*, 368.
29. At the time Ibn Hazm wrote his *Fada'il* (about 1027) he did not appear to have delved into the sciences, their meaning, and interrelationship. It was only in his later works that he came to articulate his views.
30. Ibn 'Abd al-Barr, *Mukhtasar*, 208; cf. Asin, *Abenhazam*, I, 287.
31. Ibn 'Abd al-Barr, *Jami'*, II, 133ff.
32. Abu Ishaq, al-Hufi (n.d.) was a traditionist.
33. Ibn 'Abd al-Barr, *Jami'*, I, 3.
34. *Ibid.*, I, 7.
35. *Ibid.*, I, 13.
36. *Ibid.*, I, 15.
37. *Ibid.*, I, 18.

38. *Ibid.*, I, 52.
39. *Ibd.*, I, 30.
40. *Ibid.*, I, 40.
41. *Ibid.*, I, 111.
42. *Ibid.*, I, 81.
43. *Ibid.*, I, 111.
44. *Ibid.*, I, 104.
45. *Ibid.*, I, 118.
46. *Ibid.*, II, 4ff.
47. *Ibid.*, I, 186.
48. *Ibid.*, I, 3.
49. *Ibid.*, I, 89.
50. *Ibid.*, I, 49ff.
51. *Ibid.*, I, 40.
52. *Ibid.*, I, 178.
53. *Ibid.*, I, 165.
54. *Ibid.*, I, 185.
55. On the relationship of knowledge and faith, see Rosenthal, *Knowledge*, 97ff.
56. *Ibid.*, 52-69.
57. *ma istayqantuh wa-tabayyantuh.*
58. Ibn 'Abd al-Barr, *Jami'*, II, 36-37.
59. *Ibid.*, II, 37.
60. *Ibid.*, II, 23.
61. *Ibid.*, II, 24.
62. Ibn Hazm, *Taqrib*, 156-162.
63. Ibn Hazm, *Fisal*, I, 4-5/II, 87.
64. Ibn Hazm, *Ihkam*, I, 14-28 and 58ff.
65. Ibn Hazm, *Akhlaq*, nos. 31ff.
66. Ibn Hazm, *Tawqif*, 41-55.
67. For Ibn Hazm's *Maratib al-'ulum*, see Chapters V and IX.
68. Ibn Hazm, *Ihkam*, I, 34.
69. *Ibid.*, I, 42; cf. his *Akhlaq*, no. 32.
70. Ibn Hazm, *Akhlaq*, no. 196.
71. *Ibid.*, no. 70.
72. *Ibid.*, no. 39.
73. *Ibid.*, no. 238.
74. *Ibid.*, no. 234.
75. *Ibid.*, nos. 235 and 236.
76. *Ibid.*, no. 237.
77. In fact, Ibn Hazm, *Ihkam*, I, 107ff., devotes a large section to the relationship of knowedge and action. For a general survey of the subject, see Rosenthal, *Knowledge*, 24ff.
78. Ibn Hazm, *Akhlaq*, no. 342.
79. Ibn Hazm, *Akhlaq*, 21-24. Numbers preceding each statement refer to the numbering used in Tomiche's edition. It should be added that most of the statements in his *Akhlaq* are reiterated in his *Maratib al'ulum*, 80/241.
80. On this point, see Rosenthal, *Knowledge*, 194ff.
81. Ibn Hazm, *Fisal*, I, 68/II, 181.
82. *Ibid.*, I, 4, 8, 67-73; V, 104, 113-118; cf. Asin, *Abenhazam*, I, 113ff.

83. *Ibid.*, I, 109. Cf. Sa'id, *Tabaqat*, and Ibn Khaldun, *Muqaddimah*, I, 168ff., both of whom held similar views.
84. Ibn Hazm, *Taqrib*, 178. It appears quite clear that the soul in Ibn Hazm's conception is actually the reasoning faculty.
85. *Ibid.*, 180; cf. his *Ihkam*, I, 46, where he defines intellect as "the use of obediences and virtues." For more details on the role of the intellect, see Gardet, *Raison;* Gardet-Anawati, *Introduction*, 345ff.
86. Ibn Hazm, *Ihkam*, I, 46.
87. Ibn Hazm, *Fisal*, V, 74/V, 250; cf. also his *Nafs*, in *Rasa'il*, 109.
88. *Ibid.*, V, 72/V, 248; cf. his *Iman*, in *Rasa'il*, 29.
89. *Ibid.*, V, 71/V, 247.
90. Ibn Hazm, *Ihkam*, I, 46; cf. his *Fisal*, V, 72/V, 248.
91. Ibn Hazm, *Iman*, in *Rasa'il*, 29.
92. Ibn Hazm, *Ihkam*, I, 5.
93. *Ibid.*, I, 14-28.
94. *Ibid.*, I, 38.
95. *Ibid.*, I, 37.
96. *Ibid.*, I, 18.
97. *Ibid.*, I, 27. It is significant to note that the consideration of the intellect as a sure basis of knowledge vis-a-vis instinct/inspiration *(ilham)*, historical information *(khabar)*, and imitation *(taqlid)* is, perhaps, unique in its presentation up to the time of Ibn Hazm. Only the expose of the heresiographer 'Abd al-Qadir al-Baghdadi (d. 1037) may approximate it. Al-Baghdadi, *Usul*, 6ff and 202, lists the roots of knowledge as consisting of sensory knowledge, historical reports, and knowledge based on reason — all of which have validity, although knowledge based on reason is more reliable than the other sources. Abu Hafs 'Umar al-Nafasi (d. 1143) lists the roots of knowledge as consisting of the senses, reliable historical report, and reason. However, al-Nafasi rejects the role of inspiration as a source of knowledge. See Wensinck, *Creed*, 250ff. and 262ff.

On the other hand, al-Ghazzali, *Ihya'*, III, 16-23, recognizes the validity of inspration *(ilham)* as a form of knowledge that is acquired without teaching and may take the form of understanding the holy texts, of an intuitive knowledge, or of a good thought. It is available to all people, although is not better than a solid intellectual preparation. See Jabre, *Certitude*, 175ff.

98. Ibn Hazm, *Fisal*, V, 108/V,308-309. Ibn Hazm's view on the necessary/self-vident/ appears to coincide with that of his contemporary and friend Ibn 'Abd al-Barr (see above.), note 59) and with that of al-Ghazzali, who refutes the Sophists for denying its existence. Cf. Jabre, *Certitude*, 350.
99. Ibn Hazm, *Fisal*, V, 108-199/V, 308-309, devotes a whole chapter to the question of whether knowledge is necessary or acquired. He states the various opinions on the subject, **concluding that knowledge is necessary/self-evident and that the method by means of which man arrives at certain knowledge is acquistion** *(fa-huwa al-talab wahdah huwa al-iktisab faqat, Ibid.,* V, 109/V, 310. He goes to some length to demonstrate that faith is a valid form of knowledge not needing demonstration, and concludes that evidence and human testimony constitute criteria of the truth.
100. *Ibid.*, V, 108ff/V, 308ff.
101. **Qur'an.** 16:80.
102. Ibn Hazm, *Fisal*, I, 4/ II, 87.
103. Ibn Hazm, *Ihkam*, I, 38; cf. above, note 94.
104. Ibn Hazm, *Fisal*, I, 80/II, 193..
105. *Ibid.*, I, 80-81/ II, 193-195, Cf. Ibn Khaldun, *Muqaddimah*, III, 307.
106. *Ibid.*, V, 108/ V, 309.

107. *Ibid.,* I, 6/ II, 89.
108. *Ibid.,* I, 108/ II, 308.
109. *Ibid.,* V, 109/ V, 310.
110. *Ibidem.*
111. *Ibid.,* I, 7/II, 90.
112. Ibn Hazm, *Ihkam,* I, 17-18.
113. Ibn Hazm, *Fisal,* I, 7/II, 90; cf. his *Ihkam,* I, 93ff.
114. Ibn Hazm, *Ihkam,* I, 18-19.
115. Ibn Hazm, *Fisal,* I, 77; cf. his *Ihkam,* I, 27.
116. *Ibid.,* II, 126ff./III, 177-192.
117. *Ibid.,* V, 109/V, 310-311.
118. *Ibid.,* I, 77. *(wa-'ilm Allah laysa huwa ghayr Allah).* Cf. *Ibid,* V, 109/V,310, where he refutes the Ash'arites for maintaining that God's knowledge and human knowledge fall under the same definition.
119. *Ibidem. (inna li-Llah ta'ala 'ilman haqiqan al mujazan).*
120. *Ibid.,* II, 128/III, 179.
121. *Ibid.,* II, 128/III, 181.
122. Ibn Hazm, *Ihkam,* I, 37.
123. Ibn Hazm, *Ihkam,* I, 45, says that *Iman* is from a linguistic vantage an attestation *(tasdiq)* by both the tongue and the heart. In its religious connotation, *iman* is the attestation by the heart of all that the Almighty God ordered through his Messenger and the utterance of that by the tongue. The use of the organs of the body in all matters of obedience is obligatory, and so is the avoidance of what is forbidden and what is reprehensible.

It should be added that the term *faith* is complex. In the Qur an, it is associated with and almost signifies the same thing as Islam. Several definitions or explanations of the term are given by Bukhari, Muslim, Abu Dawud, and other traditionists. **One Tradition calls it:** "Believing in Allah, His angels, His books, His apostles and the last day, and believing in the decree, the good and evil thereof." (Wensinck, *Creed,* 35). To the Mu'tazilah, faith is a verbal confession and performance of prescribed duties. To al-Ash'ari: "Faith is believing in Allah and His Apostles in accordance with what Traditions report concerning them; and this belief is not sound unless it rests on knowledge of Allah," as quoted by Wensinck, *Creed,* 134.

For more details on faith see *SEI* under *Iman;* Gardet-Anawati, *Introduction,* 331ff., and Wensinck, *Creed,* index.

124. Ibn Hazm, *Iman,* 30-31' cf. his *Fisal,* V, 109ff./V, 311f. It appears that Ibn Hazm does not conceive faith as knowledge, but as a recipient or depository of knowledge not requiring demonstration. In this connection, 'Abd al-Qadir al-Baghdadi, *Usul,* 254ff., summarizes well the nature of *iman:* "Our friends say that he who believes the foundations of religion on the authority of others, without the knowledge of the **arguments on** which they are based, does not thereby belong to a fixed category. If he admits the possibility of doubt of the foundations, saying I am not sure whether they may not be such doubts as will shake them, such a one is neither a believer in Allah nor **obedient** to Him, nay, he is an infidel. If, however, he believes the truth without being acquainted with the arguments on which it is based, and if he believes, further, that his faith is free from doubts that could shake it, there is a difference of opinion: some say that he is faithful and in conformity with the standard of Islam and obedient to Allah by virtue of his obedience and his other works, although he transgresses insofar as he neglects the intellectual methods that bring knowledge concerning the arguments on which the foundations of religion are based." As quoted by Wensinck, *Creed,* 135.

125. Ibn Hazm, *Iman,* 39-40. It should be noted that there is a general belief among Muslims that faith is a gift from God. To the rationalist Mu'tazilah, however, faith

is not a divine gift which is bestowed upon some and denied others. The Mu'tazilite argument rests on the belief that man is the author of his own deeds — good, evil, obedient or disobedient. Ash'ari, *Maqalat*, I, 234; cf. Wensinck, *Creed*, 81ff.

126. Ibn Hazm, *Akhlaq*, nos. 234, 235, and 318.
127. Ibn Hazm, *Talkhis*, 169.
128. Ibn Hazm, *Ihkam*, I, 34-35; cf. his *Fisal*, V, 109/V, 310.
129. Ibn Hazm, *Fisal*, IV, 38.
130. *Ibid.*, III, 32ff./IV, 180ff.
131. Ibn Hazm, *Taqrib*, 180.
132. *Ibid.*, 181.
133. Ibn Hazm, *Fisal*, V, 110/V, 312.
134. *Ibid.*, Iv, 38; cf. Asin, *Abenhazam*, I, 146.
135. *Mu'min 'alim haqqan siwa' istadalla aw lam yastadill.*
136. Ibn Hazm, **Fifal**, V, 111-112/V, 314.
137. Ibn Hazm, *Iman*, in **Rasa'il, 30 and 36.**
138. Ibn Hazm, Fisal, V, 113/V, 317.
139. *Ibid.*, V, 114-115/V, 319-321.
140. *Ibid.*, IV, 38; cf. Asin, *Abenhazam*, I, 146-148.
141. *Ibid.*, II, 91ff.; cf. Asin, *Abenhazam*, I, 149.
142. Cf. note 178 below on the possible relationship between the views of Ibn Hazm and al-Ghazzali. Cf. also al-Ghazzail, *Tahafut*, 42ff.
143. **Qur'an** 11:34 and 26:126.
144. Ibn Hazm, *Fisal*, I, 158. The relationship between philosophy and religion, or reason and revelation, had been the subject of heated deliberations among Muslim philosophers and religious scholars. Although philosophers and theologians shared, by and large, a common ground in questions related to some metaphysical aspects, they had seemingly irreconcilable differences in their approach to reconciling the truth contained in the revelation and that arrived at through demonstrative proofs. A number of opinions emerged in the process ranging from extreme rationalism, to a conciliatory middle course of harmonization, to extreme fundamentalism. The so-called rationalist movement of the Mu'tazalites gave prominence to reason for explaining revelation, whereas the puritans relied wholly on the religious texts. In midst of this kind of polarization, attempts were made to resolve the conflict between the two opposed groups. The tenth century al-Ash'ari, who started as a Mu'tazilite, sought reconciliation through the rational method for explaining the articles of faith. In spite of al-Ash'ari's enormous impact on Muslim theology, the area of conflict between revelation and reason was never resolved satisfactorily. Four major views emerged in the skirmish: (1) that of the philosophers, who insisted on philosophy for explaining and solving human **problems;** (2) that of the theologians, who adhered staunchly to divine ordinances and defended them against the encroachment of the philosophers; (3) that of the Shi'ites, who advocated the infallible authority of an inspired leader **(imam) as the** transmitter of and spokesman for the truth; and (4) that of mystics (Sufis), who believed in personal communion with God for attaining the absolute certainty. These trends are summarized well by al-Ghazzali in his *Munqidh*, 66ff. For more details on the relationship between revelation and reason, see Arberry, *Revelation*, 89ff., Gardet, *Raison;* Gardet-Anawati, *Introduction*, 303ff. For the position of Ibn Hazm on the intellect, see Arnaldez, *Raison*.
145. Although Muslim philosophers attempted to be conciliatory toward the revelation, they do not appear always to have been successful. The attempts of Ibn Sina (Avicenna) at harmonizing revelation and reason were not convincing. He appears to uphold some fabrication in the religious beliefs to which Ibn Hazm addresses himself. Although it is not certain that Ibn Hazm knew of Avicenna's work. It appears

that the problem of fabrication was quite common among certain philosophers. In this connection, Avicenna argues that it would have been useless for a prophet to preach a purely spiritual resurrection if the common people were to be moved to practice virtue. He says: "Physical pleasure and physical pain is what they understand; true happiness and spiritual pleasure are not comprehended by them at all and have no place whatever in their understandings, even though some may make verbal pretense of it." Arberry, *Avicenna,* 64; cf. his *Revelation,* 53.

In this connection, al-Ghazzali enjoins Ibn Hazm in the refutation of those philosophers, who deny the religious law or **consider it fabricated** ordinances and trickeries (Ghazzali, *Tahafut,* 40). One may assume that because of this and other negative views of the philosophers toward religion, al-Ghazzali devoted his *Tahafut (incoherence)* to show that philosophers are guilty and in error in questions pertaining to metaphysics.

146. Ibn Hazm, *Fisal,* I, 94-95/II, 206-208.
147. *Ibid.,* I, 97/II, 209ff.
148. It should be reiterated that Ibn Rushd, *Fasl,* 26, was not only a strong advocate of harmony of philosophy and revelation, but made pleas to accept the truth even if it were enunciated by infidels. He argues that inasmuch as the Ancients delved into rational demonstration *(al-qiyas al-'aqli)* and made great strides toward the attainment of truth, it is necessary to take their writings into consideration, accepting what is correct in them and questioning or rejecting what is not correct.

Ibn Tufayl has shown in his *Hayy* the powerful role of human faculties for attaining the truth contained in the revelation. In light of this and the impressive data bearing on Ibn Hazm's positive attitude toward the intellect, philosophy and demonstrative reasoning, Arberry's observation on the possibly negative influence of **Ibn Hazm's doctrine on his successors** is not warranted in this statement: ". . . had the advocacy of the narrow Zahiri attitude toward reason won the day, it is difficult to see how the brilliant Spanish school of Avempace (d.533/1138), Ibn Tufail (d.581/1185), and Averroes (d.595/1198) could ever have flourished" (Arberry, *Revelation,* 66). For Ibn Hazm's attitude twoard reason, see Asin, *Abenhazam,* I, 158; his *Averroismo;* and Arnaldez, *Raison.*

149. Ibn Hazm, *Akhlaq, no. 185.*
150. *Ibid., no. 188.*
151. *Ibid., no. 186.*
152. *Ibid., no. 43.*
153. *Ibid., no. 191.*
154. Shahrasanti, *Milal,* I, 30.
155. For more details on the position of the intellect in Islam, see Gardet-Anawati, *Introduction,* 345ff; *Gardet,* Raison.
156. Ibn Hazm, *Ihkam,* I, 14-28.
157. Cf. above. note 97.
158. Kindi, *Rasa'il,* 104.
150. *Ibid.,* 244.
160. Ghazzali, *Ihya',* I, 73ff.
161. *Ibid.,* I, 76; cf. Jabre, *Certitude,* 383.
162. Ibn 'Aqil, *Funun,* 562; also quoted by Makdisi, *Scholastic Method,* 654.
163. In this connection, it should be noted that Ibn 'Aqil was contemporary of al-Humaydi (d. 1095), a pupil and staunch follower of Ibn Hazm, whom he may have met. See Makdisi, *Ibn 'Aqil,* 506.
164. Ghazzali, *Ihya',* I, 107; Jabre, *Certitude,* 014.
165. See below, Chapter VI.
166. Ghazzali, *Ihya',* I, 108.

167. *Ibidem.* Cf. Jabre, *Certitude,* 226.
168. Ghazzali, *Ihya',* I, 20ff.
169. Kindi, **Rasa'il,** 372-373.
170. Ibn Hazm, *Ihkam,* I, 38.
171. On prophecy, see Guillaume, *Prophecy;* Madkour, *Falsafah,* 81-147; For al-Ghazzali's conception of prophecy, see his *Ihya',* I, 178; see also Jabre, *Certitude,* Chapter VI; cf. below, Chapter VI.
172. See above, note 141.
173. Ibn Hazm, *Fisal,* I, 8ff./II, 92ff.
174. *Ibid.,* I, 9ff/II, 94ff.
175. *Ibid.,* I, 23ff./II, 113ff.
176. *Ibid.,* I, 25ff./II, 115ff.
177. *Ibid.,* I, 94ff./II, 203ff.
178. Ghazzali, *Munqidh,* 73ff. cf. Jabre, *Certitude,* 57ff.
179. Nicholson, *Idea,* **41;** Arberry, *Revelation,* 29. See also Ghazzali, *Munqidh,* 97ff.

CHAPTER V
THE SCIENCES AND THEIR CLASSIFICATION

1. The titles of the works of al-Kindi, al-Farabi, al-Khuwarizmi, and Ibn Hazm on the subject of the sciences appear to reflect this tendency.
2. See above, Chapter IV, notes 5ff.
3. 'Amiri, *I'lam,* 84-97. Cf. Rosenthal, *Heritage,* 63ff.
4. *Ibid.,* 85ff.
5. Mahdi, *Ibn Khaldun,* 171ff.
6. See below, notes 126ff.
7. See Chejne, *Arabic,* 73. One may add the names of Tashkopruzadeh (d. 1561), the author of the encyclopedic work *Miftah,* and Hajji Khalifah (d. 1657), the author of the valuable bio-bibliographical dictionary entitled *Kashf.*
8. For the Division of the sciences, see Gardet et Anawati, *Introduction,* 85ff.; Rosenthal, *Heritage,* 54ff.; Chejne, *Arabic,* 72ff.
9. For the works of al-Kindi, see Ibn al-Nadim, *Fihrist,* 255ff.; Qifti, *Tarikh,* 366ff.; Ibn Abi Usaybi'ah, *'Uyun,* I, 206ff; and Atiyeh, *Kindi,* 148ff.
10. The two treatises of al-Kindi are entitled **Ma'iyah** and *Aqsam.*
11. Farabi, *Ihsa',* the work was translated into Latin under the title of *De Scientis,* which was edited by Gonzalez Palencia. Cf. Gardet et Anawati, *Introduction,* 102-108; Rosenthal, *Heritage,* 54-55.
12. Farabi, *Ihsa'* (Gonzalez edition).
13. *Ibid.,* 7-8.
14. Farabi, *Madinah* and *Siyasah.*
15 **Rasa'il.** I, 262.
16. *Ibid.,* I, 346.
17. *Ibid.,* I, 348.
18. *Ibid.,* I, 266.

272

19. *Ibid.,* I, 266-275; cf. Gardet et Anawati, *Introduction* 108-109; Rosenthal, *Heritage,* 55-58.
20. Khuwarizmi, *Mafatih,* 4.
21. *Ibid.,* 132. Al-Khuwarizmi recognizes also the theoretical *(nazari)* and the practial *('amali)* sciences.
22. Ibn al-Nadim, *Fihrist;* cf. Gardet et Anawati, *Introduction,* 112-113.
23. On Ibn Sina, see Qifti, *Tarikh,* 413ff; Ibn Abi Usaybi'ah, *'Uyun,* II, 2ff. and Afnan, *Avicenna.*
24. Ibn Sina, *Danesh-name,* 22.
25. Ibn Sina, *Najah,* 74.
26. Ibn Sina, *Danesh-name,* 25.
27. Ibn Juljul, *Tabaqat.*
28. Sa'id, *Tabaqat.*
29. Ibn Hazm, *Fada'il.*
30. See above, Chapter IV, notes 27ff.
31. Ibn 'Abd al-Barr, *Jami',* II, 37-40.
32. See note 32, Chapter IV.
33. The chain of transmitters is deleted here.
34. Medicine does not fit the description given by Ibn 'Abd al-Barr. In all likelihood he is referring to the natural sciences.
35. Ibn 'Abd al-Barr, *Jami',* I, 37-30.
36. Ibn Bashkuwal, *Silah,* no. 540, appears to be the only source of information regarding the relationship of Sa'id and Ibn Hazm as student and teacher. While this relationship is quite possible, the difficulty arises from the lack of information regarding the whereabouts of Ibn Hazm and of Sa'id from 1035 onward. This notwithstanding, Sa'id appears to be knowledgeable about Ibn Hazm and his works. Cf. Dabbi, *Bughyah,* 311; Yaqut, *Irshad,* V, 84; and Khan, *Hispano-Arabic Source.*
37. The Arabic title is *al-Ta'rif bi-akhbar 'ulama' al-umam min al-'Arab wa-l-'Ajam.*
38. *Kitab jami' akhbar al-umam.*
39. Sa'id, *Tabaqat.*
40. Ibn Hazm, *Tawqif,* 50. In his *Fisal,* I, 109 as well as his *Fada'il,* 163, Ibn Hazm does take into account the influence of the environment.
41. Ibn Khaldun, *Muqaddimah,* I, 168ff.
42. Sa'id, *Tabaqat,* 2. Cf. Ibn Hazm, *Maratib al-'ulum,* 78/240, who also says that law, history, and language distinguish one nation from another.
43. *Ibid.,* i.
44. *Ibid.,* 11
45. *Ibid.,* 8-9. Although Ibn Hazm, *Maratib al-'ulum,* 79/240, does not pass judgment on the inherent quality of people, he says that Turks, Khazars. Black, and Northern people do not possess sciences or works on them. On the other nd, he concedes that Indians and Chinese are people of sciences although there is no satisfactory information available about them.
46. *Ibid.,* 11.
47. *Ibid.,*
48. *Ibid.,* 19-23.
49. *Ibid.,* 23-26.
50. *Ibid.,* 27.
51. *Ibid.,* 26-43.
52. *Ibid.,* 43-49.
53. *Ibid.,* 53-103.

54. *Ibid.*, 60.
55. *Ibid.*, 89.
56. Ibn Hazm, *Tawqif*, 43-55.
57. *Ibid.*, 43.
58. *Ibid.*, 44-45.
59. *Ibid.*, 45.
60. *Ibid.*, 46.
61. *Ibid.*, 47.
62. *Ibidem*.
63. *Ibid.*, 48.
64. *Ibid.*, 48-49.
65. *Ibid.*, 53.
66. *Ibid.*, 51.
67. *Ibid.*, 54.
68. See below, chapter VIII, 44ff.
69. Khuwarizmi, *Mafatih*, 92, defines *qat'* as the cutting of dates from trees *(qat' "al-tamr min al-shajar)*.
70. Ibn Hazm, *Taqrib*, 201-203.
71. Ibn Hazm, *Talkhis*, in *Ibn al-Naghrilah*, 187-193.
72. *Ibid.*, 150.
73. *Ibid.*, 160-167.
74. *Ibid.*, 168-170.
75. For instance, his *Akhlaq*, nos. 51 and 54.
76. It is difficult, if not impossible, in light of the data available to determine the date of composition of the work. Nowhere, as far as can be ascertained, is the work mentioned in his extant works. This leads to the assumption that the *Maratib* was composed late in life.
77. See below, Chapter IX.
78. Ibn Hazm, *Maratib al-'ulum*, 64/232.
79. *Ibid.*, 66/234.
80. *Ibid.*, 68/235.
81. *Ibid.*, 71/236.
82. *Ibid.*, 71/237.
83. *Ibid.*, 71/237.
84. *Ibid.*, 72/237.
85. *Ibid.*, 74/238.
86. *Ibid.*, 76/239.
86a. *Ibidem*.
87. *Ibid.*, 80/241.
88. ***Ibidem***.
89. *Ibid.*, 81/242.
90. *Ibid.*, 83/243.
91. *Ibid.*, 84/243-244.
92. *Ibid.*, 85/244.
93. *Ibid.*, 87/245.
94. *Ibidem*.
95. *Ibid.*, 90/246.
96. See above, Chapter I, note 136.
97. This search is well stated by al-Ghazzali himself in his *Munqidh, 5*, which constitutes his own confession. See Asin, *Algazel;* and Jabre, *Certitude*.

98. *Ibid.,* 61.
99. *Ibid.,* 75.
100. *Ibid.,* 68.
101. *Ibid.,* 98.
102. See al-Ghazzali, *Tahafut,* 38, where he articulates this point.
103. Ghazzali, *Munqidh,* 64.
104. *Ibid.,* 92.
105. *Ibid.,* 92.
106. *Ibid.,* 76.
107. Ghazzali, *Ihya*
108. *Ibid.,* I, 5ff. and 13-42.
109. *Ibid.,* I, 5-11.
110. *Ibid.,* I, 12.
111. *Ibid.,* I, 12-13.
112. *Ibid.,* I, 13 and 18.
113. *Ibid.,* I, 15-16. Al-Ghazzali, *Ihya',* I, 35, adds that the religious sciences consisting of the knowledge of God, His attributes, and acts are praiseworthy whether taken in small or great quantity; in fact, the more the better, since knowledge of them is sought for arriving at happiness in this and the next world. On the other hand, the study of language, grammar, and lexicography should be pursued only to the extent of their relevance to and proper understanding of the Holy Scriptures.
114. *Ibid.,* I, 20.
115. *Ibid.,* I, 17-18.
116. *Ibid.,* I, 20. The components of philosophy are: (1) geometry and mathematics; (2) logic; (3) metaphysics; and (4) the natural sciences — all of which are worthy of pursuit, but not at the expense of the religious sciences.
117. *Ibid.,* I, 15.
118. *Ibid.,* I, 26. The religious sciences are equated with beauty, but magic, talisman, and astrology are equated with ugliness and bad character. As such, they are blameworthy and lack any usefulness in this world and in the Hereafter. To the question of how any knowledge could be blameworthy, al-Ghazzali retorts that knowledge per se may not be blameworthy except in one of three ways: (1) causing harm to its pursuers and others; (2) causing harm to oneself; and (3) indulging in the minutiae of certain discipline without the knowledge of their basic principles. *(Ibid.,* I, 34).
119. On Averroes, see Gauthier, *Ibn Rochd;* Hourani's translation of the *Fasl;* and Renan, *Averroisme;* and Asin, *Averroismo.*
120. Ibn Rushd, *Fasl,* 30ff., 55, and 67.
121. Ibn Rushd, *Tahafut,* II, 527.
122. Ibn Rushd, *Kashf,* 61 ff; and 71ff.
123. Ibn Rushd, *Fasl,* 30-31, 55, and 58.
124. *Ibid.,* 31-32. In fact, Ibn Hazm uses identical expressions, see Ibn Hazm, *Risalatan,* 114; cf. above, Chapter III, note 139.
125. *Ibd.,* 67.
126. See Mahdi, *Ibn Khaldun.* However, nowhere does he suggest the possibility of Ibn Khaldun's indebtedness to Ibn Hazm.
127. Ibn Khaldun, *Muqaddimah,* II, 436.
128. *Ibid.,* II, 411ff.
129. *Ibid.,* II, 346-347.
130. *Ibid.,* II, 311ff.
131. *Ibid.,* I, 351.

132. *Ibid.,* I, 355ff.
133. *Ibid.,* III, 111.
134. *Ibid.,* III, 35.
135. *Ibid.,* III, 37.
136. *Ibid.,* III, 38.
137. *Ibid.,* III, 252.
138. See Ibn Hazm, *Maràtib al-'ulum,* 78/240.
139. Ibn Khaldun, *Muqaddimah,* III, 41.

CHAPTER VI
HIS RELIGIOUS IDEAS AND DOCTRINE

1. See above, Chatper V, notes 70 and 86.
2. See above, Chapter V, notes 73 and 89.
3. See below, notes 43ff.
4. Ibn Hazm, *Qur'an;* see Appendix.
5. Ibn Hazm, *Qira'at,* see Appendix.
6. Ibn Hazm *Nasikh;* see Appendix.
7. Ibn Hazm, *Jami',* see Appendix.
8. Ibn Hazm, *Sunan;* see Appendix.
9. Ibn Hazm, *Sharh;* see Appendix.
10. Ibn Hazm, *Ijma';* see Appendix.
11. Ibn Hazm, *Maratib al-ijma',* see Appendix.
12. Ibn Hazm, *Iman* and *Durrah;* see Appendix.
13. Ibn Hazm, *Tawqif* and *Nasa'ih;* see Appendix.
14. Ibn Hazm, *Salah;* see Appendix.
15. Ibn Hazm, *Hijjah and Manasik;* see Appendix.
16. Ibn Hazm, *Alam;* see Appendix.
17. Ibn Hazm, Arwah and *Nafs;* see Appendix.
18. Ibn Hazm, *Sima'* and *Ghina';* see Appendix.
19. Ibn Hazm, *Fisal, Ibtal, Kashf* and *Yaqin;* see Appendix.
20. Ibn Hazm, *Fisal, Izhar* and *Ibn al-Naghrilah,* see Appendix.
21. Asin, *Abenhazam,* II, 34ff., has vign an analysis of the work.
22. Dhahabi, *Tadhkirah,* III, 321; Ibn Hajar, *Lisan,* IV, 194.
    Ibn Qudamah (1146-1223) was a Hanbalite jurist.
23. Muhammad Rashid Rida (1865-1935) a modern religious scholar and founder of the journal *al-Manar.*
24. In the introduction of the edition of Ibn Hazm's *Muhalla.*
25. See above, Chapter IV, notes 128ff.
26. See above, Chapter IV, notes 114ff.
27. See above, Chatper IV, notes 55ff.

28. Ibn Hazm, *Fisal,* I, 3/II, 10. In attempting to prove the necessity of revelation, Ibn Hazm, *Fisal,* I, 69/II, 182, refutes the Brahmans for denying the validity of revelation, which is a reality and within God's power as it appears in the Qur'an. He also refutes the allegation of some Jews who deny the abrogation of the revealed law, saying that it is God' prerogative. Furthermore, abrogation is attested to by the facts of history *(Fisal,* I,100/II,213ff). This leads Ibn Hazm to argue, further, that the dictates of reason require that what is affirmed about a thing must be affirmed about another — that is, if Moses is credited with miracles, the same credit should be given to Jesus and Muhammad. The same is the case for Zoroastrians, who believe in the divine mission of Zoroaster, but deny that of Moses and that of Muhammad *(Fisal,* I, 102/II,217).

29. *Ibid.,* I, 71/II, 187. To Ibn Hazm, prophets are chosen people who possess the best qualities among mortals. In this connection, he takes up the question of whether angels, saints, or prophets are the most excellent beings. In the light of the various opinions, particularly of those who place saints over prophets and even contemporary individuals over Muhammad, he asserts that this is unbelief and offers the following hierarchy of beings: angels, messengers of God, ordinary prophets, and companions of the Prophets *(Fisal,* V, 20ff./V, 182ff).

On the question of whether a prophet could be a sinner or lacking in excellence, Ibn Hazm refutes such allegations and takes issue with some Sufis who maintain that there could exist among the friends of God people who are more excellent than God's messengers and His prophets *(Fisal,* V,226/V,140.).

30. Ibn Hazm, *Muhalla,* no. 13.

31. For more details on the miracles of the Prophet, see Ibn Hazm, *Fisal,* I,104-105/ II,220-221; V,7/V,158-159; also, his *Muhalla,* nos. 65 and 108; and his *Jawami',* 7-14, where he lists thirty-seven miracles of the Prophet.

It is interesting to note that Ibn Hazm discusses miracles along with magic and talisman *(Fisal,* V, 1ff/V, 147). His intent becomes quite clear when he establishes the difference between magicians and soothsayers, on the one hand, and prophets on the other. He refutes the allegation that magicians, soothsayers, and saints are able to transmute the essence of things or to produce miracles. It is God alone Who can change the essence of things through miracles and make them manifest through His prophets, thus excluding magicians, soothsayers, and saints; for if miracles were possible for beings other than prophets, the possible and the impossible would be the same, and the essence of all things would be destroyed *(Fisal,* V, 3/V,149). Natural changes resulting from semen, grains being transformed into plants, and the like should not be confused with transmutation of the essence of things Cf. Ibn Khaldun, *Muqaddimah,* I, 190, who expresses a similar idea, saying that if miracles were to be produced by liars, "proof would become doubt, guidance misguidance and, I might add, the confirmation of truthfulness untruth. Realities become absurdities, and essential qualities would be turned upside down."

32. Ibn Hazm, *Muhalla,* no. 68. Ibn Hazm, *Fisal,* V,12ff./V,168, admits the existence of jinns or spirits in that it is within God's power to create. Furthermore, the Qur'an and the majority of the Islamic community recognize the existence of jinns. To Ibn Hazm, jinns are made of fire and air, and inhabit fire, air, and earth. They are transparent, colorless, and invisible to ordinary mortals; they are intelligent, discerning, capable of religious feelings, and subject to rewards and punishments. In pre-Islamic times, they inspired soothsayers and poets. The prophet himself was said to have been possessed by them. Subsequently, they were thought to take corporeal forms and even engage in marital intercourse with mortals. See MacDonald, *Attitudes,* 130ff.; *SEI* under *Djinn.*

Despite all this, jinns are incapable of producing miracles, which are assoicated with prophets only. They are different from wonders *(khawariq)* that can be produced by magicians. He reproaches the Sufis and Christians who claim that miracles can be produced by saints. Likewise, the refutes the Shi'ites for claiming that 'Ali, the

son-in-law of the Prophet, had made the sun come back twice to the horizon. *(Fisal,* V,4/V,150), Cf. Ibn Khaldun, *Muqaddimah*, I, 191, who does not seem to make a distinction between miracles *(mu'jizat)* and wonders *(khawariq)* except that the wonders of the prophets are good and those of the sorcereres are bad.
33. Ibn Hazm, *Fisal,* I,78-79/II,190ff. Here Ibn Hazm refutes a Mu'tazilite who maintained that God had sent prophets to different species of animals including fleas and lice. To Ibn Hazm, this is the height of absurdity since animals lack the gift of rationality which man, jinn, and angels possess. Nowhere is there any indication that God ever addressed Himself to anything except those who have the ability of understanding *(Fisal,* I,80/II,193). To the question whether prophecy is feasible among women, Ibn Hazm does not consider this seriously except to mention that some Cordovan theologians pondered on it, some denying its feasility while others admitted it. To him, women are not only eligible to receive prophecy, but had actually been beneficiaries of it, as attested by scriptural testimony. *(Fisal,* V,17ff/V,175ff).
34. Ibn Hazm, *Fisal,* I,83/II,197.
35. *Ibid.,* I,90-91/II,199.
36. Ibn Hazm, *Muhalla,* nos.9,13,85. In his *Fisal,* V, 17/V,176-77, Ibn Hazm defines prophecy *(nubuwah)* as derived from a root meaning "to inform," "to give news," or "to teach." In its true meaning, it is the deliberate purpose of God to instruct the inspired person *(nabi)* and inculcate in him a necessary and veritable knowledge of the truth of what God inspires or reveals to him. This inspiration can be communicated through an angel as intermediary, or through direct communication of God with the soul of the inspired.

Once more, Ibn Hazm contrasts this prophetic inspiration with natural phenomena, conjecture, assumption, divination, and foretelling the future by a magician or soothsayer. Cf. Ibn Khaldun, *Muqaddimah,* I, 184ff.; MacDonald, *Attitude,* 41ff.; and Guillaume, *Prophecy.*
37. Ibn Hazm, *Muhalla,* nos. 50,84,85.
38. *Ibid.,* no. 12.
39. *Ibid.,* no. 72.
40. *Ibid.,* no. 1070.
41. *Ibid.,* no. 1908.
42. *Ibid.,* no. 44.
43. Ibn Hazm, *Fisal,* II,16/III, 248. For bibliographical studies of the Qur'an, see *SEI* under *Kur'an.*
44, *Ibid.,* II,3-7/III,241ff. Here Ibn Hazm discusses at great length the Qur'an as the Word or language of God. The great majority of Muslims agree that God has a language, but theologians differ on the nature of that language and on the Word of God. Although Ibn Hazm agrees with the orthodox view that God's language is his own science and eternal, he takes issue with the Mu'tazilites, who maintain that God's language is created. He also takes issue with the Ash'arites, who maintain that it is an eternal attribute, but different from God. He also refutes the Ash'arites for affirming that God has *one word* only; but adding the qualification that that word was not revealed to the soul of Muhammad, being only an *expression* of it. To Ibn Hazm, such assertions constitute impiety since the Qur'an is the Word of God and since its terms and the Word are one and the same idea. Furthermore God's Word is more than one since the Qur'an has 114 chapters consisting of some 6000 verses, each of which is made of words. Thus, the Qur'an or the Word is read in mosques and at home and contained in a book form. This should not be confused, however, with the materials of which words are made: ink, paper, air, sound, and the like, which are created. Cf. also *Fisal,* V,211/V,114.
45. *Ibid.,* II, 3ff./III,16ff.
46. This view is inspired by the Qur'anic verse 17:90. The question of the inimitability of the Qur'an occupied the attention of a great number of theologians and philol-

ogists. Among the predecessors of Ibn Hazm were Ibn Qutaybah, the author of the *Ta'wil* and Baqillani, author of the famous *I'jaz*. Ibn Hazm, *Fisal*, II,16-17/ III,247-252, held the common orthodox view that the Qur'an is inimitable now and will remain so until the Day of Judgment. It is so because God Himself has forbidden its imitation, and not because it possesses the ultimate of human eloquence. If this were the case, its eloquence would not surpass the level achieved by the works of Hasan al-Basri, Sahl Ibn Harun, and al-Jahiz. In consequence, the view attributed to al-Ash'ari that the Qur'an is co-eternal with ١ but it is not the Qur'an we possess, constitutes an absurdity since such a view would do violence to the miraculous nature of the Qur'an as well as to its inimitability.

47. Ibn Hazm, *Muhalla*, no. 21. To Ibn Hazm, *Fisal*, I, 75/III,119ff., the authenticity of the Qur'an is beyond any question and is, unlike the Old and New Testaments, attested to by the facts of history. Its verses are clear and do not lend themselves to allegory or the like as is the case in the Old and New Testaments, which are in addition filled with interpolation, omission and lies. He dismisses the discrepancies found in the various readings and recensions as minor, and discounts the allegation of some Shi'ites who claim that the text of the Qur an is corrupt and contains numerous interpolations and omissions (*Fisal*, V,182/V, 57).
48. *Ibid.*, no. 1444.
49. Ibn Hazm, *Fisal*, I,82/II,195; cf. his *Muhalla*, nos. 22 and 93.
50. Ibn Hazm, *Ihkam*, II,206.
51. *Ibidem.*
52. Ibn Hazm, *Muhalla*, no. 1444.
53. *Ibid.*, nos. 1135 and 1266.
54. Ibn Hazm, *Ihkam*, I,80ff.; Abu Zahrah, *Ibn Hazm*, 284ff.
55. *Qur'an* 6:38.
56. Ibn Hazm, *Ihkam*, I, 85.
57. *Ibid.*, I, 87ff. On the general subject of Traditions, see *SEI;* Wensinck, *Handbook;* Guillaume, *Traditions.*
58. Ibn Hazm, *Fisal*, II, 83-84; also his *Nubadh*, 28. Cf Asin, *Abenhazam*, I, 172-173.
59. Ibn Hazm, *Ihkam*, I, 87ff.
60. *Ibid.*, II, 208.
60. *Ibid.*, II, 208.
61. *Ibid.*, IV, 402.
62. *Ibid.*, I, 88; VIII, 1057.
63. *Ibid.*, III, 362.
64. Ibn Hazm, *Nubadh*, 8-9.
65. Ibn Hazm, *Mufadalah.*
66. Ibn Hazm, *Ihkam*, IV, 494.
67. Ibn Hazm, *Muhalla*, no. 96.
68. Ibn Hazm, *Nubadh*, 10.
69. *Ibid.*, 13.
70. Ibn Hazm, *Muhalla*, no. 98.
71. Ibn Hazm, *Nubadh*, 38.
72. Ibn Hazm, *Muhalla*, no. 99; cf. his *Ihkam*, IV, 495.
73. Ibn Hazm, *Ihkam*, IV, 494 and 550.
74. *Qur'an*, 4: 59.
75. Ibn Hazm, *Ihkam*, IV, 498.
76. *Ibid.*, IV, 495.
77. *Ibid.*, I, 5.

78. *Ibid.,* I, 6.
79. Ibn Hazm, *Fisal,* I, 82/ II, 122. Cf. Asin, *Abenhazam,* I, 174-175.
80. Arnaldez, *Grammaire,* 37-47.
81. *Ibid.,* 266. Al-Ash'ari (873-935), a leading scholar, had a powerful influence on the formulation of orthodox theology. See his *Ibanah;* and *Maqalat;* cf. MacDonald, *Theology,* 189; Makdisi, *Ash'ari;* McCarthy, *Theology.*
82. *Ibid.,* 283.
83. Ibn Hazm, *Fisal,* II, 149. For instance, *Qur'an* 3:119, 154; *Qur'an* 4: 12, 26, 176.
84. Ibn Hazm, *Ihkam,* I, 39 Cf. Arnaldez, *Grammaire,* 83ff. By the time of Ibn Hazm, there were numerous followers of al-Ash'ari some of whom may not have adhered closely to al-Ash'ari's doctrine.
85. Ibn Hazm, *Fisal,* II, 75. Cf. Asin, *Abenhazam,* I, 177-178.
86. Ibn Hazm, *Ihkam,* I, 28ff. Cf. Arnaldez, *Grammaire,* 37-47; Chejne *Arabic,* 10.
87. *Qur'an* 14: 4.
88. *Qur'an,* 26: 195.
89. Ibn Hazm, *Nubadh,* 25.
90. Ibn Hazm, *Ihkam,* III, 259 and 294ff.; His *Nubadh,* 28ff.; Arnaldez, *Grammaire,* 53ff. and his *Ahbar.*
91. *Ibid.,* III, 260; cf. his *Nubadh,* 25ff.
92. Ibn Hazm, *Ihkam,* III, 263ff.
93. *Ibid.,* III, 340.
94. *Ibid.,* III, 341.
95. *Ibid.,* III, 328.
96. *Ibid.,* III, 329.
97. *Ibid.,* III, 329.
98. Arnaldez, *Grammaire,* 79.
99. Ibn Hazm, *Ihkam,* III, 272.
100. Arnaldez, *Grammaire,* 80.
101. Ibn Hazm, *Ihkam,* III, 272.
102. *Qur'an* 14:4.
103. Ibn Hazm, *Ihkam,* III, 290.
104. *Ibidem.* 'A'ishah had fought 'Ali at the famous Battle of the Camel following his succession to the Caliphate. Henceforth, his followers looked upon her with disfavor.
105. Arnaldez, *Grammaire,* 101-102.
106. Ibn Hazm, *Ihkam,* V, 676 cf. Arnaldez, *Grammaire,* 158ff.
107. *Ibidem.*
108. *Ibid.,* VI, 722-1170.
109. Ibn Hazm, *Ibtal,* 38-39.
110. *Ibid.,* 44.
111. *Ibid.,* 42. For a general view of Islamic jurisprudence, see Coulson, *Law;* Lopez, *Derecho;* Melliot, *Introduction;* Schacht, *Introduction,* and *Origin.* Also *SEI* under *Fikh.*
112. Ibn Hazm, *Ihkam,* V, 722-744.
113. Ibn Hazm, *Fisal,* I, 48ff. and 98ff.
114. Ibn Hazm, *Ihkam,* V, 745-756. *Ihtiyat* appears to have been condoned by some legal schools. Cf. Schacht, *Introduction,* 123.
115. *Ibid.,* V, 749
116. *Ibid.,* V, 755.
117. *Ibid.,* V, 756.
118. *Ibid.,* VI, 757ff.

119. Ibn Hazm, *Ibtal*, 5. Cf. *SEI* under *Istihsan*. Schacht, *Introduction*, 299, defines *istihsan* as "approval," a discretionary opinion in breach of strict analogy.
120. Ibn Hazm, *Ihkam*, VI, 757.
121. *Qur'an* 39:18.
122. Ibn Hazm, *Ihkam*, VI, 758.
123. *Ibid.*, VI, 762. CF. his *Ibtal*, 5 and 50ff. It appears that Ibn Hazm does not take into consideration, as other jurists did, the question of welfare *(istilah,* or *maslahah)* as one of the determining factors for arriving at legal decisions. Cf. *SEI* under *istihsan*.
124. For his discussion of *taqlid*, see his *Ihkam*, VI, 793-883. His *Ibtal*, 6; his *Nubadh*, 54; and his *Iman*, 2ff. Cf. *SEI* under *Taklid*.
125. Ibn Hazm, *Ihkam*, I, 37.
126. Ibn Hazm, *Muhalla*, no. 99.
127. *Ibid.*, nos. 99 and 103.
128. Ibn Hazm, *Ihkam*, VI, 793-794.
129. *Ibid.*, VI, 797.
130. *Ibid.*, VI, 800.
131. *Ibid.*, VI, 803.
132. *Ibid.*, VI, 813.
133. *Ibid.*, VI, 821
134. *Ibid.*, VI, 801.
135. *Ibid.*, VI, 836.
136. Ibn Hazm, *Fisal*, IV, 36; 111-115; cf. Asin, *Abenhazam*, I, 180-181.
137. Ibn Hazm, *Ihkam*, VI, 765-792; his *Ibtal*, 22ff.; and his *Nubadh,* 40ff. See *SEI* under *Ra'y*.
138. Ibn Hazm, *Ibtal*, 22.
139. *Qur'an* 3:5, Ibn Hazm, *Ihkam*, VI, 765; his *Muhalla*, no. 100; his *Ibtal*, 55ff.
140. Ibn Hazm, *Muhalla*, nos. 103 and 124.
141. *Qur'an*, 42:38.
142. Ibn Hazm, *Ihkam*, VI, 769.
143. *Ibid.*, VI, 770.
144. *Ibid.*, VI, 774.
145. *Ibid.*, 792.
146. Ibn Hazm, *Ibtal*, 4.
147. *Ibid.*, 56.
148. Ibn Hazm, *Ihkam*, VII, 887-928; his *Ibtal*, 52ff. Cf. Arnaldez, *Grammaire*, 58ff.
149. Ibn Hazm, *Ihkam*, I, 42.
150. *Ibid.*, VII, 887.
151. *Ibidem.;* cf. Arnaldez, *Grammaire*, 162.
152. Ibn Hazm, *Ibtal*, 5 and 68ff.; his *Ihkam*, VII, 929-1109; his *Muhalla*, nos. 100, 104, 133; and his *Nubadh*, 44ff; cf. Arnaldez, *Grammaire, 165-193*. See *SEI* under *Kiyas*.
153. Ibn Hazm, *Ihkam*, VI, 762.
154. Ibn Hazm, *Ibtal*, 30.
155. The use of analogy was a point of contention among early philologists, with those of al-Kufah supporting it while those of al-Basrah denied its validity. Cf. Chejne, *Muslim Spain*, 83, and his *Arabic*, 48.
156. Ibn Hazm, *Ihkam*, VII, 1034.
157. *Ibid.*, VII, 1034-1035.
158. *Ibid.*, VII, 1109.
159. *Ibid.*, VIII, 1110-1155; his *Ibtal*, 5; his *Nubadh*, 48. Cf. Arnaldez, *Grammaire*, 185-193.

160. Ibn Hazm, *Ihkam*, I, 41; VIII, 1126.
161. Ibn Hazm, *Ibtal*, 5-6.
162. Ibn Hazm, *Ihkam*, VIII, 1110.
163. Ibn Hazm, *Ibtal*, 47.
164. *Ibid.*, 49.
165. Ibn Hazm, *Ihkam*, VII, 1112.
166. *Ibid.*, VIII, 1110.
167. Ibn Hazm, *Maratib al-'ulum* 65/233, where he warns the student against studying causation.
168. Ibn Hazm, *Ihkam*, VIII, 1122.
169. *Ibid.*, VIII, 1123.
170. *Ibid.*, VIII, 1127.
171. *Ibid.*, VIII, 1128-1129.
172. *Ibid.*, VIII, 1130.
173. Ibn Hazm, *Muhalla*, nos. 1774 and 1776.
174. *Ibid.*, nos. 1775, 1800, 1802, 1807.
175. *Ibid.*, 1792.
176. Ibn Hazm discusses the importance of *ijtihad* in his *Ihkam*, V, 648ff; *Fisal*, III, 250; *Ibtal*, 41ff.; *Muhalla*, nos. 103, 108, 109. For a general view of *ijtihad*, see *SEI*.
177. See Arnaldez, *Grammaire*, 124.
178. Ibn Hazm, *Ibtal*, 41-42.
179. Ibn Hazm, *Muhalla*, nos. 103.
180. *Ibid.*, no. 109, where he says, "al-haqq min al-aqwal wahid wa-sa' iruha khata'."'
181. Arnaldez, *Grammaire*, 181.
182. Ibn Hazm, *Ihkam*, V, 653; his *Fisal*, III, 248, 250, 258. cf. Asin, *Abenhazam*, I, 182.
183. Ibn Hazm, *Ihkam*, V, 648, says, "Ma'jur 'ala ijtihadih al-ladhi huwa al-haqq li-annahu talaba al-haqq wa-laysa qawl al-qa'il bi-ra'yih ijtihadan wa-imma khata' fa-laysa ma'juran 'alayh."
184. *Ibid.*, II, 233-234.
185. *Ibid.*, VI, 873. Cf. *Muhalla*, no. 108.
186. *Ibid.*, VI, 774.
187. *Ibid.*, V, 658' VI, 699.
188. *Ibid.*, V, 704, where he says, "fa-l-istidlal wa-l-ijtihad shay' wahid." Thus, it would appear that *ijtihad* in Ibn Hazm's conception does not mean exerting oneself to form an opinion through the application of analogy as the Shafi'ites imply, but to search for the proper evidence as found in the Qur'an and Traditions. For the various connotations of *ijtihad*, see MacDonald, *Theology*, 315-351; and SEI.

CHAPTER VII
BELLES-LETTRES, LANGUAGE, AND HISTORY

1. Ibn Shuhayd, *Tawabi'*, 77. Abu-l-Qasim al-Iflili (d. 1049) was a prominent philologist of Cordova.
2. Ibn Hazm's *Ta'aqqub* (lost) would shed a better light on the difference separating traditional philology and the modern trend in Cordova.
3. See Ibn Shuhayd's *Tawabi'*.
4. Ibn Hazm, *Fada'il*.
5. See Ibn Hazm's poem in Ibn Bassam, *Dhakhirah*, I:i, 145. For the place of Ibn Hazm in Arabic Literature, see Chapter I.
6. Ibn Hazm, *Fasahah;* see Appendix. It is significant to point out that "rhetoric" and "eloquence" occupied the attention of a great number of Arab philologist, literary critics, and religious scholars. Their significance had bearing not only on the concept of linguistic purity and elegant expressions in general, but on the belief in the inimitability of the Qur'an by any mortal. Because of this pregnant religious significance with respect to style and content in addition to clarity of ideas and easy rendition, rhetoric and eloquence had definite bearing on Ibn Hazm's Zahirite doctrine. In consequence, it is probable that Ibn Hazm devoted his attention to the subject in a more prolix form than the laconic account appearing in his *Taqrib*, 204-205. In this connection, Ibn Hazm follows the format of Aristotle's *Organon*. On the other hand, in all probability he took into consideration the views of his predecessors such as al-Jahiz (d. 869), Ibn al-Mu'tazz (d. 887), Ibn Qutaybah (d. 889), Qudamah Ibn Ja'far (d. ca. 920), and perhaps al-'Askari. On the subject of rhetoric, see Mehren, *Rhetoric;* Dayf, *Balaghah;* Dayah, *Naqd;* Mubarak, *Nathr;* and Trabulsi, *Critique*. Also, Grunebaum, *Theory;* and Cantarino, *Poetics*.
7. Ibn Hazm, *'Arud*, see Appendix. Versification *('ilm al-'arud)*, dealing with metrics and rhymes, was an important science in Muslim education. Khalil Ibn Ahmad (d. 786), its supposed founder, is said to have written on the subject, followed by a larger number of Arab philologists. The Andalusian Ibn 'Abd Rabbihi (d. 940) devoted section 19 to it in his *'Iqd*, lucidly summarizing the discipline as it was known among Eastern writers. In his capacity as a poet, it is probable that Ibn Hazm delved into the subject. See Weil, *Metren*, and *'Arud* in EI.[2]
8. Ibn Hazm, *Tasmiyah;* see Appendix.
9. Ibn Hazm, *Shu'ara';* see Appendix.
10. Ibn Hazm, *Maratib al-'ulama';* see Appendix.
11. Ibn Hazm, *Za';* see Appendix.
12. Ibn Hazm, *Sad;* see Appendix.
13. Ibn Hazm, *Fada'il*. See Appendix.
14. Ibn Hazm, *Akhlaq*. See Appendix.
15. Ibn Hazm, *Tawq*, 51.
16. *Ibid.*, 31. For the importance and significance of the *Tawq*, see the articles by Husayn, Levi-Provencal, Marcais, and Garcia Gomez.
17. Nykl, *Poetry*, 78, suggests 1022 as the date of its composition. He was followed by Garcia Gomez, *Tawq*, 51. The year 1022 must be discounted on the ground that the data indicate that in 1022 Ibn Hazm appears to have been residing in Cordova, which he did not leave until about 1025.
18. Ibn Hazm, *Tawq*, 100.
19. Ibn Dawud wrote his *Zahrah* in 1,000 verses.

20. Ibn Hazm, *Tawq*, 67.
21. *Ibid.*, 98-99.
22. *Ibid.*, 100.
23. *Ibid.*, 130.
24. *Ibid.*, 223.
25. See Castro, *Espana*, 396ff; Garcia Gomez, *Tawq*, 72.
26. He is Ahmad Ibn al-Husayn al-Hamadhani (d. 1088), author of several *Maqamat*. He was followed by al-Hariri (d. 1122), who immortalized this genre in his famous *Maqamat* consisting of fifty episodes.
27. Ibn Hazm, *Tawq*, 309; cf. 91-92.
28. See above, Chapter III, notes 125ff.
29. Humaydi, *Judhwah*, 309.
30. Ibn Hazm, *Tawq*, 110.
31. Mainly Humaydi, *Judhwah;* Ibn Bassam, *Dhakhirah;* Ibn Sa'id, *Mughrib;* Yaqut, *Irshad;* Dhahabi, *Siyar;* and Maqqari, *Nafh*.
32. Ibn Khayr, *Fahrasah*, 417, and 410.
33. Subki, *Tabaqat*, II, 184; Ibn Kathir, *Bidayah*, XI, 247ff. 'Abbas, *Tarikh*, 370-74, reproduces the whole poem.
34. Ibn Bassam, *Dhakhirah*, I:i, 145-146.
35. *Ibid.*, I:i, 143-144.
36. Yaqut, *Irshad*, V, 95.
37. Ibn Hazm, *Tawq*, 299ff., where he has two long poems on the excellence of chastity.
38. Ibn Bassam, *Dhakhirah*, I:i, 145.
39. Hassan Ibn Thabit (d. 673) made his mark at the Ghassanid court and is considered to be among the leading poets. See Nallino, *Litterature*, 56-57; also Blachere, *Literrature*, II, 313.
40. Ka'b Ibn Malik (d. 670), a leading pre-Islamic poet of the Khazraj tribe. Like Hassan Ibn Thabit, he espoused the cause of Muhammad. See Blachere, *Litterature*, II, 312.
41. 'Abdallah Ibn Ruwahah was a pre-Islamic poet of the Khazraj tribe, and became a staunch defender of Islam. See Blachere, *Litterature*, II, 312.
42. Salih Ibn 'Abd al-Quddus (d. 783) was a poet and a preacher whose poetry contained moralizing maxims. He was put to death by the 'Abbasid caliph al-Mahdi on charges of heresy.
43. Ibn Hazm, *Maratib al-'ulum*, 65/233; his *Talkhis*, 163.
44. 'Antarah Ibn Shaddad was a pre-Islamic poet of the tribe of 'Abs and distinguished himself as a great warrior who fought ceaselessly to gain the hand of his cousin 'Abla.
45. 'Urwah Ibn al-Ward was also a pre-Islamic poet of the tribe of 'Abs who displayed great courage in war. See Blachere, *Litterature*, II, 287.
46. Sa'd Ibn Nashib (d. ca. 728) was a poet of Basrah. See Zirikli, *A'lam*, III, 139.
47. Ibn Hazm, *Maratib al-'ulum*, 66-67/233-234, Cf. Chejne, *Muslim Spain*, 171.
48. *Ibid.*, 68/235.
49. Ibn Hazm, *Taqrib*, 206.
50. *Ibidem*.
51. *Ibidem*.

52. Ibn Hazm, *Maratib al-'ulum*, 67/234. In spite of the preeminent position of poets and poetry in pre-Islamic and Islamic times, there developed an uneasiness toward them from the time of Muhammad. This ambivalence remained quite prevalent among a good number of religious scholars. Partly as a consequence of Muhammad's confrontation with poets and partly as a result of literary criticism, poetry came to be conceived as something conveying a subjective rather than an objective state. This criterion can be traced back to Muhammad, who placed poets and poetry in a bad light. (Q 52:30; Q 69:40 etc.) The literary critic Qudamah, *Naqd*, 26, quotes the saying that "the best poetry is that which is the most untruthful" *(ash'ar al-shi'r akdhabuh)*. Al-'Askari, *Sina'atayn*, 146, maintained that most poetical compositions are based on lies and absurdity of attributes; slander, false testimony and calumny. The Andalusian belletrist Ibn 'Abd Rabbihi, *'Iqd*, Sec. 19, gives the pros and cons and relates that the best poet is the one who is able to make a true thing appear false and a false thing appear true.

This negative attitude toward poetry was, however, nullified by its profuse use by the same people who criticized its merit. The reason for this seeming contradiction was that poetry was considered not only the archives of the Arabs, but the most reliable tool for elucidating grammatical and lexical points in the Qur'an and Traditions. Furthermore, poetry was related intimately to the concept of rheotric and eloquence. In light of this multiple significance, Ibn Hazm could hardly rule out the inclusion of poetry in his hierarchy of the sciences and even in the education of the young. For more detailed information concerning the position of poetry and the critical approach to it see Trabulsi, *Critique*, who deals for the most part with the views of Ibn Qutaybah, Ibn al-Mu'tazz, Qudamah and al-'Askari. A more recent treatment is that of Cantarino, *Poetics*, 35ff.

53. Ibn Hazm, *Talkhis*, 162.
54. *Ibidem*. In spite of this ambivalence, Ibn Hazm could hardly exclude poetry from his division of the sciences (see his *Taqrib)*, 201; and his *Maratib al-'ulum*, 80/241). His predecessors such as al-Farabi, the Brethren of Purity, al-Khuwarizmi, who were probably influenced by Aristotle's *Organon* made provision for it in the divisions of the sciences.
55. Abu Tammam (d. 846) was a neoclassical poet of the 'Abbasid period. He compiled the famous anthology of poetry known as *Diwan al-hamasah*.
56. Al-Buhturi (d. 897) was an able poet and compiler of a poetical anthology.
57. Ibn Hazm, *Tawq*, 232-233.
58. Abu Nuwas (d. ca. 800) was a famous poet of wine, song and panegyric.
59. Ibn Hazm, *Tawq*, 253.
60. Ibn Darraj al-Qastalli (d. 1030) was one of the great poets of al-Andalus. See Blachere, *Ibn Darraj;* Nykl, *Poetry*, 61-64; Peres, *Poesie;* Vernet, *Literatura*, 89; Monroe, *Poetry*, 146ff.
61. Bashshar Ibn Burd (d. 784), one of the prominent poets under the 'Abbasids, was put to death on charges of Heresy.
62. Habib refers to Abu Tammam; see above, note 55.
63. Al-Mutanabbi (d. 965) was one of the most gifted of Arab poets. His popularity has been great throughout the centuries. On him, see Blachere, *al-Mutanabbi*.
64. Ja'far Ibn 'Uthman al-Hajib (d. 978) was a competent poet who served the caliphs 'Abd al-Rahman III and al-Hakam II in the capacity of chamberlain. On him, see Nykl, *Poetry*, 49.
65. Ahmad Ibn 'Abd al-Malik Ibn Marwan was a tenth century Andalusian poet who served at the court of the caliph 'Abd al-Rhaman III.
66. Aghlab Ibn Shu'ayb was also a tenth century Andalusian poet who served at the court of the caliph 'Abd al-Rahman III. See Dabbi, *Bughyah*, no. 579.
67. Muhammad Ibn Shukhays (d. 1009) was the court poet of al-Hakam II. See Nykl, *Poetry*, 43.

68. Ahmad Ibn Faraj (d. 970) served at the court of al-Hakam II, for whom he composed his *Book of Gardens*, a poetical anthology. See Nykl, *Poetry*, 43.
69. 'Abd al-Malik Ibn Sa'id al-Muradi was an Andalusian court poet. See Humaydi, *Judhwah, no. 631; Dabbi, Bughyah, no. 1067*.
70. Ibn Hazm, *Fada'il*, 178; Chejne, *Muslim Spain*, 159-160.
71. Ibn Hazm, *Fada'il*, 178. Cf. Monroe's introduction to Ibn Shuhayd, *Tawabi'*, 18.
72. Zuhayr Ibn Abi Sulma was a pre-Islamic poet of panegyric. See Nicholson, *History*, 116-119.
73. He is Abu Tammam, see above, note 55.
74. Jarir was the court poet of al-Hajjaj, viceroy of the Umayyad caliph 'Abd al-Malik.
75. Al-Hasan Ibn Ahmad Abu 'Ali al-Farisi (d. 987).?
76. Imru'-l-Qays was one of the most prominent pre-Islamic poets and author of one of the seven famous *Mu'allaqat*.
77. 'Ali Ibn 'Abbas al-Rumi (d. 896) was a prominent Baghdadi poet. Cf. Zirikli, *A'lam*, V: 110.
78. Qudamah Ibn Ja'far (d. 948), author of the *Naqd al-Shi'r* of which Ibn Hazm appears to approve, was a leading literary critic.
79. Abu 'Ali al-Hatimi (d. 998) was a literary critic. Cf. Brocklemann, GAL, I:195.
80. "wa kawn al-mar' sha'iran laysa muktasaban la-kinnaha hilah" ("the raison d'etre for a man being a poet or not made resides in that poetry is an artifice" is signifcant in that it appears to place poetry outside the hierarchy of the sciences and the crafts which are, by necessity, acquired through teaching. Thus poetics, as opposed to the art of versification *('ilm al-'arud)*, is not acquired but constitutes a natural gift. Thus, it follows that the production of poetry is the result of a natural disposition *(Tab')* and not of mere craftsmanship. Earlier the ninth century literary critic Ibn Qutaybah, *Shi'r*, 78, 90, distinguished between the "natural poet" and the "artificial poet" *(masnu')*, saying that the artificial poet is one who amends his poems, whereas a natural poet's poetry flows easily and he who has complete control over its rhymes. In other words, the true poet is not a mere craftsman, but one who has a natural gift of inventiveness and creativity. Cf. Monroe's introduction to his translation of Ibn Shuhayd's *Tawabi'*, 18ff.
81. Ibn Hazm, *Taqrib*, 206-207. In his *Maratib al-'ulum*, 66/233, Ibn Hazm says that poetry consists of transmission, the nicety and defects of meaning, different kinds, meters, and composition. He states in his *Taqrib*, 202, that its source is what had been heard from the Arabs with respect to meters and with respect to what people had agreed upon as good or bad concerning nice and sweet expressions, meaning, proper metaphors, sweet allusion, and beautiful versification.
82. *Ibid.*, 204-205, Cf. not 6.
83. Ibn Hazm, *Ihkam*, I, 17-18; III, 290.
84. Al-Jahiz (d. 868) was a leading prose writer and author of numerous belletristic works. In all likelihood, Ibn Hazm was familiar with his *Bayan, Hayawan* and *Bukhala'*.
85. Hasan al-Basri (d. 728) is known for his piety and his eloquence.
86. Sahl Ibn Harun (d. 830) was a major prose writer who tended to show the superiority of the non-Arabs over the Arabs.
87. 'Abdallah Ibn al-Muqaffa' (d. 757) was an able prose writer and translator of the famous book of fables entitled *Kalilah wa-Dimnah*.
88. Ibn Hazm, *Taqrib*, 204ff.
89. Ibn Hazm, *Maratib al-'ulum*, 80/241; cf. his *Taqrib*, 203.
90. Ibn Hazm, Taqrib, 205.
91. Ibn Hazm, *Maratib al-'ulum*, 80/241

92. By the time of Ibn Hazm, the inimitability of the Qur'an had been firmly established. Among early works on the subject are the *Ta'wil of Ibn Qutaybah and the I'jaz* of al-Baqillani.
93. Ibn Hazm, *Taqrib*, 205.
94. Ibn Hazm, *Fisal*, III, 55ff./III, 241ff., where he says that the Qur'an is beyond human eloquence (wa-laysa min naw' balaghat al-nas).
95. Ibn Hazm, *Talkhis*, 160. For the intimate relationship between language and Zahirism, see Arnaldez, *Grammaire;* and Chapter VI.
96. *Qur'an* 16:103, *Qur'an :* 26:195. On the religious significance of Arabic, see Chejne, *Arabic*, 8ff. For the linguistic movement in al-Andalus, see Mutlaq, *Harakah*.
97. Ibn Hazm, *Talkhis, 161*.
98. Ibn Hazm, *Ihkam*, V, 693.
99. Ibn Hazm, *Talkhis*, 161-163
100. Ibn Hazm, *Maratib al-'ulum*, 64-65/232-233; *Talkhis,*163; *Taqrib*, 202.
101. Al-Zubaydi (d. 989) was a leading philologist of Spain and author of several works on the language.
102. Muhammad Ibn al-Sariy Ibn Sahl Ibn al-Sarraj (d. 929), a leading philologist. Cf. Brokelmann, *GAL;* Supp. 174.
103. Ibn Hazm, *Taqrib*, 202.
104. Abu 'Ubayd al-Qasim Ibn Sallam, a leading philologist.
105. Khalil Ibn Ahmad (d. 789) was a leading philologist of Basrah and author of *Kitab al-'ayn*.
106. Thabit Ibn Abi Thabit, a philologist and follower of Abu 'Ubayd. See Yaqut, *Irshad*, II, 396-397.
107. Muhammad Ibn al-Qasim Ibn Bashshar al-Anbari (d. 940). Cf. Borckelmann, *GAL.*S, 122 Zirikli, *A'lam*, VII, 226-227.
108. Dawud al-Dinawari (d. 895). Cf.Zirikli, *A'lam*, I, 119.
109. For studies of some of his historical works, see above Chapter I, notes 90ff.
110. Ibn Hazm, *Maratib al-'ulum,*78/240. History occupied an important place in Islamic culture and constitutes a large portion of Arabic literature. Ibn Hazm considers it significant for inclusion among the sciences.
111. Ibn Hazm, *Jawami';* see Appendix.
112. Ibn Hazm, *Hijjah;* see Appendix.
113. *Ibid.*, 43.
114. *Ibid.*, 44.
115. Ibn Hazm, *Asma'* in *Jawami'*, 275-315.
116. Ibn Hazm, *Ashab* in *Jawami'*, 319-335.
117. Ibn Hazm, *Mufadalah*.
118. Ibn Hazm, *Jumal Jawami'*, 339-350.
119. Ibn Hazm, *Ghazawat*.
120. Ibn Hazm, *Imamah*.
121. See above, Chapter II, notes 77ff.
122. Ibn Hazm *Siyasah*.
123. Ibn Hazm *Asma' al-khulafa';* in *Jawami'*, 353-381.
124. Ibn Hazm, *Nuqat*.
125. Ibn Hazm, *Dhikr*.
126. Ibn Hazm, *Jamharah*.

127. Ibn Hazm, *Nasab.*
128. Ibn Hazm, *Fada'il.*
129. Ibn Hazm, *Shu'ra'.*
130. Ibn Hazm, *Tasmiyah.*
131. Ibn Hazm, *Maratib al-'alama'.*
132. Ibn Hazm, *Fahrasah.*
133. Ibn Hazm, *Fisal.*
134. Ibn Khaldun, *Muqaddimah,* I, 327.
135. Maqqari, *Nafh,* I, 327
136. Ibn Sa'id, *Mughrib,* I, 44; Maqqari, *Nafh,* I, 342.
137. Ibn al-Khatib,*A'mal,* 26.
138. *Ibid.,* 14.
139. Marrakushi, *Mu'jib,* 49.
140. *Ibid.,* 5; also Ibn al-Abbar, *Hullah,* I, 203; Maqqari, *Nafh,* I, 385.
141. Ibn al-Abbar, *Hullah,* II, 3; Marrakushi, *Mu'jib* , 106.
142. Ibn al-Khatib, *A'mal,* 142-143.
143. Marrakushi, *Mu'jib,* 57.
144. *Ibid.,* 61.
145. *Ibid.,* 63 and 65.
146. *Ibid.,* 73, 74, 80, 84. Cf. Ibn Sa'id, *Mughrib,* I, 132 and 164; Ibn al-Abbar, *Hullah,* I, 126, 128, 206 and 221; Maqqari, *Nafh,* II, 10, 237 and 519; III, 67, IV, 76.
147. Sakhawi, *I'lan* in Rosenthal, *History,* 333-334, 396, 430, 523, and 527.
148. Ibn Hazm, *Taqrib,* 202. He adds: "Its source is based on premises guaranteeing the continuity of transmission and its soundness without leaving any shred of doubt." *(Ibidem.)*
149. Ibn Hazm, *Maratib al-'ulum,* 87/240, appears to imply here that the student should not waste precious time investigating historical problems, but rather should occupy himself only with things whose veracity had been demonstrated.
150. Ibn Hazm, *Maratib al-'ulum,* 71/237. History occupied an important place in Muslim education and scholarship and in the intellectual development of Islam because history recorded the great moments of Islam - its inception, expansion, and impact on a large area of the world in the religious, intellectual, and political spheres. History had immediate bearing on the religious life of Islam, and along with religion and language was considered a principal factor in differentiating one nation from another. Because of this preeminence, history finds a legitimate place in Ibn Hazm s division of the sciences (his *Maratib al-'ulum,* 78/240, also his *Taqrib,* 201).Although the philosophers al-Farabi and Ibn Sina did not make provision for history in their division of the sciences - probably because of the impact of the Greek precedent, which overlooked history- other Muslim scholars such as the Brethren of Purity, al-Khuwarizmi, Ibn al-Nadim, and al-Ghazzali, to mention only a few, did make provision for it. See Rosenthal, *History,* 30ff.
151. *Ibidem;* cf. Rosenthal, *History,* 36ff.
152. *Ibid.* 88/240; cf. Chejne, *Muslim Spain,* 172ff.
153. Ibn Hazm, *Jamharah,* 2; *Maratib al-'ulum,* 79/242. Cf. Rosenthal, *History* note 3, 26.
154. Ibn Hazm, *Jamharah,* 3. Cf. Bosch, *Ibn Hazm.*
155. Ibn Hazm, *Maratib al-'ulum,* 88-89/240-241. Cf. Rosenthal, *History,* 37 and 117.
156. Ibn Hazm, *Fisal,* I, 73ff./II, 91ff.
157. *Ibid.,* I, 7-8.
158. Ibn Hazm, *Ihkam,* I, 94-97.

159. *Ibid.*, I, 94.
160. *Ibid.*, I, 95.
161. *Ibid.*, I, 123.
162. See above, Chapter VI, notes 58ff.

CHAPTER VIII
THE PHILOSOPHICAL SCIENCES

1. On the various divisions of the sciences, See Chapter V, notes 11ff. In fact, al-Ghazzail excludes philosophy altogheter from his division of the sciences, stating that philosophy is not a discipline in itself but comprises the natural and metaphysical sciences. Cf. Chapter V, 116.
2. See Chapter V, note 86,
3. Ibn Hazm, *Maratib al-'ulum* 78/240.
4. He is Alexander of Aphrodisia, commentator on Aristotle's works.
5. Ibn Hazm, *Tawqif*, 43. Al-Kindi, *Rasa'il*, 97, considers philosophy the noblest craft consisting of the knowledge of things in their realities to the limit of human power.
6. *Ibidem.*
7. *Ibid.*, 47.
8. *Ibid.*, 55.
9. See Chapter III, note 41.
10. Ibn Hazm, *Maratib al-'ulum,* 71/237.
11. Ibn Hazm, *Hatif,* 10.
12. See Chapter IV, note 143.
13. See Chapter IV, notes 113ff.
14. Ibn Hazm, *Taqrib,* 202.
15. Ibn Hazm, *Maratib al-'ulum,* 71/237.
16. See Chapter III, notes 14ff.
17. See Chapter I, notes 72 and 78.
18. Ibn Hazm, *Akhlaq,* no. 12.
19. Ibn Hazm, *Nafs,* see Appendix.
20. Particularly his *Fisal, Tawqif,* and *Talkhis.*
21. Ibn Hazm, *Kindi;* see Appendix.
22. Ibn Hazm, *Razi;* see Appendix. See Kraus, *Opèra,* 175-176.
23. See Chapter V, note 88.
24. Ibn Hazm, *Maratib al-'ulum,* 89/241. On mathematics, see Suter, *Mathematiker;* Mieli, *Science;* and Millas Vallicrosa, *Estudios.*
25. *Andrumakhis,* is mentioned by Ibn Juljul, *Tabaqat,* 34, as a Greek physician.
26. Ibn Hazm, *Tawqif,* 44.
27. Ibn Hazm, *Talkhis,* 164. Al-Farabi, the Brethren of Purity, and al-Khuwarizmi, among others, gave mathematics a prominent place in their division of the sciences. Cf. Chapter V, nots 19ff.

289

28. Ibn Hazm, *Taqrib*, 202.
29. Ibn Hazm, *Maratib al-'ulum*, 67/235.
30. Ibn Hazm, *Tawqif*, 44; *Maratib al-'ulum*. 68/235.
31. Ibn Hazm, *Maratib al-'ulum*, 68/235. On Astronomy, see Suter, *Mathematiker*.
32. Lunkhas may be a typographical error for Ibbarkhas (Qifti, Tarikh, 69) who is associated with Ptolomy.
33. Ibn Hazm, *Tawqif*, 45.
34. Ibn Hazm, *Talkhis*, 164; also his *Maratib al-'ulum*, 82/242.
35. See Chapter III, notes 14ff.
36. See Chapter III, notes 41ff.
37. Mainly his *Fisal*, V,9/v,162; *Tawqif*, 45; *Maratib al-'ulum*, 88/245; *Akhlaq*, nos. 36 and 41. Cf. Garcia Gomex, *Medicina;* Samso, *Medicina*.
38. Ibn Hazm, *Tawqif*, 45-46. In his *Maratib al-'ulum*, 88/245, Ibn Hazm reiterates the same point about the state of medicine in primitive society. Cf. Ibn Khaldun, *Muqaddimah*, III, 149ff.

On Arab medicine in general, see Campbell, *Medicine;* Leclerc, *Histoire;* and and Mieli, *Science*.
39. Ibn Hazm, *Taqrib*, 202.
40. Ibn Hazm, *Maratib al-'ulum*, 79-80/241.
41. *Ibid.*, 82/242.
42. Ibn Hazm, *Talkhis*, 164.
43. Ibn Hazm, *Maratib al-'ulum*, 75/239.
44. Ibn Hazm, *Maratib al-'ulum*, 71/237.
45. For the development and place of logic in Muslims scholarship, see Rescher, *Development,* and his *Studies;* Madkour, *Organon;* Grunebaum, *Logic,*
46. Nashshar, *Manahij,* 181ff; and Rosenthal, *Legacy,* 75.
47. This point is discussed at some length in his *Maratib al-'ulum*.
48. In his *Taqrib,* 200, Ibnn Hazm states: "We composed this book of ours and many others while we were in exile and far away from the homeland, family and offspring." This could not have taken place during his first exile (1023-25) while he was still young. Cf. his *Tawq,* 251. It is likely that he composed it during his second exile that took place in 1025, after which he returned to Cordova in 1029 remaining until 1035 when he was exiled for the third time never to return to his native Cordova.
49. See below, note 131.
50. Mainly, Sa'id, *Tabaqat,* 101; Ibn Hayyan as quoted by Ibn Bassam, *Dhakhirah,* I:ii, 140; and Ibn Sa'id, *Mughrib,* I, 354.
51. Mainly, Yaqut, *Irshad,* V, 87; Dhahabi, *Siyar,* 438, who depended on Sa'id and Ibn Hayyan.
52. Ibn Hazm, *Fisal,* III, 68; V, 70.
53. Ibn Hazm, *Ihkam,* 9, 15, 17, 18, 69, 110, 314, 315, 414, 448, 492, 635, 657, 677. etc.
54. Ibn Hazm, *Tawqif,* 4ff.
55. Ibn Hazm, *Maratib al-'ulum,* 71/236, 79/241, 89/246.
56. See Madkour, *Organon,* 3; Rescher, *Development,* 15ff.
57. See S. Van Den Berg in *EI*[1] under *Mantik*.
58. The Arabic terminology of some of these titles differs among Muslim authors, who more often than not give the Greek terminology and their Arabic equivalents. This procedure was adopted by Ibn Hazm. Cf. below, notes 153ff.
59. Ibn al-Nadim, *Fihrist,* 249, credits 'Abdallah b. al-Muqaffa', the translator of the famous book of Fables, *Kalilah wa-Dimnah,* as one of the early translators of logic. However, it is likely that it was his son Muhammad. Cf. Rescher, *Development,* 93ff.

60. *Ibid.*, 294; cf. Rescher, *Development*, 103ff.
61. *Ibid.*, 285; cf. Rescher, *Development*, 111ff.
62. *Ibid.*, 263.
63. *Ibid.*, 264; cf. Rescher, *Development*, 130ff.
64. *Ibid.*, 255; Atiyeh, *Kindi;* Rescher, *Development*, 100ff.
65. *Ibid.*, 248ff.; Rosenthal, *Sarahsi,* 54.
66. *Ibid.*, 263ff.; Rescher, *Development*, 263ff.
67. *Ibid.*, 299ff.; Rescher, *Development*, 117ff.
68. Qifti, *Tarikh,* 413ff.; Rescher, *Development,* 149ff.
69. Rescher, *Studies,* 16; Brunschwig, *Logic,* 10ff; Madkour, *Organon,* 16.
70. Sa'id, *Tabaqat,* 88.
71. *Ibid.*, 107. Cf. Rescher, *Development,* 135ff.
72. *Ibid.*, 91. Cf. Rescher, *Development,* 144ff.
73. *Ibid.*, 87.
74. *Ibid.*, 103.
75. *Ibid.*, 98.
76. *Ibid.*, 98ff.
77. Ibn Hazm, *Fadl,* 175.
78. On Ibn Fathun (d. ca. 1010), see Humaydi, *Judhwah,* no. 478; Sa'id, *Tabaqat,* 92; Dabbi, *Bughyah,* no. 813; Rescher, *Development* 143.
79. On Ibn al-Kattani, see Humaydi, *Judhwah,* no. 35; Ibn Juljul *Tabaqat,* 109; Dabbi, *Bughyah,* no. 81.
80. Humaydi, *Judhwah, no. 813.*
81. Ibn Hazm, *Maratib al-'ulum,* 83.
82. Ibn Hazm, *Fadl,* 175.
83. Cf. note 28.
84. Ibn Juljul, *Tabaqat,* 113.
85. *Ibid.*, 110.
86. Humaydi, *Judhwah,* no. 148, mentions him as a famous poet.
87. *Ibid.*, no. 149.
88. Sa'id, *Tabaqat,* 108. There are also: Abu-l-Hasan 'Abd al-Rahman b. Khalaf b. 'Asakir al-Darimi (d. 1070) and the physician Abu 'Uthman Sa'id b. Muhammad b. Baghunish (d. 1052). See Rescher, *Development,* 164 and 148.
89. See Nashshar, *Manahij,* 89ff.; van Ess, *Theology,* 21ff.
90. Ibn Khaldun, *Muqaddimah,* III, 115, states the problem succinctly saying that "theology merely wants to fight heretics."
91. Ibn Hazm, *Taqrib,* 197; cf. Ibn Rushd, *Fasl,* 63ff.; Ghazzali, *Munqidh,* 68ff.
92. Ibn Hazm, *Taqrib,* 198. This attempt of putting logic at the service of theology is often credited to al-Ghazzali. Cf. Madkour, *Organon,* 263ff.
93. Tawhidi, *Imta',* I, 105-128, preserves the text of the debate, which is analyzed by Mahdi, *Language,* 51ff.
94. *Ibid.*, 109; cf. Mahdi, *Language,* 81.
95. 'Amiri, *I'lam,* 89ff; cf. Rosenthal, *Legacy,* 67ff.
96. Nashshar, *Manahij,* 181ff. Ibn al-Salah al-Shafi'i (d. 1245), *Fatawa* 35, gave the following reply to the question of whether occupation with logic is permissible: "Logic is an introduction *(madkhal)* to philosophy; thus, the introduction to evil is evil, making occupation in teaching and learning it not condoned by God, or anyone of the Companions." Subsequently, the great reformer Ibn Taymiyyah devoted his *Radd* refuting logicians. Cf. Rescher, *Development,* 40ff. Nashshar, *Manahij,* 191ff.

97. Judging by the enormous number of titles on the secular sciences attributed to al-Kindi, it is unlikely that he would have omitted logic from his classification of the sciences.
98. Khuwarizmi, *Mafatih*, 140ff.
99. Farabi, *Ihsa'*, 7.
100. Ikhwan al-Safa', *Rasa'il*, I, 204.
101. Khuwarizmi, *Mafatih*, 130. Cf. Madkour, *Organon*, 49ff.
102. Farabi, *Ihsa'*, 22.
103. As translated by Rosenthal, *Legacy*, 69.
104. As translated by Rescher, *Studies*, 9.
105. *Ibid.*, 59.
106. Mainly his *Shifa'*, *Najah*, and *Danesh Nameh*. For Ibn Sina's approach to logic, see Madkour, *Organon*.
107. Ibn Sina, *Danesh-Nameh*, I, 25.
108. Ghazzali, *Maqasid* (leiden, 1888), 6. In His *Mustasfa*, I, 10, al-Ghazzali says: "One cannot rely absolutely on the knowledge of the one who did not master logic." Cf. Jabre, *Certitude*, 97ff.
109. Ibn Hazm, *Taqrib*, 5.
110. *Ibid.*, 9, 10, 35, 78.
111. *Ibid.*, 6.
112. *Ibid.*, 8.
113. *Ibid.*, 32, 44, 46, 50, 81. Ibn Taymiyyah, *Radd*, 131, suggests that Ibn Hazm followed Matta b. Yunus.
114. *Ibid.*, 9, 10, 35, 78.
115. *Ibid.*, 8.
116. *Ibid.*, 115ff.
117. *Taqlid, qiyas,* and other methods used in jurisprudence remained anathema to Ibn Hazm's Zahirite doctrine. See his *Ibtal;* and *Ihkam*, 798ff.
118. Ibn Hazm, *Taqrib*, 202.
119. Ibn Hazm, *Maratib al-'ulum*, 79/241.
120. *Ibid.*, 71/236; cf. his *Fisal*, I, 4.
121. *Ibid.*, 72.
122. Ibn Hazm, *Taqrib*, 186.
123. *Ibid.*, 10.
124. Ibn Hazm, *Maratib al'ulum*, 89/246.
125. Ibn Hazm, *Taqrib*, 3ff.
126. *Ibid.*, 6. Ibn Hazm reiterates the same point in his *Fisal*, II, 95 and his *Tawqif*, 41.
127. *Ibid*, 6ff.
128. *Ibid.*, 7.
129. *Ibid.*, 9. His categorization of people according to their ability is reiterated in his *Tawqif*, 36.
130. Cf. above, note 5.
131. *Taqrib*, 27, 65, 180, 202.
132. *Fisal*, I, 47, III, 68, 90; V, 70.
133. Cf. above, notes 9, 10, 11, and 12.
134. Humaydi, *Judhwah*, no. 708.
135. Sa'id, *Tabaqat*, 101.
136. As quoted by Ibn Bassam, *Dhakhirah*, I:ii, 140.
137. Ibn Sa'id, *Mughrib*, I, 354.

138.	Yaqut, *Irshad*, V, 87.
139.	Qifti, *Tarikh*, 232-233.
140.	Ibn Khallikan, *Wafayat*, III, 13-14.
141.	Dhahabi, *Siyar*, 438.
142.	For instance, C. van Arendonk in EI[1] under Ibn Hazm; and Nashshar, *Manahij*, 81.
143.	For instance, Madkour, *Organon*, 243; and Jabre, *Certitude*, 108. Both of their works were written before the edition of the *Taqrib*. On the other hand, Asin Palacios, *Abenhazam*, I, 250, considers Ibn Hazm the precursor of al-Ghazzali, although he suggests that Ibn Hazm may have modeled his *Taqrib* after the works of Ibn Sina.
144.	Cf. above, notes 66 to 72.
145.	*Taqrib*, 12.
146.	*Ibid.*, 15.
147.	*Ibid.*, 17.
148.	*Ibid.*, 17. Ibn Hazm appears to have composed a separate treatise on the subject of definition and description.
149.	*Ibid.*, 20, *jawhar* corresponds to the *jins al-ajnas* of al-Khuwarizmi, *Mafatih*, 141. Ibn Hazm, Ibid, 44ff, deals with it at great length when discussing the ten expressions of the *Categories* and considers it the principal expression, being the rest mere ancillaries.
150.	*Ibid.*, 31.
151.	*Ibid.*, 20. The term *ashkhas* was already used by the Brethren of Purity, *Rasa'il*, I:1, 3313 in addition to Porphyry's *quinque voce*. Cf. Madkour, *Organon*, 74.
152.	*Ibid.*, 32-34.
153.	*Ibid.*, 67. Khuwarizmi, *Mafatih*, 143ff., uses the following corresponding expressions; *jawhar, kamm, kayf, idafah, mata, ayna, wad'/nusbah, lahu, yanfa'il*, and *yaf'al*. Cf. Ibn Hazm, *Ibid.*, 23.
154.	*Ibid.*, 75.
155.	*Ibid.*, 75.
156.	*Ibid.*, 79.
157.	The term *khabar* in the sense of a "proposition" appears to have been used prior to the time of Ibn Hazm. Cf. Rescher, *Studies*, 35; and van Ess, *Theology*, 30.
158.	Ibn Hazm, *Taqrib*, 39.
159.	Cf. Khuwarizmi, *Mafatih*, 146, who calls it *qadiyah salibah*.
160.	*Ibid.*, 146, calls it *qadiyah mahsurah*.
161.	It should be pointed out that the discussion of propositions falls under *Qiyas* (Analytics). Cf. Khuwarizmi, *Mafatih*, 149. Also, Ibn Hazm, *Taqrib*, 106ff discusses them in the Book of *burhan*.
162.	Ibn Hazm, *Taqrib*, 105.
163.	*Ibid.*, 106.
164.	*Ibid.*, 106.
165.	*Ibid.*, 117ff.
166.	*Ibid.*, 124ff.
167.	*Ibid.*, 145ff.
168.	*Ibid.*, 149ff.
169.	*Ibid.*, 158.
170.	*Ibid.*, 161.
171.	*Ibid.*, 162ff.
172.	*Ibid.*, 165.

173. *Ibid.,* 166. Cf. van Ess, *Theology,* 34ff. Prior to Ibn Hazm, theologians appear to have inferred the "hidden" from the "visible" *(al-istidlal bi-l-shahid 'ala al-gha'ib)* as an extension of analogy *qiyas* to which Ibn Hazm addresses himself in vehement terms.
174. *Ibid.,* Ibn Hazm, *Ibid.,* 162, also rejects the vicious circle *(burhan al-dawr)* and the definition of the unknown on the basis of the unknown *(bayan al-majhul fi-l-majhul).*
175. *Ibid.,* 167ff.
176. *Ibid.,* 169. Cf. van Ess, *Theology,* 34ff., Nashshar, *Manāhij,* 88.
177. *Ibid.,* 171.
178. *Ibid.,* 172.
179. *Ibid.,* 173.
180. *Ibid.,* 173ff.
181. *Ibid.,* 176ff.
182. *Ibid.,* 182ff.
183. *Ibid.,* 183.
184. Cf. above, note 47. This section on *disputatio* constitutes, on the whole a veritable treatise on the conduct *(adab)* of disputants.
185. Ibn Hazm, *Taqrib,* 185ff. Cf. note 49. Such investigation *(bahth)* requires that the individual study all views, opinions, the natures of things, and the different proofs presented. *(Ibid.,* 197(
186. *Ibid.,* 185.
187. *Ibid.,* 190.
188. *Ibid.,* 195ff. He argues that reputable authorities can err.
189. Qudamah b. Ja'far (d. 848), a rhetorician and author of various works among which is the *Naqd al-nathr.* Cf. *EI.*
190. Hasan al-Basri (d. 728) was a noted ascetic and theologian. Cf. *EI.*
191. Sahl b. Harun (d. 830) was a famous prose writer. Cf. *EI.*
192. 'Abdallah b. al-Muqaffa' (d. 757) was prominent prose-writer and translator of of the famous book of fables, *Kalilah wa-Dimnah.*
193. Ibn Shuhayd (d. 1034) was a close friend of Ibn Hazm, and wrote a book of rhetoric, which Ibn Hazm confesses not to have seen. (Cf. Ibn Hazm, *Taqrib,* 204).
194. Ibn Hazm, *Taqrib,* 204.
195. *Ibid.,* 207.
196. Rescher, *Studies,* 30.
197. Khuwarizmi, *Mafatih,* 145ff. Cf. Rescher, *Studies,* 64ff.
198. Farabi, *Ihsa',* 46-50.
199. Ibn al-Nadim, *Fihrist,* 248.
200. Rescher, *Studies,* 35, considers *khabar* as a seemingly obsolete Arabic equivalent of the Greek *logos apophantikos,* i.e., Proposition.
201. Farabi, *Ihsa',* 50.
202. Ibn Hazm, *Taqrib,* 185ff., cf. also his *Ihkam,* 19ff.
203. *Ibid.,* 81.
204. *Ibid.,* 106.
205. *Ibid.,* 52 and 54. He also remarks *(Ibid., 63)* that Latin makes distinction between the present and future tenses, whereas Arabic ordinarily does not.
206. *Ibid.,* 92.
207. *Ibid.,* 95. For one, Madkour, *Organon,* 243, credits al-Ghazzali for the coinage of *'amm* and *khass.* Cf. Ghazzali, *Mihakk,* 30.
208. Ibn Hazm, *Radd,* 10.

209. Ibn Hazm, *Fisal*, II, 95.
210. Cf. above, note 100. It should be added that the nexus of Ibn Hazm and al-Ghazzali cannot be ruled out since al-Ghazzali himself acknowledges Ibn Hazm's authority with respect to the beautiful names of God. See al-Ghazzali, *Maqsad*, 126; Dhahabi, *Siyar*, 402. One may add that Ibn Taymiyyah, *Radd*, 131-132, mentions Ibn Hazm's involvement in logic.
211. Ibn Bajjah wrote among other things Commentaries of al-Farabi's Commentaries on logic. See Brockelmann, *GAL*, I, 460; Rescher, *Development*, 171ff.
212. The philosopher-physician Ibn Tufayl does not appear to have written on logic. However, his *Hayy Ibn Yaqzan* cover the whole intellectual process where the intellect plays a most important role in perceiving the truth.
213. Ibn Rushd wrote Commentaries on the *Organon* and the *Eisagoge*, and other works bearing on logic. Cf. Rescher, *Development*, 177ff.
214. Among other Andalusians, who concerned themselves with logic may be cited: Abu-l-Salt (d. 1134) of Denia, author of the *Taqwim* on logic (Cf. Rescher, *Development*, 167ff.); Ibn Tumlus (d. 1223), author of *Madkhal*, who lamented the negligence of logic in al-Andalus, and defended it in a language similar to that used by Ibn Hazm. (Cf. Rescher, *Development*, 188ff.); and the mystic Ibn Sab'in (d. 1270). Cf. Rescher, *Development*, 201ff.
215. Cf. Chejne, *Muslim Spain*, 319. It is interesting to note that in his *Madkhal*, Ibn Tumlus does not make any mention of Ibn Hazm nor of any of his Andalusian predecessors. Instead, he gives the impression that logic was totally unknown in al-Andalus and that he came to discover it on his own. However, he acknowldges his indebtedness to al-Farabi and al-Ghazzali. The gist of Ibn Tumlus; claim follows: the majority of the disciplines had been overworked, so that he wanted to write about something which has not been treated before. After much research, he discovered that logic was the neglected subject among the various disciplines. In fact, people dissassociated themselves from it because of fear of being accused of heresy; he could not find anyone around who was familiar with the subject, except those who denigrated it without even knowing one single letter of logic. This state of affairs prompted him to pursue the discipline and find out by himself its nature and purpose. He soon discovered that logic is one of the noble sciences deserving of study and a manual that will be available to all who are concerend with the truth.

CHAPTER IX.
THE SPURIOUS SCIENCES.

1. Ibn Hazm, *Maratib al-'ulum*, 59/231; cf. Chejne, *Muslim Spain*, 169-170.
2. *Ibid.*, 60/231.
3. For a general treatment of music, see Erlanger, *Musique*; and Farmer, *History*. It should be pointed out that Ibn Hazm's predecessors and contemporaries considered music an integral part of the mathematical sciences and wrote voluminous works on it. The philosopher al-Kindi wrote three treatises on it (see Atiyeh, *Kindi*, 169) and probably included it in the division of the sciences which he classified. He was followed by his pupil al-Sarakhsi, who is reported to have written four treatises on the subject. They were followed by al-Farabi and other Muslim thinkers.
4. Jabir Ibn Hayyan, who flourished in the second half of the eighth century, was an early proponent of alchemy. A number of works are attributed to him. On him, see Kraus, *Jabir*. Cf. Mieli, *Science*, 59ff., and Ruska, *Alchemister*.

5. Rosenthal, *Heritage*, Chapter XI.
6. Ibn Khaldun, *Muqaddimah*, III, 112, lists the philosophical sciences as being seven: logic, mathematics, geometry, astronomy, music, physics, and metaphysics. Ibn Hazm's predecessors such as al-Farabi, the Brethren of Purity and al-Khuwarizmi made ample provision for music under the general heading of mathematics. On the other hand, al-Ghazzali appears to overlook it in his *Ihya'*, but includes it in his *Ladunniyyah*, 30, under the mathematical sciences. Cf. above, Chapter V, notes 11ff.
7. Ibn Hazm, *Maratib al-'ulum*, 60/231.
8. Ibn Hazm, *Ghina'* in *Rasa'il*, 93-101. On the question of the legitimacy or illegitimacy of music in general in Muslim society, see Ibn 'Abd Rabbihi, *'Iqd*, VI, 43ff; Farmer, *History*, 20ff.
9. Ibn Hazm, *Muhalla*, nos. 500 and 553.
10. *Ibid.*, nos. 553 and 1565.
11. *Ibid.*, no. 1565.
12. *Ibidem*.
13. *Ibid.*, no. 144.
14. *Ibid.*, no. 32.
15. It is interesting to note that al-Farabi does not include alchemy in his *Inventory of the Sciences*. The Brethren of Purity mention it along with magic and incantation, but under the general heading of belles-lettres; al-Khuwarizmi calls it a craft, but includes it under the foreign sociences, and Ibn al-Nadim places it among night chats, magic, and fables.
16. Ibn Khaldun, *Muqaddimah*, III, 228. For Ibn Bishrun's *Risalah*, see Ibn Khaldun, *Muqaddimah*, III, 230-245.
17. Ibn Hazm, *Maratib al-'ulum*, 60/231,
18. Ibn Khaldun, *Muqaddimah*, III, 227ff.
19. *Ibid.*, III, 245.
20. *Ibidem*. Ibn Khaldun says that it is only in miracles that a change in the essence of things takes place. Cf. Chapter VI, notes 31ff.
21. Ibn Khaldun, *Muqaddimah*, III, 267.
22. *Ibid.*, III, 270.
23. *Ibid.*, III, 274.
24. Ibn Hazm, *Maratib al-'ulum*, 79. Ibn Hazm appears to follow the practice of his predecessors in considering astronomy and astrology together.
25. See Atiyeh, *Kindi*, 188ff., cf. Khuwarizmi, *Mafatih*, 225.
26. Farabi, *Ihsa'*, 66.
27. Ibn Hazm, *Tawqif*, 45.
28. Ibn Hazm, *Fisal*, I, 96/II, 164ff.; V, 36/V, 186.
29. *Ibid.*, V, 37/ V, 189.
30. *Ibid.*, V,. 38/ V, 190.
31. *Ibidem*.
32. Ibn Hazm, *Maratib al-'ulum*, 68-69/235-236.
33. **Ibn Hazm**, *Fisal,* V, 38ff./V, 191ff.
34. Ibn Hazm, *Maratib al-'ulum*, 68/235.
35. Ibn Khaldun, *Muqaddimah*, III, 112.
36. *Ibid.*, III, 116ff.
37. *Ibid.*, III, 258.
38. *Ibid.*, III, 260.

39. *Ibid.*, III, 261.
40. *Ibid.*, III, 262ff.
41. *Ibid.*, III, 263ff.
42. The inclusion of magic *(sihr)*, talisman *(tilasmat)*, dreams *(manamat)*, and vision —*ru'ya)* under one heading may be justified by the assumption of Arabic authors that all of them, including prophecy and miracles (cf. above, Chapter VI, notes 31ff.), are concerned with the perception of the unseen. From antiquity, the world of spirtis consisting of Gods and other ethereal beings were the object of both magic and religion and hence were the concern of magicians, soothsayers, and prophets. In fact, reference to magic and to persons possessed by jinns, particularly soothsayers and poets, abound in the Qur'an and Traditions. Cf. Qur'an 2:102; 5:110; 7:6; 10:76, etc.)
43. The suggestion that Muhammad was possessed by a jinn and that he was under a magical spell caused spirited deliberations among Qur'anic commentators, theologians, philologists, and philosophers. As a result, magic, talismans, dreams visions, and their ancillaries were included among the "sciences." However, there was no agreement among scholars as to the place they should occupy in the hierarchy of the sciences — some scholars deleted them altogether, whereas others assigned them a place among the sciences. For instance, al-Farabi overlooked them in his *Ihsa'*, and so did al-Khuwarizmi in his *Mafatih*. On the other hand, Bretheren of Purity *(Rasa'il,* I, 266ff. ch. above, Chapter V, note 19) included magic and talisman among the practical sciences and dream interpretation among the religious sciences. Ibn al-Nadim, *Fihrist,* 308ff. included divination, magic, and astrology among night chats and fables, giving several titles on the subject of magic and incantation. The theologian al-Ghazzali, *Ihya',* I, 15 and 16, included magic, talisman and juggling among the religious sciences, but labeled them as blameworthy. However, al-Ghazzali did not discourage people from having a knowledge of them, on the ground that knowledge will enable the individual to distinguish them from miracles. Finally, Ibn Khaldun, *Muqaddimah,* II, 6, included magic and alchemy among the philosophical sciences, but reserved separate and ample sections for their refutation. For magic *(sihr)* and talismans, see *SEI* under *sihr* and *hama'il*; MacDonald, *Attitude,* 95ff. Also, Thorndike, *History.*
44. Ibn Hazm, *Muhalla*, no. 68. It is obvious that Ibn Hazm wanted to make a clear distinction between magic and talisman, on the one hand, and prophecy and miracles, on the other. To him, prophecy and miracles are divine instruments of unquestionable validity and should not be exposed to the encroachment of magicians and soothsayers.
45. Ibn Hazm, *Fisal,* V, 2-12/V, 147-168.
46. *Ibid.*, V,4/V, 151ff. Talisman has been in common use among the Islamic peoples for centuries, and had serious implications for religious beliefs and practices. It consists of the use of amulets in the form of shells, bones, astrological symbols, or letters; objects on which are ordinarily inscribed prayers, verses of the Qur'an or holy names; and figurines of all sort. Amulets, as Ibn Hazm is inclined to concede, are supposed to fulfill one's wishes for either gaining a favor or averting a disaster.

    Several treatises on talisman were written by Muslims. Maslamah al-Majriti (d. ca. 1007) is said to have dealt with the subject. Cf. Ibn al-Nadim, *Fihrist,* 308ff.
47. *Ibid.*, V,5/V, 153.
48. *Ibid.*, V,6/V, 156.
49. Although Ibn Hazm does not include visions *(ru'ya)* and dream interpretation *('ilm al-'ibarah)* among the principal sciences, he does say that dream interpretation, like rhetoric (see Chapter V, note 87) is the result of two or more sciences. Inasmuch as dreams *(manamat)* and visions have a bearing on the intercourse

with the unseen, particularly with good spirits and divine inspration, they occupied the attention of a goodly number of Muslim authors. The Brethren of Purity, *Rasa'il* I, 202, list dream interpreation *('ilm ta'wil al-manamat)* under the religious sciences, and Ibn Khaldun, *Muqaddimah*, I, 194ff., refers to them as *'ilm tafsir al-ru'ya* and places them with prophecy and soothsayings under one heading. To him, as to Ibn Hazm, dreams and visions have a reality of their own, since they had been experienced by prophets and other venerable men of Islam. For works on the subjects of dreams and visions, see Ibn al-Nadim, *Fihrist*, 316ff.; Band in *JRAS*, XVI, 153. Cf. MacDonald, *Attitude*, 77ff.

50. Ibn Hazm, *Maratib al-'ulum*, 82/242. Also, his *Taqrib*, 203, where Ibn Hazm says that the source of dream interpretation is derived from things related by the Messenger of God and by virtuous men who had had experience in this science. No doubt Ibn Hazm was influenced by the strength of various Traditions supporting the validity of dreams and visions.

The *Mishkat al-masabih*, III, 962ff., a compendium of Traditions comprising some of the traditions transmitted by the traditionists al-Bukhari, Muslim, al-Tirmidhi, and others, contains several traditions attributed to the Prophet. The gist of some are: "He who sees me in a dream has seen me"; "A good vision comes from God and a dream *(hulm)* from the devil", "When the last hour draws near, a believer's vision can hardly be false. A believer's vision is a forty sixth part of prophecy, and what pertains to prophecy cannot be false."

51. Ibn Hazm, *Fisal*, V, 19-20/V, 180-182.
52. Ibn Khaldun, *Muqaddimah*, III, 159.
53. *Ibid.*, III, 169.
54. *Ibid.*, III, 170.
55. *Ibid.*, III, 156.
56. *Ibid.*, III, 157.
57. *Ibid.*, III, 159.
58. *Ibidem*.
59. *Ibid.*, III, 160.
60. *Ibid.*, III, 161.
61. *Ibid.*, III, 161.
62. *Ibid.*, III, 163.
63. *Ibid.*, III, 167.
64. *Ibid.*, III, 103-110.

CHAPTER X
IBN HAZM'S MARATIB AL'ULUM:
THE MANUSCRIPT

1. See Chapter V, notes 76ff.
2. Humaydi, *Judhwah,* no. 708; Dabbi, *Bughyah,* 1204; Ibn Khallikan, *Wafayat,* III, 13; Hajji Khalifah, *Kashf,* no. 11750.
3. Asin, *Abenhazam,* I, 247-248.
4. Asin, *Codice.*
5. *Ibid.,* 46-56.
6. 'Abbas, *Rasa'il.*
7. Mu'nis, *Classificacion.*
8. Chejne, *Muslim Spain,* 168-174.
9. Rosenthal, *Heritage,* 58-61.
10. Cf. Khuwarizmi, *Mafatih,* 242. *Lawiyy* refers probably to war songs.
11. *Ibid.,* 243. *Taniniyy* is probably soft music or "humming." Cf. Lane, under *tanin.*
12. See Chapter Vii, note 101.
13. See Chapter VII, note 102.
14. Sibawayh (d. ca. 800) was a leading grammarian.
15. See Chapter VII, 104.
16. See Chapter VII, note 105.
17. See Chapter VII, note 106.

18. See Chapter VII, note 107.
19. Abu 'Ali al-Qali (d. 967) was an emigre from Baghdad who settled at the court of 'Abd al-Rahman III and excelled in philology and belles-lettres.
20. See Chapter VIII, note 108.
21. See Chapter VII, note 39.
22. See Chapter VII, note 40.
23. See Chapter VII, note 41.
24. See Chapter VII, note 42.
25. See Chapter III, note 44.
26. See Chapter VII, note 45.
27. See Chapter VII, note 46.
28. The *Almagest* was the work of Ptolemy.
29. See Chapter III, note 45.
30. It is his *Fisal.* See above.
31. This view contrasts with that held by Ibn Khaldun, *Muqaddimah,* III, 288ff., who viewed the superabundance of books as detrimental to learning.
32. Rosenthal, *Heritage,* 60, translates *batt* as "lancing boils," when actually it means opening incisions.
33. See Chapter III, note 41.
34. *Qur'an,* 5:3.

LIST OF PERIODICALS

AJSLL.	American Journal of Semitic Languages and Literature
Andalus.	Al-Andalus.
BEO.	Bulletin d'etudes orientales.
BH.	Bulletin Hispanique.
BRAH.	Boletin de la Real Academia de Historia de Madrid.
BSOAS.	Bulletin of the School of Oriental and African Studies.
BUG.	Boletin de la Universidad de Granada.
CE.	Cultura Espanola.
EI.	Encyclopedia of Islam (4 vols., Leiden, 1913-1914; 2nd ed., Leiden, 1954—
Hesperis.	
IC.	Islamic Culture.
IO.	Islam et Occident.
Islamica.	
IS.	Islamic Studies.
JA.	Journal Asiatique.
JAOS.	Journal of the American Oriental Society.
JNES.	Journal of Near Eastern Studies.
JQR.	Jewish Quarterly Review.
JRAS.	Journal of the Royal Asiatic Society.
Majma'.	Majallat al-majma' al-'ilmi al-'arabi (Damascus).
MS.	Medieval Studies.
MW.	Muslim World.
REI.	Revue des etudes islamiques.
RH.	Revue hispanique.
RIEEI.	Revista del Instituto de Estudioes Islamicos (Madrid)
RIEI.	Revista del Instituto de Estudios Islamicos (Madrid).
RO.	Revista de Occidente.
RT.	Revue Thomiste.
SEI.	Shorter Encyclopedia of Islam (Cornell, 1953).
SI.	Studia Islamica.
Speculum.	
ZDMG.	Zeitschrift der Deutschen Morgenlandischen Geseltschaft.

APPENDIX

THE WORKS OF IBN HAZM

(1) *'Adad:*   *'Adad ma li-kull sahib fi musnad Baqi* (the Number [of Traditions] of Each Transmitter as They Appear in the *Musnad* of Baqi).*
Dhahabi, *Siyar,* 436.
*Baqi Ibn Makhlad (d. 886) whom Ibn Hazm admires as religious scholar.

(2) *Adwiyah:*   *Kitab fi-l-adwiyah al-mufradah* (Book of Simple Drugs)
Dhahabi, *Siyar,* 436.

(3) *Ihkam:*   *Ahkam al-din* (The Dicta of Religion)
Ibn Hazm, *Taqrib,* 97.

(4) *Ahl al-shaqa':*   *Risalah 'an hukm man qala inna arwah ahl al-shaqā' al-mu'adhdhibah ila yawm al-din* (Treatise Concerning the Decision of Those Who Maintain That the Souls of Wretched People Continue to Suffer Until the Day of Judgment). Cf. Asin, *Codice,* 24-25.
Afghani, *Ibn Hazm,* 56.
Ibn Hazm, *Fisal,* III, 83, has *Baqa' Ahl al-Jannah wa-l-Nar Abadan* (The Eternal Duration of the People of Paradise and Hell). These two titles may refer to the same work. Cf.
(Arwah (11)

(5) *Ajwibah:*   *Ajwibah* (Replies)
Afghani, *Ibn Hazm,* 51.

(6) *Akhlaq:*   *al-Akhlaq wa-l-siyar* (Character and Conduct), Cairo, 1908. Spanish Translation b. M. Asin Palacios, Madrid, 1961;
Edited with French Translation by N. Tomiche, Beirut, 1961. Tomiche's edition is being used.

The work appears to be the same as the one entitled *Risalah fi mudawat al-nufus wa-tahdhib al-akhlaq wa-l-zuhd fi-l-radha'il* (Treatise for the Cure of the Soul and the Education of Character and Frowning on Vices), ed. by I. 'Abbas in *Rasa'il,* 113-173, among others (Cairo, 1913; and 1962; and Medina, 1975). Cf. *Siyar* (122a) below; Asin, *Codice,* 18; Nykl, *Treatise.*

(7) *Akhlaq al-nafs/*   *Akhlaq al-nafs* (The Characters of the Soul).
Ibn Hazm, *Taqrib,* 72, 180, 181.
Yaqut, *Irshad,* V, 95.
Afghani, *Ibn Hazm,* 51
This work may be the same as the preceding.

(8) *Alam:*   *Risalah fi alam al-mawt,* in *Rasa'il,* 103-106. Cf. Asin, *Codice,* 20-24; Afghani *Ibn Hazm,* 57, has *hal al-mawt alam am la.*

(9) *Anajil:*   *Ta'lif fi-l-radd 'ala anajil al-nasara* (A Composition Refuting the Gospels of the Christians).
Dhahabi, *Siyar,* 436.

(10) *'Arud:*   *Kitab fi-l-'arud* (A Book on Prosody).
Dhahabi, *Siyar,* 436, has *Shay' fi-l-'arud* (Something on Prosody).

(11) *Arwah:*   *Risalah fi arwah al-ashqiya'* (Treatise Concerning the Souls of Wretched People). It is mentioned by 'Abbas in *Rasa'il,* and may be identical with *Ahl al-shaqa'* mentioned bove (4).

(12) *Ashab:*   *Ashab al-futya min al-Sahabah wa-man ba'dahum* (People of Expert Legal opinions from among the Companions and Those Who Followed Them). In *Jawami',* 319-335.

(13) *Asma' al-khulafa':*   *Asma', al-khulafa' wa-l-wulah* (The Names of Caliphs and Governors), in *Jawami',* 353-381

(14) *Asma' Allah;*   *Asma' Allah al-husna* (The Beautiful Names of God) Dhahabi, *Tadhkirah,* 3:1147

(15) *Asma' al-Sahabah:*   *Asma' al-Sahabah wa-l-ruwah wa-ma li-kull minhum min al-ahadith* (The Names of Companions and Transmitters and the Traditions Attributed to Each of Them), in *Jawami',* 275-315

(16) *Athar:*   *Kitab al-athar al-lati zahiruh a al-ta-'arrud wa-nafi al-tanaqudd 'anha* (The Book of Extant Traditions That Contracited each other and Those Which Did Not). Dhahabi, *Siyar,* 433, says that it consisted of 15,000 folios, and the work was still incomplete.

(17) *Bulghah:*   *Bulghat al-hakim* (The Competency of the Physician) Dhahabi, *Siyar,* 436

(18) *Dhikr:*   *Dhikr awqat al-umara' wa-ayyamihim bi-l-Andalus* (A Narrative of the Time and Days of the Emirs of al-Andalus).
'Abbas, *Ibn al-Naghrilah,* 5.

(19) *Diwan:*   *Diwan* (Poetical Collection) compiled by his pupil al-Humaydi, *Judhwah,* no. 708, 309.

(20) *Durrah:*   *Al-Durrah fima yalzam al-muslim (The Pearl Dealing with What is Expected of a Muslim).*
Ibn Hazm, Muhalla, no. 54
Dhahbi, *Siyar,* 435. Asin, *Codice,* 7-8.

(21) *Fada'ih:*   *al-Fada'ih* (The Scandals) presumably referring to the revolts of the Berbers, and other lawlessness.
'Abbas, *Ibn al-Naghrilah,* 5.

(22) *Fada'il:*   *Risalah fi fada' il al-Andalus wa-dhikr rajaliah* (Treatise Dealing with the Merits of al-Andalus and Narration about Its Men), in Maqqari, *Nafh,* III, 156-179. French translation by Pellat in *Al-Andalus,* 19(1954), 53-102.

(23) *Fahrasah:*   *Fahrasat shuyukh Ibn Hazm* (The List of Ibn Hazm's Teachers).
Ibn Khayr, *Fahrasah,* 429.
Cf. Asin, *Abenhazam,* I, 272.

(24) *Fara'id:*   *Kitab al-Fara'id* (The Book of Religious Duties) Dhahabi, *Siyar,* 434.

(25) *Fasahah:*   *Bayan al-fasahah wa-l-balaghah* (Elucidation of Eloquence and Rhetoric).
Dhahabi, *Siyar,* 436. cf. Dayah, *Naqd,* 210.

(26) *Fisal:*   *al-Fisal fi-l-milal wa-l-ahwa' wa-l-nihal* (The Solution Concerning Religions, Sects, and Denominations). Cairo, 1347-1348 A. H. Spanish Translation by Asin Palacios, 5 Vols. Madrid, 1927-1932.
Ibn Hazm, *Ihkam,* 16, 17, 25, 36, 86, 94, 97, 129, 132,

	344, 414, 445, 453, 472, 492, 659, 1147, 1148. _____ *Taqrib,* 27, 65, 180, 202. Cf. Asin, *Abenhazam,* I, 267
(27) *Ghazawat:*	*Ghazawat al-Mansur Ibn Abi 'Amir* (The Expeditions of al-Mansur Ibn Abi'Amir). Dhahabi, *Siyar,* 436.
(28) *Ghina':*	*Risalah fi-l-ghina' al-mulhi: a-mubah hu am mahzur* (Treatise on Distracting Singing: Is It Permissible or Forbidden). Ed. by 'Abbas, in *Rasa'il,* 91-101. Cf. *Sima'* (121) below. Asin, *Codice,* 25-26.
(29) *Hadd:*	*al-Hadd wa-l-rasm* (On Definition and Designation). Dhahabi, *Siyar,* 436
(30) *Hadd al-tibb:*	*Kitab hadd al-tibb* (Book of the Definition of Medicine) Dhahabi, *Siyar,* 436
(31) *Hatif:*	*Risalah fi-l-radd 'ala hatif min bu'd* (Treatise refuting the Invisible Caller Shouting from Far Away). Ed. by 'Abbas, in *Rasa'il,* 5-17; cf. Asin, *Codice,* 13-15.
(32) *Hijjah:*	*Hijjat al-wada'* (The Farewell Pilgrimage). Ed. by Mamduh Haqqi, Damascus, 1959; second edition Beirut, 1966. Dhahabi, *Siyar,* 433, says it has 120. folios. Cf. Asin, *Abenhazam,* I, 263.
(33) *Hudad:*	*al-Hudud* (On Definitions). Afghani, *Ibn Hazm,* 55. It may be the same *al-Hadd wa-l-rasm* (29)
(34) *Ibn Hafsun:*	*Risalah fi dhalika (al-fasahah wa-l-balaghah) li-Ibn Hafsun** (Treatise Concerning That Eloquence and Rhetoric) of Ibn Hafsun). Dhahabi, *Siyar,* 436. *It may refer to the rhetorical speeches of Ibn Hafsun, a ninth-tenth centuries rebel, who defied the central government.
(35) *Ibn al-Ifilli:*	*al-Radd 'ala Ibn al-Iflili fi shi'r al-Mutanabbi** (Refutation of Ibn al-Iflili Concerning the Poetry of al-Mutanabbi). Mentioned by *'Abbas* in *Ibn al-Naghrilah,* 5. *Ibn al-Iflili (d. 1049) was a traditional philologist of Cordova whom the poet Ibn Shuhayd redicules in his *Tawabi',* 76.
(36) *Ibn Ishaq:*	*al-Radd 'ala Ibn Ishaq* (Refutation of Ibn Ishaq)* Ibn Hazm, *Fisal,* III, 10. Cf. Khalifah, *Ibn Hazm,* 132. *Ibn Ishaq may be the same as the philosopher al-Kindi and the treatise the same as *al-Kindi* (64) below. Or, possibly his friend whom he mentions in this *Tawq,* 112, 113, 121.
(37) *Ibn al-Naghrilah:*	*al-Radd 'ala Ibn al-Naghrilah al-Yahudi* (Refutation of The Jew Ibn Naghrilah). Ed. 'Abbas in *Ibn al-Naghrilah,* Cairo, 1960. Dhahabi, *Siyar,* 435, has *al-Radd 'ala Isma'il al-Yahudi al-ladhi allafa fi tanaqud ayat al-nasa'ih al-munjiyah* (Refutation of the Jew Isma'il Who Wrote a Composi-

tion Criticizing the Qur'anic Verses Dealing with Admonitions That Lead to Salvation).
Cf. Asin, *Codice,* 13; Garcia Gomex, *Polemica.*

(38) *Ibn al-Rqwandi:* *Kitab al-tarshid fi-l-radd 'ala kitab al-farid li-Ibn Rawandi fi i'tiradih 'ala al-nubuwat** (Book of Guidance Dealing With the Refutation of the "Unique Book" of Ibn Rawandi Who Opposed Prophecies).
Dhahabi, *Siyar,* 435.

*Ibn al-Rawandi is probably Ahmad Ibn Yahya. Ibn Ishaq al-Rawandi (d. 910), author of numerous works of heretical leaning. Cf. Zirikli, *A'lam,* III, 252.

(39) *Ibtal:* *Ibtal al-qiyas wa-l-ra'y wa-l-istihsan wa-l-taqlid wa-l-ta'lil* (The Invalidation of Analogy, Personal Opinion, Preference, Imitation, and Interpretation).
Ed. by S. al-Afghani, Damascus, 1960; Beirut, 1969.
Cf. Goldziher, *Zahiriten,* who analyzed the salient points. Cf. Asin, *Abenhazam,* I, 259

(40) *Ihkam:* *al-Ihkam li-usul al-ahkam* (The Establishment of the Roots of Legal Decisions).
Printed in 8 vols. Cairo, 1345-1348 A. H. Reprinted in two volumes (Cairo, n.d.) with continuous pagination. The latter is being used.
Ibn Hazm, *Fisal,* III, 76, 254.
The work is mentioned by the majority of Ibn Hazm's biographers.

(41) *Ijma':* *Kitab al-ijma'* (Book Dealing With the Consensus).
Dhahabi, *Siyar,* 434, adds that it consists of two volumes. Humaydi, *Judhwan,* no. 708, 309, has *al-Ijma' wa-masa' iluh* (The Consensus and The Questions Pertaining Thereto).
Cf. Asin, *Abenhazam,* I, 259.

(42) *Ikhtilaf:* *Kitab ikhtilaf al-fuqaha' al-khamsah: Malik wa-Abi Hanifah wa-l-Shafi'i wa-Ahmad wa-Dawud* (The Book Dealing with the Difference Separating the Five Jurists: Malik, Abu Hanifah, al-Shafi'i, Ahmad, and Dawud).
Dhahabi, *Siyar,* 434.
This work may be identical with *Malik* (66) below.

(43) *Imamah:* *al-Imamah wa-l-mufadalah* (The Imamate and Preference).
Ibn Hazm, *Fisal,* IV, 72-129; Asin, *Codice,* 19-20.
Cf. Khalifah, *Ibn Hazm,* 130; cf. *Siyasah* (122b) below.

(44) *Iman:* *al-Bayan 'an haqiqat al-iman* (Elucidation of the Reality of Faith).
Ed. by 'Abbas, in *Rasa'il,* 19-40; cf. Asin, *Codice,* 5.
It may be the same as *Mas'alat al-iman* listed by Dhahabi, *Siyar,* 435.

(45) *I'rab:* *Kitab al-i'rab 'an al-hirah wa-l-iltibas al-mawjudayn fi madhahib ahl al-ra'y wa-l-qiyas* (The Book Showing the Confusion and Ambiguity Existing in the Schools That Advocate Personal Opinion and Analogy).
Ibn Hazm, *Ihkam,* 567; also his *Muhalla,* 9:503.
It may be the same as *Kashf* (61) below.

(46) *Isal:* *al-Isal ila fahm kitab al-khisal al-jami'ah li-mahsal shara'i' al-Islam fi-l-wajib wa-l-halal wa-l-haram* (Arriving at Understanding "The Book of Properties" Comprising the Way for Arriving at the Legal Precepts of Islam Concerning What is Obligatory, Permissible, and Forbidden).

Ibn Hazm, *Ihkam*, 456, 520, 553, 629, 814; also his *Fisal*, I, 114 and IV, 172; and *Muhalla*, I:30. It is also mentioned by the majority of his biographers, among whom Yaqut, *Irshad*, V, 90, says that it consists of twenty-four volumes. Dhahabi, *Siyar*, 433, says that the work consists of 15,000 folios. Cf. Asin, *Abenhazam*, I, 260.

(47) *Istijlab:*   *Kitab al-istijlab* (Calling Attention to). Dhahabi, *Siyar*, 435.

(48) *Istiqsa':*   *al-Istiqsa'* (Careful Examination). Afghani, *Ibn Hazm*, 51.

(49) *I'tiqad:*   *al-I'tiqad* (On belief). Dhahabi, *Siyar*, 405. Afghani, *Ibn Hazm*, 57.

(50) *Ittisal:*   *al-Ittisal* (The Link) Hajji Khalifah, *Kashf*, II:258. Cf. Afghani, *Ibn Hazm*, 51.

(51) *Izhar:*   *al-Izhar li-ma shunni'a bih 'ala al-Zahiriyyah* (Demonstrating or refuting the Repulsive Things Attributed to Zahirism) Dhahabi, *Siyar*, 435.

(52) *Jalinus:*   *Kitab ikhtisar kalam Jalinus fi-l-amrad al-haddah* (Book Summarizing the sayings of Galen Concerning Acute Diseases). Dhahabi, *Siyar*, 436.

(53) *Jamharah:*   *Jamharat ansab al-'Arab* (Collection About the Genealogy of the Arabs). Ed. by E. Levi-Provencal, Cairo, 1948; also by 'Abd al-Salam Harun, Cairo, 1962.

(55) *Jami':*   *al-Jami' fi sahih al-hadith bi-ikhtisar al-asanid wa-l-iqtisar 'ala asahhiha wa-ijtilab akmal al-faziha wa-asahh ma'aniha* (The Comprehensive Book on Sound Traditions with Abridgment of Chain of Transmission, Selection of the Most Authentic Having the Most Complete Text and the Most Precise Meaning). Mentioned by most biographers, mainly, Yaqut, *Irshad*, V, 94; Dhahabi, *Siyar*, 434, and his *Tadhkirah*, III, 1252. Cf. Asin, *Abenhazam*, I, 255-256.

(56) *Jawab:*   *Risalah fi-l-jawab 'amma su'ila 'anhu su'al ta'nif* (Treatise Responding to Questions of Rebuke). 'Abbas, in *Rasa'il*, in Introduction.

(57) *Jawami':*   *Jawami' al-sirah* (Comprehensive Information about the Life of Muhammad). Ed. I. 'Abbas, Beirut 1956

(58) *Jumal:*   *Jumal futuh al-Islam* (The Sum of the Conquests of Islam) Ed. I. 'Abbas, in *Jawami'*, 339-350.

(59) *Kalam:*   *al-Durrah fi tahqiq al-kalam* (The Pearl Dealing with Ascertaining Theological Problems). Afghani, *Ibn Hazm*, 55. 'Abbas, in Rasa'il, Introduction.

(60) *Kalb:*   *Mas'alat al-kalb* (The Question about the Dog). Afghani, *Ibn Hazm*, 57. Asin, *Codice*, 15.

(61) *Kashf:*   *Kashf al-iltibas lima bayn al-Zahiriyyah wa-ashab al-qiyas* (The Uncovering of Ambiguity between Zahirism

(62) *Khawlani:* and the Followers of Analogy).
Yaqut, *Irshad,* V, 95:
Dhahabi, *Tadhkirah,* III, 1153;
Afghani, *Ibn Hazm,* 58;
Cf. Asin, *Abenhazam,* I, 259.
Cf. above, *I'rab* (45).
al-I'tab 'ala Abi Marwan al-Khawlani (The Censure of Abi Marwan al-Khawlani).* Dhahabi, *Siyar,* 435.

*Al-Khawlani may be the same as Abu Muslim 'Abdallah Ibn Thuwab (d. 682), who was an ascetic. Cf. Zirikli, *A'lam,* IV, 203.

(63) *Khisal:* *Kitab al-khisal* (The Book of Properties).
Of unknown authorship but commented on by Ibn Hazm's *Isal* (46) above.

(64) *Kindi:* *al-Radd 'ala al-Kindi al-faylasuf* (Refutation of the Philosopher al-Kindi).
Ed. I. 'Abbas, *Ibn al-Naghrilah,* 187-235.

(65) *Majalis* (Literary Sessions). Being, according to Yaqut, *Irshad,* V, 94, minutes of some of his polemics.
V, 94, minutes of some of his polemics.

(66) *Malik:* *Kitab ma infarada bih Malik aw Abu Hanifah aw al-Shafi'i* (Book Dealing with the Differences Separating Malik, Abu Hanifah, and al-Shafi'i).
Dhahabi, *Siyar,* 434. However, Dhahabi, *Tadhkirah,* 3:1152, gives the titel *Fi-ma khalafa fih Abu Hanifah wa-Malik wa-l-Shafi i jumhur al'-ulama' wa-ma infarada bih kull wahid wa-lam yusbaq ila ma qalahu* (Concerning What Abu Hanifah, Malik, and al-Shafi'i Disagreed on with the Majority of Scholars, and Concerning the Particular Stand of Each One of Them Without Having Had a Precedent).

This work may be identical with *Ikhtilaf* (42) above.

(67) *Malikiyyah:* *Kitab fi-ma khalafa fih al-Malikiyyah al-tawa'if min al-sahabah* (Book Concerning the Differences of the Malikite School with Some of the Companions).
Ibn Hazm, *Muhalla,* under *Fara'id*
'Abbas, in *Ibn al-Naghrilah,* 5.

It may be similar if not identical in content to *Ikhtilaf* (42) and *Malik* (66) above.

(68) *Ma'na:* *Risalah fi ma'na al-fiqh wa-l-zuhd* (Treatise Dealing with the Meaning of Jurisprudence and Asceticism).
Dhahabi, *Siyar,* 435.

(69) *Manasik:* *Manasik al-hajj* (The Rites of Pilgrimage)
Cf. Asin, *Abenhazam,* I, 262-263

(70) *Maratib al-Ijma':* *Maratib al-ijma' fi-l-'ibadat wa-l-mu'amalat wa-l-i'tiqadat* (The Categories of the Consensus Concering Acts of Worship, Transaction, and Beliefs). Cairo, 1357 A.H. Ibn Hazm, *Ihkam,* 200, has *Kitab al-maratib.*

(71) *Maratib al-'ulama':* *Maratib al-'ulama' wa-tawalifihim* (The Categories of Scholars and Their Writings).
Dhahabi, *Siyar,* 435

(72) *Maratib al-'ulum:*	*Maratib al-'ulum wa-kayfiyat talabiha wa-ta'alluq ba'diha bi-ba'd* (The Categories of the Sciences, the Manner of Studying Them, and Their Relation to One Another). Ed. I. 'Abbas, in *Rasa'il,* 59-90 Cf. Asin, *Codice,* 46-56. Rabat manuscript no. 209 which is being edited here. Ordinarily, pagination in the notes refer to 'Abbas' edition and to the Rabat manuscript.
(72a) *Masa'il:*	*Masa'il usul al-fiqh.* Cairo, 1332 A.H.
(73) *Mufadalah:*	*Fi-l-mufadalah bayn al-sahabah* (On Preference among the Companions). Ed. by Afghani, Damascus, 1940.
(74) *Mughallis:*	*Mukhtasar al-muwaddah li-Abi al-Hasan al-Mughallis al-Zahiri* (Abridgment of "The Explicative" by Abu-l-Hasan al-Mughallis al-Zahiri). Dhahabi, *Siyar,* 434. *He is Abu-l-Hasan 'Abdallah Ibn Ahmad Ibn Muhammad (d. 918), follower of Dawud, the founder of the Zahirite school.
(75) *Muhalla:*	*al-Muhalla bi-l-athar fi sharh al-mujalla bi-l-ikhtisar* (The Adorned Book Regarding Extant Material Commenting in a Summary Fashion on the Book "The Exalted"). Printed in 11 vols. Cairo, 1351 A.H. Ibn Hazm, *Ihkam,* 629 Dhahabi, *Siyar,* 433, says it consists of 8 volumes.
(76) *Mujalla:*	*al-Mujalla sharh al-muhalla* (The "Exalted" Regarding the Commentary of "The Adorned One"). Ibn Hazm, *Muhalla,* 5.
(77) *Mukhtasar:*	*Mukhtasar fi 'ilal al-hadith* (Abridgment Concerning the Deficiencies of Traditions) Dhahabi, *Siyar,* 435
(78) *Muntaqa:*	*Kitab muntaqa al-ijma' wa-bayanuh min jumlat ma la yu'raf fih ikhtilaf* (Book on the Careful Examination of the Consensus and Elucidation of Those Questions in Which There Is Unanimous Agreement). Yaqut, *Irshad,* V, 94 Cf. Asin, *Abenhazam,* I, 258
(79) *Muraqabah:*	*Muraqabat ahwal al-imam min tark al-salah 'amdan* (The Censure of the Conditions of the Imam with respect to Forsaking Prayer Intentionally). Dhahabi, *Siyar,* 435. Cf. *Tarik* (123) below.
(80) *Nafs:*	*Risalah fi ma'rifat al-nafs bi-ghayriha wa-jahliha bi-dhatiha* (Treatise Concerning the Cognition of the Soul of Things Other than Itself and Its Ignorance of Itself). Ed. by 'Abbas, in *Rasa'il,* 107-111; Asin, *Codice,* 6-7.
(81) *Nasab:*	*Nasab al-Barbar* (The Genealogy of the Berber). Dhahabi, *Siyar,* 435.
(82) *Nasa'ih:*	*Kitab al-nasa'ih al-munjiyah min al-fada'ih al-mukhziyah wa-l-qaba'ih al-murdiyah min aqwal ahl al-bida' min al-firaq al-arba' al-Mu'tazilah wa-l-Murji'ah*

(83)	Nasikh:	

wa-l-Khawarij wal-l-Shi'ah (Book of Admonitions Leading to Salvation Concerning the Shameful Sandals and Abominable Ugliness in the Doctrines of Heretical People from among the Four Sects: the Mu'tazilah, The Murji'ah, The Khawarij, and The Shi'ite Groups).
Ibn Hazm, *Fisal,* II, 116 mentions its. In addition, he appears to insert it in the same work, *Fisal,* IV, 178-227. Cf. Asin, *Abenhazam,* I, 266-267

(83) Nasikh: *Ma'rifat al-nasikh wa-l-mansukh* (The Knowledge of the Abrogating and the Abrogated).
Printed on the margin of Suyuti, *Jalalayn,* Cairo, 1308-1321 A.H.

(84) *Nihal:*   *Mukhtasar al-milal wa-l-nihal* (Abridgement on Religions and Denominations).

(85) *Niqafur:*   *Jawab qasidat Niqafur za'im al-Rum al-lati wajjaha bi-ha ila al-Muti'li-Lah Amir al-Mu'minin* (Reply to the Ode of Nicephorous, Ruler of the Romans, Which He Addressed to the Commander of the Faithful, al-Muti' li-lah).
Subki, *Tabaqat,* II,. 184, where the poem is found; also Ibn Kathir, *Bidayah,* XI, 247-252.
'Abbas, *Tarikh: 'Asr Qurtubah,* 374-382

(86) *Nubadh:*   *Al-Nubadh fi usul al-fiqh al-zahiri* (Sections on the Roots of Zahirite Jurisprudence).
or
Nubdhah   Ibn Hazm, *Muhalla,* I: 54.
Ed. by Muh. Zahid al-Kawthari, Cairo, 1940.

(87) *Nuhhal:*   *Maqalat al-nuhhal* (Treatise on the Slender Person)
Dhahabi, *Siyar,* 436.

(88) *Nukat:*   *al-Nukat al-mujazah fi nafy al-ra'y wa-l-qiyas wa-l-ta'wil wal-l-taqlid* (Witty and Brief Remarks Denying Personal Opinion, Analogy, Interpretation, and Imitation).
Ibn Hazm, *Muhalla,* I:54.
Dhahabi, *Siyar,* 435; and His *Tadhkirah,* 3:1149.

(89) *Nuqat:*   *Kitab nuqat al-'arus fi akhbar al-khulafa' Bani Umayyah fi-l-Andalus* (Embroidery of the Bride Concerning the History of the Umayyad Caliphs in al-Andalus).
Ed. by C. F. Seybold in *Revista del Centro de Estudios Historicos de Granada,* 3/4(1911); also by Sh. Dayf, in *Majallat Kulliyat al-Adab* (Cairo), 3(1959); cf. Seco de Lucena, *Andalus* 6(1941), 357-375. Cf. Asin, *Abenhazam,* I, 269-272. Dayf's edition is being used here.

(90) *Qasr:*   *Qasr al-salah* (On the Brevity of Prayer).
Dhahabi, *Siyar,* 435.

(91) *Qawa'id:*   *Dhu-l-qawa'id* (The Book on the Fundaments of Jurisprudence).
Ibn Hazm, *Ihkam,* 614.
Dhahabi, *Siyar,* 434, has the lengthier title of *Kitab al-imla' fi qawa'id al-fiqh* (The Book Completing the Fundaments of Jurisprudence), which consists of a thousand folios. It is mentioned in Abu Bakr Ibn al-'Arabi's *'Awasim.*

(92) *Qira'at:*   *al-Qira'at al-mashhurah fi-l-amsar* (Famous Qur'anic Readings in the Great Metropolis).

(93) *Qismah:* Ed. 'Abbas, in *Jawami'* 269-271
Ibn Hazm, *Muhalla,* 3:253, 9:228; 10:300, has *Qira'at.*
Qismat al-khums fi-l-radd 'ala Ismail al-qadi (Apportionment of the Fifth Refuting the Judge Isma'il)* Dhahabi, *Siyar,* 433
*Isma'il was most probably the founder of the 'Abbadid dynasty in Seville (1023-1091). He died in 1023.

(94) *Qur'an:* *Risalah fi-l-Qur'an laysa min naw' balaghat al-nas* (Treatise That The Qur'an Is Not Part of Human Rhetoric)
Ibn Hazm, *Fisal,* I, 107; cf. Asin, *Abenhazam,* I, 265.

(95) *Radd:* *Kitab al-radd 'ala man i'tarada 'ala al-Fisal* (Refutation of Those Who Criticise the *Fisal*)
Dhahabi, *Siyar,* 434.

(96) *Radd 'ala:* *Kitab al-radd-'ala man kaffara al-mu' awwalin min al-muslimin* (Book Refuting Those Who Labeled Heretics Some of the Early Converts to Islam).
Dhahabi, *Siyar,* 534.

(96a) *Rasa'il:* *Rasa'il Ibn Hazm,* Ed. by I. 'Abbas, Cairo, 1952, and 1954. See content in Bibliography under 'Abbas.

(97) *Razi:* *al-Tahqiq fi naqd kitab al-'ilm al-ilahi li-Muhammad Ibn Zakariya' al-tabib* (Determination Concerning the Refutation of "The Book of Metaphysics" by the Physician Muhammad Ibn Zakariya' $_{[}$al-Razi$_1$).
Ibn Hazm, *Fisal,* I, 3, 34, and V, 70.
Dhahabi, *Siyar,* 435, has *"al-Radd 'ala Ibn Zakariya' al-Razi,* in one hundred folios."
Cf. Asin, *Abenhazam,* I, 252-253.

(98) *Risalah:* *al-Risalah al-lazimah I li-uli al-amr* (The Necessary Treatise Concerning the Most Outstanding Leaders Whose Decisions are Binding).
Dhahabi, *Siyar,* 435.

(99) *Risalah:* *Risalat al-mu'aradah* (Treatise on Polemics)
Dhahabi, *Siyar,* 435.

(100) *Risalatan:* *Risalatan lahu ajaba fi-hima 'an risalatayn su'ila fi-hima su'al al-ta'nif* (His Two Treatises in Which He Responded to Two Treatises Posing Stern Censure against Him).
Ed. by 'Abbas, in *Ibn al-Naghrilah,* 83-133.
Cf. Asin, *Codice,* 15-18.

(101) *Ruh:* *Mas'alah fi-l-ruh,* (Question on the Soul).
Dhahabi, *Siyar,* 435

(102) *Sa'adah:* *Maqalat al-sa'adah* (Treatise on Happiness)
Dhahabi, *Siyar,* 436, lists it among Ibn Hazm's medical works.

(103) *Sad:* *Mu'allaf fi-l-sad wa-l-dad* (Composition On the Letters S and D).
Dhahabi, *Siyar,* 436.

(104) *Sadi':* *Kitab al-sadi' wa-l-radi' fi-l-radd 'ala man kafara ahl al-ta'wil min firaq al-Islam wa-l-radd 'ala man qala bi-l-*

		taqlid (The Book that Prevents and Tears to Pieces Refuting the Heretic Upholders of Interpretation and Those Upholders of Imitation).
		Yaqut, *Irshad*, V, 94.
		Dhahabi, *Tadhkirah*, 3:1152
		Cf. Asin, *Abenhazam*, 258
(105)	Salah:	*Kitab al-salah* (The Book on Prayer)
		Ibn Hazm, *Fisal*, V, 14.
		Cf. Asin, *Abenhazam*, I, 262
(106)	Sawad:	*Mas'alah hal al-sawad lawn aw la* (Questions as to Whether Blackness Is Color or Not). Dhahabi, *Siyar*, 436.
(107)	Sharh:	*Sharh ahadith al-Muwatta' wa-l-kalam 'ala masa' ilih* (Commentary on the Traditions of the *Muwatta'* of Malik and Discussion of Its Problems.)
		Yaqut, *Irshad*, V, 94.
		Dhahabi, *Siyar*, 434, has *Kitab imla' fi sharh al-Muwatta'*, in one thousand folios Cf. his *Tadhkirah*, 3:1152, Cf. Asin, *Abenhazam*, I, 256.
(108)	Sharh-fusul:	*Sharh fusul Buqrat* (Commentary on Hippocrates' Aphorism).
		Dhahabi, *Siyar*, 436, lists it among Ibn Hazm's medical works.
(109)	Shifa':	*Maqalah fi shifa' al-did bi-l-did* (Treatise Concerning Cure with Its Opposite).
		Dhahabi, *Siyar*, 436, lists it among Ibn Hazm's medical works.
(110)	Shu'ara':	*Kitab fi-l-shu'ara* (Book of Poets)
		Dayah, *Naqd*, 310. It may be different from *Tasmiyat* (134) below.
(111)	Shuyukh:	*Tasmiyat Shuyukh Malik* (The Names of Malik's Teachers)
		Dhahabi, *Siyar*, 436.
(112)	Sima':	*Mas'alat al-sima'* (The Question of Singing). Cf. *Ghina'* (28) above.
		Hajji Khalifah, *Kashf*, 3:617.
		Cf. Asin, *Abenhazam*, I, 163.
(113)	Siqilli:	*al-Risalah al-balqa' fi-l-radd 'ala Muhammad 'Abd al-Haqq Ibn Muhammad al-Siqilli* (The Bright Treatise Refuting Muhammad al-Siqilli (The Sicilian)
		Dhahabi, *Siyar*, 434, says it consists of two small volumes. *not able to identify.
(114)	Sirah:	*al-Sirah al-nabawiyyah* (The Biography of the Prophet Muhammad). Ed. by 'Abbas, in *Jawami'*. 1-266.
(114a)	Siyar:	*al-Siyar wa-l-akhlaq* (Conducts and Characters) It may be identical with *Akhlaq* (6) above.
(114b)	Siyasah:	*al-Siyasah* (On Politics)
		It may be the same *Imamah* (43) above.
		Ibn Hazm, *Taqrib*, 181, simply has *Siyasah*.
(115)	Sunan:	*Muhim al-sunan* (The Most Important Deeds (Traditions) of the Prophet.
		Hajji Khalifah, *Kashf*, 6:278, no. 13473.
		Cf. Asin, *Abenhazam*, I, 254-255.

(116) *Tabdil:*   *Izhar Tabdil al-Yuhyd wa-l-Nasara al-Tawrah wa-l-Injil wa-bayan tanaqud ma bi--aydihim min dhalika mimma la yahtamil al-ta'wil* (Book Demonstrating the Alterations of the Jews and Christians in the Bible and the Gospel and the Proof of the Contradictions in the Books They Possess Which Do Not Admit of Any Interpretation).
Ibn Hazm, *Fisal,* I, 116-217, where the treatise appears to be inserted in part or in full. Cf. Asin, *Abenhazam,* I, 266; Humaydi *Judhwah,* no. 708, 309; Dhahabi, 3:1147; Hajji Khalifah, *Kashf,* I, 346, no. 888.

(117) *Tabyin:*   *Kitab tabyin fi hadd 'ilm al-Mustafa a'yan al-munafaqin* (Book Showing the Definition of the Knowledge of the Prophet Muhammad among the Major Hippocrites).
Dhahabi, *Siyar,* 434.

(118) *Ta'kid:*   *Risalat al-ta'kid* (Treatise on Certainty).
Dhahabi, *Siyar,* 435.

(119) *Talkhis:*   *al-Talkhis li-wujuh al-talkhis* (Abridgement Dealing with the Various Aspects of Salvation).
Ed. by 'Abbas, in *Ibn al-Naghrilah,* 137-183.
Dhahabi, *Siyar,* 435, has *al-Talkhis fi a'mal al-'ibad* Concerning the Actions of the People), which may be the same. However, Dhahabi, *Siyar,* 434, has another title, *al-Talkhis wa-l-takhlis fi-l-masa'il al-nazariyyah* (Abridgement and Salvation Concerning Speculative Questions), which evidently appears to be a different work having philosophical rather than religious content. Cf. Asin, *Abenhazam,* I, 251. Cf. Asin, *Codice,* 27-46.

(120) *Tamr:*   *Maqalah fi-l-muhakamah bayn al-tamr wa-l-zabib* (Treatise Dealing with Deciding Whether to Use Dates or Raisins for Cure).
Dhahabi, *Siyar,* 436, has it among Ibn Hazm's medical works.

(121) *Tanwir:*   *Tanwir al-miqbas* (Lighting the Lamp of Knowledge) Afghani, *Ibn Hazm,* 54.

*(122) *Taqrib:*   *al-Taqrib li-hudud al-mantiq* (Introduction Defining Logic). Ed. by 'Abbas, Beirut, 1959.
Ibn Hazm, *Fisal,* III, 68, 90; and V. 70.d His *Ihkam.* 9, 15, 17, 18, 69, 110, 314, 315, 414, 448, 492, 635, 657, 677, 793, 951. The work is mentioned by the majority of Ibn Hazm's biographers and often in a bad light.

(123) *Tarik:*   *Kitab anna tarik al-salah 'amdan hatta yakhruj waqtuha la qada' alayh fi-ma qad kharaja min waqtih* Dealing with the One Who Abandons Prayer intentionally until It Is Due Is Not Accountable with Respect to the Expired Time). 'Abbas, *Ibn al-Naghrilah,* 5.

(124) *Tasaffuh:*   *Kitab tasaffuh fi-l-fiqh* (Book Scrutinizing Jurisprudence). Dhahabi, *Siyar,* 434.

(125) *Tasmiyah:*   *Tasmiyat al-shu'ara' al-wafidin 'ala Ibn Abi 'Amir).* (The Names of the Poets at the Court of Ibn Abi 'Amir).

(126) *Tawq:*   *Taq al-hamamah fi-l-ulfah wa-l-ullaf* (The Dove's Ring Dealing with Love and Lovers).

	Ed. by D.K. Petrof (Leiden, 1914; various printings in Cairo, 1950 and Damascus (n.d.) English translation A.R. Nykl (Paris, 1931) and A.J. Arberry (London, 1953). French trans. by L. Bercher (Algiers, 1949). Russian Trans. A. Salil (Moscow & Leningrad. 1933). German trans. Max Weisweiler (Leiden). Italian trans. F. Gabrieli (Bari, 1949). Spanish trans. E. Garcia Gomez (Madrid, 1952). The Spanish translation by Garcia is being used.
(127) *Tawqif:*	*Risalat al-tawqif 'ala shari' al-najah bi-ikhtisar al-tariq* (Treatise for Setting up the Way of Salvation in a Brief Manner). Ed. by 'Abbas, in *Rasa'il*, 41-45. Cf. Asin, *Codice*, 9-13.
(128) *Tibb:*	*Fi-l-tibb al-nabawi* (On Prophetic Medicine). Dhahabi, *Siyar*, 436.
(129) *Usul:*	*Masa'il usul al-fiqh* (The Questions of the Roots of Jurisprudence). Printed (Cairo, 1332 A.H.)
(130) *Usul-furu'*	*al-Usul wa-l-furu'* (The Roots and Branches of the Law). Asin, *Codice*, 2. Afghani, *Ibn Hazm*, 52. It may be the same as the preceding work.
(131) *'Uthman:*	*Tartib su'alat 'Uthman al-Darimi li-Ibn Ma'in).* (The Arrangement of the Questions of Uthman al-Darimi by Ibn Ma'in.)* Dhahabi, *Siyar*, 435. *'Uthman al-Darimi (d. 894) was a traditionist and author of a *Musand*. Yahya Ibn Ma'in (d. 848) was a famous Baghdadi traditionist.
(132) *'Uthman Ibn Sa'id:*	*Bayan ghalat 'Uthman Ibn Sa'id al-A'war fi-l-musnad wa-l-mursal* (Showing the Mistakes of 'Uthman Ibn Sa'id al-A-'war (The One Eyed) Concerning Traditions with Unbroken and Broken Shains of Transmissions).* Dhahabi, *Siyar*, 435. *Uthman Ibn Sa'id is probably the same as 'Uthman al-Darimi above (131).
(133) *Wa'd:*	*Risalah fi-l-wa'd wa-l-wa'id wa-bayan al-haqq fi dhalika min al-sunan wa-l-Qur'an* (Treatise Dealing with Reward and Punishment Showing the Truth of That on The Basis of Traditions and The Qur'an). 'Abbas, in *Ibn al-Naghrilah,* 3. Dhahabi, *Siyar,* 435, has *al-Risalah al-Sumadihiyyah fi-l-wa'd wa-l-wa'id* (The Sumadihite Treatise on Reward and Punishment). It is probable that the treatise was dedicated to a member of Banu Sumadih who ruled for a time in the eastern part of al-Andalus, mainly in Almeria.
(134) *Yaqin:;*	*Kitab al-yaqin fi-l-naqd 'ala al-mulhidin al-muhtajjin 'an Iblis al-la'in wa-sa ir al-kafirin* (The Book of Certainty Refuting the Heretics Who Rely on the Accursed Devil and Unbelievers). Ibn Hazm, *Fisal*, III, 206 and V, 206-207; Cf. Asin, *Abenhazam*, I, 264. Dhahabi, *Siyar,* 434, has *Kitab al-yaqin fi naqd tamwih al-mu'tadhirin 'an Iblis wa-sa'ir al-mushrikin* (The Book of Certainty Refuting The Confusion of Those Who Rely on the Devil and Polytheists).

(135) *Za':* *Mu'allaf fi-l-za' wa-l-dad* (Composition on the Letter Z and D). Dhahabi, *Siyar,* 436.
(136) *Zahiriyyah:* *Ma Waqa'a bayn al-Zahiriyyah wa-ashab al-qiyas* (What Took Place between the Zahirite School and the Upholders of Analogy). Dhahabi, *Siyar,* 435.
(137) *Zajr:* *Zajr al-ghawi* (Rebuking the Dabbler). Dhahabi, *Siyar,* 435, in Two Parts.

BIBLIOGRAPHY

NOTE: The bibliography includes abbreviations for titles which appear in the notes.

'Abbas, I. (ed.)
Ibn al-Naghrilah: *al-Radd 'ala Ibn al-Naghrilah al-Yahudi wa-rasa' il ukhra li-Ibn Hazm.* Cairo, 1960.
It contains: *Ibn al-Naghrilah, Risalatan, Talkhis* and *Kindi.* For the full corresponding titles see under Ibn Hazm in the Appendix.

———(ed.) *Jawami':* *Jawami' al-sirah wa-khams rasa' il ukhra.* Cairo, n.d. It contains: *Jawami', Qira'at, asma' al-sahabah, Ashab, Jumal,* and *Asma' al-khulafa'.*
For the full corresponding titles, see under Ibn Hazm in the Appendix.

———(ed.) *Rasa'il:* *Rasa'il Ibn Hazm.* Cairo, 1952 and 1954.
It contains: *Hatif, Iman, Tawqif, Maratib al-'ulum, Alam, Nafs,* and *Akhlaq.*
For the full corresponding titles, see under Ibn Hazm in the Appendix.

———*Tarikh:* *Tarikh al-adab al-andalusi: 'Asr siyadat Qurtubah.* 2nd. ed., Beirut, 1969.

'Abd al-Baqi, Muh. *al-Mu'jam al-mufahras ı li-l-alfaz al-qur'aniyyah,* Cairo, A.H. 1364.

'Abd al-Jalil, J.M. *Histoire: Histoire de la litterature arabe.* Paris, 1960.

'Abd al-Qadir al-Baghdadi: *Usul: Kitab usul al-din.* Istanbul, 1928.

Abu Dawud al-Isfahani, *Zahrah:* *Kitab al-zahrah.* Ed. A. R. Nykl and I. Tuqan, Cairo, 1932.

Abu-l-Khashab, I. Tarikh: *Tarikh al-adab al-'arabi fi-l-Andalus.* Cairo, 1966.

Abu-l-Salt al-Dani. *Taqwim/* *Taqwim al-dhihn.* Ed. and Spanish Trans. A. Gonzalez Palencia, Madrid, 1915.

Abu Zahrah, Muh. *Ibn Hazm:* *Ibn Hazm: hayatuh wa-'asruh.* Cairo, 1954.

Addison, J. T. *The Christian Approach: The Christian Approach to Moslems.* New York, 1942.

Afghani, Sa'id. *Ibn Hazm: Ibn Hazm al-andalusi wa-risalah fi-l-mufadalah bayn al-sahabah.* 2nd ed. Beirut, 1969.

Afifi, A. *Ibnul 'Arabi: The Mystical Philosophy of Muhyid din Ibnul Arabi.* Cambridge, 1939; reprint (Lahore, n.d.)

Afnan, A.M. *Avicenna:* *Avicenna, His Life and Works.* London, 1958.

al-'Amiri, Abu-l-Hasan. *I'lam:* *al-I'lam bi-manaqib al-islam.* Ed. A. 'A. Ghurab. Cairo, 1967.

Arberry, A. J. *Revelation:* *Revelation and Reason in Islam.* London, 1965.

Archiprest of Hita: *El libro de buen amor,* ed. J. Corominas. Madrid, 1967.

Arnaldez, R. *Ahbar:* "Ahbar et Awamir chez Ibn Hazm de Courdoue", *Arabica* 2(1955), 211-227.

———. *Controverses:* *Controverses theologiques chez Ibn Hazm de Courdoue et Ghazali.* Madris de Dar el-Salam, 1953.

Arnaldez, R. *Grammaire:*	*Grammaire et theologie chez Ibn Hazm de Cordoue.* Paris, 1956.
———. *Guerre:*	"La guerre Sainte selon Ibn Hazm de Cordoue" in *Etudes d'orientalism dediees a Levi-Provencal,* Paris, 1962, II, 445-459.
———. *Raison:*	"La raison et l'identification de la verite selon Ibn Hazm de Cordoue." in *Melanges Massignon,* I, 1956, 111-112.
al-Ash'ari. *Ibanah:*	*al-Ibanah 'an usul al-diyanah.* English trans. W.C. Klein, New Haven, 1940.
———. *Maqalat:*	Maqalat al-islamiyyin wa-ikhtilaf al-musallin. 2 vols., ed. H. Ritter, Istanbul, 1929-30.
Asin Palacios, M. *Abenhazam:*	*Abenhazam de Cordoba y su historia critica de las ideas religiosas.* 5 vols. Madrid, 1927-1932. See *Fisal* under Ibn Hazm in the Appendix. Reference to the translation is ordinarily made following the pagination of the Arabic text.
———. *Abenmasarra:*	*Aben Masarra y su escuela.* Madrid, 1914.
———. *Algazel:*	*Algazel.* Zaragoza, 1901.
———. *Averroismo:*	"El Averroismo teologico de Santo Thomas de Aquino", in *Homenaje a Don Fracisco Codera,* Zaragoza, 1904, 271-331.
———. *Caracteres y conducta.*	See *akhlaq* under Ibn Hazm in the Appendix.
———. *Codice:*	"Un codice inexplorado del Cordobes Ibn Hazm", *Al-Andalus,* 2 (1934), 1-56.
———. *Cordobes:*	"El Cordobes Abenhazam, primer historiador de las ideas religiosas", lecture before *La Real Acedemia de la Historia,* Madrid, 1942.
———. *Historia:*	*Historia y filologia arabe,* II & III Madrid, 1948.
———. *Indiferencia:*	"La indiferencia religiosa en la Espana musulmanan segun Abenhazam, historiador de las religiones y los cultos, *"Cultura Espanola,* 5(1907), 297-320.
———. *Moral:*	*"La moral gnomica de Abenhazam,"* Cultura Espanola. 13(1909), 41-61 and 17-340.
———. *Obras:*	*Obras Escogidas.* 2 vols. Madrid, 1946
———. *Origen:*	"El Origen del lenguage y problemas conexos," *Al-Andalus,* 4(1949), 253-281; also in *Obras,* 357-388, and in *Historia,* 377-378.
'Askari. *Sina'atayn:*	*Kitab al-sina'aıtayn.* Cairo, 1971.
Atiyeh, G. *Kindi:*	*al-Kindi: The Philosopher of The Arabs.* Rawalpindi, 1966.
Averroes, see Ibn Rushd.	
Badi' al-Zaman. *Maqamat:*	*Maqamat.* Ed. Muh. 'Abduh, Beirut, 1889
al-Baghdadi, 'Abd al-Qadir. *Farq:*	*Kitab al-farq bayn al-firaq.* English trans. Part One by K. C. Seelye, New York, 1920. Part Two by A. S. Halkin, Tel-Aviv, 1936.
———. *Mukhtasar:*	*al-mukhtasar.* Ed. P. K. Hitti, Cairo, 1924.
al-Balawi, Yusuf. *Alif:*	*Kitab alif ba'.* 2 vols. Cairo, A.H. 1287.
Baqillani. *I'jaz:*	*I'jaz al-Qur'an.* Cairo, A. H. 1347.
———. *Tamhid:*	*Kitab al-tamhid wa-l-radd 'ala al-mulhidah wa-l-mu'attilah wa-l-rafidah wa-l-mu'tazilah.* Cairo, 1947.
Bercher, L. *Tawq:*	"A propos de Tawq al-hamamah d'Ibn Hazm,", in *Melanges William Marcais. Paris, 1950, 29-36.*

_____.	See his translation of the *Tawq* under Ibn Hazm in the Appendix.
Bergdolt, *Ibn Hazm/*	"Ibn Hazm's Abhandlung uber die Farben," *Zeitschrift fur Semitistik und Verwandte Gebiete,* 19(1933), 139-46.
Blachere, R. *Histoire:*	*Histoire de la litterature arabe des origines a la fin du XVe siecle.* 3 vols., Paris, 1952-1966.
_____. *Ibn Darraj:*	"La vie et l'oeuvre de poete-epistolier andalou Ibn Darraj al-Qastalli," *Hesperis,* 16(1933), 99-121.
_____. *Mutanabbi:*	"Le poete al-Mutanabbi et l'occident musulman, *"Revue des Etudes Islamiques,* (1929), 127-135.
Boer, T. de. *History:*	*History of Philosophy in Islam.* London, 1903.
Bosch, Vila. *Ibn Hazm:*	"Ibn Hazm, genealogista," in *IX Centenario de Aben Hazm,* Cordoba, 1963.
Briffault, R. *Troubadours:*	*The Troubadours.* Bloomington, Ind., 1965.
Brocklemann, C. *Beitrage:*	"Beitrage zur Kritic und Erklarum on Ibn Hazm's 'Tawq al-Hamama'," *Islamica,* 5(1932), 462-474.
_____. *GAL:*	*Geschichte der arabischen Literatur.* 2 vols. and 3 Supls. Weimar & Leiden, 1898-1942.
Brunschvig, R. *Logic*	"Logic and law in classical Islam", in Grunebaum *Logic,* 9-20.
_____. *Polemiques:*	"Polemiques medievales autour du rite de Malik", *Al-Andalus,* 15(1950), 377-435.
Bukhari. *Sahih:*	*Sahih al-Bukhari.* Cairo, 1932.
Campbell, D. *Medicine:*	*Arabian Medicine and its Influences in the Middle Ages.* 2 vols. London, 1926.
Cantarino, V. *Poetics:*	*Arabic Poetics in the Golden Age.* Leiden, 1975.
Capellanus,A.*Courtly Love:*	*The Art of Courtly Love.* English trans. J.J. Parry, New York, 1964.
Cardaillac, D. *Polemique:*	*La polemique anti-chretienne du manuscrit aljamiado No. 4944 de la Bibliotecue Nationale de Madrid.* 2 vols. Montepellier, 1972.
Casiri, M. *Bibliotheca:*	*Bibliotheca Arabico-Hispana Escurilensis.* 2 vols. Madrid, 1760-1770.
Castro, A. *Espana:*	*Espana en su historia: cristianos, moros y judios.* Buenos Aires, 1948. English trans. unter The *Structure of Spanish History,* E. L. King. Princeton, 1954.
_____. *History:*	*History of Religious Intolerance in Spain.* London, 1953
_____. *Realidad:*	*La realidad historica de Espana.* Mexico, 1954
Chejne, A. *Arabic:*	*The Arabic Language: Its Role in History.* Minneapolis, 1969.
_____.*Ibn Hazm:*	"Ibn Hazm and His Palce in the Intellectual History of Islam", in *SI*
_____. *Muslim Spain:*	*Muslim Spain: Its History and Culture.* Minneapolis, 1974.
_____. *Succession:*	*Succession to the Rule in Islam.* Lahore, 1960.
_____. *Islamization:*	"Islamization and Arabization in al-Andalus," in *Islam and Cultural Change in The Middle Ages.* Wiesbaden, 1975, 59-86.
_____. *Role:*	"The Role of al-Andalus in the Movement of Ideas," in *Islam and the Medieval West.* Binghamton, 1980.
_____.	*The Moriscos Through Their Literature* (In Press).
Corbin, H. *Ibn 'Arabi:*	*Creative Imagination in the Sufism of Ibn 'Arabi.* London, 1969.

Coulson, N.J. *Law:*	*Islamic Law.* Edinburgh, 1964.
Cruz, Hernandez, M. *Filosofia:*	*La filosofia arabe.* Madrid, 1963.
———. *Historia:*	*Historia de la filosofia espanola.* 2 vols. Madrid, 1957.
Dabbi, Ahmad. *Bughyah:*	*Bughyat al-multamis.* Madrid, 1884.
Daniel, N *Islam:*	*Islam and the West.* Edinburgh, 1960.
Dayah, Muh. *Naqd:*	*Tarikh al-naqd al-adabi fi-l-Andalus.* Beirut, 1968.
Dayf, A. *Balaghah:*	*Balaghat al-'Arab fi-l-Andalus.* Cairo, 1924.
Dayf, Sh. *Balaghah:*	*al-Balaghah: tatawwur wa-tarikh.* Cairo, 1965.
———. *Naqd:*	*al-Naqd.* Cairo, 1954.
Dhahabi. *Tadhkirah:*	*Tadhkirat al-huffaz.* 4 vols. Hyderabad, 1955-58.
———. *Siyar:*	*Siyar al-nubala'.* The portion on Ibn Hazm is ed. by S. Afghani, in *Majma' al-'ilmi al-'arabi* (of Damscus) X (1941), 433-449.
Denomy, A. *Arabic Influence:*	"Concerning the Accessibility of Arabic Influence to the Earliest Provencal Troubadours," *Medieval Studies,* 15 (1953), 147-158.
———. *Fin Amors:*	"Fin Amors: The Pure Love of the Troubadours. Its Amorality and Possible Source," *Medieval Studies* 7 (1945), 139-179.
———. *Heresy:*	*The Heresy of Courtly Love.* Gloucester, Mass., 1965.
Dickie, J. *Ibn Shuhayd:*	"Ibn Shuhayd: A biographical and Critical Study," *Al-Andalus,* 29 (1964), 243-310.
Dozy, R. *Histoire:*	*Histoire des mususlmans d'Espagne jusqu'a la conquete de l'Andalousie par les Almaravides.* New edition by E. Levi-Provencal, Leiden, 1932. English trans. Francis Griffin Stokes under Spanish Islam, New York, 1913.
———. *Recherches:*	*Recherches sur l'histoire et la litterature de l'Espagne pendant le moyen age.* 2 vols. Paris, 1881.
———. *Supplement:*	*Supplement aux dictionnaires arabes.* 2 vols. Leiden-Paris, 1927.
Erlanger, R.D. *Musique:*	*La Musique arabe,* Paris, 1930-1959.
Epalza, M. de. *Tuhfa:*	*La Tuhfa, autobiografia polemica islamica contra el cristianismo de 'Abdallah al-Taruman* (fray Anselmo Turmeda), Rome, 1971.
Fada'il:	*Fada'il al-Andalus wa-ahliha.* Ed. S. al-Munajjid. Beirut, 1968.
Farabi, Abu Nasr. *Fusul:*	*Fusul al-madani.* Ed. D. Dunlop. Cambridge, 1961.
———. *Ihsa':*	*Ihsa' al-'ulum.* Ed. and translated into Spanish A Gonzalez Palencia. Madrid, 1953.
———. *Madinah:*	*al-Madinah al-fadilah.* Ed. F. Najjar, Beirut, 1964.
———. *Siyasah:*	*al-Siyasah al-madaniyyah.* Ed. A. Nader, Beirut, 1959.
Farmer, H. G. *History:*	*Hitory of Arabian Music,* London, 1931.
Friedlander, I. *Komposition:*	"Zu Komposition von Ibn Hazm's Milal wa-n-Nihal," in *Noldeke Fetschrift Orientalische Studien,* 1896, I, 267-277.
———. *Heterodoxies:*	*The Heterodoxies of the Shi'ites According to Ibn Hazm.* Hew Haven, 1923.
Gabrieli, F. *Amore:*	"Un trattato d'amore moresco," in *Storia e civilta musulmana.* Naples, 1947, 90-98. See under Ibn Hazm for his translation of *Tawq*

_____. *Storia:*	*Storia della litteratura araba.* Milan, 1951.
Garcia Gomez, E. *Abenalcotia:*	"Abenalcotia y Abenhazam," in *Revista de Occidente,* 48 (1927).
_____. *Medicina:*	"El collar de la paloma" y la medicina occidental", *Homenaje a millas Vallicrosa I* (Barcelona, 1954), 701-706.
_____. *Polemica:*	"Polemica religiosa entre Ibn Hazm e Ibn al-Nagrila," *Al-Andalus,* IV (1936-1939), 1-28.
_____. *Poemas:*	*Poemas arabigo andaluses.* 5th ed. Madrid, 1971.
_____. *Tawq:*	"El 'Tawq' de Ibn Hazm y el 'Diwan al-sababa.' " *Al-Andalus,* 6 (1941), 65-72. See under Ibn Hazm for his Spanish translation of the *Tawq.*
_____. *Traduccion:*	"En torno a mi traduccion de 'El collar de la paloma'," *Al-Andalus,* 17 (1952)m 457-521.
_____. *Tres Capitulos:*	"Tres capitulos del 'collar de la paloma'," *Revista de Occidente,* 137 (1934).
Gardet, L. *Raison:*	"Raison et foi en Islam," *Revue Thomiste,* 1937-1938.
Gardet, L. and M. Anawati. *Introduction:*	*Introduction a la theologie musulmane.* Paris, 1948.
Gauthier, L. *Ibn Rochd:*	*Ibn Rochd.* Paris, 1948. See under Ibn Rushd for his French translation of Ibn Rushd's *Fasl.*
_____. *Ibn Tofail:*	*Ibn Tofail: sa vie et ses oeuvres.* Paris, 1909.
Gayangos, P.	See Maqqari's *Nafh.*
Ghazzali. *Ihya':*	*Ilhya''ulum al-din.* 4 vols. Cairo, 1933.
_____. *Iqtisad:*	*al-iqtisad fi-l-i'taqad.* Cairo, n.d.
_____. *Maqsad:*	*Kitab al-maqsad al-asna.* Cairo, A.H. 1332.
_____. *Mihakk:*	*Mihakk al-nazar.* Cairo, n.d.
_____. *Mi'yar:*	*Mi'yar al-'ilm.* Cairo, 1927.
_____. *Munqidh:*	*al-Munqidh min-l-dalal.* Ed. J. Saliba. 6th. ed. Damascus, 1960.
_____. *Risalah:*	*al-Risalah al-ladumiyyah.* In *Jawahir al-Ghawali,* Cairo, 1934.
_____. *Tahafut:*	*Tahafut al-falasifah.* Ed. M. Bouyges, Beirut, 1927.
Gibb, H. A.	*Arabic Literature.* Oxford, 1963.
Goldziher, I. *Dogme:*	*Le dogme et la loi de l'Islam.* French trans. Arin, Paris, 1920.
_____. *Ibn Toumert:*	*Le livre de mohammad Ibn Toumert.* Algiers, 1903.
_____. *Vorlesungen:*	*Vorlesungen uber den Islam.* Heidelberg, 1910.
_____. *Zahiriten:*	*Die Zahiriten.* Leipzig, 1884. Cf. *Ibtal* under Ibn Hazm.
Gonzalez Palencia, A. *Historia:*	*Historia de la literatura arabigo-espanola.* 2nd. ed. Barcelona, 1932.
_____. *Islam:*	*Islam y occidente.* Madrid, 1931.
Grabmann, M. *Geschichte:*	*Die Deschichte der scholastichen Methode.* 2 vols. Reprint, Graz, 1957.
Grunebaum, G. E. (Ed.) *Logic:*	*Logic in Classical Islamic Culture.* Wiesbaden, 1970.
_____. *Theory:*	*A Tenth Century Document of Arabic Literary Theory and Criticism.* Chicago, 1950.
Guillame, A. *Prophecy:*	*Prophecy and Divination.* London, 1938.

———. *Tradition:*	*Traditions of Islam.* Oxford, 1924.
Hajiri, T. *Ibn Hazm:*	*Ibn Hazm: surah anddalusiyyah.* Cairo, n.d.
———. *Tarikh:*	*Fi tarikh al-naqd wa-l-madhahib al-adabiyyah.* Alexandria, 1953.
Hajji Khalifah. *Kashf:*	*Kashf al-zunun.* Ed. G. Flugel, 7 vols. Leipzig-London, 1835-58.
Handler, A. *Zirids:*	*The Zirids of Granada.* Miami, 1974.
Hariri. *Maqamat:*	*Maqamat al-Hariri.* Beirut, 1886. English Transl. Pt. I by T. Chenery, London, 1867; and Pt. II, by F. Steinglass, London, 1898.
Haykal, A. *Adab:*	*al-Adab al-andalusi min al-fath ila suqut al-khilafah.* Cairo, 1968.
Hitti, P. K. *History:*	*History of the Arabs.* New York, 1958.
Horten, M. *Systeme:*	*De philosophischen Systeme der speculativen Theologen in Islam.* Bonn, 1912.
Hourani, G.	See Ibn Rushd's *Fisal.*
Huart, C. *Litterature:*	*Litterature arabe.* Paris, 1902.
Huici Miranda, A. *Valencia:*	*Historia musulmana de Valencia.* 3 vols. Valencia, 1970.
Humaydi, Muh. *Judhwah:*	*Judhwat al-muqtabis.* Ed. Mt. T. Tanji. Cario, 1952.
Husayn, T. *Hubb:*	"Fi-l-hubb". *Al-Kitab al-Misri*, 5(1946), 3-18.
Husik, I. *History:*	*A History of Medieval Jewish Philosophy.* Philadelphia, 1941.
Husri. *Zahr:*	*Zahr al-adab.* Ed. Z. Mubarak. 2 vols. Cairo, n.d.
Ibn al-Abbar. *Hullah:*	*al-Hullah al-siyara',* ed. Husayn Mu'nis. 2 vols. Cairo,1963
———. *I'tab:*	*I'tab al-kuttab* ed. A. al-Ashtar. Damascus, 1961.
———. *Takmilah:*	*al-Takmilah li-kitab al-silah,* ed. F. Codera, Madrid,1887-1890
Ibn 'Abd al-Barr. *Bahjah:*	*Bahjat al-Majalis wa-uns al-mujalis.* First pt. ed. Muh. al-Khuwli, Cairo, n.d.
———. *Intiqa':*	*al-Intiqa' fi fada'il al-thalathah al-fuqaha'.* Cairo, A.H. 1350.
———. *Jami':*	*Jami' bayan al-'ilm wa-fadlih.* Cairo, A. H. 1320.
———. *Mukhtasar:*	*Mukhtasar Jami' bayan al-'ilm.* Cairo, A.H. 1320.
Ibn 'Abd al-Malik. *Dhayl:*	*al-Dahyl wa-l-takmilah,* ed. Ihsan 'Abbas, pts. 4 and 5, Beirut, 1964-1965.
Ibn 'Abd Rabbihi. *'Iqd:*	*al-'Iqd al-farid,* ed. A. Amin et al. 7 vols. Cairo, 1948-1953.
Ibn 'Abdun. *Risalah:*	*Risalat Ibn 'Abdun fi-l-qada' wa-l-hisbah,* ed. E. Levi-Provencal. Cairo, 1955.
Ibn Abi Usaybi'ah. *'Uyun:*	*'Uyun al-anba' fi tabaqat al-atibba',* ed. A. Miller. 2 vols. Cairo, 1882-1884.
Ibn al-'Arabi al-Ishbili. *'Awasim:*	*al-'Awasim min al-qawasim,* Algiers, A.H. 1346.
Ibn 'Arabi, Muhyy-l-Din. *Fusus:*	*Fusus al-hikam.* Cairo, A.H. 1252. French trans. by T. Burckhardt under *Sagesse de prophetes* (Paris, 1955).
———. *Futuhat:*	*al-futuhat al-makiyyah.* 4 vols. Cairo, A.H. 1295.
Ibn 'Asakir. *Tabyin:*	*Tabyin kadhb al-muftari fi-ma nusiba ila-l-imam Abi-l-Hasan al-Ash'ari.* Damascus, A. H. 1347.
Ibn al-Athir. *Kamil:*	*al-Kamil fi-l-tarikh,* ed. C. J. Tornberg. 14 vols. Leiden 1851-76.

Ibn Bashkuwal. *Silah:*	*al-Silah*, ed. 'I. 'I, al-Husayni, 2 vols. Cairo, 1955.
Ibn Bassam. *Dhakhirah:*	*al-Dhakhirah*, pt. I:i, Cairo, 1939-1942.
Ibn al-Faradi. *Tarikh:*	*Tarikh 'ulama' al-Andalus*, ed. 'I. 'I. al-Husayni 2 vols. Cairo, 1954.
Ibn Farhun. *Dibaj:*	*al-Dibaj al-mudhahhab*. Cairo, A.H. 1351
Ibn Gabirol. *Yanbu':*	*Yanbu' al-hayah*. Abridged English trans., H.E. Wedeck, New York, 1962.
Ibn Hajar al'Asqalani.*Lisan:*	*Lisan al-mizan*. 6 vols.Hyderabad, A.H. 1329-1333.
Ibn Hanbal, *Musnad:*	*Musnad Ibn Hanbal*. 3 vols. Cairo, n.d.
Ibn Hayyan. *Muqtabis:*	*al-Muqtabis*, portion of which was edited by A. Melchor, Paris, 1937 and another portion by 'Abd al-Rahman al-Hajji, Beirut, 1965.
Ibn Hazm al-Ansari.*Minhaj:*	*Minhaj al-bulagha' wa-siraj al-udaba'*. Tunis, 1966.
Ibn Hazm.	See Appendix above.
Ibn 'Idhari. *Bayan:*	*al-Bayan al-mughrib*, ed. G.S. Colin, E. Levi-Provencal, and I. 'Abbas, 4 vols. Paris, 1930-1967.
Ibn al-'Imad. *Shadharat:*	*Shadharat al-dhahab fi akhbar man dhahab*. 4 vols. Cairo, A.H. 1350.
Ibn Juljul. *Tabaqat:*	*Tabaqat al-atibba' wa-l-hukama'*, ed. F. Sayyid. Cairo, 1955.
Ibn Khaldun. *Muqaddimah:*	*al-Muqaddimah*. English trans. F. Rosenthal. 3 vols. New York, 1958.
Ibn Khallikan. *Wafayat:*	*Wafayat al a'yan*, ed. Muh. Muhyy-l-Din 'Abd al-Hamid. 5 vols. Cairo, 1948.
Ibn Khaqan. *Matmah:*	*Matmah al-anfus*. Constantinople, A.H. 1302.
———. *Qala'id:*	*Qala'id*. Bulaq, A.H. 1283.
Ibn Kathir. *Bidayah:*	*al-Bidayah wa-l-nihayah*. 14 vols. Cairo, A.H. 1351-1358.
Ibn al-Khatib. *A'mal:*	*A'mal al-a'lam fi man buyi'a qabl al-ihtilam min muluk al-Islam*, ed. E. Levi-Provencal. Rabat, 1934; Beirut, 1956.
———. *Ihatah:*	*al-Ihatah fi akhbar Gharnatah*, ed. Muh. 'Inan, one vol. Cairo, 1955.
Ibn Khayr, Muh.	*Fahrasah*, ed. F. Codera and J. Ribera. Saragossa, 1893.
Ibn Mada. *Radd:*	*Kitab al-radd 'ala al-nuhah*, ed. Sh. Dayf. Cairo, 1947.
Ibn Manzur. *Lisan:*	*Lisan al-'Arab*. 20 vols. Bulaq, A.H. 1300-1307.
Ibn al-Muqaffa'. *Adab:*	*al-Adab al-kabir*. Beirut, 1898.
———.	*Kalilah wa-Dimnah*, a work translated by him.
Ibn al-Nadim. *Fihrist:*	*al-Fihrist*, ed. G. Flugel. Leipzig, 1871-1872.
Ibn Qayyim al-Jawziyyah	*Rawdah: Rawdat al-muhibbin wa-nuzhat al-mushtaqin*. Damascas, A.H. 1349.
Ibn Qutaybah. *Shi'r:*	*Kitab al-shi'r wa-l-shu'ara'*. Cairo, 1966.
Ibn Rashiq. *'Umdah:*	*al-'Umdah fi sina'at al-shi'r wa-naqdih*. 2 vols. Cairo, A.H. 1344.
Ibn Rushd. *Fasl:*	*Fasl al-maqal*, Ed. G. Hourani (Leiden, 1959) and English Trans. by the same (London, 1961). The edition of Muh. 'Amrah (Cairo, 1972) is being used here.
———.*Kashf:*	*Kash al-manahij*. Cairo, A.H. 1313 and 1328.
———. *Rasa'il:*	*Rasa'il*. Hyderabad, 1947.
———. Tafsir:	*Tafsir ma ba'd al-tabi'ah*. Beirut, 1938.
———. Tahafut:	*Tahafut al-tahafut*. Ed. S. Dunya. 2 vols. Cairo, 1964-1965. English trans. S. van den Bergh, 2 vols. Oxford, 1954.

Ibn Sa'id. *Mughrib:*	*al-Mughrib fi hula al-Maghrib,* ed. Sh. Dayf. 2 vols. Cairo, 1954.
Ibn al-Salah. *Fatawa.*	*Fatawa Ibn al-Salah.* Cairo, 1348 A.H.
Ibn Sayyid. *Hada'iq:*	*al-Hada'iq fi-l-matalib al-'aliyah al-falsafiyyah,* ed. Muh. al-Kawthari. Cairo, A.H. 1365.
_____. *Hulal:*	*al-hulal fi sharh abyat al-jumal* (in manuscript, Dar al-kutub, Cairo)
_____. *Insaf:*	*al-Insaf fi-l-tanbih.*Cairo, A.H. 1319.
_____. *Intisar:*	*al-Intisar min man 'adala 'an al-istibsar,*ed. H. 'Abd al-Majid. Cairo, 1955.
_____. *Iqtidab:*	*al-Iqtibad fi sharh al-kitab,* Beirut, 1901.
_____. *Sharh:*	*Sharh saqt al-zand.* 5 vols. Cairo, 1945-1948.
Ibn Shuhayd. *Diwan:*	*Diwan Ibn Shuhayd.* Beirut, 1063.
_____. *Risalah:*	*Risalat al-tawabi' wa-l-zawabi',* ed. B. al-Bustani. Beirut, 1951. English trans. J. Monroe. Berkeley, 1971, Pagination of the translation is being used here.
Ibn Sidah. *Muhkam:*	*al-Muhkam wa-l-muhit al-a'zam.* 3 vols. Vairo, 1958.
_____. *Mukhassas:*	*al-Mukhassas,* 17 parts, Cairo, A.H. 1316-1321.
Ibn Sina. *Aqsam:*	*Fi aqsam al-'ulum al-hikmiyyah.*
_____. *Isharat:*	*Kitab al-isharat wa-l-tanbihat,* ed. Froget, Leiden 1892.
_____. *Mantiq:*	*Mantiq al-mashriqiyyin.* Cairo, A.H. 1328.
_____. *Najat:*	*al-Najat,* ed. M.S. al-Kurdi. Cairo, 1944.
Ibn Taymiyyah. *Naqd:*	*Naqd al-mantiq,* ed. Muhammad Hamid, al-Faqi. Cairo, 1951.
Ibn Tufayl. *Hayy:*	*Hayy Ibn Yaqzan.* Beirut, 1962. English Trans. S. Ockley (London, 1708) and A.S. Fulton (London, 1929); German trans. G. Pritius (Frankfurt, 1726); Spanish trans. A. Gonzalez Palencia (Madrid, 1934); French trans. L. Gautier (Beirut, 1936).
Ibn Tumart. *A'azzu:*	*A'azzu ma yutlab.* ed. J.D.Luciani. Algiers, 1903.
Ibn Tumlus. *Madkhal:*	*Kitab al-madkhal li-sina'at al-mantiq,* ed. and Spanish trans. M. Asin Palacios. Madrid, 1916.
Ibn al-Zubayr. *Silah:*	*Silat al-silah,* ed. E. Levi-Provencal. Rabat, 1938.
Ibrahim, Zakariya.	*Ibn Hazm al-andalusi.* Cairo, 1958.
Ikhwan al-Safa. *Rasa'il:*	*Rasa'il Ikhwan al-Safa,* ed. K. al-Zirikli. 4 vols. Cairo,A.H.1347.
'Inan, Muh. 'A. *Dawlah:*	*Dawlah al-'amiriyyah.* Cairo, 1958.
_____. *Duwal:*	*Duwal al-tawa'if.* Cairo, 1960.
Jabre, F. *Certitude:*	*La notion de certitude selon Ghazali.* Paris, 1958.
Jahiz. *Bayan:*	*al-Bayan wa-l-tabyin,* ed. 'Abd. al-Salam Harun. 4 vols. Cairo, 1961.
_____. *Bukhala':*	*al-Bukhala',* ed. van Vloten. Leiden. 1900.
_____. *Hayawan:*	*al-Hayawan,* ed. 'Abd al-Salam Harun. 7 vols. Cairo, A.H. 1323-1325.
Jawami':	See 'Abbas and Ibn Hazm in the Appendix.
Jeanroy, A. *Poesie:*	*La poesie lyrique de troubadours.* 2 vols. Toulouse-Paris, 1934.
Kalilah wa-Dimnah.	Ed J. E. Keller and R. White Linker. Madrid, 1967. Cf. Ibn al-Muqaffa'.
Khafajah, Muh. *Qissah:*	*Qissat al-adab al-'arabi fi-l- Andalus.* Cairo, 1966.

Khalifah, 'Abd al-Karim.
Ibn Hazm: Ibn Hazm al-andalusi: hayatuh wa-adabuh. Beirut, n.d.
Kahhalah, 'U. Mu'jam: Mu'jam al-mu'allifin. Damascus, 1957.
Khalis, Salah, Ishbiliyah: Ishbiliyah: fi-l-qarn al-khamis al-hijri. Beirut, 1965.
———. Ibn 'Ammar: Muhammad Ibn 'Ammar al-andalusi. Baghdad, 1957.
———. Mu'tamid: al-Mu'tamid Ibn 'Abbad. Baghdad, 1958.
Khan, M.S.
Hispano Arabic Source: An Eleventh Century Hispano-Arabic Source for Ancient Indian Sciences and Culture, Calcutta, 1975.
Khuwarizmi. Mafatih: Mafatih al-'ulum, ed. G. von Vloten. Leiden, 1895.
Kilani, K. Muqaddimah: Muqaddimat diwan Ibn Zaydun. Cairo, 1932.
———. Nazarat: Nazarat fi tarikh al-adab al-andalusi. Cairo, 1924.
Kindi. Aqsam: Kitab aqsam al-'ilm al-unsi (Not extant).
———. Ma'iyah: Kitab fi ma'iyat al-'ilm al-unsi (Not extant).
———. Rasa'il: Rasa'il al-Kindi al-falsafiyyah, ed. M.A. Abu Rida. 2 vols. Cairo, 1950-1953.
Kraus, P. Jabir: Jabir Ibn Hayyan. Cairo, 1942.
Kraus, P. Opera: Razis Opera Philosophica. Cairo, 1939.
Kula'i. Ihkam: Ihkam san'at al-kalam, ed. Muh. al-Dayah. Beirut, 1967.
Lane, E.   Arabic-English Lexicon. Edinburgh, 1863.
Laoust, H. Ibn Taymiyyah: Essai sur les doctrines sociale et politique de Taki al-Din Ahmad Ibn Taimiya. Cairo, 1939.
Leclrec, L. Histoire: Histoire de la medicine arabe. 2 vols. Paris, 1876.
Le Gentil, P. Poesie: La poesie lyrique espagnole et portugaise a la fin du moyen age. Rennes, 1949-1953.
Levi-Provencal, E.
Civilication: Le civilization arabe en Espagne. 3rd. ed. Paris, 1961.
———. Collier: "En relisant le'Collier de la colombe'." Al-Andalus, 15 (1950), 335p360.
———. Histoire: Histoire de l 'Espagne musulmane. 3 vols. Paris, 1950-1953.
Lopez Ortiz J. Derecho: Derecho musulman. Barcelona-Buenos Aires, 1932.
MacDonald, D. B.
Theology: Development of Muslim Theology, Jurisprudence and Constitutional Theory. New York, 1903.
———. Attitude: The Religious Life and Attitude in Islam. London, 1909.
Madkour, I. Organon: L'Organon d'Aristote dans le monde arabe: ses traductions, son etude, et ses applications. Paris, 1934; 1969.
Mahdi, M. Ibn Khaldun: Ibn Khaldun's Philosophy of History. London, 1957.
Maimonides, M. Guide: Guide to the Perplexed. English trans. M. Friedlander. New York, 1956.
Makdisi, G. Ash'ari: "Ash'ari and the Ash'arites in Islamic Religious History," Studia Islamica, XVII-XVIII (1962), 37-80 and 19-39.
———. Dialectique: "Le livre de la dialectique d'Ibn 'Aqil," Bulletin d'etudes Orientales, 20 (1967), 119-206.
———. Ibn 'Aqil: Ibn 'Aqil et la resurgence de l'Islam traditionaliste au XIe siecle. Damascus, 1963.

———. *Institution:*	"Muslim Institution of Learning in Eleventh Century Baghdad," *BSOAS,* XXIV (1961), 1-56.
———. *Method:*	"The Scholastic Method in Medieval Education," *Speculum,* XLIX (1974), 640-661.
Malik Ibn Anas. *Muwatta':*	*al-Muwatta'.* Cairo, A.H. 1939.
Maqqari. *Azhar:*	*Azhar al-riyad,* ed. Muh. al-Saqqa et al. 3 vols. Cairo, 1939-1942.
———. *Nafh:*	*Nafh al-tib,* ed. I. 'Abbas, 8 Vols. Beirut, 1968. Partial English trans. P. de Gayangos under the title of *The History of the Mohammedan Dynasties in Spain.* 2 vols. London 1840-1843.
Marcais, W. *Tawq:*	"Observations sur le texte du 'Tawq al-hamama'," *Fets.* *Henri Basset.* Paris, 1938, II, 59-88.
Marrakushi. *Mu'jib:*	*al-Mu'jib fi talkhis akhbar al-Maghrib,* ed M. S. 'Iryan. Cairo, 1963.
Matteo, I. de. *Pretese:*	*Le pretese contradizioni della S. Scrittura secondo Ibn Hazm.* Rome, 1923.
McCarthy, R. C. *Theology:*	*The theology of al-Ash'ari.* Beirut, 1953.
Mez, M. *Renaissance:*	*The Renaissance of Islam.* London, 1937. Spanish trans. (Madrid, 1936).
Mieli, A. *Science:*	*La science arabe.* New ed. Leiden, 1966.
Millas Vallicrosa, J. M. *Estudios:*	*Estudios sobre la historia de la ciencia espanola.* Barcelona, 1949.
Milliot, L. *Introduction:*	*Introduction a l'etude du droit musulman.* Paris, 1953.
Monroe, J. *Poetry:*	*Hispano-Arabic Poetry: A Student Anthology.* Berkeley, 1974.
———. *Tawabi':*	See under Ibn Shuhayd.
Mubarrad. *Kamil:*	*Kitab al-kamil fi-l-lughah wa-l-adab,* ed. Abu-l-Fadl Ibrahim. 4 vols. Cairo, 1956.
Mu'jam: *Mu'jam fiqh Ibn Hazm.*	2 vols. Damascus, 1966.
Mu nis H. *Clasificacion:*	"Clasificacion de las ciencias segun Ibn Hazm." *Revista del Instituto Egipcio de Estudios Islamicos,* 13 (1956-1966), 7-16.
Munk, S. *Melanges:*	*Melanges de philosophie juive et arabe.* Paris, 1859.
Muslim. *Sahih:*	*Sahih.* 4 vols. Cairo, A.H. 1330.
Mutanabbi. *Diwan:*	*Diwan,* ed F. Dietrici. Berlin, 1861.
Mutlaq, A. H. *Harakah:*	*al-Harakah al-lughawiyah fi-l-Andalus mundh al-fath al-'arabi hatta nihayat 'asr muluk al-tawa' if.* Sidon-Beirut, 1967.
Nallino, Ca. A. *Litterature:*	*La litterature arabe des origines a l'epoque de la dynastie Umayyade.* Paris, 1950.
al-Nashshar, 'A. *Manahij:*	*Manahij al-bahth 'ind mufakkiri al-islam.* Cairo, 1966.
Nicholson, R. *History:*	*A Literary History of the Arabs.* Cambridge, 1956.
Nuwayri. *Nihayah:*	*Nihayah.* 18 vols. Cairo, 1923-1955. The Portion on Spain was translated into Spanish by M. Gaspar Remiro in *Revista del Centro de Estudios Historicos,* 2 (1917-1919).

Nykl, A. R. *Ibn Hazm:*	"Ibn Hazm's Treatise on Ethics," *American Journal of Semitic Languages and Literatures*, XL (1923), 30-36.
———. *Influence:*	"L'influence arabe-andalouse sur les troubadours," *Bulletin Hispanique*, 41 (1939), 305-315.
———.*Poetry:*	*Hispano-Arabic Poetry and Its Relations with Old Provencal Troubadours.* Baltimore, 1946.
———.*Troubadour:*	*Troubadour Studies.* Cambridge, Mass., 1944.
Ocana Jimenez, M. *Notas:*	"Notas sobre la Cordoba de Ibn Hazm," *IX Centenario de Aben Hazem.* Cordoba, 1963.
———. *Tablas:*	*Tablas de conversion.* Madrid-Granada, 1946.
Pearson, J.D. *Index:*	*Index Islamicus.* Cambridge, 1958.
Pellat, Ch. *Ibn Hazm:*	"Ibn Hazm biobliographe et apologiste de l'Espagne muslmane," *Al-Andalus*, 19 (1954), 53-102. Cf. *Fada'il* under Ibn Hazm.
———. *Langue:*	*Langue et litterature arabe.* Paris, 1970.
Peres, H. *Poesie:*	*La poesie andalouse en arabe classique un XIe siecle.* Paris, 1937.
Perlmann, M. *Authors:*	"Eleventh-Century Andalusian Authors on the Jews of Granada." *Proceedings of the American Academy for Jewish Research*, 18 (1949).
———. *Ibn Hazm:*	"Ibn Hazm on the Equivalence of Proofs," *The Jewish Quarterly Review*, 40 (1950)
Pons Boigues,F. *Dos Obras:*	"Dos obras importantisimas de Aben Hazam," en *Homenaje a Menendez y Pelayo.* Madrid, 1899, 509-523.
———. *Ensayo:*	*Ensayo bibliografico sobre los historiadores y geografos arabigo-espanoles.* Madrid, 1898.
Prietoy Vives, A. *Reyes:*	*Los reyes de taifas, estudio historico numismatico.* Madrid, 1926.
Qali. *Amali:*	*al-Amali.* 2 vols. Cairo, 1953-1954.
Qifti. *Tarikh:*	*Tarikh al-hukama'.* ed. A. Muller. Leipzig, 1903.
Qudamah Ibn Ja'far. *Naqd:*	*Kitab naqd al-shi'r*, ed S. A. Bonebakker. Leiden, 1956.
Rasa'il:	*Rasa'il Ibn Hazm*, see 'Abbas.
Rasa'il:	*Rasa'il Ikhwan al-Safa'*, see Ikhwan al-Safa'.
Renan, E. *Averroes:*	*Averroes et l'averroisme.* Paris, 1852.
Rescher, N. *Development:*	*The Development of Arabic Logic.* Pittsburgh, 1964.
———. *Studies:*	*Studies in the History of Arabic Logic.* Pittsburgh, 1963.
Ribera y Tarrago, J. *Ensenanza:*	*La ensenanza entre los musulmanes espanoles.* Zaragoza, 1893.
———. *Disertaciones:*	*Disertaciones y opusculos.* 2 vols. Madrid, 1912.
———. *Musica:*	*Musica de las Cantigas.* Madrid, 1922.
Rikabi, J. *Adab:*	*Fi-l-adab al-andalusi.* 2nd ed. Cairo, 1966.
Rosenthal, F. *Heritage:*	*The Classical Heritage in Islam.* Berkeley-Los Angeles, 1975.
———. *History:*	*History of Muslim Historiography.* Leiden, 1968.
———. *Knowledge:*	*Knowledge Triumphant.* Leiden, 1970.

_____. *Sarahsi:*	Ahmad b. at-Tayyib as-Sarahsi. New Haven, 1943.
Ruska, J. *Alchemisten:*	Arabische Alchemisten. 2 vols. Heidelberg, 1924.
Sa'id. *Tabaqat:*	Tabaqat al-umam. Cairo, n.d.
Sakkaki. *Miftah:*	Miftah al-'ulum. Cairo, A.H. 1317.
Salem, A. *Khawarij:*	Political Theory and Institutions of the Khawarij. Baltimore, 1956
Samso, Julio. *Medicina:*	"En torno al collar de la paloma" y la medicina," Al-Andalus, 49 (1975), 213-19.
Sanchez Perez, J.A. *Ciencia:*	La ciencia arabe en la edad media. Madrid, 1954.
Sarton, G. *Introduction:*	Introduction to the History of Science. 3 vols. Baltimore, 1927-1948.
Schack, A. F. *Poesie:*	Poesie und Kunst der Araber in Spanien und Sizilien. Berlin-Stuggart, 1865-1877.
Schacht, J. *Introduction:*	Introduction to Islamic Law. Oxford, 1964.
_____. *Origins:*	The Origins of Muhammadan Jurisprudence. Oxford, 1950.
Schreiner, *Beitrage:*	"Beitrage zu Geschichte der theologischen Bewegun in Islam." ZDMG, LII and LIII (1899).
Seco de Lucena, L. *Naqt:*	"Sobre el "Naqt al-'arus" de Ibn Hazm de Cordoba," Al-Andalus, 6 (1941), 357-375. Spanish translation in Boletin de la Universidad Granada (1941).
Sezgin, F. *Geschichte:*	Geschichte des arabischen Schriftums. Leiden, 1967.
Shabibi, Muh. *Adab:*	Adab al-Magharibah wa-l-Andalusiyyin. Cairo, 1961.
Shafi'i. *Fiqh:*	Fiqh al-akbar. Cairo, A.H. 1324.
_____. *Risalah:*	Risalah fi usul al-fiqh. Cairo, A.H. 1321.
Shahrastani. *Milal:*	Kitab al-milal wa-l-nihal. Cairo, n.d.
Shalaby, A. *History:*	History of Muslim Education. Beirut, 1954.
Shaqundi. *Risalah:*	in Maqqari, Nafh, III, 186-222. Spanish trans. by E. Garcia Gomez under Elogio del Islam espanol. Madrid-Granada, 1934.
Sharif, M. *History:*	History of Muslim Philosophy. 2 vols. Wiesbaden, 1963-1966.
Sharishi. *Sharh:*	Sharh al-maqamat al-haririyyah. 2 vols. Cairo, A.H. 1314.
Sibawayh. *Kitab:*	al-Kitab. 2 vols. Cairo, A.H. - 1316-1317.
Simonet, F.J. *Historia:*	Historia de los mozarabes de Espana. Madrid-Granada, 1897-1903.
Steinschneider, M. *Literatur:*	Polimische und apologetische Literatur in arabischen Sprache, zwischen Muslimen, Christen und Juden. (Abhandlungen fur die Kunde des Morgenlandes, VI, no. 3), Leipzig, 1877.
Subki. *Tabaqat:*	Tabaqat al-shafi'iyyah. 3 vols. Cairo, A.H. 1324.
Suter, H. *Mathematiker:*	Die Mathematiker und Astronomen der Araber und ihre Werke. Leipzig, 1900.
Suyuti. *Bughyah:*	Bughyat al-wu'ah fi tabaqat al-lughawiyyin wa-l-nuhah. Cairo, A.H. 1326.
_____.*Muzhir:*	al-Muzhir. 2 vols. Cairo, 1958.
_____. *Tafsir:*	Tafsir al-jalalayn. Cairo, A.H. 1308-1321.
Tabari. *Akhbar:*	Akhbar al-rusul wa-l-muluk. 3 vols. ed. M.J. De Goeje et al. Leiden, 1879-1901.

———. *Tafsir:*	*Tafsir al-Qur'an.* 30 vols. Cairo, n.d.
al-Tawhidi. *Imta':*	*al-Imta' wa-l-mu'anasah.* Ed. A. Amin and A. Zayn, 3 vols. Cairo, 1939-44.
Tha'alibi. *Yatimah:*	*Yatimat al-dahr.* 4 vols. Damascus, A.H. 1304.
Thorndike, L., *History:*	*History of Magic and Experimental science* 2 vols., Cambridge, 1927.
Ticknor, G. *History:*	*History of Spanish Literature.* 3rd ed. Boston, 1866.
Tirmidhi. *Sunan:*	*Sunan.* 2 vols. Cairo, A.H. 1291.
Tomiche, *Epitre morale:*	See *Akhlaq* under Ibn Hazm.
Tourneau, R. Le. *Almohad:*	*The Almohad Movement.* Princeton, 1969.
Trabulsi, A. *Critique:*	*La critique poeitque des Arabes.* Damascus, 1956.
Tritton, A.S. *Ibn Hazm:*	"Ibn Hazam, the Man and the Thinker," *Islamic Studies,* III (1964), 471-84
———. *Theology:*	*Muslim Theology.* London, 1947.
Turtushi. *Siraj:*	*Siraj al-muluk.* Cairo, A.H. 1287.
Tyan, E. *Histoire:*	*Histoire de l'organization judiciaire en pays de l'islam.* 2 vols. Paris, 1938-43.
van Hess, J. *Theology:*	"The logical Structure of Islamic Theolgy." In Grunebaum, *Logic,* 21-50.
Vernet, J. *Literatura:*	*Literatura arabe.* Barcelona, 1968.
Wensinck, A.J. *Creed:*	*Muslim Creed.* London, 1965.
———. *Handbook:*	*A Handbook of Early Muhammadan Traditions.* London, 1927.
Wulf, M. de. *Histoire:*	*Histoire de la philosophie medievale.* Lovain, 1922.
Wustenfeld, F. *Geschichtschreiber:*	*Die Geschichtschreiber der Araber und ihre Werke.* Gottingen, 1882.
Yafi'i. *Mir'at:*	*Mir'at al-janan.* 4 vols. Heyderabad, A.H. 1337-1339.
Yaqut. *Irshad:*	*Irshad al-arib.* 7 vols. ed. D. S. Marogliouth, Leiden-London, 1907-1927.
———. *Mu'jam:*	*Mu'jam al-buldan.* 8 vols Beirut, 1955.
Zaydan, J. *Tarikh:*	*Tarikh adab al-lughah al-'arabiyyah.* 4 vols. Cairo, 1957.
Zirikli. *A'lam:*	*al-A'lam.* 10 vols. Cairo, 1954-1959.
Zubaydi. *Istidrak:*	*Kitab al-istidrak 'ala Sibawayh,* ed. I. Guidi. Rome, 1890.
———. *Mukhtasar:*	*Mukhtasar al-'ayn* (in manuscript).
———. *Tabaqat:*	*Tabaqat al-nahwiyyin wa-l-lughawiyyin,* ed. Muh. Ibrahim. Cairo, 1954.

INDEX

'Abbaids, 29
'Abbas, I, 11, 13, 170, 190
'Abbasid Caliph, 94, 146
'Abadolah (emir), 147
'Abdallah Ibn Qasim, 44ff.
'Abd al-'Aziz, 29
'Abdallah Ibn Ruwahah, 137, 196
'Abd al-Malik Ibn Sa'id al-Muradi, 139
'Abd al-Rahman III, 23, 36
'Abd al-Rahman V (al-Mustazhir), 27
'Abd al-Rahman al-Murtada, 26
'Abd al-Rahman Sanchol, 23
'Abd al-Rahman b. Isma'il b. Zayd, 160
Abridgement (Ibn Al-Sarraj), 195
Abu 'Abdallah b. Mas'ud, 161
Abu 'Ali al-Hatimi, 139, 175
Abu Bakr, b. Bishrun, 180
Abu Bakr, 145
Abu Bakr Ibn Hazm, 24
Abu Hanifah, 8, 111, 125, 126, 127, 131
Abu Hayyan, 15
Abu Hurayrah, 145
Abu Ishaq al-Hufi, 90
Abu-l-Mughirah, 27, 32
Abu-l-Salt, 178
Abu-l-Walid Yunus Ibn 'Abdallah, 199
Abu Nuwas, 140
Abu Sulayman (son of Ibn Hazm), 30
Abu Tammam
Abu 'Ubayd, 8, 143, 196
Abu Zahrah, 13
Acts of the Council of Toledo, 40
Acts of Martyrs, 40, 51
Adam, 112, 192
'adl, 63, 116
adna, 64, 127
Adomites, 183, 198
afanin, 207
afdal al-'ulum, 100
afdal al-umam, 145
al-Afghani, 11
Afudiqtiqa (Apodictics), 172
al-Aghlab, 28
Aghlab Ibn Shu'ayb, 139
al-aghzal wa-l-raqiq, 137, 196
Agriculture, 88, 102
ahkam, 97, 102 (of *hukm*)
Ahkam al-nujum, 181
ahl al-nazar, 47
ahl al-shaghab, 174
ahl al-ra'y, 99
Ahmad B. Hafsun b. 'Abdallah, 161
Ahmad Ibn 'Abd al-Malik Ibn Marwan, 139

Admad Ibn Dawud al-Dinawari, 143
Ahmad Ibn Faraj, 139
Ahmad Ibn Hazm (father), 20, 21ff.
Ahmad Ibn Ishaq, 8
Ahmad Ibn Rashiq, 28, 29
ahsana, 123
ahsan al-aqwal, 123
'A'ishah, 121, 145
'ajam, 20
ajnas (jins), 96, 170
ajr 'azim, 142
akhbaq, 93, 154, 157
akhbar (cf. khabar), 102
akhbar daruriyah, 101
al-akhdh al-mursal, 124
Akhlaq, 11, 30, 32, 63, 64, 154
a'ala, 64
'a la zahirih, 113, 121
alah, 159, 162, 163
'alamah, 129ff.
Alchemy, 88, 89, 94, 100, 108, 155, 179, 180ff, 192
Alcira, 178
Alexander, 150, 153, 206
Alexandria, 37
alfaz, 170
Algarve, 20
Algeciras, 34
'Ali, 9, 125, 145, 151
'Ali Ibn 'Abbas al-Rumi, 140
'Ali Ibn Hammud, 25
'Ali Ibn Mujahid, 29
Aljamiado Texts, 19
'alim, 118
'allamah, 62
Almagest, 156, 197
Almeria, 25, 26, 31, 36, 51
Almohad Dynasty, 16, 108
Almohad rulers, 16, 107
Almohads, 17
Alpuente, 27, 28, 31, 51
'amal, 9
amarah, 47
al-'Amiri, 57, 84, 96, 104, 162, 163
'Amirid, 21, 22, 25; 'Amirids, 23, 25;
'Amiri dictatorship, 36
'amm, 177
Ammonites, 150, 183, 198, 206
amr (cf. command), 47, 119, 171
Analogy (cf *qiyas*)
Analytics *(qiyas)*, 159, 172, 173ff, 176
'anasir, 172

INDEX

Anawati, 12
anbiya' (cf. Prophets), 112
Ancients (philosophers), 6, 164, 171, 173, 174, 177
al-Andalus (cf Muslim Spain), 2, 3, 6, 7, 11, 19, 20, 22, 23, 27, 32, 35, 37, 44, 55, 57, 85, 89, 94, 123, 133, 146, 149, 150, 159, 160, 161, 178, 180, 186, 206
Andalusian; cities, 36; culture, 42; poets, 145; scholars, 57, 107, 147; society, 1, 2, 22, 134
Andalusians, 35, 39, 89, 90, 94, 159, 160
Andreas Cappelanus, 19
Andrumakhish, 155
Angelology, 87
Anselmo Turmeda, 19
'Antarah, 137, 196
Anulutikiya, 172; cf. Analytics
anwa' 96 (cf. *naw'*)
Apodictics *(burhan)*, 160, 172ff., 176
Appolonius, 94
'aqibah, 123
'aqil, 70, 80, 81, 105
'aql, 47, 68, 69, 70, 79, 80, 105, 116, 120, 131
'aqliyy, 102
aqsam, 83
Aquila, 183, 199
Aquinas, ST., 105
aqwal basitah, 176
Arab; aristocracy, 22; scholars, 13ff., world, 5
Arabian Peninsula, 27
Arabic; culture, 181; grammar, 27, 45, 114, 126, 142ff.; language, 1, 21, 39, 45, 52, 53, 56, 62, 86, 87, 94, 97, 98, 103, 117ff., 127, 130, 134, 142ff., 153, 157, 160, 162, 177, 212; literature, 56, 134, 136; lexicography, 127, 142ff.' logic, 159 ff., 160, 169; lyrical poetry, 12; philology, 83, 160; science, 21, 83, 85, 98, 88, 95, 212; works, 19
Arabs, 20, 62, 93, 98, 141, 142, 146, 149, 159
a'rad (cf. *'arad),* 96, 170
'arad, 70, 96, 119
Arberry, 12
Archimedes, 94
Archpriest of Hita, 19
Ardashir Ibn Babak, 150, 202, 206
Aristotle, 39, 86, 94, 140, 153, 154, 159, 164, 169, 170, 172, 174, 175, 176, 177

Aristotelian logic, 160, 168; methodology, 162
Arnaldez, 12, 117, 118
Art of Courtly Love, 19
Art of Reading, 86, 88
Art of Writing, 86, 87
'arud, 133
ashab al-alfayn, 145
al-Ash'ari, 1, 53, 117ff., 162
Ash'arite, 16, 113
al-ashbah wa-l-ula, 127
ashkal al-burhan, 173
ashkhas, 96, 170
Asin, 11, 15, 18, 21, 52, 190
asl (usul), 47, 106, 110, 113, 114, 119, 143
al-asma' al mufradah (of categories), 171
al-asma' al-mukhtalifah, 171
al-asma' al-musthtaqqah, 171
al-asma' al-mushtarikah, 171
al-asma' al-mutaradifah, 171
al-asma' al-mutawati'ah, 171
Assyrians, 183, 198
Astrologers, 184ff., 199, 213
Astrology, 88, 89, 91, 94, 96, 107, 155, 179, 181ff., 198ff., 209
Astronomy, 38, 86, 88, 89, 90, 91, 94, 96, 97, 99, 108, 153, 154, 156, 206
al-athar al-'ulwiyyah, 87
Athens, 66
athim, 131
Averroes (cf. Ibn Rushd)
awa'il al-'aql, 98
awamir (cf *amr)*
Awqaf Collection, 190
al-Awza'i, 8
awzan, 98
'ayn, 119
al-Azdi, 40
Aznalcazar (husn al-Qasr), 26, 31
Badajoz, 36
Badı' al-Zaman, 134
bahth, 162, 173, 175
al-Baji, 29, 54
balaghah (cf Rhetoric), 97, 103, 120, 133, 140
Balat al-Mughirah, 24, 33
Balawi, 5
balaya, 167
Banu Hazm, 20, 21
Baghdad, 37, 135, 146
Baqiyy Ibn Makhlad, 147
bara ah, 140, 175
barahim (cf. *burhan)*
Bari Arminiyas (cf Hermeneutics), 171
Bashshar, 139
Basrah, 37, 143, 145
batil, 47

INDEX

al-batil batil, 123
batin, 18, 76, 120
batiniyyah, 79, 105
batt, 157, 206
bayan, 47, 113, 119, 133
bazi, 129
belles lettres, 37, 89, 133 ff.
Berbers, 23, 24, 25, 26, 27, 93, 94, 146
Bercher, 12
bida' (cf. bid'ah)
bid'ah, 1, 18, 44, 47, 116, 127
bi-fi'l, 87; fi'l, 106
bi-iktisab, 71
bi-muqaddimat raji'ah, 72
Biography, 88, 89
bi-quwwah, 87
Black: Africa, 69; communities, 150, 206; people, 97, 150
Bobastro, 34
Book of Good Love, 19
Book of Poetry, 134, 147
Books, 101ff., 203ff.
Bosch, 12
Botany, 88
Brahmans, 81
Brahmins, 201
Brethern of Purity, 4, 83, 87ff., 99, 163, 179
Brockelman, 13
Buddhism, 3
al-Buhturi, 139
burhan (barahin), 16, 46, 47, 54, 70, 77, 79, 96, 113, 123, 153, 162, 165, 168, 172, 174, 176
Byzantine Emperor, 137
Caliphate (abolished), 24ff., 28, 36, 146, 149
Caliphs, 146
Calligraphy, 85
Categories, 160, 171, 176
Categories of Nations (Sa'id) 93ff
Categories of Scholars (Ibn Hazm) 134, 147
Categories of the Sciences, (cf *Maratib al-'ulum*) 1, 4, 11, 39, 61, 64, 96, 99ff.
Causatin, (cf *ta'lil*)
Ceuta, 25
Chaldeans, 93, 94
Chejne, 12, 190
Chemistry, 180
China, 61, 150, 183, 186, 198, 206
Chinese, 93, 150, 183, 198
Christianity, 3, 18, 19, 53, 105, 110, 122
Christian Liturgies, 40,51
Christians, 1, 19, 23, 35, 51, 81, 111, 122, 124, 159, 202
City Management (Farabi), 87
Classification of the sciences, 83ff.
Clear Book (Zubaydi), 195
Commands, 113, 114, 116, 119ff., 122

Commentary, 85
Common people, 78
Companions, 1, 3, 43, 112, 115ff., 124, 125, 126, 145, 149, 150
Companions Who Made Legal Decisions (Ibn Hazm), 145
Consensus (cf. *ijma'*)
Copts, 93, 158, 183, 198, 205
Cordova, 13, 23, 24, 26, 27, 29, 31, 36, 41, 51, 94, 135, 147
Crafts, 88, 90, 155
Curriculum, 100ff.
al-Dabbi, 5, 7
Dad and Za', (Ibn Hazm) 134
daha', 79
da'if, 127
dahriyyun, 82
dalal, 78, 123
dala'il (cf. *dalil*), 123
dalalah, 63
dalil (dala'il), 47, 81, 115, 120, 121, 131, 132, 136
dalil al-khitab, 47, 121, 126
dall, 47
Damascus, 18, 145, 146, 151
Danesh-name (Ibn Sina), 89
daribah, 34
da'wa al-ilham, 124
Darius Ibn Darius, 150, 206
dawahi, 10
Day of Judgement, 61
Dayah, 13
Daylamites, 97
Deliver From Error (Ghazzali), 106
Demonstration *(cf. istidlal),* 75, 88, 108
Denia, 28, 31, 36, 60
Denominations (of Muslim sects) 97, 111, 147
al-Dhahabi, 5, 7, 8ff., 11, 15, 18, 42, 111, 157, 169
dhat allah, 9
dhat al-aswar, 172
dhikr, 60
Dhu-l-Qi'dah, 24
Dialectics (cf. *jadal* and *disputatio*) 76
didd, 177
Di Matteo, 12
din, 31, 92
Dioscorides, 157
disputatio (cf. *jadal*), 46ff., 88, 106, 107, 172, 175
Divination, 8, 88, 89
Divine Revelation, 16, 17, 46, 54, 68, 75, 76, 80, 81, 82, 88, 95, 97, 107, 111, 116, 143, 151, 201
Don Quijote, 35
Dove's Ring (Ibn Hazm) (cf. *Tawq*), 134
Dozy, 12, 20
Dreams, 185ff.
Dream Interpretation, 88, 97, 99, 108, 185, 207
dun-istidlal, 75

329

INDEX

dururi, 62
East, 14, 15, 34, 35, 40, 41, 84, 146, 152, 159, 160, 181
Eastern al-Andalus, 29, 46, 60; authors 5, 134; Islam, 35, 159, 161
Edomites, 150
Education, 36ff., 49, 99ff., 103
Egypt, 37, 147
Egyptians, 93, 94
Eisagoge, 159ff., 163, 170ff., 176
Eloquence and Rhetoric (Ibn Hazm), 134
Empedocles, 94
Euclid, 6, 39, 52, 94, 154, 156, 197
English, 190
Ethics, 86, 94
Ethiopia, 144
Europe, 136
European language, 19
European thought, 4
Europeans, 136
Evidence, see *hujjah*
Excellence of Al-Andalus (Ibn Hazm), (cf. *Fada'il),* 134
al-fa''alah al-mudabbirah, 70
fada'il (cf. *fadl),*
fada'il al-nafs, 94
fadihah, 34
Fadl (fada'il) (Ibn Hazm), 28, 38, 64, 74, 75, 139, 146ff., 161, 169
Fadl, son of Ibn Hazm, 10, 30
fahm, 63, 72, 116, 167
Fahrasah (Ibn Hazm), 40
fa'il, 171
faith (cf. *Iman),* 46, 109, 110, 111
falsafah (cf. philosophy), 153
Falsehood, see *batil*
al-faqih al-muntahi, 8
far' (furu'), 7, 8, 47, 106
Farabi, 4, 86ff., 89, 94, 96, 154, 158, 160, 163, 176, 179, 180, 181
Farewell Pilgrimage (Ibn Hazm), 144
fard, 47
fard 'ayn, 106
fard kifayah, 106, 142, 156
faridah, 61
fasiq, 55, 124
fasl, 107, 170
Fatih Mosque, 11, 190
fawr, 47
fi dhatih, 124
Fihrist, (Ibn al-Nadim), 89
fikrah, 62
fiqh (of jurisprudence), 87, 127

Firaq, 196
Fisal, (Ibn Hazm), 11, 18, 34, 46, 51, 52, 63, 98, 100, 110ff., 121, 122, 144, 146, 147, 151, 159, 169, 181, 184, 185, 202
fitnah, 22, 32, 33
Foreign sciences, 83, 88, 89
Friedlander, 12
funun, 94
furu' (cf. far')
futya, 97, 165
Gabriel, 144
Gabrieli, 12
Galen, 39, 94, 154, 157
Galicians, 94
Garcia Gomez, 12, 21, 135
Gardet, 12
Genealogy, 62, 89, 102, 146ff., 149ff., 206
General Library of Rabat, 190
Geometry, 88, 89, 94, 97, 99, 107, 108, 198
gha'ib, 62
gharad, 47, 129ff.
gharib, 97
al-gharib al-musannaf, 143, 196
ghayr burhaniyy, 155
Ghazzali, 1, 8, 15, 80ff., 85, 104ff., 162, 164, 170, 177
Gibb, 12, 13
God, 10, 32, 48, 52, 53, 61, 64, 65, 67, 71, 73, 74ff., 80, 81, 90, 92, 97, 99, 100, 101, 108, 110 111ff., 116ff., 121, 122, 125ff., 138, 167, 171, 180, 184, 185, 186, 197, 201
Gogs and Magogs, 93
Goldziher, 12, 15
Gospels, 40
Grammar, 85, 88, 89, 97, 98, 99, 100, 106, 195ff., 206
Granada, 26, 27, 31
Greek, 39, 56, 83, 153, 162, 170, 171
Greek logic, 162
Greek philosophers, 144, 154, 159
Greeks, 93, 94, 150, 155, 157, 206
Guide to the Knowledge of the 'Abbadids (Fadl Ibn Hazm), 30
Habib, 139 (see Abu Tammam)
Habib Ibn 'Aws, 140
hadd (hudud), 47, 96, 170, 176
hadith, 102, 144; cf. Traditions
hajib, 22
Hajjaj, 52
Hajji, 13
Hajji Khalifah, 6

INDEX

Hajiri, 13
Hakam I (emir), 147
Hakam II (caliph), 21, 22, 36, 45, 147, 160
hal, 123
halal, 122
haml, 170
Hammudids, 25ff., 147
Hanabalism, 3
Hanbalite, 18, 43
Hanifism, 3
Hanfiite, 43, 123
haqa'iq al-ashya', 72
haqq, 47, 54, 70; cf. truth
al-haqq haqq, 123
al-haqq taqlidan, 125
Haqqi, 11
harakah iradiyah, 71
haram, 47, 122, 139
Harun, 11
Hasan, 140
Hasan al-Basri, 65, 141, 175
Hassan Ibn Thabit, 137, 196
hayawan, 87
Haykal, 13
Hayy (Ibn Tufayl), 17
Hazmiyyah, 15
Hebrew, 39, 53
Hebrews, 93
Hell, 61
Hereafter, 100, 191, 194, 196, 210, 214
Hermeneutics, 160, 176
hifz, 8
High March, 24
hija', 138, 197
Hijjah (Ibn Hazm), 11
hikam wa-khayr, 137
Hinduism, 3
Hippocrates, 38, 154, 157
Hisham I (emir), 147
Hisham II (caliph), 21, 22, 23, 24, 25, 30, 33
Hisham III (caliph), 27, 28
Hispano-Arabic: authors, 5; manuscripts, 4; society, 1
Hiss, 63, 69, 71
hissiyy, 102
History, 37, 88, 89, 96, 97, 100, 107, 143ff., 200ff., 206ff.
hiyal, 185
Holy Texts, 117, 142; cf. *nass*
Horten, 12
hudud, 96; cf. *hadd*
hudud al-kalam, 165

hudud al-mantiq, 153
hujjah (hujaj), 8, 47, 54, 71, 79, 116, 131
hukama', 67
hukm, 47, 123, 130
Humam Ibn Ahmad, 41
Humaydi, 5, 7, 15, 28, 40, 42, 136, 137, 144, 161, 169
humq, 70, 79
Hunayn Ibn Ishaq, 160
huruf wa-rumuz, 164
al-ibanah wa-l-tabyin, 47
'ibarah (cf. Hermeneutics), 96, 160, 171
Ibn al-Abbar, 5, 149
Ibn 'Abd al-Barr, 4, 15, 28, 29, 36, 40, 42, 60ff., 63, 90ff., 95, 96
Ibn 'Abd Rabbihi, 58, 59, 61
Ibn 'Add Rahman al-Nasir, 6
Ibn 'Abd al-Warith, 40
Ibn Abi 'Abdah, 40
Ibn Abi 'Amir al-Mansur, 21, 22ff., 94ff., 146, 147
Ibn al-Anbari, 143, 196
Ibn 'Aqil, 79, 80
Ibn 'Arabi, Muhyi al Din, 5, 15, 17
Ibn 'Arabi, Abu Muhammad, 15
Ibn al-'Arabi al-Ishbili, (lAbu Bakr) 5, 9ff., 14, 15, 41
Ibn Asbagh, 42
Ibn Bajjah, 1, 11, 178
Ibn Bashkuwal, 5
Ibn Bassam, 5
Ibn Dahhun, 41
Ibn Darraj al-Qastali, 139
Ibn Dawud, 135
Ibn Dawud al-Dinawari, 196
Ibn al-Faradi, 40
Ibn Gabirol, 11
Ibn Fathun al-Saraqusti, 161
Ibn Hajar, 6
Ibn Hawwat, 6
Ibn al-Haytham, 38, 157
Ibn Hayyan, 6, 20, 21, 24, 27, 36, 169
Ibn Hazm, 1, 2, 3, 4, 6; works, 11, 11ff.; His influence on 14ff; doctrine, 15; genealogy, 20; his family, 22f.; in Mallorca, 28ff.; In Eastern Andalus, 29; death, 36; on society, 31ff.; on revolt, 32; on Cordova, 33; on Caliphate, 33ff.; on Rulers, 35; on al-Andalus, 35; education of, 37ff.; teachers of, 39ff.; Zahirite, 43ff.; Palemics 46ff.; on rules of disputatio, 48ff.; on knowledge, 57ff.; and al-Ghazzali. 80ff., 104ff., classification, 96ff.

INDEX

98ff.; and Ibn Khaldun, 108ff.;
Ash'ari, 117ff.; on language, 117ff.;
human criteria, 121ff.; *ijtihad* 130ff.;
love, 135; belles lettres, 133ff.;
Poetry, 137ff.; Rhetoric, 137ff.;
Language, 142ff.; History, 143ff.;
Philosophy, 153ff.; on Mathematics,
155ff.; on Astronomy, 156; on Medicine, 156ff.; on Natural science,
158; on logic, 158ff.
Ibn al-Iflili, 133
Ibn al-'Imad, 6, 7
Ibn al-Jallad, 160
Ibn al-Jassur, 40
Ibn Juljul, 89
Ibn al-Kattani, 39, 41, 51, 103, 154, 157, 161, 180
Ibn Khaldun, 6, 18, 85, 93, 104, 108ff., 147, 174, 181, 184ff., 187ff.
Ibn Khallikan, 5, 7, 169
Ibn Khaqan, 5
Ibn al-Khatib, 6, 147
Ibn Kathir, 5, 7
Ibn Khayr, 137
Ibn Muflit, 41, 45, 46
Ibn al-Muqaffa', 141, 160, 175
Ibn al-Nadim, 4, 83, 89, 96, 98, 176, 179
Ibn al-Naghrilah, 11, 53
Ibn Nami, 42
Ibn Nubati, 42
Ibn Qudamah, 111, 140
Ibn Rushd, 1, 11, 15, 16, 17, 79, 85, 107ff., 154, 162, 178
Ibn al-Saffar, 41
Ibn Sa'id, 5, 147, 169
Ibn al-Samh, 180
Ibn al-Sarraj, 143, 195
Ibn Shuhayd, 5, 13, 27, 36, 133ff., 140, 175
Ibn Sidah, 28, 29, 36, 160
Ibn Sina, 83, 89, 96, 154, 158, 160, 163ff., 180, 181, 190
Ibn Taymiyah, 18
Ibn al-Tubni, 42
Ibn Tufayl, 1, 16, 17, 79, 85, 107, 178
Ibn Tumart, 16ff.
Ibn Tumlus, 178
Ibn 'Uthman, 42
Ibn Wajh al-Jannah, 42
Ibn al-Waqshi, 161
Ibn Zaydun, 36
Ibn Zur'ah, 163
ibtal, 11, 18, 121

'id al-adha, 180
'id al-fitr, 180
idafah, 171
idan, 180
Ideal City (Farabi), 87
idrak, 69
Idris b. Yahya b. 'Ali b. Hammud, 34
b,i-idtrar, 71
idtirariyyah, 72
ihkam, 98
Ihkam (Ibn Hazm), 11, 46, 47, 53, 63, 110ff., 121, 128, 151, 159
ihsa', 83
Ihsa' al-'ulum (Farabi), 163
ihtiyat, 12ff., 47, 121
ijazah, 37
ijma', 1, 43, 44, 47, 102, 110, 113ff., 115ff., 123
al-ijma' al-sahih al-mutayaqqan, 115
ijtihad, 3, 8, 18, 43, 45, 47, 68, 105, 130ff., 162, 175
al-ijtihad al-muqayyad, 8
ijtihad al-ra'y, 126
ikhlas, 92
ikhtilaf, 115
ikmal al-din, 115
ilahiyyun, 82
al-'ilaj bi-l-fikr, 91
'ilal (see *'illah),* 98, 110
ilham, 47, 70ff., 180, 173
'illah (see *'ilal),* 10, 47, 128, 143
al-'illah wa-l- ma'lul, 171, 174
'ilm, 47, 57, 103, 106, 118, 163
'ilm al-adab, 88
'ilm al-a'dad, (cf. mathematics), 88, 102
'ilm ahwal al-qalb, 106
'ilm Allah, 73
'ilm a'la, 90
'ilm al-alfaz, 86
'ilm asfal, 90
'ilm al-athqal, 86
'ilm awsat, 90
'ilm al-badihiyat, 72, 74
'ilm al-hay'ah, (cf. astronomy), 102
'ilm al-handasah, 86
'ilm hada'iq al-umur, 105
'ilm al-hiyal, 86
'ilm al-'ibarah (cf. dreams), 103
al-'ilm al-ilahi, 86
'ilm al-istidlal, 85
'ilm al-jazr wa-l-fa'l, 88

INDEX

'ilm al-khabar (cf. *khabar* and history), 148
'ilm al-khalq, 73
'ilm al-lisan, 86
al-'ilm al-madani, 87
'ilm madhmum, 106
'ilm mahmud, 106
'ilm al-manazir, 86
'ilm al-mantiq, see logic
'ilm al-mu'amalah, 106
'ilm al-mukashafah, 106
'ilm al-musiqa, 86
'ilm al-nafs, 102
'ilm al-nujum (cf. astronomy), 86, 102
'ilm qawanin al-ash'ar, 86
'ilm qawanin al-kitabah, 86
'ilm qawanin al-qira'ah, 86
'ilm al-qiyas, 90
'ilm al-ta'alim, 86
al-'ilm al-tabi'i, 86
bi-'ilm yaqiniyyin, 105
'ilm al-tibb (cf. medicine), 102
al-'ilm al-yaqin, 105
al-'ilm wa-l-adab, 58
al-'ilm wa-l-'amal, 64
ilzam, 47
imam, 9, 47, 68, 73, 79, 80
al-imam al-ma'sum, 105
imamate (cf. Caliphate), 146
Imamate and Politics (Ibn Hazm), 146, 208
Imitation (cf. taqlid)
Imru'u al-Qays, 140
'inad, 47
inbittat al-ma', 127
Incantation, 185ff.
India, 150, 156, 183, 198, 206
Indians, 93, 94, 150
al-ins wa-l-jinn, 112, 149
insan, 70
intellect *('aql)*, 58, 62, 70ff., 73ff., 109
Inventory of the Sciences (Farabi), 86ff.
al-'Iqd al-farid (Ibn 'Abd Rabbihi), 58, 59, 61
iqna', 47
i'rab, 97
Iraq, 37
'ird, 31
Isal (Ibn Hazm), 111
Ishaq Ibn Hunayn, 160
isharat, 89, 164
Islam, 1, 2, 3, 4, 5, 51, 54, 55, 78, 79, 92, 105, 109 111, 143, 144, 148, 150, 153, 179
Isalamic; community, 14, 34, 43, 110, 124, 130, 145, 150, 206; culture, 42, 85, 157, 164, 179; conquests, 145; dynasties, 147; experiences, 148, 150
Islamic; history, 1, 143; law 43; religion, 200; sects. 2. 46; sciences: . 83; theology, 162; world, 190
ism, 120, 172
Isma'il Ibn Yunus, 26, 39
Israelites (cf. Jews), 206
Istanbul, 4, 11, 190
istidlal, 49, 62, 72, 79, 132
al-istidlal bi-l-shahid 'ala al-gha'ib, 173
istihsan, 1, 47, 121, 123
istikhbar, 171
istilah, 118
isti'mal al-hawas, 72
istinbat, 47, 12, 127
istiqna', 173
al-istiqra' al-madhmum, 174
istithna', 47, 115
ithbat hujuj al-'uqul, 79
i'tiqad, 10, 47, 71, 73, 80, 106
ittiba', 62
'iyafah, 91
'izzah, 10
jabbar, 118
Ja'far Ibn 'Uthman al-Hajib, 139
al-jadal al-madhmum, 46
al-jadal al-mahmud, 79
jadal wa-jadal, 47
jadal wa-munazarah, 173; cf. *disputatio*
Jahiz, 141
jahl, 32, 47, 54, 63, 87
jaliy, 62
Jamharah (Ibn Hazm), 149
Jami' (Ibn 'Abd al-Barr), 60, 61, 63, 90, 93
jami'ah, 173, 177
Jarir, 140
Jativa, 27, 28, 29, 31, 51, 135
Jawami' (Ibn Hazm), 11
jawahir, 70; cf. *jawhar*
jawhar, 70, 96, 170, 171
jawr, 63
Jesus, 112
Jewish writings, 51
Jews, 19, 35, 51, 53, 81, 97, 111, 122, 124, 147, 150, 159, 202
jihad, 1, 99, 120
jins (ajnas), 170
jism, 119
jubn, 63
jud, 63
Judaism, 3, 18, 19, 110, 122, 202
Judhwah (Humaydi), 15, 53
Jurisprudence, 88, 89, 90, 95, 102, 107, 108, 110, 206, cf. *fiqh*

INDEX

juz', 177
Ka'b Ibn Malik, 137, 196
kalam, 80, 81, 102; cf. theology
kalam Allah, 113
Kalilah wa-Dimnah (Ibn al-Muqaffa'), 141
kalimah, 172, 176
Kamil (Mubarrad), 147
kammiyyah, 171
karahah, 47
kawn, 9
al-kawn wa-l-fasad, 87
kayfiyyah, 171
Key of the Sciences (Sakkaki), 85
Keys of the Sciences (Khuwarizmi), 88
khabar, 71ff., 98, 171, 176. cf. History
al-khabar al-sahih, 114
al-khabar al-mursal, 127
khabar tawatur, 151
Khadijah, 145
khafiy, 62
Khalaf al-Husri (pseudo-caliph), 34
Khalifah, 11
Khalil Ibn Ahmad, 143
khalq al-insan, 196
Kharijite, 9
khass, 177
khassah, 92, 170
khata', 47
khayr, 67
khayl, 129
Khayran, 25ff., 30
Khazars, 93, 150, 206
khilaf, 47
Khisal (Ibn Hazm), 111
khitab, 126
khitabah, 175; cf. rhetoric
khusus, 47, 115, 117
khutut al-kaff, 91
Khuwarizmi, 4, 83, 88ff., 96, 163, 176
khuyala', 129
kidhb, 32, 47, 54
Kindi, 39, 80, 81, 83, 86ff., 89, 94, 154, 160, 163, 176, 179, 180, 181
Kitab, (Sibawayh), 121, 143
Kitab al-akhbar, 171; cf. Hermeneutics
Kitab al-arithmatiqi (Andrumakhish), 155
Kitab al-'ayn (Khalil Ibn Ahmad), 143
Kitab al-balaghah, 175; cf. Rhetoric
Kitab al-burhan, 172; cf. Apodictics
Kitab al-shi'r, 175; cf. Poetics
Kitab al-zahrah (Ibn Dawud), 135
Knowledge, 56ff., 203ff; 208; cf. *'ilm*
Kufah, 37, 145
kufr, 47, 116, 164

kull, 177
kull dhi hiss salim, 78
kull qa'il, 54
kunayah, 47
kunyah, 20
kutub al-awa'il, 160, 177
la adri, 63
la hukm illa bi-l-lah, 9
la hukm illa bi-l-yaqin wahduh, 122
lafz, 47, 127
lahn, 114
Language, 86, 87, 96, 97, 118ff., 133, 142ff., 206; cf. Arabic
laqab, 146
Latin, 19, 39, 94, 177
lawiyy, 192
Legal decisions, 97; cf. *futya*
Levi-Provencal, 11
Lexicography, 86, 88, 89, 97, 98, 99, 100, 102, 106, 115, 195ff., 206; cf. *lughah*
Linguistic intuition, 120
Logic, 38, 57, 86, 88, 89, 94, 96, 97, 100, 107, 108, 153, 154, 158, 199ff., 201, 206; cf. *'ilm al-mantiq*.
Loving numbers, 187
lubb, 166
lughah, 47, 93, 102; cf. Lexicography
Lunakhas, 156
ma ba'd al-tabi'ah, 87
ma istahsanna, 123
ma istahsanu, 123
ma'adin, 87; cf. Minerology
ma'ani, 85, 102
ma'arif, 72
ma'asi, 79
ma'azif, 180
MacDonald, 12
madhhab, 62
madhahib, 97
Madhiji, 161
madhmum, 56
Maghrib, 9
Maghribi script, 190
Magic, 88, 89, 100, 107, 155, 179, 185ff., 192
mahmud, 56
Maimonides, 11
majalis, cf. *majlis*
majaz, 120
majlis, 7, 37
majmu'ah, 11, 190
Majriti, 180
ma'jur, 156
makan, 171
makhsusah, 172

INDEX

makus wa-qabalat, 142
mala lengua, 52
Malaga, 27, 34
Malik Ibn Anas, 3, 8, 41, 43, 111, 125, 126, 132
Malikism, 3, 41, 43
Malikite (s), 16, 41, 107, 123
Malikite jurisprudence, 29, 41
Mallorca, 15, 28, 29, 31, 46, 51, 54
ma'lul, 129
ma'lum, 47
ma'lumat, 62, 173
Ma'mun, 94
ma'na (ma'ani), 119
man tamantaqa tazandaza, 162
Manahij (Ibn Rushd), 107
Manichaeans, 97
Manichaeism, 201
al-mansus 'alayh, 126
Manta Lisham, 20, 30, 31
mantiq, 116 cf. logic
mantiai. 54
Maqqari, 27
al-Maqsur wa-l-mamdud wa-l-mahmuz (Qali), 196
Maqulat, 160, 171; cf. Categories
maratib, 83
Maratib al-'ulum (Ibn Hazm), 147, 154, 159,177 181, 189ff., 191; translation of, 191-215; edition of, 216ff.
ma'rifah, 61, 74, 96
al-marju' ilayh, 97
Marrakushi, 5, 7, 10, 14, 20, 147
Mars, 184
ma'siyah, 47
al-maskut 'anhu, 126
maslahah, 209
Mathematics, 38, 84, 86, 88, 89, 90, 91, 94, 96, 97, 99, 107ff., 153, 154, 155, 197ff., 206
matn, 102
Matta b. Yunus, 160, 162
mawadi' qard al-farufi al-khaylan, 91
mawali, 20
mawdu'ah, 78
mawhibah, 74
mawjudat, 69
maysar, 180
mazamir, 180
Mecca, 144, 145, 149, 156
Mechanics, 87, 88, 89

Medicine, 39, 85, 88, 89, 90, 91, 92, 94, 96, 97, 98, 108, 153, 154, 206, 213
Medina, 37, 116, 144, 145, 149
Mediterranean, 36
Messengers, (cf. *rusul),* 112
Metaphysics, 84, 94, 108, 153
Medieval European thought
Messenger of God, see Prophet
Middle Ages, 4
miftah, 83, 170
Mihakk (Ghazzali), 177
milk 171
min ghayr dhikr, 112
al-minhaj al-'aqli, 13
al- minhaj al-islami, 13
Miracles, 111ff., 143, 151, 185ff.
misahah, 156
mithl, 127
Mi'yar, (Ghazzali), 177
Moabites, 150, 183, 198, 206
Morocco, 4
mu'addib, 40
mubah, 107, 122
Mubarak, 13
Mubarrad, 147
mudawah, 96
mudabbir, 77
al-Mudhakkar wa-l-mu'annath (Ibn al-Anbari), 196
Mufadalah (Ibn Hazm), 77
Mufradat, 176
mufassal, 47
mufassar, 47
muftarad 'alayna, 115
mufti. 126
mughayyabat, 187
al-Mughni, (Ibn Qudamah), 111
Muhalla (Ibn Hazm), 11, 18, 46, 110ff., 121
al-mu'allim al-awwal, 86
Muhammad, see Prophet
Muhammad, 'Abbadid ruler, 30
Muhammad I (emir), 147
Muhammad b Abdun, 161
Muhammad b. Idris Ibn 'Ali b. Hammud, 34
Muhammad b. Isma'il, 160
Muhammad b. Maymun. 161
Muhammad Ibn 'Abdun, 160
Muhammad Ibn al-Hasan, 209
Muhammad Ibn Ishaq, 25
Muhammad Ibn Shukhays, 139
Muhammad b. al-Qasim, b Hammud, 34
Muhammad al-Mahdi, 23, 24

INDEX

Muhammad al-Mustakfi, 27
muhmalah, 172
mujahid, 28, 29, 31, 60
Mujalla (Ibn Hazm), 111
mujibah, 172
al-Mujiz (Ibn al-Sarraj), 143
mu'jiz, 141
mu'jizat, (cf. miracles), 112, 185
mujmal, 47
mujtahid, 31, 45, 131ff.
al-mujtahid al-mukhti', 131
al-mukhassas: 124
muktasab, 62
Mukhtasar al-'ayn (Zubaydi), 196
mukus, 32
Muladies (cf. Muwalladun)
mulk al-jinn, 91
mu'min, 80, 81
al-munazarah wa-l-jadal, (cf. *jadal)* 165
munkasi', 166
Mundhir Ibn Sa'id, 45
Mundhir Ibn Sa'id al-Balluti, 147
munfa'il, 171
munqati', 114
Munqidh (Ghazzali), 80
Mu'nis, 190
munshi', 78
Munyat al-Mughirah, 20
muqaddamat, 106
Muqaddamatan, 173
Muqaddimah (Ibn Khaldun), 108
al-muqallid al-musib, 131
mursal, 114
musabbab, 130
musamahah, 174
mushawarah, 126
mushtabahat, 122, 174
Music, 86, 89, 91, 94, 100, 155, 179ff., 192
Muslim; jurists, 13; philosophers, 83; 144, 153, 154; philosophy, 86; scholars, 4, 14, 56, 68, 83, 85, 92, 151, 155, 160, 185; sects, 144; Spain (cf. Andalus), 1, 2; thought, 14; world, 1, 39, 133
Muslims, 1, 19, 32, 52, 55, 78, 94, 131, 135, 139, 142, 150, 153, 159, 187, 206
mutaqaddimun (cf. Ancients), 164, 174, 177
Mustazhir, 147
Mu'tadid, 30, 33, 137
mudabbir, 118
mutakallimun (cf. Theologians), 76, 81
Mutanabbi, 133, 139
mutammamat, 107

mutanazaran (disputants), 48
al-muwaqqif al-awwal, 120
Mu'tazilah, 73, 113, 117
Mut'tazilism, 16
Mu'tazilites, 73, 79, 118
Muwatta' (Malik), 43
Muwalladun, 20
al-Muzaffar, 23
Mysticism (cf. Sufism), 105
nabat (cf. Botany), 87
nadb, 47, 120
nafi 'amm, 177
nafi khass, 177
nafiyah, 172
nafs, 87
nafsuh al-natiqah, 72
nahw (cf. grammar), 102
nahy (nawahi) (cf. prohibition), 47, 117
Najah (Ibn Sina), 89
najamah, 91
najdah, 63
Naqd al-shi'ir (criticism of poetry) (Ibn Qudamah), 140
naqid 'amm, 177
naqid khass, 177
naql, 7, 173
Names of Caliphs (Ibn Hazm), 146
Names of Companions (Ibn Hazm), 145
nasbah, 182
naskh, 47
nasab, (cf. genealogy), 102, 198
al-nasikh wa-l-mansukh, 143
nass (nusus), 2, 3, 7, 8, 44, 46, 47, 70, 81, 116, 117, 120, 131
natijah, 173, 177
Natural Sciences, 84, 86, 88, 100, 107, 153, 158, 199ff.
naw', 170, 180
Nawadir (Qali), 147
nawahi, (cf. *nahy)*
naw' al-anwa', 170
nazar, 80
nazar fi-l-katf, 91
Near East, 155
Negroes, 93
New Testament, 40, 51, 122
Nicephorous, 137
Nicholson, 13
nida', 171
Niebla, 20
niyyah, 47
Nomads, 120
North Africa, 150, 205,

INDEX

Northerners, 94, 150, 206
Nubadh (Ibn Hazm), 11, 110, 121
nubuwwah (cf. prophecy), 47, 96
Nukat al-Islam (Ibn Hazm), 10
Nu'm, 26, 136
nur, 105
nusbah, 171
nu'ut, 172
Nuwayri, 5
nusus (cf. nass), 1
Nykl, 12

Old Testament, 40, 51, 122, 183, 198
Optics, 86
Organon, 86, 159, 163, 164ff., 170ff., 171ff., 176
Orthodox Caliphs (cf. Rashidun), 124

Pellat, 12, 13
Pentateuch, 53
Peres, 12
Perlman, 13
Persians, 93, 94, 150, 183, 198, 206
Petrof, 12
Philosophers, 57, 73ff., 75ff., 81, 82, 83, 90, 91, 95, 96, 97, 103, 105, 108
Philosophical sciences, 38, 57, 84 85, 88, 94, 95, 108, 153ff.
Philosophy, 76ff., 81, 89, 94, 95, 96, 107, 111, 153, 206
Physicians, 203, 213
Precedence Among the Companions (Ibn Hazm), 145
Plato, 39, 65, 94, 153, 154
Platonic, neo, 160
Poetical Science, 86
Poetics, *(sh'ir)*, 160, 175, 176
Poetry, 37, 86, 88, 89, 90, 97, 98, 196ff., 206
Poets at the Court of Ibn Abi 'Amir (Ibn Hazm), 134
Polemics (cf. *jadal),* 46ff.
Politics, 87, 88, 94
Pons Boigues, 12
Porphyry, 154, 159, 164, 170, 175, 176, 177
Portugal, 20
Practical Sciences, 86, 88
Preference (cf. *istihsan)*
Precaution (cf. *ihtiyat)*
Prohibitions, 113, 114, 116, 119ff., 121
Prophecy, 39, 80, 96, 101, 111ff., 143, 151, 154, 184, 186, 201, 209

Prophets, 67, 68, 92, 112, 151, 185, 186
Prophet (Muhammad) (Cf. Muhammad), 1, 6, 17, 32, 43, 51, 62, 64, 68, 75, 80, 81, 90, 92, 97, 101, 108, 111ff., 114, 120ff., 123, 124, 125, 126, 127ff., 129, 131, 138, 144, 149, 150, 151, 156, 187, 192, 201, 212
Prosody, 86, 88, 134
Ptolemy, 6, 39, 52, 94, 154, 156
Psychology, 88
Pythgoras, 94
qaba'ih, 53
qa'id, 59
qada', 102, 187; cf. astrology
al-qada' bi-l-kawakib, 181
qadamah, 171
qadaya, 99, 171; cf. *qadiyah*
qadim, 171
qadiyah (qadaya), 126, 172
qadiyatan, 173, 177
Qali, 147, 196
qalladtu fulanan al-amr, 124
qarinah, 173
qasidah, 137
Qasim Ibn Hammud, 26
qat', 99
Qatighuriyas; cf. Categories
qawl, 172
al-qawl bi-l-batin, 9
al-qawl bi-l-zahir, 9
Qayrawan, 35, 37
qayyasun, 174
qiblah, 156, 208
Qifti, 5, 161
qira'ah, 102
qiyas, 1, 18, 43, 46, 60, 118, 121, 122, 124, 126ff., 165, 172, 173ff.
Qudamah Ibn Ja'far, 140, 175
Qur'an, 1, 6, 8, 16, 17, 18, 22, 37, 43, 44, 52, 56, 60, 63, 87, 92, 97, 101, 103, 107, 110, 112ff., 117, 119, 122, 123, 125, 126, 127ff., 131, 141, 142, 143, 195, 201, 206, 208.
Qur'anic commentary, 45, 108
Qur'anic reading, 97, 99, 108, 208
Qur'anic studies, 38, 41, 89, 165
Quraysh, 23, 33, 34
Qurayshite, 149
quwah, 185
quwat al-'aql, 70
quwat al-tafkir, 72
Rabat, 4
Rabat manuscript, 190ff.

INDEX

radd 'ala, 51
raghbah, 171
rajul husri, 33
Ramadan, 127, 180, 190, 212
Rasa'il, (Ibn Hazm), 11
Rasa'il Ikhwan al-Safa, 87ff.
rasm, 47, 170
rasf, 8
Rashid Rida, 111
Rashidun, 3
Rationalists, 76; cf. philosophers
Rawfid, 121
ra'y, 1, 47, 52, 60, 121, 123, 125ff.
raza'il, 79
Razi, 39, 94, 155, 160
Reading, 194ff.
Reason, 46, 111; cf. *'aql*
Religion, 73ff., 87, 97, 107
Religious laws, 206, 211; cf. *shara'i'*
Religious scholars, 55, 57, 63, 75ff., 85, 90, 91, 92, 95, 102
Religious sciences, 8, 38, 56, 63, 84, 88, 96, 108, 110, 153, 202ff., 210ff.
Revivification of the Religious Sciences (Ghazzali), 106
Rhetoric, 85, 86, 88, 97, 99, 137ff., 160, 175, 186, 206, 209; cf. *balaghah* and *khitabah*
ri'asah, 8
risalah, 47
Risalatan (Ibn Hazm), 11, 54
Ritter, 11, 190
Rituriqa, 175; cf. Rhetoric
riwayah, 98
Romance, 39
Romans, 93, 183, 198
Rosenthal, 12, 156, 61, 190
ruqyah, 186
ruh, 70
Rulers, 203
Russians, 93
rusul, 112; cf. Prophets
rutbah, 8
Rutbat al-hakim and Majriti), 180
ru'us al-'ulum, 91
ruwah, 102; cf. *riwayah*
ru'yah, 186
sabab, 47, 128ff.
sad and dad
Sa'd Ibn Nashib, 138, 196
sadaqah, 208
safsatah, 174; cf. sophistics
Sagitta, 91

sahabah, 115; cf. Companions
shahawat, 174
sahib, 40
Sahl Ibn Harun, 141, 175
Sa'id al-Baghdadi, 22
Sa'id Ibn Hazm, 20ff.
Sa'id of Toledo, 4, 6, 7, 10, 15, 20, 59, 89, 90, 93ff., 95, 96, 160, 169
sa'iq, 59
saj', 135
Sakhawi, 147
sakhif, 9
Sakkaki, 85
salaf, 166
Salie, 12
Salih Ibn 'Abd al-Quddus, 137, 196
sam'i, 79
Saqalibah; cf. Slavs
saqit, 122
Sarakhsi, 160, 180
Sarton, 13
Sasanid, 183, 198
Satan, 187
Saturn, 183, 184, 199
sawab, 47
sawt, 170
Schack, von, 12
Shreiner, 12
Sciences of the Ancients, 96; cf. *'ulum al-awa'il*
Seco de Lucena, 12
Secular Sciences; cf. philosophical sciences
Seville, 9, 29, 30, 31, 34, 36, 51, 137
Sezgin, 13
Sha'ban, 20
Shafi'i, 8, 9, 41, 43, 111
Shafi'ism, 3, 43
Shafi'ite(s), 16, 43, 123, 126
shaghab, 47, 124
shahwah, 123
shahid, 62
shartiyyah, 172
Shaqundi, 5, 7
Shar'ani, 15, 18
shar', 115
shara'i', 79, 121
shar'i, 54
shari'ah, 3, 16, 44, 47, 76, 101, 102, 103, 110, 113, 206; cf. Religious law
shart, 47
shaykh, 40
Shifa' (Ibn Sina), 89
Shi'ism, 16, 18

INDEX

shi'r, 103; cf. poetry
shirk, 47
shitranj, 180
shuhh, 63
Sibawayh, 121, 143, 195
sidq, 47
sifah, 113, 128
sifat, 172, 176
Siffin, 9
Simonet, 21
sina'ah, 140, 163, 175
sina'ah 'ammah, 157
Sinai Peninsula, 147
Sarafi, 162
Siyar (Dhahabi), 7, 11
Slavs, 23, 25, 69, 93, 97
Socrates, 94
Solomon, 59
Sophistics (mughalatah), 160, 172
173, 174ff., 176
Sophistry, 88
Sophists, 81, 111
Sorcery, 179, 185ff.
Southerners, 94
Spanish ancestry, 20
Spanish Christians, 20
Spanish Islam, 54
Spanish language, 190
Speckles of the Brides (Ibn Hazm), 146
Specialists, 212
Speech guide; cf. *dalil al-khitab*
Steinschneider, 12
Stoic, 160
Style, 85
Subki, 5, 53, 137
Sufi (s), 16, 82, 105, 107
Sufism, 41, 85, 88, 108
Sulayman al-Musta'in bi-llah, 24, 25
sullugismus, 177
sunnah (sunan), 1, 47, 92, 114; cf. Traditions
sur, 172
surah, 49, 87, 170
suwar, 93
Suyuti, 85
Syntax, 85
Syria, 150, 206
Syrians, 150
Syriac, 39
Syriac people, 150, 206

ta'ah (ta'at), 47, 69, 74, 79
Ta'aqqub (Ibn Hazm), 133
tab', 140, 141, 175
taba'i' wa-mahiyah, 72

tabaqat, 102
Tabari, 10, 141
tabi'ah, 47
tabi'ah daruriyah, 71
tabi'iyyat, 100
tabi'iyyun, 82
Tadhkirah (Dhahabi), 7
tafsir, 97; cf. Commentary
tafsir wa-sharh, 47
Tahafut (Ghazzali), 82, 102
tajribah, 85, 99, 155, 157, 181
takhlit, 32, 155
takhyir, 120
takzib bi-l-qadar, 92
Talamanki, 41
ta'lil, 122, 127ff.
Taliq, 42
Talisman, 88, 94, 100, 107, 108, 155,
179, 185, 192
Talkhis (Ibn Hazm), 10, 99, 100, 121
Talmud, 40, 51
Tamimi, 42, 149
tamwih, 124
tamyiz, 69, 72, 100, 116
tanabir, 180
taniniyy, 192
taqlid, 1, 8, 17, 41, 44, 47, 60, 71,
80, 117, 121, 123ff., 165
taqlid al-imam, 105
Taqrib (Ibn Hazm), 11, 38, 46, 51, 63, 97,
100, 137, 154, 159, 161, 163, 164ff.,
167ff.
tarakhi, 47
tasarruf, 126
tasawwur, 89
tasdiq, 89
tashih, 100
tashih al-istidlal, 172
tasmiyah, 91
Tawabi' (Ibn Shuhayd), 134
tawaqquf, 123
tawhid, 17
ta'wil, 1, 17, 47, 119
Tawq (Ibn Hazm), 11, 19, 28, 31, 38, 133,
134ff., 139, 169
Tawqif (Ibn Hazm), 63, 96, 100, 118, 159
tayaqqun, 63
Teaching, 97, 193ff.
Thabit, 196
Thabit Ibn Thabit, 143
Thawri, 8
The Book (Sibawayh), 195
Theologians, 105, 108

INDEX

Theology, 38, 80, 88, 89, 108, 110, 210, cf. *kalam*
Theoretical sciences, 86
tibb al-ajsam, 102
al-tibb al-nabawi, 156
Toledo, 36, 159
Topics, 160, 172, 175, 176; cf. *jadal*
Torah, 202
Traditions (Prophetic), 1, 15, 17, 18, 38, 41, 43, 44, 51, 52, 59, 60, 62, 63, 74, 87, 90, 97, 98, 99, 102, 107, 110, 113ff., 117ff., 122, 123, 126ff., 131, 142, 143, 151, 165, 180, 206, 208
Treatise on Good Conduct (Ibn Hazm), 134 Cf. *Akhlaq*
Tritton, 12
Truth, 107, 110, 113, 116; cf. *haqq*
Tubiqa, 172; cf. Topics
Tughra'i, 181
tuhmah, 122
Tunis, 170
Tunisia, 37
Turks, 93, 94, 97, 150, 206

'Ubaydallah Ibn 'Abd al-Rahman, 6, 42
'ud, 6
'Udhri, 42
ukhluqah, 33
'ulum al-'ajam, 88
al-'ulum al-'aqliyyah, 89
al-'ulum al-'arabiyyah, 88
'ulum al-awa'il, 96, 153' cf. Philosophical Sciences
al-'ulum ghayr al-shar'iyyah, 107 cf. Secular Sciences
al-'ulum al-naqliyyah al-wad 'iyyah, 108 Cf. Religious Sciences
al-'ulum al-riyadiyyah, 88
al-'ulum al-shar'iyyah, 106 Cf. Religious Sciences
al-'ulum al-tabi'iyyah, 108
'Umar, 125
'Umar, b. Yunus b. Ahmad al-Harrani, 161
Umayyad dynasty, 42, 146
Umayyad family, 20
Umyyad house, 22, 25, 35
Umayyads 22, 25, 35, 136, 146, 151
'umum, 47, 115, 117, 120
'Urwah Ibn al-Ward, 138, 196
ustadh, 40
usul, see *asl*
Valencia 26, 27, 29, 31, 36, 51
Veterinary medicine, 88

Vision, 184ff., 209; cf. *ru'yah*
al-Wadih (Zubaydi), 143
wad', 170
Wahrani, 42
wahy, 80, 112
wahy matluw, 114
wahy marwi, 113
wali, 81
wara', 47
wazn al-anqar, 91
Weisweiler, 12
West, 14, 15, 34, 35, 152, 181
Western Islam, 108
Western scholars, 11ff.
Western thought, 19
wizarah, 7
Writing, 194ff.
wujub, 9
wuquf, 9
Wustenfeld, 12
Yafi'i, 5
Yahya b. 'Adi, 160, 163
Yahya b. Hammud, 26, 27
Yahya b. Mujahid al-Fazari, 199
Yahya b. Zakariya, 58
yaqin, 80, 115, 122, 162
Ya'qub (Almohad ruler), 31
Ya'qub b. Hazm, 30
Yaqut, 5, 7, 170
Yeminites, 149, 150, 183, 198, 206
zahir, 3, 18, 44, 77, 120
Zahirah, 24
Zahirism, 9, 16, 41, 42ff., 110ff., 135, 143
Zahirite, 7, 51, 55, 127
Zahirite doctrine, 7, 11ff., 116, 117ff., 141, 142; cf. Zahirism
Zahirites, 9, 111, 152
Zahrawi, 38, 39, 157
zajr, 90
Zakarias, 202
zaman, 171
zann, 60, 72, 112, 122, 169
zann wa-shakk, 115
Zaytunah Mosque, 170
zindig, 53
Zion, 202
Zirid ruler, 26, 27
Zoroastrianism, 3, 202
Zoroastrians, 97, 111, 202
Zoology, 88
Zubaydi, 143, 147, 195, 196
Zuhayr b. Abi Sulma, 140